SECOND EDITION

The English Language

A Linguistic History

LAUREL J. BRINTON & LESLIE K. ARNOVICK

OXFORD
UNIVERSITY PRESS

OXFORD
UNIVERSITY PRESS

8 Sampson Mews, Suite 204, Don Mills, Ontario M3C 0H5
www.oupcanada.com

Oxford University Press is a department of the University of Oxford.
It furthers the University's objective of excellence in research, scholarship,
and education by publishing worldwide in

Oxford   New York
Auckland   Cape Town   Dar es Salaam   Hong Kong   Karachi
Kuala Lumpur   Madrid   Melbourne   Mexico City   Nairobi
New Delhi   Shanghai   Taipei   Toronto

With offices in
Argentina   Austria   Brazil   Chile   Czech Republic   France   Greece
Guatemala   Hungary   Italy   Japan   Poland   Portugal   Singapore
South Korea   Switzerland   Thailand   Turkey   Ukraine   Vietnam

Oxford is a trade mark of Oxford University Press
in the UK and in certain other countries

Published in Canada by Oxford University Press

Library and Archives Canada Cataloguing in Publication
Brinton, Laurel J.
The English language : a linguistic history / Laurel J. Brinton & Leslie
K. Arnovick.—2nd ed.

Includes bibliographical references and index.
ISBN 978-0-19-543157-5

1. English language—History—Textbooks. I. Arnovick, Leslie K., 1957– II. Title.

PE1075.B75 2011   420'.9   C2010-907703-2

Cover image: Ford Madox Brown (1821–1893), The Seeds and Fruits of
English Poetry. The Ashmolean Museum, University of Oxford. WA1920.3.

Oxford University Press is committed to our environment.
This book is printed on permanent (acid-free) paper ∞.

Printed and bound in Canada

2 3 4 – 14 13 12

Contents

7 The Grammar of Old English   194

8 The Rise of Middle English: Words and Sounds   240

12 Modern English   404

List of Tables, Figures, and Sample Texts

Tables

Figures

Sample Texts

Preface

Introduction

This text surveys the development of the English language from its Indo-European past to the present day. It begins with a discussion of attitudes toward language change and of motivations for and mechanisms of linguistic change. Considering next the prehistoric changes from Proto-Indo-European to Germanic, the text then examines the structure and vocabulary of English through its major periods: Old English, Middle English, Early Modern English, and Modern English. The text focuses on changes in sounds (*phonology*), in forms of words and their endings (*morphology*), in sentence structure (*syntax*), in spelling (*orthography*), in meanings of words (*semantics*), and in vocabulary (*lexicon*). Attention is also given to social and political factors affecting the language.

This text is addressed to all students interested in English, including those whose primary area of interest is English language, English literature, theoretical and applied linguistics, stylistics, the Middle Ages, English as a second language, or secondary English education. The text does not assume any background in language or linguistics; all necessary terms and concepts are taught in the text, and the International Phonetic Alphabet (IPA), which students are required to use, is carefully introduced. The text assumes the perspective of North American English, especially in its discussion of the national and regional varieties of English.

Upon completion, students should have acquired

- a comprehension of the mechanisms of language change and an acceptance of the inevitability of language change;
- a knowledge of the origins of English and its place in respect to other languages of the world;
- a recognition of the major stages in the language and important changes in the development of English from a synthetic to an analytic language; and
- an understanding of how the current state of the English language has resulted from historical change.

Recommended web links (covering external history, pronunciation guides, grammar reviews, supplemental exercises, sample manuscripts and texts, maps, etc.) are given at the end of each chapter. Recommendations for further reading, both to aid in understanding the chapter material and to allow students to pursue topics further, are also given at the end of each chapter.

Most of the examples presented in the text are taken from literary sources, especially Chaucer and Shakespeare for Middle and Early Modern English, respectively. While these examples will be of interest to students of literature, they have been chosen because both writers incorporate a range of registers, from high to low, and a variety of genres—both prose and poetry; moreover, they represent speech, which we assume may approximate actual conversation. Their works are readily available in searchable electronic corpora, which we have taken advantage of to provide fresh illustrations of the grammatical phenomena under discussion.

The text includes self-testing exercises, incorporated throughout each chapter, that are designed to help students learn the skills and concepts embodied in each chapter. The answers to these questions are located in an answer key at the end of the book.

The second edition features a convenient guide (see below) for reference and review as well as a comprehensive timeline of the major events (linguistic, literary, historical, and social) in the development of English. In addition to fully updated print and web references directing students to the latest research, the new edition also offers enhanced discussion of a number of topics: the effects of media (radio, television, and computers) on the language; the socio-cultural causes of change; the Great Vowel Shift (illustrated in detailed figures); the expansion of the vocabulary of Modern English during the Renaissance; and the sources and dialects of Canadian English, including consideration of the effects of immigration on the language (illustrated with maps). We have reorganized the book in order to devote a separate chapter to varieties of English. In addition, a more comprehensive treatment of sounds from Proto-Indo-European and Germanic to the modern day, illustrated with consonant and vowel charts for each period, makes it easier to trace phonological changes. Additional literary texts focusing on contemporary attitudes toward language are included for each stage of English. New primary-source analyses, along with study questions, provide links from the textbook to readings on the companion website (see below).

Quick Reference Guide

The new Quick Reference Guide, located at the end of the text, functions both as a study aid and a reference for the student. The guide begins with an overview of the line of descent of English and of the International Phonetic Alphabet. Phonological inventories are then gathered together to allow the student to trace change over time: these include vowel charts from Proto-Indo-European, Germanic, Old English, Middle English, Early Modern English (including the Great Vowel Shift), and Present-Day English along with consonant charts from Proto-Indo-European and Germanic (Grimm's Law), Old English, Middle English, and Modern English. The guide also provides a synthesis of morphological changes discussed in the textbook. Visual schema show

- the sources of English inflections,
- the sources of English pronoun forms,
- the sources of English verbal constructions, and
- the chronology of English clause types.

Companion Website

An accompanying website contains additional resources for both students and instructors (www.oupcanada.com/BrintonArnovick2e).

On the website, students will find the following materials:

1) Three different tutorials for using the search functions of the online *Oxford English Dictionary*—these tutorials give students practice searching for words of foreign origin, for literary coinages, and for syntactic constructions.
2) Additional self-testing exercises and answers (modeled on those given in the text) for all of the chapters, providing students with further opportunities for practice and review.
3) Websites for further investigation.
4) Spoken performances of the following Old, Middle, and Early Modern English literary works with accompanying written texts:
   - Old English: *The Wanderer*
   - Middle English: a selection from the *Alliterative Morte Arthur* and a selection from Geoffrey Chaucer's *Troilus and Criseyde*
   - Early Modern English: William Shakespeare's Sonnet 18 and Sonnet 29; selections from Shakespeare's *King Richard II* and *King Henry V*; John Donne's 'Song' ('Go and catch a falling star'), 'Holy Sonnet 6', and 'A Hymn to God the Father'; Ben Jonson's 'On My First Son' and 'Epitaph on Elizabeth, L.H.' and a selection fr'*The Silent Woman*.

Students are directed to these readings at the appropriate place in the textbook with the following icon 🌐. In-text study questions focus on linguistic features of the readings.

Instructors will find sample syllabuses for using the textbook in a quarter (10-week), semester (16-week), or year-long course. In addition, three different versions of the 10-week syllabus are given, with a general, medieval, and modern focus.

A Note on Punctuation

For this text we have used various punctuation conventions which students may not be familiar with.

It is the practice to distinguish between words (or parts of words) which are 'mentioned' rather than used. Using words is what we do whenever we speak, but mentioning words is what we do when we refer to words as words or to the forms of words, rather than evoking their meanings. For example, try reading the following sentences:

> The word grammar has seven letters.
> Bank has several different meanings.
> The feminine suffix -rix is almost obsolete.
> The clause when you arrive home is an adverbial clause.

Readers may have difficulty understanding such sentences because they contain word forms which are mentioned rather than used. The convention in printed texts is to italicize these mentioned forms, as follows:

> The word *grammar* has seven letters.
> *Bank* has several different meanings.
> The feminine suffix *-rix* is almost obsolete.
> The clause *when you arrive home* is an adverbial clause.

This convention should make these sentences much easier to read. This use of italics differs from the use of quotation marks to repeat the exact words of a spoken or written text (for example, 'convention' occurs two times in the previous paragraph) or to give the meaning or gloss for a word (for example, the word *garrulous* means 'tiresomely talkative').

Italics denote all linguistic forms which are used as examples within a sentence. When the actual sound of the word is being referred to, the International Phonetic Alphabet (IPA) is used. The IPA is a set of symbols used to transcribe, that is, to represent in writing, speech sounds in a precise and technical way. The IPA will be introduced in detail in Chapter 2 (see also Appendix A). To distinguish such representations from regular writing, they are enclosed in square brackets (or slashes), for example:

> The word *read* is pronounced [rɛd] or [rid]

The practice of this textbook is to use square brackets to represent sounds, as will be explained in Chapter 2.

Acknowledgments

We would like to thank our colleagues at the University of British Columbia, Siân Echard, Bryan Gooch, Steve Partridge, and Gernot Wieland, who expertly recited the samples of Old, Middle, and Early Modern English texts that can be heard on the website. Other colleagues who deserve thanks are Ina Biermann, Niall Christie, Anthony Dawson, Stefan Dollinger, Margery Fee, John Wilson Foster, Patricia Merivale, Laura Moss, Tiffany Potter, and Richard Unger. Gernot Wieland also supported the project from the beginning and lent us his Old English wisdom on a number of occasions. Our graduate student, Ben Packer, wrote or adapted many of the self-testing exercises. Gary Holland of the University of California, Berkeley, provided the passage of Vedic Sanskrit. Henry Ansgar Kelly of the University of California, Los Angeles, commented on the first edition; we benefited from his always thoughtful observations. John Considine of the University of Alberta provided extensive — and always astute — commentary on our revised text. Our thanks to Robert Weyeneth of the University of South Carolina and Ralph Brands of the University of British Columbia for assistance and support. Virginia Evans read, with a keen eye, several iterations of the distance learning course, which served as a basis for this text. Our thanks to the Office of Learning Technology of the University of British Columbia for permission to use the content of our English 320 course in this textbook. Finally, we would like to thank our undergraduate students, who continue to teach us ways to make the history of the English language meaningful.

We dedicate this book to our professors at the University of California, Berkeley, who inspired our research and teaching. This second edition is for Donna, Louise, Susan, and Gregory.

At Oxford University Press, we would like to thank all of the editors who worked on the first edition, especially Eric Sinkins. For the second edition, we extend our thanks to Peter Chambers, Jacqueline Mason, and in particular Janice Evans for her keen eye and meticulous copyediting. We owe a debt of gratitude to our anonymous reviewers, who were generous with their comments.

Abbreviations

The following abbreviations are used in this text:

AAVE	African American Vernacular English		NZE	New Zealand English
acc.	accusative case		O	object
ADJ	adjective		obj.	objective case
ADV	adverb		OE	Old English
AusE	Australian English		OF	Old French
AUX	auxiliary		OHG	Old High German
BCE	Before the Common Era		ON	Old Norse
BE	British English		p.	person
CanE	Canadian English		part.	participle
CE	Common Era		PDE	Present-Day English
CONJ	conjunction		PIE	Proto-Indo-European
dat.	dative case		pl.	plural
EModE	Early Modern English		pres.	present tense
fem.	feminine		pret.	preterit tense
Fr.	French		q.v.	quod vide ('which see')
gen.	genitive case		RP	Received Pronunciation
Ger.	German		S	subject
Gk.	Greek		SAE	South African English
Gmc.	Germanic		sg.	singular
Go.	Gothic		Skt.	Sanskrit
HE	Hiberno-English		SSE	Standard Scottish English
IE	Indo-European		subj.	subjunctive mood
ind.	indicative mood		s.v.	sub verbo ('under the word')
instr.	instrumental		USEng	United States English
Lat.	Latin		V	verb
LSE	Liberian Standard English		WE	Welsh English
masc.	masculine		WISE	West Indian Standard English
ME	Middle English		1st p.	first person
ModE	Modern English		2nd p.	second person
N	noun		3rd p.	third person
NAE	North American English		>	changes to, becomes
neut.	neuter		<	derives from
nom.	nominative case		Ø	no ending or form

Studying the History of English

OVERVIEW

Beginning with a number of reasons for studying the history of English, this chapter offers a definition of language and surveys its component parts. Next it gives an overview of the recognized periods in the history of English, providing a sample text from each. It then focuses on several concrete examples of change in Shakespearean sonnets, contrasting Early Modern English with Modern English. The chapter argues for the inevitability of linguistic change, claiming that this is brought on by the conventional or arbitrary nature of language. We speculate briefly about the origin of language, and explore the popular notion that language change entails linguistic corruption. After analyzing the reasons for such an attitude, we look at prescriptive approaches to grammar and the belief in standards of linguistic correctness. The chapter ends with a discussion of the resources available for studying the history of the English language.

OBJECTIVES

After completing this chapter, you should be able to

- give a general definition of language and its components;
- identify the names and dates of the historical periods of the English language;
- point out where the language in a passage from an earlier period of English differs from Modern English in respect to sounds, word forms, syntax, and meaning;

- understand the relation between the linguistic sign and language change; and
- explain reasons for the predominant attitude toward language change and recognize examples of this in popular literature.

Why Study the History of English?

Some reasons for studying the history of English are intrinsic to the language as it has developed and been studied over time, and some are intrinsic to the student's individual educational interests.

We have over 1,200 years of recorded history for the English language. Although such a period pales in comparison to the recorded histories of such languages as Hebrew, Chinese, and Greek, it is nonetheless a substantial and unbroken time span over which we have good documentary evidence. We are fortunate to have this record when we consider that for many of the world's languages, we have only very sparse records, making linguistic study much more challenging. The many Native languages of North America, for example, did not come to be recorded until relatively recently, when some were already endangered or lost.

Although the changes that English has undergone in its history are not unique, they are nevertheless dramatic. English has experienced a significant change in the way in which it encodes grammatical meaning—what linguists call 'typological' change—from being a highly inflected (or *synthetic*) language to one that relies primarily on fixed word order and function words to convey meaning (an *analytic* language). Moreover, the English language has been subject to equally dramatic external influences—for example, the Norman Conquest of England—which have changed the vocabulary of English and, to a lesser extent, its grammar and speech sounds (*phonology*).

The processes of change in the English language have been illuminated by a considerable amount of scholarship. This attention to English is in a way accidental: scholars of historical linguistics working early in the nineteenth century focused on the Germanic and Indo-European language families, and in this way revealed much about the history of English. In spite of thorough study, however, important areas remain open to debate and inquiry.

For reasons that are historical and political rather than linguistic, English has become one of the most widely spoken languages in the world and has attained the status of a global language. Of course, there is nothing linguistically superior about English, and it would be wrong to engage in linguistic jingoism. Certainly, English has a cosmopolitan vocabulary, one of the characteristics often cited as an attribute of a world language, but there is no evidence that its lack of inflections contributes to grammatical simplicity and ease of use by non-native speakers. For example, a speaker of a Chinese language might well find English processes of word formation and grammatical marking very complex.

The global importance of English results from two historical factors: British colonialism, which peaked in the nineteenth century, and the emergence of the

United States as an economic and military power in the twentieth century. Because of this political dominance, English is now the primary or official language in more than sixty countries, spread over every continent of the globe. English serves as a *lingua franca*, a common language used for commerce, government, academia, culture, and tourism by people who may not speak it as their first or even second language. As a legacy of imperialism, English is the language of government, law, civil service, and education in many countries. It is used as a neutral means of communication between different ethnic groups (for example, in India). It is the language of air traffic control, maritime traffic, and emergency services, and it is frequently used on the Internet, on home computers, and for video games. In short, it has become a 'pluricentric' language, 'whose norms are focused in different local centres, capitals, centres of economy, publishing, education and political power' (Romaine 1998:27).

On a disciplinary level, studying the history of English is a way to become familiar with the methods and principles of linguistics. More particularly, the history of English informs our understanding of the language's current state; modern spelling and pronunciation, for example, result from historical developments, and irregularities (as well as regularities) can be explained by reference to the language's past. Principles of semantic change operating in English can tell us, for example, how the meaning of the word *nice* developed from 'foolish and ignorant' to 'pleasing or agreeable'. The history of English can also provide insight into the literary works of great writers: a full appreciation of a writer such as Shakespeare depends upon knowledge of the grammar, phonology, and vocabulary of Early Modern English, just as an appreciation of Chaucer depends upon a knowledge of Middle English.

Finally, studying the history of English helps us trace the origin of the standard English we use today, whether at university or at work, and enables us to distinguish between prescriptive and descriptive rules of English grammar. Study of historical developments in any language can lead us to recognize that linguistic change is inevitable and that patterns of change that began in the past are likely to continue into the future. Such study should lead to greater self-consciousness about the language we use and to an awareness that 'everyone speaks a dialect', that standard English is but one of a number of Englishes, including regional and national varieties, none of which is inherently superior to any other. Ultimately, study of the history of English reveals that language is, above all, a cultural construct.

A Definition of Language

Human language is a system. In other words, it is highly structured and operates according to a set of principles. Every language is governed by rules for the formation of words and sentences; these rules constitute its grammar. In order for us to learn a language, the set of rules must be finite in number, but with these rules we can produce an infinite number of sentences and understand sentences which we have never heard before. Theoretically, we could also produce sentences of infinite length, though there are practical limits imposed by memory and the physiology of speech. It is for these reasons that we say that human language is infinite or creative.

Language consists of meaningful signs, things that stand for or represent something else. In general, the relationship between the linguistic sign and the thing it represents is symbolic—that is, it is conventional, or arbitrary, since there is no natural or necessary relation between a sequence of sounds and an object in the real world. We will consider the arbitrary nature of the sign in greater detail below, as it is a fundamental principle underlying language change.

Since human language is primarily vocal (oral and aural), speech comes prior to the written word in both the history of humankind and the history of the individual: we learn to speak before we learn to write. Writing is a secondary, and in many ways imperfect, means of recording speech, although both speech and writing make certain distinctions that the other medium cannot make.

Human language is now thought to be innate: we have an inborn capacity for language acquisition. That is, we are genetically equipped to learn a language (not a specific language, but human language in general). In other words, every child is capable of acquiring any language to which he or she is exposed. However, because a person must be exposed to a language to acquire it, we may also say that language is *learned*. Human language has multiple functions, from communicating ideas to expressing emotion and maintaining social cohesion. It is one of several communicative means that human beings possess, including gesture, facial expression, body movement, and tone of voice.

Language is generally agreed to be uniquely human, differing from animal communication in being systematic, creative, conventional, both innate and learned, and possibly displaced in time and space from its stimulus. Another reason to say that language is human and an innate feature of the human brain is the existence of a number of universal features shared by all languages. Consider the following phenomena (adapted from Fromkin et al. 2007:28–9):

- All human beings have language.
- All languages are creative and symbolic.
- All languages use finite sets of discrete sounds.
- All languages are governed by finite sets of rules (i.e. grammar).
- All languages have similar grammatical categories (noun, verb).
- All languages contain semantic universals ('male', 'female', 'animate', 'human').
- All languages make grammatical distinctions, such as past time, plural number, and negation.
- All language may be used to perform various speech acts, such as asking questions, issuing commands, and making promises.
- There are no primitive languages, except perhaps contact languages (i.e. pidgins).
- All languages change over time.

The Components of Language

For purposes of linguistic study, language is divided into levels, or components. Although we treat these components separately, they are interrelated in a complex way in the system of language.

The first component is *phonology* (from Gk. *phōnē* 'sound'). Phonology is the study of the sound system of a particular language: the distinctive speech sounds, the combinations of sounds that are possible, and the prosodic features that operate in the language.

The second component is *morphology* (from Gk. *morphē* 'form'). Morphology is the study of the form and formation of words in a particular language. It considers the arrangement of sounds into minimal meaningful units (called *morphemes*), the processes by which words are built, the grouping of words into classes, and the nature of the vocabulary.

The third component is *syntax* (from Gk. *suntaxis* 'ordering'), which is the study of how words are arranged into higher units, such as phrases (e.g. noun or verb phrases), clauses (e.g. main or subordinate clauses), and sentences (e.g. interrogative/declarative/imperative or positive/negative or active/passive sentences). The arrangement of words, or *word order*, typically concerns the major functional elements—subject (S), verb (V), and object (O)—and their usual patterning in the language.[1]

Phonology will be treated in detail in Chapter 2. With regard to morphology, it is important here to introduce a number of technical terms that will be developed later. Morphemes may be either 'bound' or 'free'. Free morphemes can stand on their own as independent words (for example, *help*). Generally they carry the major meaning of the word and are called *roots*. Bound morphemes must be attached to some other form. While there are some *bound roots* (such as *mit* in *commit* or *fer* in *refer*) which carry the principal meaning but cannot stand independently as words, bound morphemes are often *affixes* (either *prefixes* or *suffixes*), such as *un-* and *-ful* in *unhelpful*, which do not carry the principal meaning of the word. Affixes perform one of two functions:

- *derivation*: they may be used to derive new words from existing words, such as *-er* in *helper*, which derives a noun from a verb, or *un-* in *unhappy*, which forms a word with a negative meaning; or
- *inflection*: they may signal grammatical distinctions, such as plural (as *-s* in *books*) or past tense (as *-ed* in *helped*).

---

1 There are numerous ways of approaching the study of syntax, which especially in the twentieth century have become highly formal and theoretical. Since the purpose of this textbook is primarily to account for a wide range of syntactic phenomena in the history of English rather than to justify a particular theoretical model, the approach toward syntax taken here will be functional, descriptive, and typological. A combination of methodologies allows us to explicate diachronic processes such as grammaticalization, which involves complex morphological, syntactic, and semantic-pragmatic changes.

Inflections can generally be added to all members of a particular part of speech; they do not change the root's part of speech or lexical meaning (its dictionary definition). The inflectional system has changed dramatically in the history of the language. In earlier English, there were numerous inflectional endings marking a wide variety of grammatical categories. In Modern English, these are limited to a few regular forms: -*s* (noun plural), -*'s* (noun possessive), -*er* (adjective/adverb comparative), -*est* (adjective/adverb superlative), -*s* (verb third-person singular present tense), -*ed* (verb past tense), -*ed* (verb past participle), -*ing* (verb present participle). In contrast, there are numerous derivational endings in Modern English, both native and borrowed. Derivation can change the part of speech of a word or affect its lexical meaning. Derivational affixes are highly idiosyncratic and can be added to only particular roots; thus, one can say *unhappy* but not *unnice*.

Derivation is an important process of word-building in English. A second important process is *compounding*, the joining of two roots into a compound word, such as *lipstick*. We will examine how both derivation and compounding function in the different stages of the English language to create new words, or *neologisms*. Other less productive or less common word-building processes (which we examine in more detail in Chapter 12) include functional shift (e.g. from the noun *fun* to the adjective *fun*), clipping (e.g. *professor* to *prof*), and blending (e.g. *guess* + *estimate* > *guesstimate*).

Morphology treats the classification of words into parts of speech. Major parts of speech (nouns, verbs, adjectives, and adverbs) express lexical meaning, while minor parts of speech, or *function words* (prepositions, articles, conjunctions, auxiliary verbs, pronouns, and particles), primarily indicate meanings related to the grammar of the sentence (*grammatical meaning*). Finally, morphology is concerned with the vocabulary, or lexicon, of a language—in other words, the inventory of words either native to the language or borrowed from other languages.

As we will see in the history of English, there is an intimate relationship between morphology and syntax. As the morphological complexity of English has been reduced, the syntactic component has expanded; grammatical distinctions that at an earlier stage were expressed by means of inflection have come to be expressed by using fixed word orders or by *periphrastic constructions*, which make use of function words.

In addition to the formal components just explained, language can be discussed in terms of its *semantic* and *pragmatic* dimensions. Semantics (from Gk. *sēmantikos* 'significant') is the study of lexical and grammatical meaning. Three sets of conceptual distinctions are used in semantics. The first is the distinction between the *intension* of a word and its *extension*. The extension is all the things to which the word refers; the extension of *dog*, for instance, includes 'all collies, Dalmatians, dachshunds, mongrels, etc., etc. that have ever lived or will ever live and every fictitious creature that is accepted as being a dog' (Kreidler 1998:132). The intension of a word is the set of properties, or defining characteristics, shared by all members of the word's extension. It is the dictionary definition of the word. Thus, the intension of *dog* is 'a four-legged mammal belonging to the genus *Canis*'.

A second distinction is made between *denotation* and *connotation*. The denotation of a word is its literal, objective meaning. Connotations are the associations or emotions that a word (and the object it names) evokes. These may be the feelings associated with the word by an individual, a group, or the culture at large. A word may have either good or bad connotations, or it may be neutral. For example, the word *December* may have as its connotations 'cold', 'bad weather', 'darkness', 'snow', 'Christmas', 'parties', 'school holidays', 'year end', and so on, some of which are positive ('parties'), some negative ('darkness'), and some neutral ('year end') (Crystal 2008:98). Synonyms (with the same intension and extension) often differ only in respect to their connotations. Note the range of connotations in the following sets of words, which could be used to refer to the same thing: *inexpensive/cheap*; *breeze/draft*; *stout/obese/fat*; *steed/horse/nag*.

The third set of distinctions involves universal semantic features, the essential components of meaning that cannot be analyzed any further. Any word in the language consists of a bundle of these features, and one word differs from any other word in respect to at least one feature. These features are stated in terms of a binary distinction, such as ±HUMAN (capitals are used to indicate that this is being used as a feature, not a word). Using a limited set of semantic features, we could analyze the meanings of the words *man* [+ANIMATE +HUMAN +ADULT +MALE], *woman* [+ANIMATE +HUMAN +ADULT −MALE], *boy* [+ANIMATE +HUMAN −ADULT +MALE], and *girl* [+ANIMATE +HUMAN −ADULT −MALE] (alternatively, ±FEMALE could be used).

Pragmatics (from Gk *pragmatikos* 'deed') is the study of language in use. It is concerned with the function of language in its social context. It covers a wide range of topics, including what the communicative intentions of speakers are; what principles speakers and hearers use in communicating; what underlying beliefs and assumptions they share; how social, cultural, and political institutions shape language use; and how discourse or communication is structured. Furthermore, pragmatics is concerned with the sophisticated means by which all of these factors become encoded in language. In this text we will touch only briefly on pragmatics. (For in-depth studies of pragmatic changes over time, see Arnovick 1999 and Brinton 1996.)

As we will see, changes occur in all of the components of a language over time. Among the components described here, changes in the vocabulary are the most obvious, but there have been equally extensive developments in the phonology, morphology, syntax, and semantics of the English language. Furthermore, what happens in one component often entails substantial changes in the others.

Exercise 1.1 Morphological and Semantic Concepts

1. Analyze the following words into *prefix* (P), *suffix* (S), and *root* (R).

    Example: retroactive – *retro* (P) + *act* (R) + *ive* (S)
              undernourished – *under* (R) + *nourish* (R) + *ed* (S)

    a. handyman _____

    b. immobilization _____

    c. fire-retardant _____

    d. biodegradable _____

    e. worldly-wise _____

    f. flightworthiness _____

    g. owner-occupied _____

    h. counterclockwise _____

    i. unforeseeable _____

    j. icebreaker _____

2. Find one example of each of the eight inflectional suffixes in the following
    paragraph.

    > God said to Noah, 'The end has come of all things of flesh; I have
    > decided this, because the earth is full of violence of men's making,
    > and I will efface them from the earth. . . .'
    >   The flood lasted forty days on the earth. The waters swelled, lifting
    > the ark until it was raised above the earth. The waters rose and swelled
    > greatly on the earth, and the ark sailed on the waters. The waters rose
    > more and more on the earth so that all the highest mountains under
    > the whole of heaven were submerged. The waters rose fifteen cubits
    > higher, submerging the mountains. And so all things of flesh perished
    > that moved on the earth, birds, cattle, wild beasts, everything that
    > swarms on the earth, and every man. . . . (Genesis 6: 13–7: 22 from *The
    > New Jerusalem Bible* 1985)

    (1) _____

    (2) _____

    (3) _____

    (4) _____

(5) _____

(6) _____

(7) _____

(8) _____

3. In the passage given in (2):

    a. What is the intension of the word *cattle*?

    _____

    b. Give the denotation and connotation of the word *efface*.

    _____

    c. Using the semantic features given in the text and any other that you feel necessary, give an analysis of *bird*.

    _____

Linguistic Change in English

The Periods of English

Although the development of the language has been gradual and continuous, we conventionally divide the history of English into either four or five periods. These periods coincide in large part with important political and social events.

The first period is that of Old English (OE). This period was previously called Anglo-Saxon, but that term is now generally reserved for the people and the society of the time rather than the language. The period dates from approximately 450 to 1100 CE, although our earliest written records date only from the eighth century. The beginning is demarcated by the arrival in England of Germanic speakers from continental Europe. For the modern-day English speaker, Old English must be learned as a foreign language. It is highly inflected with variable word order and a primarily Germanic vocabulary. The literature in Old English is quite rich, including Germanic heroic poetry such as *Beowulf,* secular prose like the *Anglo-Saxon Chronicle* (a record of events in early English history), and religious poetry and prose that includes saints' lives, sermons, and Bible translations. Most of the Old English literature that survives is written in a dialect known as West Saxon.

The second period is that of Middle English (ME), beginning with the conquest of England by French speakers from Normandy in 1066 and continuing through to almost 1500 CE. For the first 200 years or so, French served as the official language of England, and the literature produced in England was mostly in French (and Latin), though English continued to be spoken by a majority of the population. When English began to be written widely in the thirteenth century, it had lost most of the inflections of Old English and much of the vocabulary, and it had been inundated with French words. In addition to the impact of French on English during this time, a second factor accounting for the extensive changes in the language before its re-emergence was the scarcity of written records in English. With few written documents to preserve a standard form of the language, changes already in progress in late Old English accelerated.

Middle English is recorded in a number of regional dialects, such as the London dialect of Geoffrey Chaucer, author of *The Canterbury Tales*, and the West Midland dialect used by the anonymous author of *Sir Gawain and the Green Knight*. For the modern-day English speaker, Chaucer's language is fairly understandable, since it is close to the dialect that evolved into standard English; in contrast, the *Gawain* poet's language is almost incomprehensible, since it was heavily influenced by Scandinavian languages and preserves Old English vocabulary. The end of Middle English is often placed at the death of Chaucer in 1400, but this is undoubtedly too early. A writer who more aptly marks the end of the period is Thomas Malory (died *c*. 1470), chronicler of Arthurian legends.

The third period is that of Early Modern English (EModE), dating from roughly 1500 to 1700 CE. It begins shortly after the introduction of the printing press to England by William Caxton (in 1476); the period includes the English Renaissance, and its end coincides with the death of poet John Dryden. The major linguistic development marking the beginning of this period is the rise of a standard dialect. The period is also marked by an important phonological change, the *Great Vowel Shift*, as well as a number of grammatical changes. Writings from this time provide little difficulty for the modern-day English speaker. The great writer of this period is, of course, William Shakespeare (1564–1616).

A fourth period often distinguished is that of Late Modern English, extending from 1700 to 1900 CE. Although linguistic changes during this time are not as dramatic as in the earlier periods of the language, several features are noteworthy, such as the beginning of English 'plain style' (as opposed to the copiousness of earlier ages) and the spread of English around the globe. However, many scholars speak simply of Modern English (ModE, 1700 to the present), which incorporates both Late Modern English and Present-Day English (PDE, 1900 to the present).

In addition, we can get a sense of what the language looked like before these recorded stages by reconstructing the language from which all the Germanic languages descend, called Proto-Germanic, as well as the language from which most of the languages of Europe and northern India descend, called Proto-Indo-European (PIE). The former was probably spoken around 200 BCE, while the latter dates from at least 4000 BCE.

Biblical material provides an especially rich source of historical material for linguistic study because the Bible has been translated in every age, and translators are particularly careful in their renderings of the 'word of God'. Moreover, biblical texts have survived due to their preservation by the early Church. Compare the four versions of Matthew 13: 24–30 (the parable of the sower and the seed) given below. The first is taken from a tenth-century Old English text, the second from a fourteenth-century Middle English text, the third from an early sixteenth-century text of Early Modern English (see Frey 1966:4, 33, 61), and the fourth from the Modern English *The New Jerusalem Bible* (1985). (You will see that a number of letters are used in writing Old English that we no longer have today: þ stands for lower case *th*; Þ represents capital *th*; and æ is a linking of *a* and *e*. We will study these in more depth in Chapter 6.)

OLD ENGLISH

Heofona rice is geworden þæm menn gelic þe seow god sæd on his æcere. Soþlice, þa þa menn slepon, þa com his feonda sum, and oferseow hit mid coccele onmiddan þæm hwæte, and ferde þanon. Soþlice, þa seo wyrt weox, and þone wæstm brohte, þa ætiewde se coccel hine. þa eodon þæs hlafordes þeowas and cwædon: 'Hlaford, hu, ne seowe þu god sæd on þinum æcere? Hwanon hæfde he coccel?' Þa cwæþ he: 'Þæt dyde unhold mann.' Þa cwædon þa þeowas: 'Wilt þu, we gaþ and gadriaþ hie?' Þa cwæþ he: 'Nese: þylæs ge þone hwæte awyrtwalien, þonne ge þone coccel gadriaþ. Lætaþ ægþer weaxan oþ riptiman; and on þæm riptiman ic secge þæm riperum: "Gadriaþ ærest þone coccel, and bindaþ sceafmælum to forbærnenne; and gadriaþ þone hwæte into minum berne."'

MIDDLE ENGLISH

The kyngdom of heuenes is maad lijk to a man, that sewe good seed in his feld. And whanne men slepten, his enemy cam, and sewe aboue taris in the myddil of whete, and wente awei. But whanne the erbe was growed, and made fruyt, thanne the taris apperiden, and the seruauntis of the hosebonde man camen, and seiden to hym, Lord whether hast thou not sowen god seed in thi feeld? where of thanne hath it taris? And he seide to hem, An enemy hath do this thing. And the seruauntis seiden to him, Wolt thou that we goon, and gaderen hem? And he seide, Nay, lest perauenture ge in gaderynge taris drawen vp with hem the whete bi the roote. Suffre ge hem bothe to wexe in to repyng tyme; and in the tyme of ripe corne Y shal seie to the reperis, First gidere the taris, and bynde hem to gidere in kyntchis to be brent, but gadere ge whete in to my berne.

Continued

EARLY MODERN ENGLISH

[T]he kingdoom of heven is lijk a man that soweth good seed in his feld, and whilest the men weer asleep his enmie cam and sowed darnel among the middest of his corn and went his wais, and when the blaad cam yp, and the corn eared out, then the darnel appeared also. Then cam the housholders servants to him and said, 'Sir, did not yow soow good seed in yor ground; from whens then hath it this darnel?'

He told them, 'The enmie did this.'

'Wil iou then', said the servants, 'that we go and weed it out?'

'Nai', quoth he, 'leest in weeding the darnel, ye pluck yp also the corn. Let booth grow togither yntil hervest, and in hervest tym I wil speek to the hervest men, "gather first the dernel and bind it in the bundels that it might be burnt, and bring the corn in to mi garner."'

MODERN ENGLISH

The kingdom of heaven may be compared to a man who sowed good seed in his field. While everybody was asleep his enemy came, sowed darnel all among the wheat, and made off. When the new wheat sprouted and ripened, the darnel appeared as well. The owner's servants went to him and said, 'Sir, was it not good seed that you sowed in your field? If so, where does the darnel come from?' 'Some enemy has done this,' he answered. And the servants said, 'Do you want us to go and weed it out?' But he said, 'No, because when you weed out the darnel you might pull up the wheat with it. Let them both grow till the harvest; and at harvest time I shall say to the reapers: First collect the darnel and tie it in bundles to be burned, then gather the wheat into my barn.' (Matthew 13: 24–30)

Exercise 1.2 Periods of English

Answer the following questions based on the biblical translations of Matthew 13: 24–30. You may need to work backwards through the passages in order to interpret some of the Old English words.

1. Find three sets of words that are the same (or nearly the same) in all four passages. Can you characterize these words?

_____

_____

_____

_____

2. Describe briefly what things are 'sown' and 'grown' in each of the four passages. Note the similarities from period to period, and the differences. Which words are nearly unchanged? Which are very different? What might this suggest about the nature of English vocabulary?

_____

_____

_____

_____

_____

_____

_____

3. The central comparison between heaven and a cultivated field is introduced in each passage in the first sentence. What changes in word order can you identify? Between which periods are these changes greatest?

_____

_____

_____

_____

_____

An Example of Linguistic Change

To exemplify the extent of linguistic change in the 400-year span between Shakespeare's time and our own (as opposed to the entire 1,200-year span of written English), let's look at a selection of Early Modern English:

> Betwixt mine eye and heart a league is tooke,
> And each doth good turnes now vnto the other.
> When that mine eye is famisht for a looke,
> Or heart in loue with sighes himselfe doth smother;
>   (from Shakespeare, Sonnet 47)[2]

_____

2 This and all subsequent quotations from Shakespeare follow the original spelling of the 1609 printed edition of the sonnets and the 1623 First Folio edition of the plays (see http://etext.lib. virginia.edu/modeng/modengS.browse.html). Our practice here is to identify citations with play titles. For a modern-spelling edition, see Evans (1997).

Despite the similarities between Early Modern and Modern English, even a quick read of these lines from Sonnet 47 reveals several differences on all levels of language (ignoring differences in spelling):

- in terms of morphology, we would say *does* not *doth* and *my* not *mine*;
- in terms of vocabulary, *betwixt* and *unto* (*vnto*) are archaic;
- in terms of semantics, *league* is now rarely used with the sense 'pact' (except in specialized expressions, such as 'in league with' and 'League of Nations');
- in terms of syntax, we would say *has been taken* not *is tooke* and *when* not *when that*, and we would require an article before *heart*; and
- in terms of word order, and even allowing for the freedom of word order in poetry dictated by the requirements of meter and rhyme, we would be much more likely now to say *smothers himself with sighs* (or if *do* is emphatic, *does smother himself with sighs*) than *with sighes himselfe doth smother*.

Another selection shows further differences:

> O no, thy loue, though much, is not so great,
> It is my loue that keepes mine eie awake,
> Mine owne true loue that doth my rest defeat,
> To plaie the watch-man ever for thy sake.
>> For thee watch I whilst thou dost wake elsewhere,
>> From me farre off, with others all too neere.
>> (from Shakespeare, Sonnet 61)

- in terms of phonology, even if we allow that rhymes in poetry need not always be exact, we can no longer rhyme *great* and *defeat* or *where* and *near* (*neere*). At the same time, we know enough about Shakespeare's English to determine that *defeat* probably had the sound we now hear in *great* and *near* had the sound we now hear in *where*;
- in terms of morphology, where Shakespeare says *thee* and *thy*, we would use *you* and *your*;
- in terms of syntax, we see the word order object–verb rather than verb–object in *my rest defeat*, and the order object–verb–subject rather than subject–verb–object in *for thee watch I*; and
- in terms of vocabulary, *whilst* is not common in North American English.

 Now listen to Shakespeare's sonnets 18 and 29 (readings 4 and 5 on the companion website) and follow along with the written text. Keep in mind that the rhyme scheme of Shakespearian sonnets is abab cdcd efef gg. Is there an instance in either poem in which this scheme seems to be violated? Could sound change be responsible, or is Shakespeare intentionally flouting the norms? (For the lack of rhyme in the pair *possessed* and *least* in Sonnet 29, sound change is the more plausible explanation; it is likely that *least* rhymed with *best*.) The word *haply* (Sonnet 29, 1. 10) means 'by chance'. It is related to the word *happily* meaning 'fortunately, luckily, gladly'. Can you explain this shift in meaning? It is likely a type of metonymic change, as we will see in our discussion of semantic change in Chapter 3.

If sixteenth-century English is significantly different from Modern English, we should not be surprised that ninth- or thirteenth-century English diverges even more radically, as seen in the selections from the parable of the sower and the seed given above. A purpose of this textbook is to examine the extent of this divergence.

Exercise 1.3 Analyzing Shakespearean English

From the perspective of a Modern English speaker, analyze the following passage from Shakespeare's Sonnet 11. Consider phonology, morphology, syntax, and vocabulary.

> As fast as thou shalt wane, so fast thou grow'st,
> In one of thine, from that which thou departest,
> And that fresh bloud which youngly thou bestow'st
> Thou maist call thine, when thou from youth conuertest.

_____

_____

_____

_____

The Nature of Linguistic Change

The study of language change is called *historical* or *diachronic linguistics*. Because there are many misconceptions, we will begin by examining the nature of language change.

The Inevitability of Change

Change in a language over time is inevitable. As the well-known Swiss linguist Ferdinand de Saussure recognizes, there is no reason for language to be exempted from the universal law of mutability; time changes all things:

> Absolute stability in a language is never found. . . . All parts of the language are subject to change, and any period of time will see evolution of greater or smaller extent. It may vary in rapidity or intensity. But the principle admits no exceptions. The linguistic river never stops flowing. (1986 [1915]:139)

All known languages have undergone and are undergoing change; only dead languages—languages which are no longer spoken—are immune from change. Even American Sign Language, the gestural and partially iconic language of the deaf, has sustained changes in word order and vocabulary. The effects of time on language are natural and perfectly normal. Language change does not result in a loss of efficacy or expressiveness (or at least no one has developed criteria by which these aspects can be measured), nor does it produce a worse system of grammar, just a different one. All linguistic systems seem equally well suited for the purposes of communication. We cannot even say that grammar becomes simplified over time because simplification in one aspect is often accompanied by elaboration in another. For example, the loss of inflections in English (which might be described as a simplification) has coincided with an increase in the use of function words to mark grammatical distinctions, resulting in such impressively complex auxiliary phrases as *That car must have been being driven* by a madman.

Even Chaucer recognized that 'in forme of speche is chaunge'. His famous statement concerning change and variation in language appears in Book II (ll. 22–28) of the fourteenth-century poem *Troilus and Criseyde*, a selection of which may be heard on the companion website (Reading 3). In the previous section, we considered Shakespeare's Early Modern English; Chaucer's Middle English dates from about 200 years earlier. Two forms that are lost by Shakespeare's time are *me nedeth* (l. 11) and *us thinketh* (l. 25). Why do you think the subject of the verb appears as *me* rather than *I* or as *us* rather than *we*? This is an impersonal verbal construction dating from Old English, as we shall discuss in Chapter 7.

Language change is largely uncontrollable. While it is thought that language change can at least be slowed down or inhibited in some way, attempts to do so have proved ineffectual. For example, language academies established in several European countries to direct the course of the language have had little success; languages seem to follow their own inevitable course. However, the rate of change and a language's susceptibility to it do vary and may be reduced by the following factors:

- geographic isolation, which protects a language from foreign influence;
- separation of a group of speakers from the main speech community, which leads to conservatism on the part of speakers who are reluctant to depart from tradition;
- political and social stability, which eliminates the need for linguistic change to meet changing social conditions;
- attitudes of ethnic and linguistic purism, which encourage the vigilance of speakers of a language against external influences and internal change; and
- a strong written tradition.

Because of its permanency, the written form exerts a conservative influence on language: it may brake, prevent, or even reverse changes. In contrast, the spoken form is ephemeral and the source of most changes. Languages therefore undergo rapid change in periods when they are not written down—recall the extensive changes during the early period of Middle English referred to earlier in this chapter. In today's world, we can add mass media as a factor that slows down change, or encourages uniformity. In general, mass communication encourages conformity, while separation encourages diversity.

Icelandic is an example of a language to which almost all of the retarding factors apply. Iceland, an island in the Atlantic Ocean, is geographically isolated. The nation has a history of political stability and promotes strong feelings of linguistic purism; vocabulary borrowings, for example, are actively discouraged, with native formations used in their place. Finally, Icelandic has had a strong, continuous written tradition since the eleventh century. As a consequence, the written form of Modern Icelandic is quite close to that of Old Icelandic or Old Norse (ON) of the eleventh century. Although there have been quite extensive phonological changes, the modern-day speaker can read and understand the ancient texts.

Sometimes people point to signs of natural linguistic change as evidence of the decay or destruction of a language, but the process by which languages die is fundamentally different. In the most common scenario, a more socially prestigious and politically powerful language gradually supplants a resident one. The latter ceases to be spoken by anyone as a native language and later even as a second language. Among the many examples of languages that have died in this way are many Native American languages, which were supplanted by English, Spanish, and French during European colonization, and some of the Celtic languages, which were supplanted by English.

The Arbitrary Nature of the Linguistic Sign

Language change is possible because of the conventional or arbitrary nature of the linguistic sign. As mentioned earlier, language is a system of signs, which may be related to the things they represent in a number of ways. The philosopher C.S. Peirce (1932) recognized three types of signs:

- *iconic* signs, which resemble the things they represent (for example, photographs, diagrams, star charts, or chemical models);
- *indexical* signs, which point to or have a necessary connection with the things they represent (for example, smoke to fire, a weathercock to the direction of the wind, or a symptom to an illness); and
- *symbolic* signs, which are only conventionally related to the things they represent (for example, a flag to a nation or a rose to love).

A very few aspects of language are iconic; onomatopoeic words, such as *cock-a-doodle-do* for the sound of the rooster or *buzz* for the sound of the bee, can be said to resemble the natural sounds they represent (even though they vary across languages and are partially conventionalized). Aspects of word order may also be iconic, as in the sequence *Susie went to Paris, London, and Rome*, where the most natural reading is that she visited the cities in the order listed. Other aspects of language are indexical (or *deictic*) since they point to the things they represent; these include demonstratives (*this/that*) and adverbs (*here/there*) that denote proximity to the speaker in space, tense markers (present/past tense) and adverbs (*now/then*) that denote proximity to the speaker in time, and pronouns (*I/you*) that denote the speaker and hearer.

Most language, however, is symbolic. The relation between the linguistic sign and the thing it represents is conventional or arbitrary. That is, the sequence of sounds constituting a word bears no natural, necessary, logical, or inevitable connection to the thing in the real world that it names. Speakers must agree that it names that thing. In English, for example, we have entered into a tacit social agreement that the word *apple* stands for a particular fruit in the real world; there is no resemblance between the sound of the word and the fruit. Like all conventions or agreements, language can be changed if speakers accept the change. English speakers, for example, could agree to call this fruit by another name. In fact, we frequently agree to substitute one name or another, especially in order to avoid giving offense; for example, *bipolar* has replaced *manic-depressive* as a name of an illness, and in Canada *First Nations* has largely replaced *Indians* as a name for certain Aboriginal peoples (although *Indian* is the official term used in some government legislation and continues to be used occasionally in Canada and to a greater degree in the United States). In a sense, then, language is like any other social agreement, such as conventions of dress or manners, for it can be changed by the general consent of the members of the agreement.

The Origin of Language

While we can say something about why languages change, and even more about how they change (see Chapter 3), we can say almost nothing of substance about how language originated. There is only speculation—and a long history of it—on this topic. In Europe until the eighteenth century, the dominant belief was in the divine origin of language: many readers are familiar with the biblical stories of Adam naming the animals in the Garden of Eden and of Babel, which explains the diversity of human languages. In the eighteenth and nineteenth centuries a number of alternative theories were proposed; the rather amusing names of these speculations suggest that none was given much credence:

- the *bow-wow* theory: words are onomatopoeic or echoic, imitating natural sounds;
- the *pooh-pooh* theory: words originate in the instinctive cries evoked by intense emotion;
- the *ding-dong* theory: words are a kind of natural resonance that humans emit when struck by an impression;
- the *yo-he-ho* theory: words derive from the grunts and groans that humans produce when exerting strong physical effort;
- the *ta-ta* theory: words are the vocal counterpart of certain gestures; and
- the *ta-ra-ra-boom-de-ay* theory: language develops from ritual incantation and dance. (See Simpson 1979:16)

These theories are based on a number of false assumptions. First, they generally see language as originating in iconic or indexical systems (based on resemblance or connection); they do not, however, account for the leap from such systems to the highly sophisticated system of human language based on symbolic representation. Second, they see languages evolving from a primitive to a more complex state. However, we have no evidence for this assumption, since the earliest recorded languages are highly complex, and so-called primitive peoples speak elaborately developed languages (see Chapter 4). Third, they imply that human beings existed—in an advanced stage of their evolution—without language. According to the thinking of contemporary science, the facility for learning language is almost certainly innate, and since language is what sets us apart from the other primates, the language capacity must have evolved along with the human brain. Human culture depends upon language for its transmission.

Exercise 1.4 The Nature of Linguistic Change

1. By listing all the features which would increase the rate of linguistic change, describe the kind of community whose language would be constantly and rapidly evolving.

    _____

    _____

    _____

    _____

    _____

2. Recalling Peirce's three types of signs, give three linguistic examples of each.

    _____

    _____

    _____

    _____

    _____

3. Explain what is meant by the 'arbitrary nature of the linguistic sign'.

    _____

    _____

    _____

    _____

    _____

    _____

Attitudes Toward Linguistic Change

Jean Aitchison (2001) describes three typical views of language change: as slow deterioration from some perfect state; as slow evolution toward a more efficient state; or as neither progress nor decay. While all three views have at times been held, certainly the most prevalent perception among the general population is that change means deterioration.

Linguistic Corruption

To judge from many schoolteachers, authors of letters to editors, and lay writers on language (such as Edwin Newman or William Safire), language change is always bad. It is a matter of linguistic corruption: a language, as it changes, loses its beauty, its expressiveness, its fineness of distinction, even its grammar. According to this view, English has decayed from some state of purity, its golden age, such as the time when Shakespeare was writing, or Milton, or Pope. People may interpret change in the language as the result of ignorance, laziness, sloppiness, insensitivity, weakness, or perhaps willful rebellion on the part of speakers. Their criticism is couched in moralistic and often emotionally laden terms. For example, Jonathan Swift in 1712 asserted that 'our Language is extremely imperfect; that its daily Improvements are by no Means in Proportion to its daily Corruptions; that the Pretenders to polish and refine it, have chiefly multiplied Abuses and Absurdities; and that in many Instances, it offends against every Part of Grammar' (1957:6). Such views have prompted critics to try to prevent the decline of the language, to defend it against change, and to admonish speakers to be more careful and vigilant.

Given the inevitability of linguistic change, attested to by the records of all known languages, why is this concept of deterioration so prevalent? One reason is a sense of nostalgia and a tendency to resist change of every kind, especially in a world that seems out of control. As speakers of our language, we feel that we are the best judges of it, and furthermore that it is something that we, in a sense, possess and can control.

A second reason is a concern for linguistic purity. Language may be the most overt indicator of our ethnic and national identity; when we feel that these are threatened, often by external forces, we seek to defend them by protecting our language. Tenets of linguistic purity have not been influential in the history of the English language, which has quite freely accepted foreign elements into it and is now spoken by many different peoples throughout the world. But these feelings are never entirely absent. We see them, for example, in concerns about the Americanization of Canadian or of British English.

A third reason is social class prejudice. Standard English is the social dialect of the educated middle and upper-middle classes. To belong to these classes and to advance socially, one must speak this dialect. The standard is a means of excluding people from these classes and preserving social barriers. Deviations from the standard (which are non-standard or substandard) threaten the social structure.

Fourth is a belief in the superiority of highly inflected languages such as Latin and Greek. The loss of inflections, which has characterized change in the English language, is therefore considered bad. A final reason for the belief that change equals deterioration stems from an admiration for the written form. Because written language is more fixed and unchanging than speech, some conclude that the spoken form in use today is fundamentally inferior.

Of the other typical views toward language change, the view that it represents a slow evolution toward some higher state finds expression in the work of nineteenth-century philologists, who saw language as an evolving organism. The Danish linguist Otto Jespersen, in his book *Growth and Structure of the English Language* (1982 [1905]), suggested that the increasingly analytic nature of English resulted in 'simplification' and hence 'improvement' to the language. Leith (1997:260) also argues that the historical study of English was motivated by a desire to demonstrate a literary continuity from Old English to the present, resulting in the misleading impression that the language has steadily evolved and improved toward a standard variety worthy of literary expression. The third view, that language change represents the status quo, neither progress nor decay, where every simplification is balanced by some new complexity, underlies the work of historical linguistics in the twentieth century and forms the basis of our text.

Prescriptivism versus Descriptivism

Underlying the view of language change as decay is a belief in a fixed standard of usage and a *prescriptive* approach to grammar. These notions arose in the eighteenth century, as we will see later. A prescriptive grammar *prescribes* (dictates) and *proscribes* (forbids) certain ways of speaking and writing. It attempts to establish and maintain a standard of correctness and to legislate usage.

In contrast, a *descriptive* grammar explains or analyzes how language works or is used, without making value judgments. It is only in a prescriptive sense that we can talk about good grammar or bad grammar, for in a descriptive sense, grammar is simply the set of rules or principles by which a language operates; all grammars in this sense are equally effective, and no language can be without one. The difference between descriptive grammars and prescriptive grammars is comparable to the difference between constitutive rules, which determine how something works, such as the rules for the game of chess, and regulatory rules, which control behavior, such as the rules of etiquette. If the former are violated, the game cannot work—or it becomes something different; if the latter are violated, social interaction continues but may be seen as crude, awkward, or rude. Prescriptive grammar dictates the forms that people should use, while descriptive grammar describes the forms that people actually use. We will consider the origin of prescriptive approaches to grammar and usage in Chapter 11, but note that in this text, the term *grammar* will always be used in a descriptive sense.

Exercise 1.5 Attitudes Toward Linguistic Change

Discuss briefly the dominant attitude toward language change, mentioning the three typical views of change and describing the basic differences between prescriptive and descriptive grammars.

_____

_____

_____

_____

_____

_____

_____

Resources for Studying the History of English

Study of the history of any language begins with its texts. In order to meet the need for records of early English, F.J. Furnivall (one of the editors of the *Oxford English Dictionary*) founded the Early English Text Society (EETS) in 1864 and the Chaucer Society in 1868. These societies helped make previously inaccessible manuscripts available to scholars by publishing these rare texts (Knowles 1997:141). Through Oxford University Press, the EETS continues to publish texts to this day, having produced close to five hundred titles, including poetry, prose, drama, court documents (wills, trial records), commercial records, and public and private letters, all of which exemplify literary and non-literary language over a vast period. This material allows the study of English in its earlier periods and contrastively as it changes over time. Increasingly, a wealth of primary and secondary material has become available online or electronically. Secondary resources include dictionaries of current English along with etymological dictionaries and period dictionaries, historical grammars of English, and concordances (word lists) to the works of major early authors. Corpora (collections of texts) spanning the history of English have also been assembled. The following discussion provides a brief introduction to some of these materials:

General Dictionaries

There are countless dictionaries of the English language. Because of its comprehensiveness, the premier dictionary of English is the *Oxford English Dictionary* (available in a third edition online, as well as earlier CD-ROM and print versions), which is based on historical usage, tracing the meanings of words from their earliest appearance in the language and illustrating usage with textual quotations (see further, Chapter 12). The recently completed *Historical Thesaurus of the Oxford English*

Dictionary (Kay et al. 2009) offers a conceptual classification of nearly one million words from an historical perspective; all the synonyms or words related to a concept may be traced chronologically from the time of Old English to the present day.

The American Heritage Dictionary of the English Language (2000) includes usage notes based on the judgments of a panel of experts and reliable etymological information which traces words back to their Indo-European roots. A ground-breaking dictionary first appearing in 1961 was *Webster's Third New International Dictionary of the English Language Unabridged*, noteworthy for its citation of the full range of English vocabulary, including slang, non-standard, and 'vulgar' terms as well as variant pronunciations. Its refusal to censor this vocabulary was highly controversial at the time. Other dictionaries are devoted to particular dialects of English, e.g. the *Canadian Oxford Dictionary* (2004).

There are many shorter dictionaries of English (such as so-called 'college' and 'desk' dictionaries) that may not contain the number of vocabulary entries nor the range of features found in the dictionaries mentioned above; these usually offer reduced coverage of etymologies, rare or obsolete meanings, and illustrative examples.

Historical and Etymological Dictionaries

Dictionaries of the historical periods of English are available. The *Dictionary of Old English* is currently being written at the University of Toronto: volumes A to G have appeared to date. An older but still invaluable dictionary of Old English is Bosworth and Toller's *An Anglo-Saxon Dictionary* (1898/1921). After many years of work, the monumental *Middle English Dictionary* (1952–2003), modeled on the *Oxford English Dictionary*, has been completed at the University of Michigan and is available online. Both the Old and Middle English dictionaries define words from the existing texts of the period. For the Early Modern English period, Schmidt's 1902 *Shakespeare-Lexicon* is available in a 1971 Dover reprint, but the *Oxford English Dictionary* remains the essential lexicographic work.

The best sources on the etymology of English vocabulary are *The American Heritage Dictionary*, Klein (1969), and Lieberman (2008), as well as the *Oxford English Dictionary*. Accessible to the lay reader is *The Barnhart Dictionary of Etymology* (1988). Calvert Watkins's appendix to *The American Heritage Dictionary* (expanded and published separately, 2000) is an excellent source of information on the Indo-European roots of English. Entries in the dictionary are coordinated with those of the appendix.

Historical Grammar and Syntax

Several multi-volume grammars of English offer historical explanations and context. Jespersen's *A Modern English Grammar on Historical Principles* (1928–49) and Poutsma's *A Grammar of Late Modern English* (1904–26) are particularly thorough and insightful discussions. Visser's *An Historical Syntax of the English Language* (1963–73) records the syntactic development of English in full detail.

Concordances and Historical Corpora

Concordances, which allow us to study the use and patterning of words by individual writers, exist for the works of many canonical authors in English. Important for historical research are the concordances of Chaucer (Oizumi's *A Complete Concordance to the Works of Geoffrey Chaucer*, 1991–2) and Shakespeare (Spevack's *A Complete and Systematic Concordance to the Works of Shakespeare*, 1968–70). A concordance to the entire Old English corpus exists on microfiche and is serving as the basis for ongoing dictionary work.

More recently, historical corpora have become available electronically. Important corpora may be accessed through the Electronic Text Center of the University of Virginia (http://etext.virginia.edu/collections/languages/english/) and the Humanities Text Initiative of the University of Michigan (http://www.hti. umich.edu/index-all.html), which includes corpora of Middle English and Early Modern English (http://www.hti.umich.edu/m/memem/), as well as many other sets of texts. These resources allow us to search for words more quickly and easily than concordances do; they have the advantage of permitting us to search for phrases and word combinations and to see these in context. The *International Computer Archive of Modern and Medieval English (ICAME) Collection of English Language Corpora* (1999) (http://icame.uib.no/newcd.htm), compiled at the University of Bergen and available on CD-ROM, contains a large number of different corpora, both historical and modern, spoken and written. The pioneer historical corpus of English, the Helsinki Corpus, is available as part of the ICAME collection. A corpus of historical American English (http://corpus.byu.edu/coha/) is now available freely online. Many libraries have also purchased the Chadwyck-Healey collections, which cover a wide range of historical periods and genres and allow for keyword searches. Check your university library for Early English Books Online (EEBO) (see http://www.proquest.com/en-US/catalogs/databases/detail/eebo.shtml) or for Literature Online (LION) (see http://lion.chadwyck.com/). The second and third editions of the *Oxford English Dictionary* can be electronically searched and used as a database for word studies in the history of English. Finally, many corpora of Modern English are available online, such as the British National Corpus (http://www.natcorp.ox.ac.uk/), the Michigan Corpus of Academic Spoken English (http://quod.lib.umich.edu/m/micase), the Corpus of Contemporary American English (http://www.americancorpus.org/), and the Corpus of Historical American English (http://corpus.byu.edu/coha/).

Exercise 1.6 *Oxford English Dictionary*

In order to familiarize yourself with the *Oxford English Dictionary*, answer the following questions. If you are using the online version of the dictionary, you will want to consult the 'Guide to *OED* Entries' (http://dictionary.oed.com/about/guide/). The print version has a preface entitled 'General Explanation' which can direct you through the information presented in each entry.

1. The first use of the word *sandwich* is in 1762. In this quotation, the word is capitalized. Why is this? Explain on the basis of the word's etymology.

   _____

   _____

2. Is the word *booty* related to the word *boot* 'shoe'?

   _____

   _____

3. If you look up the word *quiz,* you will find many definitions for the noun and more than one entry for the verb. Which definition means 'an oral exam'?

   _____

   _____

4. What language does the word *slogan* derive from? What is its earliest meaning in English? When is the last recorded use of the word with this meaning in the *OED*?

   _____

   _____

5. The word *stomach* has a complex route of transmission into English. Trace this route.

   _____

   _____

6. What is the earliest spelling for the word *eerie*? When did it first occur with its modern spelling?

   _____

   _____

7. List two obsolete meanings of the word *nice.*

   _____

   _____

8. Give the positive and negative connotations of the word *ritzy.*

   _____

   _____

RECOMMENDED WEB LINKS

The following sites give general overviews of the web resources in the history of the English language:

> http://www.uni-due.de/SHE (Raymond Hickey's web page)
> http://ebbs.english.vt.edu/hel/hel.html (D.W. Mosser's web page)
> http://www.towson.edu/~duncan/hellinks.html (Edward Duncan's web page)

The following site provides links to a wide spectrum of sites associated with English literature:

> http://andromeda.rutgers.edu/~jlynch/Lit/

This website provides further definitions of linguistic terminology:

> http://www.ucl.ac.uk/internet-grammar/frames/glossary.htm

The Survey of English (University of London) maintains an online grammar of Modern English:

> http://www.ucl.ac.uk/internet-grammar/

'Glottopedia', a free dictionary of linguistics (modeled on Wikipedia) that is under the direction of Martin Haspelmath, is:

> http://www.glottopedia.de/index.php/Main_Page

FURTHER READING

An extremely interesting, very readable, and beautifully produced account of the English language is:

> Crystal, David. 2003. *The Cambridge Encyclopedia of the English Language*. 2nd edn. Cambridge: Cambridge University Press.

The standard reference work on the history of English is:

> *The Cambridge History of English*. 1992–1999. Vols. I–VI (Vol. I ed. by Richard M. Hogg, Vol. II ed. by Norman Blake, Vol. III ed. by Roger Lass, Vol. IV ed. by Suzanne Romaine, Vol. V ed. by Robert Burchfield, Vol. VI ed. by John Algeo). Cambridge: Cambridge University Press.

Traditional and more contemporary textbooks of the history of English include:

> Algeo, John. 2010. *The Origins and Development of the English Language*. Based on the original work of Thomas Pyles. 6th edn. Boston: Thomson-Wadsworth.
> Barber, Charles, Joan C. Beal, and Philip A. Shaw. 2009. *The English Language: A Historical Introduction*. 2nd edn. Cambridge: Cambridge University Press.
> Baugh, Albert C., and Thomas Cable. 2002. *A History of the English Language*. 5th edn. Upper Saddle River, NJ: Prentice Hall.
> Gelderen, Elly van. 2006. *A History of the English Language*. Amsterdam and Philadelphia: John Benjamins.

Millward, C.M. 1996. *A Biography of the English Language*. 2nd edn. Fort Worth: Harcourt Brace.

Singh, Ishtla. 2005. *The History of English: A Student's Guide*. London: Hodder Arnold.

For more on English as a global language, see:

Crystal, David. 2006. 'English Worldwide'. *A History of the English Language*. Ed. by Richard M. Hogg and David Denison, 420–39. Cambridge: Cambridge University Press.

Romaine, Suzanne. 1999. 'Introduction'. *The Cambridge History of the English Language. Vol. IV: 1776–1997*. Ed. by Suzanne Romaine, 1–56. Cambridge: Cambridge University Press.

The most complete contemporary grammars of English include:

Biber, Douglas, Stig Johansson, Geoffrey Leech, Susan Conrad, and Edward Finegan. 1999. *Longman Grammar of Spoken and Written English*. Harlow: Pearson.

Huddleston, Rodney, and Geoffrey K. Pullum. 2002. *The Cambridge Grammar of the English Language*. Cambridge: Cambridge University Press.

Quirk, Randolph, Sidney Greenbaum, Geoffrey Leech, and Jan Svartvik. 1985. *A Comprehensive Grammar of the English Language*. London and New York: Longman.

For a basic introduction to linguistics, see:

Finegan, Edward. 2008. *Language: Its Structure and Use*. 5th edn. Boston: Thomson-Wadsworth.

Fromkin, Victoria, Robert Rodman, and Nina Hyams. 2007. *An Introduction to Language*. 8th edn. Toronto: Harcourt Canada.

An introduction to English linguistics is:

Brinton, Laurel J., and Donna M. Brinton. 2010. *The Linguistic Structure of Modern English*. Amsterdam and Philadelphia: John Benjamins.

Curzan, Anne, and Michael Adams. 2009. *How English Works: A Linguistic Introduction*. 2nd edn. New York: Pearson.

Helpful introductions to morphology, syntax, semantics, and pragmatics include:

Bauer, Laurie. 1983. *English Word-Formation*. Cambridge: Cambridge University Press.

Carstairs-McCarthy, Andrew. 2002. *An Introduction to English Morphology: Words and Their Structure*. Edinburgh: Edinburgh University Press.

Griffiths, Patrick. 2006. *An Introduction to English Semantics and Pragmatics*. Edinburgh: Edinburgh University Press.

Kreidler, Charles W. 1998. *Introducing English Semantics*. London and New York: Routledge.

Mey, Jacob. 2001. *Pragmatics: An Introduction*. 2nd edn. Malden, MA and Oxford: Blackwell.

Morenberg, Max. 2002. *Doing Grammar*. 3rd edn. Oxford and New York: Oxford University Press.

A useful dictionary of linguistic terms and concepts is:

Crystal, David. 2008. *A Dictionary of Linguistics and Phonetics*. 6th edn. New York: Wiley Blackwell.

More information on electronic corpora and corpus linguistics can be found in:

Biber, Douglas, Susan Conrad, and Randi Reppen. 1998. *Corpus Linguistics: Investigating Language Structure and Use*. Cambridge: Cambridge University Press.

FURTHER VIEWING

A video introduction to linguistic study is:

Discovering the Human Language: Colorless Green Ideas, from *The Human Language Series*. South Carolina ETV, Equinox Films, 1995.

For an exploration of various theories of language origin, see:

Episode 1: 'Let There Be Words'. *Speaking in Tongues: The History of Language*. Directed and researched by Christene Browne. Toronto: Syncopated Productions, 2007.

A lavishly produced series of eight programs on the history of English language, stronger, perhaps, on the external history of the language than on its linguistic aspects, is:

The Adventure of English: 500 AD to 2000 AD. Written and produced by Melvyn Bragg. London: LWT Production for Granada International, 2002–3.

The Sounds
and Writing
of English

OVERVIEW

This chapter introduces the sounds used in English speech and the use of the phonetic alphabet in transcribing English vowels and consonants. We then review the system of accent and stress in the language. The second part of the chapter explores the history of writing and the development of the English alphabet.

OBJECTIVES

The primary objective in this chapter is to learn the rudiments of English phonology. After completing this chapter, you should be able to

- identify the consonant and vowel sounds of English;
- understand the accentual system;
- describe how to articulate a sound represented by a phonetic symbol and be able to produce that sound; and
- transcribe Modern English words phonetically with the stressed syllable marked, and pronounce Modern English given in broad transcription.

This knowledge will later enable you to comprehend the sound systems at earlier stages of the language and the types of sound changes that have occurred. You will also understand what it means to say that our writing system is alphabetical and be able to trace the origin of the alphabet.

The Sounds of English

The Phonetic Alphabet

It would be very difficult to discuss the sounds of English with only the orthographic symbols (the letters of the alphabet) used in writing. There is an imperfect correspondence between the written symbols and the sounds they represent. One letter may stand for a variety of sounds:

c   *c̲ar*, *c̲ity*, *c̲ello*
a   *a̲pe*, *sa̲t*, *wa̲s*, *fa̲ther*

Conversely, one sound may be represented by a variety of letters:

[f]   *f̲ollow*, *p̲h̲one*, *coug̲h̲*, *of̲f̲*
[i]   *m̲e̲at*, *ke̲y̲*, *e̲vil*, *prett̲y̲*, *m̲e̲et*, *pe̲ople*, *ce̲iling*

As you can see, there is a great variety of ways in which each of the sounds of English is written. A number of factors contribute to this disparity between sound and symbol, including sound changes in the history of English such as the Great Vowel Shift (see Chapter 10), the influence of French-speaking scribes (see Chapter 8), loan words, and the conservative nature of the writing system. We are all familiar with complaints about the inconsistency of English spelling. However, Leith (1997:36) comments that one of the 'strengths' of English spelling is that it favors no one dialect—'we are all equally disadvantaged by it.'

Thus, to signify pronunciation, we need to use a *phonetic alphabet*, a system in which each symbol represents only one sound, and each sound is represented by only one symbol. The recording of speech using a phonetic alphabet is called *transcription*. In the sections that follow, as a means of transcription, we will use the International Phonetic Alphabet (IPA), which uses a mixture of some symbols from the Latin and Greek alphabets, some symbols used in writing Old English, and some that are specially invented. There are variant versions of the IPA; this textbook uses a modified American system. When we use a phonetic symbol, we indicate that we are representing a sound rather than a spelling by enclosing the symbol in square brackets [ ] or virgules (slashes) / / (the difference between these is discussed below).

The Phoneme

Before we look specifically at the sounds of English, we need to introduce a basic concept of phonological study: the phoneme. A phoneme is a distinctive sound that makes a difference in the meaning of a word. For instance, the words *peat, pit, pate, pet, pat, putt, put,* and *pout* are pronounced identically except for one sound. The first and last consonants are the same, and only the vowel differs. One way to isolate phonemes is to focus on two words, such as *peat* and *pat*, that are distinguished by a single sound. We call these two words a *minimal pair*. We conclude that all of the medial vowel sounds in the series are phonemes, since they change the meaning of the word. Similarly, the series of words *pat, bat, cat, sat, mat, gnat, fat, that, vat, chat*, and *rat* contains minimal pairs, since the vowel and final consonant are the same and only the initial consonant differs. The initial consonants are thus all phonemes as well.

Strictly speaking, phonemes are abstractions representing classes of sounds, called allophones ('other sounds'). These are variants of phonemes that are actually spoken. In contrast to phonemes, allophones do not make a difference in meaning. We therefore describe them as *nondistinctive*. For example, the [t] sounds in *top* and *stop* are slightly different: the first is followed by a slight puff of air (or *aspiration*), whereas the second is not. Whether the [t] is aspirated or not is entirely predictable by the position of the sound in the word and by the surrounding sounds, known as the *phonetic environment*. Moreover, if *top* were pronounced with an unaspirated [t], or *stop* with an aspirated [t], we would not produce different words, just slightly odd-sounding words. Hence, the aspirated and unaspirated [t] are allophones of one distinctive sound, which we record as /t/.

Similarly, the [k] sounds in *cat* and *cot* are slightly different: the first is pronounced with the tongue more forward in the mouth than the second. The type of [k] we pronounce, however, is entirely dependent on the quality of the vowel that follows and does not change the meaning of the word. Therefore, these are simply allophones of the phoneme /k/. The [l] sounds in *look* and *feel* are likewise articulated with the tongue either farther forward or farther back in the mouth, respectively. Note that the use of the different [l] sounds is predictable because it depends on the position of the sound in the word, here whether it is initial or final. This is an important feature of allophones: they are predictable variants of a phoneme that occur in certain phonetic environments. All of the allophones of a phoneme count as the same sound and are described as being members of the same class or set.

It is worth noticing how these phonemes and allophones are distributed. When we looked at minimal pairs above, such as *peat* and *pat*, we focused on their medial vowels. The vowels are said to be in 'parallel distribution' because they occur in the same position in each word. Allophones, as we have seen, depend on their particular phonetic environment: they must either show up in different positions (as with [l] in *look* and *feel*) or be surrounded by different sounds (as with [k] in *cat* and *cot*). Where one allophone occurs, the other does not, so they are said to be in *complementary distribution*. They are mutually exclusive.

Allophones and phonemes are transcribed differently. The normal way to represent an allophone or other nuance of pronunciation is to enclose the phonetic symbol in square brackets, as in [tʰ] for the aspirated 't' sound. This is called *narrow transcription*. In its counterpart, *broad transcription*, the phonetic symbol is enclosed in slashes, as in /t/. As broad transcription records the larger characteristics of speech and represents phonemes, it can also be called *phonemic transcription*. In the history of the language, certain sounds have undergone a change from predictable variant to contrastive sound—that is, from allophone to phoneme—and so to avoid confusion we enclose all of our transcriptions in square brackets.

The Production of Speech

Speech is an adaptation of the respiratory system for the purposes of communication. We produce English speech sounds when we exhale. The stream of air moves from the lungs through the trachea, and then passes through the larynx (or voice box), entering the vocal tract, where it is shaped by the articulators (the tongue, the teeth, the roof of the mouth, the lips). See the diagram of the organs of speech given in Figure 2.1. We will refer specifically to the functions of the articulators when we describe how consonants and vowels are formed.

In practice, one discrete speech sound leads into another, producing a continuous sequence or chain of sound known as a *phonetic continuum*. For analysis, however, we often break the speech chain into syllables. A syllable consists of a nucleus, a vowel or vowel-like sound that is the most prominent part of the syllable phonetically. Along with the nucleus we find associated consonants. Superimposed on the syllable are the features of stress and intonation. We will now examine the sounds individually, beginning with consonants.

Consonants

Consonants are speech sounds articulated with a certain amount of constriction of the airflow that has come from the lungs through the trachea. They are classified by four qualities: voicing, orality/nasality, place of articulation, and manner of articulation.

Voicing refers to the state of the vocal cords, which are two muscles found in the larynx. The vocal cords may be tensed and set in motion, opening and closing

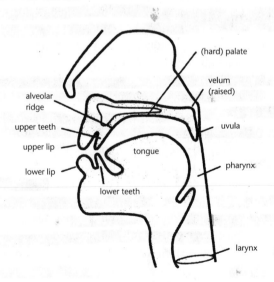

Figure 2.1 The Organs of Speech

rapidly, vibrating against one another. When they are vibrating, the sound produced is called *voiced*; when they are relatively open and still, the sound produced is called *voiceless*. You can feel the vocal cords vibrate by placing your fingers against your Adam's apple or cupping your hands over your ears and saying the two sounds *s* and *z* in sequence (these are the sounds at the end of *bus* and *buzz*, respectively). The first sound is voiceless and you should not feel any vibration, but the second sound is voiced and you should feel a slight vibration.

The *orality* or *nasality* of the sound refers to the tract through which the air passes. If the soft palate (or velum), which is a muscular flap on the roof of the mouth in the back, is raised up against the back of the throat (or pharynx), passage into the nose (the nasal tract) is blocked off; air is then allowed to pass only through the mouth (the oral tract). The sound produced is called an *oral sound*. However, if the velum is relaxed or lowered, air is allowed to pass into the nasal cavity. We produce a *nasal sound* when we block off the oral tract so that air passes only through the nasal tract. We can also allow air to pass through both the nasal and the oral tracts, producing what is called a 'nasalized' sound. The majority of sounds in English are oral; although nasalized sounds occur, they are not distinctive (in the sense of altering a meaning) as they are in French or Portuguese.

The term *place of articulation* refers to the place where the air is constricted when a consonant is articulated—specifically, the position of the lips or the tongue in respect to the teeth or the roof of the mouth. Working from the front to the back of the mouth, the following places of articulation are used in English to restrict the flow of air:

- *bilabial* – The lips are brought together.
- *labiodental* – The lower lip is brought up against the upper teeth.
- *interdental* – The tongue protrudes slightly between the upper and lower teeth or touches the back of the upper teeth.
- *alveolar* – The tip of the tongue is brought to the ridge on the roof of the mouth behind the upper teeth called the alveolar ridge.
- *alveolopalatal* – The front of the tongue is brought to the area on the roof of the mouth just behind the alveolar ridge.
- *palatal* – The front of the tongue is brought to the high domed area of the roof of the mouth, called the hard palate.
- *velar* – The back of the tongue is brought to the back area of the roof of the mouth, called the velum, or soft palate.
- *glottal* – The vocal cords are brought together and function as articulators.

The term *manner of articulation* refers to the amount and type of restriction in the airflow which occurs when a consonant is articulated. The following manners of articulation are used in English:

- *stop (oral stop)* – The flow of air through the oral tract is blocked by completely closing the articulators; the velum is raised, and no air passes through the nasal tract either.

- *nasal* (*nasal stop*) – The flow of air through the oral tract is blocked by completely closing the articulators, but at the same time the velum is lowered to allow air to flow out the nasal tract.
- *fricative* – The flow of air is constricted by bringing the articulators close enough to create turbulence or friction (a hissing sound) but not so close that complete obstruction of the airflow occurs.
- *affricate* – The complete blockage of airflow characteristic of a stop is followed by a constricted passage of airflow characteristic of a fricative; a stop is released slowly into a fricative (some linguists analyze affricates as the sum of two sounds).
- *approximant* – The flow of air is not constricted in the central part of the mouth; the articulators only *approximate*, or come close to, one another but do not come sufficiently close to create turbulence.

As if that were not enough terminology, approximants are further divided into *liquids* and *glides*. The liquids include the lateral, which is articulated by closing off the flow of air in the central portion of the mouth but allowing the flow of air around the sides, and the retroflex, which is articulated by curling the tip of the tongue back slightly toward the roof of the mouth. To articulate glides, the tongue moves from one position to another with a relatively unrestricted flow of air. Glides are sometimes called *semivowels* because they correspond in articulation to vowels, but they are technically consonants because they begin or end syllables.

Consonants are traditionally described in terms of their voicing quality first, followed by their place of articulation and finally their manner of articulation. Linguists use a grid to record the phonetic symbols representing the consonants (see Figure 2.2), with place of articulation as the horizontal axis and manner of articulation as the vertical axis. It may help to visualize the consonant chart as an abstract view of the mouth in side profile, with the lips and nose to the left and the back of the mouth to the right. The top of the chart represents the maximum closure of the mouth, and the bottom its maximum opening. Theoretically, there could be a symbol in every box in the grid (though practically, some of these sounds would be difficult or even impossible to articulate). Every language uses only a limited set of the possible consonant sounds. Figure 2.2 displays the consonants of Present-Day English, with the addition of four sounds found in historical stages of the language.

The Consonant Sounds of English

We will look now at the different ways of articulating consonants, beginning with the class called *stops*. English has three pairs of stops, each consisting of a voiceless and a voiced counterpart. The first pair of stops is made by bringing the lips together and is therefore called *bilabial*. These stops are represented by the IPA symbols *p* and *b*. If you were to pronounce the stop [p] by itself, you would in fact not hear it because the air is stopped completely. We hear stops only when we release them by

Manner of Articulation

Manner of Articulation		Place of Articulation							
		Bilabial	Labiodental	Interdental	Alveolar	Alveolo-palatal	Palatal	Velar	Glottal
Stop	Voiceless	p			t			k	ʔ
	Voiced	b			d			g	
Nasal		m			n			ŋ	
Flap					ɾ				
Fricative	Voiceless		f	θ	s	š	ç	x	h
	Voiced	β	v	ð	z	ž		ɣ	
Affricate	Voiceless					č			
	Voiced					ǰ			
Approximant	Lateral				l				
	Retroflex				r				
	Glide (or Semivowel)						j	w	

Figure 2.2 The Consonants of English and Germanic (Note: Symbols displayed in gray represent sounds found only in Germanic and Old and Middle English.)

opening the articulators; then they are called *plosives*. The bilabial plosives have the following sounds: [p] for the voiceless, as in *pat*, *tap*, *open*, and [b] for the voiced, as in *bat*, *tab*, *labor*.

The next pair of stops is made by bringing the tip of the tongue against the alveolar ridge and is therefore called *alveolar*. The alveolar stops are represented by the IPA symbols *t* and *d*. When these are released as plosives, they make the voiceless [t] sound, as in *tell*, *eat*, *after*, and the voiced [d] sound, as in *dome*, *mad*, *rudder*. Note that when [t] occurs between vowels, most North American speakers (in normal, unselfconscious speech) produce a voiced sound, rather than a voiceless sound; this is called a flap [ɾ]. For these speakers, pairs of words such as *bitter/bidder*, *metal/medal*, and *coated/coded* are homophones (that is, they are pronounced the same).

The final pair of stops is made by bringing the back part of the tongue up against the velum and is therefore called *velar*. The voiceless velar stop is represented by the IPA symbol *k* and the voiced velar stop by the IPA symbol g. When released as plosives, the voiceless sound is [k], as in *cat*, *lock*, *tickle*, and the voiced sound [g], as in *good*, *log*, *rugged*. These sounds are actually made over quite a range, from the palatal to the velar region. We articulate the [k] sounds in *keep*, *cape*, and *cap* more in the palatal region, while the ones in *coop*, *cope*, and *cop* are articulated more in the velar region. However, these variations do not make a difference in meaning: they are allophonic rather than phonemic.

English also has one unpaired stop—the glottal stop—which is articulated by bringing the vocal cords together to close off the flow of air. This is the sound found twice in the negative *uh-uh* following the vowel. It is represented by a symbol that resembles a question mark [ʔ].

The next class of consonant sounds is the *nasals*. These have the same place of articulation as the stops, differing only in having the velum lowered so that air can pass out through the nose. The nasals are all voiced. The bilabial nasal corresponding to [b] is [m], as in *mad*, *thumb*, *timer*, represented by the IPA symbol *m*. The alveolar nasal corresponding to [d] is [n], as in *nose*, *tin*, *liner*, represented by the IPA symbol *n*. To feel the velum lowering, put your tongue into position to say a [d] and then say [n]. The last nasal is the velar nasal, represented by the symbol called *eng*, which is an *n* with a tail: [ŋ]. To make this sound, put your tongue into position to pronounce a [g] and then lower the velum. Doing this in isolation can be rather difficult for English speakers since the sound never begins a word in English. It is the medial sound in *singer* and the final sound in *king*.

English is unusual among languages in that it has a very large and diverse class of *fricatives*. These all occur in voiced/voiceless pairs except for *h*. The first pair found in Modern English—the labiodental—is made by bringing the lower lip up against the upper teeth and restricting but not quite cutting off the flow of air. The voiceless labiodental fricative is represented by the IPA symbol *f*, the voiced labiodental fricative by the IPA symbol *v*. They have the following sounds: [f] as in *farm*, *off*, *offer*, and [v] as in *vat*, *love*, *over*.

The second pair of fricatives—the interdental—is made by protruding the tip of the tongue between the upper and lower teeth, or by putting the tongue against the back of the upper teeth. The voiceless interdental fricative is represented by the IPA symbol theta θ (from the Greek letter theta). The voiced interdental fricative is represented by the IPA symbol called *eth* or barred *d*: ð. The sound [θ] occurs in *thin*, *froth*, *author*, while the voiced [ð] occurs in *that*, *lathe*, *lather*. The difference between the voiceless and voiced interdental fricatives is sometimes difficult to hear. Say the following sets of words and listen carefully to the distinction (the fricative is voiceless in the first word and voiced in the second): *bath/bathe*, *ether/either*, and *thin/then*.

The third pair of fricatives—the alveolar—is made by bringing the tip of the tongue close to the alveolar ridge. The voiceless alveolar fricative, represented by the IPA symbol *s*, is pronounced [s], as in *sin*, *miss*, *blister*, and the voiced alveolar fricative, represented by the IPA symbol *z*, is pronounced [z], as in *zoo*, *Oz*, *miser*.

The fourth pair of fricatives—the alveolopalatal—is made by bringing the tongue up toward the region between the alveolar ridge and the palate. They are represented by the IPA symbols *š* and *ž*, with 'wedges' (or háčeks) above them; thus the symbols are called 'wedge *s*' or 'wedge *z*'. The voiceless alveolopalatal fricative is pronounced [š], as in *shirt*, *mesh*, *mission*, and the voiced alveolopalatal fricative [ž], as in *genre*, *beige*, *measure*. To perceive the position of your tongue more clearly, first say [s] and then [š], noting how the tongue moves back. You will also note that your lips round; this is called *labialization*. Now say the voiced versions, [z] and then [ž]: you should observe the same two changes. The sound [ž] never begins a word in English except those borrowed from French, such as *genre* or *gendarme*, and other languages.

The last fricative in Modern English is the voiceless glottal fricative represented by the IPA symbol *h* and pronounced [h], as in *hat*. The 'h' sound is analyzed by some linguists as a voiceless glottal fricative (made by bringing the vocal cords close together), but by others as a breathing sound made before a vowel, or a *voiceless approximant*.

In addition to the symbols for fricatives in Modern English, we must discuss four symbols for fricatives found in earlier stages of the language but subsequently lost. One is the voiced bilabial fricative represented by the IPA symbol β (the Greek letter beta). To make this sound, put your lips together as if you were articulating [b], but open them slightly. You will feel a slight vibration in your lips. This sound is found today in other languages, as in the second *v* in the Spanish word *vivir* ('to live'). Other important symbols represent the palatal and velar fricatives. The voiceless velar fricative is represented by the IPA symbol *x*, and is the sound [x] found in the German *Bach* and the Scottish *loch*. Practice making it by putting your tongue into position for [k] but allowing some air to pass through. Because the sound is not found in Modern English (except in Scottish Standard English), English speakers often approximate it with [k]. A slightly more forward version of this sound is found in the German word *ich*; this is the voiceless palatal fricative, represented by the IPA symbol ç (called *c*-cedilla), a letter used in the writing of French. Finally, the voiced velar fricative is the sound found in German *Bogen*, and is written with the IPA symbol ɣ (the IPA symbol differs slightly from Greek gamma). It is pronounced like a [g] but with some escape of air.

The next class of sounds found in Modern English is the *affricates*. We have one pair of voiceless and voiced alveolopalatal affricates. The voiceless is represented by the IPA symbol č and the voiced by a ǰ. The sound [č] occurs in <u>ch</u>ur<u>ch</u>, it<u>ch</u>, pit<u>ch</u>er; [ǰ] occurs in <u>j</u>u<u>dge</u>, a<u>ge</u>, lo<u>dge</u>r. (These sounds are actually complex sounds consisting of a stop released into a fricative: [č] is [t] followed by [š], while [ǰ] is [d] followed by [ž]. If you say the separate sounds in increasingly rapid succession you will produce the affricates: [t][š] > [tš] > [č]; [d][ž] > [dž] > [ǰ].

The remaining consonants, known as the *approximants*, are all voiced. Two approximants are classified as liquids and two as glides. The first liquid is the alveolar lateral, represented by the IPA symbol *l* and pronounced as in <u>l</u>ot, a<u>ll</u>, ru<u>l</u>er.[1] The second liquid, the alveolar retroflex, is produced by curling the tip of the tongue back in the mouth and is represented by the IPA symbol *r*. This sound [r] is found in <u>r</u>oad, ti<u>r</u>e, fe<u>r</u>al.

The two glides in English are represented by the IPA symbols *j* and *w*. The first, [j], is palatal, as in <u>y</u>ear, while the second, [w], is velar, as in <u>w</u>on. The velar glide is more precisely analyzed as labiovelar since in addition to the tongue being raised in the velar region, the lips are also noticeably rounded. Some speakers also produce a voiceless labiovelar fricative in words such as *where* and *which*. This will be transcribed [hw] (though the IPA symbol is ʍ). If you pronounce *where/wear* and *which/witch* the same, then you use [w] in both.

Consonants generally serve to begin and end a syllable, with a vowel being the high point, or nucleus, of the syllable. Certain consonants, however, may stand alone in a syllable without a vowel; these function as vowels and are said to have a *syllabic function*. The nasals [m, n] and the liquids [l, r] may all function syllabically, as in the second syllables of pris<u>m</u>, butto<u>n</u>, bott<u>le</u>, and butt<u>er</u>, where there is no vowel sound (even though the word may be spelled with a vowel), only the consonant. The nasal [ŋ] rarely has a syllabic function, though you might use it in the second syllable of *Jack and Jill* in rapid speech. A syllabic consonant is indicated by a tick under the letter: [,] as in [l̩], [r̩], or [n̩].

---

1 At the beginning of words, we find a 'clear *l*' as in *look, life, laugh,* and *lot*. In contrast, the variant found after vowels and [r], as in *feel, pull, meal,* and *pearl,* is known as the 'dark *l*', because it is articulated deep in the velar region. Say the words *look* and *cool* and note the position of your tongue. The variation between the clear and dark *l* is merely allophonic, making no difference in meaning (so not transcribed here).

Exercise 2.1 Consonants

Three cautions are necessary before beginning the exercises in this chapter. First, you must try, as much as possible, not to be influenced by the spelling of a word; pay attention, instead, to the way in which you pronounce the word. Remember that there may be very little resemblance between sound and spelling. Second, you must, in every case, decide how *you* pronounce the word. Your pronunciation may be slightly different from the information given in the chapter. This is normal and should not concern you. You will probably find more discrepancies in the pronunciation of vowels than in that of consonants, since vowels show great dialectal variation. Third, if you have already learned a phonetic alphabet, you will probably find some differences between the system introduced here and the one that you have learned. There is not one universally agreed-upon system of transcription.

The introduction to the phonetic alphabet may have seemed very rapid. Try not to be intimidated or overwhelmed by the material. We will be making use of the phonetic alphabet throughout the text, and there will be ample opportunities to review and to increase your understanding of English phonology. For now, just do your best to learn the symbols and the sounds they represent.

1. Give the phonetic symbol for the following articulatory descriptions.

    a. voiceless glottal fricative [_____]

    b. voiced bilabial stop [_____]

    c. labiovelar semivowel (or glide) [_____]

    d. alveolar nasal [_____]

    e. voiceless alveolopalatal fricative [_____]

    f. voiced alveolar fricative [_____]

2. Give the articulatory descriptions of the following phonetic symbols.

    a. [t] _____

    b. [s] _____

    c. [k] _____

    d. [ð] _____

    e. [r] _____

    f. [j] _____

3. Write the phonetic symbol for the *initial* consonant sound of the following words.

   a. shoot [_____]

   b. kid [_____]

   c. zone [_____]

   d. notion [_____]

   e. youth [_____]

   f. jewel [_____]

   g. Jacques [_____]

   h. sugar [_____]

4. Write the phonetic symbol for the *final* consonant sound of the following words.

   a. raise [_____]

   b. fire [_____]

   c. reign [_____]

   d. beige [_____]

   e. porch [_____]

   f. allege [_____]

   g. mourning [_____]

   h. resign [_____]

5. Write the phonetic symbol for the *medial* consonant sound of the following words.

   a. lotion [_____]

   b. latter [_____]

   c. offer [_____]

   d. leisure [_____]

   e. rugged [_____]

   f. talker [_____]

   g. yo-yo [_____]

   h. sojourn [_____]

Vowels

Whereas a consonant involves constriction of the airflow, a vowel is articulated with the air flowing through the vocal tract relatively unhindered. The mouth is open, and the articulators are not in contact; the tongue is somewhat humped or convex-shaped. Different vowels are produced by changing the shape and position of the tongue; doing so alters the shape of the resonating chamber, resulting in sound waves with different frequencies or pitches. A single vowel sound, with the pitch constant in a syllable, is called a *monophthong*; note the constant pitch of the vowel in *meet*. A complex vowel sound produced by moving from one vowel element to another, with a vowel and a glide (semivowel) in a single syllable, is called a *diphthong*; diphthongs are characterized by a change in pitch, as you hear in the diphthong in *might*. Vowels in English are generally voiced, although they may be partially devoiced if they follow a voiceless consonant, as in *his* (but this is not distinctive).

Vowels are more difficult to describe than consonants because the tongue, which functions as the articulator, does not assume discrete positions that can be easily separated and labeled. Instead, we have to consider where the tongue moves, or specifically where the high point of the tongue is, relative to both the roof of the mouth and the front of the mouth ('front' meaning the palatal region, quite far back in respect to consonant articulation). We therefore describe the high point of the tongue as *front*, *central*, or *back* (with two positions for each of these heights), and *high*, *mid*, or *low*. The jaw works in conjunction with the tongue, so that when the tongue is high, the jaw is relatively closed, and when the tongue is low, the jaw is relatively open. On the vowel grid (see Figure 2.3), height is charted on the vertical axis while the front–back dimension is charted on the horizontal axis, as though the chart were a side view of the mouth, facing left.

			Monopthongs		
			Front	**Central**	**Back**
High (close)	Tense	i (seat)	y (Fr. tu)		u (pool)
	Lax	ɪ (sit)	ʏ (Ger. Hütten)		ʊ (put)
Mid	Tense	e (OE fēt)			o (OE fōt)
	Lax	ɛ (set)		ə (sun, soda)	ɔ (port)
Low (open)		æ (sat)		a	ɑ (father)
			Diphthongs		
		eɪ (late)		aɪ (file)	oʊ (loan)
		ɪu (cute)		aʊ (fowl)	ɔɪ (foil)

Figure 2.3   The Vowel System of English (Note: Symbols displayed in gray represent sounds found only in Germanic and Old and Middle English.)

It is often necessary to specify other features of vowels: whether the lips are pursed (rounded) or not (unrounded); whether air is allowed to pass through the nasal tract (*nasalized*) or just out the oral tract (*non-nasalized*, or *oral*); whether the vowels are articulated for a longer or shorter period (*long* or *short* vowels); or whether the vowels are articulated with more or less tension on the tongue (*tense* or *lax* vowels). We will see that in English, the back vowels are generally rounded and the front and central vowels unrounded. Nasalization of vowels occurs only before nasal consonants, as in *ban*, *bang*, and is hence a predictable, or allophonic, variation. In Modern English, the length of vowels is also allophonic, determined by the consonants that follow the vowel (for example, the vowel in *sea* or *seed* is long, while the vowel in *seat* or *ceased* is short). However, in Old and Middle English, length is a distinctive feature of vowels. A vowel's length may be marked by a macron, or long mark, over the vowel, as in [ǣ] or [ē]. In Modern English, the distinction between tense and lax is primarily a means of sub-dividing each of the three main height positions (high, mid, and low) into two further positions: upper and lower. For monophthongs, tense means upper and lax means lower. All diphthongs are tense.

Diphthongs consist of a vowel and a glide. However, when acting as part of a diphthong, the glides [w] and [j] may be written as vowels, namely as [ʊ] and [ɪ], respectively. If the diphthong begins with a vowel and ends with a glide, it is called *falling* because the acoustically louder and more prominent vowel falls off to the softer glide; there is a corresponding fall in pitch. If it begins with a glide and ends with a vowel, it is called *rising*. Note that rising and falling do not refer to upward or downward movement of the tongue. In Modern English, all but one of the diphthongs are falling.

The Vowels of English

Vowel sounds show a wide range of individual and dialectal variation, so you should be aware that your own vowel sounds may differ slightly from the representative examples given in this section. You will probably find the vowel symbols more difficult to learn than those for the consonant sounds, although there are fewer of them; one aid in remembering the different vowels is to memorize a sample word containing each vowel, such as those on your chart or one that in your dialect contains the appropriate sound. When you encounter a new vowel sound that you wish to transcribe, you may then see if it rhymes with your sample word.

The front vowels in Modern English are all unrounded. There are two high front vowels: first, the sound in the word *seat*, which is tense, and represented in the IPA by a lowercase *i*, (or [i], when referring specifically to the sound); and second, the sound in the word *sit*, which is lax, and represented in the IPA by a small capital *I*, or [ɪ]. Try saying the two high front vowels in succession and note the lowering of your tongue: [i], [ɪ]. There are also two mid-front vowels, but only the lower (lax) one is found as a pure vowel in its own right. The mid-front lax vowel is represented in the IPA by the Greek letter epsilon, ɛ, and occurs in the word *set*, [ɛ]. The sound is sometimes called an open *e*. If you say the three front vowels in succession, you will notice how the tongue lowers and the jaw opens: [i], [ɪ], [ɛ].

In earlier stages of English we find a mid-front tense vowel (the close *e*), represented in the IPA by lowercase *e*, but in Modern English the sound is present only in the diphthong [eɪ] (for this reason, no sample Modern English word is given on the vowel chart). In articulating this diphthong, the tongue is not in a constant position but moves from mid-front to high front (the [j] glide). Listen to the vowel sound in the word *gate*, and now pronounce the sound [eɪ]. Note that toward the end of this sound, the tongue rises and the jaw closes somewhat. In pitch and acoustic prominence, this is a falling diphthong. Finally, the low front vowel is the sound found in the word *sat*, [æ]. It is represented in the IPA by the Old English symbol *ash*, which is a ligature, or combination of the letters *a* and *e*. Despite the combination of written letters, ash represents a single sound, not a diphthong. This vowel is lax. Now try saying all of the front vowels in sequence from top to bottom, [i], [ɪ],[e], [ɛ], [æ], noticing the movement of tongue and jaw.

The Modern English vowels articulated in the central position are also unrounded. The only one we need to distinguish is the mid-central lax vowel found in the word *sun* or in the second syllable of *soda*. This sound is made with the tongue in the most neutral, or rest, position, so it is sometimes considered a *reduced* vowel. It is represented in the IPA with a lowercase *e* rotated 180 degrees, hence [ə]; the sound is called by the Hebrew name *schwa*. We will see that it is an important vowel in the development of English.[2] Note as well that the low central [a] is used only as the starting point of a diphthong.

The back vowels pose more difficulties for description. With one exception, the vowels articulated in the back of the mouth are rounded. If you say the high back tense vowel, which is the sound in the word *pool*, [u], you will notice a rounding of your lips. The high back lax vowel, represented in the IPA by the Greek letter upsilon ʊ, is the sound [ʊ] found in the word *put*. There is no pure mid-back tense vowel in English today, although it existed in earlier English. It is represented in the IPA by a lowercase *o* and sometimes called a 'close *o*'. As with the mid-front tense vowel [e], the sound [o] lives on in a Modern English diphthong in which the tongue moves from the mid-back to the high back position (the [w] glide). This is the [oʊ] sound found in the word *load*; when you say this diphthong, your tongue rises and your lips round more markedly at the end. This is a falling diphthong.

The remaining back vowels show wide dialectal variation. For most speakers of Canadian English, the open *o*, a sound represented in the IPA by a reverse *c* [ɔ], is

---

2 Some students of linguistics may be familiar with the symbol caret [ʌ], which represents a stressed mid-central vowel; in the broad transcription system used in this text, [ə] represents both the stressed and unstressed mid-central vowel.

found in its pure form only before [r], as in the word *port* (although the sound also shows up within a diphthong, as we will see later). This is a mid-back vowel (variably tense or lax depending upon dialect). The low back vowel, represented in the IPA by a script *a*, [ɑ], is the sound in the word *father* or *part*. It is the only unrounded vowel articulated at the back of the mouth. This sound is subject to variation, including a rounded form, [ɒ], and a more centralized form, [a]. While some speakers of North American English distinguish between the words *caught* and *cot*, pronouncing [ɔ] in the first and [ɑ] or [ɒ] in the second, many people make no such distinction, articulating [ɑ] in both. In this book, the script [ɑ] should be understood as a compromise transcription allowing for some variation in the actual sound.

In addition to the vowel symbols needed for Modern English, we must add two IPA symbols necessary for describing the vowel sounds of earlier English. These are for the two high front rounded vowels. The high front tense rounded vowel is represented in the IPA by a lowercase *y* [y]. You can produce this sound by first articulating the high front tense unrounded vowel [i] and then rounding your lips. It is found in the French *tu* or German *für*. The high front lax rounded vowel is represented by a small *ʏ*. To make the sound [ʏ], first articulate the high front lax unrounded vowel [ɪ] and then round your lips. The front rounded vowels are found in Old English.

You have already been introduced to two diphthongs, [eɪ] and [oʊ]. There are four additional diphthongs in Modern English. Two of them begin in the low central region with a sound represented in the IPA by the lowercase printed [a]. The first moves from low central to high front (the [j] glide); it occurs in the word *file*, and is transcribed as [aɪ]. The other moves from low central to high back (the [w] glide); it

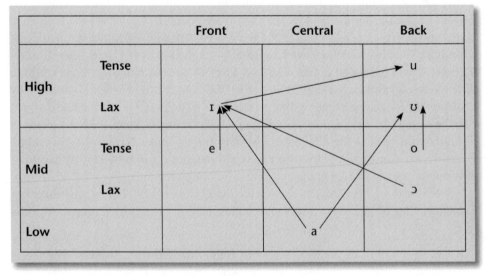

Figure 2.4   Starting and Ending Points of English Diphthongs

is the sound found in the word *fowl*, [aʊ]. Another diphthong begins with open *o* and moves forward to the [j] glide; it may be described as mid-back to high front. This is the sound in *foil*, [ɔɪ]. All of the diphthongs discussed so far have been falling. Last is the rising diphthong in the word *cute*, [ɪu]. This sound begins in the high front position (the [j] glide) and ends in the high back tense vowel; it may be described as high front to high back. Figure 2.4 shows the starting and ending points of the diphthongs in English.

Exercise 2.2 Vowels and Transcriptions of Words

1. Give the phonetic symbol for the following articulatory descriptions of vowels.

    a. low front   [_____]

    b. mid-back tense   [_____]

    c. high front lax   [_____]

    d. low central   [_____]

2. Give the articulatory descriptions of the following phonetic symbols of vowels.

    a. [u] _____

    b. [ɛ] _____

    c. [ɑ] _____

    d. [y] _____

3. Give the phonetic symbols of the following articulatory descriptions of diphthongs.

    a. low central to high back lax   [_____]

    b. mid-front tense to high front lax   [_____]

    c. high front lax to high back tense   [_____]

4. Give the articulatory descriptions of the following phonetic symbols of diphthongs.

    a. [aɪ] _____

    b. [ɔɪ] _____

    c. [oʊ] _____

5. Give the English words indicated by the following phonetic transcriptions.

    a.   [saɪn]   _____

    b.   [wɪšt]   _____

    c.   [bɪld]   _____

    d.   [koʊm]   _____

    e.   [ðeɪ]   _____

    f.   [kraʊdəd] _____

    g.   [briðd]   _____

    h.   [ɛr]   _____

    i.   [rɪč]   _____

    j.   [vɔɪd]   _____

    k.   [jə̆ŋk]   _____

    l.   [hɪuj̆]   _____

6. Give complete transcriptions of the following words.

    a.   soft   _____

    b.   parochial   _____

    c.   enough   _____

    d.   masculine   _____

    e.   though   _____

    f.   museums   _____

    g.   carve   _____

    h.   ineligible   _____

    i.   height   _____

    j.   debauchery   _____

    k.   carriage   _____

    l.   moisturize   _____

    m. roof   _____

    n.   quintessential _____

    o.   dumb   _____

    p.   parliamentary _____

7. Each of the following examples contains one error in transcription—that is, it indicates an impossible pronunciation of the word for a native speaker of English of any variety. Indicate the error and supply the correct symbol.

			Error	Correction
a.	these	[θiz]	_____	_____
b.	wishing	[wɪshɪŋ]	_____	_____
c.	hijacking	[haɪjækɪŋ]	_____	_____
d.	umbrella	[umbrɛlə]	_____	_____
e.	manage	[mænæj̆]	_____	_____

Stress

In addition to vowels and consonants, speech consists of features that extend over more than one sound—or *segment*—within a word. These are called *suprasegmental features*. One such feature is *intonation*, variations in pitch which differentiate sentence types such as questions and statements. A second is *accent*, meaning the prominence given to a particular syllable in a word.[3] Prominence can be achieved in a number of ways. In English, it is a matter of increasing the volume of air expelled when articulating the syllable, thereby increasing its loudness. We call this phenomenon 'stress' or 'stress accent'. Every word spoken in isolation contains one syllable bearing primary stress; in words with more than one syllable, another syllable may bear a weaker accent called secondary stress, and still other syllables will be unstressed. Primary stress is indicated by an acute accent mark over the vowel ['] and secondary stress by a grave accent mark ['`]; unstressed syllables are not marked at all.

English inherits from Germanic a system of initial syllable stress, where stress is fixed and predictable, as in *ápple*, *fáther*, *háppy*, *góldmine*, *bláckbird*. Only prefixed verbs like *forgét*, *understánd*, and *belíeve* break this rule by having stress on the root rather than the first syllable of the word. However, because English has borrowed a large number of words from French and Latin, we have acquired an additional stress system called the 'Romance stress rule'. The rules for assigning stress in Romance words are very complicated, based on factors such as the number of syllables in a word, the type of sounds in the final syllable, and the grammatical category of the word. For example, in *disdáin* and *delíght* the final syllable is stressed because it contains a diphthong or tense vowel, while *collápse*, *exíst*, and

---

3 Another sense of *accent* is 'the phonetic features attributable to a person's regional or social dialect'.

adópt have final syllable stress for an entirely different reason: the consonant cluster at the end of each word. In contrast, *admónish*, *cáncel*, *elícit* have stress on the second-to-last syllable because they end with a single consonant.

Some polysyllabic words have both a primary and a secondary stress (as in *rèvolútion*, *pronùnciátion*), while others have only primary stress (as in *cómplicate*, *fáshionable*). Compounds such as *góldmìne* and *bláckbìrd* have secondary stress on the second root. In some cases the position of stress depends on the part of speech: compare the verb *impórt* with the noun *ímport*, the verb *recórd* with the noun *récord*.

There is a tendency in English for unstressed vowels to be reduced in their articulation, that is, to be centralized and laxed to [ə]. Compare the following words; the underlined syllable is stressed in the first column and unstressed in the second:

impl<u>i</u>cit	*impl<u>i</u>cation*
expl<u>ai</u>n	*expl<u>a</u>nation*
emph<u>a</u>tic	*emph<u>a</u>sis*
inv<u>oke</u>	*inv<u>o</u>cation*

The unstressed vowel is usually [ə] in these cases. Not all unstressed vowels undergo this change, though; in the following words, the first syllable is unstressed while the vowel is full: *citation*, *vocation*, *fantastic*, and *simplistic*. There is considerable variation between [ə] and [ɪ] in unstressed syllables in words such as *attitude*, *compensate*, *demonstrate*, and *predator* (though most speakers would distinguish [ə] in *Lennon* and [ɪ] in *Lenin*). Which vowel do you use in the second syllable of these words? We will see later that vowel reduction in unstressed syllables has had important consequences in the history of the language. Vowel reduction is best seen not as the result of laziness or sloppiness on the part of speakers, but rather as a natural phonetic tendency.

Below is a phonetic transcription of a short poem written in Present-Day English. Can you read it and write it down? (The answer is given at the end of the chapter.)

[soʊ məč dɪpɛndz əpɑn ə rɛd (h)wilbɛroʊ gleɪzd wɪð reɪn wɑrər bɪsaɪd ðə waɪt čɪkənz]

Exercise 2.3 Stress

Indicate the primary stress in the following words.

a. parenthesis   _____

b. insensibility   _____

c. parenthetical   _____

d. accent (noun)   _____

e. absolve   _____

f.   accented   _____

g.   absolute   _____

h.   accentuate   _____

i.   absolution   _____

j.   numerous   _____

k.   timeless   _____

l.   numerical   _____

The Writing of English

So far we have limited our discussion to the speech sounds of English, but we turn now to the way in which sounds are represented in the writing system (*orthography*) of English. There exist a number of writing systems used to record the languages of the world. Some languages (Japanese, for example) are recorded in more than one system. English uses an alphabetic system whereby individual sounds are represented by discrete symbols. In the section below, we will trace the history of this alphabet. We will begin with a brief exploration of the origin of writing systems in general and distinguish writing from other forms of pictorial representation.

The History of Writing

It is tempting to regard the petroglyphs (carvings) and pictographs (paintings) left behind on cave ceilings, cliff faces, and small objects as embryonic forms of writing. Because these images are prehistoric, dating from a time before written records, we do not in fact know what most of them mean or what function they had. Archaeologists sometimes venture educated guesses as to their purpose, inferring, for example, from the appearance of a fish glyph on a boulder submerged by the sea at high tide that the image may have had some magical function for the fisherman. In other cases, more recent peoples' practices may shed some light. For example, a birthing site used by native Hawaiian women in the modern period has petroglyphs in the shape of shallow indentations carved into the lava rock. Traditionally, the mother placed the umbilical cord of her newly delivered infant in the depression for the spirits to remove or preserve in order to guarantee long life for the child. Scholars suspect that the ancient site has long been associated with such a ritual. Similarly, a cave in the Santa Barbara mountains of California is said to have been used by Chumash Native peoples, who recorded in pictographs the spirit dreams given to them during adolescent rites of passage. Despite such interpretations of what is often generically called rock art, we do not know its original meaning or use. Perhaps the cave paintings at Lascaux in France were intended purely as art; surely they merit that label for their sophistication and beauty alone.

Whatever the communicative function of rock art might have been, if indeed it sometimes had one, it does not constitute written language. Even when pictorial images seem to be representational—that is, icons or indices of objects and ideas— scholars have been unable to reconstruct any conventional or symbolic system of communication. Moreover, archaeologists and linguists have never found a 'missing link' that marks the transition of rock art into written language. In other words, when evidence of written language is found, the writing functions quite clearly as language: it employs a symbolic system of representation. Even such early writing systems as Hittite cuneiform, Chinese ideograms, and Egyptian hieroglyphics display a consciousness toward language that distinguish them from rock art. We can define writing, then, following Diringer (1962), as a conscious and complete system for the conveyance of ideas or sounds by marks on some suitable medium.

There are three major types of writing systems: *ideographic*, *logographic*, and *phonographic*. In ideographic writing, the sign is a picture of something. There is a one-to-one correspondence between the symbol and the object it depicts, and the spoken name given to the object does not matter. This kind of writing has the advantage that a speaker of any language could, in theory, decode the written message, using his or her words for the objects represented. Out of an ideographic system may arise a logographic system, in which a word becomes associated with the picture to the point that the sign functions as a word. Hittite and hieroglyphic Egyptian, although they do not fit any system perfectly, could be described as largely logographic with ideographic bases.

The development of phonographic writing arises from the need to express words and sounds that cannot adequately be expressed by pictures. In a phonographic writing such as Chinese, sounds (deriving from the word people use for an object depicted by the sign) come to be associated with a sign. Only people who speak the particular language can decode the written sign. Diringer sees phonographic writing as the graphic or visual counterpart of speech, because the signs in the written language correspond to sounds in the spoken one.

Depending on the unit of sound represented, phonographic writing may be described as either *syllabic* or *alphabetic*. The orthographic symbol in a syllabic writing system—or *syllabary*—represents a nucleus (containing a vowel) and associated consonants. A syllabary thus requires numerous signs to stand for the many possible syllable combinations that appear in a language. For example, the form of cuneiform (a writing system found on clay tablets and consisting of wedge-shaped impressions) used by the Babylonians employs symbols for 97 simple, or open, syllables (e.g. *di*, *du*, *da*) and 200 or more complex, or closed, syllables (e.g. *dad*) (Diringer 1962:42). Alphabetic writing proves more economical because it represents the individual sounds of a language, which are much less numerous than possible sound combinations used to form syllables.

The different kinds of writing just reviewed are not mutually exclusive: they may be combined within a single system. Sumerian cuneiform, for example, uses both phonographic and ideographic script. Because ambiguity at times arises, and a sign could represent both an object and at the same time a sound meant to be pronounced (in an entirely different word), this writing system also makes use of a special set of signs called determiners, indicating which reading is intended, sound or object. Likewise, the Babylonians, who adopted the cuneiform system from the Sumerians, combined phonographic signs with six vowel symbols as well as approximately three thousand ideograms (Diringer 1962:42). This example also shows that a single writing system can be adapted from one language to another. In the following section, we will also see that the alphabetic form of writing has been adapted to the representation of a wide variety of languages.

The Origin of the Alphabet

We begin with the rather amazing claim that all the alphabets that the world has known descend from a single, common ancestor alphabet. As distinct as the Greek alphabet, Devanagari (the script of India), the Russian (Cyrillic) alphabet, the runic alphabet, the Hebrew alphabet, and the Arabic alphabet may seem, all derive from a single original source. We do not know the precise identity of the alphabet's inventors, but the first known alphabet seems to have belonged to a group of Northwest Semitic speakers living in Palestine around 1800–1700 BCE. That alphabet is abstract and geometrical, rather than pictographic, containing 22 symbols that represent consonant sounds. Speakers who read the alphabetic inscriptions would automatically supply the missing vowel sounds belonging to the pronunciation of a word. In order to help people remember the alphabet, each letter was also given a name, e.g. *aleph* and *beth* for the first two letters.

Along with their names and phonetic values, the shape and order of the alphabetic letters traveled out of Palestine from one civilization to another. Just as dialects of a language may develop into separate languages, the alphabet changed over time as it was adopted by different groups of speakers. A number of important variants of the original alphabet emerged but we will focus here on the immediate ancestors of the English alphabet (see Figure 2.5). In brief, around the tenth or ninth century BCE, the Greeks borrowed the North Semitic alphabet, adding new signs to represent vowel sounds. Before the Early Greek alphabet stabilized as Classical Greek, it was borrowed by the Etruscans, who were the predecessors of the Romans in Italy and came from a very different (non-Indo-European) linguistic tradition. Before falling into disuse, the Etruscan alphabet, like the Semitic alphabet before it, developed several offshoots, two of which are relevant to English: the runic alphabet and the Latin alphabet.

Although experts debate the point, the runic alphabet of the Northwest Germanic tribes may have been based on a first-century BCE Etruscan version of the North Semitic alphabet. Runes came to England with the North Sea invaders. They were apparently first used for ritual or magical purposes, since *rune* in Old Icelandic

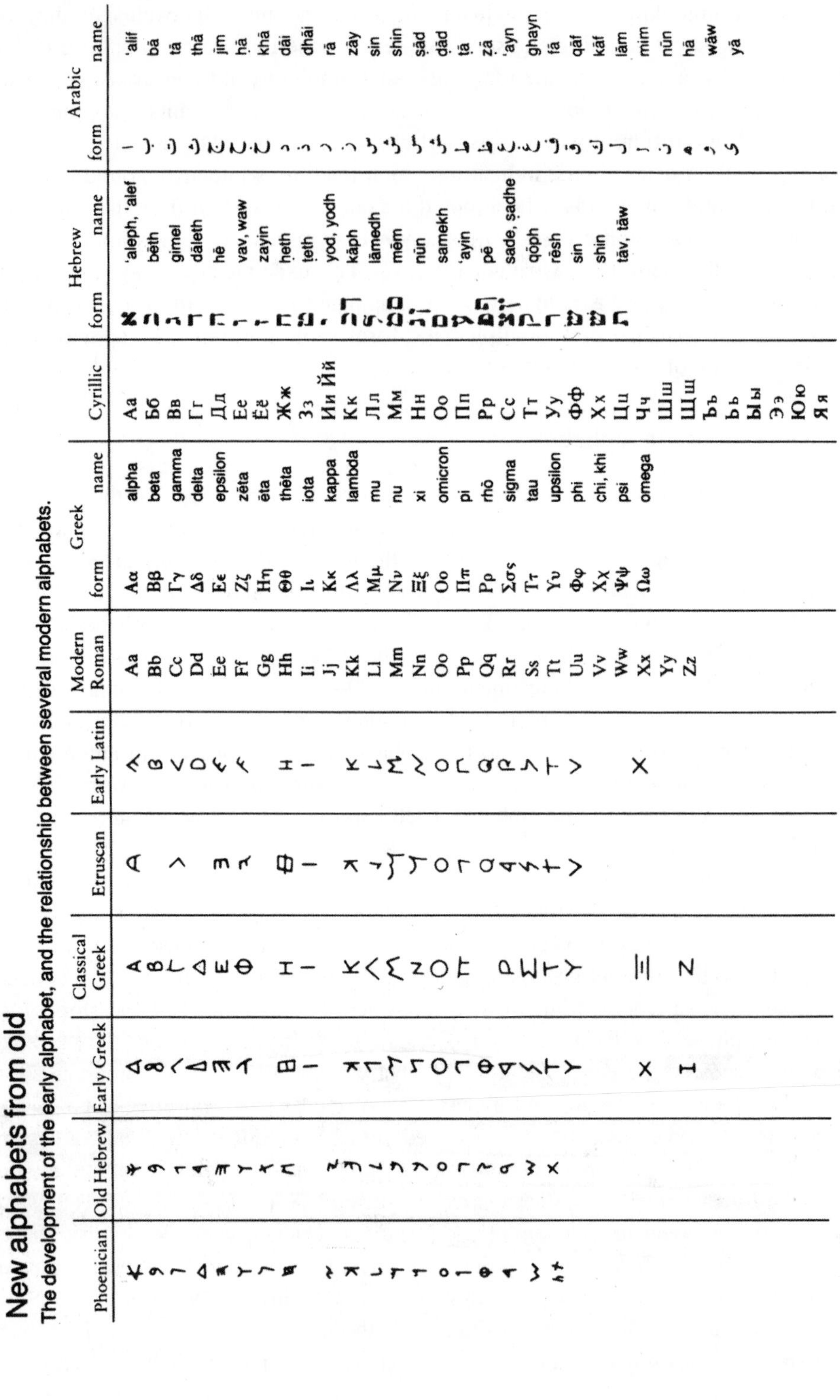

New alphabets from old

The development of the early alphabet, and the relationship between several modern alphabets.

Figure 2.5 Development of the Alphabet (from David Crystal, *The Cambridge Encyclopedia of Language*, 1st edn. [Cambridge: Cambridge University Press, 1987], p. 202, reprinted with the permission of Cambridge University Press)

means 'secret'. Similar to the way in which our alphabet is called by its first two letters (*alpha* and *beta* in Greek), the runic alphabet is known by its first six letters as the futhorc (f-u-th-o-r-c). Runic symbols are angular because the alphabet was designed for engraving or inscribing on stone and wood. (It is significant that the word *write* originally meant 'to scratch, carve, engrave, inscribe'.) Although most of the wood inscriptions have not survived, quite a number of inscriptions on stone using this alphabet have been found, from Scandinavia to northern Italy, and about forty runic inscriptions on coins, memorial stones, weapons, and household objects have been located in England. One of the most extensive inscriptions is the Anglo-Saxon poem 'The Dream of the Rood', found in part on the Ruthwell Cross. Another interesting runic inscription appears together with depictions of Germanic and Christian scenes on the Franks Casket, a small whalebone box now located in the British Museum. The illustration (see Figure 2.6) shows the front of the box, which depicts a scene from the legend of Weland the Smith on the left and the Adoration of the Magi on the right. The runic inscription in the upper left corner has been transliterated as 'FISC.FLODU', which means literally 'fish flood'.

The runic alphabet was used by the Germanic people until they acquired the Latin alphabet, a second adaptation of the Etruscan version. Roman legionnaires took both the Latin language and the Latin alphabet throughout the Roman Empire; later on, church missions took them even farther afield. The Latin alphabet provided the basic system used for writing Old English, but runes continued to be used sporadically even after the Latin alphabet was adopted. In fact, as we will see in Chapter 6, two runic symbols remained part of the Old English writing system. In the medieval period, the Latin alphabet was modified. In the late Middle Ages, once the letter *w* came into existence, and the letters *j* and *v* separated from *i* and *u* respectively, the system stabilized into the 26 letters of the Latin alphabet as we know it today.

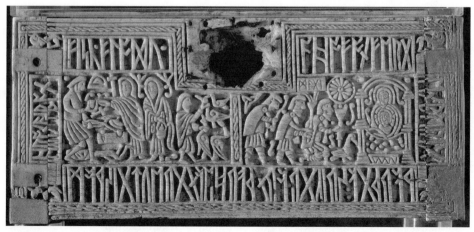

Figure 2.6 The Franks Casket, 8th Century CE, Northumbria (© The British Library)

Exercise 2.4 Writing Systems

1. Name and define the three major types of writing systems.

    _____

    _____

    _____

    _____

    _____

    _____

2. Briefly describe the nature and origins of the two alphabets important in the history of English.

    _____

    _____

    _____

    _____

    _____

    _____

RECOMMENDED WEB LINKS

The website of the International Phonetic Association is:

   http://www.langsci.ucl.ac.uk/ipa/

Peter Ladefoged's online version of his books *A Course in Phonetics*, 5th edn, and *Vowels and Consonants*, 2nd edn, provides a wealth of material on English phonology, including pronunciations:

   http://hctv.humnet.ucla.edu/departments/linguistics/VowelsandConsonants/index.html

Useful courses on English phonetics, containing text and some exercises, are:

   http://www.umanitoba.ca/faculties/arts/linguistics/russell/138/notes.htm
   http://www.chass.utoronto.ca/%7Estairs/phthong/phthong100.html

The following website provides an interactive lesson on places and manners of articulation:

   http://www.chass.utoronto.ca/%7Edanhall/phonetics/sammy.html

The Linguistic Society of America (LSA) has a brief discussion of the relationship between writing and speech:

http://www.lsadc.org/info/ling-fields.cfm (Writing)

Simon Ager's website provides useful illustrations of writing systems of the world:

http://www.omniglot.com/writing/

The runic alphabet (in several different versions, including the Anglo-Saxon futhorc) may be seen at the following website:

http://www.omniglot.com/writing/runic.htm

To see the Franks Casket with its runic inscription in more detail, go to the British Museum website:

http://www.thebritishmuseum.ac.uk/compass/

FURTHER READING

Peter Ladefoged's books are also available in print:

Ladefoged, Peter. 2005. *A Course in Phonetics*. 5th edn. Boston: Thomson-Wadsworth.
Ladefoged, Peter. 2004. *Vowels and Consonants: An Introduction to the Sounds of Languages*. 2nd edn. Malden: Blackwell.

For help with the various phonetic alphabet symbols and diacritics, the following text is an invaluable guide:

Pullum, Geoffrey K., and William A. Ladusaw. 1996. *Phonetic Symbol Guide*. 2nd edn. Chicago and London: University of Chicago Press.

For further information about the development of writing, see:

Coulmas, Florian. 1996. *The Blackwell Encyclopedia of Writing Systems*. Oxford and Cambridge, MA: Blackwell.
Crystal, David. 2003. 'The Writing System'. *The Cambridge Encyclopedia of the English Language*. 2nd edn. Cambridge: Cambridge University Press.
Diringer, David. 1962. *Writing*. London: Thames and Hudson.
Gelb, I.J. 1963. *A Study of Writing*. Rev. edn. Chicago and London: University of Chicago Press.
Rogers, Henry. 2004. *Writing Systems: A Linguistic Approach*. Cambridge, MA: Blackwell.

FURTHER VIEWING

On the emergence and development of various writing systems, see:

Episode 4: 'Civilization to Colonialization'. *Speaking in Tongues: The History of Language*. Directed and researched by Christene Browne. Toronto: Syncopated Productions, 2007.

ANSWER

The answer to the transcription reading given on p. 48 is:

so much depends
upon

a red wheel
barrow

glazed with rain
water

beside the white
chickens

(Poem XXI by William Carlos Williams, from 'Spring and All I–XXVIII', commonly known as 'The Red Wheelbarrow'; see Williams 1938:127)

3 Causes and Mechanisms of Language Change

OVERVIEW

This chapter examines linguistic change, what causes it, and how it happens. We begin by identifying both *internal* and *external* causes of change, that is, those that are inherent in the language and those that are brought about by contact with other languages or dialects. We then explore the mechanisms of phonological, morphological, syntactic, and semantic change. After suggesting how the sounds of an earlier stage of a language may be deduced from written records, we treat various types, or *mechanisms*, of sound change. Next, in studying morphological and syntactic change, we examine the processes of analogy (and false analogy) and of grammaticalization. We then distinguish between innovative and conservative changes in language. The chapter describes certain types of semantic change, including generalization/specialization, pejoration/amelioration, and strengthening/weakening. We explain the kinds of figurative shifts that words undergo (metaphor, metonymy, synecdochy, and synesthesia) and then briefly discuss invited inferences. Finally, we look at the effects of cultural and social factors on the meanings of words and conclude with a few generalizations about semantic change.

OBJECTIVES

The primary objective in this chapter is to learn why and how languages change. After reading the chapter, you should be able to identify examples of these different causes at work and be able to

■ describe the change from one sound to another in terms of articulation, and

■ identify what type of sound change(s) a word has undergone if given an older and a newer form of a word or a word in which the spelling reveals an older pronunciation.

In addition, you should understand the principle of analogy and be able to recognize processes of analogy at work in the language. You should also understand the process of grammaticalization and be able to recognize examples of it. If told the older meaning of a given word, you should be able to describe the type(s) of semantic changes the word has undergone by using knowledge of its current meaning.

Causes of Change

While we know that language change is inevitable, we are less certain of its causes. The American linguist Leonard Bloomfield claimed that the causes of language change are unknown: 'Every conceivable cause has been alleged: "race", climate, topographic conditions, diet, occupation and general mode of life, and so on' (1933:386). There are two extreme views of the causes of change. The first view is that change is unmotivated, random, and fortuitous, much like changes in fashion, which are non-functional and purely stylistic. The other view is that change is always functionally motivated, serving the expressive needs of speakers. The fact that the same kinds of changes can be observed in many different languages and that there appear to be constraints on the types of changes possible seems to invalidate the first view. On the other hand, the fact that many linguistic changes appear to have no functional value seems to invalidate the second. We need not be entirely pessimistic about understanding language change, however, for we are able to adduce a number of factors, both internal and external, which contribute to linguistic change.

Internal

Internal causes of change are those inherent to the system of a language. There are a number of factors contributing to change of which the speaker is more or less unconscious:

• *ease of articulation* – The speaker exerts the least effort in articulating sounds, leading to the assimilation of neighboring sounds, to omissions, and to clipped forms; taken to the extreme, this principle would lead all speech to the sound [ə].

- *perceptual clarity* – The hearer requires that sounds be maximally distinct (this principle works against the previous one).
- *phonological symmetry* – Phonological systems tend toward structural balance, as evidenced by the pairing of voiced and voiceless consonants or front and back vowels; thus, a language will acquire sounds to fill gaps and eliminate sounds that cause asymmetries in the system. For example, in English, the voiced sound [ž] was added to match the voiceless sound [š] already existing.
- *universal tendencies* – Certain developments commonly occur in the evolution of a language, such as the devoicing of final consonants and the loss of final *n*'s, or the development of function words and inflections from full words. These tendencies generally occur in just one direction: grammatical items derive from lexical items and not the reverse.
- *efficiency or transparency* – Although language always contains a certain amount of redundancy, when a grammar becomes overly complicated or irregular, it may undergo change to make it more accessible, that is, to achieve a one-to-one relationship between grammatical form and meaning; this has been called the 'Transparency Principle' (Lightfoot 1979). For instance, English has moved in the direction of having noun plurals always indicated by *-s*.

There are also a number of factors contributing to change of which the speaker is more or less conscious:

- *spelling pronunciation* – The speaker pronounces a word as it is written rather than as it is conventionally pronounced; for example, the speaker may pronounce the *t* in *often* (but compare *listen, soften*), the *l* in *almond* and *falcon* (but compare *walk* and *salmon*), the *h* in *forehead*, or the *p* in *clapboard* (but compare *cupboard*). Spelling pronunciations have the effect of giving the written form a life of its own.
- *hypercorrection* – The speaker may correct a mistake (which is not, in fact, a mistake); for example, the speaker who wishes to avoid the North American feature of flapping (voicing of intervocalic [t]) in words such as *voter* may incorrectly say [čɛtər] for *cheddar*. On the grammatical level, a speaker may say *between you and I* on the false belief that *me* is incorrect following *and*.
- *overgeneralization* – The speaker overgeneralizes a linguistic rule, applying it in contexts where it does not hold; for example, the speaker who knows that *pro* is often pronounced [proʊ] in *process* and *progress* may extend this pronunciation to *product*, which is normally pronounced [prɑdəkt]. The past participle *boughten* might be generated by applying the rule that all English past participles have the inflectional suffix *-en*, when in fact only some do. Although the results of hypercorrection and overgeneralization may appear the same, the motivations for these changes differ.
- *analogy* – The speaker alters a form by analogy with another form with which it is related, thus eliminating irregularities in the language. While it is questionable how conscious speakers are of this kind of change, it takes a number

of different forms and is an important force. For example, a speaker may produce the past tense form *teached* on analogy with the vast majority of verbs (e.g. *walked*) which form their past tense in this fashion, or the past tense form *pled* from *plead* on analogy with *lead/led* or *feed/fed*.

- *renewal* – Both emphatic forms (a kind of overstatement) and euphemisms (a kind of understatement) are constantly in need of renewal as they cease to convey emphasis or fail to be recognized as euphemisms. Thus, *very* is weakened and may be replaced by *totally, hugely, massively, awfully,* or *terribly.* The term *intercourse*, originally a euphemism (meaning 'interaction') for the sexual act, would now be considered either technical or overly direct, and is typically replaced with a less direct term such as *sexual relations*.

- *reanalysis* – Language users develop a new understanding of the structure of certain phrases. For example, the phrase *according to him* originated as a participle, *according,* accompanied by a prepositional phrase, *to him*. However, it has been reanalyzed as consisting of a complex preposition, *according to,* and an object, *him*.

Most of the scholars known as 'generative linguists' base their views about the causes of language change on this idea of reanalysis. According to them, a child builds a grammar of the language on the basis of the input he or she receives, and linguistic change results from children forming somewhat different grammars than their parents used.

For example, an adult saying the sentence *He is going to see her* might analyze the structure as:

[He] [is going] (motion verb) [to see her] (purpose clause).

A child might hear this as:

[He] [is going to] (future marker) [see her] (main verb).

The child has introduced a grammatical change here by developing a new future, *be going to*; the new future form thus becomes part of the grammar of the next generation of speakers. Earlier versions of this hypothesis proposed that there is 'imperfect' learning by children, who may overgeneralize a specific rule or fail to learn a difficult one, or that lazy speakers take shortcuts in the grammar (Leith 1997:98). However, if this were always the case, then language change would necessarily lead to simplification; we know that, on the contrary, grammars often become more complex over time.

External

External causes of change come about through encounters with other languages or different dialects of the same language. This is called *language contact*, and it may occur in any number of situations, including military invasion, colonization, immigration, or commercial interaction. The extent of language contact may be influenced by the cultural and social prestige of one language. Traditionally scholars agreed that external causes of change are less important than internal causes; in fact, some have argued that the external ones do not 'cause' change at all, but simply speed up changes already underway in the language, exploiting imbalances or weaknesses already present in the internal system of the language and encouraging the choice of one variant form over another. This view may underplay the extensiveness of the changes brought about by external influences, which operate indirectly over long periods of time and are difficult to assess, but the argument is nevertheless a useful antidote to the popular view, which tends to attribute far too many changes to external causes.

According to Thomason (2001:10), the effects of other languages can be divided into three types:

- contact-induced language change;
- extreme language mixture (leading to pidgins, creoles, and bilingual mixed languages); and
- language death.

Pointing out that death does not refer to the gradual alteration of a language over time (as we see in the case of Latin developing into the Romance languages), the linguist Jean Aitchison (2001) divides language death into 'suicide' and 'murder'. In the case of suicide, speakers import new forms from a prestige language until features of their original language are no longer recognizable; their language demolishes itself or destroys its own identity. The best-known cases of suicide are creoles 'devoured' by their parents in a process called decreolization (e.g. Guyanan Creole). In the case of murder, one language is supplanted by another, dominant one, which speakers adopt for various social and political reasons. Well-known examples include some of the Celtic languages and many Native North American languages, now replaced by English or French.

One response to these 'murders' has been an attempt to preserve and even resurrect the endangered language through various kinds of 'artificial life-support', such as school curricula or community language programs. Some of these attempts have proved fairly successful, such as the revival of Hebrew and the resurgence of Welsh; (a Celtic language) however, attempts to bring back Cornish or Manx (extinct Celtic languages) have only proved anachronistic. Many Native North American languages are seriously endangered (such as Abenaki in the Algonquian language family or Sechelt and Squamish in the Salish language family) or have been murdered (such as Tagish in the Athapaskan family). A concerted effort to teach Musqueam (a Salish language) is currently underway in the First Nations Languages Program at the University of British Columbia.

In tracing the history of English, we will be concerned only with contact-induced language change, not with the more extreme forms of language contact. While all components of a language may be affected by external factors, the vocabulary is the most vulnerable to change, being augmented by borrowings or loan words. (As Jean Aitchison [2001:141] points out, borrowing is a misnomer, since what we really do is 'copy it'.) There are several reasons for borrowing vocabulary: we may lack the word for a thing or a concept, the foreign term may be shorter or simpler, the foreign term may capture a nuance of meaning that we lack, or the language from which the word comes may carry prestige or dominate in a particular field. Loan words are generally assimilated quickly into the language, becoming anglicized both phonologically and morphologically: non-native sounds are replaced or modified, and inflectional and derivational affixes are added. Since words are detachable elements, borrowing foreign words does not fundamentally change the structure of the language. The phonology and grammar typically remain untouched by the borrowings. Even when sounds, grammatical forms, or syntactic structures are borrowed, which occurs much less frequently, there is a tendency for the borrowings to fit the patterns already existing. For example, English borrowed the phoneme [ž] from French in words such as *azure* and *beige*; this likely occurred only because English already had the sound [š] and was beginning to develop [ž] anyway. Borrowing [ž] removed an asymmetry in the fricative series, since [š] had been the only unpaired fricative.

Scholars have proposed a number of different models to explain the effects of language contact. In the traditional model, contact is seen to work in three ways. First, in a *substratum*, the language of the dominated (immigrant or conquered) group influences that of the dominant group. An example of a substratum would be the minor influence of the Celtic languages on English or of Aboriginal languages on North American English. Second, in a *superstratum*, the language of the dominant group influences the language of the dominated group. An example of a superstratum would be the influence of English upon the German, Ukrainian, Italian, Hindi, and so on, spoken by immigrant groups in North America. Third, in an *adstratum*, there is a mixture of languages spoken by groups of equal political and social power. This often occurs in border areas or in confined geographical areas, such as the Balkan peninsula, where a number of languages are spoken. Features spread freely from one language to another; for example, tones have been transferred among the languages of Southeast Asia (Chinese, Thai, Vietnamese); clicks have been transferred among the languages of South Africa (Khoisan languages to Zulu), retroflexes among the languages of India (Dravidian, Indic), and perhaps uvular *r* between German and French. (Tones, clicks, and retroflexes are special phonological features or sounds, none of which are found in English.)

Leonard Bloomfield (1933) has proposed an alternative model. When one language group borrows a cultural item from another along with the name for that item, *cultural borrowing* occurs. The effects of cultural borrowing are felt primarily in the vocabulary. This kind of borrowing is generally one-sided, from the language with more prestige to the one with less (such as the effect of Latin on English).

At times, however, a language will borrow from another language with equivalent status because some aspect of its culture is pre-eminent. For example, English has borrowed seafaring terms from Dutch and musical terms from Italian, though neither the Dutch nor the Italian language necessarily has more prestige than English.

When two languages are spoken in the same geographical area, a situation of diglossia exists. In such cases, there is generally a politically or socially 'upper' (prestige) language and a corresponding 'lower' (stigmatized) language. If the lower language survives, it will show a strong influence from the upper (such as English after the Norman Conquest). Here, *intimate borrowing* may occur. Intimate borrowings may affect the structure of the language as well as its vocabulary. If the upper language survives, however, it will show little influence from the lower (such as Old English in respect to Celtic). In extreme cases, the lower language will not survive at all.

Finally, *dialect borrowing* occurs between dialects of the same language. Scholars are debating the extent to which this kind of dialect-mixing, especially in the context of colonialization, is socially motivated.

Scholars have proposed a finely tuned model of borrowing based on the following scale:

1. *casual contact* (borrowers need not be fluent in the source language, and/or [there are] few bilinguals among borrowing-language speakers): only non-basic vocabulary borrowed . . .
2. *slightly more intense contact* (borrowers must be reasonably fluent bilinguals, but they are probably a minority among borrowing-language speakers): function words and slight structural borrowing . . .
3. *more intense contact* (more bilinguals, attitudes, and other social factors [favor] borrowing): basic as well as nonbasic vocabulary borrowed, moderate structural borrowing . . .
4. *intense contact* (very extensive bilingualism [exists] among borrowing-language speakers, [and] social factors strongly [favor] borrowing): continuing heavy lexical borrowing in all sections of the lexicon, heavy structural borrowing . . . (see Thomason 2001: 70–1, based on Thomason and Kaufman 1988).

As we will see, the major external influences on English, namely French and the Scandinavian languages, fall between 2 and 3 on this scale.

Historical Sociolinguistics

In recent years, a subfield of study which considers a wide range of external causes of language change has evolved. Termed 'historical sociolinguistics' or 'sociohistorical linguistics', this field merges the study of language change with the methods of sociolinguistics.

Sociolinguists study the many 'extralinguistic' determinants—including ethnicity, socioeconomic class, sex and gender, age, and group membership (social networks) as well as register and style—that are thought to underlie a speaker's choice of a 'linguistic variable'. A linguistic variable is the set of variant forms that can be used to serve a given function ('a number of ways to say the same thing'). For example, a speaker could say *I have to write a paper for this class* or *I've got to write a paper for this class* or *I must write a paper for this class* or even *I got to write a paper for this class*. What dictates whether the speaker chooses *have to*, *have got to*, *got to*, or *must*? The choice of one variant over another is largely determined by the speaker's extralinguistic characteristics—the most pervasive of which are age, sex, and social class.[1]

We see variation in all areas of language:

- orthography, e.g. the variation between *-ize* and *-ise* spellings;
- phonology, e.g. the variation between [ɪn] and [ɪŋ] for the *-ing* suffix or the variation between [aʊ] and [əʊ] in words such as *out* and *mouse*;
- grammar, e.g. the variation between *I don't want anything* and *I don't want nothing*;
- pragmatics, e.g. the use of tag questions; and
- lexicon, e.g. the variation between *soda/pop/soft drink* or *running shoe/runner/ sneaker*.

The frequency of variants is relative, not absolute. Individual speakers or groups of speakers typically use a range of variants in different proportions at different times and in different contexts. Language change can occur only if such variables exist and are used in face-to-face conversations among speakers. It is possible to identify four stages of change: the actuation of the change (based in variation), the transition as one form replaces another, the embedding of the form in linguistic and social contexts, and the social evaluation of the form by speakers. We must also keep in mind that there are grammatical and phonological constraints on the possible changes that can occur in a language (Weinreich, Labov, and Herzog 1968, as summarized in Nevalainen and Raumolin-Brunberg 2003:1).

Sociolinguists have shown that all language change starts with variation, but that not all variation leads to language change. In some cases, linguistic variables are relatively stable over time, as in the case of *-ing*, which has had the same variants for hundreds of years. In other cases, one variant is displacing another, as in the case of the modal expressions given above, where *have to* is displacing *must* in some contexts. Here, then, we have an instance of 'language change in progress', that is, a language change that we can actually witness (see Tagliamonte and Smith 2006). A major goal of sociolinguistics is to identify changes in progress in the present-day

---

1 The method of determining this choice used in sociolinguistics today is the face-to-face 'sociolinguistic interview'. In such an interview, which is typically audio-recorded (and later transcribed), the sociolinguist collects data on the informant's language choices and on his or her social characteristics.

language and to distinguish change from stable variation. To identify such changes, sociolinguists correlate social variables with linguistic data.

Some of the earliest studies which looked systematically at the influence of social determinants on language change in progress were those undertaken by William Labov (1972b). These are 'apparent-time studies': when new, incoming linguistic forms are found to be more common with younger speakers and old, outgoing forms more common with older speakers, it can be extrapolated that as the younger speakers age, the forms they use will ultimately displace the forms that their parents use. Labov's work highlights the different effects of socioeconomic groups on change in progress as well as speakers' attitudes toward and awareness of language use. In a study of [r] use, Labov found that the 'non-rhotic' speakers of New York City, where many speakers omit [r] in words like *part* and *far*, often consider the omission of [r] to be stigmatized. As a consequence, speakers insert [r] as a sign of prestige. Labov concludes that '[m]iddle-aged, lower-middle-class speakers tend to adopt the formal speech patterns of the younger, upper-middle-class speakers' (141). He terms this 'change from above' (the level of consciousness) since it is a matter of deliberate choice. He also discovered that change from above is more common in women than in men: young females are often the prime agents of change.

By contrast, Labov observes 'change from below' in Martha's Vineyard, where speakers are not overtly conscious of the choices that they make. First, a group of fishermen living 'up-island' exaggerate a pronunciation already existing (but somewhat recessive) in their dialect, namely the raised diphthongs ([əʊ] and [əɪ] in words such as *out* and *night*—that is, they begin the articulation of the diphthongs in the mid-central position rather than the expected low-central position, as in [aʊ] and [aɪ]) (cf. Chapter 13 on 'Canadian raising'). Then, people of English descent residing on the island (in the 30- to 45-year-old age range) begin to imitate these sounds—apparently subconsciously—in order to show their identification with 'traditional' Yankee values. They adopt this pronunciation in a desire to identify themselves as true islanders rather than as the despised summer visitors, who they perceive as consumer-oriented and indolent. The process is repeated as new age and ethnic groups start to follow the lead of this initial group (Labov 1972b, as summarized by Aitchison 2001:60–66).

Studying groups of speakers in Belfast, James Milroy attributes change not merely to social class but to what he calls 'social networks' among speakers in a community. He distinguishes between weak and strong ties within a network. In communities characterized by close-knit networks (e.g. Iceland), linguistic change is *less* likely to occur, whereas in communities characterized by loose-knit networks (e.g. England), change is *more* likely to occur (1992:196).

It is assumed (by the so-called 'uniformitarian principle') that if linguistic variables exist in present-day languages, they must have existed in the past as well. That is, if principles of linguistic change are detected on present-day data, then the same principles apply to older stages of the language as well. In contrast to apparent-time studies, then, 'real-time studies' used by historical sociolinguists examine language change and the social variables underlying it over time and in real historical contexts. For example, we are able to use written documents to trace the use of the second-person plural pronouns as polite forms and the relegation of the singular forms to familiar use (with their eventual loss) in the Early Modern period (see Chapter 10). In addition, we can see how variant past tense forms such as *clomb/climbed* or *swole/swelled* in Early Modern English eventually stabilized into the system of past tense forms we see today (see Chapter 10).

We can also make assumptions about the relationship between class and language change. As members of the transitional classes (lower-middle class and upper-working class) are behind much change in the modern period, it is likely that these same groups of people led change in earlier periods. We know that the nominative form *ye* was eventually replaced by the objective form *you* (except in fixed expressions such as 'Hear ye, hear ye'; see Chapter 10) between the first half of the sixteenth century and the beginning of the seventeenth century, proceeding outwards from London and promoted by upper-class usage (see the work of Nevalainen and Raumolin-Brunberg 2003). As we will see in Chapter 11, the eighteenth-century appeal to authority which leads to the standardization of Modern English is as much social and historical as it is linguistic in nature (and it does indeed lead to changed usage); changes in this case were promoted primarily by educated upper-middle-class speakers.

But how can we determine the social and cultural influences on language change in historical periods when written texts bear only silent witness and information on the social characteristics of speakers is often fragmentary or non-existent? In medieval England, John of Trevisa (writing *c.* 1387) notes the 'straunge wlafferynge, chiterynge, harrynge, and garrynge grisbayting' of certain speakers (translation of *Polychronicon*, see Chapter 8), but such comments allow us to conclude little about actual pronunciation. From the fifteenth century onwards, however, sociolinguistic study begins to be truly possible (Nevalainen 2006c:358). Increased literacy, the existence of private correspondence (especially letters), and a much wider range of other 'speech-based' texts (such as trial proceedings, witness depositions, wills, business records, newspapers, and dramatic and fictional dialogue) allow for more accurate information about the social factors underlying language use and change.[2] Aided by research in social, economic, and cultural history, we are now able to study a large variety of linguistic changes in the history of English from a social perspective.

One very important finding of both sociolinguistics and historical sociolinguistics is the effect of gender. Women—to the extent that they have the same educa-

---

2 We now have electronic corpora (see Chapter 1) of these texts, including *A Corpus of English Dialogues 1560–1760* (Kytö and Culpeper with Archer and Walker; see http://www.engelska.uu.se/corpus.html) as well as the *Corpus of Early English Correspondence c.* 1410–1663 (Nevalainen et al.; see http://www.helsinki.fi/varieng/domains/CEEC.html).

tion and levels of literacy as men—can be seen as the leaders in language change. Women tend to favor new, standard, and 'supralocal' forms, while men tend to favor nonstandard and 'local' forms (Nevalainen 2006c:360–61). A rich and rewarding area of diachronic study has thus opened up.[3]

The possibility of attributing language change to social factors allows us to extrapolate more readily about the causes of change in the past. We may also consider how social networks played a role in the past. The effect that social prestige has on pronunciation and usage as well as on the rest of the grammar (including pragmatics) cannot be underestimated. Language is, after all, an artifact of culture.

---

3 *The Handbook of Historical Sociolinguistics* (Hernández-Campoy forthcoming) gives a good idea of the scope of this study. Another important source of information is the Historical Sociolinguistics Network (http://www.philhist.uni-augsburg.de/hison/).

Exercise 3.1 Causes of Change

1. Give brief definitions of the following concepts of internal causes of language change.

   a. ease of articulation _____

   _____

   b. perceptual clarity _____

   _____

   c. phonological symmetry _____

   _____

   d. universal tendencies _____

   _____

   e. efficiency or transparency _____

   _____

   f. spelling pronunciation _____

   _____

   g. hypercorrection _____

   _____

h. overgeneralization _____

_____

i. analogy _____

_____

j. renewal _____

_____

k. reanalysis _____

_____

2. Using the above list, indicate by letter which concepts answer the following questions.

a. Which are more or less unconscious processes? _____

b. Which are more or less conscious processes? _____

c. Which two act in opposition to each other? _____

d. Which two seem to explain similar changes? _____

e. When a child says 'She rided the bike' instead of 'She rode the bike', which process is being applied? _____

f. Which two processes may describe the two pronunciations of *often* as [ɑfən] or [ɑftən]? _____

g. Which process explains the pairing of such sounds in English as [t]/[d], [f]/[v], and [p]/[b]? _____

h. Which concept can explain the application of *-d* or *-ed* to create the past tense of new borrowings in Modern English? _____

i. Which process could explain the creation of new slang adjectives, like *harsh, rad,* or *random,* for emphasis? _____

Given our understanding of language change—that gaps tend to be filled and irregularities removed—we can hypothesize about future changes in a language, but we cannot be sure which changes will actually occur. We best understand change in the phonological component, which seems to be quite regular. As time progresses, we are also understanding more about developments in the morphological, syntactic, semantic, and pragmatic components.

Mechanisms of Phonological Change

Determining Sounds from Written Records

Before we can even begin to talk about phonological change in a language, we must determine the sounds of earlier stages of the language. Unfortunately, for pre-modern languages we have no sound recordings, so we must work exclusively from the written records. As we have seen for Modern English, orthographic symbols are often an inexact representation of the sounds in speech, in part because changes in sound were not recorded in writing after English spelling became fixed, around 1500. Determining the sounds of a form of the language no longer spoken is a kind of detective work, where a variety of clues must be pieced together:

- the statements of contemporary grammarians, lexicographers (dictionary makers), and other writers;
- puns, word plays, and rhymes in the literature (though these must be used with caution, since the sounds of words entering into these combinations may not correspond exactly, as in slant rhymes and eye rhymes);
- the representation of natural sounds in onomatopoeic words (though, again, caution is needed here because these words are at least partially conventionalized);
- scribal variations and non-standard spellings that often reflect actual pronunciations;
- the development of a sound in closely related languages—for example, we can use French, Spanish, and Italian to extrapolate the nature of a sound in the parent language, Latin; and
- the structure of the hypothesized phonological system, for we assume that such a system will be like modern sound systems in, for example, tending toward symmetry, pairing voiced and voiceless consonants or back and front vowels.

The Nature of Sound Change

One school of linguists in the nineteenth century claimed that sound change is absolutely regular, that it operates without exception. They spoke in terms of 'laws' of sound change (we will learn about Grimm's Law and Verner's Law in Chapter 5). While we now believe this to be an overstatement, we still consider sound change to be highly regular and to be reducible to a set of rules.

Sound changes fall into two classes: conditioned and unconditioned. An *unconditioned* change is one in which every instance of a particular sound changes, regardless of its phonetic environment (i.e. the surrounding sounds or position in a word). The sound changes independently of, or in isolation from, any neighboring sound. In an unconditioned sound change it is common for an entire class of sounds—for example, all stops—to change; such a systematic change is called a *sound shift*. There have been important unconditioned sound shifts in the prehistory of the English language, including the First Sound Shift (where all Germanic stop consonants shifted) and the Great Vowel Shift (where all Middle English long or lengthened vowels shifted). The other type of change—*conditioned*—is one in which a particular sound changes only in certain phonetic environments; the operation of the change depends upon the neighboring sounds, known as the *conditioning environment*. We can state such changes in terms of phonetic rules; the formal presentation of these rules need not concern us here except to note that the symbol > is used to indicate a change; thus [b] > [p] means that the sound [b] becomes the sound [p].

Types of Sound Change

Within the two broad classes of sound changes, we can identify a variety of different mechanisms or types. Most of the following types of change are conditioned.

Assimilation

By assimilation a sound becomes similar to an adjacent sound in voicing, manner of articulation, or place of articulation. Assimilation is motivated by ease of articulation. Two sounds may become identical, or simply alike, in respect to some articulatory features. For example, when *-ling* is attached to *goose* or *-band* to *house*, resulting in *gosling* and *husband*, the final [s] of the root is voiced to [z] to match the voicing quality of the following [l] or [b]; this is partial assimilation. When *-man* is attached to *wif*, giving us the Middle English *wimman*, the [f] becomes [m] to match the following [m]; this is complete assimilation. Try to identify which of the following examples show partial or complete assimilation:

> *con- + plete > complete*
> *con- + late > collate*
> *con- + rect > correct*

It is common for a sound to come to resemble whatever follows it. The process by which this happens is called regressive assimilation because one sound reaches back to affect the preceding one, as the speaker anticipates the articulation to come. For example, in the case of *incongruous* and *Vancouver*, we anticipate the velar consonant [k] by changing the alveolar nasal to a velar nasal. Less often a sound becomes like the one that precedes it, which is progressive assimilation; here, one sound reaches forward to affect the following sound. An example of this kind of assimilation occurs with the past tense marker *-ed*, where the [d] becomes [t] when the preceding sound (the final consonant of the verb) is a voiceless consonant, as in *rushed*, *missed*, *kicked*, *hoped*, *matched*, etc. The sound to which another sound assimilates is usually the immediately adjacent one, but it may also be a sound in the neighboring syllable. This kind of assimilation, called distant assimilation, occurs in the process of umlaut (to be discussed in Chapter 6).

Dissimilation

By dissimilation a sound becomes dissimilar to an adjacent sound. Dissimilation is motivated by the need for perceptual clarity. It is much less common than assimilation, occurring most often with liquids ([l] and [r]) and nasals. For example, the Modern English *pilgrim* derives from the Latin *peregrinus*, but the first *r* in the Latin word has dissimilated to become an [l] sound. A similar change occurs in ModE *purple*, which had two [r] sounds in the original Latin word, *purpur*. The two *r*'s are changed (to *r* and *l*) to make them acoustically more distinct. Two fricatives may dissimilate as well, as in OE *þeofþ* (*þ* represents a voiceless interdental fricative), which has become ModE *theft*, with the shift [fθ] > [ft].

Addition of a Sound

The addition of a sound (or *intrusion*) is usually prompted by the difficulty of coordinating articulatory movements. It is quite common for a stop to be inserted in sequences of nasals, liquids, and fricatives. The stop is generally articulated in the same place as (or said to be *homorganic* with) the nasal or liquid, as in the following examples:

> [d] inserted between [n] and [r]: OE *þunor* > ModE *thunder*
>   [n] and [l]: OE *spinel* > ModE *spindle*
>   [l] and [r]: OE *ealre* > ME *alder*
>
> [b] inserted between [m] and [l]: OE *þȳmel* > ModE *thimble*
>   [m] and [r]: ME *slūmere* > ModE *slumber*

A stop may also be inserted to break up the sequence of a nasal and a fricative, as in the pronunciation of *prince, sense, dense*, and *mince* with [t] between [n] and [s], rhyming with *prints, cents, dents*, and *mints*. Another example is the pronunciation of *warmth* with [p] between [m] and [θ] or *length* with [k] between [ŋ] and [θ]. A consonant added at the end of a word is especially common after [s] or [n], such as OE *betwihs* > ModE *betwixt*, ME *soun* > ModE *sound*, or *vermin* yielding the dialectal variant *varmint*. This is called an excrescent stop. Another common addition is schwa, as in *ath[ə]lete, chim[ə]ney*, or *fil[ə]m*.

Loss of a Sound

The loss of a sound is very common, motivated in most cases by ease of articulation. The loss of an initial vowel occurs in *opossum* > *possum* or *about* > *'bout*. The loss of a medial vowel is called syncope, as in *mem(o)ry*, or *ev(e)ning* and the names *Barb(a)ra* or *Britt(a)ny*; and the loss of a final vowel is called apocope, as in OE *nama* > ModE *name* (where the *e* is silent) or OE *sunu* > ModE *son*. Consonants may be lost in all three positions as well. If the consonant which is lost occurs adjacent to other consonants, we have what is called simplification of a consonant cluster. All final consonants, since they are weakly articulated, are prone to loss. Here are some examples of consonant loss:

initial: OE *hnutu* > ModE *nut*
the loss of [k] in ModE *knit*
the loss of [g] in ModE *gnat*

medial: OE *godspel* > ModE *gospel*
OE *weorðscipe* > ModE *worship*
the loss of [t] in ModE *castle*
the loss of [l] in ModE *chalk*
the loss of [d] in ModE *handsome*

final: the loss of [b] in ModE *dumb*
the loss of [n] in ModE *hymn*
the loss of [d] in ModE *drowned*
the loss of [g] in ModE *sing*

Metathesis

Metathesis is the reversal or reordering of two sounds. This is especially common with sequences of liquids and vowels or of fricatives and stops:

liquid + vowel > vowel + liquid: Spanish *tronada* > ModE *tornado*
vowel + liquid > liquid + vowel: OE *beorht* > ModE *bright*
fricative + stop: OE variants *ascian* 'to ask' and *axian* (x = [ks]) (this alternation is still heard in dialects of PDE)

A more recent instance of metathesis is the pronunciation [nukjələr] for *nuclear*. Sometimes, people even move a word division so that, for instance, *an other* becomes *a (whole) nother*, with the [n] of the article becoming attached to the beginning of the noun following it. This is called metathesis of juncture.

Other Types of Sound Change

The types of sound changes given above affect only individual lexical items and do not generally alter the phonological system itself. However, other changes may affect the language's inventory of distinctive (or contrastive) sounds:

- If two sounds merge completely or if one sound splits into two then the inventory of sounds in the language may be depleted or increased. For example, in Middle English, the OE long vowels [ē] and [ǣ] merged as [ē], as in OE *gēs* and *strǣt* (ModE *geese, street*), decreasing the number of vowel phonemes as [ǣ] was lost from the inventory. In Early Modern English, the short vowel [ʊ] split into two, [ʊ] and [ə], as in *push* and *putt*, but since [ə] already existed in the language, this split caused no increase in the inventory of sounds.

- When an allophone becomes a phoneme, the number of distinctive sounds in the language increases. In English, voiceless and voiced fricatives such as [s] and [z] were originally allophones of the same fricative phoneme. They have since become separate phonemes, contrasting in such pairs as *sip* and *zip*. This is called phonemicization.
- Simple losses or additions of sounds also occur; for example, the consonants [x], [ç], and [ɣ] have been lost from English and [ž] acquired.

Apart from the changes already discussed, any aspect of the articulation of a vowel or a consonant may be altered. Vowel changes may be qualitative, producing a different kind of sound, such as when the tongue is moved by raising (e.g. [o] > [u]) or lowering (e.g. [o] > [ɔ]) or by fronting (e.g. [o] > [e]) or backing (e.g. [æ] > [ɑ]), or the position of the lips is changed by rounding (e.g. [i] > [y]) or unrounding (e.g. [y] > [i]). A monophthong may gain a glide (e.g. [o] > [oʊ], [e] > [eɪ]) in a process called *diphthongization*, while a diphthong may lose a glide ([æɪ] > [æ]), which, rather unsurprisingly, is called *monophthongization*. A tense vowel may become lax (e.g. [e] > [ɛ]), or be both centralized and laxed to become [ə] in a move known as *reduction*. This particular vowel change, as we will see, has had profound effects on the grammar of English.

Other vowel changes are quantitative, as the length of articulation of the vowel is increased (*lengthening*) or decreased (*shortening*). Often when a consonant is lost, the preceding vowel will be lengthened to compensate. For example, when [n] was lost in the Proto-Germanic word for 'goose', *gans, the resulting Old English form, *gōs*, had a long vowel. (But compare *gander* in which the *n* was not lost).

Consonants may change in the place or manner of articulation, or in their voicing. Such changes are usually the result of assimilation of the consonant to an adjacent sound. Some of the possible consonant changes are:

- *labialization* – The lips become round, as in the [l] sound of *loom* and *loose* (in anticipation of the rounded vowels that follow) as opposed to the [l] sound of *lace* and *lime* (where the following vowels are unrounded).
- *velarization* – The consonant is articulated more in the velar region of the mouth, as in the [l] sound of *feel* and *pail* (following a vowel or [r]) as opposed to the [l] sound of *leave* and *lap*.
- *palatalization* – The consonant is articulated more in the palatal region of the mouth, as in [s] > [š] (moving back from alveolar to alveolopalatal) or [x] > [ç] (moving forward from velar to palatal). We see the change from [s] > [š], for example, in the rapid articulation of *miss you* because we anticipate the palatal glide in *you*. Palatalization may involve a change in manner of articulation as well, as in the change of a stop to an affricate: [t] > [č] or [k] > [č], as in *kirk* and *church*. Palatalization is an important process, discussed in chapters 6 and 10.

- *fricativization* (or *spirantization*) – A consonant, usually a stop, is changed to a fricative, as in the final consonant in the related words *democrat* and *democracy* where [t] > [s].
- *rhotacism* – A consonant, usually [s], becomes [r], as in the related words *genus* and *generic*.
- *lenition* – A 'weakening' of a consonant occurs between vowels; a stop consonant > fricative (e.g. OE *mōdor* > ModE *mother*), a fricative > approximant (OE *hālgian* > ModE *hallow*), voiceless > voiced (e.g. the voicing of [t] in words such as *butter* or *matter*).
- *vocalization* – A consonant becomes a semivowel or vowel, as in OE *hafoc* > ModE *hawk*.
- *voicing or devoicing* – A consonant becomes voiced, as in the verb *house* compared to the noun *house,* or a consonant becomes voiceless, as in the [l] sound in *please* or the [r] sound in *pray* which are partially devoiced because they follow voiceless consonants.

Exercise 3.2 Mechanisms of Phonological Change

1. Give complete phonetic descriptions of the following symbols, then name the sound change.

   a. [z] > [ž] _____

   _____

   b. [u] > [aʊ]_____

   _____

   c. [b] > [p]_____

   _____

   d. [y] > [i]_____

   _____

   e. [ɪ] > [ə] _____

   _____

2. Say each of the following words and observe the way(s) in which the spelling and the pronunciation differ. Disparities of this sort are often the result of sound change. Name the sound change or changes in each case.

   a. February _____

   _____

   b.   yolk _____

   _____

   c.   irresponsible (from *in* + *responsible*) _____

   _____

   d.   every _____

   _____

   e.   bright _____

   _____

3.   Compare the older and newer forms and determine the sound change(s) undergone by each word:

   a.   ME claps, ModE clasp _____

   _____

   b.   OE andswaru, ModE answer _____

   _____

   c.   ME kinred, ModE kindred_____

   _____

   d.   ME launde, ModE lawn_____

   _____

   e.   OE hlid, ModE lid_____

   _____

Mechanisms of Morphological and Syntactic Change

It is difficult to separate morphological and syntactic change because change in one component is often accompanied by or entails change in the other component. We will treat them together.

Analogy

The motivating force in morphological change, and to a lesser extent in syntactic change, is analogy. Analogy is a process by which one form becomes like another one with which it is somehow associated (such as having the same function). Analogy often works by a kind of proportion: *a* is to *b* as *c* is to *x* (with the new or changed form being *x*). For example, following the pattern of *bus* pluralizing to *buses*, we might form the plural of *ox* as *oxes*. If *oxes* were to displace the inherited plural *oxen*, then *analogical extension* would have taken place. In this case, analogy makes the language more transparent by working toward the end that *-(e)s* always expresses the plural and that the plural is always expressed by *-(e)s*. An important effect of analogy is the removal of irregularities or anomalous forms. Jean Aitchison refers to analogy as a 'tidying up' process (2001:176). However, it is important to keep in mind that analogy may be ad hoc and sporadic and does not always work in a systematic way.

There are two types of morphological analogy—one that affects stems and one that affects affixes. Analogy in stems works to remove irregularities in the root of different inflected forms of a word, irregularities which generally come about through sound change. Such irregularities are, in fact, quite infrequent in English. However, one example is the irregular plural formation in *knife/knives*, *life/lives*, *wife/wives*, *loaf/loaves*, *leaf/leaves*, etc., where the singular root ends in a voiceless fricative and the plural root in a voiced fricative. While many of these plural forms have resisted analogy, some of the nouns have acquired analogical plurals, producing such forms as *scarfs*, *hoofs*, and *wharfs* against the irregular, inherited forms *scarves*, *hooves*, and *wharves*. Certain newer words such as *reef* (in the sense of a 'narrow ridge of rock, sand, coral, etc.') have only the regular plural form, *reefs*.

Analogy in affixes is much more common. It generally refers to the way in which an inflectional ending will extend its domain so as to be added to words which originally took different endings. Table 3.1 presents the example of noun plurals in Old English, where the plural is indicated by a variety of different endings, depending on the class to which the noun belongs.

In English, the *-as* plural ending (which becomes *-s* by regular phonetic change) evolves as the analogical plural ending; it spreads to nouns which originally took different plural endings. It is as if an analogical proportion is set up: *stone* is to *stones* as *hand* is to *x*, with *x* then being formed as *hands*. The form chosen as the analogical ending is usually the most widespread one; in this case, *-as* is the plural ending of the largest class of nouns in Old English. The analogical ending becomes the regular, or productive, ending: it may eventually be added to all nouns, and it is added to any new nouns entering the language. However, a few of the older forms remain, such as *foot/feet*, *ox/oxen*, *child/children*, and *sheep/sheep*, which have non-productive plural endings. These endings are found in only a few remnant, or 'frozen', forms; they are hardly ever used as a means for pluralizing new words in the language.

Language change is neither complete nor consistent, as evidenced by these remnant forms. It tends to be slow at first, rapid in the middle, and slow at the end, with a few forms resisting change. In addition, words of very high frequency tend to resist analogical change and to be the most irregular forms of the language. It is said

Table 3.1 Analogy in English Plural Endings

OE sg.	OE pl.	OE plural marker	ModE pl.	ModE plural marker
stān	stānas	-as	stones	-s
hand	handa	-a	hands	-s
cwēn	cwēne	-e	queens	-s
ēage	ēagan	-an	eyes	-s
lim	limu	-u	limbs	-s
gēar	gēar	Ø	years	-s
lamb	lambru	-ru	lambs	-s
bōc	bēc	ō > ē	books	-s

that 'analogy works where memory fails', since we may have difficulty remembering the forms of less frequently used words; we do not have any difficulty remembering the irregular forms of words we use constantly (such as, for example, forms of the verb *to be*). Occasionally, even when an analogical form spreads, the irregular form survives in a restricted context. Thus, while the regular plural of *brother* is now *brothers*, the remnant form *brethren* is preserved in religious contexts, while the remnant plural of *cow* (*kine*) is still used occasionally in poetry.

We will see many examples of analogical change, for example, the replacement of the strong (irregular) past tense which uses a vowel change (e.g. *glid, glad*) with the weak (regular) past tense which uses a dental suffix (*glide, glided*). The power of analogy can also be seen in the types of false analogy at work in the language. For instance, analogy frequently underlies children's mistakes, such as when they form the past tense of *bring* as *bringed*, the plural of *foot* as *foots*, or the comparative of *good* as *gooder*. In each case, they are simply applying the productive inflection. Unlike the way analogy operates in language change, however, children create these forms for very common words.

A second kind of false analogy is *back-formation*, where speakers derive a morphologically simple word from a form which they analyze as morphologically complex. Hence, following the very productive pattern in which *-er* may be added to a verb to create an agent noun (e.g. *work* + *-er* > *worker*; *sing* + *-er* > *singer*), speakers 'back-form' the (previously non-existent) verbs *burgle* from *burglar*, *lech* from *lecher*, *babysit* from *babysitter*, and *orate* from *orator*. Or they analyze the *-y* as being a suffix in *jelly* and *lazy*, as it is in many other words, and create the verbs *jell* and *laze*. Other examples include *coeducate* (from *coeducation*), *window-shop* (from *window-shopping*), *mass-produce* (from *mass-produced*), *megalith* (from *megalithic*), and *peeve* (from *peevish*).

Closely related to back-formation is false morphological analysis, which is also based on analogy. For example, the singular forms borrowed from Old French *pease* and *cerise* were falsely analyzed as containing plural *-s*, by analogy with regular noun plurals ending in *-s* in English, and the singular forms *pea* and *cherry* were created. Similarly, the OE form *rædelese* was reanalyzed as a plural, and the singular form *riddle* was derived. By the same reasoning, the *-s* of the root is analyzed as a plural marker in the OE singular form *ælmesse* and the ME singular form *richesse*, giving plural ModE forms *alms* and *riches*.

Folk etymology is also based on analogy. Here, a word which is unfamiliar or has become unfamiliar (because it is an older English word or a borrowing from a foreign language) is associated with a more familiar word. Its referent remains the same, but its phonetic form is often modified by analogy and it is given a new history. For example, the word *female* has nothing to do with *male*; rather, the diminutive *-elle* ending of the French word *femelle*, meaning 'woman', was unfamiliar to English speakers, so they altered the form of the word to resemble their native word *male*. Similarly, *helpmate* has nothing to do with *mate*, but because the Middle English form *meet*, meaning 'suitable', had become unfamiliar, the form of the word was altered to something more recognizable. Some other examples of folk etymology include the following:

- *earwig* < OE *wicga* 'one that moves about, a beetle', hence 'a beetle thought to crawl into the ear' (nothing to do with wigs)
- *kittycorner* < Fr. *quatre* 'four', hence 'the diagonal' (nothing to do with cats)
- *bridegroom* < OE *guma* 'man', hence 'the man of the bride' (nothing to do with the tender of horses)
- *hangnail* < OE *ang* 'painful', hence 'a painful nail' (nothing to do with hanging) (cf. Ger. *Angst*)
- *wedlock* < OE *wedd* 'pledge' + *lāc* 'offering' (nothing to do with locking)
- *shamefaced* < OE *sceam* 'shame' + *fæst* 'fixed' (nothing to do with faces)
- *sockeye* < Salish *sukkegh* (nothing to do with socks or eyes)

Grammaticalization

A second important kind of change in morphology and syntax is called grammaticalization, a process by which a word with full lexical meaning becomes a lexically empty grammatical marker. It may also be reduced phonetically and become an inflection. Words are often grammaticalized to replace inflections which are lost or weakened. For example, the *to* that marks the infinitive of the verb (e.g. *to eat*) was originally in Old English a full preposition that took a (verbal) noun object. However, in this situation, *to* no longer functions as a preposition in Modern English but serves as a grammatical marker signaling the non-finite form to follow, and it is often phonetically reduced to [tə].

The conversion of a full verb into an auxiliary verb is an example of grammaticalization. For example, the Modern English markers of the future, *shall* and *will*, began life as full lexical verbs in Old English (called *preterit-present* verbs, as will be discussed in Chapter 7) with the meaning of 'obligation' and 'intention', respectively. In the course of Middle English, these meanings faded in some contexts to become pure markers of the future tense, conveying only prediction. Their syntactic status also changed from full verb (a verb which can stand alone in a sentence) to auxiliary verb (a verb which must accompany another verb and is subordinated to it). A more recent example of the grammaticalization of a future marker is the construction *be going to* (as in *I am going to be rich some day*), which no longer carries any sense of direction or motion (compare the full verb *I am going home some day*). It is likewise a grammaticalized form of the main verb *go* (in the progressive form *be going*) followed by an infinitive, which develops into an auxiliary phrase *be going to*, often unified as *gonna*. In addition, many verbs have been grammaticalized as auxiliary verbs, to replace lost inflections on the verb: *have* comes to mark the perfect; *be* and *get* come to mark the passive; *be* comes to mark the progressive; the modal auxiliaries (e.g. *should*, *could*, *must*, *may*), which were full verbs in Old English, come to mark subjunctive mood; and *do* serves as a substitute auxiliary.

The conversion of prepositions into markers of case is another example of grammaticalization. For example, in Modern English, genitive (possessive) case may be expressed by an inflection (e.g. *the table's leg*) or by a prepositional phrase (e.g. *the leg of the table*); in this use, *of* has lost its original meaning 'off, from' and has become a pure marker of the possessive. Similarly, dative case (the indirect object) is marked in Modern English by the preposition *to*, whose meaning of 'direction or motion toward' is considerably weakened or abstracted: compare *I gave the book to Maria* (indirect object) and *I drove the truck to New York* (motional goal). Since the inflection of the dative in nouns no longer survives in Modern English, prepositional phrases with *to* or *for* (e.g. *I wrote the poem for Maria*) and word order (e.g. *I gave Maria the book*) are the only available means for marking this case.

Later we will examine in more detail these and other instances of grammaticalization: of the adverbs *more* and *most* as markers of degree (even though the inflections -*er* and -*est* survive), of the preposition *by* as marker of the agent in a passive sentence, of the OE demonstrative *that* as the definite article *the*, and of the OE numeral *one* as the indefinite article *a/an*.

Conservative and Innovative Changes

Analogical change and grammaticalization alter the means for marking various grammatical distinctions, but they do not generally make a difference to the total number of such distinctions in the language. In the spread of the -*s* plural marker in nouns, for example, there is no change in the distinction made (plural number continues to be expressed), just a change in the particular formal marker used, -*s* rather than the Old English inflections -*a*, -*ru*, -*an*, etc. In the grammaticalization of the *of* marker for the possessive, there is likewise no change in the distinction made (genitive case), only a change in its formal marking. These are called conservative changes (Benveniste 1968), and the majority of changes in the language appear to be of this sort (a fact which should calm the fears of those concerned about language 'deterioration').

Some changes, however, cause a grammatical distinction to be added to or lost. These are innovative changes. We will see a number of losses in the grammar of English: of dual number, of grammatical gender, of the second-person singular pronoun, of certain consonant and vowel sounds, of the distinction between long and short vowels, of the distinction between accusative and dative case in the pronoun forms, etc. However, many losses are partial (e.g. we have lost many strong verbs yet still retain a core of them), or are partially replaced by some other aspect of the grammar (e.g. we have lost most person and number distinctions on the verb but now require an overt subject in all but imperative sentences). True additions to the system of a language are difficult to find, primarily because it seems that grammatical distinctions do not rise out of a vacuum; often they are already present in the language in a somewhat different form. Nonetheless, we can point to several such additions, discussed in later chapters: the progressive, an article system, a gender system based on animacy, the 'dummy' subject *it*, and perhaps the future tense.[4]

---

4 In the case of the future tense, we see the difficulty of identifying additions. While Old English does not have any overt verbal marking of the future, either inflections or auxiliary verbs, it does have future adverbs, or a future meaning that may be inferred from context. Can we say, then, that Old English does not have the future?

Exercise 3.3 Mechanisms of Morphological and Syntactic Change

Consider the following words and determine the processes of morphological and syntactic change that differentiate them. Where relevant, say whether the change is conservative or innovative.

a. the verb *sculpt* and the noun *sculptor* _____

_____

b. auxiliary verb *may* from the OE verb *magan* 'to be able' _____

_____

c. EModE *skeates* (pl.) 'ice skates' in the seventeenth century from Dutch *schaats* (sg.) 'skate, stilt' _____

_____

d. *charterhouse* 'charitable institution', originally meant 'a Carthusian monastery'

_____

_____

e. OE *ic* 'I', *wit* 'we two', *we* 'we all' have become ModE *I* (sg.), *we* (pl.) _____

_____

f. OE *wīfmann* 'woman' and *wīfhād* 'womanhood' are masculine; their ModE equivalents are feminine and neuter respectively _____

_____

g. ModE *acorn* from OE *æcern* 'field fruit, mast (fallen nuts)' (OE *æcer* 'field' > ModE *acre*) by way of ME *akkorn*, which is believed to be a combination of *ake* 'oak' and *corn* 'kernel' _____

_____

h. ModE *oakum* 'loose fiber often used in caulking' from OE *acumba* 'flax fibers separated by combing' (*a-* 'out' + *cemba* 'to comb') _____

_____

Mechanisms of Semantic Change

Semantic change is an alteration in the lexical meaning of words and morphemes. Of all the components of language, lexical meaning is most susceptible to change. Semantics is not rule-governed in the same way that grammar is because the connection between sound and meaning is arbitrary and conventional. Furthermore, although we look to dictionaries to give us the one correct meaning of a word, meanings are in fact very flexible and fluid. Some words (such as *much* or *many*) are inherently vague; others are used vaguely. Meanings are also subjective, with individual speakers often holding different notions about the meaning of a word. For some speakers of English, *decimate* means 'to destroy or remove one in every ten', while for others it means 'to destroy or remove a large proportion' or 'to subject to severe loss'. Finally, semantic change is more obviously linked to cultural, social, and political changes than are phonological, morphological, and syntactic changes.

The meaning of a word often departs radically from its original or etymological meaning. This should not surprise us, nor should we, like the eighteenth-century grammarians, insist upon the sanctity of the etymological meaning, which is simply the first recorded definition of the word. Sometimes it is difficult to see how the etymological meaning relates to the present one. For example, the word *snack* originally meant 'dog bite' but comes to mean a 'light refreshment'. At other times, as shown in Figure 3.1, we can construct a logical chain of shifts in meaning from the earliest to the latest meaning of a word, as in the case of *silly* (OE *gesælig*). Until we construct this chain, however, the shift from the OE meaning of 'happy, blessed' to the current sense of 'foolish, senseless, stupid' might be incomprehensible.

Types of Semantic Change

In semantic change, as we will see, the intension or the extension of a word may change. Words may change either their denotation or their connotations, and may either add or delete semantic features. Although it is often difficult to say why word meanings change and usually impossible to say if or when they will change, we can say something about the direction, mechanisms, and types of semantic change.

Generalization and Specialization

Generalization is the widening in scope of a word's meaning, allowing it to denote a greater variety of referents. For this to happen, specific parts of the denotation must be dropped; as a result, there is a reduction in the number of semantic features. For example, the word *holiday* originally referred only to 'holy days', but now it can refer to days without any religious significance which are set aside as non-work days, such as Labor Day, or we can go on 'holidays' when we take a vacation. Thus, the feature of holiness has been deleted. Similarly, a *sanctuary* originally referred to a 'holy place', which was therefore a safe place, but now the word refers to any safe, but not necessarily holy, place, such as a bird sanctuary or a political sanctuary. Other examples of generalization are:

> *box*, formerly 'a small container made of boxwood'
> *butcher*, formerly 'one who slaughters goats'
> *scent*, no longer exclusively 'an animal odor used for tracking'
> *carry*, formerly 'to transport in a vehicle'
> *junk*, formerly 'worn out pieces of rope'
> *crisis,* formerly 'a turning point of a disease'
> *divest*, formerly 'to take off one's clothes'
> *bonfire*, formerly meaning 'fire of bones'

A more common process than this is specialization, the narrowing in scope of the meaning of a word. The number of semantic features of the denotation increases, and hence the number of referents of the word decreases. The word ends up naming a subcategory of the category it originally named. Specialization sometimes occurs in tandem with borrowing: a native word is specialized, and a borrowed word takes over the more general meaning. For example, the native word *lust* originally meant 'desire in general' (as the cognate word still does in Modern German), a meaning now expressed by the French borrowing *desire*, with *lust* specialized to

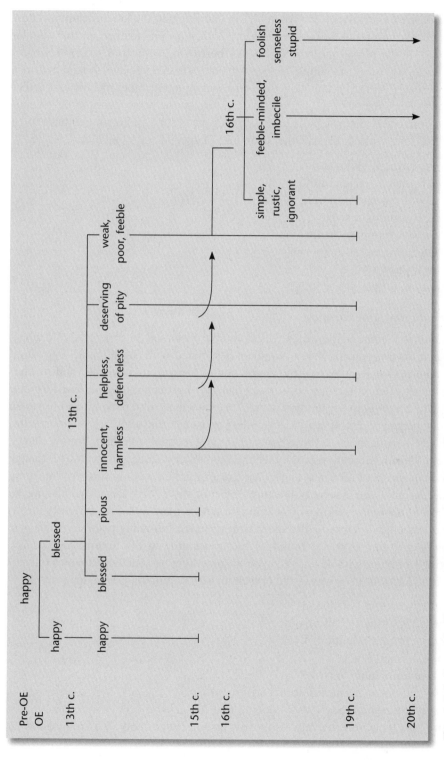

Figure 3.1 Semantic Changes of *silly* (from M.L. Samuels, *Linguistic Evolution with Special Reference to English* [Cambridge: Cambridge University Press, 1972], p. 66, reprinted with the permission of Cambridge University Press)

'sexual desire'. *Free* meant 'free or noble' in Old English; the latter meaning is now expressed by the French borrowing *noble*. *Feather* meant 'feather' in the singular but 'wing' in the plural until the Old Norse borrowing *wing* took over the word's plural meaning. *Stool*, meaning 'a seat for one person', became specialized to a backless seat, with the French loan word *chair* taking on its other meaning. Whether this process is a matter of the borrowed word forcing the native word to be specialized or, conversely, the specialization causing a need for a more general term to be borrowed is not entirely clear. Other examples of specialization include:

> *acorn*, formerly 'wild fruit'
> *gum*, formerly 'inside of the mouth'
> *sermon*, formerly 'a speech, discourse'
> *adder*, formerly 'a snake'
> *adventure*, formerly 'happening'
> *cellar*, formerly 'a storehouse'
> *meat*, formerly 'food'
> *gestation*, formerly 'carrying'

Pejoration and Amelioration

Pejoration is the acquisition of a less favorable meaning. In a pejorative change, there is a lowering in the value judgment associated with the referent. Pejoration is a complex change, affecting the denotation of a word, its referents, and its connotations. It often combines with specialization. For example, a *villain* formerly referred to a 'low-born or common person', a *clown* to a 'rural person', an *idiot* to an 'ignorant person', a *blackguard* to a 'scullery assistant', and a *hussy* to a 'housewife' (< OE *hūs* + *wīf*). In all of these cases, there is a recognizable direction of change to a less valued referent. Words other than nouns also undergo pejorative change by the acquisition of a negative meaning: for example, *cunning*, formerly meaning 'knowledgeable'; *coy*, formerly meaning 'quiet or shy'; *carp*, formerly meaning 'to talk, boast'; *admonish*, formerly meaning 'to advise'; and *immoral*, formerly meaning 'not customary'. Observe the specialization in the following pejorative changes: *grumble*, changing from 'to mumble' to 'to mumble in discontent' and *addict*, changing from 'one who devotes himself to something' to 'one who devotes himself to harmful substances or ways'. Other examples of pejoration can be seen in:

> *harlot*, formerly 'vagabond'
> *expletive*, formerly 'filling out'
> *poison*, formerly 'potion, drink'
> *smug*, formerly 'neat'
> *sly*, formerly 'able to strike'
> *surly*, formerly 'masterful, lordly (from *sir*)'
> *corpse*, formerly 'body'
> *rustle*, no longer exclusively 'to move with soft fluttering or crackling sound'

A rather recent change involving pejoration is the word *judgmental*, which originally meant 'inclined to make judgments', whereas today it is almost always used pejoratively to mean 'inclined to make uncharitable or negative judgments, overly critical'.

In contrast, amelioration is the acquisition of a more favorable meaning, again involving change in intension, referent, and connotations. There is an elevation in the value judgment involved in the referent. Amelioration also often accompanies specialization. For example, a *steward* formerly referred to the 'overseer of the pig sty' (< OE *stig* + *weard*), an *engineer* to a 'plotter, schemer', a *boy* to a 'rascal, servant', and a *mansion* to a 'house, dwelling'. Examples of amelioration in other parts of speech are *esteem*, formerly 'to put a value on'; *bare*, formerly 'useless, worthless'; and *jolly*, formerly 'arrogant, wanton, lustful'. Other examples include:

> *marshal*, formerly 'horse servant, groom'
> *epicure*, formerly 'a person devoted to sensual pleasure and luxury'
> *success*, formerly 'outcome, result'
> *rapture*, formerly 'abduction'
> *shrewd*, formerly 'wicked'
> *spill*, formerly meaning 'to shed blood'
> *revolution*, formerly 'rolling over'
> *compliment*, formerly 'filling up'
> *nice*, formerly 'silly, simple'

Weakening and Strengthening

We sometimes use words which are weaker or stronger than required by the circumstances. Use of a weaker word than is required by the context is a kind of understatement that may lead to strengthening of that word; employing a stronger word, on the other hand, is a kind of overstatement that may result in its weakening. For example, the word *molest*, originally used as a more socially accepted word, or *euphemism* (from the Greek word meaning 'to speak favorably'), for rape has led to that word acquiring the denotation 'to subject to unwanted or improper sexual activity'. On the other hand, in the expression *awfully nice*, the word *awfully*, which once held a sense of 'causing dread and awe', is a hyperbole that has become weakened to 'very'. Where weakening or strengthening occurs, the words often end up being replaced.

We tend to avoid the direct terms for topics that we find difficult to talk about, such as unpleasant jobs, parts of the body, sex, pregnancy, birth, bodily functions, disease, old age, and death; this avoidance is called a linguistic taboo. Instead, we use euphemisms, which can be formed by a variety of means:

- *generalization* – use of a wider or more general term, such as *growth* for 'cancer', *condition* for 'disease', *procedure* for 'operation', *person of interest* for 'police suspect', and *voiding* for 'defecation or urination'

- *splitting features* – lessening the impact by dividing the semantic features between two words (each innocuous on its own), such as *job action* for 'strike', *ethnic cleansing* for 'pogrom, genocide', and *pre-owned* for 'used'
- *borrowing words* – use of a neo-Latin or Greek pseudo-technical term, such as *perspire, expire, abdomen, mortuary, expectorate, sputum,* or *halitosis*
- *figure of speech* – use of a metaphor, such as *belly button* or *pass (away)*, or a metonymy, such as *glow* for 'sweat' or *in his cups* for 'drunk'
- *semantic shift* – use of the name of one part of the process to denote another part, such as *to sleep with, to make love with/to,* or *to go to the bathroom*
- *phonetic distortion* (or *taboo deformation*) – alteration of the phonetic form of the word, such as *gad, darn, doggone, son of a gun,* or *shoot*
- *diminutives* – addition of a diminutive suffix, such as *fanny, tummy,* or *tipsy*, or the use of reduplication, such as *wee-wee, pooh-pooh*
- *acronyms or initialisms* – such as *VD* for 'venereal disease', *TB* for 'tuberculosis', *DTs* for 'delirium tremens', and *SOB* for 'son of a bitch'

Euphemisms are in continual need of renewal. If the euphemism displaces the original word completely, then it may itself come to be considered too strong or direct a word and thus need to be replaced. The word *toilet* is a euphemism deriving from the diminutive of the French word for the 'towel, cloth' covering a dressing table, *toilette*. However, this word is today associated with the actual plumbing fixture and thought too direct, so a range of euphemisms are substituted: *washroom, bathroom, WC, loo, ladies' room, lavatory, comfort station, gents, the necessary*, etc.

A primitive attitude toward language seems to underlie euphemism, one that sees an essential link between the word and the thing denoted; this makes the word very powerful because it evokes the thing named. Apart from delicacy or squeamishness, euphemisms may result from deliberate political deception, as with words like *pacification, relocation camp,* or *final solution*. However, the oldest euphemisms in the language are motivated by fear or awe. Out of respect, religious people often do not use a personal name for their god, but refer instead to a Father, Lord, or Master. (The word *god* originally meant 'the invoked one'.) Respect may also prevent us from calling our parents by their personal names. Animals may be the object of superstition and hence referred to indirectly, perhaps out of fear of summoning them: the Germanic word for 'bear' means 'the brown one', while its Slavic equivalent means 'the honey eater'. Similarly, the word for 'wolf' in Indo-European undergoes phonetic deformation as a result of taboo. In a different realm, the left side is often the source of superstition, since it is associated with ill omens or bad luck. We see this in the Latin word *sinister*, meaning 'on the left' but also 'unfavorable, unfortunate, unlucky, inauspicious'. It is interesting that the two euphemisms used for 'left' in Classical Greek are *aristerós* (from *aristós* 'best, noblest') and *eu⁻onumos* ('well-named').

The opposite of the understatement found in euphemisms is the hyperbole which is especially common with a class of adverbs called intensifiers (e.g. *very*). These undergo a continual process of weakening, and progressively stronger words must replace them. Apart from *awful* mentioned earlier, adjectives such as *fabulous* ('fabled'), *marvelous* ('causing wonder or astonishment'), *outrageous* ('exceeding the limits'), and *incredible* ('not to be believed') have all been turned into intensifiers and semantically weakened to 'very'. Weakening can be observed in other words as well:

adore from 'worship as divine' to 'like'
swelter from 'faint from excessive heat' to 'be hot'
fascinate from 'bewitch by spell' to 'interest strongly'
starve from 'die' to 'be hungry'

We have many expressions involving hyperbole of this kind: *I'm dying to* (= 'I want to'), *I'm freezing* (= 'I'm cold'), *I'm famished* (= 'I'm hungry'), *I'd love to* (= 'I'd like to'), *that's terrible* (= 'that's bad') etc.

Figurative Shifts

Figurative shifts in meaning involve a kind of sideways leap, a transfer of meaning from one referent to another. When two things resemble each other in respect to at least one feature, then the name for one can be transferred to the other. There are a number of different types of figurative shift. The most widely known is metaphor, which contains an implied comparison based on similar semantic features of two referents; the qualities belonging to the first referent become associated with the second, as in 'love is a rose' or 'John is a rat'. When a metaphor dies—that is, when the metaphorical meaning is no longer recognized but has become part of the denotation of the word (either replacing or supplementing the original denotation)—then a semantic change has taken place. Metaphors are pervasive, and metaphorical shifts underlie much of the meaning in language. The dead metaphors involving parts of the human body hint at the extent of metaphorical meaning originally present: *mouth of a river*, *lip of a glass*, *legs of a table*, *head of a nail*, *hands of a clock*, *shoulder of the road*, *ribs of a ship*, *eye of a storm*, *tongue of land*, and *guts of a machine*.

A shift from concrete to abstract meaning, often from physical to mental, occurs frequently in metaphor. Many Latinate words undergo such a shift: *translate* meant 'to carry across', *report* 'to carry back', *deduce* 'to lead away', *abstract* 'to draw away from', *compose* 'to put together', *affirm* 'to make firm', *conceive* 'to catch', and *explain* 'to make flat'. Native vocabulary can be used in the same way: *grasp a point*, *get the joke*, *catch one's meaning*, *search one's soul*, *wrestle with an idea*, *a shallow notion,* and *a deep thought*. The opposite direction of change, from abstract to concrete, does occur, but much less commonly. For example, an *essay* was originally an 'attempt or a trial' but is now used to name the concrete results of writing. Another common metaphorical shift is from spatial to temporal meaning, as in *the days to come*, *days gone by*, *long ago*, *a short time*, *shortly*, *the days ahead*, *a brief encounter*, and *next week*.

Three figurative shifts similar to metaphor, known by rather fancy classical names, are *synecdoche*, *metonymy*, and *synesthesia*. In synecdoche, the name of a part is used for the whole, as in the expressions *new blood* ('a person'), *an old face* ('a person'), *a rhyme* ('a poem'), *a roof* ('a house'), *the paper* ('the newspaper'), and *bread* ('food'). A proverbial saying containing synecdoche is *Many hands make light work*. Often, a thing is named by the substance which composes it: *a glass, a fur, an iron*, or *woolens*. In metonymy, something is named by an object associated with it, for example *the bar* ('the legal profession'); *the throne, the scepter*, or *the crown* ('the king/queen etc.'); *the pen is mightier than the sword* ('writing is more powerful than fighting'); *blood, sweat, and tears* ('hard work, self-sacrifice'); the White House ('the president of the US and the president's advisors'); *Ottawa* ('officials in the Canadian government'); *runners* ('shoes used for running'); *room and board* (in which *board* is the 'table at which one eats'); and *the block* ('people who live on the block'). In synesthesia, a word referring to one sense is transferred to another or to a non-sensual domain, as in *a flat note, a quiet color, a bitter reproach, a bright idea, a broad style, a cool reception, hot news*, and *a coarse person*.

In a final kind of figurative shift, a word naming an internal psychological state is used to refer to an external object evoking that state, or vice versa. An example of such a shift is *dreadful* in the phrase *a dreadful occasion*; *dreadful* formerly referred to the subjective experience of a person who was 'full of dread' but came to refer to an objective situation 'causing dread or fear'. Similarly, *complexion*, originally meaning 'physical constitution', now means the external 'natural appearance of the skin'. An example of this shift in reverse, from objective to subjective, is *happy* in *a happy person*; *happy* formerly described a lucky occurrence, but came to refer to a person's state evoked by such good fortune. Similarly, *nauseous* in the expression *a nauseous feeling* changes the objective meaning 'inducing nausea' to the subjective meaning 'suffering from nausea'.

Invited Inferences

Semantic change may also come about by a process of what has been called pragmatic strengthening. Here, meanings which arise in context 'on the fly' and must be inferred by hearers become part of the conventional, denotational meaning of the word. These meanings are known as conversational implicatures, or 'invited inferences'. The word *since* originally had a temporal meaning, as in *Since dinner, I have been reading a novel*. However, in certain contexts, one might infer a causal meaning, as in *Since he left, I have been unhappy*. Here, *since* may be interpreted as 'after' or 'because'. In this context, the new causal meaning is said to be defeasible or revocable, because one could deny it by adding *but it is not because he left that I have been unhappy*. Elsewhere, the causal meaning seems to have become part of the denotation of the word, as in *Since you are rich, why don't you buy a new house?* Here, *since* must mean 'because', not 'after'. A semantic change has occurred. Similarly *while*, originally meaning 'during', may invite the interpretation 'although', as in *While he is away, we are staying at his house.* In a sentence such as *While I don't agree with you, you may do as you wish*, it is clear that the new meaning has become part of the denotation of *while*, and is the only interpretation possible.

Cultural Change

The word *picture* has long meant a 'visual representation' but, because of technological advances, can now refer to much more than a painting. Cinematic movies, X-rays, a television image, a photograph, and a computer-generated graphic are just a few of the things that may now be called a *picture*. Cultural changes such as these may result in changes to a word's referents, even though the function of the referent usually remains the same and the denotation of the word remains more or less the same. A *satellite* is still an 'entity that orbits a celestial body' but now includes those that are man-made as well as those that are natural. The 'physical means of ground warfare', *artillery*, has changed from catapults and crossbows to mortars and howitzers. *Oil* once referred exclusively to olive oil, but now includes sunflower oil, safflower oil, palm oil, canola oil, rape seed oil, etc. Notice that this type of change will often involve generalization of the meaning of a word. In the case of *paper* (< *papyrus,* 'a reed'), the word has undergone a synecdochal change and then cultural change as paper ceased to be made from reeds. The term *bed/table linen* dates from a time when sheets and tablecloths were made from linen (synecdoche), but they are now made from a variety of fabrics (cultural change). The expression *a tin*, referring to 'a tin can', shows the same two types of semantic changes because cans are no longer made entirely of tin.

Social Change

Social factors also motivate semantic change. We see these influences at work when prestige or technical words enter the general vocabulary, as people imitate the usage of the upper classes or of authorities such as psychologists or psychoanalysts. These days, an outgoing person is *an extrovert*, a shy person is *inhibited*, an interested person is *obsessed*, a confused person is *neurotic*, a careful person is *compulsive*. All of these specialized terms have undergone generalization in the process of being popularized. The language of sociology has also been generalized: our friends are our *peer group*, our way of living is our *lifestyle*, the person we admire is our *role model*. Most recently, computer language has begun to be used pervasively: we *interface* or *network* with one another and we *input* or *access* information.

People may also imitate the usage of the lower classes by adopting slang. Slang is the specialized language of any vcohesive group (such as a class, an age group, a professional group, etc.), serving to mark group solidarity and exclude outsiders. It more often involves the attribution of a new meaning to an existing word than the creation of a new word. Clipping off part of the word is common in slang. While slang is quite ephemeral, it sometimes enters the general vocabulary; examples are *bigot*, *jazz*, *job*, *mob*, *proposition* (in the sense of 'request sexual favors'), and *leak* ('disclose information').

Exercise 3.4 Mechanisms of Semantic Change

When unsure of particular meanings, use the *OED* or another etymological dictionary.

1. The following words are listed with their former meanings. Name the semantic change each has undergone to reach its present meaning.

    a. *shroud* 'garment, clothing' _____

    b. *allergic* 'physical sensitivity to a substance' _____

    c. *aisle* 'passage between pews of a church' _____

    d. *brook* 'to enjoy, make use of' (now 'to tolerate') _____

    e. *fame* 'rumor, report' _____

    f. *business* 'state of being busy' _____

    g. *go* 'walk' _____

2. Name the figurative changes exemplified by the following expressions.

    a. *four sheets to the wind* _____

    b. *turn over a new leaf* _____

    c. *a sour note* _____

    d. *elect a new board* _____

3. Give the means by which the following euphemisms are formed.

    a. *STD* 'sexually transmitted disease' _____

    b. *jesum crow* 'Jesus Christ' _____

    c. *enjoys his drink* 'a drunkard' _____

    d. *confinement* 'the lying-in of a woman in childbirth' _____

    e. *SAD* 'seasonal affective disorder' _____

    f. *bowel movement* 'defecation' _____

4. Indicate whether the following terms are the result of imitating higher or lower social class usage.

    a. *flat foot* 'policeman' _____

    b. *anal* 'inclined to fuss over details' _____

    c. *metaphysical* 'outside of immediate need or concern' _____

    d. *loonie* 'Canadian dollar coin depicting a loon' _____

    e. *loony bin* 'asylum' _____

Some Generalizations about Semantic Change

The first generalization to be made about semantic change is that it occurs very quickly—so quickly, in fact, that dictionaries cannot entirely keep up with it. An example is the word *desultory* in a sentence such as *He walked along in a desultory manner*. Many speakers of contemporary English would say that the word means something like 'slowly, aimlessly, despondently'. There are numerous citations over the last 25 years attesting to such a meaning. However, even dictionaries published fairly recently stick to the word's older senses; for example, *The American Heritage Dictionary* (2000) lists the first definition of *desultory* as 'moving or jumping from one thing to another' (see Justice 1987 for a fuller discussion of the treatment of this word in older dictionaries). Similarly, the word *peruse* is now commonly used in the sense 'to skim or read casually', fast superseding the standard dictionary definition 'to read thoroughly or carefully'. When dictionary editors do notice semantic changes, they often track them for several years before including the emerging definition, so even the newest books can be behind the times.

Apart from this generalization, it seems difficult to determine absolutes about semantic change because it so often entails contradictory or opposing trends. Joseph Williams (1975) was able to identify the following directions of change: that abstract words tend to develop out of concrete ones (e.g. *understand*), that neutral words tend to become polarized (*esteem*), that words with strong emotional content tend to weaken (*awful*), that words of insult come from the names of animals or low-class people (*rat, villain*), and that metaphorical uses of words are drawn from everyday experience (*mouth of a river*).

Recently, scholars have argued that semantic change is more regular than once thought. For example, Traugott and Dasher (2002:3–4) point out that the greatest degree of regularity exists in grammaticalization, but that verbal, adjectival, and adverbial forms may also change according to consistent patterns. They also argue that irregular meaning changes seem to occur primarily with nouns, which are 'particularly susceptible to extralinguistic factors'.

The passage below (adapted from Algeo and Butcher 2005:244–5) serves as a review of semantic change. Its humor depends on the discrepancy between the current and former meanings of the italicized words.

> He was a happy and *sad girl* who lived in a *town* forty miles from the closest neighbor. His unmarried sister, a *wife* who was a vegetarian teetotaler, ate *meat* and drank *liquor* three times a day. She was so fond of oatmeal bread made from the *corn* her brother grew that she *starved* from overeating. He fed nuts to the *deer* that lived in the branches of an *apple* tree which bore pears. A *silly* and wise *boor* everyone liked, he was a *lewd* man whom the general *censure* held to be a model of chastity.

Below are the former meanings of the words which allow for a coherent reading of the passage:

sad – 'sober'	*starved* – 'died'
girl – 'youth'	*deer* – 'animal'
town – 'small enclosure'	*apple* – 'fruit'
wife – 'woman'	*silly* – 'blessed'
meat – 'food'	*boor* – 'farmer'
liquor – 'liquid'	*lewd* – 'lay'
corn – 'grain'	*censure* – 'opinion'

The changes undergone by the words are various:

- specialization: *girl*, *wife*, *meat*, *liquor*, *corn*, *deer*, *apple*, *starved*
- weakening: *starve* (in the sense of 'be hungry')
- perjoration: *silly*, *boor*, *lewd*, *censure*
- metonymy: *sad* (since sadness may be associated with sobriety), *censure* (as criticism may be associated with the giving of opinions)
- cultural change: *town*

RECOMMENDED WEB LINKS

You may wish to explore the archives of the Histling listserve, where a variety of topics related to historical linguistics have been discussed online:

> http://listserv.linguistlist.org/archives/histling.html

For brief discussions of language contact, language variation and change, and endangered languages, see the Linguistic Society of America website:

> http://www.lsadc.org/info/ling-fields.cfm ('Languages in Contact', 'Language Variation and Change', 'Endangered Languages')

FURTHER READING

General (very accessible) introductions to historical linguistics include:

Arlotto, Anthony. 1972. *Introduction to Historical Linguistics*. Boston: Houghton Mifflin.

Jeffers, Robert J., and Ilse Lehiste. 1979. *Principles and Methods for Historical Linguistics*. Cambridge, MA and London: The MIT Press.

Schendl, Herbert. 2001. *Historical Linguistics*. Oxford: Oxford University Press.

Trask, R.L. 1994. *Language Change*. London and New York: Routledge.

For a discussion of types of sound changes specifically in English, see:

Minkova, Donka, and Robert Stockwell. 2009. *English Words: History and Structure*. 2nd edn. Cambridge: Cambridge University Press.

For a lively discussion of the social factors in language change, see:

Aitchison, Jean. 2001. *Language Change: Progress or Decay?* 3rd edn. Cambridge: Cambridge University Press.

For more on language contact, you may want to look at:

Thomason, Sarah G. 2001. *Language Contact: An Introduction*. Washington, DC: Georgetown University Press.

Thomason, Sarah G. and Terrence Kaufman. 1988. *Language Contact, Creolization and Genetic Linguistics*. Berkeley, Los Angeles, and London: University of California Press.

For further information on sociolinguistics, see:

Labov, William. 1972. *Sociolinguistic Patterns*. Philadelphia: University of Pennsylvania Press.

Milroy, James. 1992. *Linguistic Variation and Change: On the Historical Sociolinguistics of English*. Oxford and Cambridge, MA: Blackwell.

A good overview of historical sociolinguistics is:

Nevalainen, Terttu. 2006. 'Synchronic and Diachronic Variation'. *Encyclopedia of Language and Linguistics*. 2nd edn. Ed. by Keith Brown, Vol. 12, 356–63.

On language death in the Celtic languages, see:

Dorian, Nancy C. 1981. *Language Death: The Life Cycle of a Scottish Gaelic Dialect*. Philadelphia: University of Pennsylvania Press.

For more on semantic change, see:

Algeo, John. 1998. 'Vocabulary'. *The Cambridge History of the English Language. Vol. IV: 1776–1997*. Ed. by Suzanne Romaine, 57–91. Cambridge: Cambridge University Press.

Lakoff, George, and Mark Johnson. 1980. *Metaphors We Live By*. Chicago and London: University of Chicago Press.

Traugott, Elizabeth Closs, and Richard B. Dasher. 2002. *Regularity in Semantic Change*. Cambridge: Cambridge University Press.

Williams, Joseph M. 1975. *Origins of the English Language: A Social and Linguistics History*. New York: The Free Press.

FURTHER VIEWING

On the principles underlying the proliferation of languages, see:

Episode 3: 'Mother Tongues'. *Speaking in Tongues: The History of Language*. Directed and researched by Christene Browne. Toronto: Syncopated Productions, 2007.

4 The Indo-European Language Family and Proto-Indo-European

OVERVIEW

This chapter examines the two major systems, typological and genealogical, used for classifying languages. We consider three different kinds of typological classification and explain the two metaphors underlying genealogical classification—the 'family tree' model and 'wave' theory. After a brief look at non-Indo-European language families, we turn our attention to the Indo-European family: to the discovery of its existence and to the different branches constituting the family. We then consider the parent language of Indo-European. After defining a proto-language, we look at how such a language is reconstructed using the comparative method, and summarize the phonological and grammatical features of Proto-Indo-European. We then consider what aspects of Proto-Indo-European society and culture can be deduced from linguistic evidence alone. Finally, we look briefly at theories concerning the date and homeland of the Proto-Indo-Europeans.

OBJECTIVES

The primary objective in this chapter is to learn about Indo-European. After reading the chapter, you should be able to

- distinguish between typological and genealogical classification of languages;
- describe the historical events leading to the discovery of the Indo-European language family;

■ identify a language as belonging to the Indo-European family or another language family;

■ identify the branch (or sub-branch) of Indo-European to which a language belongs; and

■ describe the general features of each of the various branches of Indo-European: the ancient languages and modern descendants, the geographical location, the age and nature of the written records, and the archaic or innovative features of the languages.

In addition, you should understand the basis for reconstructing a proto-language, especially the ways in which cognates are differentiated from loan words. You should also be able to describe the linguistic features of Proto-Indo-European, the Indo-European process of ablaut and its reflexes in Modern English, and aspects of the society, culture, and homeland of Proto-Indo-European that can be deduced from its vocabulary.

Classification of Languages

Languages are classified according to two different systems. A typological classification is based on particular structural features found in languages, with no regard to the derivation of the languages. A genealogical (or genetic) classification employs the metaphor of the family tree and is based on the common origin of and historical relations among languages. While typologically related languages resemble one another structurally, genetically related languages may exhibit many differences, especially if separated widely in time or location. Geographic proximity is not a factor in either classificatory system, although change may travel from one language to another adjacent language or languages (what is called areal change).

Typological Classification

Linguists have proposed at least three different ways of classifying languages by type. The first is based on the number of morphemes (or meaningful units) per word and dates from the early nineteenth century. It recognizes the following types of languages:

1. **An isolating language generally has one morpheme per word.** Words do not vary their form, use no affixes, and are frequently monosyllabic. Heavy reliance is put on word order. Vietnamese is such a language:

Khi	tôi	dến	nhà	bạn	tôi,	chúng	tôi	bắt	dầu	làm bài
when	I	come	house	friend	I,	pl.	I	begin	do	lessons

'When I arrived at my friend's house, we began to do lessons.'

2. An agglutinating language has several morphemes per word; every word consists of a root and a number of affixes. Each morpheme remains distinct and identifiable, and one meaning is expressed per morpheme. As the name suggests, the parts of the word are 'glued together'. Turkish is a good example:

Yap-tığ-ım   *hata yı*   *memleket-i*   *tanı-ma-ma-m-a*   *ver-ebil-ir-siniz*
made-*part.*-my mistake-*obj.* country-*obj.* know-not-*gerund*-my-to give-can-*tense*-you
'You can ascribe the mistake I made to my not knowing the country.'

3. An inflecting language likewise has a number of morphemes per word, a root and affixes. In contrast to agglutinating languages, the morphemes in inflecting languages may be fused, modified, or irregular, and each affix expresses a number of different meanings, as in Latin:

Arm-a   *vir-um-que*   *can-ō*
weapon-*neut.pl.obj.*   man-*masc.sg.obj.*-and   sing-*1ˢᵗsg.pres.ind.active*
'Arms and the man I sing.'

(The three examples are taken from Trask 1996:125–6.)

A difficulty with this particular method of classifying by type is that it often assumes a progression from a 'primitive' isolating language to a more sophisticated agglutinating type to a most 'advanced' inflecting type. Although there are certainly instances in which independent words develop into affixes and originally separate affixes may fuse into inflections (thus giving the progression isolating > agglutinating > inflecting), there is nothing primitive about isolating languages—we also find evidence of languages changing in the opposite direction. In fact, English has developed from a highly inflected language to one which shows more agglutinating and isolating characteristics.

A different, broader kind of typological classification not resting on ideas of progression is proposed by Edward Sapir in his classic 1921 book, *Language*. It makes three distinctions: analytic, synthetic, and polysynthetic. An *analytic* language, such as Modern English, is one which either does not combine inflectional morphemes or does so sparingly; grammatical relations are indicated primarily by word order and function words, only to a limited extent by affixing. A *synthetic* language is one which expresses grammatical relations primarily by affixing; both inflecting and agglutinating languages count as synthetic. Finally, a *polysynthetic* language is one which combines a large number of morphemes, including the major parts of a sentence, into a single word, but keeps the morphemes distinct. Work on polysynthetic languages has further challenged the idea of the superiority of inflecting languages. Consider the example of Nootka (Nuu-Chah-Nulth), a polysynthetic language:

tl'imsh-ya-'is-ita-'itl-ma
boil-ed-eat-ers-go for-he does
'He invites people to a feast.'

(This example is taken from Whorf 1956:243.)

Sapir sees these categories as useful not so much for classifying languages as for defining the changes they undergo. We shall see that the major development in the English language is a movement from synthetic to analytic.

Finally, a recent typological classification has been developed based not on the number of morphemes per word, but on the order of elements in the sentence, specifically on the position of the subject (S), the verb (V), and the object (O). It has been found that the languages of the world fall primarily into three basic types (SVO, SOV, and VSO) while the other three orders (VOS, OSV, and OVS) are much rarer. Furthermore, other word-order tendencies arise from the basic order of object and verb (subjects are not as important typologically), as shown in Table 4.1. Modern English is an example of an SVO language, Japanese or Turkish of an SOV language, and Welsh or biblical Hebrew of a VSO language. At a much earlier stage, English had SOV word order and that it has undergone a change to SVO. However, while we know that a language may change its basic word order over time, many questions remain about how this occurs—for example, whether the position of object and verb changes first and then the order of the other elements, or vice versa, and whether change happens first in main clauses and then subordinate clauses.

A major difficulty with all typological schemes is that there is no such thing as a 'pure' type. All languages are mixed or inconsistent. Modern English simultaneously exhibits features of isolating, agglutinating, and inflecting languages. In word order, while English appears to be quite consistently VO, it goes against VO tendencies by typically placing adjectives and genitives before their nouns (e.g. *the large house*, *the table's leg*; on the other hand, we do find the expected VO orders in the less common constructions *the house at the corner*, *the leg of the table*). Some linguists see languages as always in a state of transition from one type to another, perhaps on a trajectory toward typological consistency (or *harmony*).

Table 4.1 Typological Features of VO and OV Word Order

VO	*OV*
use of prepositions	use of postpositions
use of suffixes	use of prefixes
auxiliary precedes verb	auxiliary follows verb
adjective follows noun	adjective precedes noun
genitive follows noun	genitive precedes noun
relative clause follows noun	relative clause precedes noun
case marking absent	case marking present

Genealogical Classification

Unlike the typological approach, where similarities among languages are seen as the result of universal features, a major assumption of genealogical classification is that these are the result of common origin. The model underlying this is the family tree, using the metaphor of genetic relationships among languages deriving from the same source. We speak of a language family, of a parent (or ancestor or mother) language and its daughter languages, of sister languages, of those descending (or deriving) from the parent, and of these being born or dying; here, language is spoken of as though it were organic. While this view is not strictly correct—languages develop gradually rather than being delivered fully formed into the world, and speakers, rather than languages, are the ones that physically die—the family tree metaphor has proved very useful in tracing descent and revealing affinities. Genealogical classification is therefore more useful than typological classification for historical work; we will employ it below.

A family tree model was proposed in 1871; just one year later, however, linguists began discussing an alternative approach to overcome some of its shortcomings. This second model, known as the wave model, recognizes that language change spreads through contact: it begins at a certain point and spreads outward like the ripples on a pond caused by a dropped stone. While more accurate than a family tree, the wave model is less convenient and less conceptually clear. An important point it underscores, however, is the difficulty of distinguishing a language from a dialect. While in theory languages are mutually unintelligible and dialects mutually intelligible, what we find in reality, because of the wave-like nature of change, is a chain of dialects. Contiguous dialects would probably be mutually intelligible, while dialects on either end of the chain would probably not be. Nonetheless, we continue to use the convenient fiction of language and dialect.

Exercise 4.1 Classification of Languages

1.   Describe the different methods of classifying languages and the general features that distinguish these methods from each other.

_____

_____

_____

_____

_____

_____

2. For the typological classifications based on morphemes per word, name the three types and describe their features.

_____

_____

_____

_____

_____

_____

_____

Language Families

Keep in mind that English is one out of approximately 6,500 languages found in the world and that Indo-European is only a single language family. A full discussion of the world's languages is outside the scope of this text. However, you should be aware of the range of language families in the world and the place of Indo-European within it. For example, many languages are spoken in the geographical area of Europe, but some are not genetically related to Indo-European. One such language is Basque, spoken today in the Pyrenees mountains of southern France and northern Spain. Basque is an orphan, or _language isolate_, not thought to be related to any other known language. (There are other language isolates in the world, such as Korean, Haida, and Ainu.) Basque speakers probably inhabited the Iberian peninsula before it was invaded by Indo-European speakers. Other non-Indo-European examples are Hungarian, Finnish, Estonian, and Lappish (all classified as Finno-Ugric), as well as languages such as Cheremis, Samoyed, and Ob-Ugric (all classified as Samoyed) spoken in countries within the former Soviet Union; together these are known as the Uralic family. Another family spoken in the southeasterly part of the European continent and continuing into Asia Minor is Altaic, consisting of Turkish, Azerbaijani, Mongolian, and a variety of languages spoken in China and in former Soviet republics. Finally, in the Caucasus mountains, a number of non-Indo-European languages, such as Georgian and Chechen, are grouped together as the Caucasian languages.

The Indo-European Language Family

The basis of the name _Indo-European_ is geographical: it includes most of the languages spoken from India in the east to Europe in the west (see Figure 4.1).

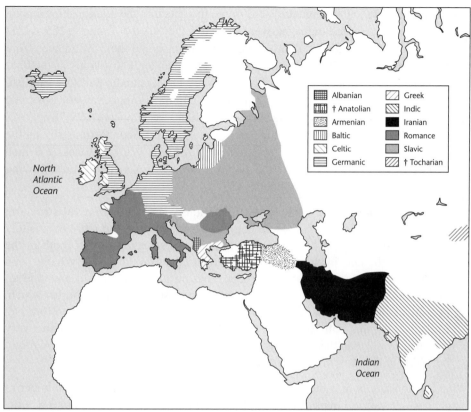

Figure 4.1   Distribution of Indo-European Languages in Present-Day Europe and Southwestern Asia (For a dead language, indicated by †, the area denoted is the place where material remains have been found.)

The Discovery of Indo-European

Because we have ancient texts in many of the daughter languages, we possess considerable knowledge of the linguistic history of the Indo-European language family. The evolution of the individual languages and the genetic relationships among them have been studied intensively since the beginning of the nineteenth century, but until then establishment of the family had been slow in coming. Linguists had to work out the connections among most of the languages of Europe and some of the languages of southwest Asia and northern India and, more importantly, recognize that the common ancestor had left no written records.

Scholars in earlier centuries had been primarily concerned with a search for the 'original language' from which all languages derived. They falsely assumed this to be one of the known languages—Latin, Greek, Phrygian, Hebrew, Chinese, even Dutch. There were also conjectures about the derivation of the different languages, ranging from a view of it as being completely haphazard (the confusion of the Tower of Babel) to the idea of an orderly progression (or degeneration) from Greek to Latin to the vernacular languages of Europe. Insights into the relationships among the European and Indic languages were at first rather spotty. Dante (1265–1321) saw the relationship among Italian, French, and Spanish and their differences from both German and Greek. In the twelfth century, an Icelander, known only as the First Grammarian, recognized the connections between Old Icelandic and Old English. And in the sixteenth century, while traveling in India, Filippo Sassetti observed similarities between numerals in Sanskrit and Italian (see Simpson 1979:78).

Not until the late eighteenth century did the nature of the connections among the Indo-European languages become apparent. In 1786, Sir William Jones, a British jurist in India, read a paper before the Asiatick Society in Calcutta. The following excerpt reveals Jones's central insights:

> The *Sanscrit* language, whatever be its antiquity, is of a wonderful structure; more perfect than the *Greek*, more copious than the *Latin*, and more exquisitely refined than either, yet bearing to both of them a stronger affinity, both in the roots of verbs and in the forms of grammar, than could possibly have been produced by accident; so strong indeed, that no philologer could examine all three, without believing them to have sprung from some common source, which, perhaps, no longer exists; there is a similar reason, though not quite so forcible, for supposing that both the *Gothick* and the *Celtick*, though blended with a very different idiom, had the same origin with the *Sanscrit;* and the old *Persian* might be added to the same family (Cannon 1990:245).

What is important here is that Jones perceived the relation among a large number of languages — Sanskrit, Greek, Latin, Gothic (by which he meant Germanic), Celtic, and Persian — but he did not include many which had in the past erroneously been included, such as Hebrew, Arabic, or Chinese. Furthermore, he considered 'forms of grammar', which we now know to be more reliable indicators than vocabulary, to be important in establishing connections among languages. Finally, he realized that the common ancestor of these languages might no longer exist.

Jones's important insights were the beginnings of the discipline of comparative philology (*vergleichende Sprachwissenschaft*), a study of the development of Indo-European languages and the reconstruction of their common source, which is called Proto-Indo-European. Men such as Jacob Grimm and Karl Verner, who figure in our discussions later, were important early figures in this discipline.

The Branches of Indo-European

Determining the branches of Indo-European took a long time. For many years, people grouped the languages into two sets sharing certain linguistic features: a western set (Germanic, Italic, Celtic, and Hellenic) known by the Latin word for 'one hundred', *centum*, and an eastern set (Indo-Iranian, Albanian, Armenian, and Balto-Slavic) known by the Avestan (an ancient Iranian language) word for 'one hundred', *satem*. In the western branch, the palatal and velar *k* of Proto-Indo-European (see below) merged as one sound (e.g. [k] in Latin), while in the eastern branch, the two sounds were kept distinct, with the palatal *k* becoming a fricative (e.g. [s] in Avestan). In the twentieth century, however, the discovery of two new branches of Indo-European, Tocharian and Anatolian, both centum languages but geographically eastern, disrupted this apparent east–west division. The traditional distinction still remains useful as a point of comparison, and moreover it is likely that Tocharian speakers moved from the west to the east after the merger of the palatal and the velar *k*'s had taken place.

We must clarify a few points. Languages are 'dead' (or extinct) when they have no current speakers. However, some dead languages, such as Latin, have modern descendants, while others, like Hittite, have none. The term *old* is problematic when discussing languages. On one hand, all Indo-European languages are equally old, in that they all derive from the Proto-Indo-European source. On the other hand, we have very old records for some languages, such as Indic, Hittite, Hellenic, and Iranian, against much more recent evidence for others, such as Celtic, Slavic, Armenian, and Germanic. We can also distinguish between archaic and innovative features: an archaic feature is one which has changed very little in the course of time, preserving a characteristic which we believe existed in Proto-Indo-European. Old Irish (spoken from the fourth to the sixth century CE) and the modern Celtic languages, as well as the modern-day Baltic language Lithuanian, preserve many archaic features. An innovative feature has changed dramatically over time, altering many of the inherited linguistic properties. Mycenaean Greek (spoken from approximately 1600 to 1200 BCE) and Hittite (approximately 1900 to 1200 BCE) show a number of innovative grammatical features. At the same time, Hittite preserves some very archaic elements, particularly in its phonology. Remember that the archaic quality of a language is unconnected with the age of its records. This mixture of old and new is perhaps typical of all languages.

What follows is a brief survey of the branches of Indo-European, beginning with the satem languages (see Table 4.2).

Satem Languages

Albanian

Albanian is a language spoken in Albania, a country on the Balkan peninsula. Records of this language date only from the fifteenth century CE. Its vocabulary is strongly influenced by the Romance languages, as well as by Slavic, Altaic, and Hellenic. Due to late and spotty evidence and the foreign influences on its lexicon, Albanian looks very different from its Proto-Indo-European origins.

Armenian

Armenian is spoken in Turkey, Iran, and the Republic of Armenia. Records, in a form called Old or Classical Armenian, date from the fifth century CE. The vocabu-

Table 4.2 The Indo-European Family

Proto-Indo-European (satem)							
Albanian	Armenian	Balto-Slavic				Indo-Iranian	
		Baltic	Slavic			Iranian	Indic
			West	South	East		
Albanian	Armenian	†Old Prussian			†Avestan		
		Lithuanian	Slovak	Serbo-Croat	Byelo-russian	†Old Persian	†Sanskrit
		Latvian	Czech	Bulgarian	Russian	Farsi	†Prakrits
			Polish	Slovenian	Ukrainian	Kurdish	Hindi · Marathi
			Sorbian	Macedonian		Pashto	Bengali · Romany
						Ossetic	Urdu · Punjabi

† = extinct language, - - - = line of descent

Continued

Table 4.2 The Indo-European Family—*Continued*

Proto-Indo-European (centum)								
Germanic			**Celtic** (Insular)		**Italic**	**Hellenic**	**Anatolian**	**Tocharian**
West	**North**	**East**	**Brythonic**	**Goidelic**				
Standard German	Swedish	†Gothic	†Cornish	†Manx	†Latin	†Mycenaean Greek	†Hittite	†Tocharian A
Yiddish	Danish		Welsh	Scots Gaelic	French	†Homeric Greek	†Luvian	†Tocharian B
Dutch/Afrikaans	Norwegian		Breton	Irish Gaelic	Spanish	†Classical Greek	†Lydian	
Frisian	Faeroese				Italian	Modern Greek	†Lycian	
Flemish	Icelandic				Portuguese			
Low German					Romanian			
English					Rhaeto-Romance			
					Catalan			

† = extinct language, - - - = line of descent

lary has a large admixture of Iranian and Greek. However, grammar, not vocabulary, indicates Armenian's distinct position within Indo-European, though it was not identified as a separate branch until 1875.

Balto-Slavic

The Baltic and Slavic languages are often linked as one branch called Balto-Slavic. The Baltic languages consist of Old Prussian (which became extinct about 1700), and Lithuanian and Latvian, spoken in the Baltic republics. While the records of the Baltic languages are not very old, dating from the sixteenth century, the languages are themselves quite archaic and hence they are important in reconstructing Proto-Indo-European.

In contrast, our oldest record of the Slavic languages dates from the ninth century, a Bible translation in what we call Old Church Slavonic or Old Bulgarian (a form that is close to Proto-Slavic). It is the language of the Orthodox Church and has long been used in writing for religious purposes. The Slavic branch is divided into three branches: West (Czech, Polish, Slovak, and Sorbian), South (Serbian, Croatian, Bosnian, Bulgarian, Slovenian, and Macedonian), and East (Byelorussian, Russian, and Ukrainian). Following the breakup of the Soviet Union, the national independence gained by countries such as Latvia and Lithuania has allowed indigenous languages to flourish.

Indo-Iranian

Indo-Iranian consists of two closely related sub-branches. The ancestor language of the Indic branch is Sanskrit, which, because of the age of the written records and the archaic nature of the language, is very important for linguistic purposes. It is first recorded in a form called Vedic Sanskrit in the *Rig Veda*, a collection of hymns, dating from 1200 to 1000 BCE. A later version, Classical Sanskrit, dating from 500 BCE, is described by the famous grammarian Pānini.

Sanskrit is the religious language of Hinduism, still used for that purpose today. The vernacular or spoken versions of Sanskrit are known as Prakrits, which are preserved in the speech of women and characters of lower caste in Sanskrit drama. One of these, Pali (*c*. 300 BCE), is the religious language of Buddhism. Prakrits are the ancestors of many modern-day Indian languages, including Hindi, Bengali, Urdu, Punjabi, and Marathi.

Meanwhile, the Gypsies (or Romani—*Gypsy* is a shortening of *Egyptian*) who migrated west into Europe, speak Romany, which is also an Indic language. Interestingly, the southern Indian languages like Tamil and Kannada are non-Indo-European, belonging instead to the Dravidian family; the Dravidian-speakers occupied the Indian sub-continent before the invasion of the Indo-European speakers.

The other half of Indo-Iranian—Iranian—can be divided into an eastern division consisting of the ancient language Avestan and a western division consisting of the ancient Old Persian. Records of Avestan (the *Avesta* is the sacred text of the Zoroastrian religion), which is closely related to Sanskrit, date from the sixth century BCE, but no modern descendants exist. Records of Old Persian, the ancestor language of Modern Persian, or Farsi, (spoken in Iran) date from approximately the same time. Other modern Iranian languages are Kurdish, Pashto, Baluchi, and Ossetic.

Centum Languages

Tocharian

Tocharian is a fairly recently discovered branch of Indo-European. At the end of the nineteenth century, bilingual texts—Buddhist tracts and monastic accounts dating from the sixth to the eighth century CE—written in Sanskrit and in an unknown language were discovered in the Chinese province of Xinjiang. In 1908, the unknown language, found in dialects labeled A and B, was proven to be Indo-European; later it was shown to constitute a separate branch. There are no modern descendants of Tocharian, nor do we know what became of the people who left these records.

Anatolian

Anatolian is also a recently discovered branch of Indo-European. Excavations near the Turkish village of Boğaz-köy in 1906 unearthed clay tablets written in cuneiform. These were bilingual texts in Akkadian (a Semitic language) and an unknown language, which was determined after careful study of its grammar to be Hittite and shown in 1915 to be Indo-European (the relationship is evident in such Hittite words as *wa-ta-ra* for 'water'). The Hittites, mentioned in the Bible, formed a powerful kingdom from 1900 to 1200 BCE. Hittite records are thus the oldest ones we have of Indo-European (some scholars believe that Hittite is close to the proto-language and refer to Indo-Hittite). Hittite preserves the Proto-Indo-European sounds called laryngeals, which have been lost in the other daughter languages. However, Hittite is innovative in its grammar, having reduced, for example, the many verb tenses of Proto-Indo-European to two, past and present. In addition to Hittite, a number of other Anatolian languages have also been discovered, including Luvian (written in hieroglyphics), Lydian, and Lycian.

Hellenic

The Hellenic branch has very old records. In the early part of the twentieth century, archaeologists working on the island of Crete and at Pylos and Mycenae on the Peloponnesian peninsula of Greece discovered clay tablets written in two unknown scripts, which became known as Linear A and Linear B. The first remains undeciphered, but Michael Ventris and John Chadwick managed, by a brilliant process of deduction and guesswork, to decipher Linear B. They determined that Linear B was an ancient, previously unknown form of Greek; because it was written in a syllabary, a system not well suited to the writing of Greek, its identification posed a great challenge. The documents proved to be storehouse records and administrative material, but fascinating for the linguist. Mycenaean Greek, as this form is now known, was spoken between 1400 and 1200 BCE; like Hittite, it is quite innovative. There is then a gap in the records of Hellenic: Homeric Greek dates from around 1000 to 800 BCE, followed by the Classical Greek dialects. These are written with an alphabetic system. The classical Attic Greek dialect, which was used throughout the Greek Empire, comes to be a kind of standard called the *koinē*, or 'common language'. The New Testament was originally written in this dialect. The sole descendant, Modern Greek, derives from the *koinē*.

Italic

The main ancient language of the Italic branch is, of course, Latin. The oldest records of Latin date from the sixth century BCE, but records are not common until 200 BCE. The great variety of Romance languages—French, Spanish, Italian, Portuguese, Romanian, and other languages without national status, such as Provençal, Galician, Sardinian, Catalan, and Rhaeto-Romance—derive not from classical written Latin (as it is currently studied) but from Vulgar Latin, the language which spread throughout western Europe as the Roman Empire expanded. We have fairly long recorded histories for many of the Romance languages: French from the ninth century; Catalan, Spanish, and Portuguese from the tenth and eleventh centuries; and Italian from the tenth century. Oscan and Umbrian, languages spoken in Italy at the same time as Latin, are considered either a sub-branch of Italic or a separate branch of Indo-European. Our records of these languages date only from the first century BCE; falling to the political dominance of Latin, Oscan and Umbrian left no modern descendants.

Celtic

The Celtic branch of Indo-European (note that Celtic as the name of a language family is pronounced [kɛltɪk], not [sɛltɪk]) has two main divisions, a continental branch and an insular branch. We have few records of Gaulish, the sole representative of the continental branch, which became extinct by the first century CE during the Roman occupation of Gaul. The insular branch is divided into two parts: Brythonic (p-Celtic) and Goidelic (q-Celtic). Brythonic consists of Welsh, Breton (spoken in Brittany in France), and Cornish (spoken previously in Cornwall, but extinct by the mid-eighteenth century). Goidelic includes Irish Gaelic, Scots Gaelic (formerly spoken also on Cape Breton Island in Nova Scotia), and Manx (spoken previously on the Isle of Man, but now extinct). The oldest records of any Goidelic variety are those of Old Irish, whose rich literary tradition begins in the fourth century CE. The oldest records of Brythonic Celtic are in Welsh of the eleventh century; Welsh is now taught in the schools in Wales and is being revived with some success. None of the other Celtic languages are faring well despite similar attempts. They may be undergoing what Aitchison calls *language murder*; fewer and fewer people learn them as a native language, favoring instead the politically dominant English and French.

Germanic

There are a number of subdivisions of the Germanic branch. East Germanic is exemplified by Gothic, the language of the Ostrogoths and Visigoths, recorded in the fourth century CE. Because the Goths were destroyed by the Huns around 700, there are no modern descendants of Gothic, although a few settlements seem to have remained in the Crimea, and a form known as Crimean Gothic was recorded in the sixteenth century.

North Germanic has a number of modern descendants: Danish, Swedish, Norwegian, Icelandic, and Faeroese (spoken on the Faeroe Islands in the north Atlantic). North and East Germanic appear to be especially close, sharing consonant clusters not found in West Germanic.

For reasons that will be discussed in the next chapter, West Germanic is divided into two branches, named according to their geographical location: a High branch, spoken in the highlands of southern Germany, and a Low branch, spoken in the lowlands of northern Germany, the Low Countries (Belgium and the Netherlands), and England. Modern Standard German (or High German) and Yiddish, which has an admixture of Hebrew and Slavic, are existing High West Germanic languages. The Low West Germanic languages are Low German (Plattdeutsch), a regional dialect of northern Germany; Dutch; Flemish, spoken in Belgium; Afrikaans, the descendant of seventeenth-century Dutch taken to South Africa; Frisian, a language spoken on the Frisian Islands in the North Sea; and English.

Exercise 4.2 The Indo-European Language Family

1. For the following languages, identify which are non-Indo-European, which have no modern descendants, which are isolates, and which is closest (genetically) to English.

    Japanese _____

    Hittite _____

    Flemish _____

    Crimean Gothic _____

    Portuguese _____

Tamil _____

Korean_____

2. Who was William Jones and what is his importance to the study of Indo-European? Identify and explain his key ideas.

_____

_____

_____

_____

_____

_____

Proto-Language

When a group of genetically related languages share a single, common source, we call it a *proto-language* (*proto-* meaning 'first'). Some of these proto-languages are attested (that is, we have written records of them), but most are not. For French, Italian, Portuguese, Spanish, and some others, the proto-language—Vulgar Latin—is attested; for many others, including English and the other Germanic languages, the proto-language is unattested. The search for the parent of the Indo-European languages was derailed for many years by the assumption that one of the ancient languages, such as Sanskrit, Greek, or Latin, was the source from which all the others devolved. However, you will recall that one of Sir William Jones's important insights was that the source of the Indo-European languages 'perhaps no longer exists', and indeed Proto-Indo-European is unattested. The common ancestor of all the Germanic languages, Proto-Germanic (an intermediate common language between Proto-Indo-European and English and the other Germanic languages), is likewise unrecorded.

Reconstruction

Linguists are often able to partially reconstruct an unattested proto-language from extant daughter languages using a deductive process called the *comparative method*. A reconstructed language is a hypothesis about the structure and vocabulary of a proto-language. Since forms in a reconstructed language are not recorded (they are theoretical constructs), we mark them with an asterisk (*). Their spelling indicates the pronunciation which has been hypothesized by modern scholars.

In the comparative method, linguists begin with languages thought to be sisters—that is, languages assumed to be genetically related descendants of a common parent. The more archaic the daughter language, the better it is for reconstructive purposes. Linguists focus on the oldest recorded forms of the sister languages, since these will usually be the most similar to the proto-language. They collect sets of presumed *cognates*, which are forms of the same word existing independently in different languages, e.g. Skt. *rājā*, Lat. *rex* (*reg-*), and OE *rīce* meaning 'king, kingdom'. These are direct continuations from a single original word in the parent language, in this case *reg in Proto-Indo-European. The word *cognate* comes from the Latin *co-* + *gnātus*, meaning 'born together' (*gnātus* containing the same root we find—without the initial *g*—in *natal, native*, and *nativity*).

Cognates are usually similar, but not necessarily identical, in meaning. And because of sound changes in a particular language over time, the form of cognates may actually vary a great deal; for instance, Eng. *hound* and Lat. *canis* are cognate, although sound change obscures their common origin in PIE *kwon. Identifying cognates thus depends on recognizing sound changes that have taken place and relating the sounds of one language with those of another (called *sound correspondences*). As we will see in Chapter 5, the sound [h] in the Germanic languages corresponds with [k] in Latin; we say that [h] is a *reflex* of [k]. Knowing the sound reflexes is key to unlocking the relationships of words and languages.

Before cognate sets can be conclusively established, linguists must eliminate words which have been borrowed from one language to another. It is not always easy to distinguish cognates from such loan words, but some guidelines exist:

1. Linguists try to restrict cognate sets to core vocabulary because these words tend not to be borrowed. The core vocabulary names everyday objects and concepts (such as body parts, familial relationships, human processes, natural phenomena, plants and animals, colors, numbers, religion, etc.) and basic actions (to sit, stand, run, come, go, eat, drink) and includes function words (pronouns, demonstratives, conjunctions, and numerals).

2. Linguists usually reject words which are identical or very close in phonetic form. Borrowed words, like ModE *regal* (from Lat. *reg-*) or ModE *canine* (from Lat. *canis*), are often phonetically closer than cognates, since cognates develop independently over a long period and are subject to sound changes in their own languages.

3. By knowing about the timing and nature of the interaction between two language groups, linguists can often identify plausible loan words. When objects or concepts are borrowed, the words naming these are usually borrowed at the same time; for this reason, linguists eliminate such words when they set out to find cognates. For example, the ModE words *tomato* (from Nahuatl) and *bagel* (from Yiddish) were borrowed to name foods acquired from other cultures. Hence, the words *bagel* in English and *bagel* in Yiddish are not cognate; English *bagel* is a loan word.

4. Linguists try to determine the earliest *attestation*—the first written occurrence—of a word. A word attested quite late in a language's recorded history is likely to be a borrowing, since native words would have existed from the very beginning. Of course, a word might exist in speech and only accidentally be absent from the written records, so caution is necessary in drawing these sorts of conclusions.

Let us look at two very simple examples of proposed cognate sets. The first set includes French *soupe* and English *soup*. These might appear to be cognates, since they are similar in form and meaning and they name quite a basic item. However, in phonetic form they are almost identical, and the first attestation for English *soup* is 1653; therefore, we might conclude that this is an English borrowing from French. The second set includes French *chien*, Latin *canis*, and English *hound*. These also name a basic item. While these words are similar in meaning (although not as close as *soupe* and *soup*), they differ in phonetic form. Moreover, the earliest attestation of *hound* in English is 897, suggesting that this is a native word; *hound* cannot be derived from either *chien* or *canis* by any known sound changes internal to English. We can therefore rule out borrowing and conclude that these are true cognates deriving from the PIE root *kwon. In contrast, the English word *canine*, which is very like the Latin word, is first recorded in 1623; we conclude that it is borrowed. Figure 4.2 illustrates a more complete example for the concept 'butter', where there are at least six cognate sets. English *butter* is borrowed from Greek via Latin.

The comparative method rests on a couple of assumptions. One assumption is that extensive similarities of form and meaning among words in different languages cannot be the product of chance, of parallel independent developments, of a natural connection between form and meaning (as, for example, in onomatopoeia), or of universal features of language, but must result from common origin. Belief in the arbitrary nature of language (see Chapter 1) underlies this assumption. A second assumption is that sound changes are regular and widespread, not haphazard or isolated, and hence forms can be reconstructed with a fair degree of certainty.

Once cognate sets are established, the task of reconstruction begins. Sound correspondences (i.e. what sound in one language corresponds to what sound in another language) are traced. Consider some Indo-European words for 'foot':

Skt.	*pad-*	Go.	*fōtus*
Gk.	*pod-*	OE	*fōt*
Hittite	*pata*	Ger.	*Fuss*
Lat.	*ped-*	Lithuanian	*péda* 'foot-track'
Fr.	*pied*	Armenian	*ot-n* 'footprint'

(See Buck 1949:241)

BUTTER

Grk.	βούτῡρον (late)	Goth.	. . . .	Lith.	*sviestas*
NG	βούτυρον	ON	*smjǫr*	Lett.	*sviests*
Lat.	*būtyrum* (late)	Dan.	*smør*	ChSl.	. . . .
It.	*burro*	Sw.	*smör*	SCr.	*maslac*
Fr.	*beurre*	OE	*butere*	Boh.	*máslo*
Sp.	*manteca*	ME	*butere*	Pol.	*masło*
Rum.	*unt*	NE	*butter*	Russ.	*maslo*
Ir.	*imb*	Du.	*boter*	Skt.	*ghṛta-, navanita-*
NIr.	*īm*	OHG	*ancho, butera*	Av.	(*raoγna-*)
W.	*ymenyn*	MHG	*buter, anke*		
Br.	*amann*	NHG	*Butter*		

Butter was a common article of food from early times in India and Iran ('melted butter') and in northern Europe, but not among the ancient Greeks and Romans, who first heard of it as a Scythian product. It is first reported by Herodotus (4.2), who describes the process of churning, later by Hippocrates (4.20), who first introduces the word βούτῡρον. Pliny (28.133) tells of *butyrum, barbararum gentium lautissimus cibus.* Schrader, Reallex 1.175 ff.

1. Grk. βούτῡρον, lit. 'cow-cheese', but either a translation or an adaptation of a native Scythian word (πῖον, ὁ βούτυρον καλέουσι, Hipp. 4.20). Hence Lat. *būtyrum*, and fr. this OFr. *burre* (> It. *burro*), Fr. *beurre*, OE, ME *butere*, NE *butter*, Du. *boter*, OHG (late) *butera*, MHG *buter*, NHG *Butter*.

2. Sp. *manteca* (also 'fat, lard'), prob. of pre-Roman orig. REW 5324a.

Rum. *unt* (also 'oil') : It. *unto*, OFr. *oint* 'fat', fr. Lat. *ūnctum* 'ointment', pple. of *unguere* 'smear, anoint'. REW 9057.

3. Ir. *imb, imm*, NIr. *īm*, W. *ymenyn*, Br. *amann*, OHG *ancho*, MHG *anke*, OPruss. *anctan* : Lat. *unguen* 'fat, oint-ment', *unguere* 'smear, anoint', Skt. *añj-* 'anoint, adorn'. Walde-P. 1.181. Pedersen 1.46.

4. ON *smjǫr*, Dan. *smør*, Sw. *smör*, OHG *chuo-smero* (lit. 'cow-grease') : Goth. *smairþr* 'fat', OE *smeoru*, OHG *smero* 'fat, grease' (NE *smear*), Ir. *smir* 'marrow', etc. Walde-P. 2.690 f. Falk-Torp 1086 f.

5. Lith. *sviestas*, Lett. *sviests*, perh. : Av. *xšvīd-*'milk'. Walde-P. 2.521.

SCr. *maslac* (beside *maslo* 'grease'), Boh. *máslo*, Pol. *masło*, Russ. *maslo* ('butter' and 'oil') : ChSl. *maslo* 'ointment, oil', *mazati* 'anoint', Grk. μάσσω 'knead', etc. Walde-P. 2.226. Berneker 2.23, 28.

6. Skt. *ghṛta-* 'clarified butter, ghee' : Skt. *ghṛta-* 'besprinkle', further connec-tions dub. Uhlenbeck 85, 100. Walde-P. 1.407.

Skt. *navanīta-* 'fresh butter', lit. 'fresh drawn' cpd. of *nava-* 'new' and pple. of *nī-* 'lead, bring'.

Av. *raoγna-, raoγnya-* 'butter' (? So Barth. 1488) or 'oil' (Darmesteter) : NPers. *rauγan* 'oil, grease', outside connections unknown.

Figure 4.2 Sample PIE Cognate Set (from Carl Darling Buck, *A Dictionary of Selected Synonyms in the Principal Indo-European Languages: A Contribution to the History of Ideas,* 1988 © copyright University of Chicago Press; reprinted by permission of the publisher)

Looking at just the consonants, we can see the following correspondences:

Sanskrit [p] : Greek [p] : Hittite [p] : Latin [p] : French [p] : Gothic [f] : Old English [f] : Modern German [f] : Lithuanian [p] : Armenian Ø

Sanskrit [d] : Greek [d] : Hittite [t] : Latin [d] : French [d] : Gothic [t] : Old English [t] : Modern German [s] : Lithuanian [d] : Armenian [t]

These sounds are reflexes of an original sound in the parent language. The original may be one of the recorded sounds, or none of them. It is not always correct to assume that the original sound is the one found in the majority of the daughter languages. We also have to consider *phonetic plausibility*, in other words the likelihood of sound change going in one direction rather than another in any of the daughter languages. Finally, we must determine whether the reconstructed sound could have existed in the phonological system of the proto-language. Deciding upon the original sound can involve a number of difficulties, such as the variation of a sound in different positions in a word. After considering these variables, we can reliably reconstruct the PIE root for 'foot' as *ped-/pod-.

By means of the comparative method, scholars have reconstructed several hundred words for Proto-Indo-European as well as a fairly complete set of word endings. Reconstruction of entire sentences, however, is much less certain.

Exercise 4.3 Proto-Language and Reconstruction

1. What is a proto-language? List the four basic guidelines for reconstructing a proto-language.

    _____

    _____

    _____

    (1) _____

    (2) _____

    (3) _____

    (4) _____

2. Explain the difference between a cognate and a loan word. Determine which of the following Indo-European words belong to the same cognate set.

English *autumn, harvest*	Latin *autumnus*
Spanish *otoño*	Serbo-Croat *jesen*
Old Norse *haust*	Romanian *toamnă*
Russian *osen'*	German *Herbst*
(See Buck 1949:1013)	

Proto-Indo-European

Linguistic Features

The phonological system of PIE is rich in consonants. The conventional reconstruction of the stop consonants is shown in Table 4.3.

For each of the back stops, there is both a velar version (*k, *g, *gh) and a palatal version indicated by the diacritic (ˆ): (*k̂, *ĝ, *ĝh). In Germanic, they fall together. The exact phonetic quality of the voiced aspirates is debatable, but we can think of them as voiced stops followed by a puff of aspiration. Some scholars reconstruct a series of voiceless aspirated stops *ph, *th, *kh/k̂h as well. Finally, there is a series of labiovelar stops *k^w, *g^w, *g^{w}h, which are pronounced as velar stops with lip rounding, as in Modern English *qu* [k^w] (*quick*) or *gw* [g^w] (*Gwen*); most of the daughter languages have simplified these, preserving either the velar or the labial sound. (It should be noted that English has no native words with *gw*, the existing words all coming from Welsh.)

Unlike English, PIE has only one fricative, *s. Like English, however, its two nasals (*m and *n), its two liquids (*l and *r), and its two glides (*w and *j) can function as both consonants and vowels, or the only sound in a syllable. In the latter case, the nasals and liquids are represented *m̥, *n̥, l̥, and *r̥ and are pronounced as in the last syllables of ModE *prism, open, cattle*, and *runner*, respectively.

Table 4.3 Stop Consonants of Proto-Indo-European

voiceless stops	voiced stops	voiced aspirated stops
*p	*b	*bh
*t	*d	*dh
*k, *k̂	*g, *ĝ	*gh, *ĝh
*k^w	*g^w	*g^{w}h

Most scholars now reconstruct another sound in Indo-European called a *laryngeal*. As far back as the 1870s, the Swiss Indo-Europeanist (and 'father' of structural linguistics) Ferdinand de Saussure, in order to account for the occurrence of long vowels in certain positions, predicted the existence of a special class of sounds in PIE. In the twentieth century, when Hittite was discovered, *h* appeared in just those places where Saussure had postulated these special sounds. It is now thought that there were three different sounds called laryngeals. While their place of articulation is unspecified, they were probably fricatives of some sort, perhaps with the phonetic value of [ɣ], [x], or [h]. The astounding correspondence between Saussure's predictions and the actual occurrence of laryngeals in Hittite provides reassurance to linguists of the accuracy of their reconstructions.

For many years, scholars found it difficult to reconstruct the vowel system of PIE because they assumed that the three-vowel system of Sanskrit [i, a, u] was close to the original system, but now with additional IE evidence, we know that the vowel system of Sanskrit is an innovation. We can discover the vowel system of PIE by considering the sets of cognates shown in Table 4.4. Compare the sounds indicated in bold in each row.

Because we have consistency among all of the languages, we would reconstruct a *u vowel for row (a), an *i vowel for row (b), and an *ɑ vowel for row (e). (There are reasons for identifying the initial vowel of the forms in row (e) as [ɑ]).

For row (c), where the vowels are a-a-e-e-ai, it would make sense to reconstruct *e to attain a balanced system of vowels. For row (d), although *a* is the majority form (a-a-o-o-a), we have already reconstructed an *ɑ, and hence we would likely reconstruct an *o here. Finally, for row (f) we have a more difficult problem since both *i and *ɑ have already been reconstructed. It would make sense to reconstruct a sound intermediate between *i* and *a*, and looking at our vowel grid, the most likely candidate is *ə.

Table 4.4 Reconstruction of the Vowels of Proto-Indo-European

	Sanskrit	Avestan	Greek	Latin	Gothic		PIE vowel
a)	yugan	yugəm	zugon	iugum	juk	'yoke'	*u
b)	idam	idəm		idem	ita	'it, that'	*i
	riktan-	ⁱrixta-	lipto-	re-lictus		'left (behind)'	
c)	daśa	dasa	deka	decem	taihun	'ten'	*e
d)	aṣṭau	ašta	oktō	octo	ahtau	'eight'	*o
e)	ajati	azaⁱti	agō	agō	aka (ON)	'drive, impel'	*ɑ
f)	pitā	pitā	patēr	pater	fadar	'father'	*ə

Source: Hans Henrich Hock, *Principles of Historical Linguistics* (Berlin, New York, and Amsterdam: Mouton de Gruyter, 1991), p. 593, reprinted by permission of Mouton de Gruyter, a division of Walter de Gruyter GmbH & Co.

	Monophthongs		
	Front	**Central**	**Back**
High	*ī *i		*ū *u
Mid	*ē *e	*ə	*ō *o
Low			*ā *a
	Diphthongs		
	*ei	*oi *ou	
	*eu	*ai *au	

Figure 4.3 The Vowel System of Proto-Indo-European (Note: Whether the low back vowel should be reconstructed as a more back vowel [ɑ] or a more central vowel [a] is problematic.)

Following similar methods, we find that the short vowels have long counterparts (except for [ə]). We can also conclude that PIE had a set of six diphthongs formed with the basic vowels *e, *o, and *ɑ, combined with the two glides. Thus, the vowel system of PIE has the shape given in Figure 4.3.

If the existence of laryngeals is accepted, it could be argued that PIE had only one original vowel, *e. When the three laryngeals preceded the vowel, they changed the quality (giving *e, *ɑ, and *o); when they followed the vowel, they changed the quantity (giving *ē, *ā, and *ō). The vowels *u and *i result from the glides *w and *j functioning as vowels; when followed by a laryngeal, these too are lengthened. The sound [ə] is a syllabic laryngeal. Subsequently, laryngeals fused with the neighboring vowels and, except in Hittite, disappeared.[1]

---

1 Two linguists from the former Soviet Union (see Gamkrelidze and Ivanov 1995) and an American linguist (Hopper 1982), working independently, have reconstructed an alternative consonant system for Proto-Indo-European. They have argued that the system traditionally reconstructed would, in fact, be very unusual because it does not resemble any extant systems. They claim that the following inventory of consonants is more likely:

*p'	*bh/b	*ph/p
*t'	*dh/d	*th/t
*k'	*gh/g	*kh/k
*k'ʷ	*gʷh/gʷ	*kʷh/kʷ

The first column shows a set of glottalized stops, produced by closing off the glottis and compressing air in the larynx. The next two columns show voiced and voiceless stops, which may or may not be aspirated (these are predictable variants in PIE). This proposed system is not fully accepted, perhaps because glottalic stops are not found in any recorded Indo-European languages; for the purposes of this text, we will rely on the traditional system.

The accentual system of Proto-Indo-European is thought to be one of free accent; the term *free* (or *floating*) is used because the accent falls on different syllables in different words (i.e. the position of accent must be learned). Moreover, the accent can move from one syllable to another syllable even within the same word because its position depends on the inflectional or derivational endings carried by the root. The Sanskrit word for 'tooth' in the accusative singular has its accent on the first syllable (*dánt-am*) and in the genitive singular on the second syllable (*dat-ás*). Free accentual systems are found in Sanskrit and Greek, but not in Germanic, which fixes accent on the root syllable. Moreover, PIE employs a pitch accent, involving higher pitch (or vocal cord vibration) on the accented syllable, rather than a stress accent using greater volume (as we have in English).

Related to the accentual system is a process called ablaut, which involves altering the vowel in a word's root in order to show something about its meaning or grammatical function. We see the remnants of ablaut in Modern English, primarily in the strong verb (see Chapter 6), but also in other parts of speech, e.g. *ring/rang/rung*, *sing/sang/sung/song*, or *sit/sat/seat/soot/sett(le)/sadd(le)*. The possible varieties of ablauted vowels in PIE are labelled *grades*, as in *e*-grade, *o*-grade, zero-grade (in which a nasal or liquid functions as a syllable), lengthened *e*-grade, and lengthened *o*-grade. In the forms for 'foot' given in the previous section (p. 112), the Latin genitive *pedis* shows the *e*-grade (the Latin nominative *pēs* shows the lengthened *e*-grade), the Greek *póda* the *o*-grade, and Germanic the lengthened *o*-grade. For another PIE root, we find forms deriving from the zero-grade *mn̥-, such as *mind*; forms deriving from the *e*-grade *men-, such as *comment*; and forms deriving from the *o*-grade *mon-, such as *admonish*.

Derivation and inflection are the typical means of forming words in Proto-Indo-European. Words have a stem consisting of a root and a derivational suffix, to which is added an inflectional ending. The root expresses the semantic core of the word; the derivational suffix expresses the part of speech or modifies the meaning of the root; and the inflectional ending expresses the grammatical categories of the word. The root and the suffix together form the stem. The PIE word *kerwos shows the characteristic structure: *ker, the root meaning 'horn'; *-wo-, a nominal suffix; and *-s, an inflectional ending indicating nominative case and singular number. The meaning is, hence, 'one with a horn' or 'a stag'. By these means, a variety of different words can be formed from the same root.

Compounding is another characteristic type of word formation in Proto-Indo-European, as it continues to be in the Germanic languages, for example:

Skt. *nr-hán*	'man-killing'
Gk. *dus-menḗs*	'one who is evil-minded'
Lat. *sacer-dōs*	'he who lays down the sacrifice, priest'
Go. *fidur-dogs*	'that lasts for four days'

Compounding is found especially in poetic diction and personal names, such as the name *Beo-wulf,* 'bee-wolf', perhaps meaning 'bear'.

Proto-Indo-European is a highly inflected language, much more so than Old English or even the classical languages. Except for the numerals from five to ten and certain small words called particles, all the PIE words take endings or employ ablaut to indicate grammatical categories. Nouns, adjectives, and pronouns express at least eight cases, three numbers, three genders, and three degrees of comparison, and they fall into different classes. Verbs express three persons, three numbers, two voices, six tenses, five moods, and three aspects. The personal pronouns have been best preserved in the daughter languages; PIE had demonstrative and interrogative pronouns, but no relative pronouns. For an example of PIE's verbal inflections, look at the paradigms for the verb 'to bear' in Table 4.5 (see Beekes 1995:232–3).

Table 4.5 Sample Verb Inflections of Proto-Indo-European

present indicative	Sanskrit	Greek	Latin	Gothic	OE	PIE
1st p. sg.	bharāmi	pherō	ferō	baira	bere	*-ō, *-mi
2nd p. sg.	bharasi	phereis	feris	bairis	beres	*-si
3rd p. sg.	bharati	pherei	ferit	bairiþ	bereþ	*-ti
1st p. pl.	bharāmas	pheromen	ferimus	bairam	beraþ	*-mes
2nd p. pl.	bharatha	pherete	feritis	bairiþ	beraþ	*-the
3rd p. pl.	bharanti	pherousi	ferunt	bairand	beraþ	*-enti

Finally, although it is much more difficult to reconstruct syntax than phonology or morphology, some scholars have argued that Proto-Indo-European has SOV (subject–object–verb) word order. The following ancient Latin inscription (*c.* 600 BCE) shows an example of SOV order (see Lehmann 1994:76):

MANIOS	MED	FHE	FHACED	NUMASIOI
Manius (S)	*mē* (O)	[vb prefix]	*fēcit* (V)	*Numeriō*

'Manius made me for Numerius'

We cannot know if PIE consistently follows the SOV pattern because all of the daughter languages appear to have undergone word order changes to some extent. While some scholars argue that Proto-Germanic is still essentially an SOV language, we will see in Chapter 7 that Old English retains only remnants of this order, having moved toward an SVO order.

Although we have no written texts of PIE, the example of Vedic Sanskrit given below provides a sense of the grammatical complexity and vocabulary of Indo-European.

índrasya	nú	vīryā̀ṇi	právocam
of Indra	now	manly.deeds	I.proclaim

yā́ni	cakā́ra	prathamā́ni	vajrī́
which	he.did	first.ones	cudgel.bearer

áhann	áhim	ánv	apás	tatarda
he.killed	serpent	through	waters	he.bored

prá vakṣáṇā	abhinat	párvatānām
belly	he.split	of mountains

I proclaim the manly deeds of Indra
which first the cudgel-bearer did
He killed the serpent, bored through to the waters
he split the belly of the mountains

(*Rig Veda* 1.32.1)

Exercise 4.4 PIE Linguistic Features

1. Explain ablaut. Give an example.

    _____

    _____

    _____

2. Describe the three structural parts of a PIE word. What is the difference between inflection and derivation?

    _____

    _____

    _____

    _____

    _____

Society

We can get a fairly complete picture of Proto-Indo-European society and culture simply from the reconstructed vocabulary. The word stock tells us about material culture, but also offers insight into non-material aspects of society in a way that archaeological evidence cannot. The linguistic information is particularly useful in the case of the Proto-Indo-Europeans because archaeology has been unable to provide conclusive evidence of the people and their lives. Different ethnic groups may have shared the same language and lived alongside one another.

The picture of Proto-Indo-European society that emerges from the vocabulary is amazingly detailed. Proto-Indo-Europeans worshipped a primary god associated with the day or clear skies. The societal structure of the gods resembled that on earth: it was patriarchal, and the chief god of the pantheon was a father figure. They had priests and seers, recited prayers and incantations, engaged in rituals, poured libations, and made offerings to the gods. The Proto-Indo-Europeans also designated a male head of the tribe or family; society was *patrilineal* (with descent traced through the male line), and *patrilocal* (with the wife going to live with her husband's family). There are terms for the family of the husband (e.g. 'his father', 'his mother', 'his brother', and even 'wife of his brother'), but no words for relatives on the wife's side of the family. The husband 'leads home' the wife in marriage and is referred to as 'master'. Rare reference to maternity and to a female god probably preserves an older non-Indo-European system. The household was the social unit. Wooden houses were built around a central hearth and entered through double doors. They were grouped in villages, which were the seat of a tribe, clan, or family. The villages often occupied hilltop locations and were enclosed or fortified.

Proto-Indo-Europeans were an agricultural society. They raised a variety of grains (rye, wheat, barley, spelt, and corn) and ground them. They cultivated crops, yoked animals for plowing, sowed seed in furrows, and gathered or harvested crops using a sickle. They kept dogs as well as a number of domesticated animals which they herded and butchered: cows, sheep, goats, and swine, but not chickens or rabbits. They milked animals. Wealth was measured in livestock, especially cattle.

The domestic skills and tools of the Proto-Indo-Europeans were advanced. They spun wool, wove cloth, and sewed clothing. They cooked and baked; they ate apples, milk, butter, cheese, meat, and fish—foods which they seasoned with salt and sweetened with honey. They also used honey to brew a fermented beverage, mead. They used the bow and arrow and the axe but not the sword. They worked various metals, including gold, silver, copper, and perhaps bronze. While there are PIE words for wheel, axle, hub, and wagon, these are not usually primary terms but secondary, metaphorical formations, suggesting that the Proto-Indo-Europeans acquired the wheel late, probably just before their dispersal. They did have a means of transportation over water, a ship which was either poled or rowed, but not sailed. They either walked or rode horses, which were to be important in their migrations.

The Proto-Indo-Europeans measured the year in agricultural terms, according to the growing seasons, the life cycle of domestic animals, and the weather. Fall was the time of harvest. They also measured time according to the lunar month, and they named the sun and other stars. They oriented themselves in terms of natural phenomena: east was associated with shining and the dawn, and west with the evening. When naming the directions, they faced the east, since south was associated with the right and the north with the left, although the left was unlucky and hence taboo. They counted using a decimal system; in fact, the numbers from one to ten show very close parallels in the daughter languages and are easily reconstructed for PIE. They may also have had a counting system based on twelve.

The Proto-Indo-Europeans had no common term for commerce but bought and sold other human beings as slaves or redeemed them from imprisonment. They had words for 'stealing' and 'thief', and they used a legal system where justice was meted out orally. Their society seems to have been based on a principle of reciprocity with great importance placed on exchange, compensation, restitution, hospitality, oath-making and gift-giving. The latter extended from rewarding retainers to paying tribute or making atonement for crimes. A system of mutual contractual obligations thus formed the basis of their legal system. We see these features of PIE social structure preserved in the daughter societies, for example, in the literature of the Greeks (in Homer) and the Germanic peoples (in *Beowulf* and the Old Icelandic sagas). Oral poetry was also very much part of Proto-Indo-European society; it seems to have possessed a special, very rich vocabulary. We can even reconstruct entire formulas which must have been part of oral poetry, such as 'rosy-fingered dawn', 'the famous deeds of men', and 'the wheel of the sun'. The poet occupied an important position in PIE life and was the 'weaver' or 'crafter' of words.

Homeland

Speakers of Proto-Indo-European apparently lived together in a common region for some period of time and then, compelled perhaps by over-population and infertile land, began to migrate into other parts of Europe, Asia, and India. The common locale is called the Proto-Indo-European homeland. The dispersal of the Indo-Europeans over a wide geographical area and the isolation of groups over time caused the development of the different branches of Indo-European.

Because we lack conclusive archaeological evidence, we again look to the vocabulary to enable us to establish the homeland of the Proto-Indo-Europeans. If we can work out what the landscape of the Proto-Indo-Europeans was like, what weather they experienced, and what flora and fauna inhabited their land, we might determine where they lived. We know that the people were familiar with snow, cloudy skies, and thunder (though words for rain differ). They knew about boggy terrain and uncultivated land or forest, and they had encountered lakes. A number of different trees (the beech, birch, aspen, oak, yew, willow, spruce, alder, and ash), animals (wolf, bear, beaver, otter, lynx, snake, turtle, hare, and mouse), birds (crane, eagle, starling, finch, sparrow, thrush, woodpecker, goose, and duck), fish (salmon and eel), and insects (wasp, bee, fly, hornet, louse, and bedbug) were native in their land. Therefore, the natural environment of the Proto-Indo-Europeans seems to be northerly; there are no terms for trees and animals exclusively indigenous to tropical or southerly climates. Working with data on the distribution of beech trees, turtles, and salmon, Paul Thieme placed the homeland of the Proto-Indo-Europeans between the Vistula River (whose mouth is at modern-day Gdansk, Poland) and the Elbe (whose mouth is at Hamburg, Germany). Two difficulties hamper the attempt to locate the homeland by these means: first, we cannot be certain that the distribution of certain flora and fauna was the same five or more millennia ago as it is today, and second, names for trees are notoriously changeable—the beech referred to in one language may be entirely different from the similarly named tree in another. Faced with so many unknown variables, some scholars have despaired of being able to locate the homeland at all.

Marija Gimbutas (1970) has argued that the Proto-Indo-Europeans can be identified with the Kurgans (named after the Russian word for 'barrow' or 'mound' because of their burial practices). This group of people lived in the area of the Black and Caspian seas roughly six thousand years ago. Their culture bears many similarities to what we know of Proto-Indo-European culture: they had domesticated cattle and horses, used wheeled vehicles, lived in fortified hilltop villages, had a stratified society, worshiped a sky god, and believed in an afterlife. These people spread into parts of Europe, Iran, and Asia Minor between 4000 and 3000 BCE, displacing an older matrilineal civilization Gimbutas calls the Old Europeans. Although this theory is intriguing, problems with dating and archeological evidence prompt much skepticism about whether the Kurgans are in fact the Proto-Indo-Europeans. Robert Beekes (1995) thinks that the Proto-Indo-Europeans were an earlier culture, called the Sredney Stog, which evolved into the Kurgans. Calvert Watkins (2000) believes that the migration of the Kurgans after 4000 BCE was too late to allow a unified language to develop into forms as different as Hittite and Myceneaen Greek; although the Kurgans clearly were Indo-Europeans, Watkins concludes that the Kurgans already spoke a differentiated dialect, not the proto-language of the larger family.

The question of the PIE homeland is still very much open. In one theory, the British scholar Colin Renfrew (1988) argues that the Proto-Indo-Europeans were an agricultural society (raising wheat and barley and herding goats and sheep) living in central Anatolia (Turkey) around 6500 BCE and dispersing slowly over the next 2,000 years. He does not see their diaspora as the result of conquest by invading warriors on horseback; they were primarily peaceful farmers moving to more fertile land required by improved agricultural technologies and expanding populations. In contrast, Gamkrelidze and Ivanov (1995) argue that the Proto-Indo-Europeans occupied eastern Anatolia and the southeastern shores of the Black Sea in the period around 4000 BCE, migrating first into central Anatolia, then to Greece, Armenia,

India, and Iran. These linguists also suggest that the proto-language was closer to Germanic, Armenian, and Hittite than to Sanskrit.

Perhaps some day this PIE puzzle will be solved.

Exercise 4.5 PIE Society and Homeland

What information about the culture and society of ancient peoples can be gleaned from studying their languages?

_____

_____

_____

_____

_____

_____

_____

Nostratic Theory

Can we find an earlier ancestor for PIE itself? Historical linguists are skeptical. Using similar techniques of reconstruction and the comparative method, certain scholars have tried to take a step back in time and have proposed the existence of an even earlier superfamily, connecting IE with the Kartvelian, Afro-Asiatic, Altaic, Dravidian, and Uralic language families. This superfamily, called Nostratic, is assumed to have existed 12,000 to 15,000 years ago, before the development of agriculture. This theory remains highly controversial since it is based on limited sets of cognates, such as the following:

'fist' Nostratic	*payngo	'to burn' Nostratic	*k'al
PIE	*pnkwstis	PIE	*k'el
Uralic	*peyngo	Afro-Asiatic	*k'al
Altaic	*p'ayngo	Dravidian	*kal
		Altaic	*qala

No grammatical reconstruction has been attempted. Most scholars believe that it is impossible to extrapolate this far back in time, as languages change radically in such a long time frame. Neither can chance similarities and borrowing be ruled out.

RECOMMENDED WEB LINKS

Two websites offering maps with the distribution of language families throughout the world are (but note that scholars do not agree entirely on particular classifications):

> http://www.zompist.com/Langmaps.html
> http://www.ship.edu/~cgboeree/languagefamilies.html

For a map of the Indo-European languages in Europe, see:

> http://linguistics.buffalo.edu/people/faculty/dryer/dryer/map.euro.ie.GIF

Two family trees of Indo-European may be found at:

> http://www.departments.bucknell.edu/linguistics/pie2.gif
> http://andromeda.rutgers.edu/~jlynch/language.html

The Indo-European Documentation Center at the University of Texas contains information on PIE phonology, grammar, and lexicon:

> http://www.utexas.edu/cola/centers/lrc/iedocctr/

An online dictionary which allows you to search for Indo-European roots by entering the English word or meaning is:

> http://www.indo-european.nl/index2.html

FURTHER READING

For a good introduction to reconstruction, the PIE language, and PIE society, see:

> Watkins, Calvert. 2000. 'Indo-European and the Indo-Europeans'. *The American Heritage Dictionary of Indo-European Roots*, vii–xxxv. 2nd edn. Boston: Houghton Mifflin.

For a readable introduction to the Indo-European language family, you may wish to consult:

> Baldi, Philip. 1983. *An Introduction to the Indo-European Languages*. Carbondale: Southern Illinois University Press.

A recent book on PIE linguistics is:

> Clackson, James. 2007. *Indo-European Linguistics: An Introduction*. Cambridge: Cambridge University Press.

For a more detailed discussion of PIE society, see:

> Benveniste, Émile. 1973. *Indo-European Language and Society*. Trans. by Elizabeth Palmer. Coral Gables, FL: University of Miami Press.

On the debate about the PIE homeland, see:

> Gamkrelidze, Thomas V., and Vjaceslav V. Ivanov. 1995. *Indo-European and the Indo-Europeans: A Reconstruction and Historical Analysis of a Proto-Language*

and a Proto-Culture. Trans. by Johanna Nichols. Berlin and New York: Mouton de Gruyter.

Mallory, J.P., and D.Q. Adams (eds.). 1997. *Encyclopedia of Indo-European Culture*. London and Chicago: Fitzroy Dearborn.

Renfrew, Colin. 1988. *Archaeology and Language: The Puzzle of Indo-European Origins*. Cambridge: Cambridge University Press.

For supplemental reading on the matriarchal pre-IE society, you may wish to look at:

Gimbutas, Marija. 1982. *The Goddesses and Gods of Old Europe*. Berkeley and Los Angeles: University of California Press.

FURTHER VIEWING

An excellent exploration of Proto-Indo-European and the Nostratic controversy is:

In Search of the First Language. NOVA with BBC Production. WGBH Educational Foundation, 1994.

On the diversification and spread of languages, see:

Episode 2: 'Constant Change'. *Speaking in Tongues: The History of Language*. Directed and researched by Christene Browne. Toronto: Syncopated Productions, 2007.

5 Germanic and the Development of Old English

OVERVIEW

This chapter examines the changes which set the Germanic languages apart from the other Indo-European languages. We look first at the existence of a common Proto-Germanic language, the development of three branches of Germanic, and the oldest recorded languages of each branch. We then concern ourselves with grammatical, lexical, and phonological changes which took place in the Common Germanic period and which distinguish Proto-Germanic from Proto-Indo-European. We pay particular attention to the consonant shifts known as Grimm's Law and Verner's Law and to the mechanisms of change involved. The chapter briefly summarizes historical events in early England important to the development of the English language: the settlement of England by Germanic tribes in the fifth century; their Christianization beginning in the late sixth century; and the invasion and colonization of England by Scandinavians in the eighth to the tenth centuries. The chapter then examines the geographical dialects of Old English in relation to the settlement patterns of the Germanic groups and the written records extant in the different dialects.

OBJECTIVES

The primary objective in this chapter is to recognize the respects in which English is a Germanic language. You should be able to describe Proto-Germanic and the development of the three branches of Germanic, recognizing the grammatical and lexical changes which occurred, and the mechanisms involved in the phonological changes, especially the First Sound Shift. Specifically, if given a PIE form, you should be able to generate the corresponding Germanic form, and vice versa. You should also be able to

■ relate the historical events in England (from the fifth to the eleventh centuries) to the development of the English language;

■ identify the different dialects of Old English; and

■ name some of the major documents of Old English.

Proto-Germanic

The modern languages belonging to the Germanic branch of Indo-European were described in Chapter 4. The parent language of all of these is known as Proto-Germanic, Common Germanic, or simply Germanic (Gmc.). We reconstruct its linguistic features on the basis of the daughter languages and some ancient runic inscriptions (see below). The speakers were a subgroup of the people who left the Indo-European homeland perhaps as early as the tenth century BCE. Because of geographical separation from other Indo-Europeans, they developed a distinct dialect, or language, over time.

Traditionally, it was thought that the first Germanic speakers lived in the area between the Elbe and Oder rivers, what is today northern Germany and Poland, but scholars believe now that the Germanic homeland extended from southern Sweden through Denmark to northern Germany. Germanic speakers (speaking a common, but not completely uniform, language) inhabited this area until the second century CE; this is known as the Common Germanic period. Toward the end of this time, however, the Germanic group began to break up. As with the Proto-Indo-Europeans, we do not know the reason for their dispersal; traditional explanations include such factors as overpopulation, comparatively infertile land, or pressure from other groups, such as the Slavs. One group migrated further north in Scandinavia, while another migrated eastward and southward as far as the Black Sea; these ultimately became the North and East branches of Germanic, respectively. Somewhat later, another group migrated southward and westward, spreading over areas originally inhabited by Celtic speakers; this ultimately became the West branch of Germanic. The different branches, with daughter languages, are represented in Table 5.1.

Although we have no written evidence of Common Germanic, the oldest records of each of the branches gives us a picture of the parent language. Here are the ancestors of the modern Germanic languages:

- **Old High German** – (Standard) German, Yiddish, Swiss German
- **Old Saxon** – Plattdeutsch (Low German)
- **Old Low Franconian** – Dutch, Flemish, Afrikaans

Table 5.1 Germanic Family Tree

Proto-Indo-European (centum)					
Common Germanic					
West Germanic			North Germanic		East Germanic
High	Low		West	East	
German	Plattdeutsch	Frisian	Norwegian	Swedish	†Gothic
Yiddish	Dutch	ENGLISH	Icelandic	Danish	†Vandalic
Swiss German	Afrikaans		Faeroese		†Burgundian
	Flemish				

† = extinct

- **Old Frisian** – Frisian
- **Old English** – English
- **Old Norse/Old Icelandic** – Norwegian, Icelandic, Faeroese, Swedish, Danish

The oldest record of East Germanic is a translation of parts of the Greek New Testament into Gothic. This translation was made around 350 CE by a Bishop Wulfila (or Ulfilas), a Visigoth who was apparently fluently bilingual in Greek and Gothic (he may have had a Greek mother) and who adapted the Greek alphabet to write Gothic. His Bible translation is linguistically a very important document giving an extensive and accurate record of an older form of this language family.

Our records of North and West Germanic are comparatively younger. Prior to Christianization, when these peoples acquired the Latin alphabet, there existed a native Germanic writing system called the runic alphabet (see Chapter 2). This system was not conducive to the writing of long documents, but we do have inscriptions in the runic alphabet in North Germanic dating from the second century and in West Germanic from the sixth century CE. The oldest records of North Germanic in the Latin alphabet are Old Norse (ON) histories, narrative sagas, and poetry dating from after 1000 CE. The oldest records of High West Germanic in the Latin alphabet date from the eighth century CE in Old High German (OHG). Records of Low West Germanic are somewhat later; they exist in Old Saxon, Old Low Franconian, Old Frisian, and Old English. These are all very closely related languages, perhaps mutually intelligible. Of these, Old English, Old Frisian, and Old Saxon are sometimes grouped together as Ingvaeonic, or North Sea Germanic. Old English and Old Frisian are especially close, and are called Anglo-Frisian. The line of descent for English is shown in Figure 5.1.

Below are three parallel versions of the Lord's Prayer (Matthew 6: 9–13) in Gothic, Old High German, and Old English (taken from Prokosch 1938:294–8). These samples show the similarity of the older Germanic languages. The Middle,

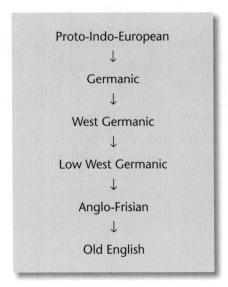

Figure 5.1   Line of Descent for Old English

Early Modern, and Modern English versions are given for comparative purposes, as is the Latin (although the Latin Vulgate is not the source for every translation) (texts taken from Fischer and Bornstein 1974:52–5 and *The New Jerusalem Bible*):

LATIN (*c*. 4th century)
Pater noster qui es in caelis, sanctificetur nomen tuum: adueniat regnum tuum: fiat uoluntas tua sicut in caelo et in terra. Panem nostrum supersub-stantialem da nobis hodie: et dimitte nobis debita nostra, sicut et nos dimit-timus debitoribus nostris: et ne inducas nos in temtationem: sed libera nos a malo.

GOTHIC (*c*. 360)
Atta unsar þu in himinam, weihnai namo þein. Qimai þiudinassus þeins. Wairþai wilja þeins, swe in himina jah anna airþai. Hlaif unsarana þana sin-teinan gif uns himma daga. Jah aflet uns þatei skulans sijaima, swaswe jah weis afletam þaim skulam unsaraim. Jah ni briggais uns in fraistubnjai, ak lausei uns af þamma ubilin. Amen.

OLD HIGH GERMAN (*c*. 840)
Fater unser thu thar bist in himile, si giheilagot thin namo, queme thin rihhi, si thin uuillo so her in himile ist, so si her in erdu. Unsar brot tagalihhaz gib uns hiutu, inti furlaz uns unsara sculdi, so uuir furlazemes unsaren sculdigon, inti ni gileitest unsih in costunga, uzouh arlosi unsih fon ubile. Amen.

OLD ENGLISH (West Saxon, *c*. 1000)
Fæder ure þu þe eart on heofonum, si þin nama gehalgod. Tobecume þin rice. Gewurþe ðin willa on eorðan swa swa on heofonum. Urne gedæghwamlican hlaf syle us to dæg. And forgyf us ure gyltas, swa swa we forgyfað urum gyltendum. And ne gelæd þu us on costnunge ac alys us of yfele; Soþlice.

WYCLIFFITE BIBLE (*c*. 1395)
Oure fadir that art in heuenes, halewid be thi name; thi kyngdoom come to; be thi wille don in erthe as in heuene; ʒyue to vs this dai oure breed ouer othir substaunce; and forʒyue to vs oure dettis, as we forʒyuen to oure dettouris; and lede vs not in to temptacioun, but delyuere vs fro yuel. Amen.

KING JAMES BIBLE (1611)
Our father which art in heauen, hallowed be thy name. Thy kingdome come. Thy will be done, in earth, as it is in heauen. Giue vs this day our daily bread. And forgiue vs our debts, as we forgiue our debters. And lead vs not into temptation, but deliuer vs from euill. Amen.

THE NEW JERUSALEM BIBLE (1985)
Our Father in heaven, may your name be held holy, your kingdom come, your will be done, on earth as in heaven. Give us today our daily bread. And forgive us our debts, as we have forgiven those who are in debt to us. And do not put us to the test, but save us from the evil one. (Matthew 6: 9–13)

Exercise 5.1 Proto-Germanic

1. a.   What are the traditional dates for the Common Germanic period?

    _____

    b.   What geographical area is currently accepted as having been inhabited by Common Germanic speakers?

    _____

    _____

    c.   What happened to this group at the end of the Common Germanic period?

    _____

    _____

    _____

    d. Give the line of descent for Old English, beginning with Proto-Indo-European.

_____

_____

2. List the cognates in the first five versions of the Lord's Prayer (given on pp. 130–131) for the following words. Don't worry about inflectional endings; cognates may not occur in all the languages in all instances.

	Lat.	Go.	OHG	OE	ME
a. father	_____	_____	_____	_____	_____
b. name	_____	_____	_____	_____	_____
c. heaven	_____	_____	_____	_____	_____
d. hallowed	_____	_____	_____	_____	_____
e. will	_____	_____	_____	_____	_____
f. evil	_____	_____	_____	_____	_____

Grammatical and Lexical Changes from PIE to Germanic

The modern Germanic languages, including English, are distinguished from other members of the Indo-European family by a number of changes which occurred in the Common Germanic period, affecting verbs, nouns, adjectives, and the overall lexicon.

The verbal system of PIE is based primarily on distinctions of *aspect*, which is an indication of whether an action is ongoing or completed. We can see an aspectual distinction in the ModE contrast between *He was writing a poem* (ongoing action) and *He wrote a poem* (completed action). In PIE, there is a three-way aspectual distinction expressed in verb stems:

- a present stem expressing ongoing action,
- a past stem expressing completed action, and
- a perfect stem expressing resultant state.

Aspect remains the primary distinction of the verb in Classical Greek and Sanskrit and many of the eastern IE languages, such as Baltic and Slavic. However, the western IE languages—Italic, Celtic, and Germanic—all evolved verbal systems based primarily on distinctions of tense. *Tense* is a formal linguistic category expressing the concept of time. It indicates whether an action is past (preterit), present, or future in respect to the moment of speaking. The system which developed in Germanic is especially simple, conflating the past and perfect stems of PIE to form the preterit tense, and retaining the present stems as the present tense. While we usually think of Modern English as having three tenses, we must keep in mind that we indicate only two tenses by simple inflection, e.g. *walk* (pres.) and *walked* (pret.), while we must use a periphrastic form, e.g. *will walk/be going to walk*, to indicate the future.

The way in which the preterit tense is expressed also changed. Germanic inherited from PIE a means of forming the preterit by ablaut (changing the root vowel) to indicate present, preterit, and past participle forms of the verb. We see evidence of this in Modern English in the *strong* (nowadays termed *irregular*) verbs such as *begin/began/begun*, *write/wrote/written*, *drink/drank/drunk*, where the preterit and past participle are distinguished from the infinitive (present) by different vowels. In Germanic, there are seven regular patterns of such vowel gradation.

In addition to IE ablaut, Germanic innovated a second means of expressing the preterit, using a dental suffix, a term used to denote the final alveolar stops in Modern English. Today's regular verbs, such as *love/loved*, *walk/walked*, *load/loaded*, form their past tense in this way, using *-d*, *-t*, or *-ed*. Jacob Grimm, a nineteenth-century grammarian (as well as a collector of Germanic fairy tales), called such verbs *weak* as opposed to strong. The origin of the dental suffix is obscure, although it is thought that it may derive from a form of the verb *do* which has become attached to the verb as a suffix. The weak pattern became the productive, or *analogical*, means of making preterit forms in Germanic. In Modern English, most verbs are weak, and any verb entering the language forms its preterit using a dental suffix. We can see this with an invented verb such as *glick*; we instinctively form the preterit as *glicked*. The once-standard IE system of ablaut (which would give us something like *glick/glack/gluck*) has given way to the Germanic innovation.

Germanic also simplified the mood and voice distinctions of the PIE verbal system. *Mood* is an indication of whether the action is viewed as fact or non-fact (for instance, possibility, probability, desire, wish, contrary-to-fact, or unreality are all *non-fact*). PIE expresses five moods by means of verbal inflection:

- indicative (fact),
- imperative (command),
- optative (wish),
- injunctive (unreality), and
- subjunctive (possibility).

Germanic retained the first two, but conflated the last three as the subjunctive, which indicates all non-factual events apart from direct commands. Since an inflected subjunctive is now quite rare in ModE (examples include *if I were*, *heaven help us*, *be that as it may*, *God shed his grace on thee*), we will treat it in more detail in Chapter 7.

Voice is an indication of whether the grammatical subject is acting, acted upon, or both. In the ModE active sentence *John broke the vase*, the subject (*John*) is acting, whereas in the passive sentence *The vase was broken*, the subject (*the vase*) is acted upon. In addition to an active voice, PIE has a middle voice inflection, comparable to the ModE reflexive form (*John burned himself*) in which the subject is both acting and acted upon. The middle voice was lost in Germanic, except in Gothic, where it was retained in a limited way, and in Old Norse. In all other cases, a new phrasal passive takes its place.

The nominal system of Germanic simplified the case distinctions of PIE. *Case* is an indication, by means of inflection, of the function of a noun in a sentence: whether it is subject, object, indirect object, and so on. As you will recall, PIE inflects nouns for eight cases. In Germanic, a number of these cases fell together, in what is called *case syncretism*, so that only five cases are marked:

- nominative (combining nominative and vocative),
- accusative,
- genitive,
- dative (combining ablative, locative, and dative), and
- instrumental.

(Don't worry if you don't understand case completely at this point; we will be discussing it in much greater detail in Chapter 7.)

Another innovation in Germanic occurred in the adjectival system. The set of adjectival endings inherited from PIE came to be used when an adjective alone modifies the noun, e.g. *gode batas* ('good boats'), but Germanic developed an additional set of adjectival endings which are used when modifiers other than an adjective, such as a demonstrative (*this*, *that*) or possessive adjective (*my*, *your*, *his*), occur with the noun, e.g. *þa godan batas* ('these good boats') (treated in detail in the discussion of Old English grammar; see Table 7.8). Jacob Grimm called the former strong, or *indefinite*, and the latter weak, or *definite*.

Finally, the vocabulary of Germanic is quite different from that of PIE. A large number of words in Germanic, perhaps one-third, are not found in any of the other IE languages. These include such common words as *brew*, *bride*, *death*, *earth*, *goose*, *gold*, *sea*, *soul*, and *weave*. While these could conceivably be IE words lost in the other branches, it is also possible that they are neologisms or loan words from a non-IE language with which Germanic came into contact during the Common period. Without any direct evidence for such a substratum, we may only speculate about how this non-IE vocabulary entered Germanic.

Exercise 5.2 Grammatical and Lexical Changes from Proto-Indo-European to Germanic

1. Briefly describe the five ways in which the PIE verbal system changed in Germanic.

(1) _____

_____

_____

(2) _____

_____

_____

(3) _____

_____

_____

(4) _____

_____

_____

(5) _____

_____

_____

2. What major change in the nominal system occurred in Germanic?

_____

_____

_____

_____

3. What major change in the adjectival system occurred in Germanic?

_____

_____

_____

_____

_____

Phonological Changes from PIE to Germanic

In addition to grammatical and lexical differences, the Germanic family is distinguished from other IE languages by certain large-scale phonological changes which occurred in the Common Germanic period.

One of the two most important sound changes affecting the history of English is the First Sound Shift (the other is the Great Vowel Shift—see Chapter 10). The existence of major consonant differences between Germanic and the other Indo-European languages was first remarked upon by the Danish scholar Rasmus Rask in 1818 and then discussed in more detail by Jacob Grimm in his grammar of German in 1828. For this reason, and because these differences result from a sound change between PIE and Germanic that was thought to have operated without exception, the change is formulated as 'Grimm's Law'. Grimm's Law describes one part of the First Sound Shift; the other, as we will see below, is described by 'Verner's Law'.

Grimm's Law

Grimm's Law posits an unconditioned sound change of massive proportions, affecting all the stop consonants of PIE. Since all of the Germanic languages show the effects of Grimm's Law, it must have operated prior to the breakup of the Common Germanic group; the shift is dated sometime between 1000 and 400 BCE. The causes of Grimm's Law are unknown, although a wide set of reasons have been suggested, including the difficulty of breathing in the high Alps—an improbable rationale. Grimm himself attributes the shift to the 'violent progress and craving for freedom which was found in Germany' (from Grimm's *Deutsche Grammatik* [1828], translated and cited by Jespersen 1922:45). Today, either a language-external cause (the influence of a substratum, or language mixture) or a language-internal cause (instability in the PIE stop system) seems more plausible. In the latter case, as a result of Grimm's Law, the consonants of Germanic are distinguished only by stopping and voicing (not by aspiration).

Recall that PIE has three sets of stop consonants: voiceless stops, voiced stops, and voiced aspirated stops. We will consider the changes undergone by these in sequence. First, by Grimm's Law, all voiceless stops in PIE become the corresponding voiceless fricatives in Germanic:

*p > *f

*t > *θ

*k > *x or *h (in initial position)

*kʷ > *xʷ or *hʷ (in initial position)

Practice describing each shift in articulatory terms and sounding it out. Note that [x] represents a voiceless velar fricative, a sound not found in Modern English, and that the superscript [ʷ] represents a sound produced with lip rounding. This shift involves no (or little) change in place of articulation and no change in voicing, only a change in manner of articulation; it is an example of fricativization.

*p > *f

Below are some examples of *p > *f (example sets are listed vertically):

PIE	*pətēr 'father'	PIE	*ped- 'foot'
Lat.	*pater*	Lat.	*pēs* (ped-)
Skt.	*pitár-*	Skt.	*pad-*
Gk.	*patĕ́r*	Gk.	*poús* (pod-)
OE	*fæder*	OE	*fōt*

Due to borrowing, we often find in Modern English both a Germanic form and non-Germanic cognates. Thus, we have ModE *father* but also *paternal* (a borrowing from Lat. *pater*) and *patriot* (from Gk. *patĕ́r*), ModE *foot* but also *pedal* and *pedestal* (from Lat. *ped-*), *pajamas* (ultimately from Skt. *pad-*), and *podiatrist* (from Gk. *pod-*).

*t > *θ

Look at the following examples of *t > *θ:

PIE	*treyes/*trei- 'three'	PIE	*tenu 'to stretch'
Lat.	*trēs*	Lat.	*tenuis*
Skt.	*trayas*	Skt.	*tanu-*
Gk.	*treîs*	Gk.	*tanaós*
OE	*þrēo* (þ represents [θ])	ModE	*thin*

Compare ModE *tertiary* (from Lat. *trēs*) and *triad* (from Gk. *treîs*); also compare *extension*, *tension*, *tenuous* (from Lat. *tenuis*), and *tendon* (from Gk. *tanaós*).

*k > *x or *h

The following examples demonstrate *k > *x or *h (in initial position):

PIE	*krewə 'raw meat, blood'	PIE	*leuk 'light, brightness'
Lat.	*cruor* (c = [k])	Lat.	*lūx* (*lūc-*) 'light'
Skt.	*kravíḥ-*	Skt.	*lōká* 'free space'
Gk.	*kréas*	Gk.	*leukós*
OE	*hrēaw* 'raw'	OE	*lēoht* 'light'

The orthographic symbol *h* in OE *lēoht* represents [x]; this sound is lost in ModE, but its prior occurrence is recorded in the conservative written form of ModE by *gh*. Compare *crude, cruel* (from Lat. *cruor*), and *pancreas* (from Gk. *kréas*); also compare *lucid, elucidate*, and *translucent* (from Lat. *lūc-*).

*k^w > *x^w or *h^w*

Look now at the following examples of *k^w > *x^w > *h^w:

PIE	*k^wod 'what'	PIE	*k^welo-s
Lat.	*quod* (*qu* = [k^w])	Gk.	*kúklos* 'circle'
OE	*hwæt*	OE	*hwēol* 'wheel'

The OE form *hwæt* is cited here because it shows the shift more clearly than the ModE form, where the spelling of the initial consonant cluster *hw-* has changed to *wh-*. Compare ModE *cycle* and *cyclone* (from Gk. *kúklos*).

Though Grimm's Law generally operates in all environments, there is one exception. When the PIE voiceless stop follows *s, it does not shift in Germanic, as in the following examples:

PIE *speu / Lat. *spuō* / ModE *spew*

PIE *stā / Lat. *stō* / ModE *stand*

PIE *skep / Lat. *scabō* / ModE *scab*

If Grimm's Law operated normally here, one would expect [sf-, sθ-, sx-] rather than [sp-, st-, sk-]; however, a sequence of two fricatives such as this is generally avoided. Compare ModE *status* and *obstacle* (from Lat. *stō*); also compare *scabies* (from Lat. *scabō*).

In the second part of Grimm's Law, all the voiced stops in PIE become the corresponding voiceless stops in Germanic. That is, there is no change in position or in manner of articulation, just in voicing. Predict the sounds in Germanic:

*b >

*d >

*g >

*g^w >

(The correct answers are *p, *t, *k, *k^w.) Look at the following examples of *b > *p. Remember that it is very difficult to reconstruct *b to PIE. Consequently, there are very few (and somewhat problematical) examples of this shift:

PIE	*kan(n)abi- 'cannabis'	PIE	*bel- 'strong'?
Lat.	*cannabis*	Lat.	*dē-bilis* 'without strength, weak'
Gk.	*kánnabis*	Skt.	*bálam* 'strength'
OE	*hænep*	Gk.	*beltíōn*
ModE	*hemp*	Dutch	*pal*

Compare ModE *cannabis* (from Lat. *cannabis*) and *debilitate* (from Lat. *dē-bilis*).

*d > *t

The following examples demonstrate *d > *t:

PIE   *dekm 'ten'   PIE   *ed- 'eat'

Lat.   *decem*   Lat.   *edō*

Gk.   *deka*   Skt.   *admi*

ModE   *ten*   Gk.   *édo*

                       ModE   *eat*

Compare ModE *decimal*, *December* (from Lat. *decem*), and *decade* (from Gk. *deka*); also compare *edible* (from Lat. *edō*).

*g > *k

Look at the following examples of *g > *k:

PIE   *genu 'knee'   PIE   *grənom

Lat.   *genu*   Lat.   *grānum*

Gk.   *gōnu*   ModE   *corn*

OE   *cnēo*

Compare ModE *genuflect* (from Lat. *genu*) and *diagonal* (from Gk. *gōnu*); also compare *grain* and *granular* (from Lat. *grānum*).

*gʷ > *kʷ

Here are some examples of *gʷ > *kʷ:

PIE   *gʷei-/gʷiu-   PIE   *gʷenā 'woman'

Skt.   *jivá* 'life'   Gk.   *gunē*

Gk.   *bíos* 'human life'   OE   *cwēn* 'queen'

Lat.   *vīvus* 'alive'

OE   *cwicu* 'living'

It is common in IE languages for the inherited labiovelars to be simplified, either to a labial sound, as in the Greek *b* in *bíos,* or to a velar sound, as in the Latin *v* in *vīvus* (pronounced [w]). However, Germanic generally retains the complex sound, as in OE *cwic* / ModE *quick*. Compare ModE *biology*, *amphibious*, and *microbe* (from Gk. *bíos*); also compare ModE *vivacious*, *survive*, and *vivid* (from Lat. *vīvus*). Note that the OE word *cwicu* is a noun meaning 'living', retained in the expression 'the quick and the dead'. Also compare *gynecology* (from Gk. *gunē*).

In the third part of Grimm's Law all the voiced aspirated stops in PIE become the corresponding voiced fricatives: *β, *ð, *ɣ. (Remember that Greek beta [β] represents a voiced bilabial fricative and Greek gamma [ɣ] represents a voiced velar fricative; neither sound is found in ModE.) Later, in most cases, the voiced fricatives become voiced stops in Germanic. The net effect is that they lose aspiration. Predict the end result:

*bh > *β >

*dh > *ð >

*gh > *ɣ >

*gʷh > *g, *w

(The correct sounds here are *b, *d, *g. The voiced aspirates develop differently in Greek, Latin, and Sanskrit. Only Sanskrit retains voiced aspirated stops, while Greek develops voiceless aspirated stops [ph, th, kh] and Latin [f] or [h].

*bh > *b

Below are examples of the shift from *bh > *b:

PIE	*bhrāter 'brother'	PIE	*bher- 'bear, carry'
Skt.	*bhrátar*	Skt.	*bhárati*
Gk.	*phrāter*	Gk.	*phérō*
Lat.	*frāter*	Lat.	*ferō*
OE	*brōþor*	OE	*beran*

Compare ModE *fraternal* and *friar* (from Lat. *frāter*); also compare *transfer, fertile* (from Lat. *ferō*), *metaphor*, and *periphery* (from Gk. *phérō*).

*dh > *d

Look at the examples of the change from *dh > *d:

PIE	*əndhero- 'under'	PIE	*reudh 'red'
Skt.	*ádhara-*	Skt.	*rudhirá*
Lat.	*īnferus*	Gk.	*(e)rúthō*
OE	*under*	Lat.	*rūfus*
		OE	*rēad*

Compare ModE *inferior* and *infernal* (from Lat. *īnferus*); also compare *rouge* and *rubella* (from Lat. *rūfus*).

*gh > *g

The following examples demonstrate *gh > *g:

PIE	*wegh 'move, ride'	PIE	*ghomon 'man'
Skt.	*váh- 'to pull'	Lat.	*homō*
Gk.	*ókhos* 'wagon'	OE	*guma*
Lat.	*vehō* 'I pull'		
OE	*weg* 'road'		

Compare ModE *vehicle* and *voyage* (from Lat. *vehō*); also compare *human* and *humane* (ultimately derived from Lat. *homō*).

*gʷh > *g or *w

For the voiced aspirated labiovelars, the development of *gʷh > *g or *w is complex:

PIE	*gʷher 'to heat, warm'
Skt.	*gharmá* 'heat'
Gk.	*thermós* 'hot'
Lat.	*formus* 'warm'
OE	*warm*

Even Sanskrit simplifies this sound. Compare ModE *thermos, thermometer* (from Gk. *thermós*), *furnace*, and *forceps* (ultimately derived from Lat. *formus*).

Grimm's Law affects only the stop consonants of PIE; it does not affect the one fricative *s, the liquids *l and *r, the nasals *m and *n, or the glides *w and *j, which remain unchanged in Germanic. The law is summarized in Table 5.2 and represented graphically in Figure 5.2.

Table 5.2 Grimm's Law

voiceless stop > voiceless fricative	voiced stop > voiceless stop	voiced aspirated stop > voiced fricative > voiced stop
*p > *f	*b > *p	*bh >*β > *b
*t > *θ	*d > *t	*dh > *ð > *d
*k > *x or *h (initially)	*g > *k	*gh > *ɣ > *g
*kʷ > *xʷ or *hʷ (initially)	*gʷ > *kʷ	*gʷh > *g, *w

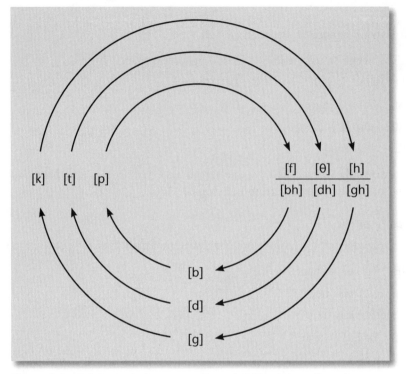

Figure 5.2 A Schematic Representation of Grimm's Law (from Jean Aitchison, *Language Change: Progress or Decay?* 3rd edn [Cambridge: Cambridge University Press, 2001], p. 184, reprinted with the permission of Cambridge University Press)

A final note: If one accepts the alternative formulation of the PIE consonant system discussed in the previous chapter, the consonant shift in Germanic is, in fact, simplified:

*p' > *p	*bh/b		*ph/p > *f
*t' > *t	*dh/d	unchanged	*th/t > * θ
*k' > *k	*gh/g		*kh/k > *x, *h
*k'ʷ > *kʷ	*gʷh/gʷ		*kʷh/kʷ > *xʷ, *hʷ

Exercise 5.3 Germanic: Grimm's Law

For each of the following samples, indicate the probable Germanic or IE form of the missing consonant, either initial, medial, or final. A ModE cognate is given for reference.

	PIE	Gmc.	ModE
a.	*mūk- 'heap'	*mū___ōn-	mow
b.	*mōd- 'assemble'	*mō___jan-	meet
c.	*gerbh- 'scratch'	*___er___an-	carve
d.	*ghalgh- 'branch'	*___al___-	gallows
e.	*a___wesī- 'axe'	*akwesi-	axe
f.	*sleu___- 'slide'	*sleub-	sleeve
g.	*s___el- 'recite'	*spellan	spell
h.	*tel- 'board'	*___il-jo-	deal (fir plank)
i.	*___ek- 'give birth to'	*θegn	thane
j.	*dhrēn- 'murmur'	*___rēn-	drone

Verner's Law

After having claimed that Grimm's Law operates without exception, we must now admit that there are certain Germanic words which appear to violate it. Grimm himself noted these exceptions but did not attempt to explain them. They were finally explained by Danish scholar Karl Verner in an article entitled 'An Exception to the First Sound Shift', published in 1875.

The exceptions that Verner examined involve reflexes of the PIE voiceless stops, which appear in Germanic as voiced fricatives (and later usually as voiced stops) rather than as the voiceless fricatives predicted by Grimm. PIE *s is also affected, shifting first to *z and then to *r. These changes are set out in Table 5.3.

Table 5.3 Verner's Law

PIE	Gmc. sound expected (by Grimm's Law)	Gmc. sound found
*p	*f	*β > *b
*t	*θ	*ð > *d
*k	*x	*ɣ > *g
*s	*s	*z > *r

These exceptions are perhaps most clearly seen in the verb paradigm, where the infinitive has the expected sound, while the past participle has the unexpected sound. Note the alternation between ð (representing an original voiceless fricative) and *d* and between *s* and *r* in the OE verbs cited below:

infinitive	past participle
snīðan 'to cut'	*sniden* '(has) cut'
cweðan 'to speak'	*cweden* '(has) spoken'
cēosan 'to choose'	*coren* '(has) chosen'
lēosan 'to lose'	*loren* '(has) lost'

We can still observe these alternations in the ModE pairs *was/were*, *lost/(for)lorn*, and *seethe/sodden*.

It is said that Karl Verner dozed off one afternoon while reading a grammar of Classical Greek and, because he had Greek forms in his mind, discovered the clue to this exception: the position of the floating accent in PIE. He realized that he was dealing with a conditioned sound change brought about by the place of the accent in the word. His explanation has come to be known as Verner's Law:

> If a PIE voiceless stop is in a voiced environment, then it will appear in Germanic as a voiced fricative (or stop) when the PIE accent does not fall on the immediately preceding syllable (i.e. vowel).

'Voiced environment' means that the sound does not begin or end the word and is not next to a voiceless sound. 'Accent does not fall on the immediately preceding syllable' means that the accent may fall on any other syllable but the one preceding the consonant. Essentially, Verner was observing that lack of stress is associated with voicing, as we still see in Modern English in the pairs *off* (a stressed adverb and hence voiceless) and *of* (an unstressed preposition and hence voiced).

If we consider the verbs given above, we can now reconcile the consonant alternations. In PIE, the accent of the infinitive is on the first syllable (as it is in Greek). Thus, the consonants found are those expected by Grimm's Law. However, the accent of the past participle is on the second syllable (as it is in Greek), not immediately preceding the consonant, and so these consonants are predicted by Verner's Law.

The Germanic words cited below show the operation of Verner's Law. Greek (or Sanskrit) forms are also cited to indicate the position of the PIE accent (on the following syllable) and the PIE consonant:

PIE *p / Gmc. *b	Gk. *heptá* 'seven'	Go. *síbun*
PIE *t / Gmc. *d	Skt. *patí* 'master'	Go. *fádi*
PIE *k / Gmc. *g	Gk. *hekurá* 'mother-in-law'	OE *swéger*
PIE *s / Gmc. *r	Skt. *snusá* 'daughter-in-law'	OE *snóru*

The difficulty in identifying the conditions for Verner's Law is caused by the shift in the position of the accent in Germanic, as discussed in the next section.

Exercise 5.4 Germanic: Verner's Law

1. The following PIE words are affected by Verner's Law. Give the Germanic sounds corresponding to the underlined sound. The OE and ModE forms are given for comparison.

	PIE	Gmc.	OE	ModE
a.	*ghaiso- 'stick'	*gai___āz	gār– 'spear'	garlic, to gore
b.	*teutā- 'tribe'	*θeu___a-	- - -	Teuton
c.	*uperi- 'over'	*u___eri	ofer	over
d.	*tekno- 'child'	*θe___naz	thegn	thane
e.	*skot- 'dark'	*ska___waz	sceadu	shade
f.	*dek- 'lock of hair'	*ta___laz	tægel	tail

2. State the conditions of Verner's Law.

    _____

    _____

Accent Shift and Ordering of Changes

As mentioned in Chapter 4, PIE has a system of free accent, which depends on variations in pitch. In such a system the accent in a word can fall on any syllable (depending on the word and how it is inflected). This accentual system is retained in Sanskrit and Classical Greek. An important change between PIE and Germanic, however, is the development of a system of fixed 'stress accent', which depends on variations in loudness. In the fixed accentual system of Germanic, the accent falls always on the first or root syllable of the word.

It is the PIE accent that dictates whether or not Verner's Law applies. Because of the change to a fixed accent system in Germanic, the conditions for Verner's Law are obscured: the accent always appears on the first syllable in Germanic, even when it was originally on another syllable in PIE. While this fixing of stress makes it difficult to determine the conditions for Verner's Law, it does allow us to order the changes involved. We can tell that they must have occurred in the following sequence:

1. Grimm's Law
2. Verner's Law
3. Accent shift

Table 5.4 summarizes these changes.

Table 5.4 The Order of Grimm's Law, Verner's Law, and the Accent Shift

	Grimm's Law	*Verner's Law*	*Accent Shift*
PIE —p–́	Gmc. —f–́	Gmc. —β–́	Gmc. –́β—
PIE —t–́	Gmc. —θ–́	Gmc. —ð–́	Gmc. –́ð—
PIE —k–́	Gmc. —x–́	Gmc. —ɣ–́	Gmc. –́ɣ—
PIE —s–́	Gmc. —s–́	Gmc. —z–́ or —r–́	Gmc. –́z— or –́r—

First Grimm's Law operates in all contexts, deriving *f, *θ, *x from PIE *p, *t, *k. Then Verner's Law operates on the output of Grimm's Law, provided the accent falls on any syllable other than the preceding one and the consonant is in a voiced environment. The voiceless fricatives are voiced, giving *β, *ð, *ɣ. Note that Verner's Law could not precede Grimm's Law since PIE has no voiceless fricatives (other than *s). Furthermore, only after Verner's Law has operated does the accent shift to the initial position. If the accent had shifted earlier, the conditions for Verner's Law could not have been met, since the accent would always have fallen on the preceding syllable.

Vowel Changes

In comparison with the consonants, the vowels of PIE underwent very few changes in Germanic. Review the vowels and diphthongs of PIE (as shown in Figure 4.3). The major changes are summarized in Figure 5.3 and exemplified below:

- Short *a, *o, and *ə merge as short *a (PIE *maghu- 'young, unmarried person' > Go. *magus*; PIE *owis 'sheep' > Go. *awistr*; PIE *pəter- 'father' > Go. *fadar*).
- Long *ō and *ā merge as long *ō (PIE *bhlō- 'bloom' > Go. *blōma*; PIE *stā- 'stood' > Go. *stōþ*).
- Long *ī and *ei merge as long *ī (PIE *su-īno- 'swine' > OHG *swīn;* PIE *skei-ro- 'shine' > OE *scīr)*.
- Long *ē shifts to long *ǣ (PIE *dhē- 'deed' > OE *dǣd)*, while a new long *ē develops from some unknown source (Gmc. *hēr 'here').
- The diphthong *eu shifts to *iu (PIE *bheudh- 'bid' > Go. -*biudan)*.

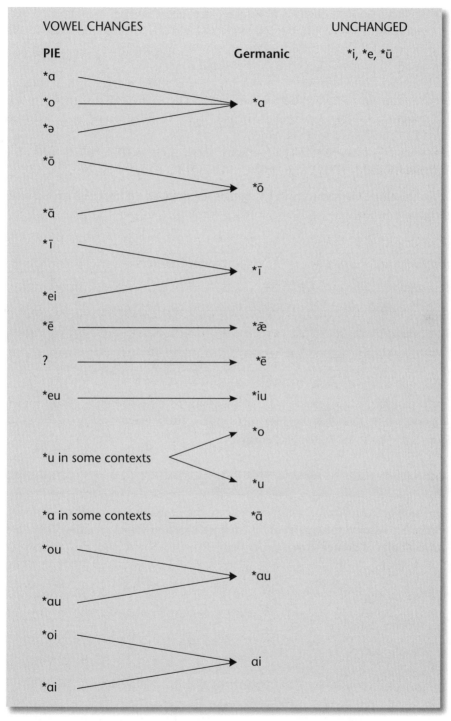

Figure 5.3   Vowel Changes from Proto-Indo-European to Germanic

- Two conditioned changes also take place: short *u becomes short *o except before a high vowel in the following syllable (cf. PIE *jugom 'yoke' > OHG *joch; PIE *bhudh 'offer' > OHG *butun* 'we offered').
- Short *a becomes long (this vowel is quite rare).
- Because of the merger of *o and *a, there is also a merger of the diphthongs *ou and *au to *au (PIE *roudhos 'red' > Go. *rauþs*; PIE *aug- 'wash' > Go. *aukan*), as well as a merger of *oi and *ai to *ai (PIE *oinos 'one' > Go. *ains*; PIE *ghaidis 'goat' > Go. *gaits*).
- Unchanged are *ū (PIE *sūro- 'sour' > OE *sūr*), *e (PIE *bher- 'bear' > OE *beran*), and *i (PIE *wid- 'know' > OE *wit-*).

The resulting Germanic vowel system is not quite as symmetrical as that of PIE, as Figure 5.4 shows.

	Monophthongs		
	Front	**Central**	**Back**
High	*ī *i		*ū *u
Mid	*ē *e		*ō *o
Low	*ǣ		*ā *a
	Diphthongs		
	*iu		*ai
			*au

Figure 5.4   The Vowel System of Germanic

Exercise 5.5 Germanic: Grimm's Law and Vowel Changes

For each of the following samples, indicate the probable Germanic or PIE form as indicated. Assume the operation of Grimm's Law and vowel changes. There are *no* examples of Verner's Law.

	PIE	Gmc.
a.	*kʷrep- 'body'	_____
b.	*albho- 'white'	_____
c.	*kīgh- 'fast'	_____
d.	*modhro- 'a color'	_____
e.	_____	*θriut- 'threat'

f. _____   *west- 'west'

g. *plokso- 'flax'   _____

Second Sound Shift and Mechanisms of Change

A later sound shift in the Germanic languages may provide a model for the mechanism of change involved in Grimm's Law (see Aitchison 2001:187–9). This is the Second Sound Shift, or High German Sound Shift, yet another unconditioned change affecting the Germanic consonants. It took place between the sixth and eighth centuries CE, beginning in southern Germany and spreading northward. Unlike Grimm's Law, the Second Sound Shift is incomplete, affecting only the voiceless stops [p, t, k], one voiced stop [d], and one fricative [θ]. The spread of this change is also incomplete; it did not reach northern Germany. In fact, this change is what distinguishes modern High German from the Low German languages spoken in the north—Dutch, Flemish, and Frisian. It also differentiates High German from English. Because the ancestors of the Anglo-Saxons left continental Europe before this sound shift took place, their language would not have felt its effects in any case.

In this shift, the voiceless stops became voiceless fricatives, the voiced stop became a voiceless stop, and the voiceless fricative became a voiced stop. Details of the shift are set out in Table 5.5.

The Second Sound Shift occurred during the Old High German period, from which we have written records, and thus we can follow its progression, observing the mechanism of the shift in operation. We know that in about 500 CE, [p], [t], and [k] shifted. Then about 600 CE, [d] shifted, and only later [θ] shifted. The mechanism involved here is called a consonantal drag chain. In a drag chain, one sound shifts, leaving a gap which is filled by the shift of another sound. The first sound thus 'drags' the second sound into its place. In this case, the shift of [t] to the cor-

Table 5.5 The Second Germanic Sound Shift

Second Sound Shift	English	German
p > pf or ff (after vowels)	pepper	Pfeffer
t > z = [ts] or ss (after vowels)	to water	zu Wasser
k > ch = [x] (after vowels)	make	machen
d > t	dream	Traum
θ > d	through	durch

responding fricative leaves a gap which is later filled by the shift of [d] into the old [t] position, and the shift of [d] leaves a gap which is later filled by the shift of [θ].

The opposite mechanism, a push chain, in which one sound begins to encroach upon the position of another sound and eventually 'pushes' it into a new position, is more common with vowel shifts because vowels can shift in incremental amounts. (We will see this phenomenon later in Chapter 10 when we discuss the Great Vowel Shift.) Because drag chains are the usual mechanism for consonantal shifts, we could conceptualize Grimm's Law as a drag chain, occurring in the sequence (somewhat simplified) shown in Figure 5.5.

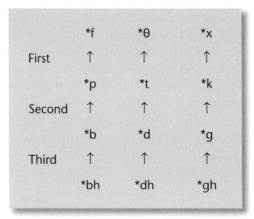

Figure 5.5 Grimm's Law as a Drag Chain

The shift of *p, *t, *k leaves a gap which can then be filled by the shift of *b, *d, *g; this in turn leaves a gap which can be filled with the shift of *bh, *dh, *gh. Though we do not know where exactly the shift began, we do know that it could not have begun with *b, *d, *g, because the shifted sounds would have merged with the original *p, *t, *k and all would have shifted together, eliminating *p, *t, *k (see Aitchison 2001:184).

If Verner's Law is taken into account, the drag chain sequence would be interrupted, as shown in Table 5.6.

Table 5.6 The First Sound Shift as a Drag Chain[a]

Step 1	*p > *f	*t > *θ	*k > *x or *h	Grimm's Law
Step 2	*f > *β	*θ > *ð	*x > *ɣ	Verner's Law
Step 3	*b > *p	*d > *t	*g > *k	Grimm's Law
Step 4	*bh > *β	*dh > *ð	*gh > *ɣ	Grimm's Law

[a]Later the voiced fricatives become voiced stops (*β > *b, *ð > *d, *ɣ > *g). (The order of the changes remains controversial and some scholars in fact believe that the changes are better accounted for as a push chain.)

A Brief History of Anglo-Saxon England

The Old English period covers a span of 617 years, from 449 to 1066 CE. Prior to this, the native population of England was Celtic. The Celts, speakers of an Indo-European language, probably entered the island during the Bronze Age. In the years 55 and 54 BCE, after successfully conquering the Celts in Gaul (modern-day France and Belgium), Julius Caesar attempted to conquer Britain; he met strong resistance and gave up the endeavor. In fact, the land was not successfully conquered by the Romans until about 43 CE, when Claudius brought 40,000 men. Even so, it remained a backwater of the Roman Empire; some Romanization occurred—roads, cities, and baths were built (the Roman baths at Bath are celebrated as 'the work of giants' in an OE poem 'The Ruin'; see text box below)—but the Romans seem to have had difficulty with inclement weather, a harsh landscape, and incursions by the Picts and Scots into the northern territory. In Hadrian's reign, a system of walls and fortifications marked the northern boundary of Roman Britain (see figures 5.6 and 5.7). During this occupation, the Romans and their subjects appear to have lived quite peacefully together; the British Celts continued to speak their own language (unlike the Celts in Gaul) and the Romans offered them some protection against the Picts. In 410 CE, however, Rome came under attack by the Visigoths (East Germanic peoples), led by Alaric, and the troops in Britain were recalled to Rome, leaving the population defenseless against the Scots (Celts who had come over from Ireland) and Picts.

Figure 5.6 Hadrian's Wall Was Built between 120 and 123 CE to Mark the Border of Roman Britain (© Mike Dodd/Amanita Photo Library)

THE RUIN

Wrætlic is þes wealstan, wyrde gebræcon;
burgstede burston, brosnað enta geweorc.
Hrofas sind gehrorene, hreorge torras,
hrungeat berofen, hrim on lime,

scearde scurbeorge scorene, gedrorene,
ældo undereotone. Eorðgrap hafað
waldend wyrhtan forweorone, geleorene,
heardgripe hrusan, oþ hund cnea
werþeoda gewitan. Oft þæs wag gebad

ræghar ond readfah rice æfter oþrum,
ofstonden under stormum; steap geap gedreas.

(from the *Exeter Book*; see Krapp and Dobbie 1936:227)

Wondrous is this wall-stone, shattered by fate.
Battlements broken, the work of giants decayed.
Roofs are fallen, ruinous are the towers,
broken the barred gate, rime on the cement,

walls broken, rent, collapsed,
undermined by age. Earth-grip stout
grasp of the ground, holds the master builders,
perished, passed away until a hundred
generations of people have departed. Often this wall survived,

grey with lichen, stained with red, withstanding the storm,
one kingdom after another; its lofty gate has fallen.

(Note: Because of the style and word order of OE poetry, our idiomatic translation does not follow the original text line-by-line.)

The Germanic Settlement of England

The traditional account of the Germanic settlement of England is given by the Vener-
able Bede, a monk in the monastery of Jarrow (on the north-east coast of England),
in his Latin history of England, the *Historia Ecclesiastica Gentis Anglorum* (*Ecclesiastical History of the English People*), finished in 731 CE. This important work was
translated into Old English in the ninth century. Bede gives the date of their coming
as the year 449; most likely, Germanic settlers began arriving twenty years before

this date. According to his account, the British Celts under a king called Vortigern 'invited' Germanic tribes to help fight the Picts and Scots; in return, these tribes were to receive the Isle of Thanet (in the Thames estuary). It is more likely, however, that the Germanic people came uninvited, pushed out of their homeland by over-population. For whatever reason they came, the first to arrive, according to Bede, were the Jutes, then the Saxons, and finally the Angles. The Jutes came from Jutland, what is now the Danish peninsula; the Angles from just south of the Jutes in modern-day Schleswig-Holstein (Germany); and the Saxons from an area to the south and west, between the Elbe and Rhine rivers (modern-day Germany and Holland) (see Figure 5.7).

Undoubtedly other Germanic tribes joined in as well, such as the Frisians, who lived in modern-day Holland and on islands in the North Sea. The first wave of Germanic tribes sent back word of the 'fertility of this land' and 'the cowardice of the British', again according to Bede. More Germanic peoples invaded England over

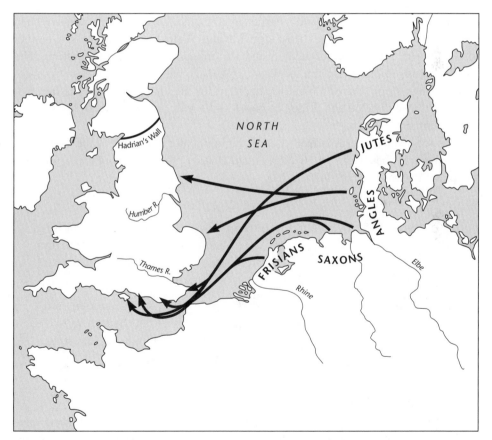

Figure 5.7   The Germanic Invasions of England (adapted from David Crystal, *The Cambridge Encyclopedia of the English Language*, 2nd edn [Cambridge: Cambridge University Press, 2003], p. 6)

the next hundred years, pushed the Picts and Scots to the north, and inhabited the southern two-thirds of the island. In the traditional account, the Jutes are said to have settled in Kent, the Isle of Wight (off the English south coast), and part of Hampshire; the Saxons in Wessex, Sussex, and Essex; and the Angles in East Anglia, Mercia, and Northumbria. The Saxons entered via the Thames and the south coast, while the Angles came via the east coast. Eventually, seven separate kingdoms formed, known as the Anglo-Saxon Heptarchy (Kent, Wessex, Sussex, Essex, East Anglia, Mercia, and Northumbria); by 800, however, only four kingdoms—Wessex, East Anglia, Mercia, and Northumbria—remained politically viable. The island came to be known as the land of the Angles, that is, *Angli-land*, with a vowel change called 'umlaut' (explained in Chapter 6) to *England*, the inhabitants of which are generally called Anglo-Saxons, after two of the three invading tribes. There continued to be contact between the new Englishmen and their relatives across the North Sea much as later colonists to North America retained contact with their English relatives across the Atlantic (Knowles 1997:34).

During this period, the island's earlier inhabitants, the Celts, seem to have been either expelled to the fringes (to Cornwall and Wales) and across the Channel to Brittany in France, or subjugated and assimilated into Germanic culture. The Anglo-Saxons referred to them as *Wealas* (Welsh), which simply meant 'foreigners', 'strangers', or 'slaves'. What is important for linguistic history is the fact that the people who invaded and settled England in the fifth century were all speakers of West Germanic dialects.

The following excerpt is from Bede's eighth-century account of the coming of the Germanic tribes (from *The Ecclesiastical History of the English People*, Book 1, Chapter 12; see Miller 1890:50).

Ða wæs ymb feower hund wintra 7 nigon 7 feowertig fram ures Ðrihtnes menniscnysse. . . . Ða Angelþeod 7 Seaxna wæs gelaðod fram þam foresprecenan cyninge, 7 on Breotone com on þrim myclum scypum. (from Bede's *Ecclesiastical History*)

Then it was about four hundred winters and nine and forty from our Lord's incarnation. . . . Then the Angles (lit. Angel people) and the Saxons were (lit. was) invited by the foresaid king and came into Britain in three great ships.

The Christianization of the Anglo-Saxons

The second linguistically important event was the Christianization of the Anglo-Saxons in the late sixth century. This took place in a two-pronged thrust from Ireland via the north and from Rome via the south. The Irish had been Christianized early in the sixth century, and by the middle of the century, Irish missionaries were spreading the religion throughout the western world, perhaps as far as Iceland and Greenland. The Irish, under St Columba, began to bring Christianity to England in 563 from the monastery at Iona, on an island off the coast of Scotland. Scotland was converted in the sixth century and Northumbria in the seventh century. Somewhat later, Pope Gregory I in Rome dispatched St Augustine to Christianize the English. The traditional account (given by Ælfric; see Chapter 7) is that Gregory saw some English boys being sold as slaves, inquired about them, and when told that they were 'Angles', thought it shameful that these fair 'angels' were heathen. St Augustine landed on the Isle of Thanet in 597 and was received by King Ethelbert (Æðelberht) of Kent, who was married to a Christian Frankish wife. In 601, Augustine was consecrated bishop of Canterbury, and later that century the Synod of Whitby decided in favor of the Roman over the Irish practices. By the beginning of the eighth century, most of England was Christian, although paganism did continue in localized areas throughout the Anglo-Saxon period.

Christianization had a number of significant effects on the English language. First, from the Irish, the Anglo-Saxons acquired the Roman alphabet. Second, Roman and Christian traditions of literacy and scholarship were imported into England; historical records were maintained by the Church. Third, many Latin loan words entered the English language and native words acquired new meanings (these topics will be discussed further in Chapter 6).

The Scandinavian Invasions of England

England was subject to a second wave of invasions beginning in the late eighth century. These were carried out by people the Anglo-Saxons called *Dene* ('Danes'), a general term indicating Norwegians and Swedes, as well as Danes. The Scandinavian invasions of England began as plundering raids in the summer by Vikings (the ON word *vikīngur* is related to *vik,* 'creek, inlet, bay', hence a *viking* is a person from the North Sea fjords). What began as isolated raids soon became more concerted attacks; by the mid-ninth century, Danes were wintering in England. In the fall of 865, a great army (*micel here*) of Vikings landed in East Anglia. By 870, Northumbria, Mercia, and East Anglia had all fallen to the Danes, and only Wessex remained in the control of the Anglo-Saxons. The West Saxons, under King Alfred, were finally victorious over the Danes, who were led by King Guthrum, in 878 at Edington. The result of this battle was a pact which allowed the Danes control over a large area of England called the Danelaw (the area north of a line running northwest from the Thames estuary across to Chester, near the northern tip of the border with Wales) but preserved Wessex for the English. A period of relative peace followed this pact, though there continued to be battles between the English and the Scandinavians, such as the Battle of Brunanburh in 937, where King Athelstan (Æþelstan), grandson of King Alfred, was victorious against assembled Scandinavian, Welsh, and Scottish forces.

Figure 5.8 The Brandon Plaque (9th century CE), Depicting St John the Evangelist with an Eagle Head (© The Trustees of The British Museum)

In the late tenth century, Scandinavians renewed attacks on the English. A famous Anglo-Saxon defeat was the Battle of Maldon in 991, commemorated in an Old English poem of the same name. Indeed, the Scandinavians even ruled as kings of England for 26 years. After the death of the ineffectual West Saxon king Ethelred, known as 'the Unready' (literally, *Æðelræd unræd* means 'Noble-counsel no counsel'), the Dane Cnut (Canute) married Ethelred's widow and assumed the throne; he was succeeded by his son Harthnacnut. West Saxon rule was restored with the accession of Ethelred's son, Edward the Confessor, in 1042.

The Scandinavian colonization of England—for that is what the Danish invasions proved to be—had important linguistic consequences. The North Germanic dialects spoken by the Scandinavians were closely enough related to the West Germanic dialects of the Anglo-Saxons to permit communication. The Scandinavians settled in significant numbers in areas of northern England (which we can determine by the Scandinavian place names in this region) and seem to have assimilated and adapted well to Anglo-Saxon society; there was undoubtedly inter-marriage between the two groups. The conditions were right, therefore, for much contact between the two languages.

The Records of the Anglo-Saxons

The Dialects of Old English

The language of the Anglo-Saxons, now generally called Old English rather than Anglo-Saxon, is recorded in a number of regional dialects. The four major dialects recognized correspond more or less to the areas settled by the different Germanic tribes (see above):

1. Kentish, spoken in Kent and part of Hampshire;
2. West Saxon, spoken in the rest of the area south of the Thames (except for Celtic-speaking Cornwall);
3. Mercian, spoken in the area between the Thames and Humber rivers (except for Celtic-speaking Wales); and
4. Northumbrian, spoken in the area north of the Humber River (except Celtic-speaking Scotland).

Mercian and Northumbrian are sometimes grouped together as Anglian, since they bear many similarities. Mercian and Northumbrian are sometimes grouped together as Anglian, since they bear many similarities and are found in areas of strong Norse influence (see Figure 5.9).

The Written Records of Old English

Most of the written records of Old English are in the West Saxon dialect. In 825, King Egbert (Ecgberht) of Wessex wrested power from the Mercian king and established Wessex as the most powerful kingdom in England, and the only one to survive the Danish invasion. Its capital, Winchester, served as a center of culture for England. The West Saxon line of kings descending from King Egbert ruled continuously until 1016. Most importantly, Egbert's grandson, King Alfred (known as 'Alfred the Great'), who ruled from 871 to 899, not only successfully fended off the Danes but also encouraged literacy and learning; many books were copied in his scriptoria. He either translated or sponsored the translation of works by Pope Gregory, St Augustine, Boethius, and Bede (his *Ecclesiastical History of the English People*). The language of the age of King Alfred is known as Early West Saxon. Due to the political power of Alfred's court and the cultural influence of his scriptoria,

Figure 5.9 Anglo-Saxon England

Early West Saxon came close to being a standard for Old English, that is, a dialect that cuts across regional differences and serves as an institutionalized norm.

A later, normative variety of Old English usually described in modern grammars is Late West Saxon. This is the language of the late tenth century, written in the reign of Alfred's great-grandson, Ethelred the Unready. Often it served as a kind of standard and was written even in areas where the regional vernacular differed. The most influential writer of this period was Ælfric, a monk at Cerne (in Dorset). Ælfric was a great scholar and a prolific writer: he wrote saints' lives and homilies (sermons and Biblical commentaries) and he translated the Heptateuch (the first seven books of the Old Testament), works by Bede, and a Latin grammar, glossary, and colloquy (texts used to teach Latin). Another important figure of the time was Wulfstan, archbishop of York, who wrote religious and legal texts.

In addition, throughout the OE period there existed a distinct poetic diction, containing a mixture of regional elements. It was primarily West Saxon-based but included some Mercian and a number of archaic features that make OE verse impossible to locate or date.

Old English literary records are extensive, although what remains is likely a fraction of the works produced, many being lost to Viking raids, fires, the dissolution of the monasteries, Reformation purges of Church libraries, and so on. Much poetry in the oral tradition was undoubtedly never written down. The earliest written texts date from about 700 CE, based on earlier literature in the pagan, Germanic, and heroic tradition, composed in alliterative verse (using repetition of initial consonants and vowels and a set number of stressed feet per line) and performed and transmitted orally. It includes the great poem *Beowulf*; the fragments 'The Fight at Finnsburg' and 'Waldere'; a shorter poem, 'Widsith' (see Figure 6.2); a number of short elegiac poems such as 'The Wanderer', 'The Seafarer', 'The Wife's Lament', 'The Husband's Message', 'The Ruin', 'Deor', and 'Wulf and Eadwacer'; charms; and riddles. These were written down by clerics after the Christianization of the Anglo-Saxons, and thus often contain Christian elements and reveal elements of literate composition. Two later poems which belong to this tradition are 'The Battle of Brunanburh' and 'The Battle of Maldon'.

The period after 600 produced diverse Christian works in Old English, written in verse and based loosely on Biblical material. The first OE writer whom we know by name is Cædmon (*c.* 670); the story of his poetic inspiration is related by Bede. A number of Biblical paraphrases in verse ('Genesis A', 'Genesis B', 'Exodus', 'Daniel', and 'Christ and Satan') can be attributed to the school of Cædmon. A second OE writer whose name we know as Cynewulf (*c.* 750) is the author of 'Christ II' and three saints' lives ('Elene', 'Juliana', and 'Fates of the Apostles').

Perhaps the most important documents in Old English for linguistic purposes are the *Anglo-Saxon Chronicles*. These may have originated as Easter tables, annals used by the clergy to determine the date on which Easter fell each year, but soon detailed entries depicting the major events of each year came to be added. There are seven versions of the *Chronicle* compiled in different places and quite divergent in the events they record, but up until 891 all of them seem to have had a common source, perhaps in southwest England, prompting the thought that King Alfred may have commissioned them. The last chronicle, the one kept in Peterborough, records events through the year 1154. The chronicles are important linguistically because they constitute a record of Old English over a long period of time, allowing us to observe changes in the language, especially in the later chronicles. Because the chronicles are not translations from Latin, their prose is unaffected by Latin style and has few literary pretensions; it is prose is of a plain, native kind—the written language in its most straightforward manifestation.

RECOMMENDED WEB LINKS

You may wish to look at Edwin Duncan's description of the seven distinctive features of Germanic:

> http://pages.towson.edu/duncan/germanic.html

For one perspective on the consonant changes of Germanic, see Scott Kleinman's web page:

> http://www.csun.edu/~sk36711/WWW/engl400/gmcsoundchanges.pdf

A large collection of scanned resources on the Germanic languages (many from the early part of the twentieth century) may be found on Sean Crist's website:

> http://www.ling.upenn.edu/%7Ekurisuto/germanic/language_resources.html

To see the territory of the Germanic tribes in 400 and 500, you may look at the following online maps:

> http://www.euratlas.com/time/nw0400.htm
> http://www.euratlas.com/time/nw0500.htm

The Applied History Research Group at the University of Calgary provides a history of the Germanic invasions of western Europe with some excellent illustrations:

> http://www.ucalgary.ca/applied_history/tutor/firsteuro/invas.html

For a translation of Bede's account of the arrival of the Germanic tribes in England, go to the following site:

> http://www.fordham.edu/halsall/basis/bede-book1.html (see chapters XV and XVI)

Numerous maps of Anglo-Saxon England are provided by Anglo-Saxons.net:

> http://www.anglo-saxons.net/hwaet/?do=show&page=Maps

For maps of the Danelaw, see:

> http://www.britannia.com/history/danemap.html
> http://www.viking.no/e/england/danelaw/ekart-danelaw.htm

A general history of Britain during the Anglo-Saxon period can be found on the Britannia website:

> http://britannia.com/history/h50.html

FURTHER READING

Readable overviews of the Indo-European and Germanic roots of English are:

> Hoad, Terry. 2006. 'Preliminaries: Before English'. *The Oxford History of English*. Ed. by Lynda Mugglestone, 7–31. Oxford and New York: Oxford University Press.
> Robinson, Orrin. 1992. *Old English and Its Closest Relatives: A Survey of the Earliest Germanic Languages*. London: Routledge.

Other reference materials available on Germanic are generally quite advanced. These include grammars of the individual older Germanic languages and the following comparative grammar:

Prokosch, E. 1938. *A Comparative Germanic Grammar*. Baltimore: Linguistic Society of America.

For enjoyment, you might wish to read some of the Old Icelandic sagas, most of which exist in translation. Of particular interest may be:

Magnusson, Magnus, and Hermann Pálsson (trans.). 1965. *The Vinland Sagas: The Norse Discovery of America*. Harmondsworth: Penguin.

For further information on Anglo-Saxon England, see:

Irvine, Susan. 2006. 'Beginnings and Transitions: Old English'. *The Oxford History of English*. Ed. by Lynda Mugglestone, 32–60. Oxford and New York: Oxford University Press.

Lapidge, Michael, John Blair, Simon Keynes, and Don Scragg. 1999. *The Blackwell Encyclopedia of Anglo-Saxon England*. Malden, MA and Oxford: Blackwell.

Mitchell, Bruce. 1995. *An Invitation to Old English and Anglo-Saxon England*. Oxford and Cambridge: Blackwell.

6

The Words
and Sounds
of Old English

OVERVIEW

This chapter begins with an introduction to the word stock of Old English, including foreign influences on it and native processes of word formation. After considering the writing system of Old English, we turn to the phonological system. First we look at what consonants appear in Old English, how they relate to the Germanic sounds, and how they are represented in writing. Then we do the same for the vowels. We also consider two important phonological processes operating in Old English: umlaut and breaking. We end our study of phonology by examining the placement of stress accent in Old English.

OBJECTIVES

After studying this chapter, you should be able to identify the sources of loan words and types of borrowing in Old English as well as the processes of word formation at work in the language. The second objective in this chapter is to understand the phonology of Old English and its relation to the writing system, recognizing differences between Old and Modern English. This chapter will show you how to

■ transcribe Old English words and mark the accented syllables; and

■ describe the operation of umlaut in Old English and its legacy in Modern English.

The Word Stock of the Anglo-Saxons

The Continuity of Germanic Vocabulary in English

The extant vocabulary of Old English is quite small (between 23,000 and 24,000 words in Old English, compared to over half a million words listed in the third edition of the *Oxford English Dictionary*) and almost purely Germanic in nature. It contains comparatively few loan words—just 3 per cent, compared to 70 per cent in Modern English (Kastovsky 1992:293–4).

The Germanic vocabulary of Old English has not survived particularly well into the current period. Just over half of the 1,000 most commonly used words in Old English poetry remain. However, the more frequently used the word, the more likely it is to have survived: of the 100 most commonly used words in Old English, 76 per cent are still used today. Function words, which serve to mark grammatical relations rather than express lexical meaning, are the best preserved of all the word classes: all of the numerals, about 82 per cent of the prepositions, 80 per cent of the pronouns, and 75 per cent of the conjunctions of Old English have survived in Modern English.[1] The major parts of speech—the nouns, verbs, adjectives, and adverbs—have been lost or replaced to a much greater extent. If preserved, Germanic words remain in one of three ways:

- with little change in meaning or form (e.g. *heofon* 'heaven', *word* 'word', *sittan* 'to sit', *beran* 'to bear', *fæst* 'fast', *nū* 'now');
- with some change to meaning or form or both (e.g. *dōm* 'judgment' giving ModE *doom*, *brēad* 'bit' giving ModE *bread*, *scieppan* 'to create' giving ModE *shape*, *sellan* 'to give' giving ModE *sell*, *uncūð* 'not known' giving ModE *uncouth*); or
- in local dialects (e.g. Scottish *aught* 'possession'), restricted contexts (e.g. OE *ang* 'painful' surviving only in *hangnail*, OE *wer* 'man' surviving only in *werewolf*), or set expressions (e.g. *Holy Ghost* from OE *gast* 'spirit', *willy-nilly* from OE *will ic, nyll* [= *ne* + *will*] *ic*).

The word stock of English has changed greatly through significant loss of OE forms and even more extensive borrowing from other languages, but it remains the case that the core vocabulary of Modern English is essentially Germanic; if you consider the 1,000 most frequently used words in Modern English, 83 per cent of them are of Old English origin.

Borrowing in Old English

Despite the essentially Germanic nature of Old English vocabulary, there was borrowing which resulted from cultural contact (as discussed in the previous chapter).

---

1 The figures are those of J.F. Madden and F.P. Magoun, Jr, cited in Cassidy and Ringler (1971:4–7).

The loan words that did enter Old English, and Germanic beforehand, often followed a complex route of transmission. For example, the Old English word *engel*
'angel' has its immediate source in Late Latin *angelus*. But the ultimate source is
Greek *angelos* 'messenger'.

Latin

The most important source of loan words in English throughout its history has been
Latin. Three separate periods of such borrowing occurred during the early years of
English. The first period of borrowing took place when the Germanic tribes came
into contact with Latin speakers, e.g. Roman merchants, on the continent of Europe
(before 449 CE). Approximately 200 words entered the language at this time. The
vocabulary borrowed reflects the nature of dealings between the two groups:

- plants: *plante* 'plant' (< Lat. *planta*)
- animals: *mūl* 'mule' (< Lat. *mūlus*)
- food: *cēse* 'cheese' (< Lat. *cāseus*)
- dress: *belt* 'belt' (< Lat. *balteus*)
- household items: *pil(w)e* 'pillow' (< Lat. *pulvīnus*)
- buildings: *weall* 'wall' (< Lat. *vallum*)
- agriculture: *sicol* 'sickle'(< Lat. *secula*)
- commerce: *cēap* 'goods' (< Lat. *caupo*)
- measure: *mīl* 'mile, 1,000 paces' (< Lat. *mīlle*)
- law: *trifot* 'tribute' (< Lat. *tribūtum*)
- learning: *diht* 'saying' (< Lat. *dictum*)
- the military: *camp* 'camp' (< Lat. *campus*)
- the Church: *mynster* 'minster' (< Lat. *monasterium*)

It appears that the Romans had a higher standard of living and more refinements
than the Germanic people, and that the contact between them was of an intimate
kind. The loan words generally refer to commonplace concrete objects rather than to
abstractions and are in a familiar rather than formal variety of language, suggesting
that the borrowings were popular and oral rather than learned and written.

The words borrowed from Latin during this period appear in both Old High
German and Old English, since the groups had not separated yet. Loan words of
this period were later subject to all sound changes in Old English and Old High
German which occurred after their adoption, and because the words underwent these
changes, we can date them as early borrowings. Table 6.1 lists some Latin borrowings during the continental period.

The second period of borrowing from Latin, the Celtic period, occurred in
England early in Anglo-Saxon times. Words may have been borrowed from Latin
by the British Celts and then borrowed by the Anglo-Saxons from the Celts, but it is

Table 6.1 Latin Loan Words in Germanic[a]

Lat.	OE	OHG	ModE	Ger.
cāseus	cēse	kāsi	cheese	Käse
cista	cist, cest	kista	chest	Kiste
coquīna	cycene	chuhhina	kitchen	Küche
cuppa	cuppe	kopf	cup	Kopf 'head'
discus	disc	tisc	dish	Tisch 'table'
piper	pipor	pfeffar	pepper	Pfeffer
pondo	pund	pfunt	pound	Pfund
prūnum	plūme	pflūmo	plum	Pflaume
sc(h)ōla	scōl	scuola	school	Schule
vīnum	wīn	wīn	wine	Wein

[a]The OE words *cēse, cist, cycene,* and *disc* exhibit evidence of a sound change called 'palatalization' (see below), where [sk] becomes [š] and [k] (before [e] and [i]) becomes [č]. Also note the effects of the Second Sound Shift (see Chapter 5) on High German words like *Kopf, Küche, Tisch, Pfeffer, Pfund,* and *Pflaume.*
Source: adapted from Theodora Bynon, *Historical Linguistics* (Cambridge: Cambridge University Press, 1977), p. 218.

also possible that Celtic and Old English took the words independently from Latin. Some examples include *port* 'harbor, gate, town' (< Lat. *portus*), *munt* 'mountain' (< Lat. *montus*), and *torr* 'tower, rock' (< Lat. *turris*).

The third period of borrowing from Latin, the Christian period, followed Christianization of the Anglo-Saxons in 597 CE by Roman missionaries. As Latin was the language of the Church, it was used in both manuscripts and artifacts of material culture in Anglo-Saxon England. For example, the gold strip from the Staffordshire Hoard, a collection of over 1,500 items of gold and silver discovered in northwestern England in 2009, shows the use of Latin. The gold strip contains the inscription *surge d[omi]ne [et] disepentur inimici tui et fugent qui oderunt te a facie tua* ('rise up, o Lord, and may thy enemies be scattered and those who hate thee be driven from thy face'), a passage from Numbers 10: 35 of the Vulgate translation of the Old Testament (see Figure 6.1).

The words that entered English from Latin at this time were usually learned borrowings concerning religion and scholarship (since the Church was responsible in

Figure 6.1   Gold Strip from the Staffordshire Hoard (bearing Latin inscription) (© The British Museum)

large part for learning and literacy in Anglo-Saxon England). Examples include the following words:

crūc 'cross' (< Lat. *cruc-em*)	*accent* 'accent' (< Lat. *accentus*)
crēda 'creed' (< Lat. *crēdo*)	*capitol(a)* 'chapter' (< Lat. *capitolum*)
mæsse 'mass' (< Lat. *missa*)	*nōtere* 'notary' (< Lat. *notārius*)
nonne 'monk' (< Lat. *nonnus*)	*tempel* 'temple' (< Lat. *templum*)
sanct 'holy' (< Lat. *sanctus*)	*organe* 'organ' (< Lat. *origanum*)

Some of these passed into general usage, but others remained restricted to scholarly contexts. The Latin borrowings of this period tend to fall into two groups: the early (entering the language by the time of King Alfred) and the later (entering at the time of the Benedictine Reform in the late tenth century).

Like all loan words, these Latin words were assimilated fully into the language and came to be inflected as if they were Old English words and combined with elements of native origin. A complex word form which consists of a native part and a borrowed part is called a *hybrid* form. These are easy to find in Old English: for instance, in the words *prēosthād* 'priesthood', *bisceopsetl* 'bishopric', *sealmscop* 'psalmist', and *cristendōm* 'Christendom', the first half is a Latin element and the second half a native OE element.

In addition to borrowing words to name Christian objects and concepts, the Anglo-Saxons adapted their own language by translating Latin into English. This process is called 'loan translation' (or 'calquing'), and the translated words are called 'calques'. The form and meaning of a foreign word becomes a model for the native construction. For example, instead of borrowing the word *patriarch*, the Anglo-Saxons translated its elements to create the native word *heahfæder* 'high father'. Consider some other examples:

OE *niwcumen* 'newcomer'	for	Lat. *novice*
OE *dyppan* 'to dip'	for	Lat. *baptize* < Gk.

OE *gōdspel* 'good word'	for	Lat. *euangelium* < Gk.
OE *eallwealdend* 'all-ruling'	for	Lat. *omnipotens*
OE *eallmihtig* 'all-mighty'	for	Lat. *omnipotens*
OE *þriness* 'threeness'	for	Lat. *trinity*
OE *ānhorn* 'one-horned'	for	Lat. *unicorn*
OE *forsetnys* 'placing before'	for	Lat. *preposition*
OE *Hālig Gāst* 'holy spirit'	for	Lat. *Spiritus Sanctus*
OE *mildheortnes* 'mild-heartedness'	for	Lat. *misericordia* 'compassion'

(Interestingly, Modern English tends to replace Old English calques with Latinate borrowings [e.g. *novice, baptize*], most of which were adopted in Middle English from French.) A similar group of words, less exact than loan translations, are *loan renditions*, in which the original is only partially translated or provides just a part of the new word (e.g. *sabbatam* 'rest' > *restedæg* 'rest day'). Finally, *loan creations* take the idea from a foreign word but contain no element that directly corresponds (e.g. *baptiszare* > *fulwian* 'to consecrate fully').

Celtic

A very minor source of loan words in Old English is Celtic. The paucity of borrowing reflects the nature of contact between the two groups: the Anglo-Saxons conquered the Celts or forced them into exile. As Bloomfield (1933) points out (see Chapter 3), there is never much impact from a language spoken by a subjugated, indigenous people (the lower language) on the one spoken by a dominant, introduced people (the upper language). Thus, we are not surprised that Old English shows little effect from Celtic (nor that in modern times the Celtic languages have almost suffered extinction because of politically dominant languages such as English and French).

The small group of Old English words that do have a Celtic origin include place names such as London, Kent, Thames, Avon, Dover, and Usk, and words such as *cumb* 'deep valley', *dunn* 'grey', and *bannoc* 'piece' from the settlement period, and *ancor* 'hermit' and *cursian* 'curse' from the Christian period.

Old Norse

A third source of loan words, Old Norse, is considerably more important. Approximately 1,000 words of Scandinavian origin entered the standard language, and even more found their way into local dialects. Although these words were undoubtedly borrowed during the late Old English period when Scandinavians and English lived in close contact, very few OE texts from the Danelaw area survive from this time. Old Norse loan words do not appear in significant numbers until Middle English and spread gradually from the northern to the southern ME dialects. As many as 1,500 place names in northern England seem to attest to Scandinavian presence (those ending in *-by*, *-beck*, *-dale*, *-thorp*, *-thwaite*, *-toft*), as do personal names ending in *-son* and *-sen* (the latter is Danish). Most words name everyday objects and actions, while some are in the specialized domains of ships, law, and warfare, in which the Scandinavians obviously excelled.

A number of things could happen when an ON word was borrowed:

- It could completely replace the OE word, as in the case of ON *taka* (ModE *take*) replacing OE *niman*.
- Both words could be retained, with one restricted to the northern dialect, as in the case of ON *kirkja* giving the Scottish form *kirk* in contrast to standard ModE *church*.
- Both words could be retained in the standard dialect, usually with some semantic differentiation, as in the case of ON *skirt* and native *shirt*. Words which derive from the same original word (in PIE) but which arrive in a language via different routes of transmission are called *doublets*. Below are some of the more certain doublets of Old English and Old Norse origin:

OE	**ON**
shirt	*skirt*
from	*fro* (as in *to and fro*)
rear	*raise*
no	*nay*
edge	*egg* 'to incite'
shatter	*scatter*
shrub	*scrub*

- Also, an OE word could be retained but acquire the meaning of the ON cognate; this phenomenon is called *semantic loan*. An example is the word *with*: the OE word *wið* 'against' came to have the meaning of the ON word *við*, which meant 'in conjunction, company with', while the OE word meaning the latter, *mid*, was lost. OE *brēad*, originally meaning 'bit', came to have the meaning of the ON *brauð* 'bread', replacing the original OE word for this, *hlāf*, which specialized to *loaf*, 'loaf, unit of bread'. OE *drēam*, meaning 'joy', took on the sense of the ON cognate *draumr* meaning 'dream'.

Because of the close relation between North and West Germanic dialects of the time, it can be difficult to determine whether a word is native Old English or an Old Norse borrowing. However, phonological features can sometimes help us. Words of Scandinavian origin do not show the Old English sound change called palatalization (discussed below); hence, they have

- [sk] rather than [š]: e.g. *scream* (< ON *skræma*), *skulk* (< ON *skulke*), *skill* (< ON *skil*), *scoff* (< ON *skof*), and *skin* (< ON *skinn*);

- [g] rather than [j]: e.g. *gift* (< ON *gift*), *guild* (< ON *gildi*), and *girth* (< ON *gjörð*); and
- [k] rather than [č]: e.g. *keel* (< ON *kjöl*), *kettle* (< ON *ketill*), and *kid 'young goat'* (< ON *kið*).

Also borrowed from Old Norse are the very common verbs *get* (< ON *geta*), *give* (< ON *gefa*), and *call* (< ON *kalla* cf. OE *ceallian*).[2]

Finally, words of Scandinavian origin have [g] following a back vowel rather than OE [ɣ], which developed into ModE [w]: e.g. *drag* (< ON *draga* [compare *draw*, which comes from native Old English]), *rag* (< ON *rögg*), and *leg* (< ON *leggr*). Note that these generalizations must be applied with caution; not all words with initial [sk], for example, are of Scandinavian origin. For instance, *sketch*, *skeptic*, and *school* are from Greek; *skillet* and *skein* are from French; and *skunk* is of North American Indian (Massachusett) origin.

In casual language contact, speakers tend to borrow nouns and verbs rather than function words such as pronouns, which are an essential part of the grammar. Only in cases of intense language contact, such as in bilingual communities, is the borrowing of function words attested. It is remarkable, then, that English borrowed the Old Norse third-person plural pronouns *they*, *their*, and *them* to replace the native forms *hi*, *hire*, and *him*. English also borrowed such basic words as the pronouns *both* (< ON *báðir*) and *same* (< ON *samr*), the preposition *fro* (< ON *frá*), the conjunction *though* (< ON *þó*), the strong verb *run* (< ON *renna*), and the ordinal number *hundredth* (< ON *hundrað*). Given the centrality of the the verb *be*, it is also surprising that English borrowed the plural form *are* from Old Norse.

The adoption of function words attests to the closeness of the interaction between Scandinavian and English speakers over a long period of time. The scholars Thomason and Kaufman conclude that Scandinavian influence was 'pervasive, in the sense that its results are found in all parts of the language; but it was not deep, except in the lexicon' (1988:302). Rather, it functioned as a kind of prestige language (1988:303). They point out that the two languages were structurally and lexically so similar that Old Norse could not have modified the basic typology of English. Yet because of the close structural similarity between the two languages, it is not inconceivable that the minor variations between them could lead to confusion and hence hastened the reduction and loss of inflectional endings in the transition from Old English to Middle English, as will be discussed in Chapter 9.

---

2 While the simplex verb *get* was a borrowing from Old Norse, Old English had the prefixed verbs *begietan* 'beget' and *forgietan* 'forgot'. In Old English these words were pronounced with [j] but later acquired a [g] pronunciation by analogy with the Norse loan *get*. The English word *give* is likely a blend of ON *gefa* and the native OE verb *giefan*; again the [g] pronunciation comes from Old Norse.

Exercise 6.1 OE Word Stock

1. List the three most common ways that OE words have remained in the language; give an example of each.

    (a) _____

    (b) _____

    (c) _____

2. In increasing order of importance give the main sources of loan words in Old English.

    _____

3. Name, and give the important highlights of, the different periods of borrowing from Latin in Old English.

    _____

    _____

    _____

    _____

    _____

    _____

    _____

    _____

    _____

    _____

Word Formation in Old English

In addition to borrowing, Old English added words to the language by two native processes of word formation: *compounding* and *derivation*. Compounding is characteristic of Germanic languages and involves combining two or more free roots into one word. Compounding continues to be productive in Modern English, but not to the extent that it is in Modern German and Icelandic, which use it in preference to borrowing. Compounds largely account for the size of the word stock in Old English, especially in poetry, where they make up one third of the vocabulary, according to one scholar's estimate (see Kastovsky 1992:354). Old English compounds follow several syntactic patterns, as shown in Table 6.2.

In addition to literal compounds such as these, Old English made use of metaphor in forming a special type of compound called a 'kenning'. Through metaphor, the word *bānhūs*, literally 'bone-house', came to mean 'body'. Similarly, *beadulēoma* is a 'battle-light' or 'sword' (since it flashes in battle), *hamora lāfa* are 'hammer leavings' or 'swords', *heaðuswāt* is 'battle sweat' or 'blood', *rōdores candel* is 'heaven-candle' or 'sun', *merehrægl* is 'sea-dress' or 'sail', and *hwælweg* is 'whale-way' or 'sea'. Kennings are common in OE poetic diction, which favors the use of synonymous expressions.

It has sometimes happened in the history of the language that a word constituting half of a compound has been lost, so that while it still looks like a compound, its composition is no longer transparent: e.g. *midwife*, in which *mid* means 'with'; *cob-*

Table 6.2 Compounding in Old English

N + N > N	*meduheall* 'meadhall', *brēostnet* 'coat of mail' (cf. ModE *lipstick*)
N (genitive) + N	*dægesēage* 'daisy' (literally, 'day's eye'), *sunnandæg* 'Sunday' (cf. ModE *bull's eye*)
ADJ + N > N	*lāðweorc* 'evil deed', *īdelhende* 'empty-handed' (cf. ModE *software*)
V (stem) + N > N	*writbred* 'writing tablet', *scearseax* 'razor' (cf. ModE *crybaby*)
ADV + N > N	*oferdrync* 'over-drinking, drunkenness', *eftcyme* 'return' (cf. ModE *background*)
ADJ + ADJ > ADJ	*tilmōdig* 'well-disposed', *glēawhȳdig* 'thoughtful' (cf. ModE *red-hot*)
N + ADJ > ADJ	*īsceald* 'ice cold', *dōmgeorn* 'ambitious (literally, praise eager)' (cf. ModE *carsick*)
ADV + ADJ > ADJ	*ūplang* 'upright', *wiþermēde* 'antagonistic' (cf. ModE *forthright*)
N + V (pres. part.) > ADJ	*lindhæbbende* 'shieldbearing', *hunigflōwende* 'flowing with honey' (cf. ModE *man-eating*)
N + V (past part.) > ADJ	*ealdbacen* 'stale', *dyrneforlegen* 'adulterous (literally, secret lying)' (cf. ModE *housebroken*)
N + V > V	*rōdfæstnian* 'to crucify (literally, to cross-fasten)', *cynehelmian* 'to crown' (ModE has only back-formations such as *babysit*)

web, in which (*āttor*)*coppe* means 'spider'; *mildew*, in which *mele* means 'honey'; and *midriff*, in which *hrif* means 'belly' (here *mid* < OE *midd* means 'middle'). When compounds cease to be recognized as such, either because the two parts fuse together or because one part has been lost as an independent word, we call them 'amalgamated compounds'. Examples include ModE *barn* deriving from OE *bere* 'barley' + *ærn* 'place', ModE *tadpole* deriving from OE *tād* 'toad' + *poll* 'head', and ModE *world* deriving from OE *werold* 'the age of man' (the word *wer* meaning 'man' is otherwise preserved only in the compound *werewolf*).

Another common means of word formation in Old English is derivation, the creation of new words by adding prefixes or suffixes to existing roots. (It became even more common with the influx of Latinate affixes in Middle English.) Historically, many affixes derive from originally independent words which have become reduced to the status of bound morphemes: for instance, *some* derives from OE *sum* 'a certain, some'. Some affixes still exist as independent words; this is especially true of OE prefixes, such as *after-*, *out-*, *under-*, *up-*, *with-*, *in-*, *on-*, *over-*, or *to-*, which occur independently as prepositions and adverbs. Below are some examples of OE prefixes:

> *æfter* 'after' + *lēan* 'reward' > *æfterlēan* 'recompense' (cf. ModE *aftermath*)
>
> *be* 'around' + *healdan* 'to hold' > *behealdan* 'to occupy, possess' (cf. ModE *befriend*)
>
> *for* 'completely' + *bærnan* 'to burn' > *forbærnan* 'to burn up' (cf. ModE *forgive*)
>
> *ge* 'with' + *fēra* 'goer' > *gefēra* 'companion' (no ModE descendant)
>
> *mis* 'defect' + *efesian* 'to cut, shear' > *misefesian* 'to cut hair amiss' (cf. ModE *mistrust*)
>
> *ofer* 'over' + *mōd* 'mood, spirit' > *ofermōd* 'pride' (cf. ModE *overconfident*)
>
> *un* 'not' + *brād* 'broad' > *unbrād* 'narrow' (cf. ModE *unholy*)
>
> *wið* 'against' + *cweðan* 'to speak' > *wiðcweðan* 'to contradict' (cf. ModE *withdraw*)

Note that prefixes change only the meaning of the root to which they are attached, by making it negative, for example, or intensive. Suffixes may change either the meaning of the root or its part of speech. Table 6.3 displays some examples of OE suffixes. This list does not exhaust the possible affixes in Old English, which has a rich derivational system. Many OE affixes have survived as productive affixes (that is, they may be added to make new words) in Modern English; for example, the *-er* suffix in *singer* (from *-ere*) is the very common agentive suffix which forms an agent noun (an actor) from a verb. Some affixes have been lost, such as an *-ing* forming nouns from adjectives, as in *earming* 'wretch' from *earm* 'poor', while others are preserved as non-productive affixes in remnant forms, such as *be-* in *bemoan* and *becalm* or *-th* in *length* and *width*.

Table 6.3 Derivational Suffixes in Old English

N (concrete) > N (abstract)	
-dōm	cyningdōm 'kingdom' (cf. ModE stardom)
-scipe	cynescipe 'royalty' (cf. ModE friendship)
-hād	cildhād 'childhood' (cf. ModE brotherhood)
V > N	
-ung	earnung 'merit' (cf. ModE the singing)
-ere	cwellere 'killer' (cf. ModE singer)
ADJ > N	
-ð	mǣrð 'glory' (cf. ModE warmth)
-nes	sārnes 'pain' (cf. ModE happiness)
N > ADJ	
-ed	hringed 'made of rings' (cf. ModE two-wheeled)
-ful	forhtful 'fearful' (cf. ModE doubtful)
-lēas	drēamlēas 'joyless' (cf. ModE fearless)
-sum	wynnsum 'joyful' (cf. ModE bothersome)
-ig	hālig 'holy' (cf. ModE thirsty)
-isc	Englisc 'English' (cf. ModE childish)
-lic	heofonlic 'heavenly' (cf. ModE princely)
N > ADV	
-weard	hāmweard 'homeward' (cf. ModE backward)

Exercise 6.2 OE Word Formation

1. For each of the Old English words in the following list, give its part of speech. Then identify which is a literal compound, an amalgamated compound, a kenning, or a derived form; which component parts are affixes or roots; and which roots are nouns, verbs, adjectives, or adverbs. (A dictionary should not be necessary for this exercise.)

    a. *firencrǣft* 'wickedness' ('sin-craft')

    _____

    _____

b.   *herewǣd* 'armor' ('war-weed')

_____

_____

c.   *holdlīce* 'graciously' ('kind-ly')

_____

_____

d.   *ofercrœft* 'fraud' ('over-craft')

_____

_____

e.   *rǣdfœstnes* 'readiness to follow counsel' ('rede-fast-ness')

_____

_____

f.   *sweordplega* 'battle' ('sword-play')

_____

_____

The Orthographic System of Old English

One of the most important effects of Christianization upon the Anglo-Saxons was their adoption of an orthographic, or writing, system designed for recording longer texts, namely, the Latin alphabet (which we still use today). The Anglo-Saxons seem to have acquired the Latin alphabet from Irish missionaries, for it shows Irish modifications and is written in an angular and upright Irish hand called the Insular script (see Figure 6.2). The Irish made the following changes to the alphabet:

- the addition of the letter *eth* (lower case ð and uppercase Ð), representing *th* and known by its Scandinavian name; and
- a special form of the letter *g* (ȝ) called *yogh*.

The Anglo-Saxons also added two symbols from their own runic alphabet:

- the *thorn* (lowercase þ and uppercase Þ), a second way of representing *th*; and
- the *wynn* (ƿ), representing *w*.

In the Insular hand, there are also special forms of *f*, *r*, and *s*, as well as the *ligature* (two letters linked together as one) of Latin *a* and *e*, *æ* (uppercase *Æ*) known by its runic name *æsc* or 'ash'. Moreover, the letters *j*, *k*, *q*, *v*, and *z* are rarely or never used in Old English. Modern editors of Old English use *æ*, *þ*, and *ð*, but substitute *g* for ʒ and *w* for ƿ.

Thus, the OE alphabet used in modern editions is:

a æ b c d e f g h i l m n o p r s t þ ð u w x y

Perhaps because vellum was very expensive, Anglo-Saxon scribes followed the common practice of the time, leaving little space between words and abbreviating common words or endings. A common abbreviation is the symbol resembling a numeral seven (7) meaning 'and' (comparable to the modern &).

For an example of how Old English was written, look at the manuscript page illustrated in Figure 6.2. The poem 'Widsith' begins with the illuminated wynn. The first three lines can be transliterated as follows:

Widsið maðolade
wordhord onleac se þe mæst mærþa ofer
eorþan folca geondferde oft he flette geþah

'Widsith spoke, unlocked his word hoard, he who of men traveled through most races and peoples over the earth'

The Phonological System of Old English

Consonants

We will now look at how the consonants of Germanic developed in Old English, how they were represented in writing, and how they differ from the modern set of consonants.

Old English has a (nearly) *phonemic* writing system: it uses each alphabetic symbol to stand for a single distinct sound (or *phoneme*). Each letter is pronounced; there are no 'silent' letters. No separate symbols represent the allophones, those non-distinctive changes in sound that depend on their phonetic environment. Thus, there may be more than one predictable pronunciation for each letter. Old English does have double consonants, however, which are thought to have been pronounced for a longer time than single consonants; we transcribe them with two phonetic symbols.

We begin our comparison between Germanic and Old English consonants with the voiceless stops, as shown in Table 6.4.

A one-to-one correspondence exists here between written symbol and sound except in the case of *c*, where the two variants are phonologically conditioned. This letter represents the voiceless stop [k] before back vowels (*a*, *o*, *u*), after back vowels at the end of a word, before consonants, and when doubled: e.g. *cumbol* 'banner', *loc*

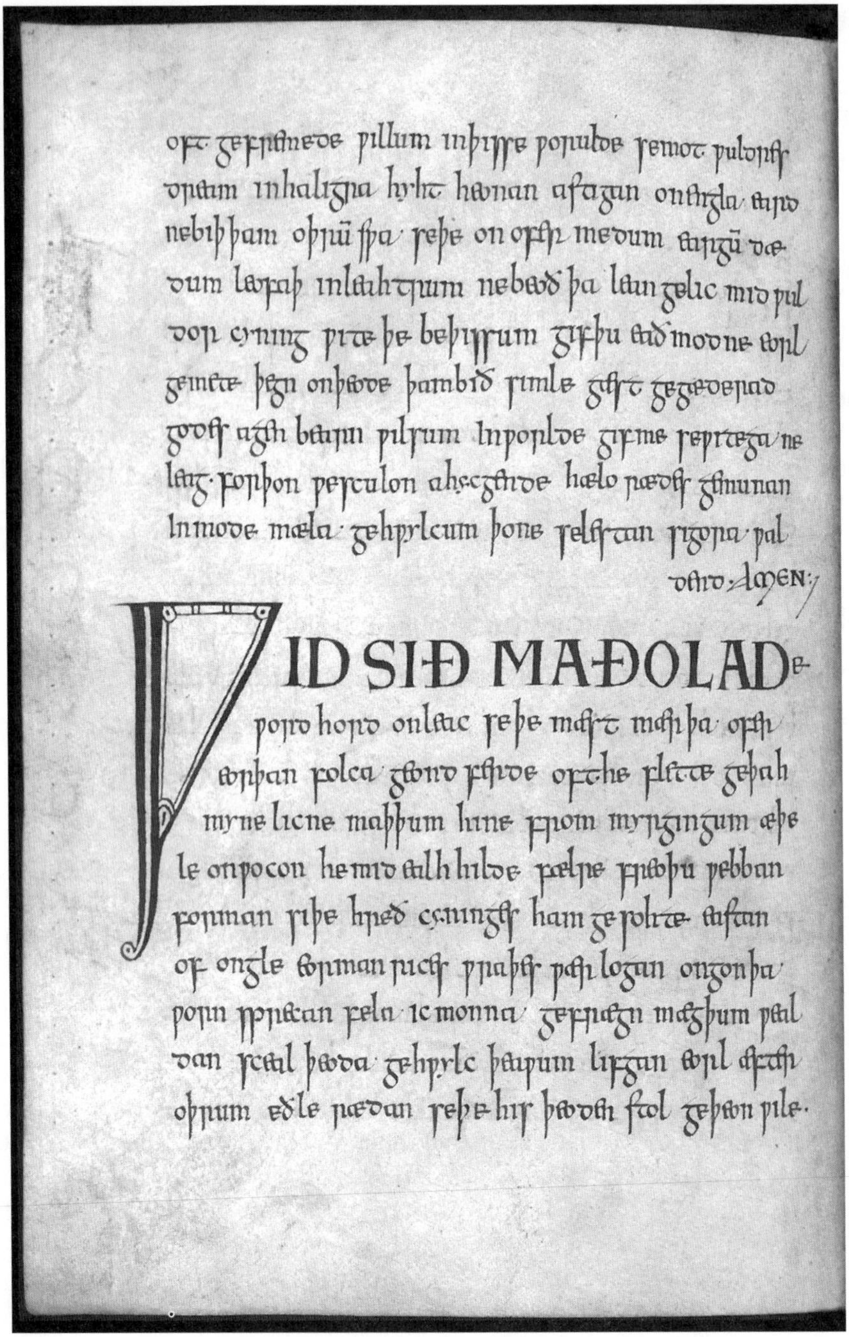

Figure 6.2   A Sample Old English Manuscript Page Containing the Opening Lines of 'Widsith', from the *Exeter Book* (10th century CE) (reprinted by permission of Dr Bernard J. Muir, Department of Language and Literature, University of Melbourne)

Table 6.4 The Germanic Voiceless Stops in Old English

Gmc. sound	OE letter	OE sound	OE sample word
[p]	p	[p]	*pæð* 'path', *pipe* 'pipe', *cēap* 'cattle'
[t]	t	[t]	*tūr* 'tower', *turtla* 'turtle', *æt* 'at'
[k]	c	[k]	*candel* 'candle', *clufu* 'clove', *bōc* 'book'
		[č]	*cinn* 'chin', *cernan* 'churn', *dīc* 'ditch'
[kʷ]	cw	[kʷ]	*cwēn* 'woman', *cwellan* 'to kill'

'lock', *cræftig* 'strong', *racca* 'part of a ship's rigging'. It represents the voiceless affricate [č] before front vowels (*i, e, æ, ea, eo*), between front vowels, and after front vowels at the end of a word: e.g. *cæfl* 'halter', *ēce* 'eternal', and *līc* 'body'. When the letter appears between a front and a back vowel, the [k] sound remains, as in *wicu* 'week' or *brecan* 'to break'. Since [k] and [č] are never found in the same phonetic environment, they are predictable variants, or allophones, of the same phoneme.

The change from [k] to [č] in the presence of a front vowel is the process known as palatalization. The front vowel (which is articulated in the palatal region) causes a sound to move either forward or backward to become more palatal in articulation (that is, from velar to palatal or from alveolar to palatal). In this case, a velar sound has moved forward.

We can now proceed to the Germanic voiced stops, as shown in Table 6.5. The voiced stop consonants also bear a one-to-one correspondence between written symbol and sound, except in the case of ȝ, or *g*. This letter represents the voiced stop [g] initially before back vowels, before consonants, when doubled, and in the sequence *ng*: e.g. *gāl* 'lust', *wegas* 'ways', *glæd* 'glad', *frogga* 'frog', and *singan* 'to sing'. Here, we find another example of palatalization, as the sound moves forward to become the palatal glide [j]; this occurs when *g* is in the context of a front vowel—that is, before a front vowel, after a front vowel, between front vowels, and after front vowels at the end of a syllable: e.g. *gēar* 'year', *wegas* 'ways', *þegen* 'thane',

Table 6.5 The Germanic Voiced Stops in Old English

Gmc. sound	OE letter	OE sound	OE sample word
[b]	b	[b]	*bedd* 'bed', *ymbe* 'about'
[d]	d	[d]	*dol* 'stupid', *hund* 'dog', *īdel* 'idle'
[g]	ȝ	[g]	*gold* 'gold', *guma* 'man', *gnēað* 'frugal'
		[j]	*gīet* 'yet', *fæger* 'fair', *dæg* 'day'
		[ɣ]	*lagu* 'law', *dragan* 'drag', *slōg* 'struck'

and *bodig* 'body'. In practically all other circumstances, such as after and between back vowels or *r* and *l*, it represents the voiced velar fricative [ɣ]: e.g. *plōg* 'plow land', *halga* 'holy', and *boga* 'bow'. Note that the Germanic voiced fricatives [β, ð, ɣ] merged with the voiced stops in most positions.

Old English preserves the Germanic fricatives as shown in Table 6.6. The fricatives do not offer the simple one-to-one correspondence between symbol and sound; instead, their pronunciation depends on the phonetic environment. The Old English letters *s*, *f*, and ð or *þ* are pronounced as voiced fricatives [z, v, ð] only between voiced sounds: e.g. *mase* 'small bird, titmouse', *efne* 'even', and *maðum* 'treasure'. The voiceless fricatives [s, f, θ] occur at the beginning or end of words or next to a voiceless consonant: e.g. *sōð* 'truth', *fūs* 'eager', *lust* 'desire', *fīf* 'five', *cræft* 'strong', and *þicce* 'thick'. The switch between voiced and voiceless here is entirely predictable, so the variations are allophones. Each set of allophones counts as only one distinctive sound, or phoneme. When doubled, the fricatives are always voiceless [ss, ff, θθ]: *cyssan* 'kiss', *offrian* 'offer', *oððe* 'or'. (This last OE word may also be spelled *oþþe*, *oððe*, or *oþðe*. The symbols ð and *þ* are used interchangeably to represent the voiced and voiceless allophones.)

The distribution of the sounds represented by the last letter, *h*, is more complex. It represents [h] at the beginning of a word before a vowel, as it did already in Germanic: e.g. *hæt* 'hat'. It represents [x] elsewhere (e.g. *dohtor* 'daughter', *þurh* 'through', and *hnutu* 'nut') except after a front vowel, where the sound undergoes palatalization, becoming the palatal fricative [ç] (e.g. *riht* 'right').

The Germanic nasals, liquids, and glides live on in Old English, as shown in Table 6.7. The [n] and [ŋ] sounds are predictable variants, allophones of the same

Table 6.6 The Germanic Fricatives in Old English

Gmc. sound	OE letter	OE sound	OE sample word
[s]	s	[s]	*sæt* 'sat', *hūs* 'house', *ēast* 'east'
		[z]	*wīse* 'wise', *frēosan* 'freeze'
[f]	f	[f]	*fisc* 'fish', *æfter* 'after', *hōf* 'hoof'
		[v]	*ofer* 'over', *lifde* 'lived'
[θ]	ð or þ	[θ]	*þæt* 'that', *tōð* 'tooth', *haraþ* 'wood'
		[ð]	*weorþlic* 'worthy', *hoðma* 'darkness'
[x]	h	[h]	*hord* 'hoard', *here* 'troop'
		[ç]	*fliht* 'flight', *mihtig* 'might'
		[x]	*mearh* 'horse', *fūht* 'damp', *hwæt* 'what'

Table 6.7 The Germanic Nasals and Approximants in Old English

Gmc. sound	OE letter	OE sound	OE sample word
[n]	n	[n]	*nytt* 'use', *ganot* 'sea bird', *ellen* 'zeal'
		[ŋ]	*hring* 'ring', *sinc* 'treasure'
[m]	m	[m]	*mund* 'palm', *plȳme* 'plum', *holm* 'sea'
[l]	l	[l]	*lamb* 'lamb', *meolc* 'milk', *cōl* 'cool'
[r]	r	[r]	*rāp* 'rope', *daroð* 'dart', *sār* 'sore'
[j]	ʒ	[j]	*gēar* 'year', *geoc* 'yoke'
[w]	ƿ	[w]	*winnan* 'win', *wund* 'wound'

phoneme. The sound [ŋ] occurs only before [g] or [k]; [n] occurs everywhere else. Remember that all consonant symbols are pronounced, so *ng* is always [ŋg] as in ModE *linger*, never just [ŋ] as in ModE *singer*.

We finish this look at the Old English consonants with the voiceless alveolopalatal fricative and voiced alveolopalatal affricate. These are spelled with digraphs (two letters representing a single sound) and consist of a stop released into a fricative:

- [š], spelled *sc*, as in *fisc* 'fish'; and
- [ǰ], spelled *cg* (*dg* in later English), as *ecg* 'edge'.

Overall, the consonant system of Old English can be represented as in Figure 6.3. Here when more than one sound is included in a single box, these represent allophones of a single phoneme. Since [k] and [č] are allophones, stops and affricates are treated together in the figure. Note also that [ɣ] is a simple fricative but must be included with [g] because the two sounds are allophones.

In addition to [kʷ], Old English has a number of other consonant clusters. The orthographic symbol *x* represented the sequence [ks] in words such as *lox* 'lynx' and *max* 'net', as it still does in words such as *box*. The symbol *z*, though infrequent, represented the sequence [ts], also written *ts*, as in *milze/miltse* 'mercy'. This cluster is still found in Modern English in loan words, e.g. *pizza*, and across morpheme boundaries, e.g. *cats*, *hits*, and *outside*. Several consonant clusters are not found today; both parts must be pronounced in *hl*, *hn*, *hw*, *hr*, *gn*, *cn*, and *wr*, as in *hl̄af* 'loaf', *hnutu* 'nut', *hwæl* 'whale', *hr̄an* 'reindeer', *gnæt* 'gnat', *cn̄eow* 'knee', and *wracu* 'revenge'. Recall that Old English orthography requires that all letters be pronounced.

Note that when a root has a prefix or a suffix or is compounded with another root, the sounds at the beginning and end of the root still behave as if they were initial or final sounds in terms of voicing and palatalization. Thus in *anhāga* 'solitary walker', where *an-* is a prefix and *hāga* is the root, the *h* in *haga* is still [h], not [x]. In *ceorfsæx*, a compound of *ceorf* 'surgeon's' and *sæx* 'knife', the *f* of *ceorf* is

Manner of Articulation		Place of Articulation							
		Bilabial	Labiodental	Interdental	Alveolar	Alveolo-palatal	Palatal	Velar	Glottal
Stop/ Affricate	Voiceless	p			t	č	k		
	Voiced	b			d	ǰ	g		
Nasal		m				n		ŋ	
Fricative	Voiceless/ Voiced		f v	θ ð	s z	š		ç x h	
	Lateral				l				
Approximant	Retroflex/ Trill				r				
	Glide (or Semivowel)						j	w	

Figure 6.3   The Consonants of Old English

[f], not [v], and the *s* of *sæx* is [s], not [z]. In *mynelicne* 'desirable', where *-ne* is a grammatical ending, the *c* is treated as a final sound and pronounced [č].

Exercise 6.3 Transcription of OE Consonants

Supply the correct phonetic symbol for the underlined consonants of the following OE words.

a. *hæcce* 'crosier'   ____

b. *hægel* 'hail'   ____

c. *prica* 'dot'   ____

d. *smēþan* 'to smooth'   ____

e. *furðor* 'further'   ____

f. *fūs* 'ready'   ____

g. *fūse* 'readily'   ____

h. *plega* 'play'   ____

i. *hafok* 'hawk'   ____

j. *þaca* 'roof'   ____

k. *nāht* 'nothing'   ____

l. *sihð* 'vision'   ____

m. *lǣce* 'physician'   ____

n. *burg* 'city'   ____

Vowels

The Germanic vowel system, shown in Chapter 5 (see Figure 5.4), changed very little in Old English.

We begin with a note on vowel length. Like Germanic, Old English has both long and short vowels, which are phonemic because they distinguish meaning, as in *god* 'god' compared to *gōd* 'good', or *wītan* 'to guard' versus *witan* 'to know'. The terms *long* and *short*, however, can lead to confusion because their strict linguistic definitions differ from the way the terms are often used by non-experts. The major misunderstanding comes when people use *long vowel* to describe a diphthong, as in the vowel sound in *kite*, which is—incorrectly, from a linguist's point of view—

sometimes called a 'long i' instead of [aɪ]. In linguistic parlance, one must stick to the definition of a long vowel as a monophthong that is pronounced for a longer time than a short monophthong. Length is often associated with tenseness, and it is generally assumed that the Old English long vowels were in fact both tense and long. In contrast, short vowels are lax (as in the difference in tenseness between *seat* and *sit* in Modern English). The concept of length is challenging because vowel length is not distinctive in Modern English; recall from Chapter 2 that although *sea* has a long vowel and *ceased* a short vowel, you could transpose the vowels with no change in meaning.

To make matters even more difficult, vowel length is usually not indicated in manuscripts, because OE speakers would have recognized the word's form and meaning from its context. Editors of OE texts often help by adding a macron to mark length, as we do when words are cited individually, though not in extended passages.

Onto the few significant changes between Germanic and Old English. The sound [ɑ] split into two sounds, [æ] and [ɑ]: [ɑ] is found before back vowels in the following syllables, before nasals, and before [w]; [æ] appears everywhere else. The sounds [ɑ̄] and [ɑi] merged as [ɑ̄]. Scholars do not agree entirely upon the exact phonetic quality of the change in the diphthongs [ɑu] and [iu], but we give the widely accepted pronunciations for Old English in Table 6.8. Note that schwa serves

Table 6.8 The Germanic Vowels in Old English

Gmc. sound	OE letter(s)	OE sound	OE sample word
[ī]	ī	[ī]	*bīdan* 'stay'
[i]	i	[ɪ]	*biddan* 'ask'
[ē]	ē	[ē]	*fēdan* 'feed'
[e]	e	[ɛ]	*tellan* 'count'
[ū]	ū	[ū]	*lūcan* 'lock'
[u]	u	[ʊ]	*wunian* 'inhabit'
[ō]	ō	[ō]	*lōcian* 'look'
[o]	o	[ɔ]	*folgian* 'follow'
[ǣ]	ǣ	[ǣ]	*ǣr* 'before'
[ɑ]	æ, a	[æ] or [ɑ]	*sæt* 'sat', *habban* 'have'
[ɑ̄] and [ɑi]	ā	[ɑ̄]	*hātan* 'command'
[ɑu]	ēa	[ǣə]	*scēawian* 'look'
[iu]	ēo	[ēə]	*scēotan* 'shoot'

Table 6.9 New Vowels in Old English

OE letter	OE sound	OE sample word
ȳ	[ȳ]	*hȳrian* 'hire'
y	[ʏ]	*yppan* 'manifest'
ea	[æə]	*ealdian* 'grow old'
eo	[ɛə]	*weorpan* 'cast out'

as a glide in Old English diphthongs. In addition, four new vowel sounds resulted from sound changes in Old English, as shown in Table 6.9. Remember that [ȳ] represents a high front rounded vowel made as if you were saying [i] but with your lips rounded; [ʏ] is the lax version of this sound. Figure 6.4 summarizes the vowel system of Old English.

Look back at the manuscript page illustrated in Figure 6.2. The first sentence can be transcribed as follows:

Widsið maðolade wordhord onleac se þe mæst mærþa ofer
wɪdsɪθ maðɔladɛ wɔrdhɔrd ɔnlæəč sɛ θɛ mæst mærðɑ ɔvɛr

eorþan folca geondferde oft he flette geþah mynelicne māþþum
ɛərðan fɔlkɑ jɛəndfɛrdɛ ɔft hē flɛttɛ jɛθɑx mʏnɛlĭčnɛ māθθʊm

		Monophthongs		
		Front	**Central**	**Back**
High	**Long Tense**	ī ȳ		ū
	Short Lax	ɪ ʏ		ʊ
Mid	**Long Tense**	ē		ō
	Short Lax	ɛ		ɔ
Low	**Long/Short**	ǣ æ		ā ɑ
		Diphthongs		
		ēə		
		ɛə		
		æə ǣə		

Figure 6.4 The Vowel System of Old English

Exercise 6.4 Transcription of OE Vowels and Consonants

Transcribe the following OE passage using the IPA. It is a late West Saxon version of the parable of the good Samaritan (Luke 10: 30–6) (Bright 1906:64–5). A gloss is provided.

Sum man fērde fram Hiērūsalem tō Hiēricho, and becōm on þā sceaðan; þā hine
A certain man went from Jerusalem to Jericho, and came upon the thieves; they him

berēafodon and tintregodon hine, and forlēton hine sāmcucene. Þā gebyrode hit þæt
robbed and tormented him, and left him half-alive. Then happened it that

sum sācerd fērde on þǣm ylcan wege, and þā hē þæt geseah, hē hine forbēah. And
a certain priest went on the same way, and when he that saw, he him passed by. And

eall swā se dīacon, þā hē wæs wið þā stōwe and þæt geseah, hē hyne ēac forbēah.
also this deacon when he was at the place and that saw he him also passed by.

Þā fērde sum Samaritanisc man wið hine; þā hē hine geseah, þā wearð hē mid
Then went a certain Samaritan man by him; when he him saw then became he with

mildheortnesse ofer hine āstyred. Þā genēalǣhte hē, and wrāð his wunda, and
compassion for him stirred up. Then drew near he, and bound his wounds and

on āgēat ele and wīn, and hine on hys nȳten sette, and gelǣdde on his lǣcehūs
poured on oil and wine, and him on his beast set, and led to his hospital

and hine lācnode; and brōhte ōðrum dæge twēgen penegas, and sealde
and him medicated; and brought on the second day two pennies, and gave

þām lǣce, and þus cwæð, Begȳm hys; and swā hwæt swā þū māre tō gedēst,
to the doctor, and thus said, 'Take care of him and whatsoever thou more besides dost,

þāonne ic cume, ic hit forgylde þāe. Hwylc þāāra þārēora þāyncð þāē þāæt
when I come, I it will repay you.' Which of the three seems to thee that

sȳ þāæs mæg þāe on ðā sceaðan befēoll?
may be that one's neighbor who among the thieves fell?

Sound Changes

The most important process that affected vowel sounds as Old English grew out of Germanic was the conditioned sound change known as *umlaut* (a name given to it by Jacob Grimm), or *i-mutation*. In umlaut, the vowel either moves directly forward in the mouth [u > y, o > e, ɑ > æ] or forward and up [ɑ > æ > e], as shown below in Figure 6.5. In this process, the speaker anticipates a high palatal sound, an *i* vowel or a *j* glide in the following syllable, by fronting or raising the vowel; that is, the vowel comes to resemble in its articulation the *i* or the *j*. (You may remember that this process is called *regressive assimilation*.) Once the vowel is fronted or raised, the *i* is either changed to *e* or lost, and the *j* is lost altogether except when it comes after *r*. These losses obscure the cause of the sound change. An example may render this more clear: when the suffix *-jan was added to the Germanic root *dōm* 'judgment'; the *j* caused umlaut of the *o*-vowel to *e* and then the *j* disappeared, yielding the Old English verb *dēman* 'to judge'. This process occurs in all Germanic languages except Gothic, apparently, where the *i* and the *j* do not vanish. The changes were completed in Old English by the time of the first written records, but we can see its results. The details of umlaut are shown in orthographic form in Table 6.10.

Umlaut is important in Old English because a number of major inflectional endings originally contained an *i* or a *j*, though this sound is no longer present. These include the plural of some nouns, the comparative of some adjectives, and certain

	Monophthongs		
	Front	**Central**	**Back**
High	ȳ	←	ū
	Y	←	ʊ
Mid	ē	←	ō
	ɛ ↑	←	ɔ
Low	ǣ		ā
	æ	←	ɑ

Figure 6.5 Schematic View of Umlaut in Old English

Table 6.10 Details of Umlaut in Old English

vowel change	example: Germanic to Old English
ū > ȳ	*rūm 'spacious' + -jan > rȳman 'to make spacious'
u > y	*full 'full' + -jan > fyllan 'to fill'
ō > ē	*gōs 'goose' + -iz > gēs 'geese'
o > e	*ofst 'haste' + -jan > efstan 'to make haste'
a > æ	*talu 'tale' + -jan > tællen 'to tell'
a > æ > e (before a nasal)	*Angel 'Angle' + -isc > Englisc 'English'
ā > ǣ	*hāl 'hale' + -jan > hǣlan 'to heal'
æ > e	*sæt 'sat' + -jan > settan 'to set'
ēo > īe	*stēor 'direction' + -jan > stīeran 'to steer'
eo > ie (later i)	*geong 'young' + -ira > giengra 'younger'
ēa > īe	*hēan 'lowly' + -iþo > hīenþ 'humiliation'
ea > ie (later i)	*eald 'old' + -ira > ieldra 'elder'

derivational endings (forming verbs from nouns, adjectives or other verbs, adjectives from nouns, abstract nouns, etc.). The legacy of umlaut in Modern English is widespread. We see its working in

- so-called irregular noun plurals (*tooth/teeth*, *foot/feet*, *mouse/mice*),
- comparatives (*old/elder*),
- transitive (causative) verbs formed from intransitive verbs (*sit/set*, *lie/lay*, *rise/raise*, *fall/fell*),
- verbs formed from nouns (*food/feed, gold/gild*),
- verbs derived from adjectives (*full/fill*), and
- adjectives derived from nouns (*Angel/English*).

Umlaut also accounts for an apparent consonant irregularity in Old English. In a word such as *gēs*, the initial sound is pronounced [g] in Old English, not [j] as one would expect if relying on the patterns described earlier in this chapter—the front vowel [e] seemingly ought to result in palatalization of the consonant. Likewise, in *cēlan* 'to cool', the initial sound is pronounced [k], not [č]. The answer to this puzzle is that the words used to contain back vowels, so the palatalization process did not apply. Only later did umlaut come to affect these words and produce the front vowels that we see in *gēs* and *cēlan*. The result is an otherwise impermissible combination of velar stop followed by front vowel. As you can see, the process of umlaut makes it difficult to ascertain the value of *c* and *g* in Old English because one must know the history of the word.

A second process that affected vowels in Old English was the source of the short diphthongs. *Breaking* (also named by Jacob Grimm) is the process by which certain vowels became diphthongized as they entered Old English. The affected vowels were the long and short *æ*, short *e*, and long and short *i*. The change occured only when these vowels preceded particular sequences of consonants, namely *r* + another consonant, *l* + another consonant, and *h* with or without a following consonant. (Only *æ* was affected in all instances; the other vowels were less consistently changed.) Some examples are shown in Table 6.11.

Table 6.11 Details of Breaking in Old English

vowel change	example: Germanic to Old English
ǣ > ēa [ǣə]	*nǣh > *nēah* 'near'
æ > ea [æə]	*hærd > *heard* 'hard', *fællan > *feallan* 'to fall'
ē > ēo [ēə]	*lēht > *lēoht* 'light'
e > eo [ɛə]	*selh > *seolh* 'seal', *fehu > *feoh* 'cattle', *herte > *heorte* 'heart'
ī > īo [īə]	*betwīh > *betwīoh* 'betwixt'
i > io [iə]	*tihhian > *tiohhian* 'to consider'

Note that the diphthong *io* merged with *eo*. For practice, try to supply the OE versions of the pre-OE forms below:

*ærm 'poor' >
*werpan 'to throw' >
*Piht 'a Pict'[3] >

---

3 The correct answers are *earm, weorpan, Pioht/Peoht*.

Exercise 6.5 Sound Changes in OE Vowels

For each Proto-Germanic form, give the written form in Old English and name the sound change between that derives OE from PGmc.

Proto-Germanic	Old English	Sound Change
a. *dāljan 'to divide'	_____	_____
b. *mūsiz 'mice'	_____	_____
c. *erðe 'earth'	_____	_____
d. *fōti 'to the foot'	_____	_____
e. *hælf 'half'	_____	_____
f. *nǣh 'near'	_____	_____

Figure 6.6   A Page from the *Cotton Vitellius* (C III, f21v, herbs, snake, and scorpion © The British Library)

Stress

Old English inherited from Germanic a system of stress accent, with the stress falling on a fixed syllable. The rules for accentuation in Old English are quite simple compared to those of Modern English: the stress falls on the first syllable or on the root syllable.

- Simple words (those consisting of a single root plus inflectional suffixes) have primary stress, indicated with an acute accent on the first syllable: e.g. *hélpan* 'to help', *gýrdel* 'belt', and *ðúrstig* 'thirsty'.
- Prefixed nouns have primary stress on the first syllable as well, except for nouns containing the prefixes *be-, for-*, and *ge-*, which never carry the accent: e.g. *mís-dǣd* 'misdeed, sin', *tố-dāl* 'division', and *ánd-swaru* 'answer'; but *be-gáng* 'worship', *for-wýrd* 'destruction', and *ge-mýnd* 'mind'.
- Prefixed verbs have primary stress on the root syllable; the prefix is never accented: e.g. *ymb-síttan* 'to besiege', *ofer-cúman* 'to overcome', and *wið-stándan* 'to withstand'.
- Compounds have primary stress on the first half and secondary stress (indicated by a grave accent) on the second half: *rű nstæ̀f* 'runic letter', *lắrhù s* 'school', *wérgèld* 'compensation for a man's life', and *góldsmìð* 'goldsmith'.

While the accentuation system of Modern English is very different from that of Old English because of the influx of Romance vocabulary in Middle English, the prefixed verbs which have been preserved show the OE stress pattern (e.g. *forgíve*, *withdráw*, *outlást*, *bemóan*), as do compounds in Modern English (e.g. *wétsùit* compared to *wét súit*). As we shall see, the accentuation system of Old English has also had an important effect on the grammar of the English language.

Exercise 6.6 Stress in Old English

Indicate the primary stress in each of the following Old English words. Derived and compounded forms are indicated.

a. hlīn-duru 'grated door'

b. hrēow-nes 'penitence'

c. bēam 'tree'

d. dēawig-feþera 'dewy-feathered'

e. ge-wrecan 'to wreak, avenge'

f.   ge-wemmed-nyss 'corruption'

g.   for-ealdian 'grow old'

h.   ǣw-fæst 'devout'

i.   be-sorg 'dear'

j.   bifian 'to tremble'

k   betera 'better'

l.   þēoden-stōl 'lord's throne'

m.   tō-weard 'toward'

n.   wālic 'lowly'

A Closer Look at the Language of an Old English Text

To conclude this chapter, let us look at a sample Old English text. In the text box below is 'Cædmon's Hymn', from Bede's *Ecclesiastical History of the English People* (Book 4, Chapter 25) (Miller 1890:344).

Nu	sculan	herigean/	heofonrices		weard	
now	*shall*	*we praise*	*heaven-kingdom's*		*guardian*	
metodes	meahte/	7	his	modgeþanc,		
creator's	*might*	*and*	*his*	*thought*		
weorc	wuldorfæder,/		swa	he	wundra	gehwæs,
work	*of the wonder-father*		*as*	*he*	*of wonders*	*each*
ece	Drihten,/	or		onstealde.		
eternal	*lord*	*the beginning*		*created*		
he	ærest	sceop/	eorþan	bearnum		
he	*first*	*shaped*	*earth*	*for men*		
heofon	to	hrofe,/	halig	scyppend;		
heaven	*as*	*roof*	*holy*	*shaper*		

þa   middangeard,/   monncynnes   weard,
the   middle-earth   of mankind   guardian

ece   Drihten,/   æfter   teode
eternal lord   afterwards   he made

firum   foldan,/   frea   ælmihtig
for men   earth   lord   almighty

('Cædmon's Hymn')

A phonetic transcription of the first sentence indicates what the Old English would have sounded like:

nū šʊlɑn hɛrɪ̈jǣən hɛəvɔnrīčɛs wǣərd
mɛtɔdɛs mǣəçtɛ ɑnd hɪs mōdjɛθɑŋk
wɛərk wʊldɔrfǣdɛr swɑ hē wʊndrɑ jɛhwǣs
ɛčɛ drɪçtɛn ɔr ɔnstǣəldɛ

We can see typical processes of Old English word formation at work in the poem. Many compounds occur:

heofonrice(s)   *wuldorfæder*

modgeþanc (literally, 'mind-thought')   *middangeard*

moncynn(es)   *ælmihtig*

Derived forms are much less common than compounds in Old English poetry. The only examples here are *on-stealde, ge-þanc, ge-hwæs,* and *scypp-end.*

We can see examples here of each of the three ways (discussed earlier) that Old English vocabulary (seen in parentheses) may survive today:

- with little change in meaning or form: *he/his, now (nu), we, after (æfter), earth (earþ(an)), and (7=and), work (weorc), wonder (wuldor), father (fæder);*
- with some change to meaning or form or both: *so (swa), shape (sceop), roof (hrofe), holy (halig), middle (middan), almighty (ælmihtig), yard (geard), shall (sculan), heaven (heofon), might (meahte), mankind (monncynn(es));* and
- in local dialects, restricted contexts, or set expressions: *bairn (bearn(um))* ('child' in Scottish English).

The OE word *weard* is cognate with *warden,* a Germanic word which was borrowed into French and then borrowed back into English from Norman French. English also borrowed *guardian* from Central French. Thus, *warden* and *guardian* are doublets. Note also the vocabulary items that no longer exist in Modern English, e.g. *frea* 'lord', *fir(um)* 'man', *herigean* 'to praise', *ford(an)* 'earth', and *drihten* 'lord'.

RECOMMENDED WEB LINKS

A full-colour image of the opening lines of 'Widsith', from the *Exeter Book* (as shown on p. 176), may be found at Bernard Muir's website:

    http://www.medieval.unimelb.edu.au/exeter/folio84v.html

Images of other Old English manuscripts may be found on the website of the Bodleian Library, University of Oxford:

    http://www.bodley.ox.ac.uk/dept/scwmss/wmss/medieval/browse.htm

To hear Old and Modern English versions of several OE poems, go to the English Companion's website:

    http://www.tha-engliscan-gesithas.org.uk/old-english-readings

The online version of Peter S. Baker's *Introduction to Old English* contains a brief discussion of Old English pronunciation, as does 'Old English Online' at the Linguistics Research Center of the University of Texas:

    http://www.wmich.edu/medieval/resources/IOE/index.html
    http://www.utexas.edu/cola/centers/lrc/eieol/engol-0-X.html

A Modern English to Old English word list may be found at:

    http://www.mun.ca/Ansaxdat/vocab/wordlist.html

Many Old English texts can be found at the following sites:

    http://www.georgetown.edu/labyrinth/library/oe/oe.html (Georgetown University's Labyrinth Library)
    http://www.ucalgary.ca/UofC/eduweb/engl401/texts/index.htm (Murray McGillivray's course website)
    http://www.utexas.edu/cola/centers/lrc/eieol/engol-0-X.html (Linguistics Research Center, University of Texas at Austin)
    (On the latter two websites, the OE texts are extensively glossed.)

For the OE text and a ModE translation of 'Cædmon's Hymn', see:

    http://rpo.library.utoronto.ca/poem/369.html

FURTHER READING

Textbooks discussing Old English sounds and word stock include:

    Hogg, Richard M. 2002. *An Introduction to Old English*. New York: Oxford University Press, Chapters 1 and 8.
    Lass, Roger. 1994. *Old English: A Historical Linguistic Companion*. Cambridge University Press, Chapters 3, 4, 5, and 8.
    Mitchell, Bruce, and Fred C. Robinson. 2007. *A Guide to Old English: Revised with Prose and Verse Texts and Glossary*. 7th edn. Malden, MA and Oxford: Blackwell, Chapters 2 and 4.
    Smith, Jeremy J. 2009. *Old English: A Linguistic Introduction*. Cambridge: Cambridge University Press, Chapters 4 and 5.

Discussions of the word stock of English include:

Barney, Stephen A. 1985. *Word-Hoard: An Introduction to Old English Vocabulary*. New Haven and London: Yale University Press.

Durkin, Philip. 2009. *The Oxford Guide to Etymology*. New York and Oxford: Oxford University Press.

Hughes, Geoffrey. 1988. *Words in Time: A Social History of the English Vocabulary*. Oxford: Blackwell.

Hughes, Geoffrey. 2000. *A History of English Words*. Malden, MA and Oxford: Blackwell.

Kastovsky, Dieter. 1992. 'Semantics and Vocabulary'. *The Cambridge History of the English Language. Vol. 1: The Beginnings to 1066*. Ed. by Richard M. Hogg, 290–408. Cambridge: Cambridge University Press.

Kastovsky, Dieter. 2006. 'Vocabulary'. *A History of the English Language*. Ed. by Richard M. Hogg and David Denison, 199–270. Cambridge: Cambridge University Press.

Serjeantson, Mary S. 1935. *A History of Foreign Words in English*. London: Routledge and Kegan Paul.

Townend, Matthew. 2006. 'Contacts and Conflicts: Latin, Norse, and French'. *The Oxford History of English*. Ed. by Lynda Mugglestone, 61–85. Oxford and New York: Oxford University Press.

For more advanced discussions of Old English vocabulary and phonology, see:

Hogg, Richard M. 1992. 'Phonology and Morphology'. *The Cambridge History of the English Language. Vol. 1: The Beginnings to 1066*. Ed. by Richard M. Hogg, 67–167. Cambridge: Cambridge University Press.

Lass, Roger. 1994. *Old English: A Historical Linguistic Companion*. Cambridge University Press, Chapters 3, 4, 5, and 8.

The *Dictionary of Old English* is partially complete:

Dictionary of Old English A–G on CD-ROM. 2008. Ed. by Antonette diPaolo Healey et al. Toronto: Pontifical Institute of Medieval Studies, University of Toronto.

A convenient student's dictionary of Old English is:

Clark-Hall, J.R. 1984. *A Concise Anglo-Saxon Dictionary*. 4th edn. Toronto: University of Toronto Press and the Medieval Academy of America.

A dual text edition of *Beowulf,* with Old English and modern translation on facing pages, will give you a feel for the poetic vocabulary of Old English:

Heaney, Seamus. 2000. *Beowulf: A New Verse Translation*. New York: Farrar, Straus & Giroux.

For more information on the intense Scandinavian influence on English, see:

Thomason, Sarah G., and Terrence Kaufman. 1988. *Language Contact, Creolization, and Genetic Linguistics*. Berkeley, Los Angeles, and London: University of California Press, 275–304.

7 The Grammar of Old English

OVERVIEW

This chapter explores Old English grammar and introduces the grammatical categories of the noun and the verb. We look at personal, demonstrative, and interrogative pronouns, the noun classes and their inflectional endings, the weak and strong declensions of the adjective, the comparison of adjectives, the formation of adverbs, and the verb classes and their inflectional endings. The chapter also discusses the grammatical process of concord and the use of cases. It ends with a consideration of Old English syntax, focusing on verbal phrases and word order.

OBJECTIVES

The objective in this chapter is to learn the fundamentals of the Old English inflectional system. After completing this chapter, you should be able to

- recognize the class and gender of a noun if given its distinctive inflected forms;
- recognize the type and class of a verb if given its principal parts;
- recognize the person, number, tense, and mood of an inflected verb if given its type and class; and
- recognize the number, case, and gender of a pronoun.

In addition, you will learn the sources of the ModE demonstrative and be able to explain why a particular case is used in a particular context. You should also be able to identify verbal periphrases and recognize the ways in which Old English syntax differs from that of Modern English. Finally, you should be able to point to examples of Old English inflections surviving in the language today.

Old English belongs to the class of inflected or synthetic languages (discussed in Chapter 4). Unlike Modern English, Old English indicates grammatical meaning primarily through the use of regular inflections (suffixes attached to the stems of words) or irregular inflected forms. When a noun, pronoun, adjective, or demonstrative is inflected, we say it is *declined*; when a verb is inflected, we say it is *conjugated*. All of a word's inflected variants together constitute its grammatical *paradigm*.

The Nominal System

We begin with the nominal system of Old English, which includes nouns, pronouns, and the modifiers of the noun (adjectives and demonstratives).

The Grammatical Categories of the Nominal System

Before we can look at the actual forms of Old English, we need to review the grammatical categories relating to nouns, pronouns, and adjectives. These are the categories of meaning expressed by the inflections; they give us information about person, number, gender, and case.

Person denotes the participants in a communicative situation: the *first person* is the speaker or speakers, the *second person* is the addressee or addressees, and the *third person* is the person(s) or thing(s) spoken about.

Number is an indication of how many things are being talked about. Modern English makes just a two-way distinction between singular and plural, but Old English distinguishes three numbers: one (singular), two (dual), and more than two (plural).

In Modern English, linguistic gender has to do with the biological sex of the entity named. Personal pronouns (*he, she, it*) indicate the real-world sex of the object referred to; in a more limited way, compounds (e.g. *boyfriend*, *girlfriend*) and derivational affixes (e.g. *heroine*, *actress*, *widower*) do so, too. This system is known as *natural gender*. However, Old English has a system called *grammatical gender*. Inherited from Proto-Indo-European, this system is still found in many modern languages, such as German, Russian, French, Italian, and Welsh. From examples such as French *le jour* 'the day' (masculine gender) and German *das Weib* 'the woman' (neuter gender), we can see that grammatical gender may have nothing to do with the real-world sex of the object; instead, it functions as a means of classifying nouns. The word *gender* in this sense is derived from Lat. *genus*, meaning 'kind'. Old English expresses three genders: masculine, feminine, and neuter.

Finally, *case* indicates the role of a noun phrase in a sentence. Old English marked as many as five cases: nominative (the subject), genitive (the possessor), dative (the indirect object), accusative (the direct object), and instrumental (the means by which something is done). For modern speakers, case may be the most difficult feature to understand because Old English expresses the role of the noun primarily by inflections, whereas Modern English relies on prepositional phrases and word order. We have lost most of the original case inflections, but in Old English, every noun, pronoun, demonstrative, and adjective contains an indicator of case.

Pronouns

The inflections of Old English are best preserved in the personal and interrogative pronouns of Modern English. This is not surprising because, as mentioned in the previous chapter, core grammatical items such as pronouns (which stand in the place of nouns) tend to resist change.

The paradigms for the OE personal pronouns (called 'personal' because they function primarily to express grammatical person) can be seen in Table 7.1. You can readily note that, apart from some phonological differences, the OE pronouns look very much like ModE ones in expressing person, number, and case; the third-person singular pronouns express gender as well.

Table 7.1 Personal Pronouns in Old English

	first person		
	singular	*dual*	*plural*
nom.	ic	wit	wē
acc.	mē (< mec)	unc (< uncet)	ūs (< ūsic)
gen.	mīn	uncer	ūre
dat./instr.	mē	unc	ūs
	second person		
	singular	*dual*	*plural*
nom.	þū	git	gē
acc.	þē (< þec)	inc (<incit)	ēow (<ēowic)
gen.	þīn	incer	ēower
dat./instr.	þē	inc	ēow
	third person		
	masculine	*neuter*	*feminine*	*plural*
nom.	hē	hit	hēo	hī
acc.	hine	hit	hī	hī
gen.	his	his	hire	hira
dat./instr.	him	him	hire	him

There are, however, a few differences between OE and ModE personal pronouns:

- Old English has complete sets of dual forms for the first and second persons meaning 'we two' and 'you two'. These have interesting uses in OE poetry, where they can express intimacy. Dual forms were lost in late Old English.
- Old English has a form indicating a single addressee and could thus distinguish between 'one of you' and 'many of you'. The second-person singular forms (*þū*, *þīn*, and *þē*) fell out of general use in Early Modern English, but they are still retained in certain religious contexts as *thou*, *thine*, and *thee* in Modern English. The second-person plural forms are still in use, but only the nominative OE form (*gē*) looks much like the ModE form (*ye* or *you*). The others acquired their modern phonological form in Middle English.
- Pronouns in Old English originally had distinct forms for the accusative and the dative cases. In the first and second persons, this distinction was lost very early, with the dative form serving both functions (in Table 7.1, for example, we see that the accusative of the first-person singular, *mec*, has been replaced by the dative, *mē*). The third-person pronouns continue to distinguish accusative and dative throughout the OE period, but eventually the two cases merge, taking the form of the dative.
- The OE third-person feminine nominative form (*hēo*) is quite different from that of Modern English. As we will see, the *she* form arose in Middle English.
- The OE third-person neuter forms all contain an initial *h*; this was lost in unstressed positions to give the modern form *it*. The OE genitive form *his* was eventually replaced in Early Modern English with the analogical form *its*. The OE dative form *him* gave way to the accusative *(h)it*.
- The OE third-person plural forms with initial *h* were all replaced with ON forms beginning with *th* (*they*, *them*, *their*) borrowed in late Old English.

In addition to personal pronouns, Old English has a set of fully inflected interrogative pronouns, which are used in asking questions (see Table 7.2).

If *hw* is transposed to *wh* (as it was in Middle English), these forms look very much like Modern English. The gender distinction in the interrogatives is between

Table 7.2 Interrogative Pronouns in Old English

	masculine/feminine	*neuter*
nom.	hwā	hwæt
acc.	hwone	hwæt
gen.	hwæs	hwæs
dat.	hwām, hwǣm	hwǣm
instr.	hwām, hwǣm	hwȳ

masculine/feminine (or animate) *hwā* 'who' and neuter (or inanimate) *hwæt* 'what'. As with the personal pronouns, the dative form eventually replaced the accusative in the masculine/feminine (*hwǣm* 'whom' replaced *hwone*), while in contrast, the accusative form replaced the dative in the neuter (*hwæt* 'what' replaced *hwǣm*). The interrogative also expresses the instrumental case, referring to the 'means or manner by which', *hwȳ*, which is the source of ModE *why*. Another instrumental form (not included above) is OE *hū*, which gives us ModE *how*. The interrogative forms were used in Old English only in asking questions. Our use of *who/whom/ whose* in relative clauses (e.g. *I met a person whom I know*; *I want a person who is willing to work*; *That is the professor whose class I attended*) is an EModE development. To form relative clauses in Old English, the invariant relative particle *þe* was used (or this particle in combination with a demonstrative, or simply the demonstrative alone).

A word of caution: the pronoun forms of Old English vary from source to source. If you compare the forms listed above with those given in any grammar of Old English, you will find a number of minor differences. This variation is typical in a language such as Old English, which has a number of different dialects, stretches across centuries, and does not have fixed spelling conventions.

Exercise 7.1 Pronouns

1. Give the person, number, case, and gender of the following Old English pronouns.

	Person	Number	Case	Gender
a. *unc*	_____	_____	_____	_____
b. *ūs*	_____	_____	_____	_____
c. *ēow*	_____	_____	_____	_____
d. *him*	_____	_____	_____	_____
e. *þın*	_____	_____	_____	_____

2. Give the Old English pronoun for each of the following descriptions.

    a. third-person neuter dative plural _____

    b. first-person nominative dual _____

    c. third-person feminine accusative singular _____

    d. second-person genitive plural _____

    e. first-person nominative singular _____

3. a. Which dual form or forms of the personal pronoun are still used in Modern English?

    _____

    b. Does Modern English still use the Old English third-person feminine nominative form?

    _____

    c. Where does the Modern English pronoun *it* come from?

    _____

    d. The Old English third-person plural forms begin with *h*. Where did the Modern English equivalents with *th* come from?

    _____

    e. The interrogative form *hwǣm* represents several case/gender combinations. What are they?

    _____

Nouns

Modern English makes only four distinctions in nouns: two of number (singular versus plural) and two of case (genitive versus non-genitive). Occasionally these distinctions result in four separate phonological forms:

man   man's   men   men's

However, usually they result in only two (note that while the apostrophe distinguishes three forms in writing, it makes no difference in pronunciation):

boy   boy's/boys/boys'

In contrast, Old English nouns distinguish two numbers (singular and plural), and five cases (nominative, accusative, genitive, dative, and instrumental); they belong to one of three grammatical genders (masculine, feminine, or neuter). Moreover, Old English has a number of noun classes, roughly correlated with gender, each with a distinct set of inflectional endings for number and case. The form of a noun does not reveal its gender or its class; when one learns a noun in Old English, one must also learn its gender and the class to which it belongs. Furthermore, the names of noun classes are rather misleading, as they are identified by the form that members of that class took at an earlier stage in their development. For example, *a*-stem nouns all had an -*a*- between the root of the noun and the inflectional ending in Germanic (the 'stem' being the root plus the characteristic vowel), but that -*a*- is nowhere to be seen in the equivalent Old English forms.

A-*stem Nouns*

The *a*-stem nouns are either masculine or neuter in gender, and 60 per cent of all nouns in Old English belong to this class. Table 7.3 is a paradigm, giving all of the inflected forms that a noun can take. The inflectional endings (in bold) are added to the stem of the noun. For example, to the stem *cyning*, an -*es* ending is added to produce the genitive singular (meaning roughly 'king's' or 'of the king'). Where the inflected form and the stem form are the same (i.e. where no ending is shown in bold), linguists say that there is a zero (Ø) ending.

Masculine and neuter *a*-stem nouns have identical endings in the singular but differ in the plural. The neuter noun paradigm may involve either a short stem or a long stem (which is one containing a long vowel or diphthong in its root or a short vowel followed by two consonants). From the neuter long *a*-stem noun declension, which has a zero plural, a number of remnant forms survive into Modern English. These are nouns such as *deer* and *sheep*, with no distinction in form between singular and plural.

In addition to being the most frequent, *a*-stem nouns are the most important historically because it is from the *a*-stem declension that we have acquired both of our regular noun endings in Modern English:

1. our -*s* plural ending derives from the masculine nominative and accusative plural ending by a process of weakening of the vowel to schwa and eventual omission (or *syncope*) of the vowel (-*as* > -*es* > -*s*), and
2. our -'*s* possessive ending derives from the genitive singular ending, also by syncope (-*es* > -*s*).

The process of analogy, described in Chapter 3, explains how these became the regular endings, replacing the less common endings of the other noun classes. Any remnant plurals of the other noun classes are now considered irregular.

Table 7.3 The *a*-Stem Noun in Old English

	a-stem					
	masculine		*neuter – short stem*		*neuter – long stem*	
	singular	*plural*	*singular*	*plural*	*singular*	*plural*
nom.	cyning 'king'	cyning**as**	lim 'limb'	lim**u**	land 'land'	land
acc.	cyning	cyning**as**	lim	lim**u**	land	land
gen.	cyning**es**	cyning**a**	lim**es**	lim**a**	land**es**	land**a**
dat./instr.	cyning**e**	cyning**um**	lim**e**	lim**um**	land**e**	land**um**

Ō-*stem Nouns*

The ō-stem nouns are the largest class of feminine nouns (25 per cent of all nouns in Old English). Looking at the example given in Table 7.4, you will notice that the short and long stems differ only in the nominative singular. Note that the genitive and dative singular endings are the same and that the genitive is without -*s*. All feminine nouns in Modern English take the analogical plural ending, -*s*, from the dominant *a*-stem declension.

Table 7.4 The ō-Stem Noun in Old English

	ō-*stem*			
	short-stem		*long-stem*	
	singular	*plural*	*singular*	*plural*
nom.	talu 'tale'	tala	ecg 'edge'	ecga
acc.	tale	tala	ecge	ecga
gen.	tale	tala	ecge	ecga
dat./instr.	tale	talum	ecge	ecgum

N-*stem Nouns*

N-stem nouns are more frequently known by the name given them by Jacob Grimm: the *weak declension*. They include masculine, feminine, and neuter nouns. As you will notice from Table 7.5, the most common ending in this declension is -*an*, but note the three (or in the case of the neuter, the four) forms in each case that do not take this ending. In Middle English, the -*an* plural ending weakened to -*en* and increased in frequency. Added to nouns which did not originally belong to the weak declension, it began to compete with the -*es* of the *a*-stem as the regular plural ending. It lost out eventually and today is preserved intact in only one word, *oxen*. The *s*-less genitive of the *n*-stem is preserved today in only a few forms such as *Lady Day* (meaning 'Lady's day', a feast in celebration of the Virgin Mary).

Table 7.5 The *n*-Stem (Weak) Noun in Old English

	n-*stem (weak)*					
	masculine		*feminine*		*neuter*	
	singular	*plural*	*singular*	*plural*	*singular*	*plural*
nom.	nama 'name'	naman	heorte 'heart'	heortan	ēare 'ear'	ēaran
acc.	naman	naman	heortan	heortan	ēare	ēaran
gen.	naman	namena	heortan	heortena	ēaran	ēarena
dat./instr.	naman	namum	heortan	heortum	ēaran	ēarum

Root-Consonant Stem Nouns

The root-consonant stem declension consists of masculine and feminine nouns. As you can see in Table 7.6, root-consonant stem nouns are characterized by umlaut in three places: the dative singular, which in pre-Old English ended in *-i, and both nominative plural and accusative plural, which used to end *-iz. Both endings caused umlaut, which (as discussed in Chapter 6) involves the fronting and/ or raising of the root vowel. Umlauted plurals are preserved in a number of Modern English nouns, including *tooth/teeth*, *goose/geese*, *mouse/mice*, and *man/men*. However, many root-consonant stem nouns came to take the analogical (*a*-stem) plural ending *-s*; instead of *bēc*, we find *books*, instead of *frynd*, we find *friends*. The umlauted plural of *cow* (*cȳ* in OE) is preserved in Modern English in the poetic word *kine*, which has acquired a second plural ending, the *-n* of the weak declension. The ModE noun *breeches*—OE *brōc* (sg.), *brēc* (pl.)—also shows a double inflection: the umlauted plural of the root-consonant stem and the *-es* of the *a*-stem declension. This doubling, which happened in Middle English, may have occurred because the original inflection ceased to be recognized as such and was assumed instead to be part of the root. Speakers therefore added a recognizable plural inflection.

Table 7.6 The Root-Consonant Stem Noun in Old English

	root-consonant stem			
	masculine		*feminine*	
	singular	*plural*	*singular*	*plural*
nom.	fōt 'foot'	fēt	lūs 'louse'	lȳs 'lice'
acc.	fōt	fēt	lūs	lȳs
gen.	fōtes	fōta	lūse	lūsa
dat./instr.	fēt	fōtum	lȳs	lūsum

Minor Noun Classes

These four are not the only noun classes of Old English; a number of minor declensions also exist, such as the *z*-stem declension, consisting of only a few common neuter nouns such as those for 'egg', 'lamb', and 'child'. The *z*-stem nouns are declined like *a*-stem neuters, except in the plural, where an *-r-* appears between the root and the rest of the inflection. This *-r-* is preserved in ModE *children*, which is doubly marked with the ME addition of the weak *-en* plural. Another minor declension, the *r*-stem declension, consists of masculine and feminine nouns denoting family relationships, such as *brōðor* 'brother', *mōdor* 'mother', and *dohtor* 'daughter'. *R*-stem nouns have umlauted forms in the dative singular and no ending in the genitive. The ModE form *brethren* has acquired both an umlauted plural of the root-consonant declension and the -*en* plural of the weak declension. From the beginning of the OE period, nouns belonging to the minor classes tended to be subsumed by the more dominant *a*-stem pattern.

Look again at the paradigms for the major noun classes in Old English. There are four generalizations that we can make about the inflectional ending of OE nouns:

- The genitive plural ending is always -*a*.
- The dative plural ending is always -*um*.
- The nominative and accusative plurals are always the same.
- The nominative and accusative singulars of neuter nouns are always the same.

These points of consistency help a bit in learning the endings.

Exercise 7.2 Nouns

1. Identify the class and gender of the following declined nouns.

   a.

	_____	_____	_____
sg. nom.	horn 'horn'	heorte 'heart'	fēond 'foe'
acc.	horn	heortan	fēond
gen.	hornes	heortan	fēondes
dat.	horne	heortan	fīend
pl. nom.	hornas	heortan	fīend
acc.	hornas	heortan	fīend
gen.	horna	heortena	fēonda
dat.	hornum	heortum	fēondum

   b.

	_____	_____	_____
sg. nom.	ǣl 'eel'	sacu 'strife'	bæð 'bath'
acc.	ǣl	sace	bæð
dat.	ǣle	sace	bæðe
pl. nom.	ǣlas	saca	baðu
acc.	ǣlas	saca	baðu
gen.	ǣla	saca	baða
dat.	ǣlum	sacum	baðum

2. The largest class of nouns in Old English, comprising approximately 60 per cent of all OE nouns, is called the *a*-stem class. Why? Which genders does this class contain?

    _____

    _____

    _____

3. Modern English has few noun inflections left. Identify them and describe their functions. Which of these inflections derive from the OE *a*-stem noun class?

    _____

    _____

    _____

4. How does *lady* in the ModE words *ladybug* and *ladyfinger* preserve a genitive form?

    _____

    _____

    _____

Demonstratives, Adjectives, and Adverbs

Demonstratives

There are two sets of demonstratives, one pointing to a referent close to the speaker (*this/these*) and one to a referent further away (*that/those*). They have a *deictic* function, which is a way of saying that their meaning depends on the speech situation and encodes the speaker's perspective. (Some other forms with deictic meaning are *here/there*, *then/now*, and *I/you*.) Demonstratives may function as either adjectives modifying a noun (*this book is mine*) or as pronouns standing in place of a noun (*this is my book*). In Modern English, demonstratives indicate the number of the noun they modify (*this book* versus *these books*), while in Old English, they also indicate the gender and case of the noun they modify. The paradigm of the 'that' demonstrative in Old English is given Table 7.7a, and the paradigm of the 'this' demonstrative is given in Table 7.7b. The demonstrative has a distinctive instrumental, but these forms have been recorded only in the masculine and neuter singular.

While the form of a noun in Old English does not indicate its gender, the demonstrative which accompanies it usually does (at least in the singlar). Thus, in the

Table 7.7 Demonstratives in Old English

a) that

	masculine	neuter	feminine	plural
nom.	se[a]	þæt	sēo	þā
acc.	þone	þæt	þā	þā
gen.	þæs	þæs	þǣre	þāra
dat.	þǣm	þǣm	þǣre	þǣm
instr.	þȳ	þȳ		

b) this

	masculine	neuter	feminine	plural
nom.	þes	þis	þēos	þās
acc.	þisne	þis	þās	þās
gen.	þisses	þisses	þisse	þissa
dat.	þissum	þissum	þisse	þissum
instr.	þȳs	þȳs		

[a]The demonstrative *se* has a long vowel when it is stressed but a short vowel when it is used as an unstressed modifier.

following examples, the demonstrative tells us that *cyning* is masculine, *heorte* is feminine, and *lim* is neuter:

> *þone cyning* 'that king'
> *þisse heortan* 'of this heart'
> *þæt lim* 'that limb'

The inflection of demonstratives bears more similarity to the inflection of the pronoun than to that of the noun, but a number of generalizations can be made concerning the two demonstratives:

- The genitive plural ends in -*a*.
- The dative plural ends in -*m*.
- The dative singular of the masculine and neuter also ends in -*m*.
- The accusative singular of the masculine ends in -*ne*.
- The genitive and dative singular of the feminine are the same.
- The nominative and accusative singular of the neuter are the same.
- The nominative and accusative plural are the same.
- Gender is indicated only in the singular.

From these many inflected forms, Modern English has retained the nominative neuter singular of each demonstrative (*þæt* > *that*, *þis* > *this*). With certain analogical additions it has also retained the nominative and accusative plural of the first demonstrative (*þā* > *those*) and the nominative masculine singular of the second demonstrative (*þes* > *these*).

Our definite article *the* grew out of the nominative singular masculine of the first demonstrative, *se* (later *þe*). This happened in Middle English, along with the emergence of the indefinite article, *a/an*, which developed from the numeral *ān*, meaning 'one'. As any non-native speaker of the language knows, the rules for the use of articles in Modern English are complex, and one or another of the articles is generally obligatory; in Old English, however, no article is required. We cannot be certain exactly when the demonstrative and numeral began to serve as articles, but it is probably best to translate the first OE demonstrative as 'that' rather than 'the', and *ān* as 'a certain one', not 'a/an'.

Exercise 7.3 Demonstratives

1. Give the number, gender, and case for the following OE demonstratives.
    Indicate duplicate possibilities.

	Number	Gender	Case
a. *se*	_____	_____	_____
b. *þā*	_____	_____	_____
c. *þǣre*	_____	_____	_____
d. *þās*	_____	_____	_____
e. *þissum*	_____	_____	_____
f. *þæt*	_____	_____	_____
g. *þisne*	_____	_____	_____
h. *þȳs*	_____	_____	_____

2. Give the OE demonstrative pronoun that fits each of the following desriptions:

    a. masculine accusative singular of *that* _____

    b. neuter genitive singular of *this* _____

    c.   feminine dative singular of *this* _____

    d.   masculine dative singular of *that* _____

    e.   dative plural of *that* _____

3. a.   Which OE demonstratives have survived into Modern English? Give the form and description of the OE source.

_____

_____

    b.   What information can a demonstrative often give you about the noun it accompanies that the noun may not give about itself?

_____

    c.   The ModE articles *the* and *a/an* developed in Middle English from which OE sources?

_____

_____

Adjectives

Old English adjectives are also inflected to show the gender, number, and case of the noun that they modify. Recall from Chapter 5 that there are two different sets of adjective endings, the strong declension (inherited from Proto-Indo-European) and the weak declension (a Germanic innovation). These inflections occur in different contexts. The weak declension is used when the noun is accompanied by any other modifier, such as a demonstrative (e.g. *that large book*), a numeral (e.g. *two large books*), or a possessive adjective (e.g. *my large book*). It is also used when the adjective is in the comparative or superlative degree (e.g. *larger book, largest book*) or appears in direct address (e.g. *John, dear son, you . . .*). The strong declension is used when the noun is not otherwise modified or when the adjective follows the verb *to be* (e.g. *That book is large*). These different contexts of use are a result of the fact that the weak declension communicates definite reference (e.g. *those large books* refers to specific or particular large books), whereas the strong declension communicates indefinite reference (e.g. *large books* refers to any large books). This complicated system has been completely lost over time; none of the adjectival endings, either from the weak or the strong declension, live on in Modern English.

The weak adjectival endings (see Table 7.8a) are very similar to the weak noun endings. The only difference between them is in the genitive plural (which may end in -*ra*). The strong adjectival endings (see Table 7.8b) are rather like the demonstrative or pronominal endings. You will find striking similarities: -*ne* in the masculine accusative singular, -*um* in the masculine and neuter dative singular, -*re* in the feminine genitive and dative singular, and -*ra* in the genitive plural.

Table 7.8 Weak and Strong Adjective Endings in Old English

a) weak				
	masculine	*neuter*	*feminine*	*plural*
nom.	-a	-e	-e	-an
acc.	-an	-e	-an	-an
gen.	-an	-an	-an	-ra, -ena
dat.	-an	-an	-an	-um
instr.	-an	-an	-an	
b) strong				
	masculine	*neuter*	*feminine*	*plural*
nom.	—	—	-u	-e (masc.), -u (neut.), -a (fem.)
acc.	-ne	—	-e	-e (masc.), -u (neut.), -a (fem.)
gen.	-es	-es	-re	-ra
dat.	-um	-um	-re	-um
instr.	-e	-e	-re	

Table 7.9 provides some examples of fully inflected noun phrases showing the different types of adjective endings. The class of the noun has nothing to do with the type of adjectival ending; a weak noun can occur with an adjective bearing a strong ending (see *gōd eare* in Table 7.9).

In addition to endings indicating the gender, case, and number of the noun, adjectives are also inflected in Old English (and in Modern English) to show degree: positive (e.g. *big*), comparative (*bigger*), and superlative (*biggest*). While the positive is unmarked in Old English, the comparative generally has an -*ra* (deriving form -*ora*) and the superlative has -*ost*; these survive as -*er* and -*est* in Modern English.

Some OE adjectival comparative endings were *-ira and *-ist in pre-Old English, which appear as -*er* and -*est* in Old English. In such cases, we also notice the effects of umlaut on the comparative and superlative forms. Table 7.10 shows two examples

Table 7.9 Examples of Fully Inflected Old English Noun Phrases

modifier + adjective (weak ending) + noun		
masculine	*neuter*	*feminine*
þǣm gōdum cyningum	þǣm gōdan lande	þǣre gōdan heortan
'to those good kings'	'to that good land'	'of/to that good heart'
[dat. pl.]	[dat. sg.]	[gen.-dat. sg.]
þone gōdan cyning	þæs gōdan landes	sēo gōde talu
'that good king'	'of that good land'	'that good tale'
[acc. sg.]	[gen. sg.]	[nom. sg.]
þāra gōdena/ra namena	þæt gōde ēare	þā gōdan lȳs
'of those good names'	'that good ear'	'those good lice'
[gen. pl.]	[nom.-acc. sg.]	[nom.-acc. pl.]
Ø + adjective (strong ending) + noun		
masculine	*neuter*	*feminine*
gōdum cyningum	gōdum lande	gōdre heortan
'to good kings'	'to good land'	'of/to good heart'
[dat. pl.]	[dat. sg.]	[gen.-dat. sg.]
gōdne cyning	gōdes landes	gōdu talu
'good king'	'of good land'	'good tale'
[acc. sg.]	[gen. sg.]	[nom. sg.]
gōdra namena	gōd eare	gōda lȳs
'of good names'	'good ear'	'good lice'
[gen. pl.]	[nom.-acc. sg.]	[nom.-acc. pl.]

each of the regular and umlauted varieties. Many umlauted forms became regularized over time (e.g. *strong/stronger/strongest*—but compare *strength*), though we preserve the umlauted *elder* and *eldest* in limited contexts.

Old English has some adjectival paradigms in which the different inflected forms not only show different endings but are formed from different roots. This is called a suppletive, or mixed, paradigm. Suppletion occurs with certain very common adjectives (and, as we will see below, verbs). Looking at the examples given in Table 7.11, you can see that the ModE suppletive paradigms *good/better/best* and *much/more/*

Table 7.10 Degrees of the Old English Adjective

positive	comparative	superlative
earm 'poor'	earmra	earm**ost**
lēof 'dear'	lēofra	lēof**ost**
grēat 'great'	grȳtra	grȳ**test**
strang 'strong'	strengra	streng**est**

most are direct descendants of the Old English forms (*sēlra* and *sēlest* have been lost). The Modern *little* has developed regular comparative and superlative forms by analogy (*littler, littlest*), while *less* and *least* exist independently. Another example of such a development is OE *nēah* 'near', *nēarra* 'nearer', and *nȳhst* 'next', which gained an analogical superlative form, *nearest*, while *next* has left the paradigm but continues to exist. Note that comparative and superlative adjectives carry two inflectional endings: following the ending indicating degree is the relevant weak adjectival ending.

In the phrases below, notice the sequence of elements is demonstrative + adjective-comparative/superlative ending-weak ending + noun:

> *se dolra cyning* 'that more foolish king' (nom.)
> *þone dolran cyning* (acc.)
> *þæs dolran cyninges* (gen.)
> *þǣm dolran cyninge* (dat.)
> *þȳ dolran cyninge* (instr.)

Table 7.11 Suppletive Adjectives in Old English

positive	comparative	superlative
gōd 'good'	betra/sēlra 'better'	betst/sēlest 'best'
lȳtel 'little'	lǣssa 'less'	lǣst 'least'
micel 'much, many'	māra 'more'	mǣst 'most'

Adverbs

Although adverbs belong to the verbal system (see below), we include them here because they are generally formed from adjectives or nouns. The old instrumental ending, *-e* (indicating *means*), may be added to adjectives: e.g. *dēop* 'deep', *dēope* 'deeply'. Over time, the *-e* ending was lost. Thus, *deep* and *slow* are historically valid adverbs, (as in *still waters run deep*) but since people perceive them as incorrect, they conventionally receive the regular ModE adverbial ending, *-ly*. Another means of forming adverbs in Old English is the combining of *-līc* (which forms adjectives) with *-e*: e.g. *heofon* 'heaven', *heofonlīc* 'heavenly', *heofonlīce* 'in a heavenly manner'; indeed, *-līce* is the source of our *-ly*. Adverbs form their comparatives with *-or* and their superlatives with *-ost* or *-est*, as in *oft* 'often', *oftor* 'more often', *oftost* 'most often'.

Exercise 7.4 Adjectives and Adverbs

1. There are two classes of adjectives in Old English. What are they called, and in what circumstances are they used?

   _____

   _____

   _____

2. Give the case, gender, number, and class for each of the following inflected adjectives. Note that there may be multiple possibilities for some; identify these as well.

	Case	Gender	Number	Class
a. *gōdra*	_____	_____	_____	_____
b. *heardes*	_____	_____	_____	_____
c. *untrumum*	_____	_____	_____	_____
d. *unforhtne*	_____	_____	_____	_____
e. *ǣmtige*	_____	_____	_____	_____
f. *mǣru*	_____	_____	_____	_____
g. *wīsan*	_____	_____	_____	_____

3. As in Modern English, adjectives in Old English were inflected for degree: positive, comparative, and superlative. Supply the missing forms in the following paradigms.

	Positive	Comparative	Superlative
a.	*earm* 'poor'	_____	_____
b.	_____	_____	*lēofost* 'dearest'
c.	_____	*dolra* 'more foolish'	_____
d.	*dēop* 'deep'	_____	_____
e.	_____	*sārra* 'more painful'	_____
f.	_____	_____	*sārlicost* 'saddest'

Agreement

We have already seen agreement between adjectives and nouns in examples such as *gōdes landes*. The phenomenon is widespread in Old English. Agreement, or concord, is a process in which the grammatical information expressed in one form must be repeated in other forms which accompany it; that is, if one form expresses masculine gender, singular number, and nominative case, then any form related to it must make the corresponding distinctions. The forms are then said to agree in gender, number, and case. Agreement in Modern English is limited because we rely on word order and prepositions for grammatical information. We find remnants today, however:

- in number between demonstratives and nouns, e.g. *this dog* (sing.), *those dogs* (pl.);
- in person and number between subjects and verbs, e.g. *he is* (3rd p., sing.), *they are* (3rd p., pl.);
- in person and number between plural nouns and their pronouns, e.g. *the men . . . they* (3rd p., pl.); and
- in person, number, and gender between singular nouns and their pronouns, e.g. *the boy . . . he* (3rd p., sing., masc.), *the girl . . . she* (3rd p., sing., fem.).

In contrast, agreement in Old English is widespread:

- demonstratives and adjectives agree with the nouns they modify in number, gender, and case, e.g. *under þæm cealdan wætere* 'under that cold water' (sing., neut., dat.);
- nouns and their pronouns agree in number, gender, and person, e.g. *se hwæl . . . he* 'the whale . . . he' (3rd p., sing., masc.), *sēo cwēn . . . hēo* 'the woman . . . she' (3rd p., sing., fem.); and
- verbs agree with their subjects in person and number, e.g. *ic eom* 'I am' (1st p., sing.), *þu eart* 'you are' (2nd p., sing.).

Demonstratives, with their many distinct forms, tend to be the most specific indicators of the gender of the nouns they modify. Inflected adjectives, especially in the weak declension, are less distinct and therefore not as reliable for this purpose. Because agreement shows us what modifies what, the word order of Old English is freer, allowing demonstratives and adjectives to be separated from the nouns they modify.

When there is a conflict between natural gender and grammatical gender, we occasionally find that agreement between nouns and their pronouns is violated in Old English. For example, we might find *þæt mægden . . . hēo* 'that maiden . . . she', not *hit* 'it' as expected, since *mægden* is grammatically neuter; or we may find *sē weall . . . hit* 'the wall . . . it', not *se* 'he' as expected, since *weall* is grammatically masculine. When such violations occur, we can conclude that the OE system of grammatical gender is beginning to be replaced by a system of natural gender.

Case Usage

Case usage in any inflected language is complex because a particular case may be used for a number of unrelated functions, or the same function may be indicated by more than one case. The complexity is in part due to the tendency for distinct Indo-European cases to fall together in the Germanic languages. (The Gmc. nominative case subsumed the nominative and vocative cases, and the Gmc. dative case subsumed the dative, ablative, locative, and instrumental cases.)

Recall that cases indicate the role of the noun in the sentence, with the primary functions as follows: the nominative marks the subject, the accusative marks the direct object, the genitive marks the possessor, the dative marks the indirect object, and the instrumental marks the means or manner of the action. However, as Table 7.12 below indicates, each case has additional functions in Old English.[1]

One can still attempt a number of generalizations:

- The objects of most verbs are expressed in the accusative case; some verbs require the genitive or dative case. The dative is used especially in situations that might be translated with a 'to' in Modern English (e.g. *derian* 'do harm to'). Similarly, adjectives that would be followed by *to* if translated into Modern English (e.g. *gelīcost* 'most like to') may take their complements in the dative case; these generally indicate nearness or emotional relationship.
- Prepositions expressing movement in space or time take their objects in the accusative, while those expressing position in space or time take their objects in the dative. The same preposition, such as *on*, may take a dative object when it expresses position ('in, on') and an accusative object when it expresses movement ('into').
- Any noun inflected in a non-nominative case can serve as an adverb. The adverbial accusative expresses extent of time or space (as in ModE *I slept all afternoon*) while the adverbial dative expresses a point in time or space (as in ModE *I saw him last night*). The adverbial genitive generally expresses frequency. It is preserved in Modern English in expressions such as *he works nights*, although the genitive is now often reanalyzed as a plural. The sound [s] found in *once, twice, thrice,* and *since* is also the adverbial genitive ending.

In addition to these generalizations, we need to take note of some additional details, as shown in Table 7.12 and discussed below.

The genitive has a number of uses unrelated to possession. The distinction between subjective and objective genitive becomes important in ambiguous ModE expressions like *John's murder*, which might imply either 'John murdered someone' (with a relation of *John's* to *murder* like one of a subject to a verb, hence a subjective genitive), or 'someone murdered John' (in which the relation of *John's* to *murder* is like one of an object to a verb, hence an objective genitive). The genitive of measure expresses some sort of measurement or extent, as in ModE expressions such as *six foot tall* or *two month long*, where what appears to be a singular (*foot, month*) is actually an old genitive plural with loss of the final *-a*. The partitive geni-

---

1 Most of the OE examples of case given in this section are taken from Quirk and Wrenn (1957:59–68).

Table 7.12 Case Usage in Old English

nominative	
subject of a sentence	**se cyning** ofslægen wæs 'the king was slain'
subject complement following a linking verb such as to be	hē is **se cyning** 'he is the king'
noun in direct address	ðū **iunga mann** 'you, young man'
accusative	
direct object of most verbs	hē ofslog **þone ealdormann** 'he killed the ruler'
object of some prepositions	þurh/geond/oþ **hine** 'through/throughout/up to him'
adverbial accusative	**ealle þa hwīle** '(for) the whole time' **þone winter** '(during) that winter'
subject of an infinitive (also object of the verb)	ne hȳrde ic **guman** þingian snotorlicor 'I have not heard a man (to) speak more wisely'
genitive	
possessive genitive	**hira** scipu 'their ships'
subjective genitive	**Grendles** dæda 'Grendel's deeds'
objective genitive	**folces** weard 'protector of the people'
genitive of measure	**þrēora mīla** brad 'three miles broad'
partitive genitive	**hūsa** sēlest 'the best of houses, the best house', sum hund **scipa** 'a hundred (of) ships', fela **tācna** 'many of the signs'
adverbial genitive	**dæges** ond **nihtes** 'day and night' **þæs** 'thereafter'
object of some verbs	benæman/wēnan **drēames** 'deprive of/expect joy'
object of a few prepositions	wið **ðæs hrōfes** 'toward the roof'
dative	
indirect object	he **him** hringas geaf 'he gave him rings'
object of some verbs	derian/miltsian/sceððan **him** 'harm/pity/injure him'

Table 7.12 Case Usage in Old English—*Continued*

complement of adjectives	lēof/lāð/nēah **hire** 'dear to/hateful to/near her'
object of some prepositions	æfter/æt/bi/on **þæm** 'after/at/beside/in that'
adverbial dative	**sumum dæge** '(on) a certain day' **hwīlum** 'at times'
instrumental	
means or manner	**handum** gebroden 'woven by hand'
accompaniment	**lytle werede** '(with) a little company'
comparison	**mærða þȳ** mā 'the more glories'
cause	**hwī** 'why', **þȳ** 'therefore'

tive expresses the whole in respect to a part, a construction used regularly in Old English with superlatives; with numerals larger than one; and with *fela* meaning 'many'. We no longer use the partitive with basic numerals (hence *a hundred ships*, not *a hundred of ships* but cf. *hundreds of ships*); otherwise, the partitive genitive is always expressed in Modern English with an *of*-phrase: *two of the members, the best of the group, many of the workers.*

The instrumental case, which is formally conflated with the dative in most instances in Old English (only a few distinct instrumentals exist in the demonstrative, pronoun, and adjective), covers a range of meanings, including means, manner, cause, and accompaniment, roughly translatable by *with* in Modern English.

Exercise 7.5 Agreement and Case Usage

A. Agreement

1. There are only a few occasions in Modern English where agreement, or concord, occurs. Describe them and give examples of each.

    _____

    _____

    _____

    _____

2. Decline the following *a*-stem noun and accompanying modifier:

    þis earme folc (neut.) 'this poor people'

    sg. nom.   _____

    acc.   _____

    gen.   _____

    dat.   _____

    instr.   _____

    pl. nom.   _____

    acc.   _____

    gen.   _____

    dat.   _____

    instr.   _____

B. Case Usage

    Identify the case and use for each italicized word in the passage given below from Bede's *Ecclesiastical History of the English People* (Book 2, Chapter 10) (Miller 1890:134–6).

Þyslic *me* is gesewen, þu *cyning*, þis andwearde *lif* manna on *eorðan*
Thus by me is seen, Thou King, this present life of men on earth

to wiþmetenesse þære *tide*, þe *us* uncuð is, swalic swa þu æt swæsendum
(in) comparison (to) that time that (to) us unknown is: as if Thou at banquets

sitte mid *þinum ealdormannum* 7 *þegnum* on *wintertide*, 7 sie fyr onælæd
were sitting with your noblemen and thanes in wintertime, and is (the) fire kindled

7 þin heall gewyrmed, 7 hit rine 7 sniwe 7 styrme ute; cume an spearwa
and your hall warmed, and it rains and snows and storms out(side); comes a sparrow

7 hrædlice þæt *hus* þurhfleo, cume þurh oþre duru in, þurh oþre ut gewite.
and swiftly the house flies through, comes through one door in, through (an)other departs.

Hwæt he on þa *tid,* þe he inne biŏ, ne biþ hrinen mid þy *storme* þæs *wintres;*
Thus, he in that time that he within is, not touched with the storm of the winter;

ac þæt biŏ an *eagan* bryhtm 7 þæt læsste fæc, ac he sona of *wintra* on þone
but that is one blink of an eye and the least interval, but he immediately from winter to

winter eft cymeþ. Swa þonne þis monna lif to medmiclum *fæce* ætyweþ;
the winter again comes. So then this of men life as (a) brief space appears;

hwæt þær foregange, oŏŏe hwæt þær æfterfylige, *we* ne cunnun.
what there goes before, or what there follows after, we (do) not know.

a. *me*   _____

b. *cyning*   _____

c. *lif*   _____

d. *eorŏan*   _____

e. *tide*   _____

f. *us*   _____

g. *þinum ealdormannum* _____

h. *wintertide* _____

i. *hus*   _____

j. *tid*   _____

k. *storme*   _____

l. *wintres*   _____

m. *eagan*   _____

n. *wintra*   _____

o. *winter*   _____

p. *fæce*   _____

q. *we*   _____

The Verbal System

To study verbs, scholars identify their principal parts, the basic forms from which the verb is inflected. In Modern English, the principal parts of a verb are the infinitive (e.g. *to walk*), the past tense (e.g. *I walked*), and the past participle (e.g. *I have walked*). Other examples include *sing/sang/sung* and *break/broke/broken*. Often the past tense and the past participle forms are the same, giving us only two distinct forms (as in the case of *bring/brought/brought*), but occasionally there may be three distinct forms (as in the case of *bite/bit/bitten*) or only one distinct form (as in the case of *put/put/put*).

Old English has four principal parts for the strong verb (see Table 7.14):

(1) the infinitive (which is also the present stem),
(2) the first/third-person singular preterit indicative (what we will call the past singular),
(3) the second-person singular and plural preterit (the past plural), and
(4) the past participle.

In OE weak verbs, the singular past and the plural past (see Table 7.13) had the same form; thus, it is necessary to list only three principal parts. Over time (in ME and EModE), there has been a tendency for the singular past and the plural past of the strong verb to have a common form as well.

Verb Classes

Like the nouns, the verbs of Old English fall into several classes. There are four major types: *weak*, *strong*, *preterit-present*, and *anomalous*.

Weak Verbs

The majority of verbs in Old English (perhaps 75 per cent) are weak, although these verbs are not necessarily the most common ones. As we saw in Chapter 5, weak verbs were an innovation of the Germanic languages, forming their preterit with a dental suffix that became the productive pattern for new verbs added to the language. Many weak verbs are derived in Germanic from other parts of speech (nouns, adjectives, or strong verbs) by the addition of a derivational suffix *-jan. As you might expect, the *-j- of this suffix caused umlaut of the root vowel, as in the following examples:

N > V *dōm* 'judgment' + *-jan > *dēman* 'to judge'

ADJ > V *cūð* 'known' + *-jan > *cȳðan* 'to make known'

V (strong) > V (weak) *dranc* (past) 'drank' + *-jan > *drencan* 'to drench'

The addition of the suffix often had the effect of making the verb causative in meaning; for example, if one adds *-jan to the adjective *hāl* 'whole, hale', one derives the causative verb *hǣlan*, meaning 'to cause to be hale' or 'to heal'. This derivational process accounts for the non-causative and causative pairs in Modern English *sit* and *set* 'cause to sit', *rise* and *raise* 'cause to rise', *fall* and *fell* 'cause to fall', and *lie* and *lay* 'cause to lie'.

Table 7.13 gives examples of the principal parts of OE weak verbs. Note that *-an* marks the infinitive, and that the preterit and past participle differ from the infinitive by the addition of a dental suffix (*-ed, -od,* or, with syncope, *-t* or *-d*). The final *-e* in the preterit is a personal ending which will be discussed in the next section. A frequent distinguishing mark of the past participle, meanwhile, is its *ge-* prefix.

Weak verbs fall into three classes (see Table 7.13). The weak class I is the most common. The vowel changes in the third and fourth examples of weak class I verbs ('to bring' *bringan/brōhte/gebrōht* and 'to seek' *sēcan/sōhte/gesōht*) result from the operation of umlaut (see Chapter 6) in the present tense forms. Most of these seemingly irregular weak verbs have been preserved in Modern English, e.g. *buy/bought/bought* and *think/thought/thought*. Class II weak verbs are distinguished from class I weak verbs by two features: an *-i-* in the infinitive and an *-o-* in the preterit and past participle. Class III consists of a few common verbs which despite some irregularities do show a dental suffix in the preterit and past participle, as in classes I and II.

Table 7.13 Weak Verbs in Old English

class	infinitive	1ˢᵗ, 3ʳᵈ p. sg. pret. ind.	past participle
I	dēman 'to judge'	dēmede	gedēmed
	lǣran 'to teach'	lǣrde	gelǣred
	bringan 'to bring'	brōhte	gebrōht
	sēcan 'to seek'	sōhte	gesōht
II	leornian 'to learn'	leornode	geleornod
	clipian 'to call'	clipode	geclipod
	folgian 'to follow'	folgode	gefolgod
III	habban 'to have'	hæfde	gehæfd
	secgan 'to say'	sægde	gesægd
	libban 'to live'	lifde	gelifd

Strong Verbs

Many of the most common Old English verbs are strong. As mentioned, strong verbs form their tenses by the IE process of ablaut, or vowel gradation. In Germanic, the ablaut grades of PIE (*e*-grade, *o*-grade. and zero grade) become regularized in the strong verbs in a number of basic patterns which underlie the seven classes of strong verbs (see Table 7.14).

Table 7.14 Strong Verbs in Old English

class/verb	infinitive	past singular	past plural	past participle
1	ī	ā	i	i
'rise'	rīsan	rās	rison	gerisen
'cut'	snīðan	snāð	snidon	gesniden
2	ēo/ū	ēa	u	o
'rue'	hrēowan	hrēaw	hruwon	gehrowen
'dive'	dūfan	dēaf	dufon	gedofen
'choose'	cēosan	cēas	curon	gecoren
3	i	a	u	u
'drink'	drincan	dranc	druncon	gedruncen
	e/eo	ea	u	o
'help'	helpan	healp	hulpon	geholpen
'die'	steorfan	stearf	sturfon	gestorfen
4	e	æ	ǣ	o
'bear'	beran	bær	bǣron	geboren
'steal'	stelan	stæl	stǣlon	gestolen
5	e	æ	ǣ	e
'avenge'	wrecan	wræc	wrǣcon	gewrecen
'sleep'	swefan	swæf	swǣfon	geswefen
6	a	ō	ō	a
'go'	wadan	wōd	wōdon	gewaden
'stand'	standan	stōd	stōdon	gestanden
7	(variable)	ēo/ē	ēo/ē	(variable)
'know'	cnāwan	cnēow	cnēowon	gecnāwen
'weep'	wēpan	wēop	wēopon	gewōpen
'sleep'	slǣpan	slēp	slēpon	geslǣpen

It might help to observe that class 3 has the structure *e* + nasal or liquid + consonant, class 4 has the structure *e* + nasal or liquid, and class 5 has the structure *e* + consonant (although the *e* does not always appear in the attested forms of the infinitive). Note, too, the breaking of *e* > *eo* and *a* > *ea* in some class 3 verb forms. Certain classes have subclasses showing slightly different vowel patterns; these are the result of phonological changes in Old English. The effects of Verner's Law, which you may recall (from Chapter 5) involves an alternation between *ð* and *d* as well as *s* and *r*, can be seen in the following verbs:

snīðan	*snāð*	*snidon*	*gesniden*
cēosan	*cēas*	*curon*	*gecoren*

The past plural and past participle have different medial consonants than the infinitive and past singular because of where the accent originally fell in Indo-European. The verb *standan* in class 6 likewise shows a difference in consonants; it contains a 'nasal infix' in the present form, the sole remnant in English of this ancient kind of inflection. Class 7 vowel gradation is quite irregular; the class is best recognized by the *ēo/ē* pattern in the preterit.

In subsequent chapters, we will look at the fate of the strong verbs in the history of English. Although many have remained strong, there has been a gradual attrition to the class of weak verbs. Even in those that have remained strong, the distinction between singular and plural past has been lost (except for the past tense of the verb *to be*).

Preterit-Present Verbs

A small but important group in Old English are the preterit-present verbs. These were all originally strong, but their preterit forms came to serve as present tense forms (hence the name of this class). This reanalysis necessitated a new preterit which was formed using the productive dental suffix. Look at the principal parts of some preterit-present verbs:

	infinitive	present	past
'may'	*magan*	*mæg/magon*	*meahte*
'can'	*cunnan*	*can/cunnon*	*cūðe*
'shall'	*sculan*	*sceal/sculon*	*sceolde*

Note the two forms of the present: the present tense was formed from the old strong preterit; therefore it retained the distinction between singular and plural found in the past of strong verbs. Because this sort of complexity was anomalous in the present, these two forms were reduced to one over time. The descendants of the preterit-present verbs are the modal auxiliaries (or helping verbs) of Modern English. The exact status of the preterit-present verbs in Old English is a matter of dispute, but they seem to have functioned more often as main verbs than as auxiliaries. Furthermore, they have undergone considerable change in meaning; for example, *may*, which originally expressed physical ability, now expresses permission or possibility.

Anomalous Verbs

The last to be discussed are those irregular verbs classified as anomalous, the verbs *be*, *do*, *go*, and *will*. These are extremely common and hence preserve their irregularities even in Modern English. In the case of the verb *be*, the present tense alone is derived from three IE roots (and so is called a 'suppletive' verb):

> *es 'to be' gives the OE forms *eom* ('am'), *is*, *sindon*, *sind*, *sint*
> *er 'to set in motion' gives the OE form *eart* ('art')
> *bheu 'to exist, grow' gives the OE forms *bēo*, *bist*, *biδ*, *bēoδ*, *bēon*

The past tense is formed with the class 5 strong verb *wesan/wǣre/wǣron*. *Was/were* are the only verb forms in Modern English to preserve the alternation of *-s* and *-r* resulting from Verner's Law.

The verb *go* is also suppletive in Old English, appearing as *gān* in the present and *ēode/ēodon* in the past. The verb remains suppletive in Modern English, but the past tense is formed with yet another verb, OE *wendan* 'to turn'. *Dōn/dyde* ('do', 'did') remains irregular in Modern English. Although anomalous in Old English, *will* has now joined the class of modal auxiliaries, in part because of its meaning of intention.

The Grammatical Categories of the Verbal System

The Old English verbs are inflected to show person and number, tense and mood. We have discussed person and number in OE pronouns. Like the pronouns, the verbs show first, second, and third person in the singular and generic person in the plural. Because a verb agrees with the subject of the sentence in person and number, subjects are often simply omitted.

The grammatical categories of tense and mood are unique to verbs. Recall that tense is an indication of the time of an event in relation to the moment of speaking and that, like all the Germanic languages, Old English indicates only two tenses, present and preterit. The preterit tense is used to express past action in Old English, just as we use it in Modern English. Old English uses the present tense differently, however; depending on the context, it may express habitual action, current ongoing action, or future action, unlike Modern English which relies on three distinct forms; thus, OE *ic helpe* corresponds to ModE *I help*, *I am helping*, or *I will help*.

In Chapter 5 we saw that Germanic has three moods: indicative, subjunctive, and imperative. Indicative is the mood of fact, used in making statements and asking questions. The imperative, a mood of non-fact, is used in making direct commands, expressing the speaker's desire or wish for the hearer (an implied *you*) to perform an action. Old English has an imperative inflection, while Modern English relies on syntax alone, e.g. *Shut the window!* The subjunctive, also a mood of non-fact, expresses possibility, probability, desire, wish, and obligation. In Old English, a simple inflection of the verb indicates these notions. The more analytic Modern English usually requires the use of modal auxiliaries such as *can, may,* and *must*:

> *God ure helpe* '(may) God help us' (Ælfric's *Lives of Saints*)
> *cild . . . sie gefulwad* 'a child must be baptised' (*Laws of Alfred-Ine*)
> *þeah man swa ne wene* 'although one might not think so' (Wulfstan's *Homilies*)

Modern English also retains a few inflected subjunctives, usually identifiable by the lack of a third-person singular present *-s* ending (e.g. *Long live the Queen*), the use of *be* for *is* (e.g. *Far be it from me*), or *were* appearing instead of *was* (e.g. *If I were rich*).

Inflectional Endings of the Verb

The inflectional endings, which show person, number, tense, and mood, differ for the strong and the different classes of weak verbs. Consider the three following examples, with their principal parts listed:

Weak (class I)	*trymman* 'to strengthen'	*trymede*	*getrymed*
Weak (class II)	*bodian* 'to announce'	*bodode*	*gebodod*
Strong (class I)	*drīfan* 'to drive'	*drāf* (sg.) *drifon* (pl.)	*gedrifen*

Table 7.15 shows how the inflected forms of these weak and strong verbs are derived from the principal parts. Here the endings indicate the combined notions of person, number, and mood. For the present tense forms of all verbs, we take the root of the first principal part, the infinitive (e.g. *drīfan* minus the *-an* ending) and then we attach the different personal endings highlighted in the table:

> *drīf* + *eð* (ind.) 'he/she/it drives'
> *drif* + *en* (subj.) 'we/you/they might drive'

(Incidentally, the doubling of the *m* in the verb *trymman* results from a less far-reaching phonological change called 'gemination'; see Cassidy and Ringler [1971:21].)

The present indicative endings for weak and strong verbs are basically the same, except that weak class II often has an *-i-* in the inflectional ending, as in *bodie* (where the weak class I has a doubled consonant). In the second and third persons of strong verbs, the *-e-* often undergoes syncope, as in *drīfst* and *drīfð,* and there is umlaut, where possible, as in *hilpst, hilpð* (from *helpan*) due to a prehistoric Germanic *-i. (You will notice that neither the strong nor the weak verbs of Old

Table 7.15 Inflectional Endings of the Verb in Old English

			weak (class I)	*weak (class II)*	*strong*
pres. ind.	sg.	1	trymme	bodie	drīfe
		2	trymest	bodast	drīf(e)st
		3	trymeð	bodað	drīf(e)ð
	pl.		trymmað	bodiað	drīfað
pres. subj.	sg.		trymme	bodie	drīfe
	pl.		trymmen	bodien	drīfen
pret. ind.	sg.	1	trymede	bodode	drāf
		2	trymedest	bododest	drife
		3	trymede	bodode	drāf
	pl.		trymedon	bododon	drifon
pret. subj.	sg.		trymede	bodode	drife
	pl.		trymeden	bododen	drifen
imperative	sg.		tryme	boda	drīf
	pl.		trymmað	bodiað	drīfað

English have the *-s* ending in the 3ʳᵈ p. sg. that we have in Modern English. This development will be explained in Chapter 9.)

Preterit tense forms of weak and strong verbs differ. In weak verbs, preterit tense is indicated by a dental suffix occurring between the root of the verb and the personal ending: *-ed* for weak class I or *-od* for weak class II. Thus, the form *trymedon* 'they performed' has the following structure:

trym (root) + *-ed* (preterit marker) + *-on* (personal ending)

In strong verbs, preterit tense is indicated by vowel alternation, e.g. present *drīf-* versus preterit *drāf-* (sg.)/*drif-* (pl.). The vowel of the singular preterit is used in the first- and third-person indicative singular, whereas the vowel of the plural preterit is used in all other indicative forms:

drāf + Ø (ind.) 'I, he/she/it drove'
drif + *-e* (ind.) 'you (sg.) drove'
drif + *on* (ind.) 'we/you (pl.)/they drove'

The personal endings of strong and weak verbs are quite different in the preterit, though the plural is always *-on*. Happily, the subjunctive endings are extremely simple: always *-e* in the singular (with no person distinctions) and always *-en* in the plural, regardless of tense or verb class. The preterit subjunctive of a strong verb is formed with the vowel of the plural preterit.

The imperative in Old English distinguishes between singular and plural, unlike in Modern English. Note that the plural imperative is identical to the plural present indicative. (There is no preterit imperative since one cannot order someone to do something in the past.)

Modern English is remarkably different; today, we have only one inflectional ending in the entire finite paradigm, an *-s* in the third-person singular, present indicative, but as it happens this ending does not descend from the *-eð* ending of Old English.

Now let us look at the non-finite forms of the verb (infinitive, present and past participles), displayed in Table 7.16. Non-finite forms are not inflected for person, number, or tense, do not agree with the subject, and cannot stand alone in the predicate of a sentence; instead, they function as adjectives (e.g. *broken chair, flowing stream*) or nouns (e.g. *to err is human*), follow auxiliaries (e.g. *have eaten, be eating, be eaten, will eat*), or follow other verbs (e.g. *let go, cause to go, see [someone] leaving, consider [something] finished*). The ending of the past participle depends on whether the verb is strong (*-en*) or weak (*-ed* for class I and *-od* for class II). The past participle in Old English also generally uses a prefix, *ge-*. The OE infinitive gives us, with loss of the *-an* ending, the ModE simple infinitive (e.g. *go, see*), but interestingly the more common ModE infinitive with *to*, as in *to go* or *to see*, comes from a different source; it is actually an OE verbal noun in the dative case following the preposition *to*.

Table 7.16 Non-finite Forms of the Verb in Old English

	weak class I	*weak class II*	*strong*
infinitive	trymm**an** 'strengthen'	bod**ian** 'announce'	drīf**an** 'drive'
present participle	trymm**ende** 'strengthening'	bod**iende** 'announcing'	drīf**ende** 'driving'
past participle	**ge**trym**ed** 'strengthened'	**ge**bod**od** 'announced'	**ge**drif**en** 'driven'
inflected infinitive	**tō** trymm**enne** 'to strengthen'	**tō** bod**ienne** 'to announce'	**tō** drīf**enne** 'to drive'

Exercise 7.6 Verbs

1. Given the principal parts, identify the type and class of the following verbs.

    a.   *tredan* 'to tread'   *træd/trǣdon/(ge)treden* _____

    b.   *fremman* 'to do'   *fremede/fremedon/(ge)fremed* _____

    c.   *dūfan* 'to dive'   *dēaf/dufon/(ge)dofen* _____

    d.   *lufian* 'to love'   *lufode/lufodon/(ge)lufod* _____

    e.   *gān* 'to go'   *ēode/ēodon/(ge)gān* _____

    f.   *wadan* 'to go'   *wōd/wōdon/(ge)waden* _____

2. Conjugate the following verbs.

    a.   Weak Class I   'to tame' *temman/temede/temedon/getemed*

        Indicative

	Present	Preterit
ic	_____	_____
þū	_____	_____
hē	_____	_____
wē, gē, hī	_____	_____

        Subjunctive

ic, þū, hē	_____	_____
wē, gē, hī	_____	_____

        Imperative

þū	_____
gē	_____
Participles	_____ _____
Infl. Inf.	_____

b.   Strong Class 7   'to blend' *blandan/blēnd/blēndon/geblanden*

Indicative

	Present	Preterit
ic	_____	_____
þū	_____	_____
hē	_____	_____
wē, gē, hī	_____	_____

Subjunctive

ic, þū, hē	_____	_____
wē, gē, hī	_____	_____

Imperative

þū	_____
gē	_____
Participle	_____ _____
Infl. Inf.	_____

Syntax

Verbal Periphrases

While tense and mood are expressed by inflection in the OE verb, other grammatical categories are expressed by periphrastic forms—that is, by separate words or phrases rather than by word endings.

1. The verbal distinction of voice indicates whether the subject of the sentence is acting (active) or is acted upon (passive), as in the distinction between *John drove the car* and *The car was driven by John*. The inflectional forms of Old English are all active in meaning; the passive is expressed by a verbal phrase. The passive periphrase of Old English is very similar to that of Modern English: it consists of a finite form of *be* + a past participle + a prepositional phrase naming the agent. Unlike Modern English, Old English could

also use a finite form of *weorðan* 'to become', and the prepositions marking the agent are *fram/from* 'from' or *þurh* 'through' rather than *by*. As in Modern English, the agent phrase is optional. The OE passive periphrase is shown in the following examples:

> *Þa hire fæder ofslegen wæs* (Alfred's translation of Bede's *Ecclesiastical History of the English People*)
> 'then her father was slain'

> *He wearð ofslegen from his agnum monnum* (Alfred's *Orosius*)
> 'he was slain by his own men'

> *þær wæron gehælde ðurh ða halga femnan fela adlige menn* (Ælfric's *Lives of Saints*)
> 'there were healed by the holy woman many sick men'

A passive sense could also be conveyed with an indefinite pronoun subject *man* 'one' and an active verb: *mon mæg giet gesion hiora swæð* (Alfred's translation of Gregory's *Pastoral Care*), 'one can still see their track' = 'their track can still be seen'.

2. Where we say in Modern English 'I have gone', forming what is called a *perfect periphrase*, Old English speakers could use a similar combination of a finite form of *have* (or *agan* 'to own') + a past participle when the participle was a transitive verb (a verb taking a direct object), as in the following examples:

> *se halga hine gehæled hæfde* (Life of Saint Giles [MS CCCC 303])
> 'the saint had healed him'

> *East Engle hæfdon Ælfrede cyninge aþas geseald* (*Anglo-Saxon Chronicle*)
> 'the East Angles had to King Alfred oaths given'

> *þa hæfde he me gebundenne mid þære wynsumnesse his sanges* (Alfred's translation of Boethius' *De consolatione philosophiae*)
> 'then he had bound me with the loveliness of his song'

However, Anglo-Saxons used a finite form of *be* (or *weorðan* 'to become') when the participle was an intransitive verb (a verb not taking a direct object), such as a verb of motion or change of state, as in the following examples:

> *þider hi þa mid firde gefaren wæron* (Alfred's *Orosius*)
> 'thither they then with an army traveled were' (i.e. 'had traveled')

> *se halga fæder wæs inn agan* (Alfred's translation of the *Dialogues of Gregory the Great*)
> 'the holy father was gone in' (i.e. 'had gone')

Ac heo wæran cumene wið Westseaxna þeode to gefeohte (Alfred's translation of Bede's *Ecclesiastical History of the English People*)
'but they were come to fight against the West Saxon people' (i.e. 'had
come')

As the last example in each set shows, the participle is sometimes inflected
as an adjective, in the first case to agree with the object and in the second to
agree with the subject. However, more often it is uninflected. (Note that the
perfect with *be* is identical in form to the passive, except that the passive is
always formed with transitive verbs.) In the history of English, *be* has gradually been replaced by *have* in the perfect; remnant *be*-perfects such as *The
cookies are all gone* or *He is arrived now* seem to describe the state of things
rather than an action.

3. Old English lacks two periphrastic forms found in Modern English, the progressive periphrase and the future periphrase. Where we use the progressive
(such as *I am writing* or *I was writing*), Old English generally uses a simple
present tense. Instances of *be* + present participle are rare in Old English, and
when they do occur, perhaps under Latin influence, the participle seems to be
functioning as an adjective, as in:

> *ðær wæron sume of þam bocerum sittende, and on hiera heortum þencende*
> (West Saxon Corpus Christi Gospel of Mark)
> 'some of the scribes were there, sitting and thinking in their hearts'

Furthermore, where we use a future periphrase with *will* or *shall*, Old English
generally uses a simple present. A future adverb will often indicate the future
meaning, or this will be clear from the context, as in this example (in which
Hrunting is the name of a sword):

> *ic me mid Hruntinge dom gewyrce* (*Beowulf*)
> 'I for myself with Hrunting [shall] achieve glory'

Willan and *sculan* are used in Old English with their full meanings of 'intention' and 'obligation', not as empty markers of the future tense.

4. Finally, Old English has a number of impersonal verbs, with no personal nominative subject. The personal subject (usually an experiencer) is expressed in
the accusative, genitive, or dative case. The following examples show the use
of impersonal verbs:

> *him* (dat.) *þyrstede*
> 'it thirsted to him' (ModE 'he was thirsty')

> *me* (acc.) *langode*
> 'there was a longing to me' (ModE 'I longed')

me (dat.) *lyst rædan*
'it pleases me to read' (ModE 'I like to read')

ælcum menn (dat.) *þuhte*
'it seemed to each man' (ModE 'each man thought')

hine (acc.) *nanes ðinges ne lyste*
'it pleased him of nothing' (ModE 'nothing pleased him' or 'he liked nothing')

Note that in translating these impersonal constructions into Modern English, either an *it* subject must be supplied or the construction must given a personal subject.

Word Order

As we have seen, a synthetic language like Old English has a much freer order of elements than an analytic language like Modern English, which relies on word order and function words rather than inflections to indicate relationships between words. Nonetheless, the word order of an inflected language is never entirely free. Generally, there is a standard (or unmarked) order for words in a declarative sentence. Special (or marked) word orders are used for other types of sentences (such as questions or negative sentences) or for special emphasis. For Old English, the fact that nominative and accusative cases are often not differentiated also contributes to the fixing of word order. When we talk about word order, we are most concerned with the position of the subject (S), the verb (V), and the object (O). The unmarked word order for Old English main clauses appears to be SVO, as in Modern English. However, there are remnants of an SOV order, which is the order generally reconstructed for Proto-Indo-European.

Word Order in Main Clauses

Main clauses in Old English have the following order:

subject + (auxiliary) + verb + (object) . . .

Ic astige min scyp mid hlæstum minum (Ælfric's *Colloquy*)
'I scaled my ship with my load'

Ic utwyrpe þa unclænan ut, and genime me clæne to mete (Ælfric's *Colloquy*)
'I throw the unclean out and take for myself the clean as food'

This category represents the unmarked SVO word order of affirmative (as opposed to negative), declarative (as opposed to interrogative or imperative), and main (as opposed to subordinate) clauses. Try to identify the S, the V, and the O in each of the examples.[2]

---

2 The correct answers are: S = *Ic, Ic*; V = *astige, utwyrpe, genime*; O = *min scyp, þa unclænan, clæne*.

Main clauses with an object pronoun have the following order:

subject + (auxiliary) + object pronoun + verb . . .

ic hine gelæde ongean to his leode (Ælfric's *Catholic Homilies*)
'I led him back to his people'

þæt hors hine bær forð, swa þæt þæt spere him eode þurh ut, and he feoll cwel-ende (Ælfric's *Lives of Saints*)
'that horse carried him forth so that that spear went out through him and he fell dying'

This category reflects the older SOV order. Look for the OV sequences in the first two sentences. (They are: OV = *hine gelæde, hine bær, him eode*.) This order is used when the object is a pronoun, not a noun. It is common with impersonal verbs. However, it is always optional; as the following example shows, the object pronoun may follow the verb:

Se cyning Wyrtgeorn gef heom land on suðan eastan ðissum lande (*Anglo-Saxon Chronicle*)
'King Vortigern gave them land on the southeast (side) of this country'

Word Order in Negative Clauses

Negative declarative main clauses have one of the following orders:

1. **negative + {auxiliary, verb} + subject + (object) . . .**
2. **subject + negative + {auxiliary, verb} + (object) . . .**

To negate a sentence in Old English, the negative particle *ne* is inserted before the verb or auxiliary. In contrast, the negative particle in Modern English follows rather than precedes the auxiliary, and negative sentences require an auxiliary verb (compare *John does not like movies* with the ungrammatical phrases **John not likes movies* or **John likes not movies*). In the following samples of Old English, *ne* precedes the verb in the first and the auxiliary in the second:

Hie ne wendon þætte æfre menn sceoldon swæ recclease weorðan (Alfred's translation of Gregory's *Pastoral Care*)
'They not think that ever men should so reckless become.'

Ic ne mæg swa fela swa ic mæg gesyllan (Ælfric's *Colloquy*)
'I not may [take] so many as I may give'

The negative particle may be contracted. In Modern English we do this by suffixing *not* to the preceding auxiliary to yield forms such as *wouldn't*, but in Old English, *ne* is prefixed to the verb or auxiliary: e.g. *ne + wæs* 'was' > *næs, ne + habban* 'have' > *nabban*, or *ne + willan* 'will' > *nyllan*. The example below contains the prefixed form *nis* (< *ne + is*):

> *Nis hyt swa stearc winter þæt ic durre lutian æt ham* (Ælfric's *Colloquy*)
> 'not-is it so stark a winter that I remain hidden at home'

Ne can also be attached to adverbs, pronouns, and adjectives in a similar fashion: *ne + an* 'one' > *nan* 'none', or *ne + æfre* 'ever' > *næfre* 'never'. When *ne* is joined to the verb or auxiliary, the contraction tends to move to the front of the sentence, resulting in an inverted word order (as in the example above).

Notice the two negative elements, *næs* and *nænig*, in the next sentence. Multiple negation is common in Old English:

> *Næs þa nænig ylding* (*Blickling Homilies*)
> 'not-was then not-any delay'

Multiple negation was proscribed in the eighteenth century because it was felt to violate rules of logic, but speakers of earlier English seem to have employed it for emphasis.

Word Order with Initial Adverb of Time or Place

Main clauses beginning with an adverb of time or place have the following order:

adverb + {verb, auxiliary} + subject + (object) . . .

> *þanne an ic it Athelfleð mine douhter* (will of Ælfgar)
> 'then grant I it to Athelfleth my daughter'

> *Her on þissum geare com Cnut mid his here* (*Anglo-Saxon Chronicle*)
> 'here in this year Cnut came with his army'

Sentences in this category invert the subject and verb after an adverb of time (e.g. *þa* 'then', *þonne* 'then', *siþþan* 'afterward', or *hēr* 'at this time') or an adverb of place (e.g. *þǣr* 'there', *þider* 'thither', or *forð* 'forth') when it begins the sentence. Such sentences occur rarely in Modern English but do exist, as with *On the table lay a magnificent feast*.

Word Order in Interrogative Sentences

Interrogative sentences have the following order:

interrogative pronoun + {auxiliary, verb} + subject + (object) . . .

> *Hwæt sylþ he þe?* (Ælfric's *Colloquy*)
> 'What gives he to you?'

> *Hwylcne cræft canst þu?* (Ælfric's *Colloquy*)
> 'Which craft know you?'

> *Hæfst þu ænigne geferan?* (Ælfric's *Colloquy*)
> 'Have you any companion?'

> *Wære þu todæg on huntnoþe?* (Ælfric's *Colloquy*)
> 'Were you today a-hunting?'

Question formation represents the third instance of inverted word order in Old English. There are two major types of questions in English: *yes/no* questions (e.g. *Did you see a movie?*) and content questions (e.g. *What movie did you see?*). In Modern English, both types require that an auxiliary verb precede the subject. In Old English, either an auxiliary or a verb precedes the subject but the auxiliary is not obligatory, as we just saw in looking at negation. Content questions contain a question word such as *what, who, where, why*, or *how* at the beginning of the sentence; the Old English question words *hwæt* and *hwylcne* can be seen above.

Word Order in Subordinate Clauses

Subordinate clauses have the following order:

subordinating conjunction + subject + (object) + verb

Gif he Godes man sy, fylgað ge him (Alfred's translation of Bede's *Ecclesiastical History of the English People*)
'if he be a man of God, follow you him'

oþþæt unc flod todraf (*Beowulf*)
'until the flood separated us'

forþam þe he his freond ys (West Saxon Corpus Christi Gospel of Luke)
'because he is his friend'

swa swa se apostol Paulus on his pistole awrat (Ælfric's *Homilies*)
'just as the apostle Paul wrote in his epistle'

swa þæt cild raðost ænig ðing specan mæge (Wulfstan's *Homilies*)
'so that a child most quickly any thing speak may'
(i.e. 'so that a child may speak any thing most quickly')

The subordinating conjunctions here are *gif, oþþæt, forþam þe, swa swa*, and *swa þæt*. As you can see, the rule in subordinate clauses is that the verb comes last. A common pattern in Old English is for the auxiliary to follow the verb and occupy the 'sentence final' position, as in the last example.

Word Order in Imperatives

Imperative sentences have the following structure:

{verb, auxiliary} + (subject) + (object) . . .

Gaþ þeawlice þonne ge gehyran cyricean bellan (Ælfric's *Colloquy*)
'go devoutly when you hear church bells'

Leofan men, gecnawaþ ðæt soð is (Wulfstan's *Homilies*)
'Dear men, know what truth is'

As in Modern English, the verb is placed first in OE imperative sentences.

Exercise 7.7 Syntax and Word Order

Describe the syntactical feature(s) represented in the following sentences (i.e. sov/svo word order, sentence type, periphrasis, impersonal verb forms).

a.   *Ualens wæs gelæred from anum Arrianiscan biscepe* (Alfred's *Orosius*)
     'Valens was taught by an Arian bishop'

     _____

     _____

b.   *hraðe heo æðelinga anne hæfde fæste befangen* (*Beowulf*)
     'quickly she one of the nobleman had firmly seized'

     _____

     _____

c.   *Is þæt deor pandher bi noman haten?* (*Panther*)
     'is that animal panther by name called'

     _____

     _____

d.   *þa wæron Seaxan secende intigan* (Alfred's translation of Bede's *Ecclesiastical History of the English People*)
     'then were Saxons seeking reasons'

     _____

     _____

e.   *men ne cunnon secgan . . . hwa þæm hlæste onfeng* (*Beowulf*)
     'no one can say . . . who that cargo received'

     _____

     _____

f.   *ic swefna cyst secgan wylla, hwæt me gemætte* ('The Dream of the Rood')
     'I of dreams (the) best to tell intend, what me dreamed'

     _____

     _____

g. *ne wæs þær huru fracodes gealga* ('The Dream of the Rood')
    'not was there certainly (a) wicked one's gallows'

    _____

    _____

h. *Hæfst þu hafoc?* (Ælfric's *Colloquy*)
    'Have you (a) hawk?'

    _____

    _____

i. *sing me frumsceaft* (Alfred's translation of Bede's *Ecclesiastical History of the English People*)
    'sing me (the) Creation'

    _____

    _____

A Closer Look at the Language of an Old English Text

Look at the following selection from Ælfric's *Catholic Homily on St Gregory* (Godden 1979:74), which is based on Alfred's translation of Bede's *Ecclesiastical History of the English People*. It is an apocryphal account of why England was Christianized. It centers on a play on words between the name of the Germanic tribe, the Angles, and the word *angel*. (The passage is partially glossed; by now you should be able to supply the missing translations.)

| Ða | gelamp | hit | æt | sumum | sæle | swa swa. | gyt | foroft | deð | (1) |
| *then* | *happened* | | | *certain* | *time* | *as* | *still* | *very often* | *does* | |

| þæt | englisce | cypmenn | brohton | heora | ware | to | romana | byrig. | | (2) |
| | | *merchants* | *brought* | *their* | *wares* | | *Rome* | *town* | | |

| and | Gregorius | eode | be | þære | stræt | to ðam | engliscum | mannum | | (3) |
| | | *went* | *along* | *the* | | | | *men* | | |

| heora | ðing | sceawigende; | Þa | geseah | he | betwux | ðam | warum. | | (4) |
| *at their* | *things* | *looking* | | *saw* | | *among* | | *wares* | | |

Continued

cypecnihtas gesette. þa wæron hwites lichaman. and   (5)
slaves   placed   who were   of white body

fægeres andwlitan   menn. and æðellice gefeaxode; Gregorius   (6)
of fair   countenance   nobly   haired.

ða beheold þæra cnapena wlite. and befran of hwilcere þeode   (7)
noticed   youths' fairness   asked   from which   nation

hi   gebrohte wæron;   Þa sæde him man   þæt hi of   (8)
they   brought   someone   from

engla lande wæron. and þæt ðære ðeodemennisc swa wlitig wære; (9)
*   nation's people   fair*

Eft   ða   gregorius   befran. hwæðer þæs landes folc   cristen   (10)
Again   asked whether   Christian

wære.   ðe   hæðen;   Him mann sæde. þæt hi hæðene wæron;   (11)
were   or   heathen

Gregorius ða of   innweardre   heortan langsume siccetunge   (12)
*   from his inward   heart   a long   sigh*

teah. and cwæð; Wa la wa. þæt swa fægeres hiwes menn   (13)
drew   said Alas   fairly   hued

sindon ðam sweartan deofle underðeodde; Eft   (14)
are   to the dark   devil   subject

he axode hu   ðære ðeode nama wære. þe hi of comon;   (15)
asked what   name   that   came

Him   wæs geandwyrd. þæt hi angle genemnode wæron;   (16)
To him   answered   Angles named

Þa cwæð he. rihtlice hi sind Angle gehatene. for ðan ðe   hi (17)
*   Rightly   are   called   because*

engla   wlite   habbað. and swilcum gedafenað þæt hi   (18)
angel's fairness have   for such   it is fitting

on heofonum engla geferan   beon; Gyt ða Gregorius befran.   (19)
in heaven   Angel's companions be   still   asked

hu ðære scire   nama wære. þe ða cnapan of   alædde wæron;   (20)
*   district   which youth   from brought*

Him   man   sæde. þæt ða   scirmen   wæron dere   gehatene;   (21)
   someone   *district men*   *Deirians   called.*

Gregorius   andwyrde.   Wel   hi   sind   dere   gehatene.   for ðan ðe   (22)
   answered   Well   *because*

hi   sind   fram   graman   generode.   and to   Cristes   mildheortnysse   (23)
   are   *wrath   delivered*   *Christ's   mercy*

gecygede;   Gyt   ða   he befran.   Hu   is   ðære   leode   cyning   (24)
called.   *the people's   king*

gehaten?   Him   wæs   geandswarod   þæt   se   cyning Ælle   gehaten   (25)
                                                  Alle

wære; Hwæt, ða   Gregorius   gamenode   mid   his   wordum   to   (26)
   Well   *played   with   words*

ðam   naman. and   cwæð; Hit   gedafenað   þæt   alleluia   sy   (27)
   name   *is fitting*   *Alleluia   be*

gesungen   on ðam   lande. to   lofe   þæs   ælmihtigan   scyppendes;   (28)
sung   in   praise   almighty's   creator

(from Ælfric's *Catholic Homily on St Gregory*)

The passage provides numerous examples of Old English inflectional morphology:

1. We note the presence of strong verbs, such as *gelamp* (1), *geseah* (4), *gesette* (5), *beheold* (7), *befran* (7), *teah* (13), *cwæð* (13), and *gesungen* (28), and anomalous verbs, such as *wæron* (5), *deð* (1), and *eode* (3), as well as the more frequent weak verbs, such as *gefeaxode* (6), *brohton* (2), *sæde* (8), *axode* (15), *andwyrde* (22), *generode* (23), and *gecygede* (24). In (4) we see a present participle *sceawigende*. Past participles are common in this passage, for example, *gesette* (5), *gefeaxode* (6), *gehatene* (17), and *geandswarod* (25); they are generally part of the passive verbal periphrasis, as in *gebrohte wæron* 'were brought' (8), also (16), (20), and (23). They often carry an adjectival ending (*-e*) agreeing with the subject. Subjunctive forms, such as *wære* (9) and *sy* (27), appear often in subordinate clauses.
2. We note a variety of case-inflected forms of the noun, such as *sæle* (dat. sg.) (1), *heofonum* (dat. pl.) (19), *hwites* (gen. sg.) (5), *cnapena* (gen. pl.) (7), *cyning* (nom. sg.) (25), and *cypecnihtas* (acc. pl.) (5), in a variety of genders, such as *siccetunge* (fem.) (12), *geferan* (masc.) (19), and *lande* (neut.) (9), and a variety of declensions, such as *a*-stem (*ðing* [4], *cypecnihtas* [5], *lande* [9]), weak (*nama* [20], *heortan* [12], *graman* [23]), root-consonant stem (*cypmenn* [2], *byrig* [2]), and *ō*-stem (*stræt* [3], *þeode* [7]).

3. We find a variety of third-person personal pronouns: *hit* (neut. nom./acc. sg.) (1), *he* (masc. nom. sg.) (4), *his* (masc. gen. sg.) (26), *him* (masc. dat. sg.) (8), *hi* (nom./acc. pl.) (8), and *heora* (gen. pl.) (4). The relative pronoun *þe* occurs as well (15).

4. We find inflected forms of the demonstrative: *þæs* (28), *þære* (3), *se* (25), and *ðam* (4).

5. Strong adjective endings occur in *sumum* (1), *hwites* (5), *fægeres* (6), and *langsume* (12), while a weak adjective ending occurs in *sweartan* (14). A comparative adjective is *innweardre* 'more inward' (12).

6. Adverbs include *foroft* (1), *æðellice* (6), *rihtlice* (17), *gyt* (19), *eft* (10), and *ða* (10), and conjunctions include *and* (3), *for ðan ðe* (17), *swa swa* (1), and *þæt* (2).

The passage shows characteristic Old English syntax:

1. There are many examples of inverted word order (ADV–V–S) in sentences with initial adverbs of time, such as (1), (4), (7), and (17). However, there are exceptions where an initial adverb does not cause inversion, as in (10), (15), and (19).

2. There are also many cases of 'verb final' word order in subordinate clauses, such as (8), (9), (11), (15), (16), and (18). Note that an auxiliary typically follows the participle, as in *gebrohte wæron* (8), although there are exceptions, as in *wæron . . . gehatene* (21).

3. The passage includes one content question (24–5).

4. There are a variety of different types of subordinate clauses, including relative clauses (5), *that* clauses (8), adverbial clauses (17), and indirect questions (20).

5. There are some sentences in which the object has been fronted, e.g. *him* (O) *mann* (S) *sæde* (V) (11); compare (16).

6. In a number of cases, periphrastic nominal constructions using prepositions occur, such as *to romana byrig* (2), whereas in other cases inflectional endings alone serve the same purpose, as in the dative case of *him* (8) meaning 'to him'.

7. The genitive precedes the noun it modifies, as in *þæs landes folc* (10).

RECOMMENDED WEB LINKS

See Murray McGillivray's online grammar of Old English:

http://www.ucalgary.ca/UofC/eduweb/engl401/grammar/index.htm

Also see Peter S. Baker's 'Old English Aerobics', which includes self-testing exercises on grammar:

http://faculty.virginia.edu/OldEnglish/OEA/

An online version of Peter S. Baker's *Introduction to Old English* is located at:
http://www.wmich.edu/medieval/resources/IOE/index.html

FURTHER READING

For more instruction in Old English grammar, you might consult one of the following grammars:

Baker, Peter S. 2003. *Introduction to Old English*. Malden, MA and Oxford: Blackwell, Chapters 4–12. For a basic review of grammar, see Chapter 3.

Hogg, Richard M. 2002. *An Introduction to Old English*. New York: Oxford University Press.

Mitchell, Bruce, and Fred C. Robinson. 2007. *A Guide to Old English: Revised with Prose and Verse Texts and Glossary*. 7th edn. Oxford: Blackwell, Chapters 3 and 5.

Smith, Jeremy J. 2009. *Old English: A Linguistic Introduction*. Cambridge: Cambridge University Press, Chapters 6 and 7.

If you wish to pursue your reading on Old English grammar, the following titles provide more complete discussions of the topic:

Denison, David. 1993. *English Historical Syntax*. London and New York: Longman.

Fischer, Olga, and Wim van der Wurff. 2006. 'Syntax'. *A History of the English Language*. Ed. by Richard M. Hogg and David Denison, 109–98. Cambridge: Cambridge University Press.

Hogg, Richard M. 1992. 'Phonology and Morphology'. *The Cambridge History of the English Language. Vol. 1: The Beginnings to 1066*. Ed. by Richard M. Hogg, 67–167. Cambridge: Cambridge University Press.

Lass, Roger. 1994. *Old English: A Historical Linguistic Companion*. Cambridge: Cambridge University Press, Chapters 6, 7, and 9.

Lass, Roger. 2006. 'Phonology and Morphology'. *A History of the English Language*. Ed. by Richard M. Hogg and David Denison, 43–108. Cambridge: Cambridge University Press.

Quirk, Randolph, and C.L. Wrenn. 1957 [Reprint 1994]. *An Old English Grammar*. 2nd edn. DeKalb: Northern Illinois University Press, Chapters 2 and 3.

Traugott, Elizabeth Closs. 1992. 'Syntax'. *The Cambridge History of the English Language. Vol. 1: The Beginnings to 1066*. Ed. by Richard M. Hogg, 168–289. Cambridge: Cambridge University Press.

FURTHER VIEWING

You may wish to view the following documentary:

Part 2, from *The Story of English*. BBC-TV coproduction with MacNeil-Lehrer Productions in association with WNET, 1986.

8

The Rise of
Middle English:
Words and Sounds

OVERVIEW

This chapter deals with the linguistic situation in England between 1066 and 1500. We review the political events leading up to the Norman Conquest and the establishment of French as the language of England. We then consider the social and political events which contributed to the increased use of English after the mid-twelfth century and its restoration as the national language by the early fifteenth century. Our central interest here is in the effects these events had on English, especially its vocabulary, which saw massive borrowing from French, some borrowing from Latin, and the loss of many native words. We also discuss the dialects of Middle English and offer texts which show contemporary awareness of language and its varieties.

The chapter then describes changes in the writing system of Middle English and phonological changes which took place during the transition from Old English. We look at consonant and vowel changes, the development of new diphthongs, and finally the lengthening and shortening of vowels.

OBJECTIVES

By the end of this chapter, you should understand the sources of loan words and the types of borrowing in Middle English, and you will be able to tell the difference between earlier and later French borrowings, between Norman French and Central French borrowings, and between levels of synonyms. You will learn to locate the dialects of Middle English and identify the most important literary records. In addition, you will discover:

- how Old English words are respelled in Middle English; and
- how the pronunciation of Old English words changes in Middle English (you will also be able to name, explain, and use phonetic notation to indicate each change).

French and English in Medieval England

The Norman Conquest

The conquest of England by the Duke of Normandy in 1066 is perhaps the single most important event affecting the linguistic development of English. As you will recall from Chapter 5, the end of the Anglo-Saxon period saw Scandinavians occupying the throne of England before the restoration of an English king (descended from King Alfred the Great). Edward the Confessor, who had been in exile in Normandy since the death of his father, Ethelred, assumed the kingship of England in 1042 after the death of King Cnut's son Harthacnut. Edward seems to have been an ineffectual king under the control of powerful earls like Godwine, Earl of Wessex (who was Edward's father-in-law). A pious and monkish man, King Edward died in January 1066 leaving no male heir. On the day of Edward's death, Godwine's son, Harold, who had been principal adviser to Edward since Edward's father's death in 1053, was elected king by the 'witan', the king's council. He became King Harold II of England.

Harold's ascension to the throne was challenged from two sides. First was King Harald Hardrada of Norway, who considered himself heir to Cnut's throne. He invaded England via the Humber River in the north, accompanied by Earl Tostig, Harold of England's brother, but their forces were defeated in the Battle of Stamford Bridge on 25 September 1066. The second threat came from Duke William of Normandy (variously called 'the Conqueror', 'the Great', or 'the Bastard'). William, who became the 7th Duke of Normandy at age six when his father, Robert the Devil, died on a pilgrimage to Jerusalem, was the illegitimate son of a tanner's daughter. However, he was second cousin to Edward (who had spent his exile in Normandy); when he had visited Edward in England, he had been led to believe he would succeed to the English throne. Perhaps he had even extracted a promise from Harold of England, who was captured in Normandy in 1064, to the effect that Harold would not oppose William's succession.

On 28 September 1066, William landed in southern England at Pevensey, near Hastings, with a large force. In order to meet this attack, Harold of England was forced to rush down from northern England immediately following the Battle of Stamford Bridge, with his army in disarray and his supporters slow in coming to his aid. The two met in battle on 14 October 1066, in what has since come to be known as the Battle of Hastings. Harold's brothers-in-law, the earls of Mercia and Northumbria, were killed in battle, and then Harold too was killed; according to legend, he was pierced through the eye by an arrow. His army then retreated. William pillaged his way through southeast England, and he was crowned king of England in Westminster Abbey in London on Christmas Day, 1066. This was the year in which Halley's Comet was visible over England; it was considered a bad omen.

Here is a translation of the account of the Conquest given in the Parker manuscript of the *Anglo-Saxon Chronicle* (Plummer 1892:Vol. 1, 194):

> **A.D. 1066**. This year died King Edward, and Harold the earl succeeded to the kingdom, and held it forty weeks and one day. And this year came William, and won England. And in this year Christ-Church [Canterbury] was burned. And this year appeared a comet on the fourteenth before the kalends of May.

The conquerors of England in 1066 came from Normandy (in present-day France), directly across the channel from England. The Normans were actually Scandinavians who had settled in France in the ninth and tenth centuries, at the same time that Scandinavians were also settling northern England. The word *Norman* is

Figure 8.1   The Bayeux Tapestry (panel 23): Harold Swears Fealty to William (copyright Reading Museum Service [Reading Borough Council]; all rights reserved)

an amalgamated compound of *North* + *man*. In 911, the leader of the Scandinavians, Rollo (Hrolfr) the Dane, signed a pact with King Charles the Simple of France (similar to the agreement that King Alfred made with the Danes in England), in which the Scandinavians acknowledged the king of France as their overlord while he ceded them the Normandy peninsula. The Scandinavians in France soon assimilated to the dominant culture: they learned French, were Christianized, and adopted Frankish customs and law. They established close relations with England during Cnut's reign, when the English nobility took refuge in Normandy.

The events of the Norman Conquest are depicted in pictures accompanied by Latin descriptions on the Bayeux Tapestry, actually a linen embroidery (see Figure 8.1). The tapestry was probably commissioned by Odo, bishop of Bayeux and half-brother of William, and made in Kent between 1076 and 1086. It is now on display in Bayeux, France.

The Establishment of French

The linguistic situation in England after the Norman Conquest is difficult to assess. William replaced most of the native English nobility with Normans in order to

reward his supporters and ensure the loyalty of his officials. By 1072, 11 of the 12 earls of England were Norman French. For a long period, there were close connections between not only England and Normandy, but also England and the rest of France. The Norman kings of England spent much of their time on French soil, and usually married French wives, through whom they gained additional French possessions. For example, Henry II, ruler of England from 1154 to 1189, gained control of two-thirds of France by his marriage to Eleanor of Aquitaine.

The Anglo-French aristocracy does not seem to have been hostile to learning English, just indifferent. It is said that William tried unsuccessfully to learn the language at the age of 43, although his youngest son, Henry I (reigned 1100–35) may actually have spoken English, since he had an English wife. Henry II understood English but did not speak it; his wife, Eleanor, needed an interpreter. The first king to have a good command of the native tongue was Edward I (1272–1307). For approximately two hundred years, then, the rulers of England were primarily monolingual French speakers. Among those without a command of English, we count the nobility and higher church officials, such as archbishops and abbots. In addition, there were French-speaking Norman troops garrisoned in England. However, as much as 90 per cent of the population continued to speak English, and this practice was tolerated by the Norman overlords. This is a situation of diglossia. In his chronicle written *c.* 1300, Robert of Gloucester tells us that 'low men hold to English and their own speech' (see text below). Because of intermarriage and the demands of business, a small group of bilingual speakers existed, including some knights, merchants, stewards, bailiffs, lesser landlords, parish priests, and monks.

The written evidence reveals three languages in use. Latin continued to be the official language of laws, petitions to parliament, official proclamations, and court records. In the late thirteenth century, commercial and city records in French also began to appear. Writings in French emanated from the monasteries in England, and French literature was cultivated in the court. There were a few English texts produced in the West Midland and South dialect areas, including the *Peterborough Chronicle*, maintained until 1154, and the *Ancrene Riwle*, a devotional guide written for three young women of high birth. The latter, written in the late twelfth or early thirteenth century, suggests that at least some of the nobility spoke English natively.

Apart from some exceptional written texts, English was for two hundred years only a spoken language; the implications of this fact are significant. You will recall from Chapter 3 that the written form is a conservative force in slowing down or preventing language change. Change originates in variation in the spoken language, and languages which are not written tend to change more rapidly than those that are. One of the strongest forces of change in Middle English, then, was the infrequency of keeping records in English during the eleventh and twelfth centuries. Moreover, English of the time was spoken in a variety of regional dialects resulting from the geographic and social isolation of the speakers; no standard dialect existed. These

Þus com lo engelond in to normandies hond

& þe normans ne couþe speke þo bote hor owe speche
          could   *then but their own*

& speke french as hii dude atom & hor children dude also teche
          they did at home   *their*

So þat heiemen of þis lond þat of hor blod come
   noblemen   *their*

Holdeþ alle þulke speche þat hii of hom nome
hold   *the same*   *they from home took*

Vor bote a man conne frenss me telþ of him lute
for unless   *knows*   *I account him little*

Ac lowe men holdeþ to engliss & to hor owe speche ȝute
but low   *their own*   *yet*

Ich wene þer ne beþ in al þe world contreyes none
I believe there is not   *no countries*

Þat ne holdeþ to hor owe speche bote engelond one
   do not hold

Ac wel me wot uor to conne boþe wel it is
but well I know that to know both is good

Vor þe more þat a mon can þe more wurþe he is.
          knows   *worthy*

(Robert of Gloucester, *Metrical Chronicle* [Wright 1887:Vol. 2, ll. 7537–47])

were undoubtedly much stronger forces in promoting grammatical change than later language interference between French and English, which, as we will see, accounts primarily for changes in the vocabulary. During this period, diglossia prevailed: English existed as a lower or socially stigmatized dialect spoken mostly by peasants, artisans, and laborers, while French, written and spoken by the ruling class, was the higher or prestige dialect, the one to be imitated.

In France, the French dialect spoken by the Norman rulers of England, known as Norman French or Anglo-Norman French, was considered inferior to the French of Paris, i.e. Central French. The stigmatization of this dialect extended to England.

By the fourteenth century, Chaucer could say ironically of the Prioress in *The Canterbury Tales* that she speaks French 'ful faire and fetisly, / After the scole of Stratford atte Bowe, / For Frenssh of Parys was to hire unknowe' (translation: 'excellently and neatly / after the school of Stratford at Bowe [i.e. Anglo-Norman], / for French of Paris is unknown to her').[1] We are to recognize that her pretension to social status is compromised by her use of an inferior French dialect.

The Re-establishment of English

A number of events contributed to the decline of French and the restoration of English as the national language in the thirteenth and fourteenth centuries. John, king of England from 1199 to 1216, lost control of Normandy in 1204 to King Philip of France. This loss forced the Anglo-Norman nobility to declare their allegiance by giving up their holdings either in Normandy or in England; Anglo–French ties consequently weakened. Then, during the reign of Henry III (1216–72), who married Eleanor of Provence, a second influx of French nobility into the English court seems to have caused resentment due to favoritism. Despite periodic revivals, Anglo-Norman French no longer appears to have been the first language of much of the English nobility; instead, the more prestigious Central French was acquired as a second language. We can deduce this from the appearance of manuals in the instruction of French from about 1300, from warnings against speaking improper French and other attempts to arrest its decline, and from a decrease in negative comments about the speaking of English, which had now become the norm. French had become a cultivated symbol of elite social status, a matter of culture and fashion rather than ethnicity. As such, it evoked resentment from an increasingly nationalistic populace and actually began to diminish in use.

In the mid-fourteenth century, the Hundred Years War broke out between England and France; open warfare continued on and off from 1337 to 1453, with important English victories under Edward III at Crécy (1346) and at Poitiers (1356) and later under Henry V at Agincourt (1415) contributing to a sense of English nationalism. The outbreak of the Black Death (likely both bubonic and pneumonic plagues), which began in 1348 in southwestern England and continued through 1349 and 1350, with periodic recurrences later on, killed up to 40 per cent of the population, mainly urban artisans and laborers. The severely depleted laboring classes gained political power because their low numbers made them more in demand. In the Peasants' Revolt of 1381 (prompted by an increase in the poll tax), they demanded higher wages and better working conditions. At the same time, the urban population of England was growing, along with the merchant and craftsman middle class. As the political power and social status of English speakers increased, so did the status of their language.

---

1 This and subsequent quotations from Chaucer are from Benson (1987).

English became, then, both the prestige language and a sign of in-group solidarity, factors that are very important in the adoption of linguistic forms. Gradually, English began to appear in official contexts. The first such document was actually the Oxford Proclamation of Henry III of 1258, but it was over a hundred years later that the official use of English became widespread, with the appearance in the second half of the fourteenth century of English guild and city records, commercial accountings, and wills and deeds. English became the language of instruction in schools and, except in the royal court, was used for judicial hearings. In the fourteenth century, writers and translators such as Robert Mannyng, John of Trevisa, and John Wyclif extolled the virtues of writing in English for 'lewed' ('unlearned') people. That century also saw a flourishing of English literature. Consistent use of English in government documents such as petitions to Parliament and court records became increasingly regular toward the second or third decade of the fifteenth century. Most scholars would say that the restoration of English was complete by the reign of Henry V (1413–22).

Exercise 8.1 External History

1. Briefly explain the linguistic significance of each of the following.

    a.   Oxford Proclamation

    _____

    _____

    b.   Godwine, Earl of Wessex

    _____

    _____

    c.   Edward I

    _____

    _____

    d.   *Peterborough Chronicle*

    _____

    _____

    e.   The Hundred Years War

    _____

    _____

f.   The written language of England during the period from 1066 to approximately 1250

_____

_____

_____

_____

2.   Identify William the Conqueror and his involvement in historical events in England in the eleventh century. Describe the effect of these events on the English language.

_____

_____

_____

_____

_____

_____

The Word Stock of Middle English

When the English language appears again in written documents of the thirteenth and fourteenth centuries, it looks very different from Old English. The most striking change is in the word stock, which shows a massive influx of French terms and a substantial loss of Old English words, especially those not belonging to the core vocabulary. In addition, borrowings from Old Norse, which occurred in the late Old English period, first show up in large numbers in Middle English texts.

French Influence

The effect of French on the native vocabulary during the Middle English period is immense. The period of greatest borrowing is the century and a half between 1250 and 1400, peaking about 1380. The grammarian Otto Jespersen, in examining when 1,000 French loan words came into English, found the distribution shown in Table 8.1 (1982 [1905]:87).

By his figures, 42.7 per cent of the loan words entered the language between 1250 and 1400, a period that probably saw the greatest bilingualism, with French speakers gradually becoming English speakers and importing items from their first language. By the time such words appeared in written English texts, they had pre-

Table 8.1 French Borrowings in the History of English

date	number	date	number	date	number
Before 1050	2	1301–1350	120	1601–1650	69
1051–1100	2	1351–1400	180	1651–1700	34
1101–1150	1	1401–1450	70	1701–1750	24
1151–1200	15	1451–1500	76	1751–1800	16
1201–1250	64	1501–1550	84	1801–1850	23
1251–1300	127	1551–1600	91	1851–1900	2

sumably been part of the oral language for some time. These words named a wide variety of everyday objects and concepts, as well as more specialized items. Before 1250, words from French had been mostly cultural borrowings, used by English speakers learning or exposed to French and relating to semantic domains such as religion or the nobility, in which the French were culturally dominant. After 1250, borrowings came from a wider variety of domains:

- government: *parliament, authority, statute*
- military: *battle, archer, army*
- law: *attorney, arrest, felony*
- economic organization: *tax, revenue, estate*
- art: *sculpture, painting, art*
- architecture: *cathedral, vault, porch*
- music: *melody, dance, music*
- literature: *volume, prose, poet*
- medicine: *surgeon, ointment, physician*
- learning: *grammar, rhyme, logic*
- fashion: *pleat, button, collar*
- food: *biscuit, bacon, dinner, fruit*
- furnishings: *lamp, blanket, couch*
- social life: *conversation, recreation, tavern*
- non-nuclear family: *niece, nephew, uncle, aunt*
- trades: *grocer, tailor, mason*

In his 1653 grammar of the language, John Wallis was the first to point out that English words are used for live animals (e.g. *ox, cow, swine, deer, sheep, calf*), whereas French words are used for prepared meat (e.g. *beef, pork, venison, mutton, veal*); many culinary terms in English are also of French origin (e.g. *feast, roast, toast, confection, sauce, sugar*).

During the Middle English period, words were borrowed from two dialects, Norman French and Central French (the source of standard Modern French). Sometimes these borrowings can be distinguished by phonetic differences. For example, Latin [k] before *a* in Norman French remains as [k], while in Central French it develops as [č], as in the following examples:

Norman French [k]	Central French [č]
carry	*charity*
carrion	*chair*
carpenter	*charge*
carriage	*chariot*
cauldron	*challenge*

Likewise, Latin [w] appears as [w] in Norman French, but as [g] in Central French:

Norman French [w]	Central French [g]
waste	*garment*
warren	*garrison*
wicket	*garland*

A number of words beginning in [w] from Norman French are ultimately of Germanic origin, such as *wage, war,* and *warden*. Occasionally, we find doublets of Norman and Central French origin, such as *cattle/chattel, cant/chant, warranty/guarantee,* and *reward/regard*. (Note that dictionaries often refer to Norman French as 'North French'.)

Using knowledge of the sound changes in the history of French, or the extent of phonetic assimilation of a word in English, we may date when a word was borrowed. The shifts in French from [č] to [š] and from [ǰ] to [ž] differentiate earlier (medieval) and later (modern) borrowings from French, as in the following examples:

earlier borrowing [č, ǰ]	later borrowing [š, ž]
champion	*chandelier*
chestnut	*chevron*
chain	*chignon*
gentle	*genre*
germ	*rouge*

The same word may be borrowed at different times, resulting in doublets such as *chief/chef* and *chain/chignon*. Another French sound change is the loss of [s] before [t]; English possesses several doublets borrowed before and after this shift:

earlier borrowing with [s]	later borrowing without [s]
feast	*fête*
beast	*bête* (noir)
hostel	*hotel*
crisp	*crêpe*
(*e*)*squire*	*equerry*

(The circumflex accent marks a change in the vowel resulting from the loss of *s*.)

The position of stress in a loan word can also permit us to distinguish earlier from later borrowings. In French words, the stress often falls on a syllable other than the first, whereas in English words, it falls on the first or root syllable. When words are first introduced from French into English, they are stressed as they would be in French; hence, many French words in Middle English have their stress on the last syllable, as in *pilgrimáge, natúre,* and *coráge* 'heart'. The longer words exist in the language, however, the more likely they are to be assimilated to the English accentual pattern, hence ModE *pílgrimage, náture,* and *cóurage*. Modern borrowings from French into English, on the other hand, may retain their French accent. The following doublets show different degrees of assimilation to the English stress pattern:

earlier borrowing (English stress pattern)	later borrowing (French stress pattern)
móral	*moróle*
géntle	*gentéel*
líquor	*liquéur*
sálon	*salóon*
drágon	*dragóon*
cáddie	*cadét*

Present-day dialects of English exhibit variation in the extent to which they have assimilated French loan words, e.g. *fíllet/fillét, cígarette/cigarétte, gárage/garáge,* and *bállet/ballét*.

Latin Influence

For much of the Middle English period, Latin served as the language in which official records were kept. Using Latin rather than English for this purpose 'represents . . . the transfer from a national standard to the prevailing European standard' (Knowles 1997:48). Words borrowed directly from Latin at this time constitute a fourth period of Latin borrowing (see Chapter 6). Often it is difficult to determine whether a word was borrowed directly from Latin or came into English via French. However, it is likely that more learned loan words, specialized vocabulary from the realms of religion, law, scholarship, medicine, science, and literature, were often borrowed directly from Latin (e.g. *immortal, scripture, client, homicide, legal, testimony, desk, formal, history, index, genius, library, conclude, depression, gesture, imaginary*). Direct Latin borrowings also tend to date from a later period than the French borrowings, particularly in the fifteenth century, when writers self-consciously and extensively used rather artificial and unusual borrowings called *aureate* terms (meaning that the words were 'gilded'). Many of these have not survived into Modern English, such as *abusion, dispone,* and *equipolent* (whereas three-quarters of the words which we can confidently identify as borrowed from French did survive).

One consequence of borrowing from both Latin and French is the introduction of new affixes (prefixes and suffixes). Speakers analyze the structure of Latinate words into their constituent parts and then extend the affix to new lexical roots. For example, ME borrowings from French such as *acceptable, agreeable, comparable, desirable,* and *reasonable* were analyzed into a root plus the suffix *-able*. Then, this suffix was added to other roots, including those of native origin, such as *believable* (appearing first in 1382), *understandable* (1475), *unthinkable* (1430), and *eatable* (1483). Likewise, ME borrowings from French such as *coward, mustard, bastard,* and *custard* were seen to have *-ard* suffixes, subsequently giving us *sluggard* (1398), *wizard* (1440), and *dullard* (1440) based on English roots. Because this two-part process of acquiring and spreading affixes takes time, many of the Latinate affixes first borrowed in word forms in Middle English do not become productive until Early Modern English (see Chapter 10).

A second consequence of borrowing from both Latin and French is the existence of two or three levels of synonyms in English. The synonyms differ in register: that is, they are formal or informal, colloquial (characteristic of the spoken language) or literary, popular or learned. When synonyms exist on all three levels, the English, the French, and the Latin, the words tend to be colloquial, literary, or learned, respectively:

English	**French**	**Latin**
rise	*mount*	*ascend*
fire	*flame*	*conflagration*
fear	*terror*	*trepidation*
holy	*sacred*	*consecrated*
kingly	*royal*	*regal*

More often, synonyms exist on only two levels:

English	**French**
hut	*cottage*
hearty	*cordial*
help	*aid*
feed	*nourish*
bill	*beak*
child	*infant*
wedding	*marriage*
wish	*desire*
meal	*dinner*
happiness	*felicity*

In addition to the distinction between colloquial and literary, these synonyms may be semantically differentiated. For example, while *help/aid* or *hide/conceal* are largely the same except in respect to formality (*aid* and *conceal* being more formal), the words *child* and *infant* reflect a difference in age; *hut* and *cottage* reflect a difference in architectural style or structure.

Exercise 8.2 Word Stock of Middle English

1. Using the following list, match the pairs of words with the best explanation (*A*, *B*, or *C*) for their forms. Then say which pairs are doublets.

> A. Norman *versus* Central French
> B. Earlier *versus* later borrowing
> C. Synonyms of English *versus* French origin

a.   negligent/negligee _____

b.   case/chest   _____

c.   folk/people   _____

d.   critic/critique   _____

e.   wimple/guimpe   _____

f.   horse/courser   _____

g.   channel/canal   _____

h.   ham/pork   _____

2. Sort the following words into synonym triplets under their most likely headings.

commence	voracious	tine
keen	even (v)	acute
hide	barb	covetous
greedy	begin	conceal
prong	level (v)	initiate
suppress	fine	equalize

English	French	Latin
_____	_____	_____
_____	_____	_____
_____	_____	_____
_____	_____	_____
_____	_____	_____
_____	_____	_____

The Written Records of Middle English

Middle English Dialects

Traditionally, Middle English is seen as existing in five regional dialects that closely correspond to the four dialect areas of Old English (see Figure 8.2). The Northern dialect, spoken north of the Humber, corresponds to OE Northumbrian; the West Midland and East Midland dialects, spoken between the Thames and the Humber with the dividing line between east and west running north from Oxford, correspond to OE Mercian; Kentish, spoken in Kent and part of Sussex, corresponds roughly to OE Kentish; and Southwestern, including the rest of the area south of the Thames, corresponds to OE West Saxon. Kentish and Southwestern are sometimes grouped together as Southern. Current scholarship on Middle English dialectology has now shown that the dialect situation was much more complex and fluid. Based on all extant written records, scholars have assembled detailed accounts and maps of Middle English dialectal features. They have found, for example, that features formerly identified as Northern may appear in pocket areas in other parts of the country (see the linguistic atlases cited at the end of the chapter).

Generally, we can describe the Northern dialect as the most innovative (that is, showing the greatest change from Old English) and the Southern dialect as the most conservative (that is, best preserving phonological and grammatical features of Old English). The Northern innovations can probably be attributed to the admixture of Scandinavian speakers. Given the diversity of dialects and the diglossia (discussed above), it is only at the very end of the Middle English period that a unified standard of English emerges.

The dialects of Middle English exhibit phonological and morphological differences. The most obvious developments in phonology affect the OE sounds [ā], [ȳ, ɣ], [eə, ɛə], and initial [f, s, and θ]. The most obvious differences in morphology are in the forms of the third-person feminine and plural pronouns, in the forms of the present participle, in the plural noun inflections, and in the third-person singular and plural present-tense verb inflections. We will examine some of these in this and the next chapter.

Writers of the time were aware of the dialect diversity in Middle English. John of Trevisa's translation of Ralph Higden's Latin *Polychronicon* provides a wealth of information about contemporary attitudes toward language (a selection taken from Babington [1865:Vol. 2, 157–63] is given below). Higden attributes the dialect diversity of English to the settlement patterns of the Germanic tribes and to mingling with the Scandinavians and Normans. He laments the resulting 'debasement' of the language—the 'straunge wlafferyng, chiterynge, harrynge, and garrynge grisbayting' (that is, 'stammering, jabbering, snarling, and chattering gnashing of teeth')—that constitutes speech for some. He sees it as a 'great wonder' that such diversity could exist in England. He also comments on the radical nature of the Northern dialect, accounting for this by the presence of strange languages and by distance from the center of political power in the south. Moreover, he points out that the use of French in schools and the acquisition of French is a means of social advancement. Trevisa's parenthetical comments in Higden's text (given below in brackets) provide fascinating information about the ways in which the status of English and French changed between the time of Higden's text, *c.* 1327, and the translation, *c.* 1387. Trevisa comments that since the plague of 1348–50, English has been used in the schools, and gentlemen's children are no longer learning French. Although he thinks they learn English quite well, Trevisa notes that 'children of gramer scole conneþ na more Frensche þan can hir lift heele' (translated: 'grammar school children know no more French than their left heel knows'). Unlike Chaucer's relatively easy-to-read English, Trevisa's Southwestern dialect (with added Midland features) is difficult to understand; reading the text out loud can help.

Figure 8.2 The Dialects of Middle English

As hit is i-knowe how meny manere peple beeþ in þis ilond, þere beeþ also so many dyuers longages and tonges; noþeles Walsche men and Scottes, þat beeþ nouȝt i-medled wiþ oþer naciouns, holdeþ wel nyh hir firste longage and speche; but ȝif the Scottes þat were somtyme confederat and wonede wiþ þe Pictes drawe somwhat after hir speche. but þe Flemmynges þat woneþ in þe weste side of Wales haueþ i-left her straunge speche and spekeþ Saxonliche i-now. Also Englische men, þey hadde from the bygynnynge þre manere speche, norþerne, sowþerne, and middel speche in þe myddel of þe lond, as þey come of þre manere peple of Germania, noþeles by comyxtioun and mellynge firste wiþ Danes and afterward wiþ Normans, in meny þe contray longage is apayred, and som vseþ straunge wlafferynge, chiterynge, harrynge, and garrynge grisbayting. This apayrynge of þe burþe of þe tunge is bycause of tweie þinges; oon is for children in scole aȝenst þe vsage and manere of alle oþere naciouns beeþ com-pelled for to leue hire owne longage, and for to construe hir lessouns and here þynges in Frensche, and so þey haueþ seþ þe Normans come first in to Engelond. Also gentil men children beeþ i-tauȝt to speke Frensche from þe time þat þey beeþ i-rokked in here cradel, and kunneþ speke and playe wiþ a childes broche; and vplondisshe men wil likne hym self to gentil men, and fondeþ wiþ greet besynesse for to speke Frensce, for to be more i-told of.

[Þis manere was moche i-vsed to for firste deth and is siþþe sumdel i-chaunged; for Iohn Cornwaile, a maister of grammer, chaunged þe lore in gramer scole and construccioun of Frensche in to Englische; and Richard Pencriche lerned þe manere techynge of hym and of oþere men of Pencrich; so þat now, þe ȝer of oure Lorde a þowsand þre hundred and foure score and fyue, and of þe secounde kyng Richard after þe conquest nyne, in alle þe gramere scoles of Engelond, children leueþ Frensche and construeþ and lerneþ an Englische, and haueþ þerby auauntage in oon side, and disauauntage in anoþer side; here auauntage is, þat þey lerneþ her gramer in lasse tyme þan children were i-woned to doo; dis-auauntage is þat now children of gramer scole conneþ na more Frensche þan can hir lift heele, and þat is harme for hem and þey schulle passe þe see and trauaille in straunge landes and in many oþer places. Also gentil men haueþ now moche i-left for to teche here children Frensche.] Hit semeþ a greet wonder how Englische, þat is þe burþe tonge of Englische men, and her owne langage and tonge, is so dyuerse of sown in þis oon ilond, and þe langage of Normandie is comlynge of anoþer londe, and hath oon manere soon among alle men þat spekeþ hit ariȝt in Engelond. [Nouerþeles þere is as many dyuers manere Frensche in þe reem of Fraunce as is dyuers manere Englische in þe reem of Engelond.]

Also of þe forsaide Saxon tonge þat is i-deled aþre, and is abide scarsliche wiþ fewe vplondissche men is greet wonder; for men of þe est wiþ men of þe west, as it were vndir þe same partie of heuene, acordeþ more in sownynge of speche þan men of þe norþ wiþ men of þe souþ; þerfore hit is þat Mercii, þat beeþ men of myddel Engelond, as it were parteners of þe endes, vnderstondeþ bettre þe side langages, norþerene and souþerene, þan norþerene and souþerene vnderstondeþ eiþer oþer.

Al þe langage of þe Norþhumbres, and specialliche at ȝork, is so scharp, slitting, and frotynge, and vnschape, þat we souþerene men may þat longage vnneþe vnderstonde. I trowe þat þat is bycause þat þey beeþ nyh to straunge men and naciouns þat spekeþ strongeliche, and also bycause þat þe kynges of Engelond woneþ alwey fer from þat cuntrey; for þey beeþ more i-torned to þe souþ contray, and ȝif þey gooþ to þe norþ contrey þey gooþ wiþ greet help and strengþe. Þe cause why þey beeþ more in þe souþ contrey þan in þe norþ is for hit may be better corne londe, more peple, more noble citees, and more profitable hauenes. (Trevisa, *Polychronicon*, Book 1, Chapter 59)

The first literary representation of dialect in English occurs in the following excerpt from Geoffrey Chaucer's 'The Reeve's Tale' from *The Canterbury Tales*. Here Chaucer parodies the Northern dialect of two students, John and Alan; Northern features in their speech include the -*s* verbal endings of *fares*, *boes*, *has*, and *werkes*; the long *a* of *na* and *ham*; and the words *boes* ('behooves'), *swa* ('so'), and *heythen* ('hence').

Aleyn spak first: 'Al hayl, Symond, y-fayth!

Hou fares thy faire doghter and thy wyf?'

  'Aleyn, welcome', quod Symkyn, 'by my lyf!

And John also, how now, what do ye heer?'

  'Symond', quod John, 'by God, nede has na peer.

Hym boes serve hymself that has na swayn,

Or elles he is a fool, as clerkes sayn.

Oure manciple, I hope he wil be deed,

Swa werkes ay the wanges in his heed;

And forthy is I come, and eek Alayn,

To grynde oure corn and carie it ham agayn;

I pray yow spede us heythen that ye may.'

(Chaucer, 'The Reeve's Tale', ll. 4022–33)[2]

A second example of the literary representation of a Middle English dialect occurs in 'The Second Shepherd's Play', a mystery play of the Towneley Cycle. When the Northern shepherd Mak imitates a Southern dialect, saying *ich* instead of the Northern form *ik* for the first-person pronoun and using the *-th* verbal ending, he is rebuked by his fellow shepherd as follows: 'Now take outt that Sothren tothe / And sett in a torde' (Cawley 1958:48). The playwright is satirizing Mak's social pretension. From these passages we can conclude that the Northern dialect was stigmatized and that the Southern dialect carried some prestige.

Middle English Literature

Middle English literature can be divided into several periods:

1. Between 1100 and 1250, literature was primarily religious, except for Layamon's *Brut*, *King Horn*, and *The Owl and the Nightengale*. Most secular lit-

---

2 The passage may be translated into ModE as follows: Alan spoke first, 'All hail, Simond, in-faith! / How fare thy fair daughter and thy wife?' / 'Alan, welcome', said Simkin, 'by my life! / And John also, how now what do you here?' / 'Simond', said John, 'By God, necessity has no equal. / It behooves him who has no servant to serve himself, / Or else he is a fool, as clerks say. / Our steward, I expect he will be dead, / So ache always the molar teeth in his head; / And therefore have I come, and also Alan, / To grind our grain and carry it home again; / I pray you speed us hence as you may.'

erature was in French. (As Knowles [1997:48] remarks, the fact that English texts were produced at all during this post-Conquest period is remarkable given that the English speakers lacked any political authority to promote use of their language.)

2.   Between 1250 and 1350, both religious and secular literature was produced, including verse romances, lyric poems, and beast epics, such as *Havelock*, the Harley lyrics, and *Dame Siriz*.

3.   Between 1350 and 1400, the great writers—Geoffrey Chaucer, John Gower, William Langland, the *Gawain* poet—were at work, and poets began using rhymed metrical verse (borrowed from the French) and also revived the native alliterative verse.

4.   Between 1400 and 1500, the literature (characterized by John Lydgate and the 'Scottish Chaucerians' Robert Henryson and later William Dunbar) was mainly derivative of the great fourteenth century works. The mystery plays (York, Towneley, Chester, Coventry) also date from this period. The writers whom we take to mark the end of the Middle English period are Sir Thomas Malory, whose Arthurian legend was completed in 1469, and William Caxton.

We have major texts written in all of the Middle English regional varieties, though Kentish texts are rare. For example, Barbour's *Bruce* and the *Wakefield Plays* are written in the Northern dialect; Layamon's *Brut*, Langland's *Piers Plowman*, and the anonymous *Sir Gawain and the Green Knight* show us the West Midland dialect; *Dame Siriz*, *The Owl and the Nightengale,* and *The Fox and the Wolf* display the Southwestern dialect; and Michel's *Ayenbite of Inwyt*, the Kentish dialect. The majority of surviving texts are written in the East Midland dialect, such as Wyclif's translation of the Bible and the *Peterborough Chronicle*. Both Chaucer and Gower wrote in the East Midland dialect, in the dialect specific to London.

 Listen to the sound recording of the *Alliterative Morte Arthure* on the companion website (Reading 2) and follow along with the written text. This poem dates from the end of the fourteenth century and probably originates in the north midlands. It is an important text within a genre called the 'Alliterative Revival', which employs both native alliteration and French rhyme. The vocabulary contains a number of Romance borrowings. Using a dictionary, you should be able to identify at least the following words as French loans in the first fourteen lines: *lege* ('liege') (2), *chamber* (3), *comfort* (4), *tenderly* (6), *langour* ('languor') (10), *destainy* ('destiny') (12), *dole* (cf. *dolour*) (12), *greve* ('grieve') (13). Consider the word *queen* in line 4. It may look like a French word, but it is actually an Old English word written according to Norman spelling conventions, as will be discussed in the next section.

Orthographic Changes

The systematic, essentially phonemic spelling system of Old English underwent a change in Middle English. In addition to replacing runic symbols with Latin

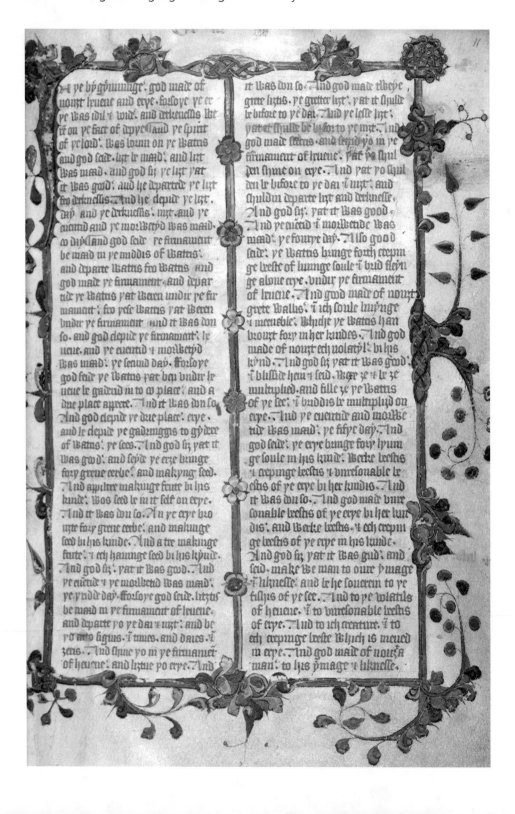

letters, Norman scribes—sometimes working with an imperfect knowledge of English—introduced a number of Romance spelling conventions. These changes initiated the confusion of English spelling in which symbols no longer correspond exactly with sounds. This lack of correspondence would later be intensified by the vowel changes of the Great Vowel Shift (to be discussed in Chapter 10). Below, Table 8.2a summarizes the most important substitutions made by the French scribes in the spelling of consonants. Note that in the French system the *h* came to indicate the fricative quality of the neighboring *s, t, c*, and *w* (the sounds [š], [θ, ð], [č], and [hw]). The symbol ð disappeared quite early but *þ* continued to be used and can be found even in some Early Modern printed texts. The letters *ch* represents [č] in French borrowings into Middle English such as *chambre, charitee*, and *chaunce*; meanwhile, *c* represents [s] before *e* and *i*, as in *circuit* and *cercle*, but [k] before *a, o*, and *u*, as in *cause, company*, and *curious*. The digraph *sc* or *sk* is reserved for [sk] in borrowed words, as in French *scorn* and *scarlet*; Old Norse *scathe, score*, and *sky*; and Latin *scripture*. In French words, *g* denotes the sound [ǰ] before *e* and *i* (e.g. *gem* and *gingre*), and *gu* denotes [g] before *e* and *i* (e.g. *guide* and *guile*).

Table 8.2b below gives the main changes in the writing of vowel sounds. For purposes of visual clarity, scribes inserted the symbol *o* in place of *u* when it appeared next to other letters written with downstrokes, as in *some, wolf, loch* (< *sum, wulf, luh*). Similarly, the symbol *y* was used in place of *i* (as in *nyce* or *lym*). The *y* was also used for long [i], and for *i* in final position (e.g. *lyf* 'life', *thy*). To show that a preceding vowel is long, scribes might add a final *e*, as in *bride*; to indicate a short vowel, they might double the next consonant, as in *dinner* (cf. *dine*). The letters *i* and *j* as well as *u* and *v* could represent both vowel and consonant sounds: in general, *i* and *u* were used medially and *j* and *v* initially. It is possible to differentiate vowels and consonants by looking at syllable structure. If the letter corresponds to the nucleus of a syllable, a vowel is being represented (e.g. *dint, lust, jre, vndo*); otherwise, a consonant is intended (e.g. *adiacent, ouer, joly, vane*). As a later addition to the alphabet, *j* is not common in Middle English, however.

Remember that these indicate spelling, not sound, changes. The use of *y* for *i* does not indicate the rounding of the vowel, nor does the use of *ou* for [ū] indicate the diphthongization of the long vowel; oddly enough, though, this vowel was diphthongized much later—in the fifteenth century—to [aʊ], so that the sound came to resemble the spelling.

Opposite. Figure 8.3   A Page from the Arundel Manuscript. From approximately 1150, English was written in a style of handwriting called Gothic hand and seen in this page from a late fourteenth-century manuscript of Wyclif's Bible (Arundel MS 104, vol. 1, f11), was still quite angular but showed a greater contrast between thick and thin strokes. The Gothic hand was replaced beginning in the mid-fifteenth century by the Chancery hand, which is the basis of modern handwriting (© The British Library).

Table 8.2 Orthographic Changes from Old English to Middle English

a) consonants		
OE orthographic symbol	ME orthographic symbol	example
ƿ	uu / w	weg
ð / þ	th	theef
hw	wh (w *in the South*, quh *or* qu *in the North*)	what
c = [č]	ch	child
c = [k]	k	knitte
cw or cƿ = [kw]	qu	queen
cg = [ǰ]	gg (*later spelled* dg)	egg 'edge'
sc = [š]	sh	shape
h = [x] or [ç]	ȝ (*later spelled* gh)	riȝt 'right'
f = [v]	v (*initially*) u (*medially*)	vice / haue
ȝ = [g]	g	good
ȝ = [j]	ȝ (*later spelled* y)	ȝeer 'year'
ȝ = [ɣ]	ȝ (*later spelled* w)	boȝe 'bow'
b) vowels		
OE orthographic symbol	ME orthographic symbol	example
æ	a / e	that, clene 'clean'
long e	e / ee / ie	ges 'geese', hie 'he'
long o	o / oo	rote 'root', doom
long u	ou / ow	hous 'house', how

Try to figure out the Middle English respelling of the underlined Old English letters:

*hw*ī*t*   *þ*ō*ht*   *o*f*er*   *æ*sc   *mū*ð*a*   *ȝ*ōd   *c*eal*c*   *c*wacian   *sc*ip[3]

3 The answers are *wh, th, ȝ, u, ash, outh, goo, ch, k, qu, sh* (ModE *white, thought, over, ash, mouth, good, chalk, quake*, and *ship*).

Exercise 8.3   Orthography

Indicate the probable Middle English spelling of the underlined letter or letters in the following Old English words. Then supply a probable Modern English reflex (word).

a. c͟niht   _____ _____   e. c͟ēosan   _____ _____

b. þ͟ēah   _____ _____   f. mu͟no͟c   _____ _____

c. rē͟fa   _____ _____   g. brō͟c   _____ _____

d. sc͟ea͟fan _____ _____   h. cū͟ð   _____ _____

Consonant Changes

The consonant inventory of Middle English remains much the same as that of Old English. However, there is an increase in the number of distinctive sounds. This came about by a process of *phonemicization*, in which sounds that are originally allophones of the same phoneme become separate phonemes. In Old English, the pairs [s] and [z], [f] and [v], and [θ] and [ð] are allophones of the same phoneme, occurring predictably in complementary phonological environments, with the voiceless variant occurring word-initially and word-finally and next to a voiceless sound, and the voiced variant occurring word-medially. In Middle English, we can no longer rely on environment to determine the sound; the allophones become unpredictable for a variety of reasons, external and internal:

- First, words were borrowed from French with initial [z] and [v], a position in which those sounds had never been found in Old English: e.g. *zest, zeal*, and *zone*; *virtue, vileinye, venim*, and *veyn*. (Words also came into the standard from the Southern dialect with initial [v]; see Table 8.3 below.)
- Second, loss of final -*e* (discussed below) caused [z], [v], and [ð] to occur in final position, where Old English would have had [s], [f], and [θ], as in *maze, groove*, and *bathe*.
- Third, simplification of the pronunciation of the double consonants [ff, ss, θθ > f, s, θ] led to the voiceless variants occurring in medial position, as in *offren* and *missen*.
- Fourth, [θ] in initial position in unstressed words such as adverbs, pronouns, demonstratives, and conjunctions became voiced to [ð], as in *then, there, they, them, this, that, though*.

In addition to the phonemicization of the voiced and voiceless fricatives, we also see that [č] became a separate phoneme from [k] (in large part because of borrowings like *change* from French which contained the sound [č] before back vowels) and [ɣ], shortly to be lost altogether, became a separate phoneme from [g] (in large part because of borrowings like *rug* from Old Norse containing [g]). The resulting consonant system of Middle English is shown in Figure 8.4. (As in Figure 6.3 when more than one sound is included in a single box, these represent allophones of a single phoneme.)

None of the other consonant changes affected the inventory of sounds in the language but were conditioned changes in particular environments; most fall under the types of sound changes we discussed in Chapter 3. As you can see in Table 8.3, these were all relatively minor, affecting small sets of lexical items; they did not alter the entire consonant system. However, one of these changes was widespread and had very important consequences for the grammar of Middle English, namely the loss of unstressed final *n*. The impact of this phonological change on inflectional endings—many of which contained *n* and were always unstressed—will be examined in the next chapter.

Table 8.3 Consonant Changes from Old English to Middle English

simplification of a consonant cluster	
[hr, hn, hl > r, n, l]	OE hrōf, hnecca, hlid > ME roof, necke, lid
[hw] > [w] (in the South)	OE hwæt > ME wat, what
[wl] > [l]	OE wlispian > ME lispe(n)
[d, t] > Ø in clusters with *s*	OE andswaru, godspell, betst > ME answere, gospel, best
loss of a consonant	
[-w-, -v-] > Ø	OE lāwerce > ME larke, OE hlāford > ME lord
[w] between a consonant and a back vowel > Ø	OE swā > ME so
[č] in unstressed syllables > Ø	OE -līce > ME -ly
[l] before [č] > Ø	OE ǣlc > ME ech, OE swulc > ME such
merger in unstressed syllables	
[m] and [n] to [n], subsequent loss of [n]	OE sittan > ME sitte, OE oxum > ME oxe

Continued

Table 8.3 Consonant Changes from Old English to Middle English—*Continued*

addition of a consonant (or intrusion)	
[d] inserted between [n] and [r], [n] and [l], [n] and [s], [l] and [r]	OE ganra, spinel, OF jaunice, OE ealre > ME gander, spindel, jaundis, alder
[b] inserted between [m] and [l], [m] and [r]	OE slūmerde > ME slumberd(e)
[p] inserted between [m] and [t]	OE ǣmtig > ME empty
excrescent [t]	OF ancien > ME ancien(t)
vocalization	
[jɛ] > [ɪ]	OE scīrgerēfa > ME shir(e)reve 'sheriff'
[ɣ] > [w] after [l] or [r]	OE belgan > ME belwen 'bellow', OE morgen > ME morwe
metathesis	
[r] + vowel > vowel + [r]	OE bridd > ME bird, OE þridda > ME third
vowel + [r] > [r] + vowel	OE fersc > ME fresh, OE þurh > ME throuȝ
stop + [s] > [s] + stop	OE wæps > ME waspe
metathesis of juncture	OF naperon, noumpere (< non + pere) > ME an apron, an oumpere 'umpire'; OE (an) ēacanama 'an also name' > ME a nickname
assimilation and dissimilation	
assimilation	OE wīfmann, hænep, lēofmann, OF confort > ME wimman, hemp, lemman, comfort
dissimilation	OE nosþirl > ME nostril
lenition	
[d] > [ð]	OE fæder > ME father, OE mōdor > ME mother
voicing	
initial [f, s, θ] in Southern dialects	OE fana, fæt, fyxen> ME vane, vat, vixen

Manner of Articulation		Place of Articulation							
		Bilabial	Labiodental	Interdental	Alveolar	Alveolo-palatal	Palatal	Velar	Glottal
Stop	Voiceless	p			t			k	
	Voiced	b			d			g	
Nasal		m			n			ŋ	
Fricative	Voiceless		f	θ	s	š	ç	x	h
	Voiced		v	ð	z			(γ)	
Affricate	Voiceless					č			
	Voiced					ǰ			
Approximant	Lateral				l				
	Retroflex/Trill				r				
	Glide/Semivowel						j	w	

Figure 8.4   The Consonants of Middle English

Exercise 8.4 Consonant Changes

Identify the consonant change in each of the following OE/ME pairs. ModE glosses are given as an aid.

Example:

OE þȳmel **ME** thimbel insertion of [b] between [m] and [l] **ModE** thimble

(Note that þ > th is merely an orthographic change)

	OE	ME	Sound Change	ModE
a.	blōstma	blosme	_____	blossom
b.	folgian	folwen	_____	follow
c.	hlāf	lof	_____	loaf
d.	cræt	cart	_____	cart
e.	lēohtlīc	līȝtli	_____	lightly
f.	behæs	behēst	_____	behest

Vowel Changes

In Middle English, we find changes both in the quality (place of articulation) and quantity (length) of vowels.

Vowel Reduction

Vowel reduction is the most important qualitative sound change we find in Middle English. Reduction is the centralization and laxing of the short vowels *a, o, u,* and *e* to schwa [ə] in many syllables other than those with primary stress. (Remember that a vowel constitutes the nucleus of a syllable.) The unstressed or weakly stressed syllables are

- the verbal prefixes and some nominal prefixes,
- every syllable other than the first in a polysyllabic word,
- the unstressed grammatical words, and,
- most importantly for the grammar, all inflectional endings.

We do not know why vowel reduction took place. The lack of stress on a vowel does not necessarily lead to its reduction to [ə]; many unstressed syllables contain full vowels in Modern English, as in *harmony* or *omit*. A fairly strong correlation does exist, however, between stressed sequences and higher or more fronted vowels, and between unstressed sequences and lower or more centralized vowels. Schwa is, of course, the most central vowel, the one which is least marked or distinguished. What cannot be doubted is that vowel reduction became a widespread feature of Middle English.

Look at Table 8.4 of OE and ME forms showing vowel reduction which occurred around the eleventh century. In every case, the vowel in the final syllable is written -*e*; on the basis of textual evidence scholars have determined that this sound is pronounced [ə]. In words longer than two syllables, such as OE *macodon* > ME *makede(n)*, all unstressed vowels could be reduced.[4]

Table 8.4 Reduction of Old English Vowels in Middle English

Old English	Middle English
talu	tāle
mōdor	mōder
tungan	tunge(n)
tūnas	tounes
bānas	bōnes
hēafod	hēved
bīndan	bīnde(n)
wicu	wēke
sceadu	schāde
gladost	gladest
dogga	dogge
stelan	stēle(n)
þrotu	thrōte

Other Qualitative Changes

The changes in vowel quality in Middle English are summarized in Figure 8.5. A number of observations concerning these changes can be made. First, the long [ȳ] merged with [ī], and the short [ʏ] with [ɪ], as a result of unrounding. (Remember,

---

4 Some of the sound changes shown in the forms in Table 8.4 are discussed later in the chapter, including open syllable lengthening in *tāle*, *wēke*, *schāde*, *stēle(n)*, and *thrōte*; the shift from [ā] to [ɔ] in *bōnes*; and the merger of [ēə] with [ē] in *hēved*.

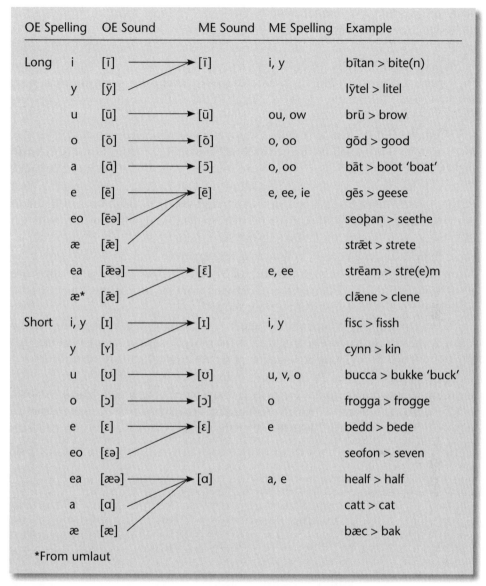

OE Spelling		OE Sound	ME Sound	ME Spelling	Example
Long	i	[ī] ⟶ [ī]		i, y	bītan > bite(n)
	y	[ȳ]			lȳtel > litel
	u	[ū] ⟶ [ū]		ou, ow	brū > brow
	o	[ō] ⟶ [ō]		o, oo	gōd > good
	a	[ā] ⟶ [ɔ]		o, oo	bāt > boot 'boat'
	e	[ē] ⟶ [ē]		e, ee, ie	gēs > geese
	eo	[ēə]			seoþan > seethe
	æ	[ǽ]			strǽt > strete
	ea	[ǽə] ⟶ [ɛ̄]		e, ee	strēam > stre(e)m
	æ*	[ǽ]			clǽne > clene
Short	i, y	[ɪ] ⟶ [ɪ]		i, y	fisc > fissh
	y	[ʏ]			cynn > kin
	u	[ʊ] ⟶ [ʊ]		u, v, o	bucca > bukke 'buck'
	o	[ɔ] ⟶ [ɔ]		o	frogga > frogge
	e	[ɛ] ⟶ [ɛ]		e	bedd > bede
	eo	[ɛə]			seofon > seven
	ea	[æə] ⟶ [a]		a, e	healf > half
	a	[a]			catt > cat
	æ	[æ]			bæc > bak

*From umlaut

Figure 8.5 Qualitative Vowel Changes from Old English to Middle English

though, that *i* and *y* are used as variants of one another in writing.) We do not see such a merger in West Midland and Southwestern dialects (in which the rounded vowel was preserved) nor in Kent and the Southeast (where the rounded vowel shifted to [e]).

Second, OE long [ā] shifted to long [ɔ] in all areas but the North (where it was preserved as [ā] and appears as [ē] in Modern Scots). Consequently, Middle English acquired two long *o*'s, written exactly the same. (Editors sometimes put a hook under the lower ǫ [ɔ̄], which is called 'open *o*'.) The only way to tell them apart is by their modern developments: the upper or 'close *o*' [ō] appears as [u], [ʊ], or [ə] in Modern English words spelled *oo*, such as *loot*, *look*, and *blood,* while the open [ɔ̄] appears as [oʊ] in Modern English words spelled *oa* or *o* plus silent *e*, such as *boat*, *moat,* and *rode*. The doublet *no/nay* is a result of the regular development of [ō] (giving *no*) and the preserved Northern form with unshifted [ā] (giving *nay*).

Third, the Old English long and short diphthongs smoothed into monophthongs as *eo* merged with *e*, and *ea* merged with *æ*. The only exception is in the Kentish dialect, which has long *eo* as a mid-front rounded vowel. Long *æ* has a complex history. It had shifted already to [ē] in all of the Old English dialects except West Saxon; in the Middle English period, the sound shifted in this dialect as well, merging with *e* and *eo* as long [ē]. The long *æ* that resulted from umlaut merged with the diphthong *ea* as long [ɛ̄]. Like long open [ɔ̄], this *e* is called 'open *e*' and is sometimes indicated with a hook by editors as ę. Modern developments do not allow us to distinguish the two long *e*'s, [ɛ̄] and [ē], of Middle English: both sounds appear as [i] in Modern English. However, words deriving from the open *e* are often respelled *ea* in later English (note the word *stream* above).

Apart from vowel reduction, the short vowels show few changes in Middle English: the merger of short *a*, *æ*, and *ea* as [ɑ] as well as the unrounding of the high front vowel and the monophthongization of the diphthongs already mentioned.

At the same time that the Old English diphthongs were lost in Middle English, a variety of new diphthongs developed. The inventory of new diphthongs is shown in Figure 8.6. The processes which produced these diphthongs are complex, and we will focus here on the principles rather than the details. There are four major sources of diphthongs in Middle English:

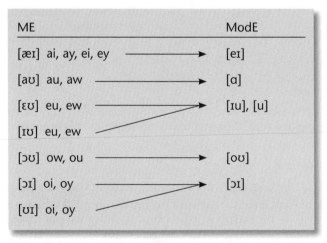

Figure 8.6 New Diphthongs in Middle English

1. borrowing – two diphthongs [ɔɪ] and [ʊɪ] from French. Examples of the former are ME *chois, noise*, and *joy* and of the latter *boilen, poysen*, and *joynen*.
2. vocalization of [w] to [ʊ] after ME [ɑ, ō, ē, ī] – this produces the diphthongs [aʊ] as in *strawe*, [ɔʊ] as in *glowen*, [ɛʊ] as in *fewe*, and [ɪʊ] as in *trewe, newe*.
3. vocalization of ȝ, either of [j] to [ɪ] after ME front vowels or of [ɣ] to [ʊ] after ME back vowels – in the first case, this produces [æɪ], as in *gray* or *leide*; in the second case, it produces [aʊ] as in *drawe* or *lawe*, and [ɔʊ] as in *bowe* or *owen*.
4. development of a glide before *h* [x], either of [ɪ] after ME front vowels or of [ʊ] after ME back vowels: in the first case, this produces [æɪ] as in *neigh* or *eighte*; in the second case, this produces [aʊ] as in *taught*, and [ɔʊ] as in *dough*.

The vowel system of Middle English can be represented as in Figure 8.7.

	Monophthongs		
	Front	**Central**	**Back**
High	ī ɪ		ū ʊ
Mid	ē ɛ̄ ɛ	ə	ō ɔ̄ ɔ
Low			ɑ
	Diphthongs		
	ɪʊ ɛʊ æɪ	aʊ	ʊɪ ɔɪ ɔʊ

Figure 8.7   The Vowel System of Middle English

Exercise 8.5 Transcription

Give phonetic transcriptions of the following ME words. The Modern English word is given for reference. Remember that *ee* = long *e*, *oo* = long *o*, *ou* = long *u* (or a diphthong).

	OE	Phonetic Transcriptions	ModE
a.	shīres	_____	shires
b.	bāne	_____	bane
c.	weie	_____	way

d. reel   _____   real

e. yclipped   _____   clept (obsolete, meaning 'called')

f. strete*   _____   street

g. chapelain   _____   chaplain

h. withouten   _____   without

i. though   _____   though

j. wight   _____   wight (obsolete, meaning 'person')

*The final -*e* in this word is scribal (not pronounced), indicating a preceding long
  vowel or diphthong.

Quantitative Changes

Quantitative changes affect the length of vowels (and sometimes consonants). They
are usually associated with changes in intonation or accent. The borrowing of large
numbers of French words with an accentual pattern quite different from the native one
could well have brought about the quantitative changes observed in Middle English.

One kind of lengthening actually predates Middle English. Old English lengthening affects certain vowels before sequences of a nasal or liquid plus stop. The most
common clusters causing lengthening are -*nd*, -*mb*, -*rd*, and -*ld*:

-nd	*blind*	>	*blīnd*
	pund	>	*pūnd* 'pound'
-mb	*lamb*	>	*lāmb*
	camb	>	*cāmb* 'comb'
	climb	>	*clīmb*
-rd	*word*	>	*wōrd*
-ld	*mild*	>	*mīld*
	feld	>	*fēld* 'field'
	gold	>	*gōld*
	bald	>	*bāld* 'bold'

In some cases, this early lengthening does not survive, as in, for example, *lamb*; if
the long vowel had survived, this word would rhyme with *comb*.

An important case of lengthening that began in the first half of the thirteenth
century is called *open syllable lengthening*. Although its conditions are in dispute,
scholars agree upon the results of the change: a short stressed vowel in an open

syllable of a two-syllable word (normally the first syllable of the word) is lengthened. An open syllable is one which ends in a vowel. Using the schematization C = consonant, V = vowel, and - = syllable boundary, we can represent open syllables in two-syllable words as follows:

- V́-CV(C)
- CV́-CV(C)

In Middle English, lengthening first affects short stressed *a, æ, e,* and *o* and later *i* and *u,* as represented in Figure 8.8. OE *æ-cer* has the structure V́-CVC and OE *ta-lu* has the structure CV́-CV; thus, the first syllable in each word is open and the vowel is lengthened. Open syllable lengthening is, incidentally, the only source of long [ɑ] in Middle English because the original long [ā] shifted to [ɔ]. Open syllable lengthening is hard to predict from Modern English forms because the loss of the final *e* sound (see the next chapter) changes open syllables to closed syllables: CVCe > CVC.

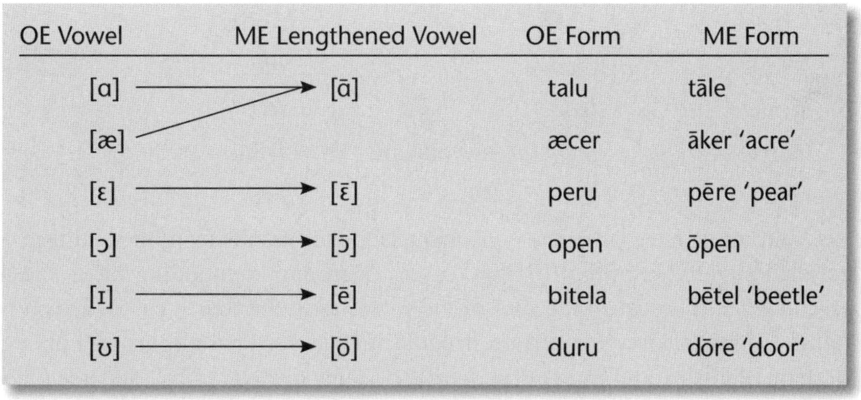

OE Vowel	ME Lengthened Vowel	OE Form	ME Form
[ɑ] ⟶	[ā]	talu	tāle
[æ] ↗		æcer	āker 'acre'
[ɛ] ⟶	[ɛ̄]	peru	pēre 'pear'
[ɔ] ⟶	[ɔ̄]	open	ōpen
[ɪ] ⟶	[ē]	bitela	bētel 'beetle'
[ʊ] ⟶	[ō]	duru	dōre 'door'

Figure 8.8 Open Syllable Lengthening in Middle English

In Middle English, open syllable lengthening led to some irregularities between singular and plural forms, e.g.:

singular	**plural**
path	*pāthes*
staf	*stāves*
wish	*wīshes*

In the singular, the short vowel is in a syllable that ends in a consonant (closed syllable, as in *staf* CCVC), but when the *-es* plural ending is added, the root syllable becomes open (as in *stāves* CCV-CVC), prompting the vowel to lengthen. In most cases, this irregularity has been removed by analogy; otherwise we would say [pæθ], but [peɪŏz]. Nevertheless, the irregularity has lived on in *staff, staves* (cf. the newer formation *staffs*).

We find the opposite process, the shortening of vowels, in three Middle English contexts. Shortening affects all unstressed long vowels:

OE	ME	ModE
mannhād	*manhod*	*manhood*
frēondlēas	*frendles*	*friendless*
āwacan	*awake(n)*	*awake*
tō morgen(ne)	*tomorwe*	*tomorrow*

The impact of this change is shown above on unstressed derivational suffixes (as in the first two cases), unstressed prefixes (as in the third case), and unstressed function words (as in the fourth case, where *to* is historically a preposition).

Stressed long vowels before a consonant cluster are shortened:

OE	ME	ModE
blēdde	*bledde*	*bled*
lǣdde	*ledde*	*led*
lēofmann	*lemman* 'sweetheart'	*leman* (archaic)
ǣfre	*ever*	*ever*

We see shortening here when the consonant sequence results from the addition of an inflectional ending (as in the first two cases) or from compounding (as in the third case), and when it is part of the root of the word (as in the fourth case). This type of shortening is responsible for certain irregularities in verb paradigms still preserved in Modern English (e.g. *bleed/bled, lead/led, keep/kept, hide/hid*, and *feed/fed*) as well as vowel alternations between compounded and uncompounded forms (e.g. *wise/wisdom* and *five/fifteen/fifty*).

Finally, the shortening process affects stressed long vowels before two or more unstressed syllables:

OE	ME	ModE
hāligdæg	*holiday*	*holiday*
crīstendōm	*Christendom*	*Christendom*
sūþerne	*southerne*	*southern*

This third type of shortening also accounts for certain irregularities in Modern English, such as *south/southern, holy/holiday*, and *Christ/Christendom*. (We might expect shortening in the word *Christ* as well, since the long vowel is followed by two consonants, but there is inconsistency before the sequence *st*.) Combined with open syllable lengthening, this type of shortening also accounts for irregularities in Middle English between singular and plural forms, as with the words for *acre*, *saddle*, and *cradle*:

singular	plural
āker	*akeres*
sādel	*sadeles*
crādel	*cradeles*

The long vowel of the singular is the result of open syllable lengthening, while the short vowel of the plural is the result of shortening before two unstressed syllables. Analogy has eliminated this irregularity in Modern English.

Exercise 8.6 Vowel and Consonant Changes

Name the vowel and consonant changes represented by the following words and show the change in phonetic symbols. Ignore orthographic changes.

Example:

OE scamu   **ME** shāme   [ɑ] > [ā] lengthening in an open syllable

[ʊ] > [ə] reduction in an unstressed syllable

	OE	ME		Changes
a.	balu	bāle	(1)	_____
			(2)	_____
b.	flēon	flē	(1)	_____
			(2)	_____
c.	hrycgas	rigges	(1)	_____
			(2)	_____
			(3)	_____
d.	wegan	weie	(1)	_____
			(2)	_____
			(3)	_____
e.	hlǣne	lēne	(1)	_____
			(2)	_____
			(3)	_____

f.	stæfas	stāves	(1) _____
			(2) _____
			(3) _____

A Closer Look at the Language of a Middle English Text

The following selection of Middle English is from 'The General Prologue' to Geoffrey Chaucer's *The Canterbury Tales*. Chaucer wrote in a London dialect close to one that became standard Modern English. The verse form used here is imported from the continent (French or Italian, according to different scholars) and is based on meter as opposed to the native system of alliteration used in Old English and in some Middle English texts, such as *Piers Plowman* and *Sir Gawain and the Green Knight*. This passage contains an abundance of French vocabulary: *perced, veyne, licour, vertu, engendred, flour, inspired, tendre, cours, melodye, priketh, nature, corages, pilgrimages, palmeres, straunge, ferne, specially, seson, devout, hostelrye, compaignye, aventure*. The assimilation of French forms into English is shown by the English derivational and inflectional affixes which are attached to the borrowings, as in *prik-eth, special-ly, engendr-ed, corage-s, pilgrimage-s*. Despite all the French, every function word in this passage remains English, with the exception of the Old Norse pronoun *they* borrowed in the late Old English period. Therefore, we find English conjunctions (*whan, and, thanne*), demonstratives (*that*), prepositions (*with, to, of, into, from, in, by*), pronouns (*his, my, every, al, swich*), articles (*the, a*), and auxiliaries (*hath, was, is, wolden*). The core vocabulary is largely English, including basic verbs (*bathed, slepen, yronne, goon, wenden, seke, bifil, come, yfalle, ryde*), nouns (*roote, holt, heeth, sonne, folk, nyght, day, felaweshipe*), adjectives (*soote, smale, seeke, hooly, redy*), and numbers (*nyne, twenty*).

> Whan that Aprill with his shoures soote
> The droughte of March hath perced to the roote,
> And bathed every veyne in swich licour
> Of which vertu engendred is the flour;
> Whan Zephirus eek with his sweete breeth
> Inspired hath in every holt and heeth
> The tendre croppes, and the yonge sonne
> Hath in the Ram his half cours yronne,

And smale foweles maken melodye,
That slepen al the nyght with open ye
(So priketh hem Nature in hir corages),
Thanne longen folk to goon on pilgrimages,
And palmeres for to seken straunge strondes,
To ferne halwes, kowthe in sondry londes;
And specially from every shires ende
Of Engelond to Caunterbury they wende,
The hooly blisful martir for to seke,
That hem hath holpen whan that they were seeke.
   Bifil that in that seson on a day,
In Southwerk at the Tabard as I lay
Redy to wenden on my pilgrymage
To Caunterbury with ful devout corage,
At nyght was come into that hostelrye
Wel nyne and twenty in a compaignye,
Of sondry folk, by aventure yfalle
In felaweshipe, and pilgrimes were they alle,
That toward Caunterbury wolden ryde.
(Chaucer, 'The General Prologue', ll. 1–27)

The following version of the first 10 lines includes length markers over the vowels:

Whan that Āprill with his shōures sōote
The drōughte of March hath pērced tō the rōote,
And bāthed every veyne in swich licōur
Of which vertu engendred is the flōur;
Whan Zephirus ēek with his swēete brēeth
Inspīred hath in every holt and hēeth
The tendre croppes, and the yonge sonne
Hath in the Ram his half cōurs yronne,
And smale fōweles māken melodȳe,
That slēpen al the nyght with ōpen ȳe

There is not complete agreement among scholars about Chaucer's pronunciation (e.g. whether unstressed *e* is pronounced [ɛ] or [ə] if at all, or whether weakly stressed words such as *of* have voiceless or voiced consonants, i.e. [ɔf] or [ɔv]). However, a likely transcription of the first 10 lines follows:

hwan ðat āprıl wıθ hıs šūrɛs sōtɛ

ðɛ drūxt ɔf marč haθ pērsɛd tō ðɛ rōtɛ

and būðɛd ɛvrı væın ın swıč lıkūr

ɔf hwıč vɛrtʊ ɛnǰɛndrɛd ıs ðɛ flūr

hwan zɛfırʊs ēk wıθ hıs swētɛ brēθ

ınspīrɛd haθ ın ɛvrı hɔlt and hēθ

ðɛ tɛndrɛ krɔppɛs and ðɛ jʊŋgɛ sʊnnɛ

haθ ın ðɛ ram hıs halvɛ kūrs ırʊnnɛ

and smalɛ fūlɛs mākɛn mɛlɔdīɛ

ðat slēpɛn al ðɛ nīçt wīθ ɔpɛn īɛ

RECOMMENDED WEB LINKS

An interactive map showing the routes of Harold, William, and the Norse invaders appears at:

http://www.essentialnormanconquest.com/battle_bevs/bev_01.htm

Additional sites on the Norman Conquest and external history of the Middle English period include:

http://www.secretsofthenormaninvasion.com/
http://britannia.com/history/hastings.html
http://www.normanconquest.co.uk/

Contemporary accounts of the Conquest have been translated on the Britannia website:

http://www.britannia.com/history/docs/battle1066.html (William of Malmesbury's account)
http://www.britannia.com/history/docs/1066.html (The *Anglo-Saxon Chronicle* for 1066)

You can find a reproduction of the Bayeux Tapestry on the following website:

http://www.bayeuxtapestry.org.uk/

The Britannia site gives a useful timeline of events for the Middle English period:

http://britannia.com/history/medtime.html

For an interesting map of the spread of the plague along trade routes, see:

http://www.ucalgary.ca/HIST/tutor/imagemid/blackdeath.gif

To hear examples of the pronunciation of Chaucer's language, go to:

http://www.courses.fas.harvard.edu/~chaucer/pronunciation/

To hear Chaucer's work read aloud, go to:

http://academics.vmi.edu/english/audio/audio_index.html
http://pages.towson.edu/duncan/chaucer/index.htm

Many Middle English texts can be found at the following sites:

http://etext.lib.virginia.edu/mideng.browse.html (University of Virginia Electronic Text Center)
http://www.hti.umich.edu/c/cme/ (University of Michigan Humanities Text Initiative)
http://www.georgetown.edu/labyrinth/library/me/me.html (Georgetown University's Labyrinth Library)

An online version of John of Trevisa's *Polychronicon*, with a glossary, can be found at:

http://www.hf.ntnu.no/engelsk/staff/johannesson/!oe/texts/imed/05imed/05_2w.htm

FURTHER READING

There are numerous books on the Bayeux Tapestry, including a recent digital edition:

Foys, Martin K. 2003. *The Bayeux Tapestry on CD-ROM*. Woodbridge: Boydell & Brewer.
Grape, Wolfgang. 1994. *The Bayeux Tapestry: Monument to a Norman Triumph*. Münich and New York: Prestel.

For additional reading on the history of medieval England, see:

Clanchy, M.T. 1993. *From Memory to Written Record, England 1066–1307*. 2nd edn. Oxford: Blackwell.
Daniell, Christopher. 2003. *From Norman Conquest to Magna Carta: England, 1066–1215*. London and New York: Routledge.
Keen, Maurice Hugh. 1990. *English Society in the Later Middle Ages, 1348–1500*. London: Allan Lane, The Penguin Press.

An accessible discussion of Middle English phonology and lexicon is:

Horobin, Simon, and Jeremy Smith. 2002. *An Introduction to Middle English*. New York: Oxford University Press, Chapters 4 and 5.

If you wish to pursue your reading on Middle English phonology, the following texts provide technical treatments of the topic:

Lass, Roger. 1992. 'Phonology and Morphology'. *The Cambridge History of the English Language. Vol. II: 1066–1476*. Ed. by Norman Blake, 23–155. Cambridge: Cambridge University Press.

Lass, Roger. 2006. 'Phonology and Morphology'. *A History of the English Language*. Ed. by Richard M. Hogg and David Denison, 43–108. Cambridge: Cambridge University Press.

Mossé, Fernand. 1952. *A Handbook of Middle English*. Trans. by James A. Walker. Baltimore and London: Johns Hopkins University Press, Chapters 2 and 3.

For a discussion of Middle English dialect diversity, see:

Corrie, Marilyn. 2006. 'Middle English—Dialects and Diversity'. *The Oxford History of English*. Ed. by Lynda Mugglestone, 86–119. Oxford and New York: Oxford University Press.

For a variety of Middle English texts, see:

Burrow, J.A. and Thorlac Turville-Petre. 1996. *A Book of Middle English*. 2nd edn. Oxford: Blackwell.

9

The Grammar
of Middle English
and Rise of a
Written Standard

OVERVIEW

This chapter begins with the consequences of vowel reduction on the grammar of Middle English. We track changes in how parts of speech were inflected, with a view to the origin of modern endings. We examine the loss of noun classes, the disappearance of grammatical gender, the development of analogical endings for the noun and the verb, and the rise of articles. We then look at resulting developments in noun and verb periphrases and changes to word order, considering theories which explain the relationship between the leveling of inflections and these syntactic changes. After a brief excursus on Middle English as a creole, we end with the establishment of a standard English dialect in the fifteenth century.

OBJECTIVES

This chapter explains certain changes in Middle English grammar that were due largely to vowel reduction. After reading the chapter, you should be able to

■ identify the inflectional forms of Middle English;
■ cite the Old English origins of these forms;

- identify their geographical distribution in Middle English;
- discuss their significance in the subsequent grammatical development of English (for example, whether they are retained as a remnant or productive form, or lost); and
- point to the differences between Middle English syntax and that of both Old and Modern English.

Understanding Middle English grammar will enable you to discuss the shift from a synthetic to an analytic system. You will have learned what is meant by a 'standard dialect', and be able to trace the development of such a standard in English.

The Effects of Vowel Reduction

Vowel reduction is one of the two factors causing the 'leveling' of inflections (i.e. merger into just a few distinct forms) and their eventual loss; analogy is the other factor. The leveling of inflections occurred in two stages:

1. the merger of unstressed *a*, *o*, and *u* with *e* and their reduction to [ə]; and
2. the silencing of final *e*'s and loss of medial *e*'s.

Table 9.1 shows the effect of the reduction of unstressed vowels on inflections in Middle English. (It also shows the shift of final [-m] to [-n] and loss of final [-n] in unstressed syllables, as discussed in the previous chapter.) Note the effects of metathesis in the case of *-ra*, *-re*, *-ne*. We will later see that the loss of final *n* is

Table 9.1 The Leveling of Old English Inflections in Middle English

OE inflection	*ME inflection*	*example OE > ME*
-a, -u, -e	-e, Ø	scipu > scipe
-an, -on, -en, -um, -ne	-e(n)	drīfan > drīven
-es, -as	-es	stānas > stōnes
-aþ, -eþ	-eth	drīfaþ > drīveth
-er, -or, -ra, -re	-er	heardra > harder
-est, -ost, -ast	-est	heardost > hardest
-ed, -od	-ed	macod > maked
-ena	-en(e)	blindena > blinden(e)
-ende	-end(e)	drīfende > drīvende
-enne	-en(e)	tō drīfenne > to drīven(e)

morphologically conditioned; final *n* is preserved in past participles, weak noun plurals, and verb plurals.

Following the reduction of vowels from the twelfth century onward, [ə] began to be silenced, even while being retained in the spelling. But as with any sound change, the loss of the reduced vowel did not occur in every case, and the *-e* has sometimes been preserved.

Final *e*'s were the first to be lost—a type of apocope. We see this first in unaccented grammatical words such as *whanne > whan* and *þanne > than*, and then (in the thirteenth century in the North and fourteenth century in the Midlands and South) in all other words, whether of native or foreign origin, e.g. *frendschipe > frendschip* and *solace > solas*. The result of this change is, of course, the loss of inflectional endings consisting of a vowel alone and of those endings in which a final *n* had previously been lost. However, final *e*'s are often retained in Middle English poetry, which is more conservative than the prose; in fact, sometimes the poet, for the purposes of poetic meter, or a scribe, adds an *-e* to a word which etymologically never had one, such as OE *lar* > ME *lore* or OE *col* > ME *cole* 'coal'. This is called an *inorganic 'e'*.

Medial *e*'s disappeared next—a kind of syncope. We find syncope affecting both suffixes and root syllables of polysyllabic words: e.g. *mægester > maister, sawol > soul(e)*, and *monaþ > month*.

The effect of vowel loss on the inflectional endings of Middle English is as follows:

- In *-es*, the *e* disappeared everywhere except—for phonological reasons—following the sibilants [s, š, z, ž, č, ǰ], as in ModE *buses, bushes, mazes, garages, churches,* and *judges.* This change started in the North; it was completed for noun plurals by 1400 and somewhat later for noun genitives and for third person singular present-tense verbs.
- In *-eþ*, the *e* was lost after long syllables in the Midlands dialects (it had already been lost in the West Saxon and Kentish dialects during the Old English period). Written evidence shows considerable variation between *-eth* and *-th* in Middle English, as in *doeth* and *doth*.
- In *-ed*, the *e* is preserved in past participles, especially when they function as adjectives, as in *blessèd, agèd,* and *learnèd.* Past tense forms do not have the *e* except, for phonological reasons, following [t, d], as in ModE *rated* and *raided*.
- In *-er* and *-est*, the *e* is preserved (even in Modern English).
- In *-en*, the past participle, we see the entire suffix preserved, as in ModE *written*.

While vowel reduction and loss occur unconsciously, analogy is a conscious cause of the loss of inflections. It operates in Middle English to spread existing inflections and to remove irregular or anomalous forms. The breakdown of the inherited inflectional system caused by both phonetic change and analogy is explored in the next section.

Grammatical Developments in Middle English

Adjectives and Nouns

Adjectives

Of all the parts of speech, adjectives show perhaps the greatest change in their inflectional system from Old English to Middle English.

   The OE adjective is fully inflected for number, gender, and case in both the strong and the weak declension. In Middle English, the effects of vowel reduction and analogical change were dramatic in both the strong and the weak declension. On the one hand, we see phonological reduction of the OE strong accusative plural adjective endings -*e* (masc.), -*u* (neut.), and -*a* (fem.), resulting in the ending -*e* [ə] in Middle English (e.g., OE *hearde, heardu, hearda* > ME *hearde*). On the other hand, analogical leveling affects the OE strong genitive singular adjective endings -*es* (masc. and neut.) and -*re* (fem.), resulting in the ending Ø (e.g., OE *heardes, heardre* > ME *hard*); phonological leveling cannot account for the change in this case, as final -*s* and -*r* would have remained. By late Middle English, the only inflectional endings left in the strong declension are Ø in the singular and -*e* in the plural. The weak declension shows a similarly dramatic loss, with only -*e* remaining in both the singular and the plural. Thus, the ME adjectival endings are as follows:

	strong	**weak**
sg.	Ø	-*e*
pl.	-*e*	-*e*

In short, the Middle English adjective is still inflected for number, but not for case or gender. Even the number distinction survives only in the strong declension, and the strong and weak declensions look identical except in the singular. Furthermore, only monosyllabic adjectives ending in a consonant, such as *leef* 'dear' or *brood* 'broad', are inflected; all other adjectives, such as *bisy* 'busy' or *hethen* 'heathen', are uninflected. The principle holds for adjectives borrowed from French: *seynt* 'holy' is inflected, but *gentil* is uninflected. Inflection of the adjective ceased altogether after the thirteenth century when the final *e*'s were lost. The exception is in the conservative Southern dialects, which kept some adjectival endings (e.g. -*ne, -es, -e, -re* in the strong and -*en* in the weak declension) throughout the period. Overall, though, we can say that Middle English shows a strong tendency toward invariable forms, i.e. forms not inflected to show grammatical differences.

   Comparatives and superlatives seem not to have altered much in Middle English, apart from regular phonetic changes: the comparative -*ra* appears as -*er,* and the superlative -*est* or -*ost* appears as -*est*. Some of the umlauted comparative and superlative forms are retained (e.g. *old/elder/eldest, long/lenger/lengest*), while others are regularized by analogy, especially in the innovative Northern dialect. We often find doubling of the final consonant of the root in the comparative and superlative, with the effect of shortening the root vowel: e.g. *greet/gretter/grettest, late/latter/lattest*. This type of irregularity has since been eliminated by analogy: *great/greater/greatest, late/later/latest*. (However, we have preserved *latter*, though it is no longer the comparative form of *late*.) From 1300, comparisons using *more* and *most/mest* became more common, as in *more noble, most wise*. This periphrastic construction originated in Old English and may have been reinforced by a comparable form in French (e.g. *le plus beau*). The Middle English version of this periphrastic form is most common with adjectives of one or two syllables (in contrast to Modern English). Double comparisons, with both the inflectional and *more/most* marker, are evident in Middle English phrases such as *most fairest*. Although these continue to be found in Early Modern English and are heard in colloquial speech today, they have been ruled out in writing since the eighteenth century. A common construction in Middle English to express high degree is the so-called *absolute superlative*, consisting of an intensifying adverb with the adjective in the positive degree, such as *ful good, wonderly sore, ryght yong*.

Nouns

Middle English nouns experienced the processes of reduction and analogy to the point that the complicated inflectional system of Old English was reduced to the basic patternshown in Table 9.2. The final -*e* of the dative singular disappeared very early in Middle English, leaving us with more or less the inflections we use today.

The genitive singular -(*e*)*s* became the analogical, or productive, genitive ending during the Middle English period, being added to nouns of all classes, including French loan words, such as *villein/villeins*. (The apostrophe we now use for the genitive is a later convention to be discussed in Chapter 10.) A few remnant genitive forms from Old English appear in Middle English texts, preserving non-productive inflections. These remnant forms include *s*-less genitives:

- from the feminine ō-stem declension, in which the genitive was originally -*e* > Ø (e.g. *soule nede* 'soul's need');
- from the weak declension, in which the genitive was originally -*an* > -*en* > -*e* > Ø (e.g. *herte blood* 'heart's blood'); and
- from the *r*-stem declension, in which the genitive was originally Ø (e.g. *doghter name* 'daughter's name').

We may also find an *s*-less genitive when the head noun begins with an *s* (e.g. *forest syde* 'forest's edge') or the possessive noun ends in -*s* (e.g. *hors feet* 'horse's hooves'). A similar variation exists in Modern English when a proper noun ends in -*s*, as in *James's* or *James'*.

Table 9.2 The Middle English Noun

sg. nom., acc.	Ø	hound
gen.	-(e)s	houndes
dat.	Ø, -e	hound(e)
pl. all cases	-(e)s	houndes

The Old English nominative and accusative plural -*as*, which by phonetic change appears as -(*e*)*s* in Middle English, became the analogical, or productive, plural ending, serving as a marker not only for all classes of nouns but also for all cases. It eventually replaced both the dative plural -*um* > -*en* and the genitive plural -*ena*, -*a* > -*ene*, -*e* from Old English. The use of such a generalized plural marker occurred early in the Northern and Midlands dialects, but somewhat later (in the fourteenth century) in the South, including London. The spread of the analogical plural ending was slowed by the existence of a rival plural marker deriving from the nominative and accusative plural of the weak declension, -*an* > -*en*. In texts from the South, especially, this plural marker is found on nouns which were not originally weak, as in the following examples:

Old English	Middle English	Modern English
dēoflas (*a*-stem, masc.)	*dev*(*e*)*len*	*devils*
word (*a*-stem, neut.)	*worden*	*words*
brōðor (*r*-stem)	*breth*(*e*)*ren*	*brothers, brethren*
cildru (*z*-stem)	*children*	*children*
cȳ (root-consonant stem)	*kīn*	*kine*

As you can see by the ModE forms *devils*, *words*, and *brothers*, the -*en* has been replaced by the analogical -*s* plural. However, -*en* is preserved in the double plurals of *children*, *brethren*, and the poetic *kine* (although this last is very rare today). The -*en* plural remained popular even up to Shakespeare's time (and in some dialects much longer) in words such as *shoen*. The ending is also preserved—legitimately—in *oxen*, a remnant Old English weak noun. Umlauted plurals of the root-consonant stem declension remain in Middle English (e.g. ME *foot/feet*), but we see these replaced gradually with analogical *s*-plurals: e.g. OE *frēond/frȳnd* > ME *freend/freendes* 'friends' or OE *burg/byrig* > ME *burʒ/burʒes* 'cities'. Similarly, endingless plurals of the neuter *a*-stem can be found (e.g. ME *swyn/swyn*) but give way to the analogical *s*-plural in later texts: e.g. ME *hors/hors, horses* or *thing/thing, thinges*. *R*-plurals of the *z*-stem declension survive in ME *lambre, calvre*, and *childre*, although often with the addition of a weak -*en* plural marker, yielding *lambren, calvren, children*. The plural of the native word for 'egg', *ǣg*, invariably appears in Middle English with a double plural inflection as *eiren*. We do not find the analogical plural *cows* until texts from the seventeenth century.

To summarize, the inflectional changes in the noun between Old English and Middle English resulted in the following:

- OE noun classes, and hence their genders, ceased to be distinct.
- Case came to be marked only in the singular. Two cases (genitive and common case) rather than four cases (nominative, accusative, genitive, and dative) were distinguished. (The instrumental case was conflated into the dative case.)

- Analogical, or productive, markers for the genitive and plural developed from the OE *a*-stem endings. These replaced many of the OE endings, although a few remnant forms continued in use.

Exercise 9.1 Adjectival and Nominal Forms

1. In the following table for the declension of the adjective *glad*, write **s** before the OE form that developed by sound change into the ME form; write **A** when the change occurred through analogy; and write **S/A** if both processes were involved. (Do not worry about the change in the root vowel from æ to *a*, which is the result of a prehistoric vowel change.)

		Old English		**Middle English**
a.	**strong**	Masc.	Fem.	
	sg. nom.	_____ glæd	_____ gladu	glad
	acc.	_____ glædne	_____ glade	
	gen.	_____ glades	_____ glædre	
	dat.	_____ gladum	_____ glædre	
	instr.	_____ glade	_____ glædre	
	pl. nom./acc.	_____ glade	_____ glade	glade
	gen.	_____ glædra	_____ glædra	
	dat.	_____ gladum	_____ gladum	

		Old English		**Middle English**
b.	**weak**	Masc.	Fem.	
	sg. nom.	_____ glada	_____ glade	glade
	acc.	_____ gladan	_____ gladan	
	gen./dat.	_____ gladan	_____ gladan	
	pl. nom./acc.	_____ gladan	_____ gladan	glade
	gen.	_____ glædra	_____ glædra	
	(alt. gen.	_____ gladena	_____ gladena)	
	dat.	_____ gladum	_____ gladum	

2. Using the following vocabulary, write the Middle English forms for the given phrases.

the 'the'

smal 'small'

wōd(e) 'wood/forest' (masc.)

nom. _____	small wood _____	the small wood
acc. _____	small wood _____	the small wood
gen. _____	small wood's_____	the small wood's
dat. _____	small wood _____	the small wood

Pronouns

Personal Pronouns

Pronouns became increasingly important with the loss of personal inflections on the verb (discussed below). They had never been obligatory sentence elements in Old English, but they became so in Middle English. We find varied forms of the personal pronoun in the dialects of the time, as shown in Table 9.3.

A number of generalizations can be made about the pronouns:

1. Middle English pronouns retained three distinct case forms: nominative, objective, and genitive. The merger of the dative and accusative case forms that began in Old English was virtually completed in that period, so we can speak of a generalized objective case based on the form of the old dative case (except in the third-person neuter, which uses the old accusative case). In texts of the Southern dialect, the accusative forms *hine* (3ʳᵈ p. sing. masc.) and *hī* (3ʳᵈ p. sing. fem.) may be found along with the dative forms.
2. The loss of the dual number (see Chapter 7) was complete by early Middle English; only a few dual pronoun forms are recorded in twelfth-century texts.
3. Variant forms of the third-person singular feminine pronoun appear in Middle English writing: first, a *he/ho* type (recorded in the Southern and West Midland dialects) which derives from the Old English form; second, a *schō* type (recorded in the Northern dialect), which perhaps derives from the Old English feminine demonstrative *sēo*; and third, a *schē/shē* type (recorded in the East Midland dialect), of obscure origin, which became the source of the Modern English *she*.
4. The Old Norse third-person plural pronouns, borrowed in the late Old English period, appear in texts along with native forms: we find the Northern dialect using the Old Norse *th*-forms in all three cases (nominative, genitive,

Table 9.3 Personal Pronouns in Middle English

	first person		
	singular		*plural*
nom.	ich, i, ic		wē
obj.	mē		us
gen.	mi(n), my		ūre, our
	second person		
	singular		*plural*
nom.	þū, þou, thou, þow		ʒe, yē
obj.	þē, thee		eow, ʒow, you
gen.	þī(n), thy		eower, ʒower, your(e)

	third person			
	masculine	*neuter*	*feminine*	*plural*
nom.	hē, ha (a)	hit, it	schō, schē/shē, he, ho, hēo	þei, þai, thai, they/hi, hy
obj.	him	hit, it	hire, hir	þeym, thaym/ hem, hom, ham
gen.	his	his	hire, here	þair(e), thair, ther/hyr, here

and objective), the Midlands dialects using the *th*-forms in the nominative but the native *h*-forms in the genitive and objective, and the Southern dialect using the *h*-forms exclusively.

5. An unstressed variant of the first-person singular pronoun developed (*i* or *y*). This form originated in the North and spread to the Southern dialect during the fourteenth century. (The uppercase *I* that we use today became standard only with the introduction of printing.) An unstressed variant of the third-person singular neuter pronoun, *it*, also grew dominant during the Middle English period. The unstressed variant of the third-person masculine pronoun, *ha* or *a*, is not as widespread.

6. The Middle English genitive form of the third-person singular neuter is *his*, derived directly from Old English. The modern form *its* is a later development.

7. Two new genitive pronoun forms appeared in the Middle English period. The old first- and second-person singular genitives, *min* and *thin*, developed additional *n*-less forms, *mi* and *thi*: the *n*-form appears before a word begin-

ning in a vowel, and the other form appears before a word beginning in a consonant (compare *an apple* as opposed to *a pear*). Middle English also uses the *n*-form in postposition, as in ModE *a friend of mine, the coat is mine*. The other persons and numbers developed additional genitive forms for use in postposition, adding a final -*s* if one was not already present: *youres, oures, theires/heres*, and *hires*. Some Middle English texts contain variants of these pronouns, with a final -*n* by analogy with *mi/min* (*hisen, heren, ouren, youren, theiren*), though these were not ultimately accepted into the standard language.

Demonstrative Pronouns

Middle English saw a severe reduction in demonstrative pronoun forms. In Old English, the two demonstratives are inflected for two numbers, three genders (in the singular), and three to five cases. Although inflected forms appear in early ME texts and sporadically in later texts, especially in the South, only five distinct forms deriving from the OE demonstrative remained by the end of the Middle English period.

Under the influence of the other *th*-demonstratives, *se*, the OE masculine singular nominative of the 'that' demonstrative developed into *þe/the*. More importantly, *the* became invariable (undeclinable) and assumed a new function. Recall that demonstratives in Old English serve a deictic function, pointing to objects close to or far from the speaker. The ME form, on the other hand, developed an *anaphoric* function, referring back to something already mentioned, or what we might call something *definite*.[1] The transition from *se* to *þe/the* and its use as a definite article began early enough to appear in the twelfth-century *Anglo-Saxon Chronicle* kept at Peterborough. This development represents an important grammatical change because the use of articles, unlike the use of demonstratives, is obligatory.

The remaining demonstrative forms continue to serve a deictic function today; the four modern forms have the following sources:

1. *That* derives from the neuter singular nominative and accusative of the OE 'that' demonstrative, *þæt*.
2. *Those* derives from the nominative and accusative plural of the OE 'that' demonstrative, *þā* (with ME shift of [ā] > [ɔ]) plus the addition of an analogical -*s* plural ending (Lass 1992:114).
3. *This* derives from the neuter singular nominative and accusative of the OE 'this' demonstrative, *þis*.
4. *These* derives by analogy with the addition of the adjectival plural ending -*e* to the masculine singular nominative form of the OE 'this' demonstrative, *þes + e*.

---

1 A good illustration of this in Modern English might be the following brief narrative: *Yesterday I saw a̲ man leading a̲n elephant down the street. T̲h̲e̲ man said that t̲h̲e̲ elephant was his pet.* It begins with the indefinite article, indicating first mention, and continues with the definite article.

Interrogative Pronouns

Apart from a spelling change (*hw > wh*) and a few phonetic changes, the interrogative pronouns appear little changed in Middle English (see Table 9.4). As with the personal pronouns, the objective forms of the interrogative pronoun derive from the masculine dative and the neuter accusative. The interrogative adverb *why* derives from the neuter instrumental.

The most common relative pronoun in Middle English is *that*, which gradually replaced the Old English relative particle *þe*: e.g. *the place that I of spak* (Chaucer's 'The Parliament of Fowls', lines 295–6) 'the place that I spoke of'. It still has this function in Modern English: *the lawnmower that was broken, the woman that answered the phone*. In the Middle English period, the interrogative pronouns began to be used as relative pronouns, first indefinitely (i.e. where we would now use a form with *-ever*: e.g. *Who hath no wyf is no cokewold* 'Whoever has no wife is no cuckold' [Chaucer's 'The Miller's Tale' A3152]), then more generally. A common occurrence in Middle English is the use of compound relative pronouns, such as *who that, whom that, whose that, which that*, and *what that*.

Loss of Grammatical Gender

Accompanying the loss of inflections in Middle English adjectives, nouns, and demonstratives was the disappearance, for internal and external reasons, of grammatical gender. Inherent difficulties exist when grammatical and natural (or biological) gender are at odds, even though grammatical gender systems are not fundamentally illogical and many languages have managed to preserve such systems. As early as the Old English period, these clashes were being resolved in favor of natural gender. Phonetic weakening is a second internal factor contributing to the loss of gender: it prompted the collapse of noun classes (which were based on gender), the loss of gender distinctions in the adjective, and the reduction of the demonstratives (either to an invariable definite article or to a form indicating number alone). An external factor was at play as well: the dual gender system of French (masculine/feminine) may have caused confusion for English speakers. Moreover, sometimes the genders

Table 9.4 The Interrogative Pronoun from Old English to Middle English

		Old English		Middle English	
masc./fem.	nom.	hwā		whō	[ā] > [ɔ]
	obj.	hwām		whōm	[ā] > [ɔ]
	gen.	hwæs		whōse	the [ɔ] is by analogy with *who* and *whom*
neut.	nom./obj.	hwæt		what	[æ] > [ɑ]
	instr.	hwȳ		whȳ	[ȳ] > [ī]

of an English noun and of its synonym in French differed, e.g. Fr. *lune* (fem.) and English *mona* (masc.). Given that the gender system was already changing in Old English, however, we might conclude that internal factors were the most important.

Exercise 9.2 Pronominal Forms

Supply the correct Middle English equivalent for each underlined Modern English pronoun in the following passages. Specify the person, case, number, and gender (for third-person pronouns) of each selection. Note the period and region of each passage.

a.   From the *Peterborough Chronicle* for the year 1137 (from Clark 1970:55)
     – Central NE Midlands (with some late OE forms)

þa þe King Stephne to Englaland com, þa macod *he*(1)   *his*(2) gadering æt
When   *came   made (called)*   *assembly*

Oxeneford. 7 þar *he*(3) nam þe biscop Roger of Serebyri 7 Alexander biscop
                 there   took (arrested)   *Salisbury*

of Lincol 7 te canceler Roger, *his*(4) neues, 7 dide ælle in prisun til *they*(5)
                the   *nephews put*

iafen up *their*(6) castles.
gave

(1) _____   (4) _____

(2) _____   (5) _____

(3) _____   (6) _____

b.   From Lawman's (Layamon's) *Brut* (ll. 11–14) (from Madden 1967:Vol. 1, 1–2)
     – *c.* 1250 SW Midlands

___*It*(1) com *him*(2) on mode: & on *his*(3) mern þonke
It came into his mind   *and into his bright (distinguished) thought*

þet *he*(4) wolde of Engle: þa æðelæn tellen;
that he would of England   *the noble deeds tell;*

(1) _____   (3) _____

(2) _____   (4) _____

c. Lyric Poem (from Stevick 1964:43)
    – Thirteenth century South

Blow, Northerne Wynd,

Send _you (sg.)_[1] _me_[2] _my_[3] swetyng!
Send   _sweeting_

    (1) _____

    (2) _____

    (3) _____

d. From Richard Rolle's _The Bee and the Stork_ (ll. 1–7) (from Allen 1931:54)
    – _c._ 1340 North

The bee has thre kyndis. Ane es, þat _she_[1] es never ydill, and _she_[2] es
                three natures One   _idle_

noghte with _them_[3] þat will noghte wyrke, bot castys _them_[4] owte and
not   _work_   _casts_

puttes _them_[5] awaye. Anothire es, þat when _she_[6] flyes _she_[7] takes
                                                                        flies

erthe in _her_[8] fette, þat _she_[9] be noghte lyghtly overhegede in the ayere
earth   _feet_   _over-heightened_   _air_

of wynde. The thyrde es, þat _she_[10] kepes clene and bryghte _her_[11]
                                          keeps

wyngez.
wings.

    (1) _____   (7) _____

    (2) _____   (8) _____

    (3) _____   (9) _____

    (4) _____   (10) _____

    (5) _____   (11) _____

    (6) _____

Verbs

Verb Classes

The verb classes of Old English appear in Middle English with few losses.

The seven classes of strong verbs remained intact, affected only by vowel shifts and open syllable lengthening (see Table 9.5). Table 9.6 shows the changes at work, placing the ME vowels next to their OE counterparts. Open syllable lengthening occurs in classes 4, 5, and 6 in the present tense and past participle. In class 2, the vowel of the past participle is lengthened and extended by analogy into the past plural. In class 3a, all forms show lengthening in front of *-nd*, *-mb*, and *-ld* (as a result of late Old English lengthening).

Ablaut appears to work according to the expected pattern in Middle English strong verbs, although analogy does operate to regularize certain forms. Vowels of the past singular, past plural, and past participle all show variation, indicating the beginning of an analogical tendency to reduce the four-way vowel gradation to

Table 9.5 Strong Verbs in Middle English

class/verb	infinitive	past singular	past plural	past participle
1	**ī**	**ǭ**	**i**	**i**
'rise'	rīsen	rōs	risen	y-risen
2	**ē (u)**	**ę̄**	**u** (later > ǭ)	**ǭ**
'rue'	rēwen	rę̄w	ruwen	y-rǭwen
'choose'	chēsen	chę̄s	curen	y-cǭren
3	**i**	**a**	**u**	**u**
'drink'	drincen	dranc	druncen	y-druncen
'climb'	clīmben	clōmb	clūmben	y-clūmbem
	e	**a**	**u**	**o**
'help'	helpen	halp	hulpen	y-holpen
4	**ę̄**	**a**	**ē**	**ǭ**
'steal'	stę̄len	stal	stēlen	y-stǭlen
5	**ę̄**	**a**	**ē**	**ę̄**
'eat'	ę̄ten	at	ēten	y-ę̄ten
6	**ā**	**ō**	**ō**	**ā**
'travel'	fāren	fōr	fōren	y-fāren
7	**(variable)**	**ē**	**ē**	**(variable)**
'weep'	wēpen	wēp	wēp	y-wopen

Table 9.6 Changes in Ablaut Grades from Old English to Middle English

class 1	OE	ī	ā	i	i	
	ME	ī	ǭ	i	i	[ā] > [ɔ]
class 2	OE	ēo	ēa	u	o	
	ME	ē	ę̄	u > ǭ	ǭ	[ēə] > [ē], [ǣə] > [ɛ̄]
class 3 a	OE	i	a	u	u	
	ME	i	a	u	u	
b	OE	eo, e	ea	u	o	
	ME	e	a	u	o	[ɛə] > [ɛ], [æə] > [a]
class 4	OE	e	æ	ǣ	o	
	ME	ę̄	a	ē	ǭ	[æ] > [a], [ǣ] > [ē]
class 5	OE	e	æ	ǣ	e	
	ME	ę̄	a	ē	ę̄	[æ] > [ā], [ǣ] > [ē]
class 6	OE	a	ō	ō	a	
	ME	ā	ō	ō	ā	
class 7	OE	var.	ēo	ēo	var.	var. = variable
	ME	var.	ē	ē	var.	

a three-way one. For example, in the case of the verb *choose* (given in Table 9.5), the change from *curen* > *chǭsen* shows the past participle's vowel extending over into the past plural (as well as an analogical change of [k] to [č]); it shows a further analogical change, namely, the replacement of the *r* (resulting from Verner's Law) with the regular consonant *s*. A number of ME verbs have both strong and weak past tense forms because the strong verbs began to take weak endings, e.g.:

> *halp* versus *helped*
>
> *crōpe* versus *crepte*

This tendency increased dramatically in the modern period, as we will see.

The other types of verbs—weak, anomalous, preterit-present, and impersonal—are retained in Middle English, but with changes:

- We find only two classes of weak verbs, rather than the three of Old English; these are characterized by two forms of the dental suffix:

  -ed(e)   (*hopen/hopede/hoped*; *lernen/lernede/lerned*)
  -de or *-te*   (*heren/herde/herd*; *tellen/tolde/told*; *mēnen/mente/ment*)

  Verbs taking *-ed(e)* include some of the OE weak class I verbs and most of the OE weak class II verbs. The remaining OE weak verbs take *-de/-te*.

- The anomalous verbs of Old English remained irregular in Middle English. The suppletive paradigm of the verb *be* is shown below:

	present		**past**
1st p.	*am/em*	*be*	*was/wes*
2nd p.	*art*	*bist/best*	*were/wore*
3rd p.	*is*	*biþ/beþ*	*was/wes*
pl.	*are(n)/arn*	*ben/beþ*	*weren/woren*

The present plural form of the verb *be* in Modern English derives from the form *aren* of the Anglian dialect of Old English.

- The preterit-present verbs underwent changes in meaning and syntactic function. They began to be used more often as auxiliary verbs than as full verbs and acquired some of the modal meanings they have in Modern English; for example, *may* expresses permission and wish, *can* expresses capacity, and *shall* expresses prediction or future. Three verbs are lost from the category of preterit-present verbs as well, with the following nine remaining: *witan* 'know', *cunnen* 'know, be able', *durren* 'dare', *shulen* 'be under obligation', *muwen* 'be able', *moten* 'be permitted', *dugan* 'avail', *þurfan* 'need', and *owen* 'own, be under obligation'.

- Impersonal verbs (verbs with no personal subject, but with the experiencer expressed in the dative) remained quite common in Middle English, perhaps reinforced by the French reflexive construction: e.g. *me mette* 'there was a dream to me', *me reweþ* 'there is regret to me', *hym nedde* 'there was need to them'. In Modern English, these have been reanalyzed as personal constructions with a nominative subject (experiencer): as *I dreamed, I regret, they needed*. Middle English uses reflexive constructions such as *she lade hir* 'she laid herself down' or *þe coc him crowe* 'the cock crows (for himself)'.

By the Middle English period, the weak pattern is the productive, or analogical, verb pattern for English. In other words, when new verbs are added to the language, they take the dental suffix for the past tense. Verbs borrowed from French, for example, assume the weak preterit ending, as in *crie/cryede/cryd* and *preye/preyede/preyd*.

Inflectional Endings

The inflectional endings of the verb undergo severe leveling in Middle English because of phonological reduction. In Table 9.7a below, you can see the inflections that would be predicted under the influence of sound change alone. Table 9.7b shows the actual endings that result from the combined forces of phonological change, analogy, and differences in dialect.

To simplify, the conservative Southern dialect develops its verb inflections as expected. The more innovative Northern dialect adopts the ending *-es* (or *-is*) every-

Table 9.7 Inflectional Endings of the Verb in Middle English

a) endings expected via phonological change				
		OE ending		*expected ME ending*
pres.	1st p. sg.	-e		-e, Ø
	2nd p. sg.	-st, -est		-est
	3rd p. sg.	-eð		-eth
	pl.	-að		-eth
		strong	*weak*	*strong*	*weak*
pret.	1st p. sg.	Ø	-e	Ø	-e, Ø
	2nd p. sg.	-e	-est	-e, Ø	-est
	3rd p. sg.	Ø	-e	Ø	-e, Ø
	pl.	-on	-on	-en	-en
b) endings of the present indicative attested in Middle English				
		North	*Midlands*	*South*
pres.	1st p. sg.	Ø	-e	-e
	2nd p. sg.	-es	-est	-est
	3rd p. sg.	-es	-eth, -es	-eth
	pl.	-es	-e(n), -es	-eth

where but the first-person singular. The Midlands dialects reach a compromise, using both the Northern ending and the inherited OE ending in the third-person singular; in the plural, it employs the Northern ending or substitutes the plural inflection from the subjunctive, which restores a distinction lost by phonetic change. Working against this is a tendency for the final *n* of the plural to be lost, opening the way for *e* to vanish as well. Strangely enough, in the singular it is the innovative Northern form *-es* which was later to become the analogical third-person singular present ending, driving out the standard *-eth*.

The endings used in the preterit indicative correspond to the expected ones. However, the only really distinct ending (since all final *n*'s and *e*'s were eventually lost) is the second-person singular of weak verbs, *-est*. Even this ending falls into disuse in the North, resulting in no preterit endings at all. The *-e* and *-en* of the subjunctive were erased by phonetic change, leading to the loss of this mood marker (although it persists overtly in a few constructions, such as *God save the Queen*, *Far be it from me*, and *If I were you*). The imperative endings sg. *-e*, *-a*, and pl. *-að* became reduced to *-e* and *-eth* and then disappeared altogether, leaving us with modern endingless forms such as *Jump!*

Non-finite verb forms in Middle English texts exhibit some interesting changes. By phonetic change, the infinitive gradually lost its ending: *-an, -ian* > *-en* > *-e* > Ø. Before this happened, there was considerable alternation between *-en* and *-e*, with the *-e* lost first in the North. This form is known as the plain or bare infinitive, as in *wol I turne* 'I will turn', and is seen in the following ModE contexts: *I will help you*, *I saw him leave*, *I made her answer the question*. The inflected infinitive of Old English also survived into Middle English, with the expected phonetic reductions: *to {V}-(i)enne* > *to {V}-en*, as in *I foryete to tellen* 'I forget to tell'. The resulting form is known as the *to*-infinitive, and is of course the usual one we use in Modern English, as in *I want to watch that movie, I wanted him to help*, and *To understand grammar is difficult*. A third infinitive form, the *for-to*-infinitive, developed in Middle English, e.g. *wenten for to sle* 'they went for the purposes of slaying *or* to slay'. While both the plain infinitive and the *to*-infinitive flourish today, the *for-to*-infinitive has been lost.

The expected form of the present participle in Middle English is *-end(e)*, but instead we find a variety of forms: *-and(e)* in the North, *-ende* and *-ing(e)* in the Midlands, and *-ing(e)* and *-ind(e)* in the South. The origin of the *-ing* form is uncertain, though it may be related to the OE gerund ending *-ung*. (A gerund is a verb functioning as a noun, e.g. *swimming is healthful*.) The ending of the past participle remained as *-en* for strong verbs (or was reduced to *-e* and eventually to Ø, cf. *written* and *rung*) and *-ed, -d*, or *-t* for weak verbs. The optional prefix of the past participle underwent reduction from [jɛ] to [ɪ] (*ge-* to *i-/y-*), as shown above in the examples of ME strong verbs. The prefix was then lost in the North (possibly due to the influence of Old Norse that had no prefix in this context) and in the Midlands, though often retained in poetry, where it served a useful purpose by supplying an additional syllable in a metrical line.

Exercise 9.3 Verbal Forms

Identify the grammatical category and dialect areas of the following verb forms. Point out the morphological changes from Old English to Middle English and discuss their relevance to the development of the language.

1. **OE** we tellað

    ME we telles, we telles/tellen, we telleth

    _____

    _____

    _____

    _____

    _____

2. **OE** hēo telleð

   ME schō telles, schē telleth/-es, hēo telleth

   _____

   _____

   _____

   _____

   _____

3. **OE** þū gehȳrst

   ME thou hēres, þū hēres(t), þow hēr(e)st

   _____

   _____

   _____

   _____

   _____

4. **OE** slǣpan, tō slǣpenne, slǣpende

   ME slēpe(n), to slēpe(n), for to slēpe(n)
   slēpand(e), slēpende, slēping(e), slēpinde

   _____

   _____

   _____

   _____

   _____

Syntax

The loss and leveling of inflections in Middle English accompanied two important changes in the grammar: the increased use of periphrasis and the development of a more fixed word order, which grew to serve the function previously filled by inflections. This is typical of a shift from a highly synthetic to an analytic language.

Periphrasis

Inflected nouns gave way to constructions that used prepositions, or to a particular word order. Verbal inflections were generally replaced by constructions using auxiliary verbs. With no distinction between nominative and accusative case in nouns, word order came to mark the subject (placed before the verb) and the object (placed after the verb):

> *a man hadde twei sones* (Luke 15: 11)
> 'a man (S) had (V) two sons (O)'[2]

With dative case no longer marked in nouns, texts show either the use of the *to*-dative construction or the positioning of the indirect object after the verb and before the direct object:

> *þe fadir seide <u>to hise seruauntis</u>* (Luke 15: 22)
> 'the father said to his servants'

> *gyue <u>me</u> the porcioun of catel* (Luke 15: 12)
> 'give me the share of the property'

The *to*-periphrasis appears in late Old English, but may have been reinforced by the comparable French indirect object construction with *à* 'to'. Likewise, the French genitive construction with *de* 'of' may have reinforced the English genitive periphrasis with *of*. Although the genitive continued to be marked inflectionally, the *of*-genitive became increasingly common in Middle English, especially to express the non-possessive genitive functions, such as subjective (e.g. *the story of Troye*), objective (e.g. *delit of synne* 'delight of sin'), or partitive (e.g. *one blodes drope* 'one drop of blood', or *al the condicioun of ech of them*).

In the verb, periphrases of the passive and the perfect already existed in Old English (see Chapter 7). These underwent minor changes in the Middle English period. In the passive, the OE verb *weorðan* > *worthe* 'become' was gradually lost, leaving only *be* as the auxiliary of the passive:

> *Ther <u>is</u> no thing <u>hid</u>, that schal not <u>be maad</u> opyn* (Mark 4: 22)
> 'There is nothing hidden that shall not be revealed'

When an agent appears in the sentence, we find it introduced with the prepositions *of*, *by*, *through*, *with*, *from*, or *mid*. The frequency of the perfect increased dramatically, though it still alternates with the simple past to indicate past action connected to the present. *Have* began to, but did not completely, replace *be* as the auxiliary of the perfect with intransitive verbs:

> *Thi brother <u>is comun</u>* (Luke 15: 27)
> 'Your brother is [has] come'

---

2 The quotations in this section are from Wyclif's fourteenth-century Bible translations (see Chadwyck-Healey's online *The Bible in English*).

Fadir, Y haue synned (Luke 15: 21)
'Father, I have sinned'

Three additional verbal periphrastic forms—the future, the progressive, and the modal subjunctive—developed in the ME period, formed with a finite auxiliary (or 'helping' verb) in combination with an infinitive or participle. Middle English does, however, allow the future to be expressed by the simple present, as in Old English:

Sone, thou art euer more with me (Luke 15: 31)
'Son, you will always be with me'

However, the future is increasingly expressed by periphrases containing the auxiliaries *will* (originally expressing intention) and *shall* (originally expressing obligation) plus an infinitive:

Y shal rise vp, and go to my fadir (Luke 15: 18)
'I shall rise up and go to my father'

lest perauenture it wole passe the termes to se the Lord (Exodus 19: 21)
'lest perhaps it will pass the bounds to see the Lord'

The progressive, a periphrase consisting of the auxiliary *be* and the present participle, developed gradually, coming into its own as a construction only in the modern period (see Chapter 11). In Middle English, we find the beginnings of the progressive in present participial constructions such as *[the seed] gaf fruyt, springynge vp, and wexynge* 'the seed gave fruit, springing up and growing' (Mark 4: 8). Because the inflectional ending for the subjunctive ceased to be distinctive and fell out of use, the OE preterit-present verbs become increasingly important for expressing non-factual actions and states, functioning as auxiliaries in combination with an infinitive:

demeden thei schulden take more (Matthew 20: 11)
'they expected they should receive more'

And he was wrooth, and wolde not come in (Luke 15: 28)
'And he was angry and was not willing to go in'

Word Order in Main Clauses

The word order of Middle English is more fixed than that of Old English but more flexible than that of Modern English. The basic, unmarked order for main clauses is the one most commonly used throughout the history of the language:

subject + (auxiliary) + verb + (object) . . .

An example of this SVO order is the following clause:

men moste have greet conseil and greet deliberacion
'men must have great counsel and great deliberation'[3]

---

3 The quotations in this section are from 'The Tale of Melibee' in Chaucer's *The Canterbury Tales*, unless otherwise noted (see Benson 1987).

We find some examples of remnant OV word order in Middle English main clauses, especially with object pronouns:

subject + (auxiliary) + object pronoun + verb . . .

I yow biseche, as hertely as I dar and kan …
'I beseech you as heartily as I dare and can'

Thre of his olde foes han it espyed, and setten laddres to the walles of his hous
'Three of his old foes had spied it and set ladders to the walls of his house'

Me thynketh it acordaunt to resoun / To telle yow al the condicioun / Of ech of hem, so as it semed me
'It seems to me that it is according to reason to tell you all the condition of each of them, so as it seemed to me' (from 'The General Prologue')

In the first example above, the object pronoun *yow* precedes the verb *biseche*. In the second example the auxiliary verb (*han*) precedes the object (*it*) and the participle follows (*espyed*). The OV order is especially common with impersonal verbs, as in *me thynketh* in the third example, where we can also see a change developing in the impersonal construction in Middle English—the appearance of a dummy *it* subject in *it semed me*.

Word Order in Negative Clauses

Negation in Middle English works differently than in Old English, following one of three patterns:

1. **subject +** *ne* **+ {auxiliary, verb} + (object)** . . .
2. **subject +** *ne* **+ {auxiliary, verb} +** *nat* **+ (object)** . . .
3. **subject + {auxiliary, verb} +** *nat* **+ (object)** . . .

He nevere yet no vileynye ne sayde / In al his lyf unto no maner wight
'He never yet no villainy not said in all his life unto no manner of person' (or, more idiomatically, 'He never said any evil to anyone in all his life') (from 'The General Prologue')

For ther nys nothyng in this world that he desireth
'For there not-is nothing in this world that he desires' (or, more idiomatically, 'For there isn't anything in this world that he desires')

These sentences are negated by placing *ne/na* before the verb and perhaps contracting it with the verb (as in *nys*). Note that multiple negation continues to be possible in Middle English; in the first sentence above, there are in fact four negatives (*nevere*, *no*, *ne*, and *no*).

The next two examples are typical of later Middle English, in which it became more common to use a reinforcing particle, such as *nat*, after the verb or auxiliary:

yet ne wolde he nat answere sodeynly
'yet he would not answer suddenly'

If I ne venge me nat of the vileynye that men han doon to me
'If I [do] not avenge myself of the villainy that men have done to me'

The post-verbal particle is an emphatic negative marker that derives from *na + wiht* 'not a thing, nothing'.

By the mid-fourteenth century, however, the pre-verbal negative was usually omitted, as in the next two examples. This did not signal the end of multiple negation (seen in the first two negative sentences given above), which remained common throughout the period. Note that, as in Old English, an auxiliary verb is not obligatory in ME negative sentences:

it folweth nat therfore that alle wommen ben wikke
'it does not follow therefore that all women are wicked'

Blisful is that man that hath nat folwed the conseilyng of shrews
'Blissful is that man that has not followed the counsel of shrews'

Listen to the sound recording of Chaucer's *Troilus and Criseyde* (Reading 3) on the website and follow along with the written text. This passage is famous because Chaucer comments on the nature of language change (ll. 22–28). You should be able to locate instances of multiple negation, as in *I nyl have neither thank ne blame* (l. 15) and *So nold I nat love purchace* (l. 33). As we saw in Chapter 1, there are also impersonal verbs, such as *Me nedeth* (l. 11) and *Us thinketh hem* (l. 25). Can you find two impersonal verbs using the dummy *it* subject?[4]

Inverted Word Order and Questions

Turning to inverted word order, we find substantial evidence in Middle English of the following pattern:

adverb + {auxiliary, verb} + subject + (object) . . .

Inversions may occur in different circumstances, e.g. when the sentence begins with an adverb of time (ME *thanne* and *now*), just as in Old English, or with a directional adverb (ME *up*):

Thanne bigan dame Prudence to maken semblant of wratthe
'Then Dame Prudence began to make semblance of wrath'

now wol I teche you how ye shall examyne youre conseil
'now I will teach you how you shall examine your counsel'

---

4 Answer: *it bitit* (l. 48) and *it so bitidde* (l. 55).

Up stirten thanne the yonge folk atones
'The young folk then came to life at once'

Inversion also takes place when the object is moved to the beginning of the sentence for emphasis (*manye freendes* below), and when the ModE sentence would begin with a *there*-subject (as in *ther is full many a man* . . . below), a construction that developed during the Middle English period.

Manye freendes have thou
'You have many friends'

Was nevere swich another as was hee
'[There] was never such another as he was' (from 'The Monk's Tale')

ther is ful many a man that crieth 'Were, were!'
'there is many a man that cries, "War, war!"'

This inversion of subject and verb is a tendency rather than a rule; the object may move to the front of a sentence while the subject and verb keep their normal order: *and þat place he clept paradys* 'and that place (O) he (S) called (V) paradise'.

In both *yes/no* and content questions, inverted word order is the rule:

(interrogative pronoun) + {auxiliary, verb} + subject + (object) . . .

Examples of questions in Middle English are given below. Note that, as in Old English, an auxiliary verb is not obligatory.

Why make ye youreself for to be lyk a fool?
'Why do you make yourself act like a fool?'

What is bettre than gold?
'What is better than gold?'

Have ye so greet envye / Of myn honour, that thus compleyne and crye?
'Have you so great envy of my honor that [you] thus complain and cry?' (from 'The Knight's Tale')

Word Order in Subordinate Clauses

The order of elements in subordinate clauses in Middle English is generally SVO, as in Modern English. However, a few remnant examples of 'verb final' order in such clauses can still be found:

subordinating conjunction + subject + (object) + verb

God forbede that it so weere!
'God forbid that it was so!'

And whan this folk togidre assembled weren
'And when this folk were gathered together'

Compare the more usual order in the following subordinate clause:

And whan this olde man wende to enforcen his tale by resons
'And when this old man went to support his tale with reasons'

Word Order in Imperative Sentences

Imperative sentences begin with the verb, as they did in Old English and still do in Modern English:

$$\{verb, auxiliary\} + (subject) + (object) \ldots$$

Trusteth me wel
'Trust me well'

Lat nat thyne eyen to moyste been of teeris
'Do not let your eyes be too moist with tears'

Ne taak no compaignye by the weye of a straunge man
'Do not take no company in the form of a strange man' (or, more idiomatically, 'Do not take any company with a strange man')

Negative imperatives are found in the last two examples.

Exercise 9.4 Syntax and Word Order

1. In which instances is SOV word order found in Middle English?

   _____

   _____

   _____

2. What conditions cause the word order to be inverted (to VS) in Middle English?

   _____

   _____

   _____

3. What is the difference between the Old English and Middle English method of expressing the future?

   _____

   _____

   _____

A Closer Look at the Language of a Middle English Text

The Old and Middle English passages from the parable of the sower and the seed first given in Chapter 1 are reprinted here so that we can review them in light of the language changes under discussion.

OLD ENGLISH

(1) Heofona rice is geworden þæm menn gelic þe seow god sæd on his æcere. (2) Soþlice, þa þa menn slepon, þa com his feonda sum, and oferseow hit mid coccele onmiddan þæm hwæte, and ferde þanon. (3) Soþlice, þa seo wyrt weox, and þone wæstm brohte, þa ætiewde se coccel hine. (4) þa eodon þæs hlafordes þeowas and cwædon: (5) 'Hlaford, hu, ne seowe þu god sæd on þinum æcere? (6) Hwanon hæfde he coccel?' (7) Þa cwæþ he: (8) 'Þæt dyde unhold mann'. (9) Þa cwædon þa þeowas: (10) 'Wilt þu, we gaþ and gadriaþ hie?' (11) Þa cwæþ he: (12) 'Nese: þylæs ge þone hwæte awyrtwalien, þonne ge þone coccel gadriaþ. (13) Lætaþ ægþer weaxan oþ riptiman; and on þæm riptiman ic secge þæm riperum: (14) "Gadriaþ ærest þone coccel, and bindaþ sceafmælum to forbærnenne; and gadriaþ þone hwæte into minum berne."' (Matthew 13: 24–30)

MIDDLE ENGLISH

(1) The kyngdom of heuenes is maad lijk to a man, that sewe good seed in his feld. (2) And whanne men slepten, his enemy cam, and sewe aboue taris in the myddil of whete, and wente awei. (3) But whanne the erbe was growed, and made fruyt, thanne the taris apperiden (4) and the seruauntis of the hosebonde man camen, and seiden to hym, (5) Lord whether hast thou not sowen god seed in thi feeld? (6) where of thanne hath it taris? (7) And he seide to hem, (8) An enemy hath do this thing. (9) And the seruauntis seiden to him, (10) Wolt thou that we goon, and gaderen hem? (11) And he seide, (12) Nay, lest perauenture ge in gaderynge taris drawen vp with hem the whete bi the roote. (13) Suffre ge hem bothe to wexe in to repyng tyme; and in the tyme of ripe corne Y shal seie to the reperis, (14) First gidere the taris, and bynde hem to gidere in kyntchis to be brent, but gadere ge whete in to my berne. (Matthew 13: 24–30)

The most obvious difference between the two passages is in vocabulary. In some cases, one English word is simply replaced with another English word (e.g. *æcere* > *feld* in verse 1). In other cases, a French borrowing has replaced an English word (e.g. *feonda* > *enemy* in verse 2). The following pairs of words are examples of some of the other changes in vocabulary evident in the two passages:

wyrt	>	*erbe* (3)
wæstm	>	*fruyt* (3)
ætiewde	>	*apperiden* (3)
þeowas	>	*seruauntis* (4)
unhold mann	>	*enemy* (8)
lætaþ	>	*suffre* (13)

Although some of the OE words in the list above have been replaced in this particular text, they remain in the modern vocabulary along with the French loan word, often with a change in meaning, as in the case of *feonda* (now in the sense 'demon', not 'enemy'). In other cases, the OE words have been lost and not replaced:

rice (1)	*eodon* (4)
geworden (1)	*þeowas* (4)
ge- (1)	*cwædon/cwæþ* (4, 7)
soþlice (3)	*þu* (10)
þa þa (2)	*(un)hold* (8)
ferde (2)	*nese* (12)
wæstm (3)	*awyrtwalien* (12)
ætiewde (3)	*for-* (14)

When we look at the grammar, we see a number of instances in which an inflectional form in OE is replaced by a periphrastic form in ME:

heofona rice	>	*the kyngdom of heuenes* (1)
þæm menn gelic	>	*lijk to a man* (1)
oferseow	>	*sewe aboue* (2)
onmiddan þæm hwæte	>	*in the myddil of whete* (2)
weox	>	*was growed* (3)
þæs hlafordes þeowas	>	*seruauntis of the hosebonde man* (4)
seowe	>	*hast . . . sowen* (5)
dyde	>	*hath do* (8)
awyrtwalien	>	*drawen vp . . . bi the roote* (12)
secge	>	*shal seie* (13)
þæm riperum	>	*to the reperis* (13)
weaxan	>	*to wexe* (13)
sceafmælum	>	*in kyntchis* (14)

The inflected demonstrative of OE is replaced with the invariable definite article:

seo	>	*the* (3)
se	>	*the* (3)
þa	>	*the* (9)
þæm	>	*the* (13)
þone	>	*the* (14)

Similarly, the relative pronoun *þe* (1) gives way to *that* (1), still used today. We see the leveling and loss of inflectional endings due to phonological reduction and the working of analogy:

heofona	>	*heuenes* (1)
slepon (strong verb)	>	*slepten* (2) (weak verb)
cwædon	>	*seiden* (4)
þinum	>	*thi* (5)
cwædon	>	*seiden* (9)
timan	>	*tyme* (13)
lætaþ	>	*suffre* (13)
minum	>	*my* (14)
gadriaþ	>	*gidere* (14)
bindaþ	>	*bynde* (14)

Verse 6 exemplifies the loss of grammatical gender in the use of ME *it* instead of OE *he*, referring to the field.

We also find changes in syntax, particularly word order:

þa com his feonda sum (ADV-VS)	>	*his enemy cam* (SV) (2)
þone wæstm brohte (OV)	>	*made fruyt* (VO) (3)
þa ætiewde se coccel hine (ADV-VS)	>	*thanne the taris apperiden* (ADV-SV) (3)
þa eodon þæs hlafordes þeowas (ADV-VS)	>	*the seruauntis of the hosebonde man camen* (SV) (4)
Þa cwæþ he (ADV-VS)	>	*he seide to hem* (SVO) (7)
Þæt dyde unhold mann (OVS)	>	*An enemy hath do this thing* (SVO) (8)
Þa cwædon þa þeowas (ADV-VS)	>	*the seruauntis seiden to him* (SVO) (9)
þa cwæþ he (ADV-VS)	>	*he seide* (SV) (11)
þylæs ge þone hwæte awyrtwalien (CONJ-SOV)	>	*lest perauenture ge . . . drawen vp with hem the whete bi the roote* (CONJ-S . . . VO) (12)
þonne ge þone coccel gadriaþ (CONJ-SOV)	>	*in gaderynge taris* (VO) (this is also a change from a finite to a non-finite clause) (12)

Finally, we also see changes in the way in which negative phrases are constructed and questions are formed:

ne seowe	*hast . . . not sowen* (5)
ne seowe þu? (VS)	*hast thou not sowen?* (AUX-SV) (5)

Change from Synthetic to Analytic

The structural changes which took place in Middle English—the leveling and loss of inflections and the development of periphrases and fixed word order—are the most significant and far-reaching grammatical changes in the history of the language. While we understand their effects, we are not certain of the causal relationships among them: did the loss of inflections lead to the periphrases and fixed order, or did the development of these analytic structures lead to the loss of synthetic markers?

The conventional view is that the inflections started disappearing first, as a result of phonetic change (i.e. vowel reduction in unstressed syllables), and that this created a need for new constructions to mark grammatical distinctions. This view sees the shift as a kind of drag chain, in which certain changes leave gaps, and other forms are 'dragged' in to fill them. A problem with this view is that it postulates either a sudden changeover from inflections to periphrases or a period in which the language may have had neither means available, since inflections had been lost but periphrases had not developed fully.

The opposite position claims that inflections were lost because they ceased to be functional, not because sound change eroded them. Periphrases predated the loss of inflections and competed with them, often providing greater clarity and utility. This view postulates a push chain, in which a more effective form 'pushes' out a weaker one. However, scholars cannot prove that inflections are inherently unclear or ineffective, and unless this assertion can be properly established, we have no reliable way to explain the loss of inflectional function.

In *Linguistic Evolution, with Special Reference to English*, M.L. Samuels (1972) tries to present a coherent view of the causal relationships involved in the shift from synthetic to analytic systems by reconciling the conventional and functional views. He wishes to account for events during the long period of overlap, when inflections and periphrases co-existed. He begins with the premise that although inflections are not intrinsically weak, we have historical evidence that they may lose their effectiveness: through phonetic reduction, through the acquisition of extended functions (rather like a word acquiring multiple meanings), and through the mergers caused by the first two factors (rather like the development of homophones). Consider the functional extension of the plural marker *-es* to all cases in the plural, or the phonetic merger of genitive and plural as *-es*. Samuels then proposes four stages of shift, first involving drag and then push:

1. The first stage is one in which pure inflections are primary. This must be a pre-Old English period in which pronouns, prepositions, and adverbs existed

but were not regularly used to mark grammatical distinctions; instead, they were used for emphasis or in special contexts.

2. The second stage, probably classical Old English, involves some weakening of inflections for the reasons given above. At this time, inflections were still the most common means of marking grammatical distinctions, but their weakening was—via a drag chain—leading to the regularization of pronouns, prepositions, and adverbs as grammatical markers.

3. The third stage, most likely corresponding to late Old English and early Middle English, sees the arrival of a push chain effect. While drag chain pressures persisted during this period, the ambiguity created by leveled inflections prompted speakers to rely on periphrases to convey grammatical information. This reliance led to the use of reduced inflections; for instance, we find in place of a fully inflected noun the use of a noun with a reduced inflection when it follows a preposition.

4. By the fourth stage, in late Middle English and Early Modern English, most inflections have been driven out of the language. Only a few reduced inflections are preserved, because of conservatism or inertia. Grammatical relations are expressed by fixed word order at the clause level and periphrases at the group level. (It makes sense to say that Modern English is still in this stage.)

The shift from synthetic to analytic processes is basically a conservative change in that the same grammatical distinctions are expressed, even though different means are used. While most noun inflections are lost, we can signal the role or case of a noun by its position in the sentence or its occurrence after a preposition; while person and number distinctions on the verb are severely reduced, we denote these by means of obligatory subjects.

Despite the major conservative shift from synthetic to analytic in the Middle English period, we can nonetheless point to a number of innovative changes. Here, some grammatical distinction was gained or lost: the dual number, grammatical gender, noun classes, and two declensions of the adjective were lost; an article system and obligatory subject place holders (*it* and *there*) were acquired.

Middle English as a Creole?

One theory (see Bailey and Maroldt 1977; Dominique 1977) explains the changes in grammar and lexicon during the Middle English period as a result of *creolization*. This is a process whereby a pidgin evolves to become a native language, or *creole*. Pidgins develop when people speaking different languages come into contact and attempt to communicate. They are functionally limited, grammatically reduced, and typically short-lived. They have instrumental functions (such as trade) but not the full range of communicative uses present in real language. Nonetheless, pidgins are not ad hoc formations, but are conventionalized and must be learned. They do not serve as the native language of any community. If children begin to learn the pidgin as their mother tongue, however, it will become linguistically more complex and expand to serve all communicative needs, thus becoming a creole.

It is proposed that Middle English is a hybrid language, a creole of French and English, whose phonology and syntax are Germanic but whose lexicon is strongly affected by French. They suggest that simplification of the grammar resulted from interference between French and English inflections. Another result of creolization, according to the theory, is the extensive borrowing of vocabulary from French.

Although intriguing, this theory has not been fully articulated nor widely accepted. The use of French in England was really quite limited; even though the aristocracy spoke French, up to 90 per cent of the population continued to speak English. The enormous influence of French on ME vocabulary is undeniable, but vocabulary is not the main criterion for determining if a language is creolized. No structural changes can be attributed directly to French. Many changes we see in Middle English were already underway in Old English (even though French contact doubtless accelerated developments) and are in keeping with a larger shift from a synthetic to an analytic language. In addition, the effects on English phonology were minimal, contrary to what one would expect in a creole. The dialects of English most in contact with French—in the South—were least changed, while the dialects least in contact—in the North—show the greatest amount of innovation.

In rejecting this theory, Thomason and Kaufmann (1988) point out that no phonemes were borrowed from French (even [ž] has a native source, namely, palatalization, see Chapter 10) and that there was no French influence on English word order or rules of concord; the impact of French was limited to lexical borrowings, derivational affixes such as *-able*, and the phonemicization of certain allophonic pairs, such as initial [f/v]. They describe the situation as one of intensive language contact, but not one of creolization, and state firmly that 'it can in no way be considered reasonable to suppose that any of the conditions for pidginization, creolization, or language mixture existed between English and French in the Middle Ages' (1988:309).

Although Middle English might not be a creole, one would not want to minimize the impact of French on English vocabulary. The linguist Angelika Lutz (2002) points out that among the most common words (the so-called 'General Service List' [GSL] with fewer than 4,000 items), Germanic vocabulary constitutes less than half; in even larger samplings, such as the *Advanced Learners' Dictionary* (*ALD*) and *Shorter Oxford English Dictionary* (*SOED*), only about a quarter of the words are Germanic. Lutz adapts figures presented by Manfred Scheler in order to give us the information in Table 9.8 below. She notes that the columns represent different stylistic levels, with the *SOED* containing the greatest proportion of rare or difficult words. Importantly, the influence of French actually increases as the vocabulary becomes more common, showing its highest percentage in the *GSL*. The influence of the other non-Germanic languages, however, decreases dramatically from the specialized to the everyday vocabulary.

Table 9.8 The Proportion of Native and Foreign Elements in the English Word Stock

	SOED (80,096 words)	ALD (27,241 words)	GSL (3,984 words)
West Germanic	22.20%	27.43%	47.08%
French	28.37%	35.89%	38.00%
Latin	28.29%	22.05%	9.59%
Greek	5.32%	1.59%	0.25%
Other Romance	1.86%	1.60%	0.20%
Celtic	0.34%	0.25%	—

Lutz concludes in the following way:

[T]he figures for Latin etc. are characteristic of cultural borrowing which makes itself felt more strongly in special sections of the vocabulary than in the general and basic vocabulary, and the percentages reflect the range and intensity of the cultural appeal of the donor language for the speakers of the recipient language. By contrast, the particularly large share of French in the basic vocabulary of Modern Standard English cannot be attributed to its cultural appeal alone but results from forced linguistic contact exerted by the speakers of the language of a conquering power on that of the conquered population. Ordinary borrowing, guided by the wish to acquire new things and concepts and, together with them, the appropriate foreign terms, could not have led to such an extreme effect on the basic vocabulary of the recipient language (2002:148).

The Rise of a Standard Dialect

While the regional dialects of Middle English were sometimes felt to differ in social prestige, their written forms all seem to have been considered suitable for recording literary texts. Moreover, although their diversity sometimes made communication difficult, there was not a strong need for a unified dialect, perhaps because Latin and later French could serve as a written standard among learned people.

After 1400, however, the situation changed. In 1476, William Caxton brought the printing press (using movable type) to England from the Low Countries, allowing for dissemination of multiple copies of books throughout England, as opposed to unique manuscripts, which had very limited distribution. The books had to be printed in a dialect and use a conventional spelling that could be understood by all; thus the language of the text became the responsibility of the publisher and might be divorced from the speech of the author (Knowles 1997:60). The major element of the Wycliffite program of religious reform in the fourteenth and fifteenth centuries was translation of the Bible into the language of the 'lewd' (unlearned) people. The Protestant Reformation which followed was based on the principle of the individ-

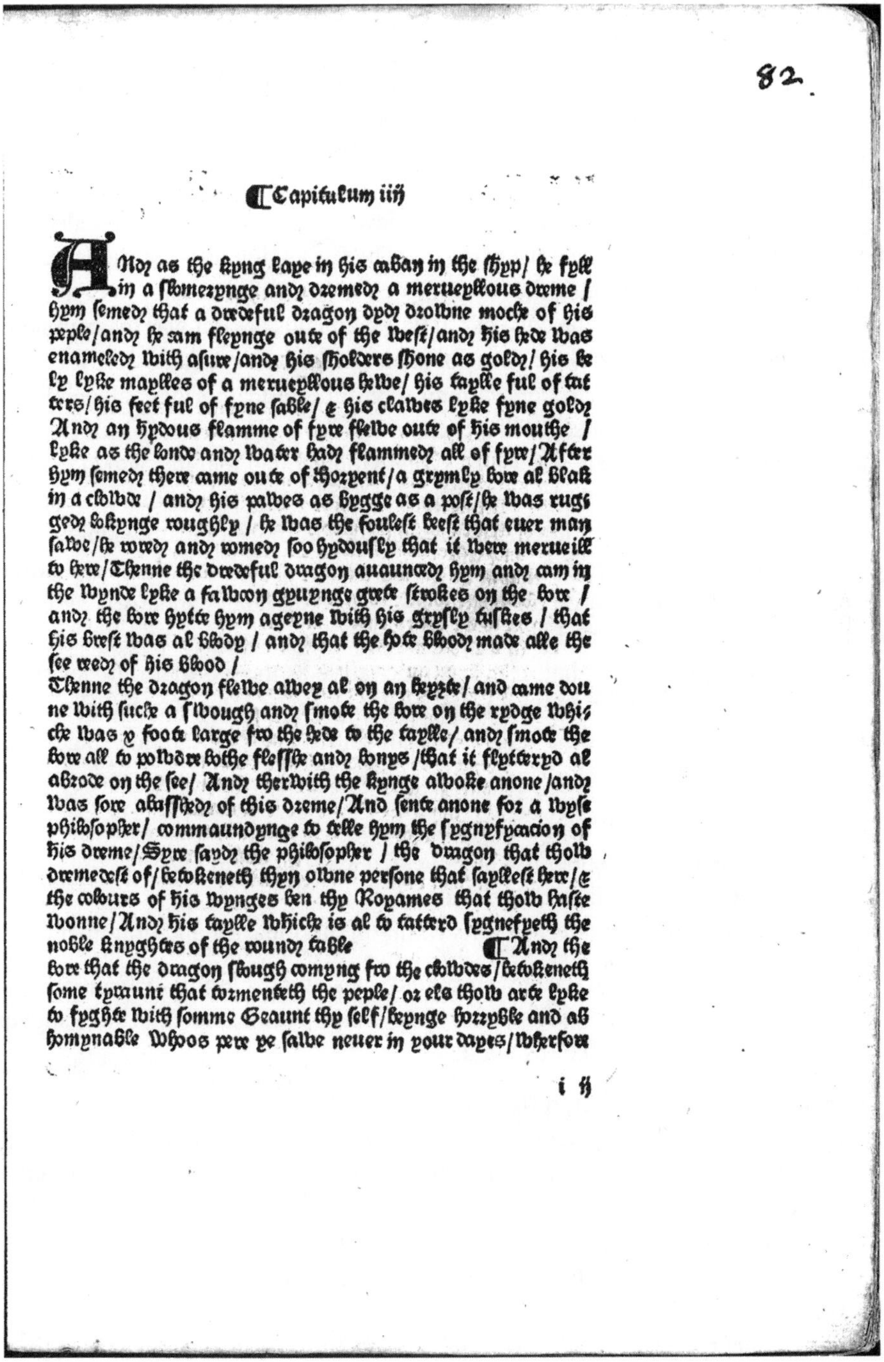

82.

¶ Capitulum iiij

And as the kyng laye in his caban in the shyp / he fyll in a slomerynge and dremed a merueyllous dreme / hym semed that a dredeful dragon dyd drowne moche of his peple / and he cam fleynge oute of the west / and his hede was enameled with asure / and his sholders shone as golde / his bely lyke maylles of a merueyllous hewe / his tayle ful of tatters / his feet ful of fyne sable / & his clawes lyke fyne golde / And an hydous flamme of fyre flewe oute of his mouthe / lyke as the londe and water had flammed all of fyre / After hym semed there came oute of thoryent / a grymly bore al blak in a clowde / and his pawes as bygge as a post / he was rugged lokynge roughly / he was the foulest beest that euer man sawe / he rored and romed soo hydously that it were merueill to here / Thenne the dredeful dragon auaunced hym and cam in the wynde lyke a falcon gyuynge grete strokes on the bore / and the bore hytte hym ageyne with his grysly tuskes / that his brest was al blody / and that the hote blood made alle the see reed of his blood /

Thenne the dragon flewe awey al on an hyghte / and came doune with such a swough and smote the bore on the rydge whiche was ȝ foote large fro the hede to the tayle / and smote the bore all to powder bothe flesshe and bonys / that it flyterryd al abrode on the see / And therwith the kynge awoke anone / and was sore abasshed of this dreme / And sente anone for a wyse philosopher / commaundynge to telle hym the sygnyfycacion of his dreme / Syr sayd the philosopher / the dragon that thou dremedest of / betokeneth thyn owne persone that sayllest here / & the colours of his wynges ben thy Royames that thou haste wonne / And his tayle whiche is al to tattred sygnefyeth the noble knyghtes of the rounde table ¶ And the bore that the dragon slough comyng fro the clowdes / betokeneth some tyraunt that tormenteth the peple / or els thou arte lyke to fyghte with somme Geaunt thy self / beynge horryble and abhomynable Whos pere ye salbe neuer in your dayes / wherfore

i ij

Figure 9.1   A Page from Sir Thomas Malory's *Le Morte d'Arthur*, Printed by William Caxton in 1485 (© The Pierpont Morgan Library, New York. PML 17560, folio [82 recto])

ual's access to the word of God. Both movements created the need for a universally understood dialect of English. A sense of English patriotism following victories of the Hundred Years War may also have encouraged a national language. A growing urban population, the result of migrations of speakers of different dialects into urban centers, especially London, made it necessary for people from different parts of the country to communicate easily.

There is strong support for the traditional view that the East Midland dialect, specifically that of London, became the standard. The East Midlands was the largest and most populous region, and also the wealthiest, with rich agricultural land and good ports. London was located at the edge of the East Midlands area; it was the commercial center, the political center, and the focus of social and intellectual activity. It is sometimes suggested that the centers of learning, Oxford and Cambridge, also enhanced the status of the East Midlands, but that Oxford was more Central and Cambridge was rather geographically isolated. The East Midland dialect had features which made it a suitable basis for the standard. A standard is not usually one pure regional dialect but a *compromise dialect*, widely intelligible and incorporating linguistic elements from other areas. It occupies a geographically central position and does not have extreme features, either of an innovative or a conservative kind. The standard is associated with prestige. The East Midland dialect had all of the necessary qualities, not being as conservative as the Southern dialect nor as innovative as the Northern. It was spoken in a central part of England, and used by those in high political and social positions.

Leith (1997:31) identifies the following four linked and overlapping stages in the process of standardization:

1. selection of a dialect as the dominant variety,
2. acceptance of that dialect by the educated and powerful classes,
3. elaboration of that dialect's functions, and
4. codification of that dialect (i.e. its fixing in dictionaries and grammars).

The traditional view of the development of standard English from the East Midland dialect, however, is undoubtedly too simplified. Samuels (1972) suggests that four competing dialects contributed:

- the early London dialect, reflecting primarily Essex features;
- a later London dialect, incorporating the dialect of different immigrant groups, first those from surrounding areas, then those from East Anglia, and later those from the Central and East Midlands;
- the dialect used by John Wyclif and the itinerant priests who distributed his Bible translation; this was a Central Midlands variety from the Oxford region; and
- the Chancery standard, the form of written English used in state documents produced at the Exchequer in Westminster (next to London on the Thames) and later in Chancery Lane in London when English began to be used for official purposes after 1430; more Central in nature, the texts of this dialect incorporate conservative West Saxon practices but few East Anglian features.

More recently, two assumptions made by Samuels have been called into question, namely that the standard developed out of a prestige dialect (the Chancery standard) and that it was centered in London. Many scholars now believe that the influence of the merchant or middle class may have been underestimated as well as that of more northerly dialects which accompanied migrants into the capital city.

Exercise 9.5 Synthetic to Analytic and Standardization

1. Discuss briefly the process of creolization. Does this process account for Middle English?

   _____

   _____

   _____

   _____

2. Discuss the main differences between a synthetic and an analytic language with reference to English.

   _____

   _____

   _____

   _____

3. Briefly comment on the following individuals and location with reference to their impact on the standardization of English.

   a. John Wyclif

   _____

   _____

   b. Geoffrey Chaucer

   _____

   _____

   c. William Caxton

   _____

   _____

   d. London

   _____

   _____

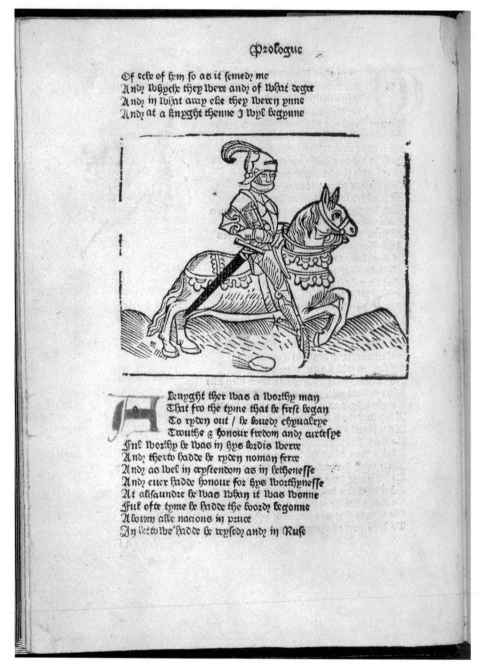

Figure 9.2   A Page from the Second Edition of Caxton's Printing of *The Canterbury Tales*, 1484 (© the British Library)

A Closer Look at the Language of a Middle English Text

We conclude this chapter with a selection from William Caxton's 'Prologue' to the *Eneydos* (1490), a translation not of Vergil's *Aeneid* but of the French *Livre des Eneyedes* by Guillaume de Roy. In his preface, Caxton discusses the problems of the translator, given dialect diversity and change in the language. He is also concerned with the selection of the proper level of diction (native or borrowed), but his choice is fairly heavily French nevertheless. The use of double or triple constructions (*delybered and concluded* [1], *fayr & straunge* [3], *olde and homely* [6], *rude and brood* [8], *vsed and spoken* [13], *waneth & dyscreaseth* [15]) is typical of the high style Caxton adopts, though it may also have served as a means of introducing and defining Latinate vocabulary. Caxton ends this selection with an amusing anecdote involving miscommunication between English speakers using different forms of the word for 'eggs' (the native English form *eyren* and the Scandinavian borrowing *egges*). The punctuation of this text will seem unusual because of Caxton's capitalization practices and his use of a slash for a comma or a period.

(1) And whan I had aduysed me in this sayd boke. I delybered and concluded to translate it

(2) in to englysshe And forthwyth toke a penne & ynke and wrote a leef or tweyne/

(3) whyche I ouersawe agayn to correcte it/ And whan I sawe the fayr & straunge termes

(4) therin/ I doubted that it sholde not please some gentylmen whiche late blamed me

(5) sayeng y^t in my translacyons I had ouer curyous termes whiche coude not be

(6) vnderstande of comyn peple/ and desired me to vse olde and homely termes in my

(7) translacyons. and fayn wolde I satysfye euery man/ and so to doo toke an olde boke

(8) and redde therin/ and certaynly the englysshe was so rude and brood that I coude not

(9) wele vnderstand it. And also my lorde abbot of westmynster ded do shewe to me late

(10) certayn euydences wryton in olde englysshe for to reduce it in to our englysshe now

(11) vsid/ And certaynly it was wreton in suche wyse that it was more lyke to dutsche than

(12) englysshe I coude not reduce ne brynge it to be vnderstonden/ And certaynly our

(13) langage now vsed varyeth ferre from that. whiche was vsed and spoken whan I was

(14) borne/ For we englysshe men ben borne vnder the domynacyon of the mone. whiche is

(15) neuer stedfaste/ but euer wauerynge/ wexynge one season/ and waneth & dyscreaseth

(16) another season/ And that comyn englysshe that is spoken in one shyre varyeth from a

(17) nother. In so moche that in my dayes happened that certayn marchauntes were in a

Continued

(18) shippe in tamyse for to haue sayled ouer the see into Zelande/ and for lacke of wynde,

(19) thei taryed atte forlond. and wente to lande for to refreshe them And one of theym

(20) named sheffelde a mercer cam in to an hows and axed for mete. and specyally he axyd

(21) after eggys And the goode wyf answerde. that she coude speke no frenshe. And the

(22) marchant was angry. for he also coude speke no frenshe. but wold haue hadde egges/

(23) and she vnderstode hym not/ And thenne at laste a nother sayd that he wolde haue

(24) eyren/ then the good wyf sayd that she vnderstod hym wel/ Loo what sholde a man in

(25) thyse dayes now wryte. egges or eyren/ (Caxton's 'Prologue' to the *Eneydos*;
Crotch 1928:108).

Caxton's language is considered a transitional variety between Middle English and Early Modern English; it is highly analytic rather than inflected. There are still significant differences between Caxton's language and our own, in morphology, syntax, and vocabulary. Some interesting features of Caxton's morphology are the use of the third-person singular verbal ending (*-eth* in *varyeth* [13, 16] and *waneth*, *dyscreaseth* [15]) as well as the use of the older form of *are*, which is *ben* (14). We find unmarked adverbs in *late* (4) and *ouer* (5).

In terms of word order, Caxton's prose resembles Modern English for the most part, though there are a number of constructions no longer found today, including:

- reflexive verbs: *aduysed me* (1), *desired me* (6), and *refreshe them* (19);
- *for-to*-infinitives: *for to reduce* (10), *for to haue sayled* (18), and *for to refreshe* (19);
- omission of the subject: *toke* 'I took'(7);
- use of relative *which* with an animate noun: *some gentylmen whiche* (4);
- an impersonal verb without an *it* subject: *happened* (17);
- passive with *of* denoting the agent: *vnderstande of comyn peple* (6);
- the older form of the negative construction without an auxiliary: *vnderstode hym not* (23);
- omission of articles: *atte forlond* (19); and
- the use of a so-called resumptive pronoun following a relative pronoun: *whyche . . . it* (3).

The *ded do shewe* construction in (9) is perhaps an emphatic auxiliary *do* followed by a causative *do*, meaning 'did (indeed) make shown'. A number of the vocabulary items are used with different senses than they have in Modern English, including *curyous* 'erudite' (5), *euydences* 'documents' (10), *reduce* 'translate' (10), *mete* 'food' (20), and *mercer* 'merchant' (20). Note also the use of *v* initially and *u* medially, and the abbreviation of *that* as y[t], where the *y* is a printer's representation of the thorn, þ.

RECOMMENDED WEB LINKS

The following site has some discussion of ME grammar:

http://courses.fas.harvard.edu/~chaucer/pronunciation/

For a detailed representation of dialect features, see *A Linguistic Atlas of Early Middle English 1150–1325*, available online:

http://www.lel.ed.ac.uk/ihd/laeme1/laeme1.html

FURTHER READING

For basic instruction in Middle English grammar, you might consult the following text:

Burrow, J.A., and Thorlac Turville-Petre. 1996. *A Book of Middle English*. 2nd edn. Oxford: Blackwell.

Horobin, Simon, and Jeremy Smith. 2002. *An Introduction to Middle English*. New York: Oxford University Press.

If you wish to pursue your reading on Middle English grammar, the following resources (in addition to works cited in the previous chapters) provide more discussion of the topic:

Denison, David. 1993. *English Historical Syntax*. London and New York: Longman.

Fischer, Olga. 1992. 'Syntax'. *The History of the English Language. Vol. II: 1066–1476*. Ed. by Norman Blake, 207–408. Cambridge: Cambridge University Press.

Fischer, Olga, and Wim van der Wurff. 2006. 'Syntax'. *A History of the English Language*. Ed. by Richard M. Hogg and David Denison, 109–98. Cambridge: Cambridge University Press.

Lass, Roger. 1992. 'Phonology and Morphology'. *The Cambridge History of the English Language. Vol. II: 1066–1476*. Ed. by Norman Blake, 23–155. Cambridge: Cambridge University Press.

Lass, Roger. 2006. 'Phonology and Morphology'. *A History of the English Language*. Ed. by Richard M. Hogg and David Denison, 43–108. Cambridge: Cambridge University Press.

Mossé, Fernand. 1952. *A Handbook of Middle English*. Trans. by James A. Walker. Baltimore and London: Johns Hopkins University Press.

Mustanoja, Tauno F. 1960. *A Middle English Syntax. Part 1: Parts of Speech*. Helsinki: Société Néophilologique.

If you do not have access to the *Middle English Dictionary*, this glossary can be very useful:

Davis, Norman, et al. 1979. *A Chaucer Glossary*. Oxford: Clarendon.

For recent views on the rise of standard English:

Nevalainen, Terttu, and Ingrid Tieken Boon van Ostade. 2006. 'Standardisation'. *A History of the English Language*. Ed. by Richard M. Hogg and David Denison, 271–311. Cambridge: Cambridge University Press.

Wright, Laura (ed.). 2000. *The Development of Standard English, 1300–1800: Theories, Descriptions, Conflicts*. Cambridge: Cambridge University Press.

For an assessment of the scholarship on Middle English as a creole, see:

Thomason, Sarah Grey, and Terrence Kaufman. 1988. *Language Contact, Creolization, and Genetic Linguistics*. Berkeley, Los Angeles, and London: University of California Press, pp. 306–15.

A representation of late ME dialects can be found in:

McIntosh, Angus, M.K. Samuels, and Michael Benskin. 1987. *A Linguistic Atlas of Late Medieval English*. Aberdeen: Aberdeen University Press.

10 The Words, Sounds, and Inflections of Early Modern English

OVERVIEW

The first half of this chapter examines borrowings, sound changes, and spelling reforms from Middle English to Modern English. We begin by discussing the extensive increase in the size of the English vocabulary in the Renaissance, primarily through Latin loan words. Next, we turn to the developments known collectively as the Great Vowel Shift, which affected long vowels. We then look at the less extensive changes affecting the short vowels and at the rise of new diphthongs, before moving on to consonant changes. We conclude this section with the etymological respellings carried out in the Renaissance.

The second half of the chapter examines grammatical changes between the two language periods in the marking of the genitive case in nouns and in the use of articles, personal pronouns, interrogative pronouns, and relative pronouns. We contrast the use of case forms in Early Modern English with their use in Modern English. We end with developments in the verb classes and personal endings.

OBJECTIVES

The first objective in this chapter is to understand Modern English pronunciation and spelling from a historical perspective. After reading the chapter, you should be able to

- give the Middle English vowel from which a Modern English vowel derives;
- explain why certain words in Modern English have acquired identical pronunciations, while other words have developed variant pronunciations;

- explain how the spellings of Modern English words often reveal the history of their pronunciation; and

- account for certain respellings and inverse spellings found in Modern English.

The second objective is to be able to identify the inflected forms of Early Modern English, including the sources and subsequent developments of forms such as the *his*-genitive, group genitive, articles, and the *thou/you* distinction.

With this chapter we begin the Early Modern English period, which corresponds roughly with the period of cultural history known as the English Renaissance. This period represents a 'revival of learning', with increased interest in the classical languages and texts, rapid developments in science and the arts, and expanding knowledge of the physical world. The great writer of this period is William Shakespeare (1564–1616), whose plays record the vibrant Renaissance vocabulary. However, we should not underestimate the influence of the King James version of the Bible (1611) on the language. Increased access to the biblical text, provided by this and earlier translations, along with the widespread publication of books and pamphlets interpreting it (often with a political polemic) provide evidence of the expansion of literacy during this period, especially to the 'lower orders of society' (Knowles 1997:95). During the Renaissance, the vocabulary underwent a major expansion, and an important phonological change called the Great Vowel Shift affected both the phonology and the orthography of English.

Early Modern English Vocabulary

According to David Crystal, 'the increase in foreign borrowings is the most distinctive linguistic sign of the Renaissance in English' (2003:60). In general, the pattern of borrowing established in the Middle English period continued during the Early Modern period. However, Latin rather than French contributed the vast majority of loan words. In fact, a search of the *OED* shows over ten times more loan words from Latin than from French in the period between 1500 and 1650. Representative borrowings from Latin and French are given below:

Latin

Sixteenth Century	Seventeenth Century
cadaver (1500)	*premium* (1601)
integer (1509)	*equilibrium* (1608)
genius (1513)	*specimen* (1610)
junior (1526)	*series* (1611)
fungus (1527)	*census* (1613)
vertigo (1528)	*vertebra* (1615)
folio (1533)	*squalor* (1621)
exit (1538)	*formula* (1638)
area (1538)	*onus* (1640)

abdomen (1541)

circus (1546)

medium (1551)

genus (1551)

species (1551)

decorum (1568)

compendium (1581)

omen (1582)

militia (1590)

sinus (1597)

virus (1599)

crux (1641)

data (1646)

copula (1650)

album (1651)

complex (1652)

pendulum (1660)

rabies (1661)

minimum (1663)

serum (1672)

stimulus (1684)

status (1693)

French

Sixteenth Century	**Seventeenth Century**
elegance (1510)	exist (1602)
elegy (1514)	epidemic (1603)
equip (1523)	accommodation (1604)
activity (1530)	ferocity (1606)
accent (1538)	adapt (1611)
erosion (1541)	erode (1612)
adopt (1548)	explicit (1613)
amplitude (1549)	evoke (1623)
absurd (1557)	annihilation (1638)
agile (1577)	latrine (1642)
escort (1579)	foible (1648)
harlequin (1590)	class (1656)

In the Renaissance, the majority of Greek words were borrowed through Latin as well, for example:

Sixteenth Century	**Seventeenth Century**
alphabet (1513)	archive (1603)
drama (1517)	onomastic (1609)
dilemma (1523)	epiglottis (1615)
hyperbole (1529)	meteorology (1620)
phrase (1530)	program (1633)
catastrophe (1540)	comma (1646)
crisis (1543)	electric (1646)
arthritis (1544)	psyche (1647)
pathos (1579)	cosmos (1650)
praxis (1581)	elastic (1653)
dialysis (1586)	euphemism (1656)
hypothesis (1596)	narcosis (1693)

The *Oxford English Dictionary* lists the following words as direct borrowings from Greek, though it may be the case that they entered English through intermediaries:

Sixteenth Century	Seventeenth Century
trophy (1513)	*anonymous* (1601)
antidote (1515)	*strophe* (1603)
barbarous (1526)	*archaeology* (1607)
idiocy (1529)	*dichotomize* (1608)
eclipsis (1538)	*enthusiast* (1609)
anarchy (1539)	*antithetic* (1610)
chronography (1548)	*calligraphy* (1613)
acrid (1550)	*exegesis* (1619)
hegemony (1567)	*epigraph* (1624)
heptagon (1570)	*diagnostic* (1625)
ephemeral (1576)	*apocalyptic* (1629)

In the Renaissance we also find a greater variety of source languages—both Indo-European and non-Indo-European—contributing to the English vocabulary than ever before. Let us first consider borrowings from Indo-European languages:

Spanish	Italian	Portuguese	Iranian Languages
armada (1533)	*archipelago* (1502)	*apricot* (1551)	*shah* (1566)
anchovy (1596)	*violin* (1579)	*coco* (1555)	*dervish* (1585)
embargo (1602)	*stanza* (1588)	*flamingo* (1565)	*caravan* (1599)
guitar (1621)	*umbrella* (1609)	*molasses* (1570)	*mullah* (1613)
cargo (1657)	*granite* (1646)	*albacore* (1579)	*shawl* (1662)

Celtic Languages	Indic Languages	German
flannel (1503) (Welsh)	*punch* (1600)	*hamster* (1607)
bog (1505) (Irish)	*nabob* (1612)	*plunder* (1632)
ptarmigan (1599) (Scots)	*guru* (1613)	*sauerkraut* (1633)
trousers (1599) (Scots)	*dungaree* (1613)	*zinc* (1651)
clabber (1634) (Irish)	*bungalow* (1676)	

Dutch	Russian	Scandinavian Languages
scone (1513)	*czar* (1555)	*rug* (1551)
dock (1513)	*beluga* (1591)	*snag* (1557)
dollar (1553)	*rouble* (1554)	*troll* (1616)
yacht (1557)	*steppe* (1671)	*fjord* (1674)
easel (1634)		*rune* (1685)

Spanish loan words began to enter the language in the sixteenth century, often via French at first, but then directly. While some Italian words entered English in the fourteenth and fifteenth centuries, again via French, they became frequent only from the sixteenth century onward. Celtic loan words were, as in earlier periods, relatively rare, and the number of Scandinavian loan words fell off substantially from the Middle English period. German loan words were beginning to appear in English, but would become more common in the following centuries. A few loan words from the Iranian languages date from the Old English period, such as *tiger* and *paradise*, and others from the Middle English period, such as *chess* and *scarlet*, but these entered via Latin and Old French respectively; direct loan words appeared only in the Renaissance. Likewise, Indic borrowings in the Old English period arrived via Latin (e.g. *panther*) and in the Middle English period via French (e.g. *sandal*), with direct borrowings appearing later.

Turning to non-Indo-European languages, we find the following loan words:

Turkish	Arabic	Hebrew
horde (1555)	*mohair* (1570)	*Jehovah* (1530)
caftan (1591)	*sheikh* (1577)	*hallelujah* (1535)
sherbet (1603)	*nil* (1583)	*shekel* (1560)
yogurt (1625)	*hashish* (1599)	*Torah* (1577)
pasha (1646)	*Ramadan* (1599)	*bethel* (1617)

Malay	Japanese	North American Indigenous Languages
bamboo (1598)	*tatami* (1614)	*raccoon* (1608)
cassowary (1611)	*miso* (1615)	*moccasin* (1612)
paddy (1623)	*shogun* (1615)	*moose* (1613)
cockatoo (1634)	*nento* (1616)	*skunk* (1634)
amuck (1663)	*sake* (1687)	*hickory* (1676)

These examples are representative; rarer examples include loan words from Hungarian (*hussar* [1532]), Tamil (*curry* [1598], *pariah* [1613], *catamaran* [1697]), Chinese (*litchi* [1588], *sampan* [1620], *yin/yang* [1671]), and South American indigenous languages (*Inca* [1594], *jaguar* [1604]). Borrowings from Arabic occurred as early as Middle English, entering through French, such as *mosque* and *sumac*. Arabic borrowings (whether direct or indirect) are often recognizable by the presence of the definite article *al-* prefixed to the root, as in *alcove* (1623), *algebra* (1541), and *alcohol* (1615). A number of Hebrew borrowings in Old English came via Latin and Greek, such as *Satan* and *amen*. Many words of non-Indo-European origin were borrowed into English via the languages of the explorers (Spanish, Portuguese, and Dutch). For example, many American indigenous words came into English through Spanish, such as *hurricane* (1555), *maize* (1565), *potato* (1565), *tobacco* (1577), *banana* (1597), *coyote* (1628), and *vanilla* (1662).

Many Latinate affixes became productive in Early Modern English. As discussed in Chapter 8, speakers tend to analyze the structure of Latinate words into constituent parts and then extend an affix to new lexical roots. For example, a number of words containing the suffix *-ation*—including *adaptation, adoration, alteration, demarcation,* and *expectation*—were borrowed in the Renaissance. This led to the creation of new forms by adding *-ation* to a Latin root, such as *verification* (1523), *valuation* (1529), *association* (1535), *cancellation* (1535), *rotation* (1555), *retaliation* (1581), *attenuation* (1594), *rumination* (1600), *authorization* (1610), *adjudication* (1623), *immigration* (1658), *experimentation* (1675), and *cultivation* (1700). The suffix was applied occasionally to English roots, including *schoolation* (1575), *blindation* (1588), *flirtation* (1718), *starvation* (1778), and *botheration* (1797). Likewise, *-ize* was extracted from complex loan words and added newly to Latinate roots to create the following forms between 1580 and 1700: *apologize, civilize, criticize, equalize, fertilize, humanize, jeopardize, monopolize, patronize, satirize, specialize, sterilize,* and *symbolize.* Again, we find *-ize* added at times to English roots: *womanize* (1593), *gospelize* (1643), *heathenize* (1681), and *tenderize* (1733).

Because of this proliferation of borrowings, a debate raged during the Renaissance between those who believed that the enrichment of English vocabulary with loan words from Latin and Greek was desirable, and those who felt that the native resources of the language were sufficient. The latter group argued that the monosyllabic words of Germanic (which they called 'Saxon') could express more truly and unambiguously the writer's meaning (cf. Knowles 1997:78ff.). For example, although his vocabulary is eclectic, Edmund Spenser (author of *The Faerie Queene* and a student of the early lexicographer Richard Mulcaster) believed in extending the meanings of existing words, coining English words, and reviving archaic words. Meanwhile, in a publication called *The Governour* (1531), Sir Thomas Elyot argued for augmenting the language with Latin borrowings. While such words might first appear 'strange and dark', he writes, they would 'once brought in custom . . . shall be as easy to understand as other words late come out of Italy and France' (see Elyot 1834:73). In the end, innovation, not convention, ruled the day in the sense that an immense number of Latin words were borrowed (a number even larger than the French borrowings in Middle English); these were learned terms deliberately introduced by writers. Some considered these words overly pedantic and ridiculed them as 'inkhorn terms' (from the traditional horn container for ink). Ultimately, a compromise emerged: many Latin borrowings, although originally objected to, were retained (such as *education, confidence, expect, maturity, dedicate, discretion, exaggerate, industrial, encyclopedia,* and *describe*), while a large number were dropped (such as *truage* 'tribute', *deruncinate* 'weed' [V], *pistated* 'baked', *homogalact* 'foster-brother', *suppeditate* 'supply', *illecebrous* 'delicate', *devulgate* 'set forth', *adjuvate* 'aid', *eximious* 'excellent', *fatigate* 'make tired', and *demit* 'send away').

We see the debate concerning native and borrowed vocabulary in the contemporary account of William Harrison in his chapter 'Of the Languages Spoken in this Iland' in Holinshed's *Chronicles of England, Scotlande, and Irelande* (1587). He considers English in the Renaissance as having evolved from its medieval origins.

> [Old English was] an hard and rough kind of speech, God wot, when our nation was brought first into acquaintance withal, but now changed with vs into a farre more fine and easie kind of vtterance, and so polished and helped with new and milder words, that it is to be aduouched how there is no one speech vnder the sunne spoken in our time, that hath or can haue more varietie of word, copie of phrases, or figures and floures of eloquence, than hath our English toong, although some have affirmed vs rather to barke as dogs, that talke like men, because the most of our words (as they doo indeed) incline vnto one syllable . . . . (Harrison, from 'Of the Languages Spoken in this Iland')
>
> [Following the reestablishment of English after French domination] afterward also, by diligent trauell of Geffray Chaucer, and Iohn Gowre, in the time of Richard the second . . . our said toong was brought to an excellent passe, notwithstanding that it neuer came vnto the type of perfection vntill the time of Queene Elizabeth . . . and sundrie and learned & excellent writers haue fullie accomplished the ornature of the same, to their great praise and immortall commendation; although not a few other doo greatlie seeke to staine the same, by fond affectation of forren and strange words, presuming that to be the best English, which is most corrupted with externall termes of eloquence, and sound of manie syllables.

The Great Vowel Shift

Nature of the Shift

Scholars argue over whether the Great Vowel Shift was really one shift or a series of separate ones that together affected all the long vowels inherited from Middle English. In any case, the changes were comparable in scope and importance to the First Sound Shift, which occurred in the pre-history of the language (see Chapter 5). Like the consonant shift, this vowel shift occurred in all phonological environments — in other words, it was unconditioned. In the Great Vowel Shift, considered as a single, complex shift, all long or lengthened (stressed) vowels were raised in articulation or, if already high vowels, were diphthongized. The shift can be schematized as in Figure 10.1.

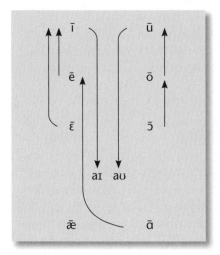

Figure 10.1 Schematic View of the Great Vowel Shift

Note that some of the vowels have been raised more than one position. We will look at the details of each of the changes in the following section. There are aspects of the shift about which we are uncertain. For example, the mechanism of change involved here may either have been a drag chain or a push chain. Traditionally, the Great Vowel Shift has been described as the former: the first sounds to change were the high vowels, [ī] and [ū], and when these diphthongized, gaps were left at the top of the vowel grid, which could be filled by lower vowels moving up. More recently, a different scenario has been proposed: [ē] and perhaps [ō] were the first sounds to change, and as they were raised in articulation, they set in motion simultaneously a drag and a push chain, pushing the high vowels out of their positions and pulling the lower vowels up.

We do not know its causes. They were probably inherent to the language, perhaps having to do with changes in the accentual or phonetic system of English. It is interesting that similar vowel shifts occurred in the other Low West Germanic languages (Dutch, Frisian, etc.) and to a lesser extent in High German. The exact chronology of the changes is also difficult to determine. The changes began perhaps early in the fifteenth century in southern England, but the complete set of changes extended over the fifteenth, sixteenth, and seventeenth centuries. Our difficulty here is that the changes are not recorded in the orthography, as we will see below, so that we can only try to deduce the sounds of the vowels from rhymes, the comments of contemporaries, and other indirect means. We know that the changes had to proceed together rather than in a series of discrete steps, because otherwise there would have been mergers of vowels and various gaps. Like all sound changes, these changes varied across space and time and did not always reach completion. Even today, we find undiphthongized [ū] (e.g. the Scottish pronunciation of *mouse*) or unraised [ē] (e.g. in some Irish pronunciations of *tea* or *sea*).

Details of the Shift

A complete chart of the Great Vowel Shift is given in Table 10.1.

Table 10.1 Details of the Great Vowel Shift

ME vowel	15ᵗʰ–16ᵗʰ century	17ᵗʰ–18ᵗʰ century
ī	əí > ə́ɪ	aɪ
ē	ī	i
ɛ̄	ē > eɪ	eɪ/i
ā	ǣ > ɛ̄ > ē	eɪ
ū	əʊ́ > ə́ʊ	aʊ
ō	ū	u/ʊ/ə
ɔ̄	ō	oʊ

1. The diphthongization of the high vowels is straightforward. In both cases a schwa glide developed in the fifteenth century before the vowel, producing the rising diphthongs [əí] and [əʊ́]. These became falling diphthongs, [ə́ɪ] and [ə́ʊ], in the sixteenth century. In most dialects, the onset of the diphthong was subsequently lowered to a low central vowel [a]. This sequence of changes is shown below:

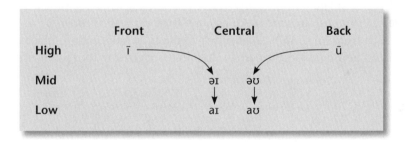

Examples: ME *ride* [rīdə] > PDE *ride* [raɪd]
ME *now* [nū] > PDE *now* [naʊ]

We should note that the earlier form of the diphthong was maintained in some dialects before voiceless consonants. These *unlowered* diphthongs are now a characteristic feature of Canadian English as well as the English spoken in some of the original American colonies (e.g. South Carolina and Virginia), where they are rather inaccurately called *raised diphthongs*. It is simply a matter of chance that the pronunciation of original [ū] came to resemble the Norman spelling *ou* or *ow*; the sound change resulting in the pronunciation [aʊ] occurred several centuries after the spelling change.

2. The shift of [ō] to [ū] occurred during the sixteenth century. Two changes have subsequently affected [u] in some words, as shown below: ū

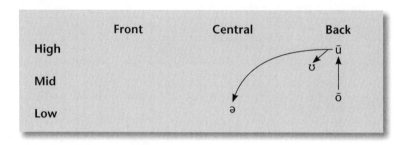

Examples: ME *fode* [fōdə] > PDE *food* [fud]
ME *foot* [fōt] > PDE *foot* [fʊt]
ME *flood* [flōd] > PDE *flood* [fləd]

The vowel [u] has laxed to [ʊ] in words such as *foot, good, book, look,* and *took,* and it has further centralized, lowered, and unrounded to [ə] in a limited number of words such as *flood* and *blood.* The tense vowel [u] is preserved especially in the presence of labials, e.g. *troop, boom, moon, coop,* and *doom.* We cannot know exactly when the laxing of [u] occurred, but Shakespeare could rhyme *food, good,* and *flood.* There continues to be variation between [u] and [ʊ] among dialects of English in words such as *hoof, roof, root,* and *broom.*

3. The shift from [ɔ] to [ō] also occurred in the sixteenth century. Since the Early Modern English period, the pure [o] has diphthongized to [oʊ] for most speakers:

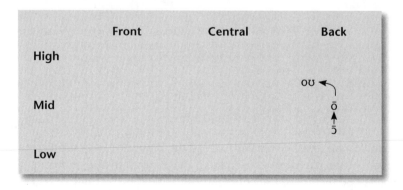

Example: ME *boot* [bɔt] > PDE *boat* [boʊt]

4. Middle English [ā] made rather a long journey forward and up: it shifted to [æ] by 1500, then to [ɛ̄] by 1600, and finally to [ē] by 1700. In Modern English the vowel [e] is diphthongized to [eɪ].

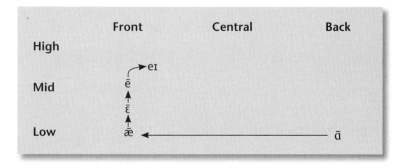

Example: ME *name* [nāmə] > PDE *name* [neɪm]

5. Middle English [ē] shifted very early to [i]; in fact, it may have been the first long vowel to shift.

```
        Front          Central          Back
High     i

Mid      ē

Low
```

Example: ME *grēne* [grēnə] > PDE *green* [grin]

6. The shift of Middle English [ɛ̄] is not quite as straightforward. During the six-teenth century, it became [ē], where it remained for some time.

   Thus, at this stage, words with original [ɛ̄] could be rhymed with words with ME [ā], since both had shifted to [ē]. This is still evident in the late seventeenth-century and early eighteenth-century writings of the Anglo-Irish satirist Jonathan Swift, who rhymed *please/bays* and *dream/name/same*; the seventeenth-century English writer John Dryden rhymed *dream/shame* and *speak/make*. Such lost rhymes may perplex readers today.

   Around the same time, however, there seems to have been a variant pronun-ciation of original [ɛ̄], namely [i]. While [i] was probably at first a pronuncia-tion avoided in educated or polite usage, we find Dryden rhyming *speak/seek* and *dream/seem* with the [i] vowel. And by the mid-eighteenth century [i] had become standard in all but a few words. In these exceptions—*steak*, *break*, *great*, and *yea*—[ē] is usually diphthongized to [eɪ] for most speakers.[1]

---

1 The older pronunciation [ē/eɪ] is also found in some personal names of Irish origin such as *Shea, Beatty,* and *Reagan;* therefore, we pronounce the name of the Irish poet Yeats with an [eɪ] but then use an [i] for the surname of English poet John Keats.

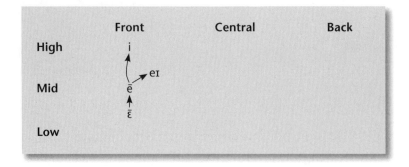

Examples: ME *leef* [lēf] > PDE *leaf* [lif]
ME *greet* [grēt] > PDE *great* [greɪt]

The shift from [ɛ̄] all the way to [i] produced a number of homophones because original [ē] had earlier also shifted to [i]:

ME [ē]	ME [ɛ̄]
meed	*mead*
heel	*heal*
reel	*real*
see	*sea*
seem	*seam*

Quite often the spelling reveals the ME source: *ee* represents an original [ē], while *ea* represents an original [ɛ̄]. For this reason, we might also expect *sweet* and *sweat* or *breed* and *bread* to rhyme. However, they do not. How can this be explained? It seems that [ɛ̄] in these words had previously shortened because the vowel preceded a dental (e.g. *death, bread, head*, and *deaf*) or an [r] (e.g. *pear, bear*, and *wear*). This shortening is not universal, though; we find [i] before a dental in *heath* and *heat* and before [r] in *shear* and *hear*, clearly showing the effects of Great Vowel Shift raising.

In conclusion, we can now highlight two important results of the Great Vowel Shift. First, it eliminated the distinction between long and short vowels that had characterized both the Old and Middle English phonological systems. The long vowels were replaced by either diphthongs or tense vowels, which contrasted with the lax short vowels. Thus, the vowel system underwent a significant change from one based on distinctions of quantity (e.g. OE *god* 'deity' versus *gōd* 'good') to one based on distinctions of quality. While Modern English does have long and short vowels (e.g. *sea* versus *ceased*), this distinction is now merely an allophonic difference, completely predictable by the voicing qualities or number of consonants that follow the vowel. Second, the Great Vowel Shift further confused English spelling. In Old and Middle English, the spellings of stressed vowels in English correspond reasonably well to their pronunciations. The arrival of the printing press in England in the late fifteenth century standardized spelling and fixed orthography to late Middle English conventions. When the long vowels shifted in the subsequent centuries, the spelling system did not change to record the new pronunciations. The spelling currently used for stressed vowels, then, is the spelling appropriate for the unshifted vowels.

Exercise 10.1   The Great Vowel Shift

1. For the following Modern English words, indicate the Middle English pronunciation of the stressed long vowel. Use phonetic symbols.

    a. down   [___]

    b. grief   [___]

    c. kind   [___]

    d. throat [___]

    e. sound [___]

    f. race   [___]

2. Using phonetic symbols, explain the pronunciations of the following homophonic pairs by showing the vowel changes from ME to ModE.

    a. see/sea _____

    _____

    b. great/grate _____

    _____

    c. hear/here _____

    _____

3. Explain why *sweet* and *sweat* do not rhyme.

    _____

    _____

4. What are two important consequences of the Great Vowel Shift?

    _____

    _____

5. Circle every word in the following passage which derives from a long vowel in Middle English. Then list **the Middle English vowel** and its **Modern English reflex**.

Example: (*We*) ME [ē]   ModE [i]

We looked up and saw headlights directly in front of us.

There was a loud crash and the car veered off the road.

By a feat of good luck, everyone made it out unhurt.

	ME	ModE
_____	[__]	[__]
_____	[__]	[__]
_____	[__]	[__]
_____	[__]	[__]
_____	[__]	[__]
_____	[__]	[__]
_____	[__]	[__]
_____	[__]	[__]
_____	[__]	[__]
_____	[__]	[__]
_____	[__]	[__]

Changes in the Short Vowels and Diphthongs

Unlike long vowels, the short vowels of Middle English have remained stable (see Figure 10.2).

Short [ɑ] moved forward to the low central position [a] and then by the late sixteenth century to the low front position [æ]. The exception to this shift occurs when short [ɑ] is followed by [l] and a consonant; the sound then becomes [ɔ] (or [ɑ] for most North American speakers). When the consonant is another [l] or a dental, the [l] is retained: e.g. *all, ball, call, small* or *malt, altar, salt, bald*. When the consonant is a velar or a nasal, the [l] is lost: e.g. *walk, talk, chalk* or *calm, palm, psalm,*

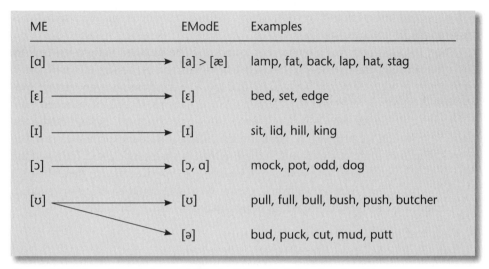

ME	EModE	Examples
[a] ⟶	[a] > [æ]	lamp, fat, back, lap, hat, stag
[ɛ] ⟶	[ɛ]	bed, set, edge
[ɪ] ⟶	[ɪ]	sit, lid, hill, king
[ɔ] ⟶	[ɔ, a]	mock, pot, odd, dog
[ʊ] ⟶	[ʊ]	pull, full, bull, bush, push, butcher
	[ə]	bud, puck, cut, mud, putt

Figure 10.2 Short Vowels from Middle English to Early Modern English

almond. However, when the consonant is a labiodental fricative, the vowel sound is [æ] and the [l] is lost: e.g. *half, calves, salve*. For some speakers and in some words [æ] also occurs when the consonant is [m]: e.g. the standard pronunciation of *salmon* [sæmən] and dialectal pronunciations of *calm* [kæm] or *palm* [pæm]. Because the *l* was never lost in the spelling, however, it has been restored in some cases by a spelling pronunciation; for example, the *l* is frequently pronounced in *alms, calm*, and *psalm*. With this information, we can account for the three variant pronunciations of *almond*: [aməmd], [almənd], and [æmənd] (the first exemplifies the standard shift, the second comes from people pronouncing the word as it is spelled, and the third has the common [æ] variant used in certain dialects).

A much later change affecting short [æ] was the late eighteenth-century shift of [æ] to [ɑ] in England; this sound change occurred after the British settlement of North America, so it is not found in most New World dialects, which preserve the older [æ] sound. This shift is far from complete in British English; in southern dialects, we find [ɑ] in *class, pass, sample, basket*, and *can't* but [æ] in identical phonological environments in *classical, passage, ample, mascot*, and *cant*.

Short [ɛ] and short [ɪ] did not change. Short [ɔ] also remained essentially unchanged, although for most North American speakers the sound has been lowered to [ɒ] or lowered and unrounded to [ɑ]. There is evidence that this sound was unrounded as early as the seventeenth century in non-standard usage: *a* is used to spell words with original *o* such as *gad* (for *god*) or *lard* (for *lord*). In a few words the *a* has become standard, leading to a spelling pronunciation with [æ], for example, *strap* (from ME *stroppe*, from which we also get the razor *strop*), *nap* (from ME *noppe*), and *drat* (from *God rot*). In addition, before [l] and a consonant, short [ɔ] became [oʊ], as in *boll, roll, toll, bolt*, or *bolster*, while the [l] has vanished before [k] and [m], as in *folk* or *yolk*. Again, spelling pronunciations have sometimes restored the [l] in these words.

Short [ʊ] split into two phonemes, [ʊ] and [ə]. The rounded variant [ʊ] usually survived between labials and [l], and between labials and [š] or [č]: e.g. *pull, push*, or *butcher*. In other contexts, we usually find [ə]. The distribution is not always predictable, because we also find [ʊ]. Certain dialects have preserved the rounded variant more fully; Swift, who was Anglo-Irish, rhymes *blush/bush, cut/put*, and *guts/puts*, all of which we presume he pronounced with [ʊ]. Remember that short *u* was respelled as *o* in some contexts in Middle English, but the sound itself followed the course of [ʊ], becoming [ə] in *come, son, wonder*, or *love*. Recall also that when [ō] shifted to [u] in the Great Vowel Shift, the raised vowel could be laxed or reduced. As a result, we find two different sets of possible sources for [ə] and [ʊ]:

[ə]   *luck* (< ME [ʊ])   *flood* (< ME [ō])
[ʊ]   *bush* (< ME [ʊ])   *wood* (< ME [ō])

Although the vowels of Early Modern English were in flux, we can represent the system circa 1600 by educated speakers as in Figure 10.3.

		Front	Central	Back
High	**Tense**	ī		ū
	Lax	ɪ		ʊ
Mid	**Tense**	ē		ō
	Lax	ɛ̄ ɛ	ə	ɔ
Low		æ	a	ɑ

Figure 10.3   The Vowel System of Early Modern English (adapted from Manfred Görlach, *Introduction to Early Modern English* [Cambridge: Cambridge University Press, 1991], p. 65)

In addition, before an [r] (at the end of a word or preceding another consonant), the short stressed sounds [ɪ], [ʊ], and [ɛ] tended to be centralized to [ə] (except in Scots; see Chapter 12):

[ɪr] > [ər]   *bird, first, shirt, dirt, girl, fir*
[ʊr] > [ər]   *hurt, turn, spur, burn, curse, cur*
[ɛr] > [ər]   *person, clerk, serve, vermin, her, were*

The original vowel has usually been preserved in other contexts, e.g. [ɛr] in *merry* and *very* or [ɪr] in *spirit* and *pyramid*, but not [ʊr] in *courage* and *furrow*. In Early Modern English, there appears to have been an alternative pronunciation for *er*, [ɑr].

For example, Swift could rhyme *served/starved*, *clerk/mark*, *deserve it/starve it*, and *verse/farse*, presumably all with the sound [ɑr]. This sound has been standardized in the case of *parson, varsity*, and *varmint* (compared to *person, university*, and *vermin*) and is heard in the British pronunciations of *clerk, Derby*, and *Kerr*. Thus, we can explain why the philosopher's name is pronounced [bɑrkli] but the university in California named after him is pronounced [bərkli]. Note that short [ɑ] and short [ɔ] tended to be retained before [r], as in *park, yarn*, and *stark*, or *horse, morn*, and *short*, though the former may appear as [ær, ɛr] in words such as *marry* and the latter as [ɑr] in *sorry* for some speakers. Do you say [sɑri] or [sɔri]?

Figure 10.4 charts the changes in the diphthongs. The [aʊ] smoothed or monophthongized to [ɔ] (or for North American speakers to [ɒ, ɑ]). The diphthong [ɔʊ] smoothed to [ɔ̄]; it then fell together with original [ɔ̄] and was raised by the Great Vowel Shift to [ō], later [oʊ]. For this reason, we have homophones such as *toe* and *tow* in Modern English: the first derives from ME [ɔ̄] and the second from ME [ɔʊ]. The exceptions to this development of [ɔʊ] occur when it precedes [xt] or [f], spelled *ght* or *gh*; in these cases it became [ɔ, ɒ, ɑ] in Modern English, as in *brought, sought*, and *thought*, or *cough* and *trough*.

The diphthong [æɪ] smoothed to [ǣ] then fell together with original [ā], which had shifted to [ǣ] and was raised by the Great Vowel Shift to [ē] > [eɪ]. For this rea-

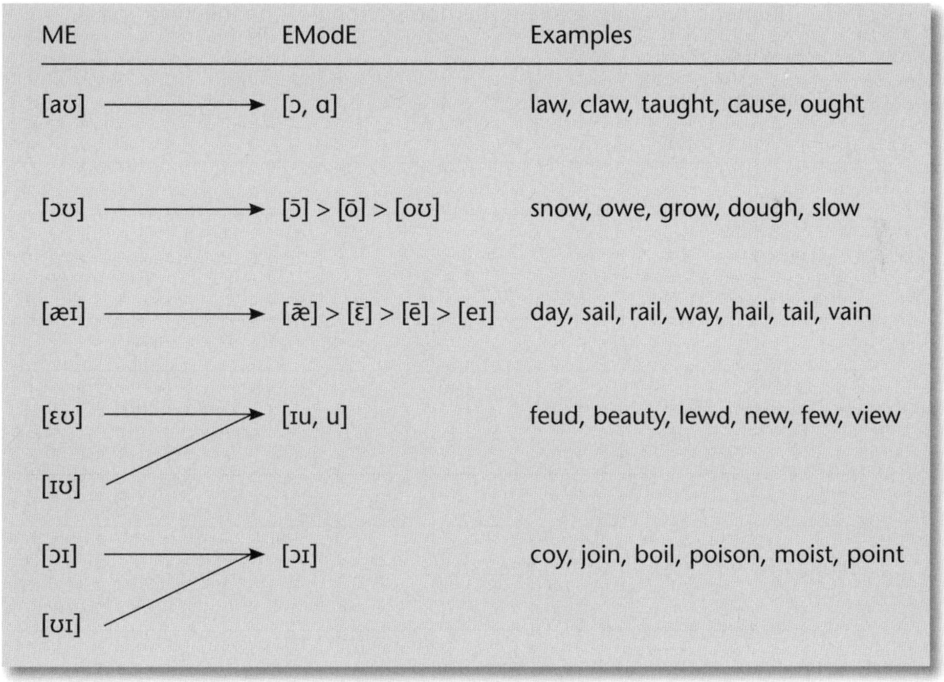

ME	EModE	Examples
[aʊ] ⟶	[ɔ, ɑ]	law, claw, taught, cause, ought
[ɔʊ] ⟶	[ɔ̄] > [ō] > [oʊ]	snow, owe, grow, dough, slow
[æɪ] ⟶	[ǣ] > [ɛ̄] > [ē] > [eɪ]	day, sail, rail, way, hail, tail, vain
[ɛʊ] ⟶ [ɪʊ]	[ɪu, u]	feud, beauty, lewd, new, few, view
[ɔɪ] ⟶ [ʊɪ]	[ɔɪ]	coy, join, boil, poison, moist, point

Figure 10.4 Diphthongs from Middle English to Early Modern English

son, we have homophones such as *made* and *maid* or *hale* and *hail* in Modern English: the first derives from ME [ā] and the second from ME [æɪ]. (As late as the eighteenth century, it was also possible to rhyme *reason/raisin*, *steal/rail*, and *unclean/again*; both ME [ɛ̄] and ME [æɪ] were at the time pronounced [ē]. Such rhymes became impossible after [ē] shifted to [i] in the case of words deriving from ME [ɛ̄].)

The diphthongs [ɛʊ] and [ɪʊ] merged in the sixteenth century as [ɪu], and this sound is preserved today. For some speakers, however, it is smoothed to [u], especially after alveolar sounds such as in *new, suit, Tuesday, produce, enthusiasm, due,* and *tune*. Note that in most dialects the diphthong is not smoothed after labials or velars or word-initially: otherwise *beauty* would be the pronounced the same as *booty, pew* the same as *pooh, cute* the same as *coot*, and *use* the same as *ooze*.

The diphthong [ʊɪ] eventually merged with [ɔɪ], but the merger was not entirely straightforward; [ʊɪ] changed first to [əɪ], at which point it was identical to an original [ī] which had also shifted to [əɪ] (see above). This permitted Swift to rhyme *child/spoil'd* and *malign/join* and Dryden to rhyme *toils/smiles*. Later, however, a spelling pronunciation of [ɔɪ] was given to this diphthong (which is usually spelled *oi* or *oy*) and the [əɪ] pronunciation was relegated to dialectal and non-standard usage.

Exercise 10.2 EModE Vowels

1. Using phonetic symbols, explain the homophony of the following pairs. Ignore consonants.

   a. sole/soul

   _____

   _____

   b. pail/pale

   _____

   _____

   c. know/no

   _____

   _____

2. Explain why *fir* and *fur* sound the same.

   _____

   _____

A Closer Look at the Language of an Early Modern English Text

Try reading William Shakespeare's Sonnet 18, 'Shall I compare thee to a summer's day?' with EModE pronunciation. Assume that the Great Vowel Shift has raised and/or diphthongized the long vowels:

shines/declines	[ī] > [əɪ] > [aɪ]
fade/shade	[ū] > [əɪ] > [eɪ]
see/thee	[ē] > [i]

Furthermore, assume that in the case of the diphthongs, Shakespeare used the intermediate pronunciations [əɪ] and [əʊ] for ME [ī] and [ū] as well as the following shifted diphthongs:

day/Maie	[æɪ] > [eɪ]
ow'st/grow'st	[ɔʊ] > [oʊ]

Although we cannot be certain, the rhyming of *temperate* with *date* suggests that the final syllable of *temperate* was pronounced [eɪt] rather than the modern [ət].

> Shall I compare thee to a Summers day?
> Thou art more louely and more temperate:
> Rough windes do shake the darling buds of Maie,
> And Sommers lease hath all too short a date:
> Sometime too hot the eye of heauen shines,
> And often is his gold complexion dimm'd,
> And euery faire from faire some-time declines,
> By chance, or nature's changing course vntrimm'd:
> But thy eternall Sommer shall not fade,
> Nor loose possession of that faire thou ow'st,
> Nor shall death brag thou wandr'st in his shade,
> When in eternall lines to time thou grow'st.
>   So long as men can breath or eyes can see,
>   So long liues this, and this giues life to thee.
> (Shakespeare, Sonnet 18)

Changes in Consonants

Changes in Early Modern English result in two significant changes in the consonant inventory: the addition of two phonemes, [ŋ] and [ž], and the loss of another (which had the two allophonic variants [x] and [ç]). Changes also affect consonant clusters; at times these are complicated by orthography.

The voiceless velar and palatal fricatives [x] and [ç] were lost in most instances by the end of the sixteenth century. All that remains today is the unpronounced *gh* spelling (from ME ʒ) in words such as *straight, thigh, right, bought, taught, dough,* and *bough*. To compensate for the loss of [ç], the preceding monophthong lengthened, which then made it subject to the effects of the Great Vowel Shift, as in *light* or *knight*. A dialectal variant of [x] was the labiodental fricative [f], found in a number of words in Modern English, including *rough, enough, draught*, and *trough*. The [f] had the opposite effect of shortening the preceding vowel. Moreover, certain words acquired *gh* in their spelling by analogy even though they never had a fricative in their pronunciation, e.g. *delight* and *haughty*. This was an unetymological respelling of these words; their pronunciation has not altered.

A number of consonant clusters became simplified in Early Modern English. Liquids were lost in certain contexts: [r] before [s] in *bass* (< *barse*), *bust* (< *burst*), *cuss* (< *curse*), and *ass* (< *arse*). As discussed in the previous section, [l] was lost after [ɔ] and [ɑ] and before laterals in combination with velars or nasals. The [w] glide was lost in [wr] sequences such as *write, wreck*, and *wrath*. Stop consonants were also lost in a number of contexts:

[gn-] > [n]	*gnaw, gnash, gnarl, gnat*
[kn-] > [n]	*know, knot, knit, knock*
[-mb] > [m]	*dumb, plumb*
[-nds] > [ns]	*handsome, landscape*
[-stl] > [sl]	*bristle, castle*
[-stn] > [sn]	*listen*
[-ftn] > [fn]	*often*

Certain sound combinations become restricted in respect to their position in a syllable (these area called *phonotactic constraints*); e.g. [gn] and [mb] can never begin or end syllables, though they may be divided across the syllable boundary, as in *magnet* and *humble*.

Note that in almost all cases the silenced consonant has remained in the spelling. Sometimes these consonants are restored through spelling pronunciations, for example *landscape* [lændskeɪp]. To complicate matters further, words were sometimes respelled in the Renaissance (see below). Here, by analogy to words such as *dumb, b* was added to the words *limb, thumb, crumb,* and *numb,* where a [b] never existed before. A different phenomenon is the addition of an excrescent *d* in words such as *sound* (from ME *soun*) or *horehound* (from ME *horhoune*). In these cases, the pronunciation as well as the spelling of the word was altered; we can hear an excrescent [d] in the non-standard but common pronunciation of *drown* as [draʊnd]. The consonant cluster [hw], which had been reduced in southern dialects of Middle English to [w] but typically spelled *wh*, was subject to a hypercorrect spelling pronunciation [hw] in Early Modern English. Even today there remains variation in the pronunciation of this cluster.

An important simplification occurred in the cluster [ŋg]. In stressed syllables, at the end of words, this cluster was simplified to [ŋ] by the loss of [g]; however, in the middle of words, the [g] was retained. In the following list, we see how each word in the first column differs in only one sound (the last) from the corresponding word in the second column, as a result of this change. Such minimal pairs show that [ŋ] has become unpredictable in its distribution, because it can occur in the same phonetic environment as [n]. This means that [n] and [ŋ] are no longer allophonic but have become separate phonemes:

sung   —   *sun*

thing   —   *thin*

king   —   *kin*

The *ng* cluster in *finger, anger*, and *hunger* and in the superficially similar *ringer, singer*, and *hanger* poses a puzzle, because the [g] is pronounced in the first set but not in the second. A consistent rule exists here, however. In the latter group of words the *-er* is a derivational suffix added to a root ending in *-ng* (hence pronounced [ŋ] with [g] lost in word-final position), i.e. *ring + -er*. In the former group, *-er* is part of the root itself; thus *anger* is a single morpheme, not **ang + -er*.

In unstressed syllables, the development of the [ŋg] cluster was different: it became [n]. We can hear this in the colloquial pronunciation of the word *nothing* as [nəθɪn] rather than [nəθɪŋ]. From the Early Modern English period well into the nineteenth century, the [ɪn] pronunciation was actually standard. Thus, Swift could rhyme *brewing/ruin, loving/sloven, picking/chicken, smelling/dwell in*, and *breathing/heathen*. We can also determine that [ɪn] was the pronunciation of the sequence *-ing* on the evidence of what are called 'inverse spellings'. When people started spelling and even saying *muzling* for *muslin* or *ruinge* for *ruin*, a kind of overcorrection is evident. Writers, aware that [ɪn] may be spelled *ing*, added *g* where it did not belong. Later, however, the spelling pronunciation of *-ing* as [ɪŋ] (perhaps reinforced by prescriptive teaching) gradually took over, to the point that [ɪn] is now considered non-standard and is restricted to colloquial speech and to certain dialects.

Palatalization, which occurred in the Old English period, became more widespread in Modern English, affecting a greater number of consonants; alveolar stops and fricatives became alveolopalatal affricates and fricatives in combination with a following palatal glide:

[t + j > č]	*posture, digestion, Christian*
[d + j > ǰ]	*individual, grandeur, residual*
[s + j > š]	*passion, tissue, mission*
[z + j > ž]	*derision, occasion, leisure*

(Remember that the palatal glide is present in the Middle English pronunciation of these words but may not be obvious in their spelling.) Palatalization can occur in the middle of a word, between a stressed syllable and an unstressed one, but dialectal variation exists in words such as *tissue, graduate, groceries*, and *immediately*, which may be unpalatalized for some speakers. In rapid speech, palatalization can also occur between words:

[č] occurs in *meet you* or *don't you*

[ǰ] in *would you* or *did you*

[š] in *pass your* or *bless you*

[ž] in *he's your* or *as yet*

Palatalization seems to have occurred quite late. Unpalatalized forms were found even in the eighteenth century when, for example, Swift pronounced the suffix *-ure* as [ər] and rhymed *venture/centre, jester/gesture, lecture/hector,* and *figure/vigour/ bigger.*

Palatalization contributes to a significant phonological development in English: it added the allophone [ž] to the sounds of the language, resulting in increased phonological symmetry, as there are now voiced and voiceless pairs of alveolo(palatal) fricatives. The existence of [ž] as a phoneme in French and its occurrence in French borrowings such as *beige, azure, garage,* and *rouge* led to its becoming a full-fledged English phoneme.

Exercise 10.3 EModE and ModE Pronunciation

1. Using phonetic symbols, show how the current spelling of the following words reveals the history of their pronunciations. Then write the ModE pronunciation followed by the ME pronunciation.

Example: ModE   ME

cough   [a, ɔ] < [ɔ̄] < [oʊ], [f] < [x]   [kɔf] or [kaf]   [koʊx]

			ModE	ME
a.	thigh	_____	[_____]	[_____]
b.	stalk	_____	[_____]	[_____]
c.	nation	_____	[_____]	[_____]
d.	hustle	_____	[_____]	[_____]

2. Given the following ME words, show their pronunciations in phonetic symbols in both ME and ModE, and then write the ModE words.

		ME Transcription	ModE Transcription	ModE Word
a.	gnawe(n)	[_____]	[_____]	_____
b.	lamb	[_____]	[_____]	_____
c.	knele(n)	[_____]	[_____]	_____
d.	goune 'official's robe'	[_____]	[_____]	_____

3.   Explain why the *g* in *Bangor* is pronounced but the *g* in *banger* is not.

_____

_____

_____

_____

_____

Renaissance Respellings

The disparity between sound and spelling brought on by the Great Vowel Shift caused a lively debate in the mid-sixteenth century. The earliest spelling reformers, Thomas Smith (1568), John Hart (1570), and William Bullokar (1580), suggested radical revisions of English spelling in an attempt to make it phonetic, including the abandonment of the Latin alphabet in favor of a completely new alphabet or the addition of symbols and diacritics to the Latin alphabet. Because these departed so far from convention, they were doomed to failure. Richard Mulcaster (1582) took a more measured approach, acknowledging custom and arguing for the importance of adopting a consistent spelling for every word. He thought, for example, that using a single spelling for *where* was more important than the particular choice of *where*, *wher*, *whear*, *whair*, or *whear*. Mulcaster's suggestions generally coincided with the way in which English spelling developed over the next century, although the extent of his influence is uncertain. Spelling in printed texts became fixed by about the mid-seventeenth century. In private documents and letters, however, it remained unfixed well into the nineteenth century.

Renaissance interest in the Latin and Greek origins of words in English did lead to respellings of borrowed words to make them correspond more closely to their etymology. Sometimes these etymological respellings were based on a mistaken conception of a word's origin. The respellings have subsequently led to new spelling pronunciations of the words in many cases.

Certain loan words from French came into Middle English without initial [h] because a sound change in French had eliminated this sound. During the Renaissance, initial *h* was then systematically restored in the spelling of these words, which were derived (or were believed to derive) from Latin. Although sometimes the *h* is unetymological or originally a variant, as in *humor* (< ME *umour* < Lat. *(h)ūmor*), in most cases it is etymologically justified. Subsequently in speech, the *h* was added by a spelling pronunciation in many cases, for example, in *host* (< ME *oste* < Lat. *hostis*), *humble* (< ME *umble* < Lat. *humilis*), and *habit* (< ME *abit* < Lat. *habitus*). Personal names *Homer, Hector, Hercules*, and *Helen* (but compare the related *Ellen*) also contain an inserted *h*. We have some cases in which the *h* is still silent, as in *honor*

(< Lat. *honor*), *hour* (< ME *(o)ure* < Lat. *hōra*), and *heir* (< ME *eir* < Lat. *hērēs*), but compare *heritage*. The variant pronunciations of *herb*, namely [hərb] or [ərb], arise out of this respelling.

An *h* was also inserted in French words derived from Greek, where the letter theta (θ, written as *th* in Latin) appeared in French as *t*. This respelling usually leads to a spelling pronunciation of [θ], as in *throne* (< ME *trone* < Gk. *thronos*) and *theme* (< ME *teme* < Lat. *thema* < Gk. *thema*), as well as in *author* (< ME *autour* < Lat. *auctour*) where the *h* is unetymological. There is alternation between [θ] and [t] in the related names *Arthur/Art, Dorothy/Dot, Katherine/Kit/Kate, Anthony/Tony*, and *Elizabeth/Betty*, while the names *Theresa* and *Thomas* have not been given spelling pronunciations (compare *Terry* and *Tom*).

French words with *f* were respelled with *ph* if they derived from Greek *phi* (φ): e.g. *phantom* (< ME *fantome* < Gk. *phantasma*) and *pheasant* (ME < *fesaunt* < Gk. *phasianos*). The pronunciation of these words did not change. Sometimes, however, *ph* was used simply as a fancy respelling of *f* in words not of Greek origin such as *nephew* (< ME *neveu*) or *Ralph* (< ME *Radolf*). Similarly, *ch* was used as a transliteration of Greek *chi* (χ) in words such as *chorus* (< Gk. *khoros*), *orchestra* (< Gk. *orkhēstra*), and *chasm* (< Gk. *khasma*); hence it was added to *schism* (< ME *sisme* < Lat. *schisma* < Gk. *skhisma*) and *schedule* (< ME *sedule* < Lat. *schedula* < Gk. *skhida*), which were ultimately of Greek origin but were pronounced with an initial [s] in Old French and hence in Middle English, too. This respelling led to various pronunciations; both [š] and [sk] in *schedule* differ from the Middle English version [s], [š] being a spelling pronunciation and [sk] being suggested by the influential dictionary editor Noah Webster.

A variety of other words were given etymological respellings in the Renaissance. Table 10.2 provides samples of these respellings. Note that the words *perfect, verdict, arctic* (sometimes), *assault, falcon, fault, vault, bankrupt, admiral*, and *baptism* were all subsequently given spelling pronunciations.

Table 10.2 Renaissance Respellings

addition of *b*	debt < ME det(te) < OF dette < Lat. debitum
	doubt < ME d(o)uten < OF douter < Lat. dubitare
	subtle < ME sutil < OF sutil < Lat. subtilis 'thin, fine'
addition of *c*	perfect < ME parfit, perfit < OF parfit < Lat. perfectus
	verdict < ME verdit < OF veirdit < Lat. -dictum
	arctic < ME artik < Lat. arcticus < Gk. arktikos
	victual [vɪtəl] < ME vitaille < Lt. victualis

Table 10.2 Renaissance Respellings—*Continued*

addition of *l*	assault < ME assaut < OF asaut < Lat. assultus
	falcon < ME faucoun < OF faucon < Lat. falco
	fault < ME faute < OF faute < Lat. fallere
	vault < ME vaute < OF vaute < Lat. volvere
addition of *p*	receipt < ME receite < OF receite < Lat. recipere, receptus
	bankrupt < OF banqueroute < Lat. -rumpere, ruptus
addition of *t*	mortgage < ME morgage < OF mortgage < Lat. mort(uus) + OF gage 'death pledge'
addition of *d*	admiral < ME admiral < OF amiral < Arabic amiral (but confused with Lat. admirari 'wonder at', cf. PDE admire)
addition of *s*	baptism < ME bapteme < OF bapteme < Lat. baptisma < Gk. baptizein

Exercise 10.4 Renaissance Respelling

Look up the following words in the *OED* or in a dictionary with etymologies. Explain their spellings and pronunciations.

a.   adventure

_____

_____

b.   indict

_____

_____

c.   calk/caulk

_____

_____

d.   adjust

_____

_____

e.   palm

_____

_____

Changes in Nominal Inflected Forms

As we have seen, the grammatical changes between Old English and Middle English consisted primarily of losses in the inflections of nouns, pronouns, demonstratives, adjectives, and verbs. In contrast, the change between Middle English and Early Modern English sees the rise of new grammatical constructions and new means of marking grammatical distinctions. Many of these changes began in late Middle English, in part to compensate for the loss of inflections. Below we examine the most important developments between 1500 and 1700.

Nouns

When the analogical plural and genitive -s endings became dominant, a few remnants of other endings survived. Early Modern English texts are more likely than Modern English ones to contain examples of genitive forms without -s or of the plural form -en in words such as *eyen, housen, shoon, fleen,* and *kneen.* Endingless genitives derive from the weak declension (e.g. *Lady Chapel*), from the *r*-stem declension naming familial relations (e.g. *father land*), and from the genitive plural, especially when expressing measure (e.g. *four yard [long], five foot [tall], seven year [span]*). Endingless genitives are also common in EModE when the noun in the genitive ends in [s] (e.g. *poore Clarence death*), the head noun begins with [s] (e.g. *for posteritie sake*), or both (e.g. *for peace sake*).

There were three new developments in the marking of the genitive in Early Modern English. The first was the rise of the so-called *his*-genitive. This construction consists of an uninflected noun (almost always naming a person or personified thing) followed by a third-person genitive pronoun: e.g. *the count his gallies, Lucilla hir company,* and *the vtopians their creditours.* The most common pronoun in this construction is the masculine *his,* which in unstressed form appears as *ys* or *is.* Speakers used this possessive even when it resulted in a gender conflict (as in *her Grace is requeste* 'her Grace his request' or *my moder ys sake* 'my mother his sake'). We are not certain how or why this construction arose; it may have first been used with foreign nouns, which could not be inflected for the genitive as a native noun would be. An Old English example such as *Nilus seo ea hire æwielme is neh þæm clife* ('that river Nile her source is near the cliff') suggests such an origin. It may also have begun as a topic-comment structure: '(speaking of) the Nile, her source is near the cliff'.

Over time, people came to regard the inherited *-s* genitive inflection as a reduced form of the possessive pronoun *his*, probably because its pronunciation, [əz], matched that of the syllabic form of the inflection occurring after sibilants, as in modern *bush's, box's, judge's,* and *church's*. In fact, we find the *his*-genitive to be especially common in Early Modern English when the possessive noun ends in a sibilant and would take the syllabic form of the ending, e.g. *King Lewes his satisfaction, Mars his heart, Moses his meekness, Augustus his daughter, Hercules his Pillars,* and *Poines his brother*. Although the *his*-genitive has not survived in Modern English, it has left a lasting mark—the apostrophe now properly found in all noun possessives. The apostrophe indicates a (presumed) contraction and began to appear in the singular genitive in the seventeenth century and in the plural genitive in the eighteenth century, at the time when the *his*-genitive was being abandoned.

The second development is called the group genitive. This construction involves a nominal group, such as a noun followed by a prepositional phrase (*the man in the back's question*) or a noun followed by a relative clause (*this man I know's wife*), or a pronoun group with *other* (*each other's friend*); as you can see, the genitive inflection is attached to the last element of the group rather than to the head noun (*man* in both cases) or pronoun. The group genitive is common in collo-quial Modern English, though it is often avoided in formal usage. In Old and Middle English, the genitive inflection is always added to the head noun; instead of *the Wife of Bath's Tale*, the earlier construction would be *the Wives of Bath Tale*, or more likely, *the Wives Tale of Bath*, with the nominal group split around the noun being modified. In Early Modern English, while older forms of the genitive may still be found (as in *the Archbishop's Grace of York*), the group genitive is common (as in *the Duke of Gloucester's niece*). Its origin is again a matter of debate among schol-ars, but it is generally agreed that its consequence was a change in the status of the genitive inflection, which became an 'enclitic', a grammatical form having an inter-mediate status between a full word and an inflection. Other examples of enclitics in English are *-n't* (cf. *not*), *-d* (cf. *had* and *would*), *-ll* (cf. *will*), and *-s* (cf. *is* and *has*).

The third development was the double genitive, a form containing both an inflected genitive and a periphrastic genitive with *of*, such as *a friend of my sister's* or *a picture of John's*. In Modern English, the first noun is generally indefinite and the second is animate; the construction has a partitive sense ('one friend from among all of my sister's friends'), and may be quite different in meaning from the single geni-tive (compare *a picture of John* and *a picture of John's*). This construction originated in the late Middle English period and became frequent in Early Modern English.

Articles

By Early Modern English, the use of the definite and indefinite articles resembled that of Modern English. The indefinite article in EModE marks the first mention of a referent, whereas the definite article refers to something already mentioned or known. Occasionally, however, the indefinite article is omitted where we would require it, as in:

> *what dreadfull noise* (Shakespeare, *King Richard III*)

> *it is pitty of her life* (Shakespeare, *Measure for Measure*)

At other times, it still has the meaning 'one', as in *both born in an hour* (Shakespeare, *Twelfth Night*). The definite article might also be omitted where we would use it, as in:

> *Since death of my deer'st Mother* (Shakespeare, *Cymbeline*)

> *foam'd at mouth* (Shakespeare, *Julius Caesar*)

> *at mercy of my Sword* (Shakespeare, *Troilus and Cressida*)

> *met him at gate* (Shakespeare, *King Lear*)

However, it also appears in some contexts where we do not include it, for example, before titles (*the Lord Northumberland*), diseases (*the gout*), and learning (*the metaphysics*). Article usage continues to be a matter of convention (that is, idiom) in Modern English as well, with the definite article omitted—for no obvious reason—in cases such as *in bed, in summer, at dinner,* or *by car*); it may also vary from dialect to dialect (*in hospital* [in England and Canada] versus *in the hospital* [in the US and Scotland]; see Chapter 12).

Pronouns

Demonstratives

The use of the demonstratives in Early Modern English also resembled that of Modern English. One difference is their combination with possessive pronouns in EModE:

> *this your perfectnesse* (Shakespeare, *Love's Labor's Lost*)

> *this my vertue* (Shakespeare, *Hamlet*)

> *that my Lord of Norfolke* (Shakespeare, *King Henry VIII*)

> *those his goodly eyes* (Shakespeare, *Antony and Cleopatra*)

In Modern English, the demonstrative is mutually exclusive with the possessive pronoun.

Personal Pronouns

Early Modern English saw changes in the forms and use of personal pronouns. The forms are shown in Table 10.3. By the end of the medieval period, the accusative

Table 10.3 Personal Pronouns in Early Modern English

	first person	
	singular	*plural*
nom.	I	we
obj.	me	us
gen.	my, mine	our, ours

	second person	
	singular	*plural*
nom.	thou	ye/you
obj.	thee	you/ye
gen.	thy, thine	your, yours

	third person			
	masculine	*neuter*	*feminine*	*plural*
nom.	he	(h)it	she	they
obj.	him	(h)it	her	them
gen.	his	his, it, its	her, hers	their, theirs

and dative had fallen together completely to yield a single objective case, leaving no distinction in form between direct and indirect objects.

Proceeding by person, we can observe the following changes:

1. At the beginning of the EModE period, the first-person genitive forms *my* and *mine* as well as the second-person genitive forms *thy* and *thine* were distinguished as in Middle English: the first of each pair would be used before nouns beginning in a consonant and the second before nouns beginning in a vowel or *h*, e.g. *my duetie, my faythe* but *mine honour, mine host*. In Shakespeare's time, however, they were used rather indiscriminately, as in *mine own* or *my own* and *thine eyes* or *thy eye*. By 1700 a new principle distinguished the forms: the first kind functioned as an adjectival genitive preceding the noun, and the second as a pronominal genitive following a preposition or verb such as *be*; the difference can be seen in Modern English *my book* compared to *the book of mine, the book is mine*. Note that the *-s* forms *hers, ours, yours,* and *theirs* also came to function as possessive pronouns; *his* and *its*, meanwhile, exhibit no distinction between the adjectival and pronominal forms.

2. The first-person plural pronoun developed two new, sometimes overlapping functions. The first is the authorial (editorial) *we* used by authors to include themselves and the readers, though this usage was already known in Old English. The second is the royal *we*. One of the earliest attestations of the royal *we* occurs in Henry III's Proclamation of 1258 (*we willen and vnnen þæt . . .*). This usage originated in the Byzantine Greek imperial court and then spread throughout Europe via late courtly Latin. It is an expression of the feudal notion that the king is the embodiment of the community. The royal *we* used to be used by British monarchs, but has fallen out of fashion.

3. The second-person singular and plural forms began to be used to make social rather than number distinctions. You are probably familiar with the social uses of second-person pronoun forms in modern European languages such as French and German. In this usage, the plural forms are used as markers of politeness, or what are called *honorifics*. The comparable use in English probably developed under French influence, first appearing in the thirteenth century; it was quite well established by the fourteenth century. The plural forms were used in addressing superiors in age, rank, and social class. Among the upper class, the plural forms were also used among equals who were not intimates. In contrast, the singular forms were used in addressing inferiors: by a king to a subject, a nobleman to a citizen, a master to a servant, a parent to a child, and sometimes even a husband to a wife. The lower classes generally relied on the singular. (On theological grounds, people also used the singular to address God.) The second-person pronoun forms can have social or interpersonal effects. When used conventionally, the plural forms indicate deference, respect, and politeness, but in cases where the singular form would be appropriate, the plural can be distancing, threatening, or reprimanding. The singular forms have two emotional uses: in intimate situations expressing tenderness, affection, or intimacy, or in situations of anger expressing disrespect or contempt. If used where inappropriate, they may be either patronizing or presumptuous. Shakespeare drew upon these possibilities for literary effect:

> *Queen*:   Hamlet, thou hast thy father much offended.
> *Hamlet*:   Mother, you haue my Father much offended.
> *Queen*:   Come, come, you answer with an idle tongue.

> (*Hamlet,* III, iv, 9–11)

In this quotation, Gertrude uses the intimate form *thou* with her son Hamlet. As is his habit, Hamlet addresses the Queen, his mother, with the seemingly respectful *you*. However, because of the nature of his reply, in which he rebukes his mother, she chides him in return by using the more distant *you*.

Although we assume Shakespeare used such words for deliberate effect, we must keep in mind that the actual usage of *thou* and *you* in Early Modern English was somewhat variable. Unlike the systems of second-person pronoun usage in French and German that held strictly until quite recently, English usage was always loose and unstable, and in many instances *you* and *thou* appear to be in free variation. *You* gradually became the neutral form of address, perhaps because its use among the upper class was emulated by all classes or because the lower-class *thou* became stigmatized. By 1700, the second-person singular forms were no longer common, the only exception being their preservation in some regional dialects, conservative formal writing (Biblical and liturgical), and among religious groups, such as the Quakers, who reject politeness markers in favor of a 'plain style' of speech.

Loss of the distinction between singular and plural in the second-person has created relatively few difficulties for English. Some dialects have attempted to restore the distinction by creating new plural forms such as *you guys, you-uns, youse, you'all*, or *y'all*, but none of these has become standard. In the eighteenth century, there was great debate about the form (number) of *be* to follow *you* in the singular since *you* was originally plural: should it be *you was* or *you were*? While *you was* was defended by Noah Webster, it eventually fell into disuse. Expressions such as James Boswell's *At night you was clear* today strike us as unclear.

4. There was a clear distinction in the early stages of EModE between the nominative and objective forms of the second-person plural pronoun, *ye* in the nominative and *you* in the objective, as in:

> *Mars doate on you for his nouices! what will ye doe?* (Shakespeare, *All's Well That Ends Well*)

But even in Shakespeare's time, the two forms seem to have been confused, perhaps because in unstressed contexts they would both be pronounced [jə]. The King James Bible of 1611, which is very conservative in its linguistic practices, maintains the distinction, but Shakespeare uses the forms fairly indiscriminately, with *you* being somewhat more common. In the following sentence, we see *ye* and *you* reversed:

> *I ha' prais'd ye, When you have well deseru'd ten times as much* (Shakespeare, *Antony and Cleopatra*)

During the course of the seventeenth century, the nominative form *ye* was lost altogether.

5. Among the third-person singular forms, only the neuter underwent significant changes in the EModE period. The unstressed forms of the nominative and objective without *h* became standard by about 1600. Sometimes we find

The Tragedie of Hamlet

Of his true ſtate.

> *Quee.* Did he receiue you well?
>
> *Roſ.* Moſt like a gentleman.
>
> *Guyl.* But with much forcing of his diſpoſition,
>
> *Roſ.* Niggard of queſtion, but of our demaunds
> Moſt free in his reply.
>
> *Quee.* Did you aſſay him to any paſtime?
>
> *Roſ.* Maddam, it ſo fell out that certaine Players
> We ore-raught on the way, of theſe we told him,
> And there did ſeeme in him a kind of ioy
> To heare of it: they are heere about the Court,
> And as I thinke, they haue already order
> This night to play before him.
>
> *Pol.* Tis moſt true,
> And he beſeecht me to intreat your Maieſties
> To heare and ſee the matter.
>
> *King.* With all my hart, and it doth much content me
> To heare him ſo inclin'd.
> Good gentlemen giue him a further edge,
> And driue his purpoſe into theſe delights.
>
> *Roſ.* We ſhall my Lord. *Exeunt Roſ. & Guyl.*
>
> *King.* Sweet *Gertrard*, leaue vs two,
> For we haue cloſely ſent for *Hamlet* hether,
> That he as t'were by accedent, may heere
> Affront *Ophelia*; her father and my ſelfe,
> Wee'le ſo beſtow our ſelues, that ſeeing vnſeene,
> We may of their encounter franckly iudge,
> And gather by him as he is behau'd,
> Ift be th'affliction of his loue or no
> That thus he ſuffers for.
>
> *Quee.* I ſhall obey you.
> And for your part *Ophelia*, I doe wiſh
> That your good beauties be the happy cauſe
> Of *Hamlets* wildnes, ſo ſhall I hope your vertues,
> Will bring him to his wonted way againe,
> To both your honours.
>
> *Oph.* Maddam, I wiſh it may.
>
> *Pol. Ophelia* walke you heere, gracious ſo pleaſe you,

Figure 10.5 A Page from the Second Quarto of Shakespeare's *Hamlet* (1604) (reproduced by permission of the Huntington Library, San Marino, California, RB 69305: *The Tragicall Historie of Hamlet*, 1604 [G1v])

even further reduction of these forms to *'t* as in *'tis, 'twere, 'twill* and also *is't, was't*. The *'t* form has not survived in Modern English except in jocular use. The genitive neuter has a somewhat complex history. We still find the historically legitimate form *his* in EModE, such as:

> *Rebellion in this Land shall lose his way* (Shakespeare, *King Henry IV, Part I*)

> *thy power had lost his power* (Shakespeare, *Venus and Adonis*)

However, this form undoubtedly caused confusion since it was identical to the masculine genitive. A number of expedients were used instead. An uninflected form *it* was used in the early part of the period, as in:

> *The innocent milk in it most innocent mouth* (Shakespeare, *The Winter's Tale*)

The periphrastic *thereof* and *of it* were also used, as in:

> *being the Queene thereof* (Shakespeare, *King Richard III*)

> *There's Magicke in the web of it* (Shakespeare, *Othello*)

The King James Bible avoids *his* but uses *of it* and *thereof*. Finally, the analogical form *its*, with the *-s* genitive ending of the noun, makes its appearance: the first known attestation of *its* comes from 1598. It appears only ten times in the 1623 Folio edition of Shakespeare, but by the end of the seventeenth century *its* had become the standard form.

Interrogative and Relative Pronouns

The interrogative pronouns have undergone very few changes in the history of English. Early Modern English inherited from Old and Middle English the interrogatives *who, whom, what, whose, why, when, where, which*, and *whether*. With the exception of *whether* and *what*, all were used in the Early Modern period as they are today. *Whether* functions in Modern English only as a conjunction, but in Early Modern English, it has as an interrogative meaning 'which of two':

> *Whether doest thou professe thyself—a knaue or a foole?* (Shakespeare, *All's Well That Ends Well*)

What has a greater range of meanings in Early Modern English than in Modern English, meaning 'who' and 'why' as well as 'what':

> *What's he comes heere?* (Shakespeare, *All's Well That Ends Well*)

> *What neede you be so boistrous rough?* (Shakespeare, *King John*)

Finally, Early Modern English possesses a number of compound interrogatives such as *wherein, wherefore, whereof, whereon*, and *whereupon*; many of these are preserved in legal English.

Relative pronouns have undergone more extensive changes. Although the usual OE relative is *þe* and the usual ME one is *that*, in Middle English, *who, what*, and *that* begin to be used as indefinite relatives (forms which today contain *-ever*, as in *Whoever enters first wins a prize*). An example of an EModE indefinite relative is Iago's line in *Othello, Who steals my purse steals trash*, or the proverbial *Who pays the piper calls the tune*. A significant expansion in relative forms began in late Middle English and progressed in the Early Modern period: the interrogative pronouns started being used as regular relative pronouns, not just indefinite ones. This occurred perhaps because *that* had assumed too many functions, as conjunction, demonstrative, and relative. The model of French, in which the interrogative form (with *que*) serves as a relative form, may also have been influential. The phenomenon began with *which, whose*, and *whom*, but only spread to *who* later in the sixteenth century. By about 1700, the relative pronoun system looked very similar to that of Modern English. The following list summarizes how this development manifests itself in Early Modern English:

1. Although today *which* is restricted to inanimate nouns, in EModE it is used frequently with animate nouns, as in:

   The Mistris <u>which</u> *I serue* (Shakespeare, *The Tempest*)

   Our Father <u>which</u> *art in heaven* (King James Bible)

2. Although today *who* is restricted to animate nouns, in EModE it sometimes occurs with inanimate nouns, as in:

   her lips, <u>Who</u> *. . . Still blush* (Shakespeare, *Romeo and Juliet*)

3. We now limit *that* to restrictive relative clauses, but in EModE it can occur in non-restrictive relative clauses, as in:

   My foolish Riuals <u>that</u> *her Father likes* (Shakespeare, *The Two Gentlemen of Verona*)

4. In formal style *that* becomes more restricted as a relative pronoun during the EModE period. However, it seems to have been the most common relative in colloquial style in Early Modern English, as it still is in Modern English. It may refer to both animate and inanimate nouns (e.g. *the book that I read, the man that I know*), despite what is often taught by prescriptive grammarians.

5. EModE uses *the which, that which*, and *as* as relative pronouns:

   Discretion; in <u>the which</u> *better part I haue saued my life* (Shakespeare, *King Henry IV, Part I*)

All <u>that</u>, <u>which</u> Henry the Fift had gotten (Shakespeare, *King Henry VI, Part III*)

those <u>as</u> sleepe, and thinke not on their sins (Shakespeare, *The Merry Wives of Windsor*)

6. Compound relative forms such as *who(m)*, *what*, *which*, or *whose* plus *that* or *so* can also occur, as in:

    these his new Honors, <u>Which that</u> he will giue them (Shakespeare, *Coriolanus*)

7. Relative pronouns may be omitted, as in:

    Try all the friends Ø thou hast in Ephesus (Shakespeare, *The Comedy of Errors*)

    My Father had a daughter Ø lou'd a man (Shakespeare, *Twelfth Night*)

While Modern English would permit the relative pronoun to be deleted in the first example above, it would not allow this in the second. Modern grammatical rules require the subject of the verb to be present, and here the relative pronoun is the subject of the verb *lou'd*. (In the first example, the pronoun *that* would function merely as an object, and both EModE and ModE grammatical rules allow it to be deleted.)

Case Usage

In Early Modern English, the only forms showing a distinction between nominative and objective case are the interrogative/relative pronouns (*who* versus *whom*) and most of the personal pronouns (*I, we, he, she, they* versus *me, us, him, her, them*). The use of these case forms was relatively unfixed and uncertain in the Early Modern period; it was not regulated until later in the eighteenth century (and then based on a Latin model rather than a natural English one, as we will see in the next chapter). In a number of contexts, EModE case usage differs from today:

1. After *and* or *but* in EModE, there is a tendency to use the nominative case, as in:

    I neuer saw a woman / But onley Sycorax my dam and <u>she</u> (Shakespeare, *The Tempest*)

    Here's none but thee, & <u>I</u> (Shakespeare, *King Henry VI, Part II*)

In ModE, the pronoun's case depends on its role in the sentence: *Edward and I* (subject) *are leaving tomorrow* but *Ralph has visited Edward and me* (object). The use of the nominative case with *and* following a preposition, which is encountered quite frequently in Modern English speech (e.g. *Let's keep this between you and I* or *He spoke to John and I about the problem*), is a hypercorrection, fixing a presumed mistake which is in fact not a mistake.

2. After *as* or *than* in EModE, the objective case is found frequently, as in:

    Is she as tall as <u>me</u>? (Shakespeare, *Antony and Cleopatra*)

    Charges she moe then <u>me</u>? (Shakespeare, *Measure for Measure*)

    In colloquial ModE, this usage continues, but rules for standard English require the nominative case, since the *as/than* clause is analyzed as elliptical, with a form of *be* omitted: e.g. *He is guiltier than she (is)*. In contrast, when *than* is a preposition, the objective form is used and a different meaning results: e.g. *He likes Susan better than her* as opposed to *He likes Susan better than she (does)*.

3. Prescriptive rules of ModE permit only the nominative case in the complement of *be* (e.g. *these are <u>they</u>; it can't be <u>he</u>*); in EModE (as in colloquial ModE) the objective case also freely occurs, as in:

    it is <u>thee</u> I feare (Shakespeare, *King Henry VI, Part II*)

    And damn'd be <u>him</u>, that first cries, 'hold, enough' (Shakespeare, *Macbeth*)

4. *Who* is used in EModE where prescriptive rules would require *whom* in standard Modern English, as in:

    Who ouercame <u>he</u>? (Shakespeare, *Love's Labor's Lost*)

    (In the sentence above, the 'he' overcame the 'who'.)

Thus, to review, in colloquial Modern English, we often violate the eighteenth-century rules of case usage by using cases in a manner close to that of Early Modern English. Prescriptive rules require the nominative case for the subject and subject complement (following the verb *be*) and the objective case for the object, indirect object, and object of a preposition. But in spoken Modern English we tend to follow a structural principle of case usage that probably also held in Early Modern English: nominative case is used in the position before the verb and objective case after the verb. The major points of conflict with prescriptive rules are in the case of the interrogative pronoun, which always precedes the verb no matter what its function in the sentence, and the case of the subject complement, which always follows the verb. Thus, using the structural principle, we say in spoken English *Who did you see?* and *It is me* rather than *Whom did you see?* and *It is I*. *Whom* is still used, although increasingly less often; it is more common as a relative than as an interrogative. The sentence *It is me* has a long history, assuming this form in the late sixteenth century.

Exercise 10.5 EModE Nominal and Pronominal Forms

1. In what contexts were the *y*-forms and the *th*-forms of the second-person pronoun used?

    _____

    _____

    _____

    _____

2. Identify the following forms. What is the significance of each to the history of English?

    a.   the kinges sone of Engeland

    _____

    b.   the Lord chamberlaine his seruants

    _____

    c.   his, of it, it, its, thereof

    _____

    d.   his fader ȝouþe 'his father's youth'

    _____

3. What is the difference between the following underlined usages and their ModE versions?

    a.   So shall you feele the loss, but not the friend <u>Which</u> you weepe for (Shakespeare, *Romeo and Juliet*)

    _____

    b.   And dogged *Yorke*, <u>that</u> reaches at the Moone (Shakespeare, *King Henry VI, Part II*)

    _____

    _____

    c.   <u>Who</u> does he accuse? (Shakespeare, *Antony and Cleopatra*)

    _____

    _____

d.   there is no man Ø can tell me what (Shakespeare, *A Midsummer Night's Dream*)

_____

_____

Changes in Verbal Inflected Forms

Verb Classes

The weak verbs of Middle English remained relatively unchanged in Early Modern English, apart from some analogical changes eliminating irregularities. The strong verbs, on the other hand, underwent a number of changes. The seven classes that remained intact during the Middle English period broke down, with the result that we now call the strong verbs *irregular*. The changes affecting the strong verbs fall into several categories:

1.   Many strong verbs became weak by analogy with the productive pattern followed by the majority of verbs. For example, the class 1 verbs *glide, abide*, and *writhe*; the class 2 verbs *creep, lose*, and *chew*; the class 3 verbs *burn, melt, swell, help*, and *climb*; the class 5 verbs *knead, weigh*, and *reap*; the class 6 verbs *heave, shave*, and *wash*; and the class 7 verbs *walk, wax* 'grow', and *weep* were among the many that became weak.

2.   By late Middle English, the distinction between singular and plural past in the strong verb was eliminated, and only three principal parts remained. In OE and ME, the singular past (e.g. OE *ic wrāt* 'I wrote') had an ablaut vowel different from the plural past (e.g. OE *wē writon* 'we wrote'). However, the two vowels were reduced to one as the language made the transition into EModE. This occurred in three ways:

     • by generalizing the vowel of the singular past, e.g. *write/wrote* (1), *sink/sank* (3), *forbid/forbad* (5), or *sit/sat* (5);
     • by generalizing the vowel of the plural past, e.g. *bite/bit* (1) or *win/won* (3); or
     • by using the vowel of the past participle in the past, e.g. *choose/chose* (2), *ran/run* (3), or *bear/bore* (4).

     The number distinction in the past has been maintained only in the verb *be* in the vowel contrast between *was* (sg.) and *were* (pl.).

3. Verner's Law alternations were removed. For example, the consonant in verbs such as *choose* (OE *cēosan/curon*), *freeze* (OE *frēosan/fruron*), and *lost* (OE *lēosan/luron*), which alternated between *s* in the present and past singular and *r* in the past plural and past participle, was regularized as *s*. The alternation has been preserved only in the past tense of the verb *be* (*was/ were*) and in the adjectival forms *forlorn* and *lovelorn* (from *lose*).

4. Certain strong past participles were retained only as adjectives. These included forms such as *cloven* (2), *sodden* (2), *molten* (3), *swollen* (3), *shorn* (4), *shaven* (6), *laden* (6), *graven* (6), *beholden* (7), *sown* (7), *mown* (7), and *hewn* (7) (compare the new weak past participles *cleaved, seethed, melted, swelled, sheared, shaved, loaded, (en)graved, beheld, sowed, mowed,* and *hewed*).

5. A few weak verbs became strong by analogy. These included both original weak verbs and borrowed verbs:

   • by analogy with the class 1 vowel pattern, e.g. *spit/spitted* > *spit/spat, chide/chided* > *chide/chid* (but more often *chided* again in ModE), *hide/ hided* > *hide/hid*, and *dive/dived* > *dive/dove* (in some dialects), and Fr. *strive* > *strive/strove*;

   • by analogy with the class 3 vowel pattern, e.g. *dig/digged* > *dig/dug, stick/ sticked* > *stick/stuck*, and *bring/brought* > *bring/ brung* (in some dialects); and

   • by analogy with the class 4 vowel pattern, e.g. *wear/weared* > *wear/wore*.

   (One notable exception to this change was in the borrowed verbs *sling, get, give,* and *take*. Since these verbs were strong in Old Norse, they remained strong in English rather than following the productive weak pattern—i.e., *sling/slung* [class 3], *get/got* [class 4], *give/gave* [class 5, changing to class 4], *take/took* [class 6].)

The transition from strong to weak verb (or vice versa) was a gradual process, taking place throughout the Early Modern English period. In some cases, the changes have subsequently been reversed. For this reason, there are many variant forms to be found in sixteenth- and seventeenth-century texts. For example, both strong and weak past-tense forms of the following verbs are found, all of which eventually became weak: *creep* (*crope/crept*), *climb* (*clomb/climbed*), *help* (*holp/helped*), *melt* (*molte/melted*), *delve* (*dolve/delved*), *heave* (*hove/heaved*), and *swell* (*swole/ swelled*). Both strong and weak past-tense forms of the following verbs are found, which nonetheless remained strong: *shake* (*shook/shaked*), *run* (*ran/runned*), *drive* (*drove/drived*), and *cling* (*clung/clinged*). A good deal of variation is common among strong past tenses, e.g. *spake/spoke* and *sot/sat*. There are also frequently alternative forms of the past participle of verbs in Early Modern English; most of these have been regularized over time. Finally, we see confusion, even in Early

Modern English, of the intransitive and transitive pairs *sit/set* and *lie/lay*; conflation of the latter two forms is virtually complete in North American English today.

Likewise, among the anomalous verbs, there are a number of alternative forms in Early Modern English. Many of the forms of *be* developed by analogy, as shown below:

	Present	**Past**
I	*am*	*was*
thou	*art*	*were, wast, werst, wert*
you (sg.)	*are*	*were, was*
he, she, it	*is*	*was*
we, you (pl.), *they*	*are, be*	*were*

The suppletive past tense of *go* in Old English, *ēode*, was replaced in the sixteenth century by another suppletive past, *went* (the past tense of the OE verb *wendan*).

Inflectional Endings

The inflectional endings of verbs in Early Modern English (see Table 10.4) are the natural development of the endings found in Middle English with dialect variants eliminated. In the present tense, the *-e* of the first-person singular was lost before the end of the ME period. The second-person singular ending became *-est* and, in a syncopated version, *-'st*, as in *thou givest* or *giv'st*. This ending was lost, however, as *thou* fell into disuse in the seventeenth century.

Listen to the sound recording of John Donne's sonnet 'Death be not proud' (Reading 9) on the website and follow along with the written text. This sonnet belongs to Donne's group of *Holy Sonnets* which date from 1609 to 1611. Also listen to 'A Hymn to God the Father' (Reading 10), dating from 1623. Notice that Donne uses the second-person *thou* throughout both poems. He uses the regular second-person verbal ending (e.g. *think'st, dost, swell'st, hast*). What forms does he use with the modal auxiliaries and with *be*?[2]

Alternative third-person singular endings are found in Early Modern English texts, including an *-es* ending deriving from the ME Northern dialect form and an *-eth* ending deriving from the ME Midlands and Southern dialects. The *-eth* ending was more common in the early part of the period, but by the beginning of the seventeenth century, *-es* had become the norm. During the period, there was considerable variation (motivated at least in part by prosodic requirements), as shown in this Shakespearian example:

> *It bless<u>eth</u> him that gi<u>ue</u>s and him that take<u>s</u>* (Shakespeare, *The Merchant of Venice*)

---

2 (Answer: *art, canst, shalt, wilt.*)

The *-eth* ending tends to be preserved in poetry and in more formal prose, and is the preferred form in the King James Bible of 1611. The *-th* was retained especially in the verbs *hath* and *doth*. Eventually this ending gave way completely to the only personal ending on the verb in Modern English, the third-person singular present indicative ending *-(e)s*.

A zero ending is characteristic of the plural from early in the modern period, although *-eth*, deriving from the ME Southern dialect, is found occasionally in sixteenth-century evidence; the originally ME Northern *-es* became fairly common in the middle of the period, and *-en*, deriving from the ME Midlands dialects, is found as a literary archaism in material from the sixteenth century:

All men doth on me looke (Boorde, *Introduction to Knowledge* [*OED*])

His teares runs downe his beard like winters drops (Shakespeare, *The Tempest*)

you thinken to be Lords of the yeare (Spenser, *The Shepheardes Calender* [*OED*])

All three remnant inflections ultimately fell out of use.

The other inflections on the verb are very similar to those of Modern English. The only distinctive ending in the preterit derived from Middle English is the second-person singular *-est* or *-'st*, as in *thou walkedst* or *thou promisedst*; again, this ending was abandoned as *thou* was lost. The present participle of Early Modern English continues the ME Southern dialect ending *-ing* and is identical to that of Modern English; the alternative *-and/-ind* endings died out. The remains of the past participial *ge-* prefix, *i-* or *y-*, were gone entirely by the Early Modern English period, but, as mentioned before, the forms of the past participle were otherwise quite variable, e.g. *drank/drunk*, *took/taken*, *wrott/wratten/written*, or *hald/holden*. Even by the end of the Middle English period, the *-e(n)* ending of the infinitive had disappeared entirely. In Early Modern English, the *for-to*-infinitive was lost, the plain infinitive was gradually restricted to a few contexts (following the modal auxiliaries, verbs of perception, and causal verbs such as *make* and *let*), and the *to*-infinitive was generalized to all other contexts.

Table 10.4 Inflectional Endings of the Verb from Middle English to Early Modern English[a]

	ME ending	*EmodE ending*
1ˢᵗ p. sg.	-e	Ø
2ⁿᵈ p. sg.	-es (N), -est, -'st	(lost as *thou* is lost)
3ʳᵈ p. sg.	-eth (S, M), -es (N)	-(e)s
pl.	-es (N), -en (M), -eth (S)	Ø

[a](N = Northern, M = Midlands, S = Southern)

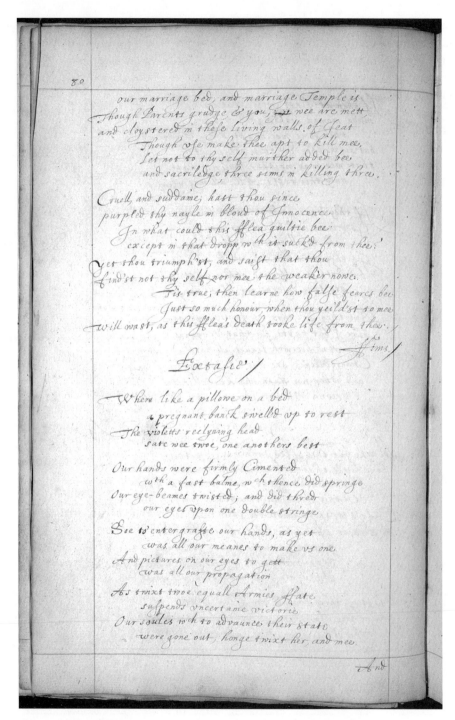

Figure 10.6 A Manuscript Page of John Donne's Poetry, Written in a Cursive Italic Hand, c. 1630 (MS 877, Trinity College Dublin, f50v, reproduced courtesy of the Board of Trinity College Dublin)

Exercise 10.6 EModE Verbal Forms

Identify the following forms and explain their place in the history of English.

a.   hopest, hopedest_____

_____

_____

b.   shave, shove, shaved, shaven _____

_____

_____

c.   ride(n), to ride(n), for to ride _____

_____

_____

d.   Let musicke sound while he *doth make* his choise;

Then if he loose he *makes* a Swan-like end,

Fading in musique   (Shakespeare, *The Merchant of Venice*) _____

_____

_____

A Closer Look at the Language of an Early Modern English Text

We will conclude this chapter by looking at a selection from the King James Bible (or Authorized Version). As well as being valued for its religious importance, this text has been praised as great literature. For a student of English linguistic history, though, the King James Bible represents a landmark in promoting the use of English. It incorporates William Tyndale's relatively recent (1526) translation of the original Hebrew and Greek testaments. Following upon James I's 1604 order for a new Bible, to be issued without interpretive annotation, some fifty clergymen and scholars undertook the new translation, which was published in 1611. The impetus behind James I's order was as much political as it was religious. In addition to putting a reliable 'word of God' into the hands of England's protestants, James also counteracted the influential 1568 Bishop's Bible by reinforcing the hierarchy of the English church, thereby also solidifying the power of the state.

12: And God looked upon the earth, and, behold, it was corrupt; for all flesh had corrupted his way upon the earth.

13: And God said unto Noah, The end of all flesh is come before me; for the earth is filled with violence through them; and, behold, I will destroy them with the earth.

14: Make thee an ark of gopher wood; rooms shalt thou make in the ark, and shalt pitch it within and without with pitch.

15: And this is the fashion which thou shalt make it of: The length of the ark shall be three hundred cubits, the breadth of it fifty cubits, and the height of it thirty cubits.

16: A window shalt thou make to the ark, and in a cubit shalt thou finish it above; and the door of the ark shalt thou set in the side thereof; with lower, second, and third stories shalt thou make it.

17: And, behold, I, even I, do bring a flood of waters upon the earth, to destroy all flesh, wherein is the breath of life, from under heaven; and every thing that is in the earth shall die.

18: But with thee will I establish my covenant; and thou shalt come into the ark, thou, and thy sons, and thy wife, and thy sons' wives with thee.

19: And of every living thing of all flesh, two of every sort shalt thou bring into the ark, to keep them alive with thee; they shall be male and female.

20: Of fowls after their kind, and of cattle after their kind, of every creeping thing of the earth after his kind, two of every sort shall come unto thee, to keep them alive.

21: And take thou unto thee of all food that is eaten, and thou shalt gather it to thee; and it shall be for food for thee, and for them.

22: Thus did Noah; according to all that God commanded him, so did he.

(Genesis 6: 12–22)

The language of the King James Bible is eloquent in terms of its simplicity, its use of native vocabulary and straightforward syntax; however, its formal style retains a number of conservative features. Morphologically, we see a number of differences from Present-Day English, including the use of the second-person singular pronoun forms, nominative *thou* (14, 15, 16, etc.), objective *thee* (21), genitive *thy* (18), and simple reflexive *thee* 'thyself' (14); the corresponding verbal form *shalt* (14, 15, 16, etc.); and the use of the third-person neuter genitive pronoun *his* 'its' (12, 20). Syntactically, there is a *be*-perfect (13), a set of sentences with the word order O-AUX-SV (14, 16, 18, 19) and a sentence with inverted word order following an adverb (22), a second-person imperative with an explicit subject (21), and an emphatic *do* (17).

RECOMMENDED WEB LINKS

For a very useful website on the Great Vowel Shift, including examples from Chaucer and Shakespeare, go to:

http://www.furman.edu/~mmenzer/gvs/

Complete online editions of the King James Bible may be found in the University of Michigan's online collection:

http://quod.lib.umich.edu/k/kjv/

The complete works of Shakespeare may be found at the following sites:

http://internetshakespeare.uvic.ca/index.html
http://the-tech.mit.edu/Shakespeare/works.html
http://www.it.usyd.edu.au/~matty/Shakespeare/

Richard Bear's online collection of Early Modern texts 1477–1799 (University of Oregon) is:

http://www.uoregon.edu/%7Erbear/ren.htm

FURTHER READING

Several basic grammars of the period include:

Abbott, E.A. 1966. *A Shakespearian Grammar*. New York: Dover [Reprint] (also available online from Perseus Digital Library: http://www.perseus.tufts.edu/).
Barber, Charles. 1976. *Early Modern English*. London: André Deutsch.
Blake, Norman. 1983. *Shakespeare's Language: An Introduction*. London: Macmillan.
Hope, Jonathan. 2003. *Shakespeare's Grammar*. London: Thomson (for The Arden Shakespeare).
Nevalainen, Terttu. 2006. *An Introduction to Early Modern English*. Edinburgh: Edinburgh University Press.

For a guide to Shakespeare's dramatic language, see:

Adamson, Sylvia, et al. (eds). 2001. *Reading Shakespeare's Dramatic Language: A Guide*. London: Thomson (for The Arden Shakespeare).

A recent glossary and companion to Shakespeare is:

Crystal, David, and Ben Crystal. 2002. *Shakespeare's Words: A Glossary & Language Companion*. London: Penguin.

For examples of primary texts from this period, including facsimiles of manuscripts and early printed books, see:

Freeborn, Dennis. 1998. *From Old English to Standard English: A Course Book in Language Variation across Time*. 2nd edn. Ottawa: University of Ottawa Press, Chapters 15–18.

For a more advanced treatment of EModE phonology and morphology, see the following resources:

Fischer, Olga, and Wim van der Wurff. 2006. 'Syntax'. *A History of the English Language*. Ed. by Richard M. Hogg and David Denison, 109–98. Cambridge: Cambridge University Press.

Görlach, Manfred. 1991. *Introduction to Early Modern English*. Cambridge: Cambridge University Press. (This book also contains an extensive selection of texts.)

Lass, Roger. 1999. 'Phonology and Morphology'. *The Cambridge History of the English Language. Vol. III: 1467–1776*. Ed. by Roger Lass, 56–186. Cambridge: Cambridge University Press.

Lass, Roger. 2006. 'Phonology and Morphology'. *A History of the English Language*. Ed. by Richard M. Hogg and David Denison, 43–108. Cambridge: Cambridge University Press.

McMahon, April. 2006. 'Restructuring Renaissance English'. *The Oxford History of English*. Ed. by Lynda Mugglestone, 146–77. Oxford and New York: Oxford University Press.

On grammatical changes in Early Modern English, see:

Nevalainen, Terttu. 2006. 'Mapping Change in Tudor English'. *The Oxford History of English*. Ed. by Lynda Mugglestone, 178–211. Oxford and New York: Oxford University Press.

Rissanen, Matti. 1999. 'Syntax'. *The Cambridge History of the English Language. Vol. III: 1476–1776*. Ed. by Roger Lass, 187–331. Cambridge: Cambridge University Press

II Early Modern English Verbal Constructions and Eighteenth-Century Prescriptivism

OVERVIEW

The first part of this chapter looks at changes in verbal constructions in Early Modern English, including impersonal verbs, reflexive verbs, the subjunctive mood, and verbal periphrases, and then considers the origin and use of the dummy auxiliary *do*. The chapter then examines the effects of prescriptivism upon the English language. We trace the rise of prescriptive grammar in the eighteenth century and the aims of the prescriptive grammarians—their desire for ascertainment of the language and calls for a language academy. We analyze the various methods used by the prescriptive grammarians in regulating the language, and look at their application in concrete examples. Finally, the chapter summarizes the work of eighteenth-century lexicographers and explains the features of a modern dictionary.

OBJECTIVES

The first objective of this chapter is to understand Early Modern English syntax. After reading this chapter, you should be able to

■ identify the sources and evolution of the verbal constructions of Early Modern English, and

- account for the function of what is called '*do*-support' in forming questions and negatives.

The second objective is to understand the social and linguistic conditions underlying the prescriptivism of the eighteenth century and the aims, methods, and results of prescriptive grammars. You will learn to

- edit English sentences to conform to the rules of prescriptive grammar (with the aid of a handbook), and
- identify the rule violated and understand its rationale.

Early Modern English Syntax

Reflexive and Impersonal Verbs

The Early Modern English period saw the gradual loss of reflexive and impersonal verbs. Reflexive verbs, common in Old and Middle English, fell out of use somewhat after Shakespeare's time, perhaps because they acquired a colloquial flavor. In their older form, reflexive verbs were followed by a simple personal pronoun:

These fiue daies haue I hid <u>me</u> in these woods (Shakespeare, *King Henry VI, Part II*)
'For five days I have hidden (myself) in these woods'

I do wish no better choise, and thinke <u>me</u> rarely to wed (Shakespeare, *Pericles, Prince of Tyre*)
'I wish for no better choice and think myself excellently wed'

Get <u>thee</u> [to] a nunnery (Shakespeare, *Hamlet*)
'Get yourself to a nunnery'

Note that in the ModE translation, if the pronoun is retained at all, it must appear in the reflexive form with *-self*. Compound pronouns with *-self* also began to appear in these constructions:

I thinke <u>myselfe</u> in better plight (Shakespeare, *The Merry Wives of Windsor*)
'I think myself in a better condition'

why hast y [i.e. thou] withdrawn <u>thy selfe</u>? (Shakespeare, *King Henry VI, Part III*)
'why have you withdrawn?'

Vnder this thicke growne brake wee'l shrowd <u>our selues</u> (Shakespeare, *King Henry VI, Part III*)
'Under this thick bracken we'll hide ourselves'

Modern English uses either no pronoun in these examples (as in *why have you withdrawn?*) or a reflexive pronoun (as in *we'll hide ourselves*). The simple pronoun is found dialectally, as in *I got me a new boat.*

The development of the impersonal verb has been more complex. While the impersonal verb construction was definitely on the decline in Early Modern English, quite a few examples can still be found in the early part of the period:

Me seemeth then, it is no Pollicie (Shakespeare, *King Henry VI, Part II*)
'it seems to me then that it is not a wise idea'

Behooues me keepe at vtterance (Shakespeare, *Cymbeline*)
'It is appropriate for me to defend to the death'

the Sun of heauen (methought), was loth to set (Shakespeare, *King John*)
'the sun in the heavens, it seemed to me, was reluctant to set'

this Lodging likes me better (Shakespeare, *King Henry V*)
'I like this accommodation better'

The impersonal verb construction evolved in two different ways. First, it developed a dummy *it* subject, as in the following EModE examples:

Behooues it vs to labor for the Realme (Shakespeare, *King Henry VI, Part II*)
'It is appropriate for us to work for the state'

It seemes to me / That yet we sleepe, we dreame (Shakespeare, *A Midsummer Night's Dream*)
'It seems to me that as we sleep we dream'

It likes me well (Shakespeare, *The Taming of the Shrew*)
'I like it a lot'

It pleaseth me so well, that I will see you wed (Shakespeare, *Pericles, Prince of Tyre*)
'I am so pleased that I will see you married'

Although we retain a number of these impersonal constructions in Modern English with *it* subjects, such as *it seems (to me) that, it happened that,* and *it pleases me that,* many have ceased to be impersonal at all. Instead of *it seems to me,* speakers now prefer *I think.* Most impersonal constructions are in fact obsolete. For example, we can no longer say *it hungers me,* but only *I am hungry.* Traditionally, the transition from impersonal to personal has been described as a reanalysis: speakers interpreted the objective noun or pronoun, which usually precedes the verb, as the personal subject of the verb. This move would have been motivated by word order change and loss of inflections. However, many scholars have not found this explanation entirely satisfactory.

Early Modern English is also characterized by a cross-categorical use of verbs. There was a strong tendency during the period to use intransitive verbs as though they were transitive. We see this especially in Shakespearian examples such as *thy flinty heart . . . Might in thy Pallace perish Elianor* (*King Henry VI, Part II*). The tendency is much weaker in Modern English.

The Subjunctive and the Modal Auxiliaries

The subjunctive endings, *-e* (sg.) and *-en* (pl.), were lost during the Middle English period by phonological change. However, in the second- and third-person singular, there remains a distinction between indicative and subjunctive: the indicative ends in *-est* or *-eth/-es,* while the subjunctive is endingless. Likewise, the verb *be* continues to be inflected in the subjunctive: the base form *be* in the present and *were* in the past. Inflected subjunctives of all verbs are on the decline in the Early Modern period but are still commonly used in subordinate clauses instead of the indicative (given in parentheses in the following examples):

> *Lest he . . . <u>confound</u>* (not *confounds/confoundeth*) *your hidden falshood* (Shakespeare, *King Richard III*)

> *though it <u>were</u>* (not *was*) *hid indeede* (Shakespeare, *Hamlet*)

> *as if it <u>were</u>* (not *was*) *the Moore* (Shakespeare, *Titus Andronicus*)

> *Not till it <u>leaue</u>* (not *leaves/leaveth*) *the Rider in the mire* (Shakespeare, *Love's Labor's Lost*)

> *though it <u>haue</u>* (not *has/hath*) *holp* [i.e. *helped*] *madmen to their wits* (Shakespeare, *King Richard II*)

The Ø-inflected subjunctive is occasionally found in EModE independent clauses expressing wishes (*Thy kingdom come, God reward me*) and exhortations (*Sit we down, Fare you well*).

The disappearance of the subjunctive form was accompanied by the increasing importance of the modal auxiliaries, which are the continuation of the OE preterit-present class, with loss of full verb status and with several changes in the inventory of verbs and verb forms. The preterit-present verbs *þurfan* 'to need', *dugan* 'to avail', and *witan* 'to know' were lost in Early Modern English, leaving the following forms:

can	dare	may	mote	shall	will	owe	need
couthe	durst	mought	must	should	would	ought	needed

Couthe acquired an unetymological *l* (*could*) by analogy with *should* and *would*. *Durst* was replaced by the regular formation *dared*. *Mought* was replaced by *might*, and *mote* was lost. Both *will/would* and *need/needed* joined the class of modal auxiliaries, neither being originally preterit-present verbs. *Owe* left the class to become a full verb. In Modern English, both *need* and *dare* have likewise left the class of modal auxiliary, except in very limited contexts. Finally, there were complex changes in the semantics of the modal auxiliaries, which we need not worry about beyond pointing out that they are now used in Modern English to express all of the notions originally expressed by the subjunctive—possibility, probability, obligation, and so on.

In the absence of mood inflection, another common means of expressing subjunctive meaning is by using the past tense, as in *I wondered if I could ask you a question*, *I wanted to talk to you*, and *We hoped that you might be free for dinner*. Here the past tense signals remoteness and hypothetical meaning. It is also a means of distancing and softening a request and adds a sense of politeness.

Verbal Periphrases

Taking up once more the phrasal constructions used to form the passive, the perfect, the progressive, and the future, we can fit the Early Modern developments into the following brief summaries.

Passive Constructions

We find the passive fully established as a verbal periphrasis in Old English. Apart from loss of the verb *weorðan* 'to become', the only change since that period has been in the preposition used to mark the agent of the passive verb: Old English uses *þurh*, *fram*, and less often *mid*; Middle English texts show *through* and *from* continuing to be used, as well as *of*, *with*, and *by*; in Early Modern English, *by, of*, and *with* appear commonly and *from* more sporadically:

Be warn'd by me then (Shakespeare, *King Henry V*)
'Be warned by me then'

those things which were done of them in secret (Tyndale, Ephesians 5: 6)
'those things which were done by them in secret'

he was torne to pieces with a Beare (Shakespeare, *The Winter's Tale*)
'he was torn to pieces by a bear'

the work is said to be done from heaven (Goodwin, *Filled with the Spirit* [*OED*])
'the work is said to be done by heaven'

Eventually, *by* won out as the sole preposition used to indicate the agent of the passive in Modern English.

The Perfect

The perfect has a long history as a periphrasic construction, with ample evidence from Middle English (and arguably even from Old English), but the ME version uses auxiliary verbs differently: *have* appears with transitive verbs and *be* with intransitive verbs. Gradually the range of verbs using *be* narrowed; we find EModE employing *be* particularly with verbs of motion (e.g. *come, depart, enter, go, meet, return*, and *run*) and verbs denoting a change of state (e.g. *become, change, grow, turn*, and *melt*):

Thy Fathers beard is turn'd white with the Newes (Shakespeare, *King Henry IV, Part I*)
'Your father's beard has turned white with the news'

The deepe of night is crept vpon our talke (Shakespeare, *Julius Caesar*)
'The deep of night has crept up on our conversation'

did he not say my brother was fled? (Shakespeare, *Much Ado About Nothing*)
'didn't he say my brother had fled?'

the world is grown so bad (Shakespeare, *King Richard III*)
'the world has grown so bad'

the King himselfe is rode to view their Bat-taile (Shakespeare, *King Henry V*)
'the king himself has ridden to see their battle'

my Cousin William is become a good Scholler (Shakespeare, *King Henry IV, Part II*)
'my relative William has become a good scholar'

However, some of the same types of verbs occur with the perfect auxiliary *have* in EModE:

I haue since ariu'd but hither (Shakespeare, *Twelfth Night*)
'I have arrived here only now'

Loue's golden arrow at him should haue fled (Shakespeare, *Venus and Adonis*)
'Love's golden arrow should have flown at him'

Where you haue neuer come (Shakespeare, *All's Well That Ends Well*)
'Where you have never come'

they must perforce haue melted (Shakespeare, *King Richard III*)
'they must by necessity have melted'

Gradually then, *have* was replacing *be* as the auxiliary of the perfect. The reasons for the generalization of *have* are complex, perhaps having to do with the potential overlap of *be*-perfects with passives (both consisting of *be* + past participle) when the same verb could be either intransitive (hence perfect) or transitive (hence passive); for example, *it is played* could be the passive of *I played it* ('it is played by me') or it could be a perfect construction equivalent to modern *it has played*. There is also potential ambiguity of the contracted form *'s*, which could be thought to represent either *is* or *has*:

I am glad he's come (Shakespeare, *The Taming of the Shrew*)
'I am glad he has/is come'

He's gone (Shakespeare, *The Tempest*)
'He has/is gone'

In Modern English, we have only a few remnant *be*-perfects, such as *he is arrived, dinner is served,* and *the leaves are turned*, but the emphasis in these constructions is on the state rather than on the action.

Verb phrases became more complex during the Middle English period with the possibility of combining the perfect and the passive as well as the perfect and the progressive along with modal auxiliaries. By the time of the Early Modern English period, modal perfect constructions were commonplace:

> *We haue not yet bin seene in any house* (Shakespeare, *The Taming of the Shrew*)

> *you haue beene mistook* [i.e. *mistaken*] (Shakespeare, *Twelfth Night*)

> *This might have been preuented* (Shakespeare, *King John*)

And here are EModE examples of the perfect progressive:

> *I haue bin drinking all night* (Shakespeare, *Measure for Measure*)

> *We haue bene praying for our husbands' welfare* (Shakespeare, *The Merchant of Venice*)

The Progressive

Unlike the passive and the perfect, the progressive is quite rare (or perhaps non-existent) in Old English, becoming common only toward the end of the Middle English period. The origin of the progressive is much debated. While it might derive from the Old English construction with *be* and the present participle (ending in *-ende*), the progressive has a different form (with a present participle ending in *-ing*) and a different meaning (expressing an action not a state). It may also derive from the Old English construction with *be* followed by the preposition *on* and a gerund (a verbal noun ending in *-ung*); this construction has the meaning 'to be in the process of, be in the midst of'. Most scholars now believe that the progressive owes its form and meaning to both constructions and was reinforced by a comparable construction in Old French and possibly by a parallel form in Middle Welsh. In any case, the progressive was established in the form *be* + present participle, with its current meaning, by Early Modern English. There are quite a few remnants in EModE of the gerund construction with *on*, which can appear as *a-* or *in*, as follows:

> *when green geese are a-breeding* (Shakespeare, *Love's Labor's Lost*)
> 'when young geese are breeding'

> *I kill'd the Slaue that was a hanging thee* (Shakespeare, *King Lear*)
> 'I killed the slave that was hanging you'

> *who was always best when he was most in talking of the world* (Brooks, *A Golden Key to Open Hidden Treasures* [*OED*])
> 'who was always at his best especially when he was talking about the world'

> *a goodly chaplet she was in making* (Hawes, *Thee Pastime of Pleasure* [*OED*])
> 'she was making a fine wreath for the head'

The Progressive Plus Passive

The one combination of verbal periphrases not found in Early Modern English is the progressive plus passive. Instead, the simple (active) progressive is used; from context, it is clear that the active form must be given a passive interpretation:

> *During the time that supper <u>was preparing</u>* (Painter, *Palace of Pleasure* [*OED*])
> 'During the time that supper was being prepared'

> *the whilst this Play <u>is Playing</u>* (Shakespeare, *Hamlet*)
> 'while this play is being performed'

> *New streets <u>are built</u> and still <u>in building</u>* (*Liverpool Municipal Records* [*OED*])
> 'New streets are built and still are being built'

As you can see from the translations here, the combination of the progressive and the passive produces two auxiliary *be*'s in one sentence; in pre-modern English there may have been a restriction on this occurring. This construction is used even beyond the EModE period, as in the following example from 1800:

> *while our dinner <u>was preparing</u>* (Carlyle, *Autobiography* [*OED*])
> 'while our dinner was being prepared'

In Modern English, we have some remnant constructions in which the active progressive has a passive meaning, e.g. *The movie is shooting in Vancouver, There is a lot owing, Trouble is brewing,* and *What's doing/cooking?*

Future Constructions

Periphrases of the future using the modal auxiliaries *shall* and *will* developed in Middle English. While these auxiliaries originally indicated 'obligation' and 'volition', respectively, they came to have pure 'predictive' meaning and thus serve as markers of the future. The following examples show how these had developed by the Early Modern period:

> *O Foole, I <u>shall go</u> mad!* (Shakespeare, *King Lear*)

> *And you say you <u>wil haue</u> her, when I bring hir?* (Shakespeare, *As You Like It*)

> *Here are the Beetle-browes <u>shall blush</u> for me* (Shakespeare, *Romeo and Juliet*)
> 'Here are the prominent eyebrows which will blush for me'

> *to-morrow, . . . it <u>will goe</u> one way or other* (Shakespeare, *Troilus and Cressida*)

Do

Perhaps the most important structural change in Early Modern English was the development of the dummy auxiliary *do*, which affected how questions and negatives were formed in English. In Old and Middle English, as we have seen, no auxiliary verb is required: speakers simply inverted the subject and verb or used the negative particle. In Modern English, an auxiliary verb is obligatory in questions and negative sentences, as well as in sentences with emphasis on the action (e.g. *He wíll so do it*, *She cán too help*). If no other auxiliary is present, *do*, a lexically empty placeholder, is inserted; this is called '*do*-support', and *do* in this function is known as 'dummy *do*'. Auxiliary *do* cannot occur together with any other auxiliary verb.

We know that by about 1700, *do* had achieved the distribution it has today, but its origin is more uncertain and its varied use during the Early Modern English period has caused scholarly controversy. There are two main sources for the dummy auxiliary:

1. a causative verb *do* meaning 'cause, make', as in *he dede Davy sadillyn an oder hors* (*Paston Letters* [Traugott 1972:140]) 'he made Davy saddle another horse'; this is common in Middle English but has given way to verbs such as *make* and *cause*; and

2. *vicarious* or *substitute do* used in place of another verb; this has existed from Old English onward, as in *he left and so did I*.

(Note that neither of these *do*'s should be confused with the lexical verb *do* meaning 'perform an action', as in *she did her homework*.)

The dummy auxiliary *do* first appears in Middle English, but seems to have been restricted to the Southern and West Midland dialects, occurring mostly in poetry (where it could function as a metrical filler). In Early Modern English, however, it became extremely common in non-poetic writing, especially court trials and sermons. Its presence or absence seems to be a matter of stylistic variation. One scholar refers to this as the 'exuberant use of *do*' (Jespersen 1928–49:Vol. 5, 505). The strikingly different use of EModE *do* is its occurrence in non-emphatic affirmative declarative sentences, where *do* never occurs in ModE. This use reached its peak in the mid-sixteenth century:

Thou shin'st in euery tear that I doe weepe (Shakespeare, *Love's Labor's Lost*)
'You shine in every tear that I weep'

your eyes do menace me (Shakespeare, *King Richard III*)
'your eyes threaten me'

vnnatural deeds / Do breed vnnatural troubles (Shakespeare, *Macbeth*)
'unnatural deeds breed unnatural troubles'

we do make our entrance seuerall wayes (Shakespeare, *King Henry VI, Part I*)
'we make our entrance in several ways'

Listen to the sound recording of Ben Jonson's 'On My First Son' (Reading 11) and 'Epitaph on Elizabeth, L.H.' (Reading 12) on the website and follow along with the written text. Can you locate the instances of *do* in affirmative (non-emphatic) sentences?[1]

Questions can be formed in EModE without *do* or any other auxiliary, as can negative sentences:

> *why looke you so vpon me?* (Shakespeare, *As You Like It*)
> 'why do you look at me in this way?'

> *Seest thou this Letter?* (Shakespeare, *Titus Andronicus*)
> 'Do you see this letter?'

> *I doubt it not* (Shakespeare, *The Comedy of Errors*)
> 'I do not doubt it'

> *Man delights not me; no, nor Women neither* (Shakespeare, *Hamlet*)
> 'Men do not delight me; no, nor do women'

> *He sends you not to murther me for this* (Shakespeare, *King Richard III*)
> 'He does not send you to murder me for this'

Over the course of the seventeenth century, the use of *do* became regulated, with *do* confined to emphatic sentences, negative sentences (including negative questions and negative imperatives), and interrogative sentences. The following EModE examples show *do* used much as it is in ModE:

> *why do you looke on me?* (Shakespeare, *As You Like It*)

> *wherefore* [i.e. *why*] *do you come?* (Shakespeare, *King Richard III*)

> *Does she loue him?* (Shakespeare, *Timon of Athens*)

> *I do not greatly care to be decieu'd* (Shakespeare, *Antony and Cleopatra*)
> 'I don't really like to be deceived'

> *O, do not slander him, for he is kinde* (Shakespeare, *Richard III*)

Interestingly, it is possible to find questions with and without *do*-support next to each other in the same line of text:

> *How didst thou scape? How cam'st thou hither?* (Shakespeare, *The Tempest*)
> 'How did you escape? How did you come to be here?'

With the eventual loss of *do* in non-emphatic affirmative declarative sentences, which may have been dictated by the eighteenth-century grammarians, the development of *do* was complete.

---

1 Answer: line 9 in 'On My First Son' and lines 3 and 6 in 'Epitaph on Elizabeth, L.H.'.

Word Order

While SVO word order was established in both main and subordinate clauses in the Middle English period, certain sentence patterns in Early Modern English differ from those of Modern English. Inverted word order was possible following a greater range of initial adverbs, including *then, now, so, yet, also, here, thus, therefore*, and adverbs of time, with no auxiliary verb necessary:

> *So haply are they Friends to Antony* (Shakespeare, *Antony and Cleopatra*)
> 'So by chance they are friends of Antony'

> *Where ne're from France arriu'd more happy men* (Shakespeare, *King Henry V*)
> 'Where never from France did happier men arrive'

> *now comes in the sweet of the night* (Shakespeare, *King Henry IV, Part II*)
> 'now the sweetness of the night arrives'

> *for so worke the Honey Bees* (Shakespeare, *King Henry V*)
> 'for so the honey bees work'

> *Neuer till this day Saw I him touch'd with anger* (Shakespeare, *The Tempest*)
> 'Never until this day did I see him touched with anger'

Inverted word order also appears in conditional clauses:

> *Were he my kinsman . . . It should be thus with him* (Shakespeare, *Measure for Measure*)
> 'If he were my kinsman, it would be so with him'

> *Take I your wish, I leape into the seas* (Shakespeare, *Pericles, Prince of Tyre*)
> 'If I were to follow your wish, I would leap into the sea'

(Note the subjunctive verb forms used in conditional clauses.) The initial clauses would usually be translated with *if* in Modern English, although we do still use an inverted word order, especially with *be, have*, and *do*, as in *Were he here/had he arrived, he would know what to do*.

Occasionally, the verb moves to the end of the subordinate clause:

> *As we his Subiects haue in wonder found* (Shakespeare, *King Henry V*)
> 'As we his subjects have discovered in wonder'

> *proclaim'd / By Richard, that dead is, the next of blood* (Shakespeare, *King Henry IV, Part I*)
> 'proclaimed by Richard, who is dead, as the next of kin'

An auxiliary and verb may be split around an object, placing the verb in final position:

A Wedded-Lady / That hath her Husband banish'd (Shakespeare, *Cymbeline*)
'A wedded lady that has banished her husband'

learned is that tongue that well can thee com(m)end (Shakespeare, *Love's Labor's Lost*)
'learned is the voice that can praise you well'

Additionally, an object may be moved to the front of a clause for emphasis, with optional inversion of the subject and verb:

But answere made it none (Shakespeare, *Hamlet*)
'But it made no answer'

Though forfeytours you cast in prison (Shakespeare, *Cymbeline*)
'Though you cast forfeiters into prison'

This did I feare (Shakespeare, *Othello*)
'This I feared'

Exercise 11.1 EModE Syntax

For each of the following examples, identify the verbal forms and constructions which differ from those of Modern English and explain their significance for the history of English.

a. When me list to sadder tunes apply me (Fletcher, *Poeticall Miscellanies* [OED])

_____

_____

_____

b. Tell him ther's a Post come from my Master (Shakespeare, *The Merchant of Venice*)

_____

_____

_____

c. Let musicke sound while he doth make his choise;
   Then if he loose, he makes a Swan-like end (Shakespeare, *The Merchant of Venice*)

_____

_____

_____

d. While the second-service was reading at the Communion Table
(L'Estrange, *The Reign of King Charles* [*OED*])

_____

_____

_____

e. Voyde sirs, see ye not maister Roister Doister come? (Udall, *Ralph Roister Doister* [*OED*])

_____

_____

_____

The Rise of Prescriptivism

In the period immediately following Early Modern English, the most significant changes came not through natural language change, but through a kind of linguistic engineering. In the eighteenth century, there emerged a profound concern for the state of the language, culminating in the publication of over two hundred grammars of English. These have had lasting and extensive effects on the grammar of formal written English and provide insight into contemporary arguments about verbal and written usage (see Hudson 1994).

Social, Linguistic, and Philosophical Reasons for Prescriptivism

While concerns about the English language focused on spelling and vocabulary in the Renaissance, it was matters of usage and grammar that most concerned society in the eighteenth century. The reasons for both the nature and the intensity of this interest are, broadly speaking, social, linguistic, and philosophical, as suggested by Elizabeth Closs Traugott (1972:163–8).

The Industrial Revolution beginning in the eighteenth century brought with it a growth in the middle class and an increase in social mobility. Especially in the cities, where class barriers were not as clearly delineated as in the country, the upper classes felt their position and authority eroding. Since language is one of the most overt behavioral signs of social class, the early grammars of the eighteenth century were written for the elite to help them maintain social distance; these grammars dictated norms of linguistic correctness for the upper class and warned against contamination of 'polite' language by the lower classes. Later in the eighteenth century, grammars began to be written for lower- and middle-class speakers who wished to rise socially by imitating the usage of their social superiors; these grammars described correct usage and advised on ways to avoid 'vulgar' forms (William Cobbett's 1819 grammar is dedicated 'especially for the Use of Soldiers, Sailors, Apprentices, and Plough-boys'). Whether they originated in elitist or democratic ideologies, the grammars seem to be based on a common assumption that language mattered and that people should be given guidance. The norm of correctness used in formal written Modern English, which we inherited from these eighteenth-century books, reflects elite usage of early eighteenth-century middle-class London, rejecting the rural regionalisms of the English working class (Knowles 1997:129). Moreover, the social basis for prescriptivism partly accounts for the moralistic tone which imbues these manuals; while some forms are described as 'uncouth', 'corrupt', 'low', 'adopted by the ignorant', 'profane', 'inelegant', 'barbaric', 'ungenteel', 'repugnant', or 'offensive', others are described as 'noble', 'refined', or 'enlightened'. We must keep in mind that these attempts to maintain social position or to rise in social status occur within the context of a social and political climate of constraint. The drive to impose linguistic conformity is in keeping with the disapproval of political and religious non-conformity also evident during the period (Knowles 1997:111).

The eighteenth century was a period not only of linguistic insecurity but also of linguistic conservatism. Broadly speaking, attitudes toward language swing over time between liberal and conservative. In liberal phases, there is concern about establishing a forceful and vigorous national idiom; improvements in the language are sought and innovations encouraged. In conservative phases, we see concern about refining and fixing the language; people express a belief that the language has decayed from an earlier, better state and that subsequent changes in the language must be prevented. Overall, attitudes were liberal in the Early Modern English period, with people feeling that the adoption of English in place of Latin and French as the medium for serious writing necessitated a rich and flexible language. As a result, we see an experimentation with language in Shakespeare and the Metaphysical poets. This playfulness continues into the eighteenth century with authors such as Laurence Sterne. But more generally, by the end of the seventeenth century, England was secure as a nation, and linguistic attitudes had swung to the conservative.

Because the eighteenth century was the age of rationalist philosophy, the so-called Age of Reason, it was believed that language, like everything else, ought to be logical, orderly, and symmetrical. The concept of a universal grammar, a medieval notion that all the different languages shared universal principles or rules, was revived; the leading eighteenth-century thinkers believed that these universal principles rested on Cartesian logic. They wanted a one-to-one relationship between form and meaning, ridding the language of alternative forms with the same meaning, or multiple meanings for the same form. Redundancies were not logically acceptable. Furthermore, verbal innovation offended against a strict sense of decorum. All aspects of language, the grammarians thought, should be under control.

Important Prescriptive Grammarians of the Eighteenth Century

The prescriptive grammarians of the age were self-appointed experts, who considered themselves qualified to make pronouncements about the structure of language. Some of these guardians of the language could boast of literary achievements (such as Ben Jonson, Daniel Defoe, Jonathan Swift, Richard Sheridan, Joseph Addison, and Samuel Johnson), while others were clergymen (such as Bishops Robert Lowth and William Ward), scientists (such as Joseph Priestley), or miscellaneous men of letters, (such as John Wallis, Lindley Murray, Nathan Bailey, George Campbell, and Noah Webster). Women occasionally contributed to the debate, one example being Ann Fisher. All of these were people of privilege and power, thus suggesting that linguistic authority was linked to social hierarchy. One of the most interesting and liberal of the eighteenth-century grammarians was Priestley (a chemist and a non-conformist minister), who published *The Rudiments of English Grammar* in 1761. More influential, however, was Lowth (a classical scholar as well as a clergyman), whose *Short Introduction to English Grammar*, first published in 1762, went through 22 editions during the eighteenth century. Lowth's approach is conservative and generally prescriptive. Samuel Johnson, a prominent intellectual in London literary society, was undoubtedly the supreme authority on language in England during the eighteenth century; in the United States, the leading figure was the lexicographer Noah Webster.

Aims of the Eighteenth-Century Grammarians

Ascertainment

Eighteenth-century pundits believed that their English language had no grammar, in the sense that it was uncodified, unsystematized, and uncertain in places. In Chapter 1, we quoted Swift's judgment that the English language was 'extremely imperfect . . . in many Instances, it offends against every Part of Grammar'. Swift was not alone; Samuel Johnson described English as being in a neglected state of 'wild exuberance', 'copious without order and energetic without rules' (1977 [1755/1773]:277). The eighteenth-century grammarians, therefore, set out to give English a grammar.

They also believed that change endangers the integrity of the language. Swift wrote that 'it is better a Language should not be wholly perfect, than that it should be perpetually changing'; he saw no necessity for a language to change 'for we find many Examples to the contrary' such as Greek, Chinese, German, Spanish, and Italian (1957:14, 9). Johnson decried the fact that 'tongues, like governments, have a natural tendency to degeneration' (1977 [1755/1773]:296). The eighteenth century looked back nostalgically to an earlier golden age, though few could agree on when this age was: using a phrase from Spenser, Johnson considered the Elizabethan period the 'wells of English undefiled' (1977 [1755/1773]:284), whereas Richard

Sheridan and Noah Webster saw the 1660 Restoration (and writers like Swift) as the high point of the language (Baugh and Cable 2002:258). They all believed that the language had decayed or been corrupted from this earlier state, and wished to reverse the harmful changes by refining, purifying, and perfecting it. Finally, heeding the warning of Alexander Pope in his 'An Essay on Criticism' that 'such as Chaucer is, shall Dryden be'(2000 [1711]:l. 483), they strove to prevent further changes in the language. (From our twenty-first-century perspective, the eighteenth-century grammarians appear unaware of linguistic history and its lessons on the inevitablity of change.) After considering the history of the English language, how-ever, Johnson concluded that it is futile to attempt to 'embalm' a language, which he considered comparable to trying to 'change sublunary nature, or clear the world at once from folly, vanity, and affectation' (1977 [1755/1773]:294).

As a consequence of these perceived faults in the language, the eighteenth-century grammarians undertook the process of ascertainment, which entailed ridding English of doubts and uncertainties. This was a tripartite process. First, they wished to standardize the language, codify the rules, settle disputed points, and establish a standard of correct usage. The question of whose speech would constitute the basis of the standard was not easily determined. James Beattie, for example, argued that it should be the 'most learned and polite persons in London and the neighbouring universities of Oxford and Cambridge' (see Figure 11.1; also see 'The Question of Usage' below). Second, the grammarians wished to refine the language, remove supposed defects and common errors, halt suspected bad tendencies, and introduce improvements if necessary. Finally, they wanted to fix the language permanently in the desired form and prevent further changes. The ambitious and remarkably con-sistent aims of the eighteenth-century grammarians may be summed up in Lowth's belief that 'the principal design of a grammar of any Language is to teach us to express ourselves with propriety in that language, and to be able to judge of every phrase and form of construction, whether it be right or not' (1762:x).

An Academy

For a period of about fifty years, it was thought that the best way to achieve ascer-tainment was by the establishment of an academy to regulate the language. In this regard, England had the model of Florence's Accademia della Crusca, established in 1582, published a dictionary of Italian in 1612, and of France, whose Académie française, established in 1636, published its dictionary in 1694. Robert Hooke, a scientist, called for the establishment of an English academy in 1660. A committee of the Royal Society was struck in 1664, perhaps under the auspices of John Dry-den, but met only three or four times. The idea of an academy had the backing of a number of influential people: Joseph Addison supported the notion in the pages of the *Spectator*, Defoe called for an academy to correct and 'purge the language of irregular additions and innovations' in his *Essay upon Several Projects* (1697), and

Scotch, accent, is no more praiseworthy, or blameable, than to be born in England, or Scotland: a circumstance, which, though the ringleaders of sedition, or narrow-minded bigots, may applaud or censure, no person of sense, or common honesty, will ever consider as imputable to any man.

Are, then, all provincial accents equally good? By no means. Of accent, as well as of spelling, syntax, and idiom, there is a standard in every polite nation. And, in all these particulars, the example of approved authors, and the practice of those, who, by their rank, education, and way of life, have had the best opportunities to know men and manners, and domestick and foreign literature, ought undoubtedly to give the law. Now it is in the metropolis of a kingdom, and in the most famous schools of learning, where the greatest resort may be expected of persons adorned with all useful and elegant accomplishments. The language, therefore, of the most learned and polite persons in London, and the neighbouring Universities of Oxford and Cambridge, ought to be accounted the standard of the English tongue, especially in accent and pronunciation: syntax, spelling, and idiom, having been ascertained by the practice of good authors, and the consent of former ages.

And there are two reasons for this preference. One is, that we naturally approve as elegant

Figure 11.1 Facsimile Page from James Beattie's 1778 *The Theory of Language* (© The British Library)

Swift asked for the patronage of the Earl of Oxford for this endeavor in *A Proposal for Correcting, Improving and Ascertaining the English Tongue* (1712). (Interestingly, Defoe's academy was to be composed of men of learning, but no teachers, clergymen, physicians, or lawyers.)

Nonetheless, the idea of a language academy never came to fruition in England. Queen Anne, who apparently supported it, died in 1714 and was succeeded by King George I, a Hanoverian who could not speak English. Then, too, the dubious results of the efforts of the French academy to keep out impurities and prevent change were already obvious. Priestley argued that an academy was unnecessary since 'the best forms will, in time, establish themselves by their own superior excellence' (1969 [1761]:vii). Most importantly, by the time his dictionary was published Samuel Johnson had come to see the futility of trying to stop language change. In the preface to his dictionary, he noted that the activities of the French and Italian academies had been in vain, because 'sounds are too volatile and subtle for legal restraints; to enchain syllables and to lash the wind are equally the undertakings of pride, unwilling to measure its desires by its strength' (1977 [1755/1773]:294). Furthermore, he believed that the 'spirit of English liberty will hinder or destroy' the dictates of an academy, should one be formed (1977 [1755/ 1773]:296). He concluded that an academy could not force a standard on the people, but only try to persuade them to adopt it.

Below is an excerpt from Swift's public letter published in 1712, in which he states that what he has 'most at heart' is a method for 'ascertaining and fixing' the English language. Although punctuation and capitalization practices in the eighteenth century differed from modern conventions and the prose style is elaborate and polite, the grammar and vocabulary of this passage closely resemble Present-Day English.

IN order to reform our Language; I conceive, My Lord, that a free judicious Choice should be made of such Persons, as are generally allowed to be best qualified for such a Work, without any regard to Quality, Party, or Profession. These, to a certain Number, at least, should assemble at some appointed Time and Place, and fix on Rules by which they design to proceed. What Methods they will take, is not for me to prescribe. Your Lordship, and other Persons in great Employment, might please to be of the Number: And I am afraid, such a Society would want your Instruction and Example, as much as your Protection: For I have, not without a little Envy, observed of late the Style of some great Ministers very much to exceed that of any other Productions.

THE Persons who are to undertake this Work, will have the Example of the *French* before them, to imitate where these have proceeded right, and to avoid their Mistakes. Besides the Grammar-part, wherein we are allowed to be very defective, they will observe many gross Improprieties, which however authorized by Practice, and grown familiar, ought to be discarded. They will find many Words that deserve to be utterly thrown out of our Language; many more to be corrected; and perhaps not a few, long since antiquated, which ought to be restored, on Account of their Energy and Sound.

BUT what I have most at Heart, is, that some Method should be thought on for *Ascertaining* and *Fixing* our Language for ever, after such Alterations are made in it as shall be thought requisite. For I am of Opinion, that it is better a Language should not be wholly perfect, than that it should be perpetually changing; and we must give over at one Time or other, or at length infallibly change for the worse (from Swift's 1712 *Proposal*; Davis and Landa 1957:13–14).

Exercise 11.2 Eighteenth-Century Prescriptivism

Give definitions of the following terms, with brief discussions of the importance of the concept in the history of English.

a.   prescriptivism and descriptivism

_____

_____

_____

_____

_____

_____

b.   vocabulary enrichment and spelling reform

_____

_____

_____

_____

_____

_____

c.   universal grammar

_____

_____

_____

_____

_____

_____

d.   ascertainment and academy

_____

_____

_____

_____

_____

Methods of the Eighteenth-Century Grammarians

Failing to establish a language academy, the eighteenth-century grammarians had to rely on their own devices to achieve their aims, including a variety of means of arbitrating linguistic matters: their own authority and the authority of the best writers, the model of the classical languages, etymology, and reason. The means themselves derived from classical grammarians, such as the Roman rhetorician Marcus Fabius Quintilian, who asserted that 'Language is based on reason, antiquity, authority, and usage' (*Institutio Oratoria*, Book 1, Chap. 6).

Authority

Often, in making prescriptions, the eighteenth-century grammarian used his personal authority as a man of learning, proclaiming simply: 'This is not English', 'I cannot conceive it to be English', 'we must not say', 'we never ought to write', or 'hardly to be approved of'. Thus, the prescriptions embodied the individual's preconceptions, prejudices, and preferences, as, for example, when Campbell declared the words *tenderheartedness, disinterestedness*, and *wrongheadedness* to be 'harsh' and 'unharmonious' and hence to be avoided (1963 [1776]:162). Lowth justifies the proscription against ending a sentence with a preposition by saying that he does not find the construction 'graceful' or 'perspicuous':

> The Preposition is often separated from the Relative which it governs, and joined to the Verb at the end of the Sentence, or some Member of it: as, 'Horace is an author, *whom* I am much delighted *with*' . . . This is an Idiom, which our language is strongly inclined to; it prevails in common conversation, and suits very well with the familiar style in writing: but the placing of the Preposition before the Relative is more graceful, as well as more perspicuous; and agrees much better with the solemn and elevated style (1762:127–8).

Here, Lowth distinguishes between 'solemn and elevated style' and 'familiar style'; note that he himself ends a sentence with a preposition in this passage ('This is an idiom . . . inclined to'). The grammarians also appealed to the authority of the best writers and men of letters. However, at the same time, they seemed to take delight in pointing out errors in other writers and in their fellow grammarians. For example, Campbell cited the following agreement error by Addison: 'Each of the sexes should keep within *its* particular bounds, and content *themselves* to exult within *their* respective districts' (1963 [1776]:185). As Webster noted, 'very eminent writers have been led into mistakes' (1951 [1789]:62).

In fact, the eighteenth-century authorities themselves did not agree on a great many points of grammar (see Bryan 1923), for example, on whether it is permissible to have the same form functioning as an adverb and an adjective (*a real test, he did {real, really} well*); whether the subject of a gerund should be in the possessive (*I object to {John, John's} drinking*); whether the objective case can be used after the verb *be* and *as* and *than* (*It is {me, I}, he is taller than {me, I}*); whether possessive pronouns as well as nouns should have an apostrophe (*your's, hi's, it's, their's, her's*); whether *whose* or *of which* should be used with inanimates (*the book whose author I know, the book the author of which I know*); whether *who* is acceptable as an objective (*Who did you want?*); whether the subjunctive should be preserved (*if I {was, were}, if it {is, be}*); whether *you* should take a plural or singular verb when referring to a singular referent (*you {was, were}*); or whether *it is* can occur with a plural noun (*it is these questions which you must answer*). Many of these points of grammatical controversy have resolved themselves in time.

Personal preference probably lay beneath most of the prescriptions of the eighteenth-century grammarians, but because they lacked the higher authority of an academy to give these preferences weight, they appealed to a number of other authorities, such as the classical languages, history, and logic.

Model of Latin

For some of the eighteenth-century grammarians, the model of the classical languages carried great weight, since they valued synthetic, or highly inflected, languages. In part, they equated inflections with grammar (as do students today who have been made to memorize Old English paradigms [Leith 1997:95]). An inflected language was for the eighteenth-century grammarians the most pure, advanced, complete, and elegant language. For example, Samuel Johnson is attributed as saying that 'every language must be servilely formed after the model of some one of the ancient' (quoted in Leonard 1929:50). By analogy with Latin, the examples given in Table 11.1 (second column) were identified as approved usage. Latin served as a model for most eighteenth-century prescriptions concerning case usage (as shown in the first three examples in Table 11.1), and these rules are still often prescribed for current written (although not spoken) English. The treatment of *as* and *than* as conjunctions rather than prepositions also dates back to that time. Those arguing for the preservation of the subjunctive in certain dependent clauses in English (*if, though, except, unless* clauses) likewise point to the use of the subjunctive in comparable clauses in Latin. Even in formal writing today, the rules concerning the use of the subjunctive have been abandoned.

Table 11.1 Use of Latin for Regulating the Language

unacceptable	*acceptable*
It is me, it is him	It is I, it is he
between you and I	between you and me
who is this for?	for whom is this?, whom is this for?
as tall as me	as tall as I (am)
taller than me	taller than I (am)
if I was	if I were

Not all eighteenth-century grammarians were slaves to Latin, however, as can be seen in the following excerpt from Noah Webster's *A Grammatical Institute of the English Language*:

> The ancient Greek and Roman languages, and the modern French and Italian, have generally been made a necessary part of a polite or learned education, while a grammatical study of their own language has, till very lately, been totally neglected. This ridiculous practice has found its way to America; and so violent have been the prejudices in support of it, that the whispers of common sense, in favour of our native tongue, have been silenced amidst the clamour of pedantry in favour of Greek and Latin (1968 [1783]:4).

Etymology

Because of their opposition to language change, the eighteenth-century grammarians believed that the etymological meaning of a word possessed a certain authority over the current one; where they found a difference, they preferred the original. For example, they argued that *beholden*, being the past participle of the verb *behold* 'to look upon, observe', should mean 'looked upon, observed'. In this they were mistaken, since the OE verb *behealdan* most commonly means 'to hold, possess', from which our meaning of *beholden* 'indebted' derives quite naturally. Similarly, because of the existence of the noun *demeanor* meaning 'behavior, deportment', they argued that *demean* must have the meaning 'to behave, conduct oneself'. In actuality, the verb and noun are derived from different sources, the noun from Fr. *de-* 'completely' + *mener* 'to lead, conduct', and the verb from the native *mean* 'intend' and a pejorative prefix *de-*. They argued that *verse*, meaning 'a turning', should be restricted to a single line of poetry (based on the meaning of Lat. *vertere* 'to turn'), while *stanza*, Italian for 'a stopping', could refer to a poetic paragraph. Other examples are given in Table 11.2.

Table 11.2 Use of Etymology for Regulating the Language

	current meaning	*etymological (preferred) meaning*
between	'in the midst of'	'between two' (cf. OE *betwēonum* 'at/by two')
alternative	'choice among possibilities'	'choice between two possibilites' (cf. Lat. *alter* 'the other two')
verbal	'oral'	'words spoken or written' (cf. Lat. *verbum* 'word')

One could easily carry etymological reasoning of this sort to absurd ends by arguing that the word *disheveled* (< Fr. *des-* 'away' + *chevel* 'hair') be restricted to hair in disarray, that *manufactured* (< Lat. *manus* 'hand' + *factus* 'made') be restricted to things made by hand, that *poise* (< Fr. *poiser* 'to weigh') refer only to things of weight or substance, or that *dilapidated* (< *dis-* 'apart' + *lapidāre* 'to throw stones', from *lapis* 'stone') be restricted to stone structures or stone things in disrepair. In the main, these etymological pronouncements had no effect on the semantics of English words.

The grammarians also determined the use of particular prepositions with verbs by appeals to etymology:

use *averse from*   not *averse to*
use *different from*   not *different than/to*

Since *averse* contains the Lat. prefix *ab-* meaning 'away from', it was argued that we should say *averse from,* not *averse to* (though we still do say the latter) (Campbell 1963 [1776]:158–9). Similarly, *different* contains the Lat. prefix *dis-* meaning 'from' and thus they thought we should say *different from*, not *different to* or *differ-*

ent than; however, both of the 'incorrect' forms are still found in Modern English. If this were carried to an extreme, we might expect to find *submit under* (< Lat. *sub-* 'under') and *prefer before* (< Lat. *pre-* 'before').

Despite the authority they granted to etymological meaning, the grammarians were ambivalent about the importance of older forms of the language. Some showed a preference for archaic forms such as *thou* and the *-st* verb ending, the distinction between *you* and *ye*, and the third-person forms *hath* and *doth*, which in the eighteenth century were quite recent losses from the language. Other writers believed that archaic or obsolete words and forms should be abandoned. For example, Campbell (1963 [1776]:166) suggested that the words *lief, dint, whit, moot, pro*, and *con*, then found only in idiomatic expressions, should be dispensed with because they were obsolete (but as you will notice, some are still current today).

Reason

Reason, in the form of logical rules, analogy, and the differentiation of forms, provided much material for the eighteenth-century grammarians. The application of logic to natural language resulted in prescriptions and proscriptions such as the following:

1. Do not use a double negative.
2. Do not use a double comparative or superlative form.
3. Do not compare 'incomparables' such as *unique, round,* and *perfect.*
4. Use the comparative degree for two things, the superlative degree for more than two.
5. Place *only* before the word it modifies.
6. Do not split an infinitive.
7. Do not end a sentence with a preposition.

As we have seen, double and even triple negatives are possible at earlier stages of the language: cf. *And that no woman has, nor neuer none / Shall mistris be of it, saue I alone* (Shakespeare, *Twelfth Night*) or *ist not enough, yong man, / That I did neuer, no nor neuer can, / Deserue a sweete looke* 'it is not enough, young man, that I never did, no, nor never can deserve a sweet look' (Shakespeare, *A Midsummer Night's Dream*). But Lowth (1762), applying rules of logic, forbade such emphatic negatives because they seemed to add up to an affirmative. Likewise, double comparatives and superlatives (such as *more happier, most fairest*), common in earlier periods, were deemed logically redundant in the eighteenth century. The rule about comparing absolutes was based on the idea that such things could not be a matter of degree; something is either perfect or not; it cannot be more or less perfect. However, we find frequent violations of this rule throughout the history of English.

Logic also dictated to the grammarians that the comparative degree be confined to two things and the superlative to three or more; nonetheless, expressions such as *the brightest of the two* appear at all stages of English. It was felt that a word should logically precede the word it modifies; this rule is applied most obviously to the placement of *only,* whose natural position in Modern English seems to be pre-verbal (as in *He only left a minute ago*). As Lowth pointed out, however, 'It is commonly said, "I only spake three words"; when the intention of the speaker manifestly requires, "I spake only three words"' (1762). He wanted to make clear that *only* restricted the number of words, not the speaking. Finally, it was argued that the infinitive marker *to* should not be separated from the infinitive by an adverb, nor should a preposition be separated from its object by being stranded at the end of the sentence. Both of these restrictions are violated frequently today (as in *to boldly go* or *What did he refer to?*).

Many rules depended on more than one rationale. For example, both etymology and logic were used to argue that *unloose* should not be used in the sense 'to free, set loose', for if *loose* means 'to free, set loose', then, the logic went, adding the prefix *un-* should reverse the meaning to 'to capture, confine'. Likewise, Campbell felt that the preposition *of* is etymologically as well as logically incorrect with *accept, admit,* or *approve* and the preposition *to* is redundant with *address* or *attain,* presumably because the verbs all contain the Latin prefix *ad-* meaning 'to' (1963 [1776]:158–9).

The eighteenth-century grammarians believed that a language should be absolutely regular, or grammatically analogous. We have already seen that analogy is a motivating force in making language regular over time. The grammarians likewise used analogy as a means of removing irregularities, as shown in Table 11.3. First, they argued that the verbs *dare* and *need* should take an *-s* third-person present singular indicative ending by analogy to all main verbs. In PDE, *dare* and *need* are borderline auxiliaries, which have no third-person singular ending in negative and interrogative contexts (e.g. *he dare not do it, Dare he do it?* but *she dares to do it*). Second, they argued that if *which* is restricted to non-human referents and *who* to human referents, then by analogy *of which* rather than *whose* should be the possessive when the referent is non-human, as in *the book, the author of which I met* rather

Table 11.3 Use of Analogy for Regulating the Language

unacceptable	*acceptable*	*by analogy with*
he dare, he need	he dares, he needs	he goes, he eats
whose (for anything non-human)	of which	who *vs* which
which (for a human being)	who	who *vs* which
toward, homeward	towards, homewards	backwards, forwards
thereabouts, hereabouts	thereabout, hereabout	about

than *the book, whose author I met*. Third, Campbell (1963 [1776]:156) argued that the forms *towards* and *homewards* should function as adverbs by analogy with *backwards* and *forwards*, where the form without -*s* functions as an adjective. In the case of *thereabout* and *hereabout*, however, Campbell asserted that the form without -*s* should be the adverbial form since there is no analogous *abouts*.

The grammarians also thought a language should be maximally transparent, with one form having one meaning, and vice versa. For example, adjectives should be distinguished from adverbs (not **real good*, but *really good*) and past tense forms from past participles (not **you should have saw*, but *you should have seen*, and not **I seen it*, but *I saw it*). When two forms with the same meaning exist in the language, the grammarians set about finding or making a distinction between them. The differentiation of forms instituted by them sometimes preserves or revitalizes historical distinctions, but may also introduce artificial distinctions. According to their rules, the following words are to be contrasted:

lie, sit, fall	*lay, set, fell*
less	*fewer*
hung	*hanged*
between	*among*
will	*shall*
can	*may*
further	*farther*
people	*persons*

Thus, *lie, sit,* and *fall* function as intransitive verbs, while *lay, set,* and *fell* function as transitive, causative verbs (e.g. *the tree is falling; I am felling the tree*); *less* is used with nouns that are not countable, *fewer* with ones that are countable (e.g. *less milk, fewer eggs*); *hung* is to be used with objects, *hanged* with people receiving capital punishment; *between* indicates two, while *among* indicates more than two; *can* expresses ability, but *may* expresses permission; *farther* indicates literal distance, *further* metaphorical distance (e.g. *farther down the road, further in the text*); and *people* denotes a group or collective, while *persons* denotes individuals.

The auxiliaries *shall* and *will* present an especially complex and interesting example of differentiation, where forms have been distinguished among different grammatical subjects and in different types of sentences, such as predictions and promises. The set of rules for the use of *shall* and *will* are based on a description by John Wallis in his grammar of English (written in Latin), *Grammatica Linguae Anglicanae*, published in 1653. In the eighteenth century, the EModE use of these auxiliaries became codified in a set of rules known as the Wallis Rules (see Table 11.4). Generations of school children learned these artificial rules, but their relevance today is further limited since *shall* is gradually falling out of use, at least in North American English. (However, many of us would still use a construction like 'Shall I take out the trash?' when we are questioning what somebody wants.)

Table 11.4 The Wallis Rules for the Use of *shall* and *will*

to promise:		to question determination/obligation:	
I will (go)	We will (go)	Shall I (go)?	Shall we (go)?
You shall (go)	You shall (go)	Will you (go)?	Will you (go)?
He/she/it shall (go)	They shall (go)	Shall he/she/it (go)?	Shall they (go)?
to predict:		to question prediction:	
I shall (go)	We shall (go)	Will I (go)?	Will we (go)?
You will (go)	You will (go)	Shall you (go)?	Shall you (go)?
He/she/it will (go)	They will (go)	Will he/she/it (go)?	Will they (go)?

Exercise 11.3 Eighteenth-Century Prescriptive Rules

1. Decide whether the following examples contain any violations of prescriptive rules based on <u>A</u>uthority, <u>E</u>tymology, <u>R</u>eason, or <u>L</u>atin Grammar. State the violation and write the relevant letter or letters next to it. If you decide there is no violation, write N for <u>N</u>one.

    a.   My house is further down the street.

    _____   _____

    b.   if I was you

    _____   _____

    c.   to hopefully return

    _____   _____

    d.   She is as old as me.

    _____   _____

    e.   I don't care who he's a friend of.

    _____   _____

    f.   Divest your coat.

    _____   _____

    g.   It is her.

    _____   _____

　　h.　Lay yourself down.

_____ _____

　　i.　This house is more perfect than that house.

_____ _____

　　j.　That book was unputdownable.

_____ _____

2.　Using your general knowledge about formal written usage in Modern English, try to correct these sentences following a prescriptive rationale.

　　a.　Van Gogh's painting is more unique than Cezanne's.

_____

　　b.　I only ate a salad for lunch.

_____

　　c.　He is so polite.

_____

　　d.　Is this assignment different than last week's?

_____

　　e.　They chose two officers, John and I.

_____

　　f.　After failing to make the appointment, I feel badly.

_____

The Question of Usage

For the eighteenth-century grammarians, the most difficult aspect of language to contend with was usage, or what they called 'custom'. We saw in Chapter 2 that *usage* is an ambiguous term, referring in a prescriptive sense to the forms that should be used and in a descriptive sense to the forms that actually are used. The Latin poet Horace decreed that 'in the hand of usage lies the judgment, the right, and the rule of speech' [*usus, quem penes arbitratum est et jus et norma loquendi*] (*Ars Poetica*, l. 71; see Horace 1978:456). He meant by this that there is no absolute standard of usage apart from the forms that are used by speakers. Regulation arises out of the forms in use and cannot be imposed from outside. While the eighteenth-century grammarians paid lip service to this Horatian view, they distrusted the usage of the majority (precisely because it was the usage of the majority [Leith 1997:56–7]), which they felt was in a very bad state; they were certainly unwilling to accept it as the arbiter. This distrust, in fact, finds its source in classical writers, as evidenced in the following passage from Quintilian:

> Usage remains to be discussed. For it would be almost laughable to prefer the language of the past to that of the present day, and what is ancient speech but ancient usage of speaking? But even here the critical faculty is necessary, and we must make up our mind what we mean by usage. If it be defined merely as the practice of the majority, we shall have a very dangerous rule affecting not merely style but life as well, a far more serious matter. For where is so much good to be found that what is right should please the majority? The practices of depilation [hair removal], of dressing the hair in tiers, or of drinking to excess at the baths, although they may have thrust their way into society, cannot claim the support of usage, since there is something to blame in all of them (although we have usage on our side when we bathe or have our hair cut or take our meals together). So too in speech we must not accept as a rule of language words and phrases that have become a vicious habit with a number of persons. To say nothing of the language of the uneducated, we are all of us well aware that whole theatres and the entire crowd of spectators will often commit *barbarisms* in the cries which they utter as one man. I will therefore define usage in speech as the agreed practice of educated men, just as where our way of life is concerned I should define it as the agreed practice of all good men (*Institutio Oratoria*, Book 1, Chap. 6).

Similar uneasiness concerning usage can be seen in Lowth's reference to the 'caprice of Custom' (1762:47). In general, the grammarians seemed to feel little compunction about ignoring or rejecting forms that were commonly used. Hence, they set about to regulate language themselves, to establish a norm of correctness and impose that on speakers.

The only eighteenth-century grammarians to follow usage with any consistency were Priestley and Webster. In his grammar of English (1761), Priestley stated that the 'custom of speaking is the original and only just standard of any language'; more importantly, he remained faithful to this principle. He believed that one cannot establish grammar by arbitrary rules. Language will change for the expedience and usefulness of its speakers. If grammarians cannot resolve a question, said Priestly, custom will do so in time. While Priestley had preferences for some structures over others, he called none wrong, but only 'stiff' or 'disagreeable', and he recognized that his preferences were 'nothing more than a conjecture' (quoted in Baugh and Cable 2002:283, 285). Webster likewise asserted that the 'basis of a standard' is 'universal undisputed practice, and the principle of analogy' (1951 [1789]:28). He criticized those grammarians who 'instead of examining to find what the English language *is*, . . . endeavour to show what it *ought to be* according to their rules' (1951 [1789]:28). However, Webster was not quite as consistent as Priestley in applying this principle, recognizing the difficulty of following custom, which, he said, is 'like fixing a light house on a floating island' (1951 [1789]:25).

In the following passage from George Campbell's 1776 *Philosophy of Rhetoric*, we hear the voice of a masterful rhetorician attempting, at his most eloquent, to define 'usage'. He begins by asserting that 'use, or the custom of speaking, is the sole original standard', but goes on to concede that 'the generality of people speak and write very badly'. Therefore, he feels it necessary to restrict usage to 'reputable', 'national', and 'present' usage.

It is in part because of his self-consciously elevated style that the passage sounds archaic to our ears. Although certain structures, such as *what that*, and some vocabulary, such as *aught* and *suffrage*, are no longer common and although Campbell's diction is at times inflated, it is sentence structure that constitutes the most obvious other difference between Campbell's language and our own. The length of sentences, their complexity (in terms of number and type of subordinate clauses and phrases embedded in the sentence), the abundance of parallel constructions, and different conventions of punctuation are very striking.

Language is purely a species of fashion (for this holds equally of every tongue) in which, by the general but tacit consent of the people of a particular state or country, certain sounds come to be appropriated to certain things, as their signs, and certain ways of inflecting and combining those sounds come to be established, as denoting the relations which subsist among the things signified.

It is not the business of grammar, as some critics seem preposterously to imagine, to give law to the fashions which regulate our speech. On the contrary, from its conformity to these, and from that alone, it derives all its authority and value. For, what is the grammar of any language? It is no other than a collection of general observations methodically digested, and comprising all the modes previously and independently established, by which the significations, derivations, and combinations of words in that language are ascertained. It is of no consequence here to what causes originally these modes or fashions owe their existence, to imitation, to reflection, to affectation, or to caprice; they no sooner obtain and become general, than they are laws of the language, and the grammarian's only business is to note, collect, and methodize them. Nor does this truth concern only those more comprehensive analogies or rules, which affect whole classes of words, such as nouns, verbs, and other parts of speech; but it concerns every individual word, in the inflecting or the combining of which a particular mode hath prevailed. Every single anomaly, therefore, though departing from the rule assigned to the other words of the same class, and on that account called an exception, stands on the same basis on which the rules of the tongue are founded, custom having prescribed for it a separate rule.

The truth of this position hath never, for aught I can remember, been directly controverted by anybody; yet it is certain, that both critics and grammarians often argue in such a way as is altogether inconsistent with it . . . .

But if use be here a matter of such consequence, it will be necessary, before advancing any further, to ascertain precisely what it is . . . .

In what extent then must the word be understood? It is sometimes called *general use*; yet is it not manifest that the generality of people speak and write very badly? Nay, is not this a truth that will be even generally acknowledged? It will be so; and this very acknowledgment shows that many terms and idioms may be common, which nevertheless, have not the general sanction, no, nor even the suffrage of those that use them. The use here spoken of, implies not only *currency*, but *vogue*. It is properly *reputable custom*.

This leads to a distinction between good use and bad use in language . . . .

Thus have I attempted to explain what that *use* is, which is the sole mistress of language, and to ascertain the precise import and extent of these her essential attributes, *reputable, national,* and *present*, and to give the directions proper to be observed in searching for the laws of this empress. In truth, grammar and criticism are but her ministers; and though, like other ministers, they would sometimes impose the dictates of their own humour upon the people, as the commands of their sovereign, they are not so often successful in such attempts as to encourage the frequent repetition of them (Campbell, *Philosophy of Rhetoric* 1963 [1776]:139–51).

Dictionaries

In addition to prescriptive grammars, the concern for linguistic correctness and a rising middle class unfamiliar with French and Latin led in the eighteenth century to the publication of complete English-to-English dictionaries for the first time. The practice of lexicography (dictionary compilation) has changed dramatically from the appearance of the first monolingual dictionary. Robert Cawdrey's *A Table Alphabetical* (1604), containing 2,500 entries, was intended to help ordinary people read the Bible and other religious texts (cf. Knowles 1997:96). Like all early dictionaries, it is a list of 'hard' words: it was not thought necessary to include many of the features we may expect to find in dictionaries today, such as common words and meanings, etymological information, syllable structures, pronunciations, parts of speech, synonyms, and antonyms. But by the beginning of the eighteenth century, many of these features came to be included. For example, John Kersey's *Dictionarium Anglo-Britannicum; or, a General English Dictionary*, which first appeared in 1715, includes definitions of common words, and Nathan Bailey's *Dictionarium Britannicum* (1730) includes as many as 49,500 entries.

The culmination of dictionary-making in the eighteenth century is Samuel Johnson's two-volume *Dictionary of the English Language*, which appeared in 1755.

It is a monumental achievement for an individual; Johnson wrote it over a period of seven years. It equals the dictionaries produced by the French and Italian academies. It has obvious faults, such as weak etymologies, unreliable pronunciations, and words that are questionably English. However, the definitions that are marred by personal prejudices (e.g. *excise* 'a hateful tax levied upon commodities') are balanced by those that have warmth and humor (*mouse* 'the smallest of all beasts; a little animal haunting houses and corn fields, destroyed by cats'). There is no doubt that it established modern lexicographic practice: Johnson was the first to use quotations from written texts in order to illustrate the usage of words and the range of their meanings in a monolingual English dictionary (see Landau 2001:64). Johnson's professed aims were to settle orthography, display analogy, regulate the structure of words, and ascertain the signification of words; he was largely successful in fixing both spelling and meaning as well as in encouraging the acceptance of Latinate vocabulary.

An American counterpart to Johnson's dictionary was Noah Webster's *An American Dictionary of the English Language*, which appeared in 1828 (see the title page reproduced in Figure 11.2). Webster intended to establish an American national norm distinct from the British standard of usage. Webster asserted, 'Our political harmony is concerned in a uniformity of language. As an independent nation, our honor requires us to have a system of our own, in language as in government' (quoted in Knowles 1997:134). (In Chapter 13, we look at Webster's influence on American spelling conventions.)

Let us look at the results of these lexicographic developments by examining some sample entries from a twenty-first-century dictionary, *The American Heritage Dictionary of the English Language*. In the entry for *lady* (see Figure 11.3), we can see a number of standard features which are described in the introductory guide to the dictionary:

- the pronunciation and stress of the word (note that North American dictionaries often use their own systems of representing pronunciation, not the IPA, and a pronunciation guide is given at the beginning and often on each page of the dictionary);
- the syllable structure of the word;
- the part of speech (here '*n.*' represents 'noun') and subclass, such as transitive and intransitive for verbs;
- the variant or inflected forms of the word (here '-dies' represents the plural form 'ladies';
- the meaning of the word, numbered and ordered from most frequent to least frequent and organized by part of speech;
- status labels such as '*Informal*' in 5b and '*Slang*' in 8 or a dialect label such as '*Chiefly British*' in 6;
- the etymology following in brackets, tracing the word back in time; this dictionary refers readers to the PIE root given in its appendix, here **dheigh-*; and
- the usage note describing the appropriate contexts for use of this word or relevant synonyms (as judged by the usage panel).

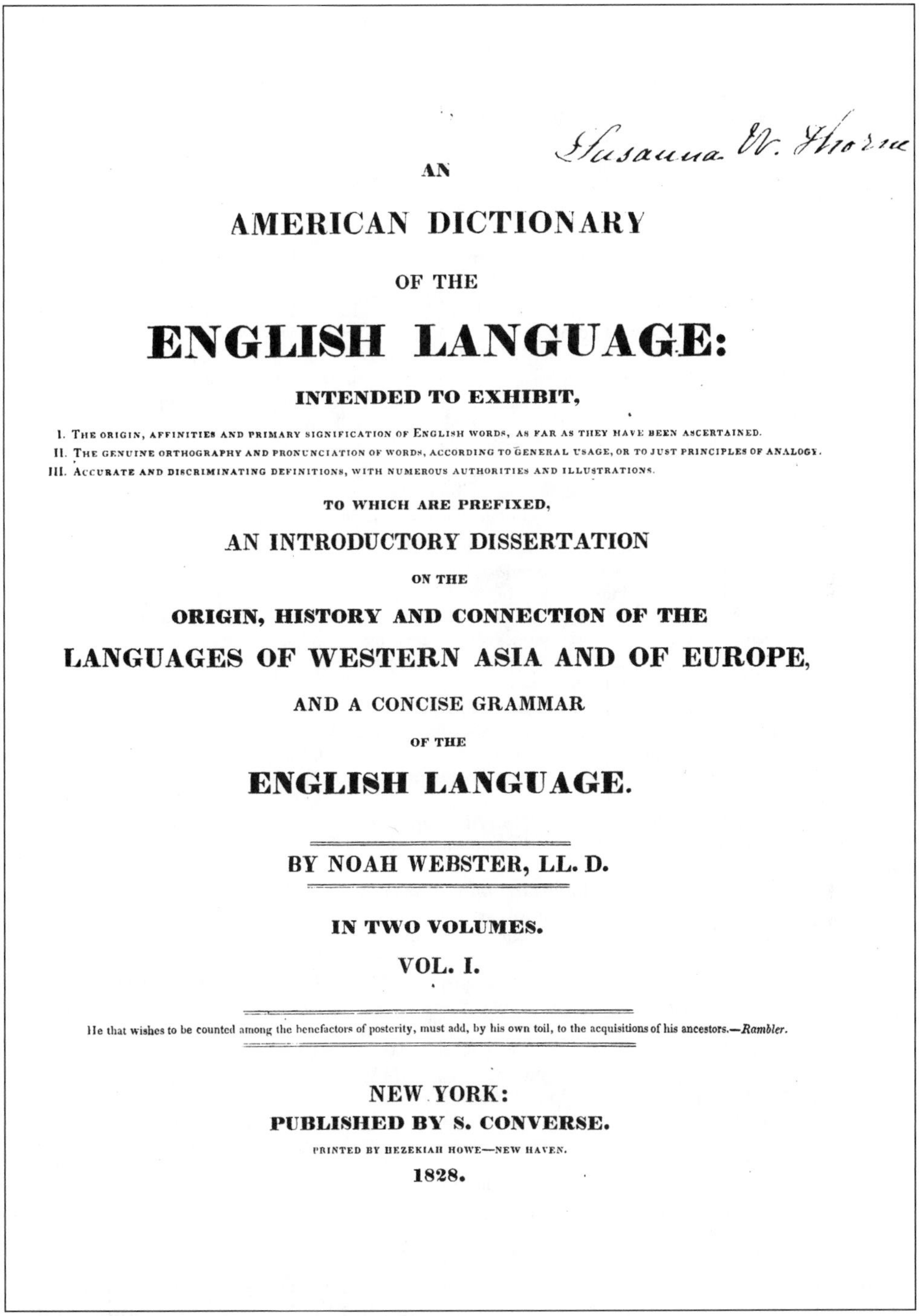

Susanna W. Thorne

AN

AMERICAN DICTIONARY

OF THE

ENGLISH LANGUAGE:

INTENDED TO EXHIBIT,

I. The origin, affinities and primary signification of English words, as far as they have been ascertained.
II. The genuine orthography and pronunciation of words, according to general usage, or to just principles of analogy.
III. Accurate and discriminating definitions, with numerous authorities and illustrations.

TO WHICH ARE PREFIXED,

AN INTRODUCTORY DISSERTATION

ON THE

ORIGIN, HISTORY AND CONNECTION OF THE

LANGUAGES OF WESTERN ASIA AND OF EUROPE,

AND A CONCISE GRAMMAR

OF THE

ENGLISH LANGUAGE.

BY NOAH WEBSTER, LL. D.

IN TWO VOLUMES.

VOL. I.

He that wishes to be counted among the benefactors of posterity, must add, by his own toil, to the acquisitions of his ancestors.—*Rambler.*

NEW YORK:
PUBLISHED BY S. CONVERSE.
PRINTED BY HEZEKIAH HOWE—NEW HAVEN.
1828.

Figure 11.2   The Title Page of Webster's *American Dictionary* (First Edition, 1828) (image courtesy of UBC Special Archives)

la·dy (lā′dē) *n., pl.* **-dies 1.** A well-mannered and considerate woman with high standards of proper behavior. **2a.** A woman regarded as proper and virtuous. **b.** A well-behaved young girl. **3.** A woman who is the head of a household. **4.** A woman, especially when spoken of or to in a polite way. **5a.** A woman to whom a man is romantically attached. **b.** *Informal* A wife. **6. Lady** *Chiefly British* A general feminine title of nobility and other rank, specifically; **a.** Used as the title for the wife or widow of a knight or baronet. **b.** Used as a form of address for a marchioness, countess, viscountess, baroness, or baroness. **c.** Used as a form of address for the wife or widow of a baron. **d.** Used as a courtesy title for the daughter of a duke, a marquis, or an earl. **e.** Used as a courtesy title for the wife of a younger son of a duke or marquis. **7. Lady** The Virgin Mary. Usually used with *Our*. **8.** *Slang* Cocaine. [Middle English, mistress of a household, from Old English *hlǣfdige*. See **dheigh-** in Appendix 1.]

Usage Note Lady is normally used as a parallel to *gentleman* to emphasize norms expected in polite society or in situations requiring courtesies: *Ladies and gentlemen, your attention please, I believe the lady in front of the counter was here before me.* The attributive use of *lady,* as in *lady doctor,* is widely regarded as condescending and inappropriate. When the sex of the person is relevant, the preferred term for this usage is *woman*. The adjectival form *female* is also acceptable; in fact, twice as many members of the Usage Panel prefer *female* and *male* to *woman* and *man* as modifiers in the sentence. *President Clinton interviewed both _____ and _____ candidates for the position of Attorney General.*

lady beetle also **la.dy.bee.tle** (lā′dē′bēt′l) *n.* See **ladybug.**
la·dy·bird (lā′dē′bûrd′) *n.* See **ladybug.**
la·dy·bug (lā′dē′bûg′) *n.* Any of numerous small, rounded, usually brightly colored beetles of the family Coccinellidae, often reddish with black spots and feeding primarily on insect pests, such as scale insects and aphids. Also called *lady beetle, ladybird.* [Probably from its seven spots being considered a symbol of the seven sorrows of the Virgin Mary.]
Lady Chapel also **lady chapel** *n.* A chapel, as in a cathedral or church, usually located behind the sanctuary and dedicated to the Virgin Mary.
Lady Day *n. Chiefly British* Annunciation, celebrated on March 25.
la·dy·fin·ger (lā′dē-fing′gər) also **la·dys·fin·ger** (lā′dēz-) *n.* A small finger-shaped sponge cake.
la·dy·fish (lā′dē-fish′) *n., pl.* **ladyfish or -fish·es** Any of several marine fishes, especially the tarpon *Elops saurus,* a game fish of tropical seas. Also called *tenpounder.*
lady in waiting *n., pl.* **ladies in waiting** A lady of a court appointed to serve or attend a queen, princess, or royal duchess.
la·dy·kill·er (lā′dē-kil′ər) *n. Slang* A man reputed to be exceptionally attractive to and often ruthless with woman.
la·dy·like (lā′dē-līk′) *adj.* **1.** Characteristic of a lady; well-bred. **2.** Appropriate for or becoming to a lady. See synonyms at **female. 3.** Unduly sensitive to matters of propriety or decorum. **4.** Lacking virility or strength. —**la′dy·like′ness** *n.*
la·dy·love (lā′dē-lûv′) *n.* A woman or girl who is someone's sweetheart.
la·dys·fin·ger (lā′dēz-fing′gər) *n.* Variant of **ladyfinger.**
la·dy·ship also **La·dy·ship** (lā′dē-ship′) *n.* Used with *Your, Her,* or *Their* as a title and form of address for a woman or women holding the rank of lady.
la·dy′s man also **la·dies′ man** (lā′dēz) *n.* A man who enjoys and attracts the company of women.
lady′s slipper *n.* Any of various orchids of the genus *Cypripedium,* having usually solitary, variously colored flowers with an inflated, pouch-like lip. Also called *moccasin flower.*

Figure 11.3   The Entry for *lady* from *The American Heritage Dictionary of the English Language,* 4th edn (copyright © 2010 by the Houghton Mifflin Company; reproduced by permission of The American Heritage Dictionary of the English Language, 4th edn)

Derived or compounded forms starting with *lady* follow this entry; whether these forms are standardly written as one word, as two separate words, or as a hyphenated word is conventional and the dictionary informs us of the accepted form. Information on capitalization is also provided.

Exercise 11.4 Eighteenth-Century Usage/Lexicography

1. Why did eighteenth-century grammarians argue whether usage (custom) provided the best basis for standard English?

   _____

   _____

   _____

   _____

   _____

   _____

2. What did Noah Webster mean when he said that following usage is 'like fixing a light house on a floating island'?

   _____

   _____

   _____

   _____

   _____

3. Who is the pre-eminent figure in eighteenth-century English lexicography, and why?

   _____

   _____

   _____

   _____

   _____

RECOMMENDED WEB LINKS

A number of primary documents by Samuel Johnson may be found on the web:

http://andromeda.rutgers.edu/~jlynch/Texts/preface.html
http://andromeda.rutgers.edu/~jlynch/Texts/plan.html

A brief discussion of prescriptivism may be found at:

http://www.lsadc.org/info/ling-fields-prescrip.cfm

A weblog entitled 'The Codifiers and the English Language' is maintained by Ingrid Tieken-Boon van Ostade, Anita Auer, et al.:

http://codifiers.weblog.leidenuniv.nl/2007/08/09/about-this-weblog

Much valuable information on English prescriptivism and standardization can be found on the Historical Sociolinguistics Network:

http://www.philhist.uni-augsburg.de/hison/index.php

You can read Robert Cawdrey's early (1604) dictionary, *A Table Alphabetical*, at:

http://www.library.utoronto.ca/utel/ret/cawdrey/cawdrey0.html

FURTHER READING

For further information on Early Modern English syntax, see:

Denison, David. 1993. *English Historical Syntax*. London and New York: Longman.
Fischer, Olga, and Wim van der Wurff. 2006. 'Syntax'. *A History of the English Language*. Ed. by Richard M. Hogg and David Denison, 109–98. Cambridge: Cambridge University Press.
Nevalainen, Terttu. 2006. 'Mapping Change in Tudor English'. *The Oxford History of English*. Ed. by Lynda Mugglestone, 178–211. Oxford and New York: Oxford University Press.
Rissanen, Matti. 1999. 'Syntax'. *The Cambridge History of the English Language. Vol. III: 1476–1776*. Ed. by Roger Lass, 187–331. Cambridge: Cambridge University Press.

A discussion of both prescriptivism and standardization may be found in:

Nevalainen, Terttu, and Ingrid Tieken Boon van Ostade. 2006. 'Standardisation'. *A History of the English Language*. Ed. by Richard M. Hogg and David Denison, 271–311. Cambridge: Cambridge University Press.

For a very good introduction to the eighteenth-century grammarians and their concerns, set in their historical contexts, see:

Baugh, Albert C., and Thomas Cable. 2001. 'The Appeal to Authority, 1650–1800', *A History of the English Language*. 5th edn. Upper Saddle River, NJ: Prentice Hall.

More detailed discussions of usage and grammar in the eighteenth century (and extending into the nineteenth and twentieth centuries) may be found in:

Finegan, Edward. 1998. 'English Grammar and Usage'. *The Cambridge History of the English Language. Vol. IV: 1776–1997*. Ed. by Suzanne Romaine, 536–88. Cambridge: Cambridge University Press.

Leonard, Sterling A. 1929. *The Doctrine of Correctness in English Usage, 1700–1800*. Madison: University of Wisconsin Press.

Michael, Ian. 1970. *English Grammatical Categories and the Tradition to 1800*. Cambridge: Cambridge University Press.

A very accessible account of the history of individual usage problems in English is:

Webster's Dictionary of English Usage. 1989. Springfield, MA: Merriam-Webster.

For a systematic survey of usage problems and their treatment in particular eighteenth-century grammars, see:

Sundby, Bertil, Anne Kari Bjørge, and Kari E. Haugland. 1991. *A Dictionary of English Normative Grammar 1700–1800*. Amsterdam and Philadelphia: John Benjamins.

For a discussion of eighteenth-century dictionaries within the larger tradition of lexicography, see:

Green, Jonathon. 1996. *Chasing the Sun: Dictionary Makers and the Dictionaries They Make*. New York: Henry Holt & Co.

Landau, Sidney I. 2001. *Dictionaries: The Art and Craft of Lexicography*. 2nd edn. Cambridge: Cambridge University Press.

FURTHER VIEWING

You may wish to view the following documentary:

Part 3, *A Muse of Fire*, from *The Story of English*. BBC-TV co-production with MacNeil-Lehrer Productions in association with WNET, 1986.

12 Modern English

OVERVIEW

This chapter studies grammatical changes since the Early Modern English period, and examines the consequences of the spread of English over a wide geographical area. We look first at modern borrowings from a variety of languages. We describe then the most complete record of the vocabulary of English, which is the *Oxford English Dictionary*, completed in the early twentieth century. We then turn to the developments in progress in Present-Day English, reviewing how new words are created and how grammar is changing. We end with a discussion of the effects of twentieth-century media (radio, television, and computer) on the English language.

OBJECTIVES

The primary objective in this chapter is to understand developments that have occurred after the Early Modern period, including:

- syntactic changes,
- modern borrowings, and
- changes in progress.

With the aid of a dictionary, you will be able to determine the source and transmission routes of a borrowing and identify the processes by which new words are formed. You will also gain a better understanding of the effects of new media upon the language from a linguistic point of view.

Grammatical and Lexical Changes since Early Modern English

While the phonological and morphological features of Modern English were fairly well established by the end of the Early Modern period, a number of grammatical changes occurred after that period. Accompanying these innovations to the grammar were additions to the vocabulary. A new dictionary of English, the *Oxford English Dictionary*, appearing in the late nineteenth century, sought among other things to record the growing vocabulary of the language.

Grammatical Changes

The Progressive Passive

The progressive passive developed as a combination of the progressive (*be* + present participle) and the passive (*be* + past participle) to yield *be* + *being* + past participle, as in ModE *The cake is being baked*. Its first evidence is from 1795 in a private letter: 'like a fellow whose uttermost grinder is being torn out by the roots by a mutton-fisted barber' (*OED*). Nineteenth-century grammarians were appalled at the construction: 'an outrage upon English idiom, to be detested, abhorred, execrated' wrote one in 1837, 'illogical, confusing, inaccurate, unidiomatic', a 'monstrosity', chided another (1871).[1] Nevertheless, it entered general usage and became common by the end of the nineteenth century. While the progressive passive is now standard, some extensions of it that have developed in the twentieth century are still only marginally acceptable in the eyes of many: the perfect progressive passive (e.g. *that man has been being worked too hard*) and the modal progressive passive (e.g. *that man should be being given a raise*).

Progressives with be

Active progressives with *be* also began to occur. First we find the combination of the progressive + *be* + a predicate adjective (e.g. *you are being wicked/candid/diligent/ clever*), which appeared at the end of the eighteenth century. The combination of the progressive + *be* + a predicate noun (e.g. *you are being a fool/a bore*) arrived a century later. The progressive with state verbs such as *know, like, live,* and *feel,* (as in *I am loving that hat* and *I am living with my parents*) seems to have been a possible construction as early as Middle English.

The get-*Passive*

The *get*-passive (or *actional passive*) developed, with *get* as the auxiliary (e.g. *He got fired/caught/hit/carried away/run over*). While the first recorded use of this construction comes from the mid-seventeenth century, it did not become usual until the nineteenth century.

---

1   See Baugh and Cable (2002:293) and Traugott (1972:178).

The *get*-passive is not synonymous with the *be*-passive. The focus in the *get*-passive is on an action, change, or a coming into being, rather than on the resulting state as is usually the case in the *be*-passive (also called the *stative passive*). The *be*-passive can be ambiguous, however. For example, if we compare *they got married* with *they were married*, we see that the first emphasizes the change of state, whereas the second could either describe a resulting or ongoing state ('they were in a married state in the past') or an action ('they weren't married and then they did something to become married'). The development of the *get*-passive has thus restored a distinction not possible since early Middle English, when *weorþan* 'to become' was lost as a passive auxiliary.

The *get*-passive is perhaps still considered colloquial, and its combination with other forms, such as a modal auxiliary and the perfect (*should have gotten arrested*), dates only from the 1950s.

The Indirect Passive

The indirect passive arose after the sixteenth century. To illustrate this construction, we can begin with an active sentence containing both a direct object (*a watch*) and an indirect object (*John*):

> *The company gave a watch to John on his retirement.*

A regular passive, which has been possible since Old English times, is formed by making the original direct object of the active sentence the subject of the passive:

> *A watch was given to John on his retirement.*

In an indirect passive, the original indirect object becomes the subject:

> *John was given a watch on his retirement.*

The Prepositional Passive

The prepositional passive, which occurred as early as the Old English period, became more frequent in the modern period. In this construction, a prepositional verb—that is, a verb combined with a preposition, such as *agree to, depend on, laugh at*—is passivized. For example, let's begin with an active sentence:

> *We agreed to the terms.*

In a prepositional passive, the object of the preposition *to* rather than a direct object becomes the subject of the passive sentence:

> *The terms were agreed to (by us).*

The result is that the preposition is separated from its object and is 'stranded'. Since the agent phrase *by us* can be omitted, the preposition often occurs at the end of the sentence, violating prescriptive rules.

Phrasal Verbs

Phrasal verbs began to proliferate. These are constructions consisting of a verb and a post-verbal particle, such as *heat up* or *run down*. They may or may not include a direct object, being transitive or intransitive:

transitive	**intransitive**
put (something) *away*	*touch down*
turn (something) *off*	*play around*
find (something) *out*	*catch on*
bring (something) *up*	*turn up*
live (something) *down*	*give in*

The neutral term *particle* is used because the grammatical status of the post-verbal word is unclear (though historically it is an adverb). Their most striking feature is that the particle can appear before or after the direct object in transitive phrasal constructions, as in *He handed over the evidence* or *He handed the evidence over*. In this respect, they differ from prepositional verbs such as *agree to, hope for, look into, work for, insist on,* and *hear of,* in which the preposition always precedes the object in an active sentence; *She hoped for better news* is possible, but not **She hoped better news for*.

The semantics of phrasal verbs is as distinctive as their syntax. The particle no longer retains its literal spatial meaning. One can *drink up* as well as *drink down* a beverage, for example, or *burn up* and *burn down* a house, or *close up* and *close down* a business. In these combinations, the particle seems to express the notion of result or completion.

Phrasal verbs first appeared in the Old English period, became increasingly common in Middle English, and finally acquired their full idiomatic properties in Early Modern English. They are highly productive in Modern English, especially in North America, but still condemned by prescriptivists as colloquial or as semantically vague or redundant; it is felt that they have displaced more elegant and expressive Romance verbs, as the following equivalents might suggest:

bring about/cause	*size up/estimate*	*look over/inspect*
egg on/incite	*give up/surrender*	*work out/solve*

Often, however, no clear Latinate equivalents exist, especially in the case of more idiomatic phrasal verbs such as *live down*. Because phrasal verbs replaced many prefixed verbs inherited from Old English (such as *forgive* or *believe*), we see again the tendency of English to become more analytic over time.

A related construction consists of a verb plus what was originally an adjective rather than an adverb; like the particle of a phrasal verb, the adjective is movable, as in:

cut open the melon ~ cut the melon open

wipe clean the counter ~ wipe the counter clean

When the adjective is in final position, it likewise expresses a sense of resultant state.

Composite Predicates

Simple verbs could be replaced by so-called composite predicates, which consist of a *quasi-auxiliary*—that is, a verb of general meaning such as *do, have, make, draw, give,* and *take*—in combination with a noun that has been formed from a verb. Below are some typical replacements:

call	*give a call, make a call*
look	*have a look, take a look*
try	*have a try*
approve	*give approval*
care	*take care*
attend	*pay attention*
dive	*do a dive*
wash	*do the wash*
refer	*make reference to*
conclude	*draw a conclusion from*
assume	*make an assumption*

Note that there are some dialect differences in the use of composite predicates; thus, British speakers say *have a seat* and *make a study* while North American speakers say *take a seat* and *do a study*.

Purists often disapprove of composite predicates, which they claim are needlessly wordy and feel are less 'active' because the action is expressed by a noun rather than a verb. However, these constructions have legitimate uses such as allowing modification (e.g. one can say *take a long bath* but not **bathe longly*).

The development of phrasal verbs and composite predicates, both consisting of a phrase rather than a single form, is consistent with the increasing analyticity of the English language.

Modal Auxiliaries

Generally, the modern period has seen the demise of the subjunctive inflection and its replacement by modal auxiliaries. In independent clauses, as we have seen, the subjunctive is retained only in fixed expressions such as *suffice it to say,* and *God bless you*. In dependent clauses, some speakers use the subjunctive when expressing a conditional sense, especially in more fixed expressions (e.g. *if I were you, though he be late*); increasingly, this is being replaced by the indicative (e.g. *if I was you, though he is late*). The subjunctive has only one productive form in North American English, as discussed in Chapter 13.

'Stacked Noun' Constructions

Modern English, particularly in technical or business writing, has developed a tendency to use so-called 'stacked noun' constructions, formed with a string of nouns functioning adjectivally as in *automobile-assembly plant, air-traffic-control officer, task-force recommendations,* and *death-penalty opponents*. These constructions could be analyzed as kinds of super-compounds, rather like the compounding in other Germanic languages (see Chapter 6).

Exercise 12.1 ModE Grammatical Changes

In each of the following sentences identify the grammatical feature(s) which have developed since Early Modern English.

a.   He was given the boot (i.e. fired) for poor performance.

_____

b.   He thought they were being ridiculous.

_____

c.   He figured he should be being considered for promotion.

_____

d.   He wanted to show them up.

_____

e.   In no time, a plan got drawn up by him.

_____

Modern Borrowings

From the Renaissance on, borrowings in English have been characterized by the diversity of their source languages. While the traditional languages—Latin, Greek, French, and Low Germanic (e.g. Dutch as well as the Celtic and Scandinavian languages)—continue to function as the source of many English loan words in the modern period, the variety of non-Indo-European and other Indo-European languages contributing to vocabulary continues to grow. Contact with these languages comes in part through the distribution of English over the globe. In North America, English was brought into contact with indigenous languages, in addition to African languages, French, Spanish, German, Italian, Portuguese, Modern Greek, Indic and Slavic languages, and Chinese, among others; in South Africa it met with Dutch (Afrikaans) and native languages such as Bantu and the Khoisan languages; in India with Dravidian and the Indic languages; in New Zealand with Maori (a Polynesian language); and in Australia with various Aboriginal and immigrant languages.

Borrowings from Latin and Greek have continued in Modern English but differ from those of earlier periods in being exclusively learned, often found in the other European languages, and frequently non-existent as words in the classical period. That is, they are neo-Latin or neo-Greek words, formed out of Latin and Greek morphemes. These borrowings constitute a large part of the technical vocabulary of the present age, the language of science, medicine, engineering, computers, and warfare. The use of Latin prefixes in deriving these words is common, as in *ultraviolet, multilateral, prenatal, intravenous, interferon, extraterrestrial, protein, counterintelligence, transformer*, and *nitroglycerine*. Some of the words, such as *television, neonatal, antibiotic, hypodermic,* and *polypeptide*, are hybrids formed from Greek and Latin morphemes. The size of the technical vocabulary of Modern English is very large. In fact, the Greek and Latin vocabulary of Modern English is larger than the vocabularies of either Greek or Latin in the classical periods. Furthermore, much of the technical vocabulary has entered general usage, such as *bronchitis, anesthetic, arteriosclerosis, enzyme, catalyst, radioactive, microprocessor, hormone, relativity, anemia,* and *ozone*.

Another feature of neo-Latin forms is the complete disregard of the grammar (inflections) of Latin forms (as usual, V stands for 'verb' here, N for 'noun', etc.):

V > N	*caret* 'it is lacking'	*deficit* 'it is lacking'	*exit* 'it departs'
	fiat 'let it be done'	*habitat* 'it dwells'	*credo* 'I believe'
	placebo 'I shall please'	*caveat* 'let him beware'	*veto* 'I forbid'
	memento 'remember!'	*recipe* 'take!'	*posse* 'be able'
	habeas corpus 'you shall have the body'		
ADJ > N	*bonus* 'good'	*quota* 'how great'	*integer* 'whole'
ADV > N	*alias* 'otherwise'	*alibi* 'elsewhere'	*interim* 'meanwhile'
	item 'just so'		

Borrowings from the other traditional sources of English loan words have been less important in the modern period. Words borrowed from French are still quite common, but less clearly assimilated into English; they often retain their original accented syllable, as in *risqué, sauté, protégé, trousseau, platoon, morale, montage, éclair, gourmet, repertoire, massage, café, plateau,* and *matinée*, or they have [ž] in initial position (where it is never found in the native vocabulary), as in *genre* or *gendarme*. Borrowings from the Celtic languages, never very frequent, refer in the modern period almost exclusively to cultural items with Celtic associations, such as *plaid, whiskey, blarney, leprechaun, shamrock, brogue, clan, cairn*, and *banshee*. Scandinavian loan words of the modern period also name items clearly bound to the parent culture, such as *saga, ski, geyser, ombudsman*, and *smorgasbord*. Finally, borrowings from Dutch, Flemish, and Low German fall into several narrowly defined semantic areas, such as food (*waffle, cookie, slaw*) and drink (*geneva* > *gin*), art (*sketch*), and sailing (*schooner*), as was true even in the earlier periods. A number of borrowings have been taken from Dutch immigrants to North America. Others, such as *veldt, trek*, and *wildebeest*, have been taken from Afrikaans, the South African development of Dutch.

Moving on to the non-traditional sources, both Indo-European and non-Indo-European, we must keep in mind that the route of transmission might be quite complex, and that we must often distinguish the ultimate source from the intermediate and immediate sources. The Indo-European languages that have contributed words to English in the modern period include Spanish, Portuguese, Italian, High German and Yiddish, the Balto-Slavic languages, and the Indo-Iranian languages.

Spanish borrowings naming landforms, food, flora, and fauna have often emerged in the New World, particularly in the American Southwest (e.g. *taco, ranch, gringo, canyon, rodeo, guerilla, silo*). Portuguese borrowings (e.g. *piranha, samba*) become much less common in the modern period.

Italian borrowings are often concentrated in particular semantic domains, including music (*piano, concert, sonata*), architecture (*stucco, cupola, piazza, studio, casino*), and food (*salami, pasta, spaghetti, artichoke*). Some Italian terms have come directly from immigrants to North America.

Borrowings from High German date primarily from the eighteenth and nineteenth centuries, usually in areas of scholarship (mineralogy, geology, linguistics, etc.) (*nickel, gestalt, leitmotif*), schooling (*kindergarten, seminar*), and food and drink (*delicatessen, strudel, pretzel*). A number of borrowings from Yiddish, a dialect of German, are found in English. Some Hebrew words have entered English via Yiddish, e.g. *schmooze, meshuga, schlemiel*.

The Slavic languages have contributed words like *borscht, vodka, borzoi*, and *intelligentsia*. In the modern period, Iranian borrowings have tended to enter English via other languages, such as *khaki* via Urdu and *jasmine* via French and Arabic, but direct borrowing is still possible (e.g. *baksheesh*). Because of eighteenth-century colonization, several words have entered English directly from the Indic languages (e.g. *shampoo, jungle, chutney, thug*).

English has borrowed freely from many non-Indo-European languages as well, from Tamil (e.g. *poppadam, mulligatawny*), Japanese (*hibachi, judo, tycoon*), Chinese (*feng shui, kow-tow, pidgin, loquat*), Malay (*gecko, ketchup, sarong*), Hungarian (*goulash, paprika*), Turkish (*fez, tulip*), Arabic (*mecca, kebab*), and Hebrew (*kibbutz, kosher*).

While words from the indigenous languages of South America usually entered English via Spanish in the seventeenth century, those from North American indigenous languages have entered English directly, as, for example, *toboggan, caribou*, *chipmunk*, *squash*, *kayak*, and *chautauqua*. Words of African origin have entered English via Spanish and Portuguese as well as via the language of American slaves (e.g. *cola*, *yam*, *gumbo*, *okra*).

While English has borrowed freely, it may also translate compound words or phrases in the process known as calquing, or loan translation, introduced in Chapter 6. In Modern English, the German compounds *Lehnwort, akademische Freiheit, Wunderkind, Weltanschauung, Zeitgeist, Weltschmerz*, and *Blitzkrieg* have been translated into English as *loan word, academic freedom, wonder child, world view, spirit of the times, world-weariness*, and *lightning warfare*; French *nom de plume* appears as *pen name*, Italian *la dolce vita* as *the good life*, and Spanish *momento de la verdad* as *the moment of truth*. A very interesting example of calquing is the set of psychoanalytic terms, *id, ego*, and *superego*; these are translations of the German terms used by Freud, *es, ich*, and *Überich*, into Latin. Their English translations would be 'it', 'I', and 'over-I', which were perhaps not considered to have the status of the Latin equivalents as technical terms. At times we use the foreign phrase along with the calque (as is the case with *Blitzkrieg* and *Zeitgeist*), whereas at other times we simply borrow the foreign phrase, as with French *joie de vivre, laissez-faire, hors d'oeuvre, de jour, à la mode, maître d'hôtel*, or *savoir faire*.

Joseph Williams (1975:116) suggests that we can distinguish two categories of borrowed words in English, and consequently two reasons for borrowing. First, the words may name objects or activities associated with another culture. This may occur even if the thing itself does not become part of an English-speaking country's general culture, as with *kibbutz, fez, geisha, samovar*, and *guilder*, although in other cases the object or activity has made the cultural leap, as with *pickle, chess, ketchup, bagel*, and *skunk*. The concept and the term may be restricted to a specialized group within the culture, such as the technical terms *umlaut, ablaut, sandhi*, and *Sprachgefühl* used by linguists. Second, borrowed words may capture a concept already existing in our culture but not previously distinguished by a name, such as Dutch *boss*, Italian *ghetto*, Scots Gaelic *slogan*, Latin *creed*, Spanish *vigilante*, Japanese *tycoon*, and Irish *blarney*. These words may have crystallized a semantic focus on a concept that used to be amorphous or not clearly delineated.

The *Oxford English Dictionary*

Although Johnson's 1755 dictionary represented a large advance in the art of lexicography, some 100 years later London's Philological Society began to discuss the deficiencies of dictionaries in terms of completeness and the historical information provided. In 1858, these philologists (the word is derived from the Latin *philologia*, meaning 'love of learning', but refers in English specifically to people who study languages) proposed a book that they intended to call a *New English Dictionary on*

Historical Principles. The following year, they entered into an agreement with Clarendon Press, part of Oxford University, for its publication.

The professed aim of the dictionary was to record every word of English and to trace its history (forms, spellings, meanings, uses, pronunciations, etymology) with a full selection of quotations. Volunteers were solicited to read texts and collect quotations on slips of paper, which were then used as evidence and illustration by the lexicographers in writing their definitions. Texts published by the Early English Text Society and by the Chaucer Society provided much of the material for earlier English. The dictionary was issued in installments beginning in 1884 and was completed

Figure 12.1 James A.H. Murray, Editor of the First Published Fascicles of the *Oxford English Dictionary*, in His 'Scriptorium' (reprinted with the permission of the Secretary to the Delegates of Oxford University Press)

in 1928, eventually comprising 10 volumes, 15,487 pages, 240,165 entries, and 1,800,000 quotations. (The entire work was supplemented in 1933 and reissued in 13 volumes. A 20-volume second edition was issued in 1989.) In the process, 5 million slips of paper had been collected, and six chief editors had overseen the project. The end result—a monumental achievement—represented a more objective and scientific approach to dictionary-writing than the personal approach of Samuel Johnson and other eighteenth-century lexicographers. The dictionary is now an electronic file that continues to be worked on, and many library computers offer access to it.

Exercise 12.2 Modern Borrowings

1. Using the *OED*, look up the following words and determine their histories. Give the year of first attestation; then, using the derived-from symbol (<), show transmission history from original languages; then give the etymological meaning. Finally, state which of these words are probably learned borrowings.

    a. taiga _____

    _____

    b. pastiche _____

    _____

    c. coyote _____

    _____

    d. plutonium _____

    _____

    e. hibernate _____

    _____

    f. decathlon _____

    _____

    g. fauna _____

    _____

    h. federalist _____

    _____

i. hammock _____

_____

j. hangar _____

_____

k. souvenir _____

_____

Changes in Progress

Neologisms

In addition to borrowing, which results from language contact, there are many means for creating new words that are internal to the language. Rarely do we invent a completely new word or morpheme; when we do so, and the word is accepted into common usage, it is called a 'coinage'. The words *googol* 'ten raised to the hundredth power' (coined in 1940 and later adapted as *Google*, the name of the Internet search engine) and *quark* 'sub-atomic particle' (coined in 1964, but associated with a term used by James Joyce in *Finnegan's Wake* in 1939) are some of the few conclusive examples of the process of coinage that can be cited. Other coinages might include onomatopoeic words such as *hiss, buzz, sizzle, meow*, and *woof*, which imitate sounds in nature, or expressions of emotion such as *ouch, phooey, boo-hoo*, and *phew*. Coinages have been attributed to various literary figures, such as Bunyan (*muckrake*), Shakespeare (*multitudinous, bump, dwindle*), Milton (*sensuous, luxurious, astonished, oblivious*), Spenser (*blatant, elfin, shiny, askance*), Byron (*blasé*), and Walpole (*serendipity*). Apart from vocabulary explicitly claimed by authors (e.g. Lewis Carroll's *jabberwocky* or J.R.R. Tolkien's *maril* 'bookbinding'), we cannot know whether an author actually invented the word or whether he or she was simply the first to record it in writing.

Rather than creating or coining words out of thin air, we much more commonly modify existing words. The major means for doing so—compounding and derivation—have already been discussed, as has the less common process of back-formation (see Chapter 3). However, one new kind of compound, verb-verb combinations (such as *kick-start, stir-fry, freeze-dry, slam-dunk, tap-dance, strip-search, force-feed, hang-glide, dive-bomb, blow-dry*) is worthy of note. This pattern finally gained acceptance in the twentieth century and is becoming increasingly productive (Wald and Besserman 2002).

In addition to the major processes, there exist a number of less common ways to create new words in the language. These processes include functional shift (conversion), commonization, clipping, acronyms and initialisms, blends, reduplication, and retronyms.

- A functional shift is the conversion of one part of speech to another without the addition of a suffix. We can convert nouns into verbs (*to shoulder, to telephone*), verbs into nouns (*a drive, a break*), adjectives into verbs (*to better, to tame*), adjectives into nouns (*the rich, a private*), nouns into adjectives (*paper shredder, office building*), adverbs to nouns (*whys and wherefores, the hereafter*), as well as particles to verbs (*to down, to up*). Some recent examples include *heritage* 'of historical, cultural, or scenic value' (N > ADJ, 1970), *to kneecap* 'to cripple by shooting in the legs' (N > V, 1975), *to boot up* 'to prepare a computer for operation' (N > V, 1980), *to chill* 'to pass time idly' (N > V, 1985), and *to green* 'to render sensitive to ecological issues' (ADJ > V, 1985).

- A special kind of functional shift is what we may call commonization, in which a proper noun (naming a real or fictional person, place, or group) is converted into a common noun (*china, mentor, sandwich, volt*), verb (*lynch, pander*), or adjective (e.g. *frank, maudlin*). A derivational suffix may be added to convert a proper noun into a common noun (*chauvinism, nicotine*), verb (*tantalize, pasteurize*), or adjective (*platonic, spartan, turquoise*). A similar process may convert a brand name into a generic or common word, such as *kleenex, band-aid, vaseline,* and *xerox*. Twentieth-century examples include *Alzheimer's disease* (1911), *Ponzi scheme* (1920), *Pilates* (1981), *Teflon* (1983), and *Nintendo* (1989).

- A clipping is the result of deliberately dropping part of a word, usually either the end (*condo < condominium, fax < facsimile*) or the beginning (*burger < hamburger, car < motorcar*) or less often both (*flu < influenza*), while retaining the same meaning and word class. Sometimes a word or part of a word in a phrase is clipped, for example, *movie < moving picture*. A clipping may preserve a prefix or suffix rather than (part of) the root, as in *ex < ex-husband/wife* or *bi < bi-sexual*. Newer clippings include *porn < pornography* (1962), *high tech < high technology* (1972), *cell phone < cellular telephone* (1984), and *crystal meth < crystal methamphetamine* (1984). The term *Wi-Fi* was invented as a clipping for *wireless fidelity* (1999). All dialects include certain distinctive clipped forms; in CanE, for example, we find *emerge < emergency room, physio < physiotherapy/ physiotherapist,* and *grad < graduation ceremony/graduation dinner-dance*.

- In an acronym, the initial letters (or syllables) of words in a phrase are pronounced as a word, as in NATO < N(orth) A(tlantic) T(reaty) O(rganization) (1949), AIDS < a(cquired) i(mmune) d(eficiency) s(yndrome) (1982), *laser < l(ight) a(mplification) (by the) s(timulated) e(mission) (of) r(adiation)* (1960), *radar < ra(dio) d(etection) a(nd) r(anging)* (1940), PIN < p(ersonal) i(dentification) n(umber) (1976), and SARS < s(evere) a(cute) r(espiratory) s(yndrome) (2003). In an initialisms, the initial letters of words in a phrase are pronounced as letters, as in *r.s.v.p. < r(épondez) s('il) v(ous) p(laît), a.m. < a(nte) m(eridiem),* and *p.m. < p(ost) m(eridiem)*. Some twentieth-century examples include *UFO < u(nidentified) f(lying) o(bject)* (1953), *PC < p(ersonal) c(omputer)* (1976) or *p(olitical) c(orrectness)* (1986), and *HTML < h(yper)t(ext) m(arkup) l(anguage)* (1994). Sometimes an initialisms may involve only a single word, as in *ID < identification* or *TV < television*.

- In a blend, two free words are combined and merged phonologically, usually by clipping off the end of the first word and the beginning of the second word (as in *smog < sm(oke) + (f)og, twirl < tw(ist) + (wh)irl, transistor < trans(fer) + (re) sistor*), although sometimes one or the other morpheme is left intact (as in *perma-frost < perma(nent) + frost, videographer < video + (photo)grapher*). Blends are sometimes called *portmanteau* words. Some more recent examples include *breathalyzer < breath + (an)alyzer* (1960), *docudrama < docu(mentary) + drama* (1961), *sit com < sit(uation) + com(edy)* (1964), *televangelist < tel(evision) + evangelist* (1973), *email < e(lectronic) + mail* (1982) (*e-* has become a productive combining form, giving us *e-journal, e-text, e-commerce, e-banking,* etc.), *webcast < web + (broad)cast* (1995), and *podcast < (i)Pod + (broad)cast* (2004).

- Reduplication is a process in which the initial syllable or the entire word is doubled, exactly or with a slight phonological change, as in *ping-pong, wishy-washy, criss-cross, mish-mash* (all 'ablaut' reduplication), *nitty-gritty, namby-pamby, fuddy-duddy* (all 'rhyme' reduplication). Reduplication is often used in children's language or for humorous or ironic effect. Similarly, two words may be brought together in a compound for the sake of rhyme or assonance: some twentieth-century examples include *culture vulture* (1945), *jet set* (1951), *rock 'n' roll* (1954), *brain drain/gain* (1963), *flower power* (1969), *no-go (area)* (1971), *date rape* (1975), *toy boy* (1981), *smart card* (1980), *hip-hop* (1982), and *heart smart* (1989).

- A retronym is a word or phrase created because an existing term once used alone needs to be modified to distinguish it from a term referring to a new development. Thus, the development of *email* leads to the retronym *snail mail,* and the invention of the *digital watch* leads to the retronym *analog watch. Decaffeinated coffee* has prompted the retronym *caffeinated/leaded/regular coffee. Fast food* (first recorded in 1951) has led to the term *slow food* (1974) to refer to more traditional means of cooking.

Concerning the acquisition of new words, the scholar John Algeo concludes:

Without relying on specific percentages, it seems clear that overwhelmingly the major source for new words in English is their composition from morphemes already present in the language, by compounding and affixation. A distant, but still clearly, secondary source is the shifting of old words to new senses and uses. Shortening, borrowing, and blending are relatively minor sources of neologism. The creation of words independently of any [etymological root] is insignificant (1998:87).

Exercise 12.3 Neologisms

Name and describe the process(es) of word formation for the following words.

a.   chocoholic   _____

b.   (on the) q.t.   _____

c.   road rage   _____

d.   do's and don'ts   _____

e.   scuba   _____

f.   sucker (v)   _____

g.   hertz   _____

h.   ROM   _____

i.   rad   _____

j.   alphabet   _____

k.   CD   _____

l.   FIFO   _____

m.   ad   _____

n.   sailplane   _____

o.   double-edged   _____

p.   herky-jerky   _____

Grammatical Changes

Grammatical changes in Present-Day English are perhaps less pervasive and obvious than lexical changes. However, a few are worthy of notice:

1. The quotative constructions, first with *go* 'say' and more recently with *be like*, are highly salient in the speech of young people, as in:

   > She <u>goes</u>, 'Mom wants to talk to you.' It<u>'s like</u>, 'Hah, hah, you're about to get in trouble.'

   > I saw her coming, and I<u>'m like</u>, 'Nooooooooooo.'

Interestingly, *be like* can be used to represent both actual speech and inferred speech or sounds—what the speaker might have been thinking or might have said or uttered, including non-speech sounds. (See Butters 1980 on *go* and Romaine and Lange 1991 on *be like*.) More recently *be all* has come to function in an analogous way, as in *I said something funny, and he's all, 'Write that down!'* The construction also functions in narrative to mark action, as in *I was all laughing at him for days!*, and *I'm all proud of myself for getting the question right*. Waksler (2001:128) argues that this construction is a marker of a speaker's 'upcoming unique characterization of an individual in the discourse'. These constructions are becoming increasingly common, but whether they will become part of the standard dialect remains to be seen.

2. Bauer (1994:51–60) reports on the increased use of periphrastic *more/most* in place of the inflected comparative or superlative in words such as *more common* (cf. *commoner*), *most humble* (cf. *humblest*), *more costly* (cf. *costlier*), *most friendly* (cf. *friendliest*), *more deadly* (cf. *deadlier*), *most bitter* (cf. *bitterest*), *more obscure* (cf. *obscurer*), *more sober* (cf. *soberer*), and *more narrow* (cf. *narrower*). The usage expert H.W. Fowler (2nd edn., 1965) thought that inflected forms were possible with *more timid* (Fowler suggested *timider*), *more dogged* (cf. *doggeder*), *most cheerful* (cf. *cheerfulest*), *most cunning* (cf. *cunningest*), *more damnable* (cf. *damnabler*), and *most awkward* (cf. *awkwardest*), yet these inflected forms seem unlikely today.

3. There is frequent conflation of the past tense and past participle forms of verbs. Usually the past tense form is extended to the past participle. This is especially common in modal + perfect constructions, as in *I would have came*, *He should have gave us*, *I'd have ate it*, and *I should have rang*. The past participle is sometimes used in place of the past tense form, as in *I come to see you yesterday* and *I seen him today*. While one might argue that this is just a case of using the 'wrong' form of the verb, it may well represent an extension of the process of reducing the principal parts of strong verbs (by analogy to weak verbs) to two.

4. Reduction in the use of the objective form of the interrogative/relative pronoun *whom* is another change in progress. This form is now uncommon in questions in contexts where it would be grammatically expected, as in *Whom did you see?* being replaced by *Who did you see?* There is a conflict between the syntactic rule for forming questions, in which the interrogative word always precedes the verb, whether it is subject or object, and a rule of SVO word order natural to English, where subject forms precede the verb and object forms follow it. The latter wins out. *Whom* more generally survives in formal speech and writing. Interrogative *whom* occurs following a preposition, as in *To whom are you speaking?*, though in colloquial usage, this question would be phrased *Who are you speaking to?* As a relative, *whom* is

more commonly retained, even when it does not follow a preposition, as in *There is the woman who(m) you spoke to*, perhaps because it does not occur in the initial position in the sentence. Variation in the use of *who* and *whom* suggests present-day speakers' uncertainty about the use of the subject and object forms. Such is the confusion about the matter that we observe hyper-corrections in such sentences as *Whom do you think you are?*, where traditionally *who* would be expected. Reduction in the use of the objective form *whom* may be seen as consistent with larger changes in English, namely, the loss of case marking and the development of invariable forms; here *whom* seems to follow the pattern of nouns rather than pronouns, which generally retain case marking (e.g. *I/me, he/him, they/them*).

5. Another change in pronoun usage may be even further advanced: the use of the third-person plural pronoun to refer back to a grammatically singular indefinite or generic subject, especially with pronouns such as *everyone* or *everybody*, as in *Everyone has to take their seat now*. By traditional rules of grammatical agreement, *everyone* is a singular form, requiring a singular verb (*has*) and a singular possessive pronoun. Having only the masculine and feminine forms *he/his* and *she/her*, speakers have tried various strategies to overcome the lack of a common-gender (animate) third-person singular-pronoun. Although *he* functioned as a generic third-person singular in earlier English, to be more sensitive to issues of gender equality, contemporary speakers have replaced the masculine with expressions such as *he/she, s/he, his/her*, or *his or her*; have used the feminine; or have alternated between the two gendered pronouns in successive examples. Another strategy is to convert the forms to plural throughout (as in *All students have to take their seats now*). There is a long history of using the third-person plural form, *they/their*, which is gender-neutral as a singular, as in the sentence cited at the beginning of this point, and there appears to be growing acceptance of this stratagem. For example, everyone would accept the sentence *Just about everyone likes ice cream, don't they?* as standard. A further change in pronoun usage is the reanalysis of *none* (< *no one*) as a plural as well as a singular.

6. The existence of such examples as *No cheque's accepted*, in which apostrophe *-s* marks a plural, and *Todays special is corned beef*, in which *-s* without an apostrophe marks a possessive, is increasingly common in standard, written English. Beginning in Middle English, the possessive and the plural fall together formally (due to phonological reduction and analogical leveling) as *-(e)s*, distinguished only by syntactic and semantic context. As a result of confusion stemming from the *his*-genitive in Early Modern English, an apostrophe came to mark the genitive (see Chapter 10) and was prescribed in the eighteenth century, thus establishing a distinction (in the

written form only) between singular and plural possessive (*boy's, boys'*) and the plural (*boys*). Today's confusion over use of the apostrophe points to its non-functionality in written English and suggests its possible loss. Hyper-correction, one explanation of *No cheque's accepted*, is itself a sign of non-functionality. The utter confusion of *it's* and *its* for many writers provides further evidence for the imminent demise of the apostrophe in this context.

7. As we saw in Chapter 3, intensifiers such as *very* are continually in need of replacement by stronger and more expressive forms such as *absolutely, awfully,* and *terribly*; the most common forms in PDE are *really* and *so*. Likewise, we see the rise of new discourse markers to supplement older ones: *well, right, like, and all that, y'know, I mean*. Though generally empty of semantic content, these pragmatic forms structure the discourse and anchor it in the communicative context. While such markers have always existed in spoken discourse, the particular forms used are ephemeral. For example, Old English made use of the form *hwæt*, Middle English the form *anon*, Early Modern English the form *prithee*, all of which are now obsolete. Some discourse markers have endured, such as *well, you know*, and *I guess*, and others have appeared as recently as the middle of the twentieth century, such as *like* (not to be confused with the quotative *like* discussed above), e.g. *Like I'm actually friends with her* (see, for example, D'Arcy 2005). Although such forms were traditionally dismissed as stylistic lapses, there is now considerable interest in their varied and complex pragmatic functions as well as their historical evolution. We can expect that, in time, forms such as *like* will themselves be replaced by newer forms.

It is frequently observed today that even in the written, standard English of educated speakers, rules of usage are commonly violated and that these violations are tolerated, if not indeed accepted. Such violations range from neglecting conventions of usage concerning split infinitives or the ending of sentences with prepositions, to ignoring formal distinctions between adjectives and adverbs (e.g. *real/really [good]*), past tenses and past participles (e.g. *have took/taken, I seen*), transitive and intransitive verbs (e.g. *lie/lay*), or the categories of mass and count (e.g. *less/fewer*), and finally to breaking grammatical rules concerning inflectional forms of case (e.g. *Me and my friend went to a movie last night*) or of degree (e.g, *more smarter, bestest*). Undoubtedly such structures have always been present in colloquial speech, but they have not been part of the written standard because the regulations of eighteenth-century grammarians became part of the school curriculum in the nineteenth century and lasted well into the twentieth century. However, debate within the field of linguistics beginning in the 1930s questioned the sanctity of standard English while legitimating variant forms of the language. This new perspective altered the teaching of grammar in the classroom: prescriptions and proscriptions ceased to be taught, and at the same time non-standard varieties gained acceptance. Today we acknowledge that standard English is a political and social artifact and question the usefulness of many of the prescriptive tenets. The result of these changing attitudes is an increased tolerance of non-standard usage and grammar, not only in spoken English but also in the written form. It may well be that in the future more of the prescriptive rules will be rejected and that we will find the written and spoken forms coming closer together.

Exercise 12.4 Grammatical Changes in Progress

In the following sentences, find and name the feature that violates prescribed standards of grammar.

a. 'Gods Cool' (painted on the window of a car)

_____

_____

b. I took my umbrella because I seen it was going to rain.

_____

_____

c. Who are you looking at?

_____

_____

d. When a student arrives, they must be seated immediately.

_____

_____

e. The line-up at the book store was like an hour!

_____

_____

f. He went, 'Hi!' And I'm like, 'In your dreams.' So then we're all uncomfortable after that.

_____

_____

The Effect of New Media on English

Commentators on language have been quick to condemn the effect of new media (including radio, television, computer, and cell phone transmissions) on language. They have been concerned that these media will lead, or have led, to a decline in linguistic standards of correctness, and they have wondered whether we all might soon be writing as follows:

> My smmr hols wr CWOT. B4, we used 2 go 2 NY 2C my bo, hi GF & thr 3 :-@ kds FTF.[2]
> ['My summer holidays were a complete waste of time. Before, we used to go to New York to see my brother, his girlfriend, and their three screaming kids face to face'.]

In contrast, linguists, while understanding that new media have a profound impact on the way we communicate, are agreed that their effects on the actual structure of the language — its phonology, morphology, and syntax — are relatively minor.

Radio

In the early years (prior to World War II), radio, especially in Great Britain, was seen as a means for standardizing and codifying spoken English. Broadcasters of the British Broadcasting Corporation (BBC) were required to use an accent — called 'Broadcast English' and later 'Received Pronunciation' (RP) — which could serve as a model for the 'best' and most socially accepted form of spoken English. Moreover, the BBC Advisory Committee on Spoken English, an organization much like a language academy (see Chapter 11), was formed to rule on matters of usage and to maintain linguistic standards. However, the expansion of radio in the 1960s and 1970s led to a breakdown of this strict regulation of language practice on British radio: a plurality of accents began to be used in order to reflect the voices of the intended audiences. In the United States, radio had a different history as it was, from the beginning, a commercial endeavor, with many local radio stations incorporating diverse accents and styles. One goal of radio was to make English accessible to the many different linguistic groups in America and hence to unite the nation culturally. However, much like the BBC, the large US radio stations (NBC, CBS) wanted announcers to speak grammatically correct, classless, 'non-accented' (not local or regional, e.g. Southern or New England) English, what is known as 'Network English'. The degree to which US broadcasters were successful in promoting this accent — and indeed the validity of this accent — is debatable. It can be

---

2 A thirteen-year-old Scottish girl is reported to have written an essay with this beginning (Thurlow 2006:16).

concluded that 'contrary to popular belief and contrary to the stated aim of early national broadcasters, the role of radio has been minimal' (Schwyter forthcoming). In fact, in both Great Britain and the United States, there has been a marked shift in the dynamic between radio stations and their listeners. Radio stations no longer see themselves as custodians of 'good English'; rather, they accommodate their language to the speech of their audience. The result has been a 'democraticization' of language on radio.

Television

Television, even more than radio, is popularly seen as an agent of change in language. Just as television is frequently understood as having a negative effect on cognition and behavior, for example by increasing violent tendencies in children watching shows depicting a high degree of violence, it is often seen as contributing to the decline of linguistic standards. But linguists do not generally share this opinion. As Jack Chambers reports, 'The sociolinguistic evidence runs contrary to the deep-seated popular conviction that the mass media influence language profoundly . . . there is no evidence for television or the other popular media disseminating or influencing sound changes or grammatical innovations' (1998:124–6). Chambers goes on to argue that television may allow speakers to experience different linguistic varieties, and it may shape attitudes toward varieties (and even lead to imitations of a prestigious dialect). It may also diffuse vocabulary items, idioms, and catchphrases. But it does not lead to linguistic change, because change typically requires face-to-face interaction (Chambers 1998). William Labov has pointed out that the influence of television does not lead to the convergence or elimination of regional dialects: 'Whatever the influence of the mass media . . . , it doesn't affect the way we speak everyday. And the regional dialects of this country [the United States] are getting more and more different' (see Siegel 2006).

However, there have been relatively few detailed linguistic studies of the effect of television language on the level of accent, morphology, syntax, or even lexis. Television is a rich and diverse medium; viewers are exposed to a wide variety of genres, registers, and styles. An interesting ongoing project (the Glasgow Media Project) is showing some effects of television on the phonology of Glasgow speakers, who are incorporating features of 'media Cockney' (such as [f] for voiceless [θ] in a word such as *think* or [v] for voiced [ð] in a word such as *brother*) portrayed in London-based television programs in their local linguistic system and imbuing them with their own linguistic and social values (see Stuart-Smith n.d.). But television does not work alone; it operates in concert with many other social factors and behaviors. Stuart-Smith (forthcoming) concludes that 'despite arriving late, television may now be admitted into the complex array of factors which together contribute to the historical linguistics of English'.

Electronic Communication and the Internet

The rise of computer-mediated communication is often heralded as a 'revolution' in language. As linguist David Crystal observes, 'we are on the brink of the biggest language revolution ever' (2006b:275). Anne Curzan expands upon this idea:

> the Internet is destabilizing our notion of text and its permanence, as well as our notion of authorship; it has already created an entirely new kind of literacy; it has widened the range and speed of written communication beyond what could be imagined with printed text; and it has the potential to change the standards of written English—whichever world variety of English this standard turns out to be' (2000:300).

Curzan even suggests that we may be witnessing the change between Modern English and the next period of English, perhaps 'Post-modern English'.

But what Crystal refers to as a 'revolution' is the development of a new medium or modality of communication, not necessarily a new variety. The Internet is thus ushering in a revolution much like that brought about by the introduction of printing (see Chapter 9). With some degree of understatement, Crystal notes, 'A new medium of linguistic communication does not arrive very often, in the history of the race' (2006b:272).

Computer-mediated discourse is a realm in which the written language seems to be approaching the spoken word. Indeed, it is typically seen as a hybrid of speech and writing. Like writing, it is text-based (typed) and hence potentially planned, formal, and edited. It does not involve physical contact between interlocutors and thus lacks paralinguistic cues (intonation, stress) and kinesics (facial expressions, gestures). At the same time, much computer-mediated discourse is interactive and displays features of orality, such as informality, playfulness, lack of planning time, and perhaps decreased syntactic length and complexity along with a reduced vocabulary. But as scholars point out, computer-mediated discourse is more than a simple amalgam of oral and written language. It 'selectively and adaptively displays properties of both' and has qualities that neither medium has (Crystal 2006b:51); it is 'distinct from either writing or speaking, sometimes as a blend of the two, but in any event subject to its own constraints and potentialities' (Herring 2001:614).

That said, it has been common to see the language of the Internet as a distinct variety, what Crystal terms 'Netspeak' (also known as 'netlingo' or 'weblish') and defines as 'a type of language displaying features that are unique to the Internet':

- a distinctive lexicon, with words having undergone semantic change from their earlier meanings (*spam* [from a type of 'canned meat' to 'unsolicited email'], *flame* [from 'ignited vapor and gas' to 'a vitriolic or abusive message conveyed over an electronic medium'], *wizard* [from 'one who practices magic' to 'a webmaster']) (see Chapter 3 on semantic change). Often they

are formed through compounding (*webmaster*, *freeware*, *bugtracker*), prefix-
ing (*hypertext*, *email*, *cybersex*), and blending (*emoticon*, *netizen*, *netiquette*)
(see above on blending) as well as playful coinages (*dubiosity*, *geekitude*,
hackification);

- abbreviations ('one of the most remarked features'), including acronyms
(*HTML*, *URL*, *lol* 'laugh out loud', *btw* 'by the way') (see above on acronyms)
and rebus-like forms (*L8R* 'later', *2d4* 'to die for');
- distinctive graphic conventions, such as capitals for 'shouting' and spacing for
'loud and clear';
- emoticons or smileys (☺), repeated vowel and consonant symbols (*soooo*
goood), exaggerated punctuation (!!!!), or verbal glosses (*haha*) for emotional
expression, forms which compensate for much richer emotional meanings sig-
naled in speech by paralanguage;
- new spelling conventions 'used without sanction' (*z* for *s* in *downloadz*, *u* for
you), deviant spellings (*phreak* for *freak*), and non-standard spellings (*nite* for
night); and
- minimalist punctuation or new punctuation conventions, such as punctuation borrowed from programming language (_Hamlet_, <groan>) (Crystal
2006b:39–40, 86–98).

In addition, language on the Internet often features various kinds of ellipses—such
as deletion of unstressed subject pronouns (Ø *hope you're feeling better*), indefinite
and definite articles, auxiliaries, and copulas—as well as contractions and uncor-
rected typos. (Of course, one could question the extent to which these features are
determined by the computer technology, that is, how the medium shapes the form of
language used. Generally, scholars feel that the degree of 'technological determin-
ism' is weaker than popularly assumed.)

Crystal's notion of 'Netspeak' has been rather vigorously criticized for a variety of reasons by scholars working in the field of computer-mediated discourse.
First, it seems to suggest that there is one homogeneous form of language that is
universal to all types of computer communication. Second, it suggests that it is a
new language distinct from standard English, one that is indecipherable to outsiders
and must thus be 'translated' for the uninitiated and codified in dictionaries. Yet
the features of Internet language are not entirely new—many of the abbreviations
have a long history, as do the non-standard spellings, thus underlining a continuity
between pre-digital and digital forms of language. Third, this view has led to simplified and misleading conceptions of computer-mediated discourse. Crispin Thurlow
(2006) refers to this as the 'fetishization' of computer-mediated discourse, where
the popular media present a restricted repertoire of hackneyed expressions with
caricatured and sometimes fictionalized examples of computer-mediated discourse,
which are then held up for ridicule and contempt (perhaps such as the Scottish girl's
lines quoted above).

We must be very careful about making overarching generalizations, because computer-mediated discourse is in fact immensely rich and varied. It is conveyed via different modes and is used in a variety of social contexts, by different configurations of interlocutors, and for a number of different purposes. In fact, Crystal (2006b) notes that there are at least six different situations of use (email, chat groups, virtual worlds, World Wide Web, instant messaging, and blogging). As Susan Herring (2007) shows, this range of 'genres', 'registers', or 'socio-technical modes' depends on the technological medium (whether the communication is synchronous or asynchronous, private, anonymous, limited in size, and so on) and on the social situation of the communication (the participant structure, the characteristics of the participants, the purpose of the interaction, the topic and tone of the communication, the language register used, etc.).

The question to ask in the context of a book on the history of English is whether computer-mediated discourse has led to, or will lead to, fundamental changes in the structure of the language. What has research revealed so far? In a very early study in 1984, not long after the appearance of email, Naomi Baron speculates about 'computer-mediated communication as a force in language change'. She hypothesizes that this type of communication will result in a general reduction (or even elimination) of register shifts, a narrower range of vocabulary, fewer subordinate clauses, and fewer markers of respect than are found in face-to-face communication. She examines the social implications of computer-mediated discourse, suggesting that it could lead to loss of functionality in language (specifically its social function), discouragement of face-to-face communication, an undermining of the social fabric as social distinctions are masked, and a supplanting of persuasion by strict logical argumentation. From a linguistic perspective, she suggests that computer-mediated discourse could have effects on the essential characteristics of both speech and writing: speech would be more objective and logical, but less persuasive and rhetorical, while writing would be clearer, but stylistically more homogeneous and less rich.

The popular press has echoed Baron's concerns and even expanded upon them. If you were to judge by accounts in the popular press, you would conclude that online communication and text messaging are leading to the obliteration of 'proper' English, and even the slow death of language. Such accounts of computer-mediated discourse are highly prescriptive, pointing to the decline of linguistic standards of spelling, punctuation, usage, and grammar and the loss of literacy, and predicting further language decay and even linguistic collapse. Thurlow, in an article entitled 'From Statistical Panic to Moral Panic: The Metadiscursive Construction and Popular Exaggeration of New Media Language in the Print Media' (2006), surveys over a hundred newspaper and magazine articles appearing between 2001 and 2005 and concludes that the popular accounts present 'notoriously inflated and methodologically questionable' statistics about the rise and spread of computer-mediated discourse (its quantity, growth, and monetary value). They also embed their discussion of the presumed harmful impact of computer-mediated discourse on standard English within larger anxieties about the decline in moral standards (especially among young people), perceived threats to the status quo, the unraveling of the social fabric, and the deleterious effects of technology generally. As we saw earlier (in Chapter 1), attitudes toward language change are often part of a more general opposition to social change and innovation.

However, empirical work on computer-mediated discourse, which dates from the mid-1990s, has shown that none of the dire changes have come to pass. Research has shown that the linguistic features of computer-mediated discourse are not the result of speakers' ignorance of the standards of English correctness, but are often a matter of 'deliberate choice' (Herring 2001:617), a flouting or manipulation of the rules for creative and expressive purposes. In a recent study of the language of instant messaging, Sali Tagliamonte and Derek Denis (2008) describe teenage instant messagers as picking and choosing from the entire repertory of stylistic variants and thus showing a skilled command—rather than an ignorance—of their linguistic system. In addition, the researchers show that the use of short forms, abbreviations, and emotional language—the stereotypical features of computer-mediated discourse—is in fact 'infinitesimally small' (2008:24). Furthermore, in respect to a number of changes in progress, instant messaging is actually less innovative than speech; it shows a wider range of variants, including a higher proportion of standard forms. They conclude that instant messaging reflects 'the same structured heterogeneity (variation) and the same dynamic, ongoing processes of linguistic change that are currently underway in the speech community' (2008:25).

Overall, it is unlikely that the features of computer-mediated discourse will migrate outside their own contexts and affect the way we speak in face-to-face interactions or write on paper, thus becoming permanent features of the language. The effects will probably be confined to the lexicon—the vocabulary of computer-mediated communication entering the general lexicon and undergoing semantic extension—and perhaps to the spelling of English, the levels of language where it is relatively easy to introduce innovation. Grammatical change is much less frequent. In fact, very few, if any, grammatical changes can be attributed to computer-mediated discourse. Davis (2000) points to the use of *whisper* as a transitive verb (as in chat groups where one participant will, in order to have an off-group conversation, say, for example, *Kelly, may I whisper you?*), but he also notes that the transitive use of *whisper* is an older form (used, for example, by Dickens).

Might we expect that written language will become less formal in general? If it does, computer-mediated discourse is not the only factor contributing to this shift. Since the eighteenth century, there has been a trend toward less-formal language generally and a tendency for the written genres to become more speech-like. Minimally, computer-mediated discourse might accelerate this trend.

We can argue that the Internet will evolve new genres, adapted to the communicative situations, with new rules and new norms of register and style (Giltrow and

Stein 2009). Awareness of the new genres evolving in computer-mediated discourse allows us to recognize the creative and expressive nature of the discourse. For example, in 2001, the *Guardian* newspaper in Great Britain held a text-message poetry contest. The winning entry, by Hetty Hughes, a twenty-two-year-old student, entitled 'Inspired by Granny. Aw Bless', comments humorously on the possible effects of texting on language:[3]

> txtin iz messin,
> mi headn'me englis,
> try2rite essays,
> they all come out txtis.
> gran not plsed w/letters shes getn,
> swears i wrote better
> b4 comin2uni.
> &she's african

More recently, we have seen the rise of Twitter haiku poetry, or 'twihaiku', as in the following poem:

> Since I fell for you / my sonnets are unfinished / and my skin is pale[4]

A much larger question concerns the dominance of English as the language of the Internet. Will the use of English as a kind of *lingua franca* by both native and non-native speakers and its prestige as the language of the Internet lead to the suppression of other, less-widely spoken languages (to their 'murder'; see Chapter 3)? While English was clearly dominant in the early decades of the Internet, this dominance has weakened considerably in the last decade, and changes are progressing at a rapid pace. By some accounts, English will soon lose its place of dominance and be equaled or surpassed by Chinese (see Paolillo 2005:48).[5] As resources (such as appropriate computer keyboards) become available for speakers of lesser-known languages, the Internet may in fact provide a place for documenting and teaching these languages and could lead to the maintenance of endangered and minority languages, which are dying at an alarming rate.[6]

---

3 For more information on the Guardian's contest, see http://books.guardian.co.uk/games/mobilepoems/0,9405,450649,00.html. On the nature of text-message poetry, see http://www.guardian.co.uk/technology/2001/mar/29/internet.poetry.

4 This poem was written by the user 'makeit2double'; see http://www.makeliterature.com/twihaiku/twitter-poetry for examples of 'twihaiku'.

5 Language use on the internet is notoriously difficult to measure. It is even uncertain what is meant by speaking of the language of the internet: language of users, for example, or the language of web pages?

6 See, for example, the Linguistic Society of America's Committee on Endangered Languages http://www.lsadc.org/info/lsa-comm-endanger.cfm.

RECOMMENDED WEB LINKS

Look at the 'Words of the Decade' section on the American Dialect Society website (http://www.americandialect.org/) and try to determine what process or processes of word formation have been used in creating some of the past words of the year: *bailout* (2008), *subprime* (2007), *to pluto* (2006), and so on.

Other records of new words include:

> http://www.theatlantic.com/past/docs/language/wordwatch.htm (*The Atlantic* online)
> http://www.worldwidewords.org/

FURTHER READING

Modern borrowings as well as neologisms are discussed in:

> Algeo, John. 1998. 'Vocabulary'. *The Cambridge History of the English Language. Vol. IV: 1776–1997*. Ed. by Suzanne Romaine, 57–91. Cambridge: Cambridge University Press.
> Ayto, John. 1999. *A Century of New Words*. Oxford and New York: Oxford University Press.
> Gramley, Stephan. 2001. *The Vocabulary of World English*. London: Arnold.

The following texts contain engaging accounts of the making of the *Oxford English Dictionary*:

> Murray, K.M. Elisabeth. 1977. *Caught in a Web of Words: James A.H. Murray and the* Oxford English Dictionary. Oxford and New York: Oxford University Press.
> Winchester, Simon. 1998. *The Professor and the Madman: A Tale of Murder, Insanity, and the Making of the* Oxford English Dictionary. New York: Viking.
> Winchester, Simon. 2003. *The Meaning of Everything: The Story of the* Oxford English Dictionary. Oxford and New York: Oxford University Press.

A good general introduction to word-formation processes in English is:

> Carstairs-McCarthy, Andrew. 2002. *An Introduction to English Morphology: Words and Their Structure*. Edinburgh: Edinburgh University Press.

On new words, see:

> Algeo, John, and A.S. Algeo (eds). 1991. *Fifty Years 'Among the New Words': A Dictionary of Neologisms, 1941–1991*. New York: Cambridge University Press.
> Barnhart, Robert K., et al. (eds). 1990. *Third Barnhart Dictionary of New English*. Bronx, NY: H.W. Wilson.

For recent discussions of Late Modern English (and into the twentieth century), see:

> Beal, Joan C. 2004. *English in Modern Times: 1700–1945*. London: Arnold.
> Mugglestone, Lynda. 2006. 'English in the Nineteenth Century'. *The Oxford History of English*. Ed. by Lynda Mugglestone, 274–304. Oxford and New York: Oxford University Press.
> Tieken-Boon van Ostade, Ingrid. 2009. *An Introduction to Late Modern English*. Edinburgh: Edinburgh University Press.

Changes in Modern English are discussed in the following texts:

Barber, Charles. 1964. *Linguistic Change in Present-Day English*. Edinburgh and London: Oliver and Boyd.

Bauer, Laurie. 1994. *Watching English Change*. London and New York: Longman.

Mair, Christian. 2006. *Twentieth-Century English: History, Variation and Standardization*. Cambridge: Cambridge University Press.

On the effects of new media on English, see:

Chambers, J.K. 1998. 'T.V. Makes People Sound the Same'. *Language Myths*. Ed. by Laurie Bauer and Peter Trudgill, 123–31. London: Penguin.

Crystal, David. 2006. *Language and the Internet*. 2nd edn. Cambridge: Cambridge University Press.

Herring, Susan C. 2001. 'Computer-Mediated Discourse'. *The Handbook of Discourse Analysis*. Ed. by Deborah Schiffrin, Deborah Tannen, and Heidi E. Hamilton, 612–34. Oxford and Malden, MA: Blackwell.

Heyd, Theresa. Forthcoming. 'English and the Media: Internet'. *Historical English Linguistics*. (*Handbücher zur Sprach- und Kommunikationswissenschaft/ Handbooks of Linguistics and Communication Science*.) Ed. by Laurel J. Brinton and Alexander Bergs. Vol. 2. Berlin and New York: Mouton de Gruyter.

Schwyter, Jürg. Forthcoming. 'English and the Media: Radio'. *Historical English Linguistics*. (*Handbücher zur Sprach- und Kommunikationswissenschaft/ Handbooks of Linguistics and Communication Science*.) Ed. by Laurel J. Brinton and Alexander Bergs. Vol. 2. Berlin and New York: Mouton de Gruyter.

Stuart-Smith, Jane. Forthcoming. 'English and the Media: Television'. *Historical English Linguistics*. (*Handbücher zur Sprach- und Kommunikationswissenschaft/ Handbooks of Linguistics and Communication Science*.) Ed. by Laurel J. Brinton and Alexander Bergs. Vol. 2. Berlin and New York: Mouton de Gruyter.

For a lively discussion of computer-mediated discourse in the popular media, illustrated with copious examples, see:

Thurlow, Crispin. 2006. 'From Statistical Panic to Moral Panic: The Metadiscursive Construction and Popular Exaggeration of New Media Language in the Print Media'. *Journal of Computer-Mediated Communication* 11(3). Article 1 (http:// icmc.indiana.edu/vol11/issue3/thurlow.html).

13 Varieties of English

OVERVIEW

This chapter describes national varieties of English. It enumerates the features which distinguish the two basic varieties of English, North American and British. Next it discusses other national or regional dialects (US, Canadian, Australian, New Zealand, South African, Liberian, and Caribbean). Following this is a look at some regional dialects of the British Isles (Welsh English, Standard Scottish English, and Hiberno-English) and of the United States (including African American Vernacular English).

OBJECTIVES

The primary objective in this chapter is to understand the effects of the spread of English upon the language. You will learn to recognize the prominent phonological, grammatical, and lexical differences between British English and North American English and be able to describe the features of the other national varieties of English as well as of the important regional varieties of the British Isles and the United States.

The Development of National Varieties

As a result of extensive colonization from the seventeenth into the nineteenth century, English spread through the British Empire, producing the national varieties of English we recognize today, including United States, Canadian, Australian, New

Zealand, South African, and West Indian (Caribbean) English, as well as second-language varieties spoken in South Asia (India, Pakistan, Bangladesh, Sri Lanka), Southeast Asia (Singapore, Hong Kong, Malaysia), the Philippines, East Africa, and West Africa. Table 13.1 presents a timeline for the spread of English outside of England, culminating in the expansion of the British Empire in the nineteenth century. Subsequent transmission of English is represented in Figure 13.1.

We use the term *national variety* as a shorthand for all the local and regional varieties in a country. A regional dialect stands in contrast to a social dialect, which is shaped by factors such as the socio-economic class, gender, age, education, and occupation of the speakers. National varieties of a language develop for a number of reasons:

- separation from the mother tongue in both space and time, engendering linguistic conservatism;
- features brought over at the time of settlement of the new land being preserved;
- regional or social dialects (often not the prestige dialect) spoken by the immigrants shaping the new national dialect;
- language contact with other immigrant groups;
- language contact with indigenous languages (though this influence may be weak); and
- the new landforms, foods, flora, fauna, etc. requiring new vocabulary.

National varieties of English differ primarily in their phonology and lexicon. The set of phonological characteristics of a variety is often called an accent as in the expressions 'a British accent' or 'an Australian accent'. Phonological differences among the national varieties of English are significant. In the lexicon, however, although people are often struck by differences in word choice, the variations are often confined to the colloquial register or to specialized domains and do not affect the structure of the dialect. Grammatical differences among the national dialects are rather limited. For these reasons, the standard written forms of the different varieties are quite similar. We read novels, poetry, history, textbooks, and so on, often without even being aware that they are written in national varieties of English different from our own.

Second-language varieties of English found globally — as well as English-based pidgins and creoles — are hybrid languages resulting from complex linguistic interaction and often depart significantly from basic English structure. In some areas, the second-language varieties of English are becoming so widespread and well-used that they are acquiring 'fixed local norms of usage' (Trudgill and Hannah 2002:124). Moreover, some of the second-language varieties are spoken by very large numbers of people; for example, Indian English is spoken by over 200 million people, not just in India but throughout the world, compared to approximately the same number

Table 13.1 Timeline of the Transmission of English

Date	Britain	North America	Africa	Australasia
1066	Norman invasion of England; some English flee to Scotland			
1169	Norman settlement in southeast Ireland			
1172	The English king becomes Lord of Ireland			
1301	First Prince of Wales			
1497		Cabot reaches Newfoundland		
1536, 1542	Act of Union with Wales			
1553			Trade with West Africa	
1584		Roanoke settlement		
1607	Plantations of Ulster	Jamestown settlement		
1611	King James version of Bible published			
1620		Plymouth settlement		
1650	Cromwellian settlements in Ireland			
1707	Act of Union with Scotland			
1745	Highland Clearances			
1763		Canada ceded to the British		

Continued

Table 13.1 Timeline of the Transmission of English—*Continued*

Date	Britain	North America	Africa	Australasia
1769				Cook circumnavigates New Zealand
1770				Cook claims east Australia for the Crown
1776		United States Declaration of Independence		
1783		British Loyalists flee the US for Canada		
1788			Period of colonization of West Africa	Botany Bay settlement
1795			Occupation of the Cape Colony	
1800	Act of Union with Ireland			
1815				Following Napoleonic Wars, British colonialization of India
1825				Singapore established as a British colony
1840				Treaty of Waitangi; Settlement of New Zealand
1842				Hong Kong established as British colony
1845	Irish potato famine			
1882			British occupy Cairo	

Source: adapted from Laurie Bauer, *An Introduction to International Varieties of English* (Edinburgh: Edinburgh University Press, 2002), pp. 17–18.

of English speakers in the US and only 60 million English speakers in the UK (see Crystal 2003:62–5 for figures).[1]

British versus North American English

Patterns of colonization and historical developments have led to the emergence of two supranational varieties: North American English and British English. The first is the basis of US and Canadian English as well as the varieties spoken in Puerto Rico, Panama, the Philippines, Hawaii, Guam, American Samoa, the US Virgin Islands, and Liberia; the second is the basis of all of the other varieties (see Figure 13.1). For this reason, we begin by considering features (primarily phonological and grammatical) that distinguish North American English (NAE) from British English (BE), accounting for features of NAE as either innovations (having developed since the settlement of North America) or preservations (preserved from the speech of the original settlers while British English has lost or changed the feature). Throughout the following discussions, we assume the perspective of North American English (rather than British English) as a basis for comparison.

North American English can generally be described as conservative. Not only does it preserve features of eighteenth-century British English, but many of the immigrants to North America came from northern England, Scotland, and Ireland, areas remote from the centers of innovation in London and southern England and hence not affected by the sound changes underway there in the eighteenth century.

Phonology

Comparing North American phonology with British is made complicated by the fact that pronunciations vary within each region. When talking about British English, scholars tend to center their discussion on the prestige dialect known as Received Pronunciation (RP), even though RP was always limited by class and has waned in England to the point that it is no longer the prescribed dialect of BBC broadcasters and is today a minority dialect. When contrasting British English with North American English, we will compare RP with what is called General American (a regional dialect of US English) and General Canadian (see below):

1. NAE is a rhotic dialect, meaning that [r] is retained before consonants and at the end of words, as in *farm* and *far*. RP is not rhotic, having lost [r] in these environments, an innovation that occurred in eighteenth-century Britain. In

---

1 While these varieties are of great importance globally, they constitute a subject of study in and of themselves and thus lie beyond the scope of this textbook. For information on second-language varieties of English, such as the English of India, Hong Kong, or the Philippines, see the 'Further Readings' section at the end of this chapter. We must also keep in mind that within each of the national varieties, there are numerous regional and social dialects beyond the scope of this text. Moreover, the intricate and sometimes controversial histories of dialects cannot be fully explored here.

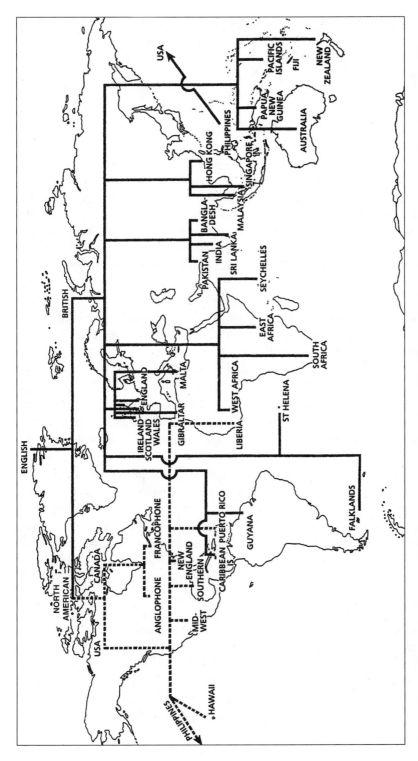

Figure 13.1   World Distribution of North American and British English (from David Crystal, *The Cambridge Encyclopedia of the English Language*, 2nd edn [Cambridge: Cambridge University Press, 2003], reprinted with the permission of Cambridge University Press)

non-rhotic dialects, a final [r] may be pronounced when it precedes a word beginning with a vowel, as in *far away*, but also sometimes when it has no etymological validity, as in 'idear' for *idea* and 'warsh' for *wash*; this is called a linking or intrusive *r*. In rhotic dialects [r] may be lost in certain contexts through a subsequent dissimilation (as in *cate(r)pillar*).

2. NAE preserves [æ] in so-called '*ask* words'. These are certain words with [æ] before [f], [f] + consonant, [s], [s] + consonant, [θ], [m] + consonant, or [n] + consonant, as in *staff, after, grass, clasp, basket, plaster, castle, fasten, path, example, dance, grant, branch,* and *demand* in which BE has changed from [æ] to [ɑ] (or [a]). This change began at the end of the eighteenth century in southern England (some New England dialects also show this shift). However, this development is not yet complete, as [æ] may be found in BE in identical phonetic environments in *gaff, gas, asp, mascot, pastel, hassle, romance, banter, scansion, stand,* and many other words.

3. NAE may preserve the distinction between [w] and [hw], that is, between the labiovelar glide and the labiovelar fricative (transcribed [ʍ]). For BE speakers, the initial sounds of *wear/where, wail/whale, wet/whet,* and *witch/which* are the same, whereas for NAE speakers, at least for older generations, the first member of each set begins with [w] and the second with [hw]. The British change of [hw] to [w] began as a vulgarism but became standard in BE by 1800; the change seems to be spreading in NAE as well.

4. NAE pronounces words derived from ME [ɔ̄], such as *goat* and *toad*, with [oʊ], whereas BE uses a more centralized diphthong [əʊ]. Similarly, NAE pronounces words derived from ME [ō], such as *loop* and *hoop*, with [u], while BE has a diphthong [ɨu] ([ɨ] is a high central vowel). In both cases, the NAE pronunciation is a preservation.

5. For words that have four or more syllables, NAE preserves a secondary stress on the second-to-last syllable when the ending is *-ary* (*legendary, necessary*), *-ory* (*explanatory, territory*), *-mony* (*ceremony, matrimony*), *-ery* (*monastery, cemetery*), and *-boro(u)gh* (*Peterborough, Edinburgh*). BE does not have this stress, and the result is that the penultimate syllable actually disappears in the pronunciation. Thus, a NAE speaker says [mɑnəstɛri] while a BE speaker says [mɒnəstri]. Again, loss of secondary stress is an innovation in BE.

6. In NAE, a [t] that occurs between vowels and follows a stressed syllable (or an [r]) is voiced to [d] or a flap [ɾ] (a speech sound made by rapidly striking the tongue against the roof of the mouth). For most NAE speakers, *latter/ladder, matter/madder, bitter/bidder, metal/medal, atom/Adam, hearty/hardy, waiting/wading* sound the same (we say they are *homophones*). This feature is actually an innovation in NAE. Another innovation is the NAE loss of [t] following [n] in words such as *winter* (a homophone with *winner*), *interesting, dentist,* and *twenty*.

7. The diphthong [ɪu] tends to monophthongize to [u] following alveolars in NAE, in words such as *tune, student, suit, duke, Tuesday, enthusiasm,* and *allude*; thus, *due/dew/do* are homophones. In other phonetic environments, the diphthong is generally preserved, as in *beauty, music, pew, few, cute,* and *argue*. The loss of the initial glide [ɪ] or [j] in the diphthong (the technical term is *yod-dropping*) is an innovation of NAE.

8. An innovation in some dialects of NAE is the merger of [ɔ] and [ɑ], so that *taught/tot, caught/cot, auto/Otto, dawn/Don, hawk/hock, offal/awful,* and *chalk/chock* are homophones, pronounced with unrounded [ɑ].

9. Most working-class dialects of BE are characterized by *h*-dropping, the loss of [h] at the beginning of words and syllables, as in *hit, happy, hedge,* and *ahead*, resulting in [h] being entirely lost in these phonemic systems. This widespread phenomenon is highly stigmatized as uneducated (Wells calls it 'the single most powerful pronunciation shibboleth in England' [1982:254]). It is not found in working-class dialects of NAE, which are conservative in retaining [h].

10. A more subtle phonological difference between NAE and BE is in intonation. Although differences in intonation are very difficult to analyze, they probably account in large part for the different 'sound' of NAE and BE. The North American variant tends to be flatter and less varied in pitch than the British English variant; rises in intonation come later in the sentence.

There are other differences in phonology between BE and NAE, but they are minor and often restricted to variant pronunciations of individual words.

Grammar

A few fairly minor grammatical features distinguish NAE from BE:

1. NAE uses an inflected subjunctive in constructions following verbs such as *insist, recommend, order, suggest,* or *move*; BE instead uses an expanded form with a modal auxiliary or an indicative. Thus, a NAE speaker says *I insist that he leave* (the third-person singular present without *-s* is subjunctive), but a BE speaker says *I insist that he must leave* or *I insist that he leaves*. Though it is likely that the use of the subjunctive is a preservation in NAE, it has been accompanied by an innovation in the negative form, with a pre-verbal *not*: *I insist that he not leave*.

2. NAE preserves the strong past participle *gotten*, while BE has regularized it to *got*, preserving the older form only in remnant adjectives such as *ill-gotten* and *forgotten*. In NAE, *have got* and *have gotten* are carefully distinguished, each having two meanings:

   have got: 'possess' or 'be obligated' (+ infinitive)

   have gotten: 'have acquired' or 'have been allowed, permitted' (+ infinitive)

3. With the verb *have*, BE preserves the older patterns of interrogation and negation without an auxiliary, as in *Have you any money?* or *You haven't any money*. NAE generally uses the auxiliary *do* in such constructions, as in *Do you have any money?* or *You do not have any money*. Also, we find the innovation *She has a dog, doesn't she?* in NAE versus *She has a dog, hasn't she?* in BE.

4. With collective nouns (nouns naming a group consisting of individuals), such as *team, herd, flock, family, committee*, and *government*, BE tends to use a plural verb, while NAE uses a singular verb. Even in NAE, however, usage varies: if the collective is seen as a unit or as an abstraction, the singular is used (e.g. *the committee agrees, the family is a dying institution*), whereas if the collective is viewed in terms of its individual members, the plural is used (e.g. *the committee are all assembled, the family are all at home*).

5. The position of *only* is more restricted in NAE than in BE, where it generally appears pre-verbally. In NAE, prescriptive rules dictate that it be placed before the word it modifies, thus *I have only two favors to ask of you* not *I only have two favors to ask of you*, because *only* modifies *two* not *have*.

6. The use of prepositions is somewhat different in BE and NAE. BE often uses *in* where NAE uses *on*: e.g. *to live in/on a street, to be in/on a team, to be in (a)/on sale*. BE also uses *different to* rather than the NAE *different than*. Both forms are considered wrong by American prescriptivists.

7. BE places the substitute verb *do* after an auxiliary, whereas NAE does not: *he could have helped and certainly might have (done)*.

8. BE omits articles in a number of instances where they have evolved as obligatory in NAE (though not for all Canadian speakers), as in *enter (the) hospital* or *be in (the) hospital*.

9. BE preserves the auxiliary *shall* more consistently than NAE does. Where NAE uses *will*, BE uses *shall*, as in the statement of prediction *I shall be there in an hour*.

10. In constructions that have pronouns as both direct object and indirect object, word order differs. BE preserves the older order of direct object followed by indirect object (e.g. *give it her*), where NAE prefers the newer analytical construction (e.g. *give it to her*).

11. BE uses a larger number of past and past participle forms ending in [t], such as *dwelt, knelt, slept, dreamt, spelt, smelt, spilt*, and *burnt*; NAE uses this ending only when the present tense of the verb has a tense vowel and the past tense a lax vowel, as in *slept* (present [slip] versus past [slɛpt]), *crept, swept, dealt*, and *felt*. Other differences in past tense forms include BE *dived, spat, sprang*, and *sank* in contrast to NAE *dove, spit, sprung*, and *sunk*.

12. NAE allows *just* with the simple past, as in *I just arrived*, whereas BE uses *(only) just* with the perfect, as in *I have (only) just arrived*. NAE is conservative here.

13. NAE permits objects with certain otherwise intransitive verbs (e.g. *wonder the same thing, stay the course, cruise the Danube*), where BE would require a preposition (e.g. *wonder about the same thing, stay on the course, cruise on the Danube*).

Lexicon

Some comparisons of lexical differences between the two varieties are shown in Table 13.2. Many more examples can be found in dialect dictionaries.

Table 13.2 Examples of Lexical Differences between British and North American English

British	North American	British	North American
dual carriageway	divided highway	nil	nothing, zero
sweets	candy	pavement	sidewalk
chemist	pharmacist	lollipop man/ woman	crossing guard
Madam	Ma'am	tights	pantyhose
maize	corn	rubber	eraser
trolley	shopping cart/buggy	saltcellar	saltshaker
pillar box	mail box	diversion	detour
nappy	diaper	high street	main street
dustbin	trash can	fringe	bangs
verge	shoulder (of road)	jumper	sweater

While it is not possible to point to particular lexical differences in terms of topic, we might point out a few patterns (see Crystal 2003:308). In some cases, entirely different words exist in the two dialects, e.g. *estate car* (BE) and *station wagon* (NAE), while in other cases, the same word exists in both dialects but has additional meanings in one of the dialects; for example, in BE *caravan* can also mean a vehicle being towed by a car. In contrast, the same word may exist in both dialects (such as *undertaker*), but one dialect may also possess a synonym (such as NAE *mortician*). Finally, words may be present in both dialects, but more common in one; hence *flat* is the more frequent term in BE and *apartment* in NAE (with *suite* also being possible in Canadian English).

Orthography

A final difference between the two varieties is in orthography. As we will see, Canadian spelling borrows from both British and US conventions, so for now we will concentrate on the innovations in US English (USEng) in comparison to BE. Noah Webster's influential 1828 dictionary was influential in establishing American spelling conventions. According to Leith (1997:241), it was Webster's belief that 'national consciousness could be stimulated by cultivating a different *look* to the language'. Among systematic changes, Webster suggested the replacements shown in Table 13.3, which are now used in USEng. Some changes, such as from *-ick* to *-ic* (*music*, *physic*, *traffic* versus *musick*, *physick*, *traffick*), have been adopted in BE as well, and we find both *-ize* and *-ise* in BE (*realize*, *civilize*, *idealize* and *realise*, *civilise*, *idealise*) but only the former in USEng. Webster also suggested that when a suffix is added to a word, the final consonant be doubled only if the final syllable is accented, thus *tráveling*, but *propélling*. Finally, he altered the spelling of a number of individual words:

curb for *kerb*	*plow* for *plough*
show for *shew*	*woolen* for *woollen*
tire for *tyre*	*ax* for *axe*
wagon for *waggon*	*gray* for *grey*

It should be pointed out that the spellings suggested by Webster were almost all variant spellings found in the eighteenth century.

Table 13.3 Orthographic Differences between US and British English

USEng	BE	USEng vs BE examples
-or	*-our*	*color, flavor, labor,* not *colour, flavour, labour* (cf. *author, doctor, mirror,* which do not have *-our* in BE)
-ol	*-oul*	*mold, smolder,* not *mould, smoulder*
-er	*-re*	*theater, center,* not *theatre, centre*
-se	*-ce*	*defense, pretense,* not *defence, pretence* (cf. *practice,* which does not have *-se* in USEng whether it is used as a noun or a verb)
-ct-	*-x-*	*inflection, connection, deflection,* not *inflexion, connexion, deflexion*
e,o	*ae, oe*	*medieval, archeology, maneuver,* not *mediaeval, archaeology, manoeuvre*

Canadian English

By the Treaty of Paris in 1763, most of Canada was ceded to Britain. An important milestone in the development of the English language in Canada was the arrival, following the Revolutionary War in 1783, of large numbers of émigrés from the newly independent United States who were loyal to the British king. The so-called United Empire Loyalists came first from New England and moved into the Maritimes. Later waves of Loyalists, coming primarily from New York, New Jersey, Pennsylvania, and eastern Vermont, moved into Upper Canada (present-day Ontario) via the St Lawrence River. The immigrants brought with them the Northern dialect of US English, fanning out from east to west. There were later migrations from the Great Lakes area and the high plains north into the prairies (see Figure 13.2).

As a result of the War of 1812, England decided to strengthen its claim in Canada by encouraging British settlements. Between 1816 and 1857, over a million people entered Canada. Canada remained a colony of Britain until the Dominion of Canada in 1867. Thus, despite its firm basis in a US dialect, Canadian English continued to feel the force of British English as a prestige dialect well into the twentieth century, with the

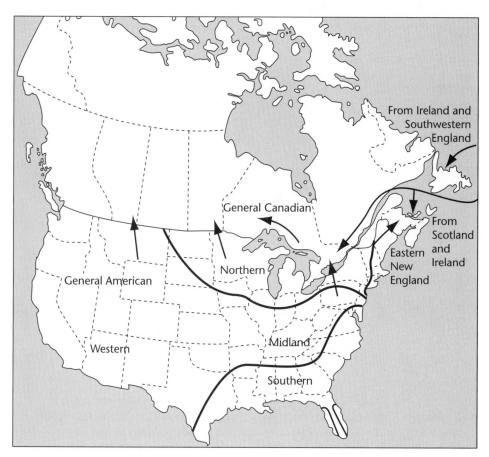

Figure 13.2 Historical Sources of Canadian English (adapted from Gerard Van Herk, 'Language in Social Contexts'. *Contemporary Linguistic Analysis: An Introduction*. Ed. by William O'Grady and John Archibald [Toronto: Pearson Longman, 2009], p. 461)

superimposition of certain British features on the original Loyalist speech. Immigration patterns also led to Scots-based enclaves of English in Canada (e.g. Cape Breton Island and Nova Scotia) and Irish-based enclaves (e.g. Newfoundland). These differences in settlement history as well as the presence of a large French-speaking population in Lower Canada (present-day Quebec) have contributed to making Canadian English a distinct variety of NAE.

The English spoken across Canada from Vancouver Island to the eastern border of Ontario, often called 'General Canadian', displays considerable homogeneity. Also identifiable is the English spoken in the Maritimes (Nova Scotia, New Brunswick, and Prince Edward Island) as well as the English spoken in Quebec, and the speech of Newfoundland, which constitutes Canada's most distinctive variety (see Figure 13.3). Subdialects such as those of the Ottawa valley, the Prairies, the West, and the Arctic North are also identifiable, as are Aboriginal English and English as a Second Language (ESL) variants. In the sections that follow, we will examine the features of General Canadian English (as it is spoken by educated, middle-

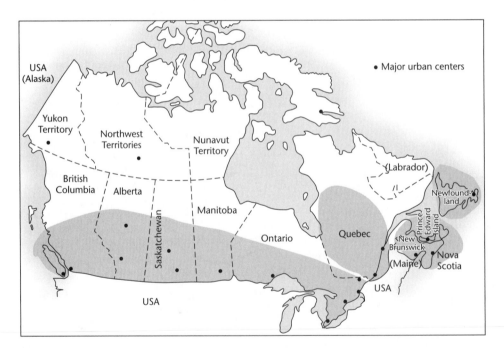

Figure 13.3 Four Major Canadian Dialect Areas (gray shading) (The northern area boundaries are arbitrary, as data is not available.) (Stefan Dollinger, 'Written Sources of Canadian English: Phonetic Reconstruction and the Low-Back Vowel Merger in the 19th Century', *Varieties in Writing: The Written Word as Linguistic Evidence*. Ed. by Raymond Hickey. [Amsterdam and Philadelphia: John Benjamins, 2010], p. 200)

class, urban Canadians). In the end, we reject the oft-held view that Canadian English is an amalgam of British and US English dialects.[2]

General Canadian English

Phonologically, Canadian English (CanE) is more or less identical to USEng in respect to being rhotic; retaining [æ] in *ask* words (though with a somewhat lower and more open [æ]); preserving [oʊ] (< ME [ɔ̄]) and [u] (< ME [ō]); keeping secondary stress in *-ary, -ory, -mony*, and *-ery* words: flapping or voicing of [t] between vowels and in certain other contexts; losing of [t] following [n]; monophthongizing of [ɪu] to [u] following [s] and increasingly after [t, d, n] as well; and merging [ɑ] and [ɔ]. CanE resembles BE more closely in the complete loss of the distinction between [w] and [hw]; the occurrence in some people's speech of [ɒ] in words such as *hot, not,* and *lot*; and the more consistent preservation of [ɔ] before [r] in words such as *sorry, tomorrow,* and *orange*.

The one truly distinguishing phonological feature of Canadian English is the raised onset of the two central diphthongs where the initial vowel of the diphthongs [aʊ] and [aɪ] in CanE is somewhat higher, or raised, to a centralized vowel [ə] giving [əʊ] and [əɪ]. This phenomenon is termed *Canadian raising*. Although raised diphthongs are not unique to Canada (they are also found, for example, in eastern Virginia, South Carolina, and Martha's Vineyard) and evidence for their spread or decline in CanE is contradictory, they are a striking feature by which even speakers without expertise in linguistics identify Canadians. The existence of raised diphthongs in CanE is usually attributed to Scottish or northern English influence. In Chapter 10, we saw that the conservative feature of the raised or 'unlowered' diphthongs represents an intermediate step in the Great Vowel Shift diphthongization of [ū] and [ī] to [aʊ] and [aɪ]. While in the sixteenth- and seventeenth-century BE raised diphthongs would have occurred in all phonological environments, in CanE they survive only in certain environments; they are allophonic, occurring only before voiceless consonants, not voiced consonants, as shown in Table 13.4. CanE is also distinguished by a predominance of rising intonation (typical of questions) in all sentence types.

A number of lexical items have pronunciations in CanE that are not typically found in either British or US English: *asphalt* [æšfɑlt], *drama* [dræmə], *bilingual* [baɪlɪŋɪuəl], *khaki* [kɑrki] (being replaced with US English [kæki]), *longitude* [lɑŋɡɪt(ɪ)ud], *opinion* [oʊpɪnjən], *docile* [dɑsaɪl], and *tomato* [təmæroʊ]. However, pronunciations of certain lexical items attest to the continuing influence of BE as a prestige dialect in Canada, e.g. *again* [əɡeɪn], *been* [bin], *decal* [dɛkəl], *herb* [hɜrb], *produce* (noun) [prɑdɪus], *senile* [sɛnaɪl], and *scone* [skɑn]. Spelling pronunciations, such as *herb* (with [h]), *arctic* [ɑrktɪk], or *often* [ɑftən], seem to be

---

2 The following discussion of Canadian English is adapted from Brinton and Fee (2001:422–40).

Table 13.4 Raised Diphthongs in Canadian English

[əɪ]/[aɪ]	[əʊ]/[aʊ]
price/prize	spouse/espouse
bite/bide	house/houses
site/side	bout/bowed
fife/five	mouth (N)/mouth (V)
tripe/tribe	blouse (N)/blouse (V)
knife/knives	lout/loud

fairly frequent in CanE, as in BE. The BE pronunciation of *schedule* [šɛdɪul] has been promoted by the Canadian Broadcasting Corporation, but the American pronunciation seems to be the preferred form for Canadian speakers. A number of British pronunciations formerly used in Canada, such as *zebra* [zɛbrə], have fallen out of use, though BE *lieutenant* [lɛftɛnənt] is still used by the Canadian military.

Apart from a few minor differences, little distinguishes CanE from its American counterpart grammatically. Widespread features include the use of *different than* rather than *different from* (the prescribed American form) or *different to* (a common British form); the noun + modifier order in phrases such as *Air Canada, Revenue Canada*, and *Parks Canada* (influenced by French); and the use of *as well* at the beginning of sentences to function as a conjunctive adverb, as in *When I get home, I have to make dinner. As well, I have to do a load of laundry.*

Without doubt, the form thought most typical (indeed stereotypical) of Canadian English is called the 'narrative *eh?*', occurring as a tag at the end of a sentence or phrase. The linguist Walter Avis (1972) distinguishes eight uses of the form, such as a tag inviting or soliciting agreement, as a reinforcement, or as a request for repetition. But, while speakers of many dialects use *eh* in all of these functions, it is the eighth use Avis mentions—narrative *eh?*—that is exclusively Canadian. It is spoken quickly and without its usual rising intonation (denoted by the question mark), and is of high frequency, as in *That was when we almost intercepted a pass, eh?* and *Stu Falkner bumped into him, eh?* Although it is said to be 'virtually meaningless' and is often stigmatized (its use is more common in the lower socioeconomic class), *eh* clearly serves connective and discoursive functions.

Like all national varieties, CanE has a set of lexical items distinctive to it. Some of the items cited in this context are borrowings from French Canadian (such as *caplin* and *coulee*), from Aboriginal languages (such as *saskatoon* 'berry' and *muskeg* 'bog' from Cree, *kokanee* 'type of salmon' from Shuswap, *sockeye* 'type of salmon' from Coast Salish, and *skookum* 'excellent' from Chinook Jargon), and from the languages of various immigrant groups (such as *pysanka* 'hand painted Easter egg' from Ukrainian). In addition to such borrowings, there are Canadianisms relating to:

- specific holidays (*Victoria Day, Canada Day*),
- French–English relations (*anglophone* 'an English-speaking person', *francophone* 'a French-speaking person', *sovereignist* 'a supporter of Quebec sovereignty'),
- Aboriginal people (*First Nation* 'Native band or community', *reserve* 'land set aside for the use of a specific group of Aboriginal people'),
- government/law/politics (*First Ministers* 'the prime minister of Canada and premiers of the provinces', *Mountie* 'a member of the Royal Canadian Mounted Police', or *RCMP*),
- finance (*GST* 'the goods and services tax', *loonie* 'a Canadian one-dollar coin depicting a loon on one side', and by analogy *toonie* 'a Canadian two-dollar coin'),
- social structure/programs (*heritage language* 'a language other than French or English spoken in Canada', *multiculturalism* 'a government policy advocating a society composed of many culturally distinct groups'),
- sports and games (*five-pin bowling* 'a variety of bowling', *shinny* 'informal pickup hockey', *crokinole*, 'a kind of board game', *three-pitch* 'a variety of softball'),
- weather (*chinook* 'a warm dry wind which blows east of the Rocky Mountains', *humidex*—blend of *humidity* and *index*—'a scale indicating the personal discomfort level resulting from combined heat and humidity'),
- education (*separate school* 'a publicly funded denominational [usually Catholic] school', *grade one* 'first grade', *March Break* 'a school holiday'),
- food and drink (*homo* 'homogenized milk with full fat content', *poutine* 'French fries topped with cheese curds and gravy', *peameal bacon* 'back bacon coated in cornmeal'), and
- miscellaneous categories (*toque/tuque* 'a close-fitting knitted hat', *parkade* 'a parking garage', *hydro* 'electricity', *garburator* 'a garbage disposal unit').

Canadian spelling conventions are a mix of those used in Britain and the United States: for example, Canadians prefer USEng *tire, jail, wagon,* and *-ize* (not BE *tyre, gaol, waggon,* and *-ise*), but BE *cheque* in the sense of 'bank draft', *grey,* and *catalogue* (not USEng *check, gray*, and *catalog*). Spelling varies from province to province and person to person. One may find *theatre* more commonly than *theater* among the same group of speakers that prefers *center* to *centre*, and vice versa. Variation also exists in people's choice of *-our* and *-or* endings in words like *labo(u)r* and *colo(u)r*; slightly more than half the population seem to choose *-our*, and this ending certainly appears more often in nationally published texts.

Newfoundland English

The distinctive features of Newfoundland English can be attributed primarily to its sparse population, geographical isolation, and continuing connection to Britain (it joined Canada only in 1949). English speakers settled in Newfoundland very early, beginning in the seventeenth century, though transient fishermen had been summering there since the sixteenth century. The earliest settlers came from the West Country of England, and beginning in the 1720s immigrants arrived from southeastern Ireland. Newfoundland became a colony of England with control over its own affairs in 1833. British immigration fell off after the first half of the nineteenth century. Newfoundland English is thus shaped by the speech of the West Country British mercantile and seafaring class, the southern Irish merchants and 'servants' (workers on fishing boats), and the British and Anglo-Irish administrators and professionals. As a result, Newfoundland English shows little influence from general Canadian English.

Two features—coalescence of [w] and [hw] and rhoticity—are characteristic of both West Country and Irish English. Particular West Country features include variable [h] (added or deleted rather arbitrarily, e.g. 'hup' for *up* or 'en' for *hen*); retroflex [r]; voicing of initial consonants (e.g. 'vir' for *fir* or 'zin' for *sin*); lowering of vowels before [r] (most noticeable are [i] > [ɛ] as in *beer*, [ɑ] > a vowel sound approximating [æ] as in *car*, and [ɔ] > a vowel approximating [ɑ] as in *hoarse*); retention of [e], especially in words spelled *ea* (e.g. *sea*); and raising of the [aɪ] diphthong to [əɪ] in all contexts (independent of Canadian raising). Particular Irish features include [t] and [d] in place of [θ] and [ð], as in 'ten' for *then* or 'fader' for *father*; realization of [θ] after a vowel as [f], as in *path*; coalescence of [tj] > [č] and [dj] > [ǰ]; rounding of [ə]; monophthongal [e] and [o], as in *bay* and *boat*; coalescence of the vowels in *cot/caught*; and [aɪ] and [ɔɪ] merger, as in *boy/buy*. Another Irish influence is the clear postvocalic [l] (instead of dark [l]), now generally found only among older speakers.

We can attribute Newfoundland's special grammatical features to the same two sources. West Country English has contributed a system of pronouns based on stress, not on case (the unstressed forms being *me, un* or *'n, (h)er, us,* and *(th)em,* as in 'Me did it'). Also from the West Country is the use of *he/she* for inanimates (*it* being reserved for dummy *it* and for mass nouns) and the use of *-s* throughout the paradigm of the present tense (*I works, you works, he/she/it works, they works*). From Irish English comes the use of the habitual *be(s)* or *don't be* (less often *does be*) and *be after* (v)-*ing* for the perfect. Other noticeable characteristics are adverbs without *-ly* and the intensifiers *real, right,* and *some* (as in *some happy*). (The use of *real* as an intensifier, as in *real happy*, is, of course, a feature of the speech of many younger speakers of NAE.)

Newfoundland English has a large, distinctive vocabulary, much having to do with fishing (e.g. *caplin* 'small fish like a smelt'), sealing (e.g. *bedlamer* 'immature harp seal'), logging (e.g. *nug* 'a chunk of wood for fuel'), and ice conditions (e.g. *clumper* 'small iceberg'). There are also many Irish borrowings (e.g. *sleeveen* 'deceitful person').

Exercise 13.1 British versus North American English

For the following words, transcribe the pronunciations most characteristic of British English (BE), United States English (USEng), and Canadian English (CanE). Ignore differences in stress.

	BE	USEng	CanE
a. class	_____	_____	_____
b. lighter	_____	_____	_____
c. primary	_____	_____	_____
d. park	_____	_____	_____
e. white	_____	_____	_____
f. router (tool)	_____	_____	_____
g. conservatory	_____	_____	_____
h. crass	_____	_____	_____
i. plenty	_____	_____	_____

Australian and New Zealand English

Australian English

After Captain James Cook's expedition to Australia in 1770, English settlement of the area began in 1787, when Captain Arthur Phillip set out with 1,100 people, 750 of whom were convicts. In 1788 he founded a penal colony at a harbor he named Sydney and annexed the eastern half of Australia. Using the island for this purpose into the late nineteenth century, England transported its social undesirables—those it considered traitors, political prisoners, union organizers, and petty criminals—to New South Wales. The first free settlers were soldiers who decided to stay following their military service. Many convicts also decided to stay in Australia after their sentences were served. Farmers came, as did government officials and those supervising prisons. Very slowly, in the first half of the nineteenth century, more free colonists arrived to look for new homes; the later gold rush brought other white settlers, and eventually most of the rest of Australia was settled. Union of the Australian colonies occurred in 1900 (Prall and Willson 1991:616–17).

The colonization of Australia with permanent white settlers represents one of the typical means by which the British Empire expanded in the nineteenth century, taking the English language with it. Because many of the first English speakers came from southern England, and London in particular, the influence of Cockney English on Australian speech has attracted attention, but many colonists came from else-where in Britain, such as Scotland. Although there is not the extent of regional varia-tion found in United States English in either Australian English or New Zealand English, there is a fair amount of social stratification within the Australasian accents. In terms of its phoneme inventory, Australian English (AusE) is very close to RP, although there is some allophonic variation. Higher prestige is associated with less variation from RP. Accordingly, at the high end of the social scale, particularly among older speakers, we find cultivated or mild speech which differs only slightly from RP. Broad accents, at the other end of the social scale, differ considerably from RP and are usually compared to Cockney.[3]

AusE is non-rhotic and has linking and intrusive *r*, its [r] being more retroflex than in British English. A [t] between vowels, as in *city*, may be voiced to the flap [ɾ], but it may also remain unvoiced. Flapping is less common in AusE than in NAE. The lateral liquid [l] tends to be dark (further back in the mouth) in all positions. AusE has /ə/ in unstressed syllables rather than /ɪ/ as RP does, as in the final syllable of *horses* and *wanted*. Like RP, AusE has [ɑ] in words such as *laugh, path,* and *grass* but (unlike RP) it has [æ] in *dance, sample,* and *plant*. (Although regional variation does occur, the pronunciation [ɑ] has more prestige in these circumstances.) Front vowels in Australian English are closer than in RP; thus [ɪ] approximates [i], [ɛ] approximates [e], and [æ] approximates [ɛ]. AusE diphthongs are wider than those in RP; this means that diphthongs are more open and have a more centralized onset. The AusE [ɑ] vowel is very front, almost [æ], in words such as *bar*. Finally, British speakers hear AusE as flatter in intonation, with less variation in pitch in neutral statements, though it is sometimes observed that rising intonation makes statements sound like questions, as in CanE.

Minimal differences separate the grammar of AusE from that of other stan-dard varieties of English. Like BE, collective nouns such as *government* and *team* take a plural verb. Like NAE, AusE usually lacks the auxiliaries *shall/should*, as in 'I *should* like to go there', and instead uses *will/would*. In AusE *do* is not rou-tinely used after an auxiliary, as it is in BE (e.g. *I may* as opposed to *I may do*). Increasingly Australian speakers add the tag *but* to the end of the sentence to mean 'however'. Australian dialects may use an infinitive rather than a participle (e.g. *to pay* rather than *paying*) in such sentences as *Some people delay to pay their tax*. The feminine pronoun, *she*, can be used to refer to inanimate nouns or in inanimate con-structions; *She'll be right* means 'Everything will be all right' (Millward 1996:388). Australians may use *thanks* rather than *please* to make a request, as in *Can I have a cup of tea, thanks?*

Even though very few Australians are of Aboriginal descent (approximately 2 per cent of the population according to the 2006 national census, but only about one in eight individuals use an Aboriginal language as their main household language[4]),

---

3 The linguistic characteristics of Australian English and New Zealand English in this and the following sections are adapted from Trudgill and Hannah (2002:15–27).

these tongues have influenced AusE, and borrowings from Aboriginal languages differentiate Australian speech from the other varieties. Of course, the flora and fauna reflect native names: e.g. *dingo, kangaroo, wallaby, koala, wombat,* and *budgerigar* 'parakeet native to Australia' (> *budgie*). From daily life, we find the borrowings *boomerang, bardy* 'edible grub', *barramundi* 'various freshwater fish', *billabong* 'blind channel of river, slough', *billy* 'container for making tea', and *yandy* 'to separate grass seed'. In Aboriginal English usage we find figurative language, *big* for 'city', and *pink-eye* for 'festival'. Australian slang contains a number of such vivid expressions: e.g. *arvo* 'afternoon', *baggies* 'baggy shorts', *bagman* 'a tramp', *boatie* or *yachtie* 'member of a crew', and *boil the billy* 'make tea'. *Bo-peep* is 'a look', *batch* 'a makeshift hut', *barney* 'noisy dispute', *biff* 'hit, strike', and *blackball* 'hard sweetmeat, humbug'. Then, too, to be *on one's bones* is to be 'hard up, destitute'. Diminutives are common in AusE, such as *barbie* 'barbeque', *cozzie* 'swimming costume', and *Chrissy prezzie* 'Christmas present'. While many of these lexical items remain uniquely applied to Australian cultural experiences, some have been exported into other varieties of English: e.g. NAE speakers may use the term *budgie* to refer to their 'parakeets'.

New Zealand English

Captain James Cook also made his way to New Zealand in his famous expedition of 1769. The islands became part of Australia (New South Wales) early on, but by 1841 they were a separate Crown colony. Unlike Australia, free white settlers, not convicts, settled in New Zealand. The settlers often encountered strong Maori resistance. New Zealand accents are very similar to those of Australia, such that outsiders often have difficulty telling mild Australian speech apart from New Zealand English (NZE). The following characteristics distinguish the two.

Much of NZE is non-rhotic, with linking and intrusive *r*. The South Island is an exception, though, with several rhotic local accents having a 'Southland burr'. (Immigrants from Scotland and Ireland may be responsible for this.) The [hw] in *which* is maintained, especially among older speakers. The voiced flap [ɾ] is heard as a variant form of the intervocalic [t] as in *city* and *better*. The word *with* has a voiceless final sound [wɪθ] where BE usually voices it as [wɪð]. The lateral liquid [l] is dark in all environments. Phonetically, the New Zealand vowel [ɪ] as in *bid* is realized as a central vowel, [ə]. This sound has in turn merged with [ʊ] after [w] so that *women* has the same pronunciation as *woman*. When unstressed at the end of a word, the RP vowel [ə] is raised slightly in NZE in words such as *butter* (the *r* being lost). The indefinite article *a* is also pronounced with this raised variant. The front vowels [ɛ] as in *bed* and [æ] as in *bad* are higher, more closely approximating [e] and [ɛ], than in AusE. Words in the set *dance, sample, grant,* and *branch* have the low back or central vowel [ɑ] or [a] rather than [æ]. Words like *laugh* and *graph*

---

4 For more details, see 'About Australia' at http://www.dfat.gov.au/facts/Indigenous_languages.html.

have [æ]. Unlike AusE, the vowel [ʊ] tends to be unrounded, so that *put* sounds like *putt*. Finally, the vowel in *bird* has considerable lip rounding.

There are only minor grammatical differences in NZE from other varieties. NZE avoids *shall* and *should* in favor of *will* and *would*, even avoiding the former in interrogatives where other dialects that lack *shall* and *should* retain them: e.g. *Will I close the window?* is a request for direction. Collective nouns take singular verbs. The indirect object requires a preposition when it follows the direct object, thus *I'll give it to him* rather than BE *I'll give it him*. Idiomatic use of prepositions differs from British and other forms of English. For example, New Zealanders say *in the weekend*, while the British say *at the weekend*, and North Americans say *on the weekend*. As in AusE, NZE has a high frequency of clipped forms in colloquial speech. Thus, we hear *beaut* 'beautiful', *ute* 'utility vehicle', and *varsity* 'university'. *Thanks* can be used in place of *please*, just as in AusE. Colloquial abbreviations often end in a diminutive even though the words may not be the same in AusE and NZE. *Postie* means 'mail delivery person'.

Because just over 13 per cent of the population of New Zealand claims Maori heritage, a quarter of whom report some fluency in their language,[5] many Maori words have come to be used by or are at least familiar to English speakers. Examples are: *whare* 'Maori hut', *waiata* 'Maori song', *tena koe* 'Maori greeting', *kia ora* 'Hi!', *Pakeha* 'a person not identifying as Maori', *kunaku* 'person', *goorie/goory* 'mongrel dog', *half-pie* 'imperfect, mediocre', *hangi* 'earth oven', *hei-tiki* 'greenstone neck ornament', *kiwi*, *moko puna* 'grandchild, niece, nephew', *pakihi* 'area of open swampy land', *taua* 'Maori army or war party', *tangi* 'dirge, lamentation', and *taongu* 'possessions, goods'. Australian loan words also make their way to New Zealand, as in *back blocks* 'land in remote area', *banjo* 'shovel', and *beg-pardon*. Distinctive New Zealand usage includes *to front* 'to show up', *to flat* 'to live in a shared flat', *a crib* 'a cabin or cottage', and *a joker* 'a guy, bloke'.

African English

As a result of colonization, English has official or semi-official status in many parts in sub-Saharan Africa, including southern Africa (Republic of South Africa, Zimbabwe, Botswana, Swaziland, Lesotho, and Namibia), eastern Africa (Kenya, Tanzania, Uganda, Malawi, and Zambia), and western Africa (Gambia, Sierra Leone, Liberia, Ghana, Nigeria, and Cameroon [where French is also official]). In both East Africa and West Africa, the non-native varieties of English are characterized by reduced vowel systems (consistent with the systems of the indigenous languages). In West Africa, a generalized West African Vernacular English has arisen with national variants, and a creolized form of English known as Krio is also widespread in Sierra

---

5 For more information, see 'QuickStats about Maori' at http://www.stats.govt.nz/Census/ 2006CensusHomePage/QuickStats/quickstats-about-a-subject/maori/.

Leone. In East Africa, the second-language versions of English bear greater similarity to the English of South Africa. Only two native varieties of English have evolved in Africa, namely, in South Africa and in Liberia. We will focus on these.

South African English

The first large group of English speakers in South Africa were the early-nineteenth-century settlers in the Eastern Cape, who came from several different dialect areas in Britain and were of a mixed social background. English was declared the official language in 1823. The early British settlers were followed in the period between 1848 and 1862 by more British immigrants to the Natal region and later in the 1870s and 1880s by those going to the diamond mines and gold fields. Dutch speakers from the Netherlands had occupied South Africa since the seventeenth century. Indians, many of whom spoke English, were imported in the 1860s as manual laborers. Indigenous populations included speakers of Bantu languages (Zulu, Xhosa, Sotho, etc.) as well as Khoisan languages. Throughout much of South Africa's history, Afrikaans and English were the two official languages, but speakers of these languages were always in an uneasy relationship (culminating in the Boer War of 1899–1902). English was the language of the socially elite and was dominant in commerce, education, science, and technology. Since 1994, English has been one of 11 official languages in South Africa. It is gaining influence in government and public affairs as it is perceived as politically more neutral than Afrikaans, which is associated with the apartheid era. The influence of English in present-day South Africa is remarkable given that it is the mother tongue of under 10 per cent of the population, though it is spoken as a second or third language by many others. As Crystal notes, 'historical, racial, tribal, and political factors have combined to produce a sociolinguistic situation of stunning intricacy' in South Africa (2003:356).

South African English (SAE) is a variant of British English (specifically southeast English); because of the relatively recent date of their transplantation, SAE, AusE, and NZE bear similarities with each other. However, one cannot really talk about a unified South African English. Lanham (1982:336–7) distinguishes three varieties based on linguistic and social variables: Conservative South African, similar to RP (spoken by British immigrants of recent descent, generally upper class, female, and over 45), a newly indigenous dialect, Respectable South African (spoken by middle- and upper-class residents of the Natal region); and Extreme (or broad) South African (spoken by lower-class residents of the Cape region and by some Afrikaaner speakers). An advanced form of Afrikaans-English is also recognized.

Like BE, SAE is non-rhotic and shows a merger of [hw] and [w] as [w]. However, it has also departed in significant ways from RP. SAE is 'alone among the "English" varieties of English' in lacking intrusive and linking *r* (Trudgill and Hannah 2002:29). The lack of *h*-dropping and the consistent pronunciation of *-ing* as [ɪŋ] rather than [ɪn] in SAE may be due to the absence of an English-speaking manual-laboring class (Wells 1982:622). Other consonant features include the following: [t] between vowels may be flapped (as in NAE); [l] is always clear; [r] can be pro-nounced as a fricative or 'tapped' with the tongue touching the roof of the mouth; [l] and [n] are not syllabic in words such as *middle* or *button*; and [tj] may coalesce to [č] and [dj] to [ǰ] in words such as *tune* and *due* (this also occurs in CanE). An interesting split affects the [ɪ] vowel: it is raised to [i] before and after velars, before [š], after [h], and at the start of words or syllables, but it is lowered to [ə] elsewhere; thus, *kit* and *mitt* do not rhyme. An apparently stigmatized feature is the lowering and retraction of certain vowels following [l]. The monophthongization of [ɪu] to [u] is common (as in USEng). The [eɪ] and [oʊ] diphthongs have centralized starting points, as in CanE, namely, [əɪ] and [əʊ]. Wells notes a 'cross-over' effect where the onset of [aɪ] is further back and that of [aʊ] further forward (1982:614). The [ɑ] vowel in *bath* is very far back and may be rounded. In broad accents [ɛ] in *dress* may be raised to [e] and [æ] in *trap* to [ɛ]. Finally, the more extreme varieties of SAE show a number of phonological features that can be attributed to Afrikaans interference, such as the lack of aspiration on voiceless consonants, devoicing of final stops as in *bad* or *bag*, the audible release of stops in clusters such as in *apt* and *picture*, the 'trilling' of [r], the voicing of initial [h] to [j], and nasalization of vowels before nasal + fricative clusters as in *dance*.

Grammatically, SAE shows little difference from the other varieties of English, though again some features may be attributed to Afrikaans influence, such as differ-ent preposition usage (e.g. *over* for 'about') or use of the *be busy* (V)-*ing* construction as a progressive. As in many forms of English, the invariant tag *is it?* is common (as in *That was a good movie, isn't it?*). Other distinctive features include the deletion of objects sometimes after transitive verbs, the use of *with* without an object (*Should I go with?*) (a construction found in some North American dialects), reduplications such as *now-now*, the appearance of *already* as a perfective particle at the end of sen-tences, the use of *must* for *shall,* and the infinitive used after an adjective instead of *of* plus a participle (*capable to understand her*).

In the lexicon, one can point to borrowings from Afrikaans (many of which occur in the broad variety of SAE and are a result of early contact), e.g. *kop/kopje* 'hill', *oud-stryder* 'veteran', *braai* 'barbeque', *in a dwaal* 'confused', *bywoner* 'poor tenant farmer', *kreef* 'crayfish', *blink klip* 'diamond', *padkos* 'provisions for a journey', *platteland* 'rural area', *broek* 'coward', *konfyt* 'fruit preserve', *boerewors* 'spiced sausage', or *sitkamer* 'sitting room, lounge'. The *OED* lists several hun-dred words from Afrikaans, but many relate to flora and fauna indigenous to South Africa. Fewer borrowings come from the Bantu languages; some examples include *impala, maas* 'thickened sour milk', *mamba* 'large venomous snake', *dagga* 'mor-tar made of mud and cow-dung', *lobola* 'bride price', *bonsella* 'surprise gift', and *muti* 'medicine'. Borrowings from the Khoisan languages are even rarer, e.g. *gnu* 'member of the antelope family', and *kierie* 'short club'. Some borrowings show complex routes of transmission, such as *dagga* 'hemp' from the Khoisan languages via Afrikaans. Certain SAE borrowings are now part of standard English, such as *basenji* 'breed of dog' (< Bantu), *veldt* (< Afrikaans), *apartheid* (< Afrikaans), *trek* (< Afrikaans), and *kraal* 'animal enclosure' (Afrikaans < Portuguese). Rather than borrowing, SAE may resort to calquing, as in the case of *monkey's wedding* 'simultaneous sun and rain' (based on Zulu expression). Some standard English words have acquired a specialized sense in SAE, including *robot* 'traffic light', *cubbyhole* 'glove compartment', *bioscope* 'movie theatre' (this one used to be in BE but is now obsolete), *cool drink* 'soft drink', *tackies* 'running shoes', *café* 'convenience store', *bell* 'to telephone', *camp* 'fenced-in portion of a farm', *just now* 'in a while', *rather very* 'somewhat', *butchery* 'butcher's shop', *bottle store* 'liquor store', and the language of apartheid (*homeland, township, endorsed out, classify, job reservation*, etc.).

Liberian English

The country of Liberia was founded in 1822. Over the next 50 years, some 15,000 freed American slaves as well as 6,000 slaves captured at sea settled there. The country became an independent republic in 1847 with a constitution modeled on that of the United States. The descendants of these original settlers, known as Americo-Liberians, were politically dominant until a coup in 1980. According to 1993 statistics, approximately 69,000 people, or 2.5 per cent of the population, spoke Liberian Standard English (LSE) as a first language. Liberia is the only country in Africa where English is the native language of black people (though increasingly blacks in South Africa are adopting English as a mother tongue). LSE has roots in southern dialects of US African American Vernacular English (also called Black English). The vowel system is more elaborate than in other West African variants; LSE distinguishes [i] from [ɪ], and [u] from [ʊ], and it uses the diphthongs [aɪ], [aʊ], and [əɪ]. Vowels can be nasalized. The final vowel of *happy* is [ɛ]. Like West African English generally, LSE favors open syllables, usually omitting a final [t], [d], or fricative. The interdental fricatives [θ, ð] appear as [t, d] initially, and as [f, v] finally. The glottal fricative [h] is preserved, as is the labiovelar fricative [hw]. Affricates have lost their stop component, thus [č] > [š]. Between vowels, [t] may be flapped as in NAE. Finally, liquids are lost at the end of words or before consonants, making Liberian Standard English a non-rhotic dialect.

Caribbean English

Beginning in the seventeenth century, various European powers, including France, the Netherlands, Spain, Portugal, Denmark, and Britain, vied for territory in the West Indies, initiating over 350 years of political and linguistic struggle in the region. Indigenous peoples of the area included Carib and Arawak speakers, to which were added groups of West African slaves, often speaking mutually unintelligible languages, brought over to work on the sugar cane plantations. There was also a European ruling class. Pidgin languages developed in order to facilitate communication, and over time, these pidgins underwent processes of creolization (see Chapter 9). The result was a set of English-, French-, Spanish-, Portuguese-, and even Dutch-based creoles spoken in the Caribbean in the seventeenth and eighteenth centuries. Where Britain exerted political power, BE became the prestige dialect (as it has remained to some degree, although US English is displacing it).

Many creoles in the Caribbean have undergone a subsequent process of 'decreolization'. This occurs when a creole and a higher prestige language—in this case, standard English—remain in contact. In this process, the creole (the substratum) is increasingly influenced by the high status language (the superstratum) and comes to resemble it more closely. This process typically involves complication (introducing irregularities and counteracting simplification) and 'purification' (in this case, removing elements derived from African languages, which are typically stigmatized, and adding more English lexicon). The result of decreolization in the Caribbean has been what linguists refer to as a post-creole continuum, a spread of dialects ranging from the 'deepest' creole to something approximating standard English. The socially most powerful variety closest to the standard is called the 'acrolect' and the variety showing the most creole characteristics is called the 'basilect'. Between these are a number of 'mesolects', showing a varying number of features of the creole or standard English.

English is now the national or official language of several countries in the Caribbean area (not all of which were originally British holdings), including Anguilla, Antigua, Barbados, Belize, the Cayman Islands, Dominica, Grenada, Guyana, Jamaica, Montserrat, Puerto Rico, St Kitts and Nevis, St Vincent, St Lucia, Trinidad and Tobago, Turks and Caicos Islands, and the British and US Virgin Islands; it is also beginning to displace French in Dominica and St Lucia. (An English-based creole, Gullah, is also spoken on islands off the coast of South Carolina and Georgia.) Because of immigration, one encounters Caribbean English in Canada, the United States, and Britain as well, and Caribbean writers have gained popularity in these countries. An example of Caribbean English can be found in the poetry of John Agard, who is originally from Guyana but moved to England in 1977. In his poem 'Listen Mr Oxford don', first published in his 1985 collection *Mangoes and Bullets*, he uses his native Caribbean creole to comment on 'mugging ["assaulting"] de Queen's English' in Clapham Common in London and respond to the hostility of language 'authorities' to his variety of English.[6]

Whether a decreolized form should be seen as a dialect of English or as a distinct language is not at all clear, especially in the light of the emergence of Caribbean islands as independent countries and growing awareness and understanding of linguistic diversity and change. What is perhaps most significant about Caribbean

---

6 Similar views on language are expressed by Jamaican poet and singer Louise Bennett (1919–2006) in her poem 'Bans a Killin' (see http://www.louisebennett.com/). See this textbook's website for a version of Bennett's poem alongside a literal Standard English translation.

Listen Mr Oxford don

Me not no Oxford don
me a simple immigrant
from Clapham Common
I didn't graduate
I immigrate

But listen Mr Oxford don
I'm a man on de run
and a man on de run
is a dangerous one

I ent have no gun
I ent have no knife
but mugging de Queen's English
is the story of my life

I dont need no axe
to split/ up yu syntax
I dont need no hammer
to mash/ up yu grammar

I warning you Mr Oxford don
I'm a wanted man
and a wanted man
is a dangerous one

Dem accuse me of assault
on de Oxford dictionary/
imagin a concise peaceful man like me/
dem want me serve time
for inciting rhyme to riot
but I tekking it quiet
down here in Clapham Common

I'm not a violent man Mr Oxford don
I only armed wit mih human breath
but human breath
is a dangerous weapon

So mek dem send one big word after me
I ent serving no jail sentence
I slashing suffix in self-defence
I bashing future wit present tense
and if necessary

I making de Queen's English accessory/ to my offence

(John Agard, from *Mangoes and Bullets: Selected and
New Poems 1972–84* [London: Serpent's Tail, 1990], p. 44)

English, no matter what form it takes, is that it is a form of English spoken natively by large numbers of people.

It may be possible to characterize a West Indian Standard English (WISE), namely, the acrolectal dialect spoken in places such as Jamaica, Trinidad, and Guyana by educated people at the top of the social scale. Description of this standard poses difficulties because it shows substantial regional variation and because one cannot know how many mesolectal features to include. Phonologically, WISE is normally non-rhotic, though [r] is articulated in Barbados and the Virgin Islands, and may be heard in Guyana and Jamaica. The [h] generally occurs (though not in the more creolized varieties), [w] and [hw] are not distinguished, and [l] is clear in all positions. The replacement of [θ] by [t] and [ð] by [d] is widespread, especially before [r]. A creole feature is the reduction of final consonant sequences, e.g. the loss of [t] in *best, left, act, pushed, hoped,* and *touched* or of [d] in *rubbed, begged, roved, breathed, wind,* and *child,* though sequences of nasal + voiceless consonant, as in *dance, ant, ink,* and *lamp* are maintained. Metathesis can occur, especially with [sk/ks] *ask/aks* and [sp/ps] *wasp/waps.* Vowel features show an even greater range of variability. However, many of the vowel mergers common in creoles (e.g. *cat/cot/ caught* as [æ], *buy/boy* as [aɪ], *bud/bird* as rounded [ʌ], *fear/fare* as [ie]) typically do not occur in WISE. Perhaps what gives Caribbean English its most distinctive sound is the full value given to vowels in unstressed syllables as well as the fact that the language is syllable-timed (syllables occurring at approximately regular intervals) rather than stress-timed (only stressed syllables occur at regular intervals). The grammar of WISE may also show some creole features.

The different varieties of Caribbean English have distinct vocabularies. A sampling of terms from Jamaican English include *janga* 'crayfish', *ganja* 'marijuana' (originally from Hindi), *bankra* 'big basket', *bandalu* 'fraud', *bakra* 'member of the ruling class', *dukunu* 'sweet cornmeal dumpling', *irie* 'cool, good, nice', *dunny* 'money', *facety* 'cheeky', *roti* 'type of bread' (originally from Hindi), and *labrish* 'gossip'. Of African origin are *duppy* 'ghost, spirit' and *burru* 'a vigorous dance'. Of French origin is *drogher* 'cooking vessel'. Standard English words may be used in specialized ways, as in *dreadlocks* 'Rastafarian hairstyle', *dread* 'terrible, excellent', *foot* 'leg and foot', *licks* 'a beating', *look for* 'to visit', *peelhead* 'bald-headed person', *a something* 'thing', *vex* 'annoyed', and *watchy* 'watchman'. Some words found in standard English were first borrowed in the West Indies, including *hurricane* (< Spanish < Carib), *savannah* (< Spanish < Carib), *manatee* (< Spanish < Carib), *iguana* (< Spanish < Carib), *calypso,* and *reggae.*

Important Regional Varieties

Within each of the national varieties of English, there exist numerous regional dialects. Because of the length of settlement of Britain by English speakers, regional dialects in this area are numerous and localized, including Cockney, West Country,

East Anglia, Birmingham, Cumberland, Devonshire, Cornwall, Dorset, Durham, Lancashire, Nothumberland, and Yorkshire, to name just a few. A particularly important present-day regional and social dialect in Britain is Estuary English, which originates as a dialect centered in London but extending throughout southeastern England and spoken by members of the lower-middle class. *Estuary English* bears certain similarities to Cockney English. It is spreading northwards and westwards and in some contexts is in competition with RP as a prestige, or at least widely accepted, dialect. While space does not permit a full discussion of all of the regional dialects of Britain, we will focus on three which have semi-national status: Welsh, Scottish, and Irish (or Hiberno-) English. We will then survey some of the important regional varieties of United States English, including African American Vernacular English.

English in the British Isles

The varieties of English spoken in Wales, Scotland, and Ireland have developed along separate paths and are distinctly different dialects of the language, yet because they are spoken in areas first inhabited by Celtic speakers, they all show some Celtic influence in their phonology, grammar, and lexicon.

Welsh English

Political and linguistic assimilation of Wales into England occurred in 1536 when English was declared the official language of Wales, and soon afterwards the use of the English Bible and Book of Common Prayer was required by law in Wales. A diglossic situation remained for some time, in which Welsh was the 'lower' and English the upper language. In the early twentieth century, English came to displace Welsh, especially in border areas, but more recent attempts to revive the Celtic language have been relatively successful, with perhaps 20 per cent of the population able to speak Welsh. (The methods of revival include compulsory instruction in the schools, funding of a Welsh-language television station, and recognition of Welsh as an official language, used alongside English on road signs and in government publications.) Nonetheless, English is the country's dominant language, and a native variety called Welsh English (WE) is identifiable. WE is not strongly affected by the Welsh substratum, though in the north and southwest, Celtic influence is most strongly evident (e.g. [z] and [ž] may be voiceless in the north while, in the southwest, an [r] after a vowel—a tapped or rolled *r*—is retained, as is [hw]).

Phonologically, WE is very similar to RP. There is a tendency to monophthongize [eɪ] to [e], especially when spelled *a* as in *made*, but this sound is distinguished from the sound in *maid* [ɛɪ] and other words spelled with *ai, ay, ei,* or *ey*. Likewise there is a tendency to monophthongize [oʊ] to [o], especially when spelled *o* or *oo* as in *no,* but this sound is distinguished from the *know* [ɔʊ] and other words spelled with *ou,* or *ow.* The diphthongs [aɪ] and [aʊ] are centered to [əɪ] and [əʊ] (as in CanE).

The diphthong [ɪu] as in *new* is often pronounced [ɪʊ]. No contrast is made between the stressed and unstressed mid central vowel; both are [ə]. Some words with [ɔ] have [o], such as *soar*, but others retain [ɔ], such as *port*. The sound in *ask* words such as *dance* is [æ] rather than [ɑ], though practice varies and may be socially determined, with [ɑ] for some speakers and in some words. Unstressed syllables are not weak and tend to be pronounced; thus *separate* is [sɛpərɛt], not [sɛprət]. For this reason, rather than [ə], unstressed orthographic *a* may be pronounced [æ], unstressed orthographic *o* [ɒ], and unstressed orthographic *e* [ɛ].

For educated speakers, WE is non-rhotic, with linking and intrusive *r*, though *r* may be retroflex, rolled, or even uvular. Voiceless stops are strongly aspirated, [l] is always clear, [t, d, n] may be dental rather than alveolar, and [w] and [hw] are not distinguished. *H*-dropping is common and [j] and [w] are lost in initial position before [i] and [u], as in *yeast* (pronounced like *east*) and *wood* (pronounced like *hood*, when [h] is also absent). At the end of words, [ž] may become [ǰ] as in *prestige*. Perhaps most distinctive in WE is the lengthening of intervocalic consonants before unstressed syllables, as in *money, chapel, missing,* and *butter*. Also, the Welsh consonants [ɬ] (a voiceless lateral fricative), spelled *ll*, and [x], spelled *ch*, may occur in place names and loan words.

In written form, WE is indistinguishable from BE. However, colloquial, oral WE exhibits some distinguishing grammatical features, including use of the invariable tag *is it?*, inversion of predicate object (e.g. *Looking for you he was*), use of negative *too* (instead of *either*) (e.g. *He wasn't on time too*), and adjective and adverb reduplication for emphasis (e.g. *it was long, long*).

There is a remarkably small number of Welsh loan words in WE. Apart from general Celtic terms, a few that may be cited are *del* and *bach*, which are terms of endearment; *eisteddfod* 'competitive arts festival'; *llymru* 'porridge dish'; *nain* 'grandma'; *taid* 'grandpa'; and *Duw* 'God', used in exclamations. The *OED* cites a handful of Welsh borrowings, such as *cynghanedd* 'a system of alliteration and rhyme in Welsh poetry', *cwn* 'a valley', *commot* 'territorial and administrative division' and *van* 'height, summit', most of which are highly localized or obsolete. A few Welsh words have entered standard English usage, such as *bard* 'minstrel', *corgi* 'breed of dog', and perhaps *gull* 'sea gull'. Some distinctive uses of standard English terms may also be noted in WE, such as *delight* 'interest', *rise* 'get, buy', *tidy* 'good, nice', and *be off* 'be angry'.

Standard Scottish English

English has been spoken in southwest Scotland since medieval times. There is a continuum of Scots English dialects spoken from the Orkney and Shetland islands of the north to the Lowlands of the south, while Scots Gaelic continues to be spoken, albeit not widely, in the north and west of Scotland. The linguistic relationship between Scotland and England has always rested on complex political and cultural factors.The union of crowns in 1603 and the union of parliaments in 1707 established

English as the official language in Scotland, but nationalism has always been strong, and the parliaments were separated again in 1999.

Scots, or Scottish (both terms are widely used), was a standardized form of the English language spoken in southern Scotland and used in government and literature until the Reformation. It derives from the Northumbrian dialect of Old English. It is the language of Robert Henryson, William Dunbar, and Robert Burns. Scots has been replaced by Standard Scottish English (SSE), which began to be used at the start of the eighteenth century. RP is not the prestige dialect in Scotland; SSE is the speech of educated, middle-class, urban Scots today. SSE is distinguished from RP primarily by its phonology, along with some lexical and grammatical features.

The phonology of SSE is conservative. Several features of the vowel system are salient. One is the preservation of short vowel distinctions before /r/ in prestige versions of SSE, which in other dialects have merged to [ə]. Thus, *first* contains the [ɪ] sound and *fern* the [ɛ] sound; also for some speakers the vowel in *horse* [ɔ] is distinguished from the vowel in *hoarse* [o]. A second striking feature is the lack of distinction between [u] and [ʊ]; thus, *pool* and *pull*, *foot* and *boot*, *full* and *fool* are all pronounced with [u] (or a slightly further forward vowel [ʉ]). Some speakers may not distinguish between *cot* and *caught*, having [ɔ] in both (rather than [ɑ] or [ɒ] found in many NAE dialects). The vowels [ɪ] and [ə] may be neutralized, so that *fin* and *fun* rhyme. As in NAE, SSE speakers do not have the distinction between [æ] and [ɑ] which distinguishes *ample* from *sample*. The sounds in *great* and *home* tend to be monophthongs, [e] and [o], though the diphthongal versions are spreading. The [aɪ] diphthong has split into [əɪ], as in *side*, and [ae], as in *sighed* (the latter in positions of length). The [aʊ] diphthong has not undergone a similar split but can be centralized to [əʊ]. (The stereotypical Scottish pronunciation of *house* with [u] shows the influence of Scots Gaelic.) In SSE, vowels are frequently long since all short vowels (except [ə] and [ɪ]) are lengthened before voiced fricatives ([v, z, ð]), [r], and at the end of a word.

In respect to consonants, SSE is a rhotic dialect. It distinguishes [hw] and [w], and may even use [hw] when not expected, as in *weasel*. The voiceless stops [p, t, k] are lightly aspirated and [l] may be dark in all positions. Despite the perception that Scots 'roll their *r*'s', *r* is more often a flap or a 'continuant' (which means that the vocal tract is only partly closed). There is no *h*-dropping in SSE. The Gaelic sound [x] is found in personal and place names and loan words (e.g. *loch, clachan* 'village') but also occasionally in English words such as *thought* or *night*. [θ] is used rather than [ð] in words such as *with, through,* and *although*. A [t] in non-initial position may become a glottal stop, though this appears to be stigmatized. In the Celtic-speaking areas (the Highlands and Isles), interference from Gaelic is obvious in the following ways: voiced stops may be devoiced, voiceless consonants may be heavily aspirated, [l] is clear, [t] and [d] may be dental, [θ] and [ð] may be missing, and voiced sibilants are devoiced.

The grammar of SSE also exhibits a significant number of distinctive character-istics (most of which are also found in Ulster English). The definite article is often used in different ways than in BE, e.g. *in the hospital* (this usage is also found in USEng), *go to the shops for the milk*, *wear the kilt*, *the now* 'just now', and *the day* 'today'. The remnant plural noun forms, *shoon/shuin* 'shoes', *eyen* 'eyes', and *kyne* 'cows', may be found, and with measure terms, plural marking on the noun may be absent, as in *ten year ago*. Some speakers continue to use the second-person singular forms, *thou/thy/thee*, but others have innovated a new plural form, *yous*. In 'broad' accents, the demonstrative forms are *thir* 'these' and *thae* 'those', which may also represent remnant forms, and the interrogative/relative forms are *at* 'that', *whae* 'who', *wham* 'whom', *whase* 'whose', and *whilk* 'which'. Resembling older usage, *that* may be used in both non-restrictive and restrictive relative clauses.

There are a number of distinctive verbal forms, including *gae/gaed/gane* 'go, went, gone', *hing/hang/hungin* 'hang, hanged/hung, hung', *lauch/leuch/lauchen* 'laugh, laughed, laughed', *do/done/done*, *tellt* 'told', *brung* 'brought', *taen* 'took', and *sellt* 'sold'. The negative particle is realized as *no* or *nae* and is typically contracted to form items such as *canno*, *didnae*, *hadnae*, or *amnae*. Multiple negatives are still pos-sible. In regard to the modal auxiliaries, *will* has virtually replaced *shall* (as in NAE), *can* or *get to* is used for permissive *may*, *should* or *want* substitutes for *ought*, and *mustn't* is common. The infinitival marker *to* may precede a modal verb, e.g. *I'd like to could do that*, and multiple modals are possible, e.g. *She'll no can give us coffee the day* (this feature is found in some dialects of United States English). Even when *have* acts as a main verb, *not* follows it; no dummy *do* is required: thus, *I hadnae a party for him* for 'I didn't have a party for him'. In contrast, *need* is always a main verb (as is the case for most speakers of NAE). The structure *needs washed* 'needs wash-ing' is found as is *wants out* 'wants to go out' (a structure also found in NAE). The agent in the passive may be marked with *frae* 'from' or *by*, as in earlier English. The progressive with state verbs is more widespread than in other varieties, as in *I'm need-ing to see you*. The past tense is used when the perfect would be expected in BE; this usage is also found in NAE, thus *Did you see the film?* 'Have you seen the film?' The tag *isn't it* (> *init*?) is common, as is the tag *e* [e], similar to *eh* in other varieties. In general, tags are widespread, even following interrogatives. Frequently, prepositional usage varies from the standard, as in *married on* 'married to' and *throw ower* 'throw out of', and the *a-* prefix is used with certain forms (*afore, aneath, aside, atween*) that standardly have a *be-* prefix (*before, beneath, beside, between*).

Scottish English has a fairly distinctive vocabulary. Scottish forms widely known outside Scotland (and found in general dictionaries of English) include *auld* 'old', *wee* 'little', *pinkie* 'finger' (now also in NAE), *aye, nay, burn* 'stream', *bonny* 'pretty', *lass*, and *ay* 'always'. SSE contains borrowings from Scots Gaelic, such as *loch* 'lake', *baudrons* 'cat', *caber* 'pole', *clachan* 'village', *coronach* 'funeral song, dirge', *dod* 'slight fit of ill humor', *droich* 'dwarf', and *strool* 'stream of liquid' (used by James Joyce), some of which have entered general usage, such as *cairn, clan, glen, sporran, plaid, whiskey*, and *ptarmigan* 'bird of the grouse family'. Moreover, quite a number of lexical items in SSE (and northern British dialects) are medieval borrowings from Old Norse, such as *kirk* 'church', *freit* 'omen', *coup* 'to barter, exchange', *brough* 'halo', *carline/carling* 'woman' (contemptuous term), *birkie* 'fellow' (jocular term), *brae* 'steep bank of a river', and *clour* 'bump on head'. Many of the forms cited in dictionaries of Scotticisms are known by relatively few present-day Scots, such as *wheen* 'many', *glaikit* 'stupid', *stoor* 'dust', *scunner* 'to disgust', and *darg* 'task', while others are unknown outside of rural, agricultural contexts, such as *grosser* 'gooseberry', *cuit* 'ankle', *skaup* 'skull', and *capoosh* 'hood'; these are usually only known to older speakers. Finally, a number of standard English words assume specialized meanings in SSE, such as *(lord) provost* 'mayor', *stay* 'to live, reside', *sort* 'to mend', *fire-raising* 'arson', *advocate* 'barrister, lawyer', *gate* 'road', *travel* 'go on foot', *scheme* 'local government housing estate', *mind* 'memory, recollection', and *sober* 'poor, miserable, humble'.

Hiberno-English

Although English has been present in Ireland since the twelfth century, Irish Gaelic retained its dominance until the 1600s. This dominance was eroded by the defeat of the Irish during the reign of Elizabeth I, an influx of English settlers during the reign of James I, efforts by Cromwell to dominate the Irish, and various plantation schemes. Under the Act of Union of 1800, Ireland became part of England and Gaelic began a steady decline. English was dominant by the mid-nineteenth century. Different settlement patterns as well as the partition of Ireland in 1921 into an independent southern Republic of Ireland and a British Northern Ireland have led to different developments of both English and Gaelic throughout the island. The language of Northern Ireland, also known as Ulster-Scots or Scots-Irish, bears strong similarities to the language of Scotland, as it results in large part from seventeenth-century Protestant immigrants from southwest Scotland. (For the most part, present-day Catholics are the descendants of the original Irish inhabitants of the area, while present-day Protestants are descendants of seventeenth-century Scots immigrants.) However, even in Northern Ireland one finds a range of accents from heavily Scots-influenced Ulster-Scots of the far north to less heavily Scots-influenced Mid-Ulster varieties in the border area. The language of the Republic of Ireland is the result of immigrants from the West Country and the West Midlands of England who settled originally in the Dublin area; their speech spread throughout the country. Considerable diversity exists between the urban, more English-like varieties and the rural, more Gaelic-influenced ones. While Irish Gaelic was much in decline by the mid-nineteenth century, it has received some support in the Republic of Ireland, where it is spoken natively by a small number of speakers in certain areas (known as the Gaeltacht), is an official language, and is taught in the schools.

We will discuss Anglo-Irish English, often called Hiberno-English (HE), in relation primarily to the dialect spoken in southern Ireland. Phonologically, the dialect is conservative, showing none of the BE or NAE innovations. As in Scottish English, RP is not the exclusive prestige dialect. For vowels, 'there is a measure of truth in the view than an Irish accent consists in the sounds of Irish imposed upon English' (Wells 1982:419). Some features stereotypically associated with HE are, in fact, recessive or found only in the speech of uneducated people, such as the failure to raise the ME [ɛ̄] vowel in *tea, steal, meat, leave, cheat, tea,* and *easy* from [e] to [i], the merger of the [ɔɪ] and [aɪ] diphthongs as [əɪ] so that *boy* and *buy* are homophones, or the pronunciation of *ol* as [aʊl] in *cold* and *old*. A feature found in contemporary HE is rounding of [ə] so that *look* and *luck, put* and *putt,* or *took* and *tuck* are nearly homophones. For some speakers, [ɛ] and [ɪ] merge as [ɛ] before [n], so that *pen* and *pin* are homophones (this feature is also found in some dialects of USEng). Also, as in SSE, vowels are not reduced before *r*, and [e] and [o] tend to be monophthongs. The vowels [ɒ] and [ɔ], which have merged in many dialects of English, are distinct in *stalked* and *stock* and generally before [p, t, k], but not elsewhere, so that *awful/offal* or *sawed/sod* are the same. The use of [æ] or [ɑ] in *ask* words is far from clear, though [æ] may certainly be heard. There are distinctive pronunciations of *many* and *any* with [æ] not [ɛ]. As in CanE, *opinion/official* have [o] rather than [ə] in the first syllable. The unstressed vowel is typically [ə], not [ɪ], so that *addition* and *edition* are not distinguished. Schwa is also found instead of [ɪu] or [o] in the unstressed syllables of *speculate* or *yellow*.

HE is a rhotic dialect, generally using a retroflex [r] as in NAE, though it may be 'darker' and it can be fricativized after [t] and [d]. The distinction between [w] and [hw] is maintained. There is no *h*-dropping, and [l] is always clear. Perhaps most distinctive among the consonant sounds is the treatment of the interdental fricatives [θ, ð]. These are realized as dentalized [t, d], so there is only a slight difference (one of place, not manner, of articulation) between, for example, the initial sounds in *thin* and *tin* or the final sounds of *breathe* and *breed*. Some speakers use dentalized stops for both. This is attributed to Gaelic influence. Concomitantly, *width* and *with* or *breadth* and *breath* may not be distinguished, while *breathed* may be disyllabic. To complicate matters, after or between vowels [t] may be a glottal stop, a voiced [t], or a flap. Final [p, t, k] are released and aspirated. In heavily Gaelic-influenced dialects, [s] > [š] and [z] > [ž], as in *star* and *wisdom*. An occasional [x] is heard in Gaelic words.

HE often has postponed stress on verbal suffixes (*educáte, prosecúte*) and in polysyllabic words on a syllable followed by consonant cluster (*algébra, charácter*), though the latter is stigmatized. This feature is found in Scottish, Caribbean, and Indian English, but is more advanced in the Hiberno-English dialect.

The influence of Irish Gaelic may be seen in a number of syntactic calques. The construction *be after* (V)-*ing*, as in *he is/was after getting up*, is used for the perfect 'he has/had just gotten up'. The construction *do* + V (including *be*) or verbal periphrase, as in *he does sing* (in the north often *he bees singing*)/*he does be happy/he does be writing*, expresses the habitual. The conjunction *and* serves as an all-purpose subordinating conjunction, meaning 'when', 'while', 'if', etc., as in *I was happy and I left* 'I was happy when I left'. It is common to see marked predicative constructions move to the front of the sentence, as in *Coming home late are you?* Sentence clefting, or division, often without any intended emphasis, is common, as in *Is it happy that you are?* rather than *Are you happy?*' People commonly reverse the usual order of subject and auxiliary in indirect questions, as in *I asked when is it due* 'I asked when it was due'. Relative pronouns are frequently omitted. Speakers ask many rhetorical questions, and they express possession with the construction *be* + *near/ at/by*, as in *There wasn't any money by that boy* 'That boy didn't have any money'.

Other features of the HE verb system include the use of *will* for *shall* (also found in NAE); occurrence of the *be*-perfect, as in *He is arrived home* for 'He has arrived home'; the more frequent use of the progressive, especially with state verbs, as in *She is liking chocolate* for 'She likes chocolate'; and the use of the present for the perfect or the past for the past perfect, as in *He's dead ten years* 'He has been dead ten years' or *He said that he paid me* for 'He said that he had paid me'. In fact, Irish people tend to avoid the perfect generally, preferring constructions like *Did you see him yet?* to mean 'Have you seen him yet' (a feature also of NAE). HE employs the forms *used be* for *used to be*, *amn't* for *aren't,* and *mustn't* for *can't*, and uses *let* for second-person imperatives, as in *Let you see to that*. We also find negative progressive imperatives, as in *Don't be saying that*. Preposition usage differs from BE: *till* is used for *to* or *until*, as in time expressions such as *quarter till five* 'quarter to five' (also used in USEng), *of* and *on* may be interchanged, and *from* is used for *since*. In the pronoun system, *yous(e)* is commonly employed for plural *you*, but with a singular verb, i.e. *youse is*. *Yes* and *no* are avoided in preference for an elliptical clause, e.g. *Are you ready? I am/I am not.*

HE contains borrowings from Irish Gaelic, for example, *spalpeen* 'rascal', *barmbrack* 'currant bun', *gombeen* 'usury', *bonny-clabber* 'clotted milk', *merrow* 'mermaid', *moulleen* 'cow without horns', *bosthoon* 'awkward, tactless fellow', *colleen* 'girl', and *lough* 'lake' (cf. Scottish *loch*), some of which have entered standard English, including *shamrock, banshee, galore* 'abundant', *leprechaun, hubbub, bog, puss* 'ugly face', *brogue* 'kind of shoe', and *smithereens* 'small fragments' (note that *-een* is a diminutive suffix in Irish). As with Scotticisms, it is likely that many terms cited as Anglo-Irish or Irish in dictionaries are not widely known among younger, urban HE speakers. Specialized Irish forms of words include *boyo* 'boy', *eejit* 'idiot', and *bejasus* 'by Jesus'. Some English words are used in specialized senses in HE, as *leaf* 'brim of a hat', *lashings* 'floods', *flake* 'to beat, flog', *ball (of malt)* 'glass (of whiskey)', *snug* 'moderately well to do', *bold* 'naughty', *yoke* 'gadget, thing', *cog* 'to cheat', *cant* 'auction, disposal of goods', and *chief(e)ry* 'office or territory of a chief'. HE has a distinctive set of directional terms: *back* 'westwards', *below* 'northwards', *over* 'eastwards', and *up above* 'southwards' (Trudgill and Hannah 2002:104).

Exercise 13.2 Vocabulary of National Dialects

Using the *OED*, supply the information requested for each word.

	Word	National Variety	Meaning	Source
a.	sasquatch	_____	_____	_____
b.	puckeroo	_____	_____	_____
c.	dowf	_____	_____	_____
d.	natty	_____	_____	_____
e.	kiva	_____	_____	_____
f.	bodach	_____	_____	_____
g.	sangoma	_____	_____	_____
h.	bywoner	_____	_____	_____
i.	coracle	_____	_____	_____
j.	potlatch	_____	_____	_____
k.	walkabout	_____	_____	_____
l.	joual	_____	_____	_____
m.	hogan	_____	_____	_____

English in the United States

Spoken varieties in the United States have been the object of intensive study. Dialect atlases, the publications of the American Dialect Society, urban surveys, and the *Dictionary of American Regional English* record evidence of regional pronunciation, grammar, and vocabulary. Yet there is little consensus as to how American dialects should be demarcated or whether boundaries should or should not be drawn upon the basis of particular evidence. For example, Pederson (2001) places New York City speech within a larger northeastern dialect along with Eastern New England, while

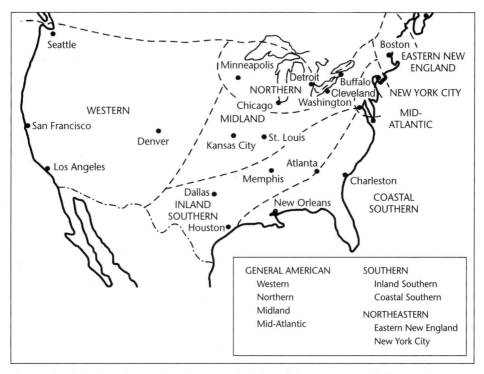

Figure 13.4 Regional Varieties of US English (adapted from Peter Trudgill and Jean Hannah, *International English: A Guide to Varieties of Standard English*, 4th edn [London: Arnold, 2002], p. 41)

Trudgill and Hannah (2002) decide that both are important and distinctive enough to constitute separate categories. Even the claim that a General American speech exists may be debated. The complex story of historic settlement, modern immigration, and continuing mobility complicate any dialect map. Variation precludes the drawing of definite dialect boundaries; at best an indistinct pattern of probable dialect distribution emerges (Pederson 2001:258). Moreover, there are other dialects that need further study, such as American-Indian English and Chicano English. We must also keep in mind that discussions of United States regional dialects often neglect the contribution of African American and Latino American ethnic speakers (e.g. in New Mexico).

With these stipulations, we may still make some generalizations. Three main dialect areas can be identified within USEng: General American, Northeastern, and Southern (see Figure 13.4). Among these three areas we find the subregional dialects enumerated below.[7]

---

7 The following account is drawn largely from Pederson (2001) and Trudgill and Hannah (2002:40–7).

General American

To some extent General American speech may be identified as much by a lack of distinguishing features as by their presence. Certainly we may contrast this dialect with the marked features of Northeastern and Southern speech.

MID-ATLANTIC

Another label for this dialect is Central Eastern, but the geographical term Mid-Atlantic is more transparent. The dialect spreads over southeastern New York State, most of New Jersey beyond the New York suburbs, eastern Pennsylvania, Delaware, and Maryland. This dialect has many features common to NAE such as rhoticity. In addition, however, it has a number of recent innovations, found among younger speakers here. Of primary importance is the behavior of the vowels [ɑ], [æ], and [ɛ], which are being moved to [æ], [e], and [ə], respectively, in accordance with the 'Northern Cities Chain Shift' (a phenomenon explained in the section on Northern speech below). Another characteristic innovation involves [eɪ] as in *bay,* which is becoming increasingly closer and narrowed to [ɛɪ]. A contrast with Southern USEng is thus developing, where the diphthong widens, as it does in AusE, NZE, and SAE. In addition, allophones of the diphthong [aɪ] which occur before voiceless consonants are being raised to [ə] to give the pronunciation *night time* [nəɪt taɪm]. Finally, we might mention that the [u] in *boot* is being fronted to a high central rounded vowel and the onset of [oʊ] in *boat* to a mid-central or mid-front rounded vowel.

An account of vocabulary in Mid-Atlantic speech proves difficult because General American lexical items often overlap. For example, from Pennsylvania Dutch country in southeastern Pennsylvania come a number of German loan translations. ('Dutch' does not refer to Holland but is a form of 'Deutsch', meaning 'German'.) We hear, for example, *fire bug* 'firefly' and *snake feeder* 'dragon fly'. Many of these words, however, are not specific to Mid-Atlantic speakers, but can be heard in other places with large numbers of German immigrants such as Milwaukee and East Texas. Such Germanisms include *fat cake* 'doughnut', *rain worm* 'earthworm', *sawbuck* 'sawhorse', *smearcase* 'cottage cheese', *clook* 'hen', and *snits* 'dried fruit'.

NORTHERN

The Northern dialect area envelopes the northern states that essentially border the Great Lakes, i.e. Minnesota, Wisconsin, Michigan, northern Illinois, northern Indiana, northern Ohio, northern Pennsylvania, northwestern New York, and west Vermont. At the core of this region are the northern cities of Minneapolis, Chicago, Detroit, Cleveland, and Buffalo. A significant sound shift is currently and recently underway here, and it constitutes the most prominent characteristic of Northern speech. In a series of linked movements in vowel space, the Northern Cities Chain Shift involves the vowels [ɑ], [æ], and [ɛ]:

1. [ɑ] moves forward to encroach upon the front vowel space of [æ]. The name *John* may thus be heard as *Jan*.
2. [æ] is in turn lengthening and moving upward through [ɛ] to [e] and may even be diphthongized to [eə] or [ɪə]. The woman's name *Ann* may be heard as the man's name, *Ian*. In this part of the shift, the degree of raising and diphthongization varies considerably from place to place, and among different words and phonological environments.
3. [ɛ] responds to the pressure from the rising of [æ] and retracts in the mouth to become a mid-central vowel closer to [ə]. *Best* may be heard as *bust*.

These speakers also contrast [oʊ] and [ɔ]:

[oʊ]	[ɔ]
mourning	*morning*
hoarse	*horse*
fourteen	*forty*

In addition, [ʊ] rather than [u] is heard in *roots*. Finally, Northern speakers predictably pronounce *greasy* with [s] and *with* with [ð].

Unique grammatical features are difficult to identify. A visitor to the Northern area might hear *wun't* 'wasn't', *be* 'am', and *hadn't aught* 'shouldn't'. A few non-standard preterites may be heard in some more rural parts of the region: *et* 'ate', *riz* 'rose', *div* 'dived, dove', and *driv* 'drove'. Among distinctively regional vocabulary we find *angleworm* 'earthworm', *swill* 'table scraps for hogs', and *johnnycake* 'cornbread'.

MIDLAND

While dialectologists argue over its historical and geographical bases, the Midland dialect is generally understood to encompass the speech of Nebraska, Kansas, western Iowa, most of Missouri, southern Illinois, southern Indiana, southern Ohio, and southwestern Pennsylvania. Neither the Midland nor the Western dialects evidence the Northern Cities Chain Shift. Certain other pronunciations may be identified as Midland regionalisms. Intrusive [r] is the most pervasive feature within the area. *Wash* may be pronounced [wɔrš] so that it rhymes with *Porsche*. Less obviously, some old, rural pronunciations also survive among educated speakers in words with vowels occurring before the fricatives [š] and [ž]. The vowel [ɪ] may be raised and tensed to [i], so that *fish* sounds like *fiche*; [ʊ] may similarly be pronounced [u], so that *push* rhymes with *douche*. In the same environment the first vowel in *special* may be pronounced [eɪ] so that it is identical to *spatial*; we hear the same vowel in *pleasure, measure, egg,* and *leg*. So too a word like *mash* is said as [mæɪš] and a word like *hush* is [həɪš].

Only a few lexical forms appear to be general to the entire region: e.g. *blinds* 'roller shades', *coal oil* 'kerosene', *hull* 'to shell beans or peas', *little piece* 'short distance', *skillet* 'frying pan'. *Sweet corn* is distinguished from *field corn*. 'Cantaloupe' is *muskmelon*. Several regional phrases occur, such as *all the further* 'as far as', and *all the ways*; the use of the preposition *till* as in 'quarter till the hour' is also common. Other constructions may be heard throughout the United States but seem to typify Midland speech, including *seen* 'saw', *boilt* 'boiled' and *clum* 'climbed'. If you were to visit the southern part of the Midlands, you might hear subregionalisms such as *pavement* 'sidewalk' (also in BE) or *fireboard* 'mantel'. The preterit and past participle forms *drink* and *shrink* may be expected, too.

WESTERN

The Western dialect is found from the Pacific coast through the Rocky Mountains (excluding New Mexico) into the Dakotas. Remarkable within this dialect are two sets of sound mergers. The first involves a sound shift that has been completed in other parts of North America (e.g. Canada) but is still in progress in the western United States. As a result, while older speakers in the West distinguish *cot* (with [ɑ]) from *caught* (with [ɔ]), among younger speakers [ɔ] is merging with [ɑ], a shift which creates the homonym pairs *taught/tot* and *sought/sot*. The second merger involves several vowels. Most notably, the vowel [æ] in *bad* has merged with [ɛ] before [r] + vowel as [ɛ], making *marry* and *merry* identical. Then, too, [ɛ] and [eɪ] may be merged in the same environment, giving both *merry* and *Mary* an [ɛ] pronunciation. A Western speaker may thus have the homonyms *marry*, *merry*, and *Mary*. Finally, in Western speech we do not generally hear a front glide [j] in words such as *new, tune*, and *due*, i.e. [nu], [tun], [du].

Because the American West has a large population, its speech is by no means uniform, and to a certain extent this area retains the dialect features of the Northern, Southern, and Midland speakers who settled west of the Mississippi. Certainly its vocabulary reflects this mixture. Moreover, because the area extending from the southwest into California was once a colony of Spain and a territory of Mexico, Spanish loan words are also to be found here. *Mesa* 'flat topped hill', *remuda* 'string of horses', and *arroyo* 'dry creek' are some examples. Loan words for food may be well known to outsiders: along with *frijoles* 'pinto beans', we find *taco, tortilla, huevo* 'egg', *chorizo*, and *enchilada*.

Northeastern

In Eastern New England and New York City we hear the subregional speech of the two main Northeastern dialects.

EASTERN NEW ENGLAND

Eastern New England speech focuses on the historically important city of Boston and includes the states of Maine, New Hampshire, Rhode Island, eastern Vermont, eastern Connecticut, and eastern and central Massachusetts. After settlement, Boston continued as a port city and thus served as a conduit through which London and southern English features moved into the United States. For this reason, the Eastern New England accent bears some resemblance to the accents of England and is differentiated from the speech of its Mid-Atlantic neighbors. The area is non-rhotic and has both linking and intrusive *r*, although younger speakers are beginning to conform with the rhoticity of General American. Like BE, Eastern New England may have the following pronunciations of vowel + *r*: *peer* [pɪə], *pair* [pɛə], and *poor* [pʊə]. It also resembles British English with a fairly fronted [a] in words such as *calm*, *father*, *dance*, and *path*. The merger of [ɔ] and [ɑ] has been completed in this area. Eastern New England speakers have [ɒ] for both; sets such as *sot*, *sought*, and *sort* become homophonous. Younger urban speakers also display Northern Cities Chain Shift pronunciations.

Especially in rural parts of this area, lexical features may be striking. *Apple dowdy* 'deep dish pie', *bonny clabber* 'curdled milk' (also in HE), *buttonwood* 'plane tree, sycamore', *comforter* 'quilt', *fritters* 'fried cakes', *hog's head cheese* 'headcheese', *spindle* 'tassel', and *pigsty* 'pigpen' are common, if not unique, to the countryside of Eastern New England. In addition to these regionalisms, many words in general use in the United States originate in this region: *chipmunk*, *firefly*, *gutter*, *kerosene*, *picket fence*, *skunk*, and *string beans*.

NEW YORK CITY

The New York City dialect area covers not only the five boroughs of the city itself, but also the areas adjoining it: Long Island, the Hudson River Valley up into Westchester County, northern New Jersey, and southwestern Connecticut (Millward 1996:356). The dialect's distinctiveness is a hallmark of the city's history. In the eighteenth century, following the initial Dutch settlement, New Amsterdam became New York and developed as an English port. The mid-nineteenth century saw Irish and German immigrants, and by the late nineteenth century, the immigration facility at Ellis Island received people from southern and eastern Europe speaking Yiddish, Polish, Italian, and other European languages. In the twentieth century, Hispanic peoples came, as did African Americans and Asians. Many local New York speech patterns result from this rich settlement pattern.

Certain pronunciations characterize New York City speech. Unlike most everywhere else in English-speaking North America, however, accents are socially stratified as they have traditionally been in Britain. Upper-class accents lack the local features found in lower-class accents. The dialect is non-rhotic, and linking and intrusive *r* are usual. As in Boston, however, younger speakers, especially among the more affluent and educated, are increasingly rhotic. New York, as does Boston, has the additional vowel long [a], but in New York it is phonetically realized as [ɑə]. This sound occurs in *bard*, *calm*, *father*, and in words like them, although it is absent in *dance* and *path*, which have [æ]. In words such as *bird* and *girl*, we often hear the diphthong [ɛɪ], though this allophone is less frequent among younger speakers. Because the vowel [ɔ] is present in New York City pronunciations, the words *cot* [ɑ] and *caught* [ɔ] are distinct. Some New Yorkers articulate [θ] and [ð] as dental stops, [t] and [d], so that *then* and *den* may be homophones, although the stop consonant is less likely among educated speakers. The Northern Cities Chain Shift is manifest in New York City speech.

As elsewhere, lexical regionalisms are less accurate benchmarks for the New York dialect. For example, a large Hispanic population has lent Spanish words like *bodega* 'a corner convenience store' into common New York parlance. But, just as we saw that German loan translations are not unique to Mid-Atlantic speech, so too are Spanish loans plentiful in many other American cities and towns. Nor is vocabulary uniform within the dialect area; usage may vary from neighborhood to neighborhood. A 'regular' coffee comes with milk and a bit of sugar in Midtown but with three heaping teaspoons of sugar in Wall Street.

Southern

Like Northeastern, Southern speech departs noticeably from General American dialects. We can divide the Southern dialect area into Coastal Southern and Inland Southern. The Coastal pattern runs from eastern Virginia to the gulf coast of Texas, including the seaboard of the South Atlantic and Gulf States. The Inland dialect extends into West Virginia, Kentucky, Tennessee, western Virginia, western North Carolina, western South Carolina, northern Georgia, northern Alabama, Arkansas, southwestern Missouri, Oklahoma, and most of Texas. Inland speech includes the mountain varieties of Appalachia and the Ozarks. Historic patterns of settlement differentiate somewhat the two southern dialects: further away from Charleston and other eastern ports, Inland speech may preserve features which, on the coast, give way to innovations brought later on by trade with London. To simplify, Inland speech remains rhotic (albeit variably), while Coastal speech is more likely to be non-rhotic, lacking the expected linking and intrusive *r*. Along the Atlantic you might also hear allophonic variants of the diphthongs [aɪ] and [aʊ]. Before voiceless consonants the centralized onsets occur: [əɪ] and [əʊ] respectively (historic forms preserved in CanE as well).

Other subregionalisms occur in this large dialect region, but a number of generalizations nevertheless seem to hold true for a Southern dialect. Southern speech has some of the most remarkable features in the United States. Both its phonemes and prosody make it generally identifiable to the outsider. *Greasy* is pronounced with [z] throughout the dialect area. We hear a contrast between [oʊ] and [ɔ] in *hoarse/horse* and *mourning/morning*. In many stressed monosyllables, the vowels [ɪ], [ɛ], and [æ] often break into diphthongs which take a [ə] glide at the end. Taken to its extreme, *bed* [bejəd], *bid* [bɪjəd], and *bad* [bæijəd] occur. Younger speakers are especially likely to have homophones in the pairs *den/din, meant/mint, pen/pin*, and *ten/tin*; in other words, [ɪ] alternates for [ɛ] before [n]. Before voiced consonants, [aɪ] and [ɔɪ] are monophthongized to long [a] as in *ride* and [ɔ] as in *oil*, respectively. The verb forms *isn't* and *wasn't* often have [d] instead of [z], yielding [ɪdnt], for example. Southern speakers put the primary stress on the first syllable of *July, September, October, November*, and *December*. Weak stress falls on the final syllable of the names for the days of the week, rendering that sound [ɪ] rather than [eɪ] as is heard elsewhere in the US.

Southern grammatical features include the well-known second-person plural pronoun, *you all* or *y'all*. The need for a second-person plural recognizably different from the singular, *you*, leads to its innovation in *you all* (cf. *youse* and *you guys* in other dialects). The doubling of modal auxiliaries occurs in the South: 'I might could do it' would not surprise a Southerner. Also stigmatized outside of the South is the widespread contracted negative *ain't* (on the complex history and usage of *ain't*, see *Webster's Dictionary of English Usage* 1989:60–4). Less frequent in educated southern speech is the perfective *done* in 'I done told you that already'. Pederson (2001) mentions the omission of the verb 'be' in expressions like 'he a puppy' and the deletion of the auxiliary in 'he done it'. Along with other originally southern features, this last feature is also heard in African American Vernacular English, because black speakers emigrating out of this area took their southern regionalisms with them. Doubtless, too, African American Vernacular English reinforces regionalisms in Southern English that might otherwise be lost to conformity with General American speech.

Despite the increasing homogenization of the United States, Southern USEng retains some regional vocabulary words. We hear of *butter beans* 'lima beans', *grits* 'milled cornmeal', *chitlins* 'hog intestines', *boiled peanuts, she crab* 'female crab', *greens* 'boiled leaf vegetables', *roasting ears* 'corn on the cob', *sweet tea* 'sweetened ice tea', and *varmint* 'small predatory animal'. *Hoppin John* (a dish of greens, black-eyed peas, and pork) is prepared on New Year's. *Barbecue* is pork pulled from the bone. If you're hungry for chicken or pork and three side servings of vegetables, you go to a *meat 'n three* and have *sweet potato pie* for dessert.

Exercise 13.3 American Regionalisms

1. Using the *Dictionary of American Regional English,* find the definitions for the following words.

    a. clophopper _____

    _____

    b. flapdoodle _____

    _____

    c. dust bunny _____

    _____

   d.   boogerman/bogeyman _____

   _____

   e.   elbow grease _____

   _____

   f.   get-go _____

   _____

   g.   doohickey _____

   _____

   h.   fraidycat _____

   _____

2.   Look up the following words in the *Dictionary of American Regional English*
     and, using the maps provided, discuss their geographical distribution in
     reference to the dialect areas identified in the text.

   a.   davenport 'sofa, couch'   _____

   _____

   _____

   b.   baby-buggy _____

   _____

   _____

   c.   creep 'crawl'_____

   _____

   _____

   d.   frigidaire 'refrigerator'_____

   _____

   _____

   e.   ethyl 'high octane gasoline'_____

   _____

   _____

African American Vernacular English

Given the number of its speakers, their diversity, and their geographical distribution, we should not be surprised that African American Vernacular English (AAVE) is by no means uniform. That is, we should expect as much variation within this speech as within any other dialect according to such factors as age, residence (urban versus rural), and income. In general, it can be identified by the salient features listed by Rickford (1999) and summarized below, many of which are not unique to AAVE. Just like any dialect or language, AAVE functions according to a system of governing principles or rules.

AAVE is a continuum of English vernaculars spoken by African Americans, and refers to essentially the same thing as the informal oral dialect known as *Ebonics* (a blend of *ebony* + *phonics*). While many speakers of AAVE use the two terms interchangeably, the word *Ebonics* carries ideological and political connotations for others. The first is a popular conviction that African American speech derives entirely from the Niger-Congo African languages brought with the slaves to North America. By eschewing a label that includes the word 'English' (such as AAVE or Black English), *Ebonics* distances the vernacular from English. The other connotation comes from the use of the term to refer to educational programs in which teachers employ African American vernacular to teach standard English in school, a pedagogical strategy which became the subject of some controversy in California in the 1990s.

Scholars have argued over the influences of Hiberno-English and Caribbean creoles on the formation of AAVE. The linguist John Rickford concludes that 'there can be absolutely no doubt that *some* pidgin/creole speech—whether homegrown (e.g. Gullah, or Sea Island Creole) or imported—was an element in the formative stage of African American Vernacular English' (1999:249). Other linguists oppose the creole hypothesis. They attribute nearly all of the features of AAVE to a dialect of (originally) British English. Salikoko Mufwene (2001) points out that AAVE must have started with the colonization of South Carolina in 1670, decades before the advent of Gullah, to which AAVE is likened. He argues that AAVE's grammar is essentially English, pointing to the features of Southern USEng it incorporates. An equally pertinent question is whether AAVE is diverging from white American vernaculars. Does the recently recorded variation amount to systematic language change?

PHONOLOGY
AAVE exhibits a number of distinctive consonant features:

1. The dialect is non-rhotic; for example, there is no [r] in the pronunciation of *sister* and *four*. Intrusive and linking *r* are not usual.
2. In preconsonantal position, [l] may be vocalized to a high back unrounded vowel represented in the IPA as [ɯ]. *Help* may be represented orthographically as 'he'p' and is pronounced [hɛɯp] and *silk* is pronounced [sɪɯk]. At times, [l] may even be lost in final position, so that *tall* is [tɔ] and *goal*,

[goʊ]. This has the grammatical repercussion of deleting the contraction *'ll* of *will* in future tense constructions.

3. Consonant clusters at the ends of words may be simplified or reduced, especially those ending in [t] or [d], as in *hand* and *passed*.
4. The interdental fricatives, [θ] and [ð], are realized as stop consonants, [t] and [d], at the beginning of words. *Them* may be [dɪm]. In medial or final position, they sometimes become the labiodental fricatives [f] and [v], as in *brother*. *Something* may be [səmfɪn].
5. Unstressed *-ing* is realized as [ɪn], not [ɪŋ], as in *walking*.
6. Deletion of initial [d] and [g] in certain auxiliaries, as in 'I'on know' for *I don't know*, or 'I'm'a do it' for *I'm gonna do it*.
7. More common among older than younger speakers is deletion of unstressed initial and medial syllables, for example, the first syllable of *afraid*.

The vowel system is also distinctive in a number of ways:

1. As in Southern USEng, [aɪ] and [ɔɪ] are monophthongized or smoothed to [a] and [ɔ], respectively, as in *buy* [ba] and *toy* [tɔ].
2. Before nasal consonants, [ɪ] and [ɛ] merge, e.g. [pɪn] for *pen* and *pin*.
3. Social separation among the races is evident in light of the fact that AAVE speakers do not seem to be participating in the Northern Cities Chain Shift, nor in the innovations found in the Mid-Atlantic dialect of General American.

In respect to prosody, AAVE tends to shift primary stress to the initial syllable (e.g. *pólice* instead of *políce*) and exhibit more varied intonation. A wider range of pitches may be employed along with more rising and level final contours.

Syntax

AAVE displays the following syntactic features:

1. *Ain('t)* functions as a general negator, replacing *am not*, *isn't*, *aren't*, *haven't*, *hasn't*, and *didn't*: e.g. *He ain' here* 'He isn't here' or *I ain't been told* 'I haven't been told'.
2. Multiple negation is not proscribed as it is in standard English, yielding sentences such as *He don't never say nothing*.
3. Appositive pronouns occur, as in *That teacher, she yell at the kids*.
4. Inflected *is* and *are* may be omitted in copulative and auxiliary constructions, as in *You sick* or *She working right now*.
5. Invariant *be* expresses continuing or repetitious action, as in *He be studyin' all the time* 'He always studies' versus *He studyin'* 'He is studying right now'.
6. Invariant *be* may also be used for the future, as in *He be here tomorrow* 'He will be here tomorrow'.
7. The past tense form may function as a past participle, as in *He had bit* instead of *bitten*.

8. Direct questions may be formed without subject-auxiliary inversion but with rising intonation, as in *Why I can't play?*

9. Indirect questions (without *if* or *whether*) may exhibit subject-auxiliary inversion, as in *He asked me could I go with him.*

10. Unstressed *been* or *bin* occurs in present perfect constructions, as in *He been sick* for 'He's been sick'.

11. The construction *it* + (*is, 's, was, ain't*) replaces *there* + (*is, 's, was, isn't*), as in *It's a school up there* for 'There's a school up there'.

12. The auxiliary *done* emphasizes the completed nature of an action, as in *He done did it* for 'He's already done it'.

13. The form *say* is used to introduce direct speech, as in *They told me <u>say</u> they couldn't go*.

MORPHOLOGY

We find several distinctive features in noun and verb inflections as well as in the use of forms:

1. When the context is clear, the noun plural marker *-s* is often omitted, as in *four dog* or *many house*.

2. When the context is clear, the possessive marker *-s* may be omitted in noun-noun possessive constructions, as in *the <u>lady</u> house* 'the lady's house' or *<u>John</u> hat* 'John's hat'.

3. The third-person present indicative verbal ending may be omitted, especially in the presence of past-time adverbs, as in *The man <u>walk</u> there every morning.*

4. Past tense endings (*-ed* suffix, ablaut, etc.) may be omitted, as in *He <u>walk</u> there yesterday* or *He <u>tell</u> me so before.*

5. The forms *y'all* and *they* are used to mark second-person plural and third-person plural genitives, as in *it's y'all ball* and *it's they house*, respectively.

LEXICON

As Geneva Smitherman (1977:59) observes, 'words have potentially two levels of meaning, one black one white' (quoted by Mufwene 2001:309). 'Counterlanguage' or camouflaged constructions disguise intended meaning from outsiders, originally white masters. Examples include *sneak* 'to attack someone off guard', *train* 'group rape', *double-bank* 'to gang up on someone', and *give some sugar* 'kiss' (Mufwene 2001:308–9). A number of English words in general use derive from AAVE, including *goober, okra,* and *yam,* loans from African languages. The etymologies of two words used well beyond the African American community are controversial: *tote* may be related to the Kikongo verb *tota* 'carry' and *hip* may derive from the Wolof word *hipi* 'be aware'. Expressions like 'givin' five' and 'Whassup' originate in the African American community, while other black cultural idioms and slang contribute *nitty gritty, cool, jam* 'to improvise', *jazz,* and *rap.*

A LOOK AT EARLY AAVE

The Negro spiritual below, 'I Know Moon-Rise', employs a call response/pattern brought with the slaves from their homes in West and Central Africa. The pattern facilitates the singing of Protestant hymns unfamiliar to the Africans: the lyrics would be called out in anticipation of the singers' next line (O'Meally 1997:6–7). We know that this song was sung by black soldiers on the Union side during the Civil War because the nineteenth-century scholar and abolitionist, Colonel Thomas Wentworth Higginson, remarks on the words, 'I lie in de grave an' stretch out my arms', writing in 1867: 'Never, it seems to me since man first lived and suffered, was his infinite longing for peace uttered more plaintively than in that line' (quoted by Johnson 1925:42).

I Know Moon-Rise

(1) I know moon-rise, I know star-rise,

(2) I lay dis body down.

(3) I walk in de moonlight, I walk in de starlight,

(4) To lay dis body down.

(5) I walk in de graveyard, I walk throo de graveyard,

(6) To lay dis body down.

(7) I lie in de grave an' stretch out my arms,

(8) I lay dis body down.

(9) I go to de jedgment in de evenin' of de day

(10) When I lay dis body down.

(11) An' my soul an' your soul will meet in de day

(12) When I lay dis body down.

As it is recorded by Johnson (1925:42), this spiritual gives us important evidence about the sound system of early African American Vernacular English. Unlike many spirituals, the texts of which survive with normalized spelling, this version preserves, through its spelling, the voiced initial stop [d] that AAVE speakers use in place of [θ]. In line (3) in place of *the* we see *de*; in (4), instead of *this* we see *dis*. We observe the absence of [ŋ] in *evenin'* (line 9). The [d] in *and* is omitted in the form *an'* (line 7).

When we turn to look at grammatical features, a characteristic absence attracts our attention. Observe the way at least one editor (e.g. O'Meally 1999:9) establishes lines 5 and 7:

I'll walk in de graveyard, I'll walk through de graveyard (1.5).

I'll lie in de grave and stretch out my arms (1.7).

Because the action is future and conditional, editors commonly restore *'ll* to the text so that the lines make sense. We know, however, that *'ll* is deleted through the vocalization of [l] after a vowel (*I*), and that the result is grammatical.

RECOMMENDED WEB LINKS

The Speech Accent Archive reproduces the accented speech of speakers from many different language backgrounds (both native and non-native English speakers) reading the same sample paragraph:

http://classweb.gmu.edu/accent/

Sound files representing a large variety of English dialects can also be found at:

http://www.uni-due.de/SVE/ACC_accents_of_English.htm

Perhaps the best place to begin studying varieties of English on the web is Raymond Hickey's site:

http://www.uni-due.de/SVE/

Below is another good site on varieties of English:

http://www.ic.arizona.edu/~lsp/

The following site provides numerous links to sites devoted to US English, AAVE, Canadian English, and Caribbean English:

http://www.evolpub.com/Americandialects/AmDialLnx.html

The following websites focus on Canadian English:

http://www.yorku.ca/twainweb/troberts/raising.html
http://www.ic.arizona.edu/~lsp/CanadianEnglish.html
http://www.chass.utoronto.ca/~chambers/dialect_topography.html (Professor Jack Chambers's dialect topography of Canadian English)
http://www.heritage.nf.ca/dictionary/ (*Dictionary of Newfoundland English Online*)

The following sites are concerned with dialects of US English and AAVE:

http://www.ic.arizona.edu/~lsp/
http://www4.uwm.edu/FLL/linguistics/dialect/ (American Dialect Survey)
http://www.ling.upenn.edu/phono_atlas/ (Atlas of North American English, University of Pennsylvania)
http://www.angelfire.com/ak2/intelligencerreport/yankee_dixie_quiz.html (Yankee/ Dixie quiz—just for fun)
http://www.une.edu.au/langnet/definitions/aave.html (AAVE)

http://www.arts.mcgill.ca/linguistics/Faculty/boberg/research.htm (Professor Charles Bobergs's McGill Dialectology and Sociolinguistics Laboratory)

This site deals with Standard Scottish English (note that there are numerous websites devoted to Scots):

http://www.scots-online.org/grammar/sse.htm
http://www.dsl.ac.uk/ (The Dictionary of the Scots Language website)

Information on Australian English may be found at:

http://www.macquariedictionary.com.au/

South African English is discussed at:

http://www.ru.ac.za/dsae (the Dictionary Unit of South African English)
http://www.mediaclubsouthafrica.com/index.php?option=com_content&view=article&id=423

Hiberno-English is discussed at:

http://www.uni-due.de/IERC/

For dialect information on regional variants of British English, including RP, Estuary English, and Cockney, see:

http://www.ic.arizona.edu/~lsp/
http://www.phon.ucl.ac.uk/home/estuary (Estuary English)
http://www.yaelf.com/rp.shtml (RP)

Statistics concerning the use of English (and other languages) worldwide may be obtained at:

www.ethnologue.com

FURTHER READING

For more on national varieties of English generally, see:

Algeo, John (ed.). 2001. *The Cambridge History of the English Language. Vol. VI: English in North America*. Cambridge: Cambridge University Press.

Bailey, Richard W., and Manfred Görlach (eds). 1982. *English as a World Language*. Ann Arbor: University of Michigan Press.

Burchfield, Robert (ed.). 1994. *The Cambridge History of the English Language. Vol. V: English in Britain and Overseas*. Cambridge: Cambridge University Press.

Cheshire, Jenny (ed.). 1991. *English around the World: Sociolinguistic Perspectives*. Cambridge: Cambridge University Press.

Crystal, David. 2003. 'World English' and 'Regional Variation'. *The Cambridge Encyclopedia of the English Language*. 2nd edn. Cambridge: Cambridge University Press.

Finegan, Edward. 2006. 'English in North America'. *A History of the English Language*. Ed. by Richard Hogg and David Denison, 384–419. Cambridge: Cambridge University Press.

Hogg, Richard M. 2006. 'English in Britain'. *A History of the English Language.* Ed. by Richard M. Hogg and David Denison, 352–83. Cambridge: Cambridge University Press.

McArthur, Tom. 2002. *The Oxford Guide to World English.* Oxford and New York: Oxford University Press.

Trudgill, Peter, and Jean Hannah. 2002. *International English: A Guide to Varieties of Standard English.* 4th edn. London: Arnold.

Wells, J.C. 1982. *Accents of English.* 3 vols. Cambridge: Cambridge University Press.

For more specialized discussions of English varieties, see:

Baumgardner, Robert Jackson (ed.). 1996. *South Asian English: Structure, Use, and Users.* Urbana: University of Illinois Press.

Burridge, Kate, and Jean Mulder. 1998. *English in Australia and New Zealand: An Introduction to Its History, Structure, and Use.* Melbourne: Oxford University Press.

Clarke, Sandra (ed.). 1993. *Focus on Canada.* Varieties of English around the World, Vol. 11. Amsterdam and Philadelphia: John Benjamins.

Clarke, Sandra. 2010. *Newfoundland and Labrador English.* Edinburgh: Edinburgh University Press.

Coupland, Nikolas, and Alan R. Thomas (eds). 1990. *English in Wales: Diversity, Conflict, and Change.* Philadelphia: Multilingual Matters.

Dollinger, Stefan. 2008. *New-Dialect Formation in Canada: Evidence from the English Modal Auxiliaries.* Amsterdam and Philadelphia: John Benjamins, especially Chapters 1 and 2.

Jones, Charles. 2002. *The English Language in Scotland: An Introduction to Scots.* East Linton: Tuckwell Press.

Kallen, Jeffrey (ed.). 1997. *Focus on Ireland.* Varieties of English around the World, Vol. 21. Amsterdam and Philadelphia: John Benjamins.

Mehrotra, Raja Ram (ed.). 1998. *Indian English: Texts and Interpretation.* Varieties of English around the World, Vol. 7. Amsterdam and Philadelphia: John Benjamins.

Roberts, Peter A. 1988. *West Indians and Their Language.* Cambridge: Cambridge University Press.

Dictionaries based on historical principles have been complied for the major regional dialects:

Australian National Dictionary. A Dictionary of Australiansims on Historical Principles. 1988. Ed. by W.S. Ransom et al. Melbourne: Oxford University Press.

Dictionary of American Regional English. 1985–present. Ed. by Frederic G. Cassidy and Joan Houston Hall. Cambridge, MA: Belknap Press of Harvard University Press.

Dictionary of Canadianisms on Historical Principles. 1967. Ed. by Walter S. Avis et al. Toronto: Gage.

Dictionary of New Zealand English: A Dictionary of New Zealandisms on Historical Principles. 1997. Ed. by H.W. Orsman. Aukland: Oxford University Press.

A Dictionary of South African English on Historical Principles. 1996. Penny Silva et al. 1996. Oxford: Oxford University Press.

Dictionary of the English/Creole of Trinidad & Tobago on Historical Principles. 2009. Ed. by Lise Winer. 2009. Montreal: McGill-Queen's University Press.

For more specialized discussions of British and American regional varieties, see:

Pederson, Lee. 2001. 'Dialects'. *The Cambridge History of the English Language. Vol. VI: English in North America.* Ed. by John Algeo, 253–90. Cambridge: Cambridge University Press.

Trudgill, Peter. 1999. *The Dialects of England.* 2nd edn. Oxford and Malden, MA: Blackwell.

For more comprehensive treatments of USEng as well as language varieties spoken in the United States other than English (e.g. Native American Languages, Spanish, American Sign Language, and creoles), see:

Finegan, Edward, and John R. Rickford (eds). 2004. *Language in the USA: Themes for the Twenty-First Century.* Cambridge: Cambridge University Press.

Wolfram, Walt, and Natalie Schilling-Estes. 2005 *American English: Dialects and Variation.* 2nd edn. Cambridge, MA: Blackwell.

For more on AAVE, as well as the Ebonics debate and other related issues, see:

Mufwene, Salikoko S. 2001. 'African-American English'. *The Cambridge History of the English Language. Vol. VI: English in North America.* Ed. by John Algeo, 291–324. Cambridge: Cambridge University Press.

Mufwene, Salikoko S., et al. (eds). 1998. *African American English: Structure, History, and Use.* London: Routledge.

Rickford, John R. 1999. *African American Vernacular English.* Malden, MA and Oxford: Blackwell.

Smitherman, Geneva. 2000. *Talkin that Talk: Language, Culture, and Education in African America.* London: Routledge.

For important, early work on sociolinguistic approaches to studying language variation and AAVE, see:

Labov, William. 1972a. *Language in the Inner City: Studies in the Black English Vernacular.* Philadelphia: University of Pennsylvania Press.

FURTHER VIEWING

Some interesting documentaries are:

Part 7, *The Muvver Tongue*, from *The Story of English.* BBC-TV co-production with MacNeil-Lehrer Productions in association with WNET, 1986.

Talking Canadian. Margaret Slaght (director). Toronto: Canadian Broadcasting Corporation, 2004.

Do You Speak American? Three parts. Narrated by Robert MacNeil. New York: WNET, 2005.

Appendix A

Quick Reference Guide

A. Line of Descent of English

Proto-Indo-European (centum) (*c.* 4000 BCE)
Common Germanic (10th century BCE–2nd century CE)
(Low) West Germanic (*c.* 2nd century CE–5th century CE)
Old English (*c.* 500–1100)
Middle English (*c.* 1100–1500)
Early Modern English (*c.* 1500–1700)
Late Modern English (*c.* 1700–1900)
Present-Day English (*c.* 1900–present)

B. Phonology

B1. IPA Charts

IPA Consonant Symbols

Manner of Articulation		Place of Articulation							
		Bilabial	Labiodental	Interdental	Alveolar	Alveolo-palatal	Palatal	Velar	Glottal
Stop	Voiceless	p			t			k	ʔ
	Voiced	b			d			g	
Nasal		m			n			ŋ	
Flap					ɾ				
Fricative	Voiceless		f	θ	s	š	ç	x	h
	Voiced	β	v	ð	z	ž		ɣ	
Affricate	Voiceless					č			
	Voiced					ǰ			
Approximant	Lateral				l				
	Retroflex				r				
	Glide (or Semivowel)						j	w	

Note: Grey symbols represent sounds not found in Modern English.

IPA Vowel Symbols

		Monopthongs		
		Front	**Central**	**Back**
High (close)	**Tense**	i (seat)	y (Fr. tu)	u (pool)
	Lax	ɪ (sit)	ʏ (Ger. Hütten)	ʊ (put)
Mid	**Tense**	e (OE fēt)		o (OE fōt)
	Lax	ɛ (set)	ə (sun, soda)	ɔ (port)
Low (open)		æ (sat)	a	ɑ (father)
		Diphthongs		
		eɪ (late)	aɪ (file)	oʊ (loan)
		ɪu (cute)	aʊ (fowl)	ɔɪ (foil)

Note: Grey symbols represent sounds not found in Modern English.

B2.   The Development of Vowels

The Vowel System of Proto-Indo-European

	Monophthongs		
	Front	**Central**	**Back**
High	*ī *i		*ū *u
Mid	*ē *e	*ə	*ō *o
Low			*ā *ɑ
	Diphthongs		
	*ei	*oi	
		*ou	
	*eu	*ɑi	
		*ɑu	

The Vowel System of Germanic

	Monophthongs		
	Front	Central	Back
High	*ī *i		*ū *u
Mid	*ē *e		*ō *o
Low	*ǣ		*ā *a
	Diphthongs		
	*iu		*ai *au

The Vowel System of Old English

		Monophthongs		
		Front	Central	Back
High	Long Tense	ī ȳ		ū
	Short Lax	ɪ Y		ʊ
Mid	Long Tense	ē		ō
	Short Lax	ɛ		ɔ
Low	Long/Short	ǣ æ		ā ɑ
		Diphthongs		
		ēə ɛə		
		æə ǣə		

The Vowel System of Middle English

		Monophthongs		
		Front	**Central**	**Back**
High		ī ɪ		ū ʊ
Mid		ē	ə	ō
		ɛ̄ ɛ		ɔ̄ ɔ
Low				ɑ
		Diphthongs		
		ɪʊ	aʊ	ʊɪ
		ɛʊ		ɔɪ
		æɪ		ɔʊ

The Vowel System of Early Modern English

		Front	**Central**	**Back**
High	**Tense**	ī		ū
	Lax	ɪ		ʊ
Mid	**Tense**	ē		ō
	Lax	ɛ̄ ɛ	ə	ɔ ↕
Low		æ	a	ɑ

(Source: adapted from Manfred Görlach, *Introduction to Early Modern English* [Cambridge: Cambridge University Press, 1991], p. 65.)

Note: Because the diphthongs are undergoing major changes during Early Modern English, they have been omitted from this table.

Long Vowels from Old English to Present-Day English

OE Vowel	OE Examples	ME Vowel	ME Letter	15th–16th Century	17th–18th Century	PDE Examples	PDE Letter
[ī] [ȳ]	rīdan līf bī mȳs	[ī]	i, y	[əí > ə́ɪ]	[aɪ]	ride life by mice	i, y
[ē] [ēa] [ǣ]	fēdan grēne bēof dēop strǣt	[ē]	e, ee	[ī]	[i]	feed green thief deep street	ee, ie
[ǣ] [ǣə]	dǣl mǣn nǣdl hǣl bēatan bēam ēast lēaf	[ɛ̄]	e, ee	[ē > eɪ]	[eɪ/i]	deal mean needle heal beat beam east leaf	ee, ea
[ā]	nama talu lanu	[ā]	a, aa	[ǣ > ɛ̄ > ē]	[eɪ]	name tale lane	a
[ū]	mūs hūs nū dūn tūn pūnd	[ū]	ou, ow	[əʊ > ə́ʊ]	[aʊ]	mouse house now down town pound	ou, ow
[ō]	fōda fōt nōn gōd brōm bōk flōd blōd	[ō]	o, oo	[ū]	[u/ʊ/ʌ]	food foot noon good broom book flood blood	oo
[ā]	hām pāl gād 'rāte tācen bāt	[ɔ̄]	o, oo	[ō]	[oʊ]	home pole goad throat token boat	o, oa

The Vowel System of Present-Day English

		Monophthongs		
		Front	Central	Back
High	Tense	i		u
High	Lax	ɪ		ʊ
Mid	Tense	e		o
Mid	Lax	ɛ	ə	ɔ
Low		æ	a	ɑ
		Diphthongs		
		eɪ	aɪ	oʊ
		ɪu	aʊ	ɔɪ

B3. The Development of Consonants

Grimm's Law (Consonants from Proto-Indo-European to Germanic)

Voiceless Stop > *Voiceless Fricative*	*Voiced Stop >* *Voiceless Stop*	*Voiced Aspirated Stop >* *Voiced Fricative > Voiced Stop*
*p > *f	*b > *p	*bh >*β > *b
*t > *θ	*d > *t	*dh > *ð > *d
*k > *x or *h (initially)	*g > *k	*gh > *ɣ > *g
*kʷ > *xʷ or *hʷ (initially)	*gʷ > *kʷ	*gʷh > *g, *w

The Consonants of Old English

Manner of Articulation		Place of Articulation							
		Bilabial	Labiodental	Interdental	Alveolar	Alveolo-palatal	Palatal	Velar	Glottal
Stop/Affricate	Voiceless	p			t	č	k		
	Voiced	b			d	ǰ	g	ɣ	
Nasal		m			n	ŋ			
Fricative	Voiceless/Voiced		f v	θ ð	s z	š		ç x h	
Approximant	Lateral				l				
	Retroflex/Trill				r				
	Glide (or Semivowel)						j	w	

Note: When more than one sound is included in a single box, these represent allophones of a single phoneme.

The Consonants of Middle English

Manner of Articulation		Place of Articulation								
		Bilabial	Labiodental	Interdental	Alveolar	Alveolo-palatal	Palatal	Velar	Glottal
Stop	Voiceless	p			t			k	
	Voiced	b			d			g	
Nasal		m			n			ŋ	
Fricative	Voiceless		f	θ	s	š	ç	x	h
	Voiced		v	ð	z			(ɣ)	
Affricate	Voiceless					č			
	Voiced					ǰ			
Approximant	Lateral				l				
	Retroflex/Trill				r				
	Glide/Semivowel						j	w	

The Consonants of Modern English

Place of Articulation

Manner of Articulation		Bilabial	Labiodental	Interdental	Alveolar	Alveolo-palatal	Palatal	Velar	Glottal
Stop	Voiceless	p			t			k	ʔ
Stop	Voiced	b			d			g	
Nasal		m			n			ŋ	
Flap					ɾ				
Fricative	Voiceless		f	θ	s	š			h
Fricative	Voiced		v	ð	z	ž			
Affricate	Voiceless					č			
Affricate	Voiced					ǰ			
Approximant	Lateral				l				
Approximant	Retroflex				r				
Approximant	Glide/Semivowel						j	w	

C. Morphology

Sources of English Inflections

	OE Source	OE/ME Form	PDE Form
Noun Possessive	*a*-stem masc./neut. gen. sg.	*-es* > *-(e)s*	*'s*
Noun Plural	*a*-stem masc. nom./acc. pl.	*-as* > *-(e)s*	*-s*
	a-stem neut. nom./acc. pl. (long-stem)	Ø	Ø (*fish*)
	n-stem (weak) masc./fem./neut. nom./acc. pl.	*-en*	*-en* (*oxen*)
	root-consonant stem masc./fem. nom./acc. pl.	umlaut	vowel change (*geese*)
Verb	3rd p. sg. pres. ind.	*-eþ*; replaced by *-es*[a] (ME) > *-s*	*-s*
	past tense	*-ed, -od* (weak) ablaut (strong)	*-ed* (*hoped*) vowel change (*wrote*)
	present participle	*-ende*; replaced by *-ing*[b] (ME)	*-ing* (*working*)
	past participle	*-ed* (weak) ablaut + *-en* (strong)	*-ed* (*hoped*) vowel change + (*-en*) (*written, sung*)
	infinitive	*-an* > *-e(n)* > Ø to V(*enne*)	bare infinitive (*go*) *to*-infinitive (*to go*)
	imperative	*-e, -a*, Ø (sg.) *-aþ* (pl.)	Ø (sg. and pl.) (*Leave!*)
Adjective	comparative	*-ra* > *-er*	*-er* (*smaller*)
	superlative	*-est, -ost*	*-est* (*smallest*)

[a] from Northern dialect
[b] from Southern dialect

Sources of English Pronoun Forms

OE Source	OE Form	PDE Form
Personal Pronouns		
1st p. sg. nom.	*ic > i* (ME)	*I*
1st p. sg. dat.	*mē*	*me*
1st p. sg. gen.	*mīn*	*my/mine*
1st p. pl. nom.	*wē*	*we*
1st p. pl. dat.	*ūs*	*us*
1st p. pl. gen.	*ūre > our* (ME)	*our/ours*
2nd p. pl. nom.	*gē*; replaced by *you* (EModE obj.)	*you* (sg. and pl.)
2nd p. pl. dat.	*ēow > you* (ME)	*you* (sg. and pl.)
2nd p. pl. gen.	*ēower > your(e)* (ME)	*your/yours* (sg. and pl.)
3rd. p. sg. masc. nom.	*hē*	*he*
3rd. p. sg. masc. dat.	*him*	*him*
3rd. p. sg. masc. gen.	*his*	*his*
3rd. p. sg. fem. nom.	*hēo*; replaced by *s(c)he*[a] (ME)	*she*
3rd. p. sg. fem. dat.	*hire*	*her*
3rd. p. sg. fem. gen.	*hire*	*her/hers*
3rd p. sg. neut. nom./acc.	*hit > it* (ME)	*it*
3rd p. sg. neut. gen.	*his*; replaced by *its* (EModE)	*its*
3rd p. pl. nom./acc.	*hī*; replaced by *þei*[b]	*they*
3rd p. pl. dat.	*him*; replaced by *þeym*[b]	*them*
3rd p. pl. gen.	*hira*; replaced by *þair(e)*[b]	*their/theirs*
Demonstrative Pronouns/Articles		
sg. neut. nom./acc. of 'that'	*þæt*	*that*
pl. nom./acc. of 'that'	*þā*; replaced by *þō + -s* (ME)	*those*
sg. neut. nom./acc. of 'this'	*þis*	*this*
sg. masc. nom. of 'this'	*þes*; replaced by *þes + -e* (ME)	*these*
sg. masc. nom. of 'that'	*se*; replaced by *þe* (ME)	*the*
numeral 'one'	*an*	*a/an*

continued

Sources of English Pronoun Forms—continued

OE Source	OE Form	PDE Form
	Interrogative/Relative Pronouns and Adverbs	
masc./fem. nom.	*hwā > whō* (ME)	*who*
masc./fem. dat.	*hwǣm > whōm* (ME)	*whom*
masc./fem./neut. gen.	*hwæs > whōse* (ME)[c]	*whose*
neut. nom./acc.	*hwæt*	*what*
neut. instr.	*hwȳ > whȳ* (ME)	*why*
'which of many'	*hwylc*	*which*
'how' (instr.)	*hū*	*how*

[a] from East Midlands dialect
[b] borrowed from Old Norse in late OE
[c] [ō] by analogy with the other interrogative/relative forms
Note: PDE pronoun forms are generally direct developments from the OE pronoun forms (with regular phonological changes such as [ā] > [ō] as in *those*, *who*, and *whose*; these are shown by the > symbol in the table). When a PDE pronoun form is <u>not</u> a direct phonological development from the OE form, the change is indicated in the table by 'replaced by'.

D. Syntax

Sources of English Verbal Constructions

Construction	Source	PDE Form
Passive	OE *bēon, weorðan* + past participle + *fram/þurh*	*be* + past participle + *by* (*was asked by*)
Perfect	OE *habban* + past participle (trans. verb) OE *bēon* + past participle (intrans. verb)	*have* + past participle (trans. and intrans.) (*have arrived, had seen*)
Progressive	EModE *be* + V-*ing* EModE *be* + *on/in* + V-*ing*	*be* + V-*ing* (*was looking*)
Future	ME *wil/shal* + V LModE *be going to* + V	*will, shall* + V (*will buy, shall write*) *be going to* + V (*am going to meet*)
Modal Subjunctive	EModE *couthe, mought, shall* . . . + V	*could, might, shall* . . . + V (*could write, might see, shall know*)

Chronology of English Clause Types

	Affirmative Declarative Main Clauses	Affirmative Declarative Main Clauses with Object Pronouns
OE	subject + (auxiliary) + verb + (object) . . . . adverb (time/place) + {verb, auxiliary} + subject + (object)	subject + (auxiliary) + object pronoun + verb . . .
ME	subject + (auxiliary) + verb + (object) . . . . adverb (time/place) + {verb, auxiliary} + subject + (object)	subject + (auxiliary) + object pronoun + verb . . .
EModE	subject + (auxiliary) + verb + (object) . . . . adverb + {verb, auxiliary} + subject . . .	subject + (auxiliary) + verb + object pronoun . . .
ModE	subject + (auxiliary) + verb + (object)	subject + (auxiliary) + verb + object pronoun . . . .

	Negative Declarative Clauses	Interrogative Clauses
OE	*ne* + {auxiliary, verb} + subject + (object) . . . subject + *ne* + {auxiliary, verb} + (object)	(interrogative pronoun) + subject + verb + (object) . . . (interrogative pronoun) + verb + subject + (object) . . . .
ME	subject + *ne* + {auxiliary, verb} + (object) . . . . subject + *ne* + {auxiliary, verb} + *nat* + (object) . . . . subject + {auxiliary, verb} + *nat* + (object)	(interrogative pronoun) + auxiliary + subject + verb + (object) . . . (interrogative pronoun) + verb + subject + (object) . . . .
EModE	subject + verb + *not* + (object) . . . subject + auxiliary + *not* + verb + (object)	(interrogative pronoun) + auxiliary + subject + verb + (object) . . . (interrogative pronoun) + verb + subject + (object) . . . .
ModE	subject + auxiliary + *not* + verb + (object)	(interrogative pronoun) + auxiliary + subject + verb + (object) . . . .

	Imperative Clauses	Subordinate Clauses
OE	{verb, auxiliary} + (subject) + (object) . . .	subordinating conjunction + subject + (object) + verb
ME	{verb, auxiliary} + (subject) + (object) . . .	subordinating conjunction + subject + (object) + verb
EModE	{verb, auxiliary} + (subject) + (object) . . .	subordinating conjunction + subject + verb + (object) . . . verb + subject + (object) . . . [conditional clause]
ModE	{verb, auxiliary} + (object)	subordinating conjunction + subject + verb + (object) . . . .

Note: See chapters 7, 9, and 11 for further details and examples.

Appendix B

Timeline of Historical, Literary, and Linguistic Events in the History of English[1]

In addition to significant linguistic events (set in italics), this timeline includes benchmarks (e.g. the death of Queen Victoria and the world wars) that provide a chronological context for the history of English. In particular, it includes political events which have shaped the cultural and literary landscape of Britain as well as developments in technology which have furthered the spread of English by increasing communication. Note that the authors and literary works included are representative. With the advent of mass literacy and printing in the modern period, the emergence of literary periods and styles allows us to speak in terms of groups of authors rather than treating individual works separately, as we do for the medieval period. Because literary types often overlap (e.g. a certain text might be considered both postmodern and postcolonial), classifications are illustrative only.

c. **1900–1200** BCE   The **first written evidence of Indo-European languages**, in Hittite, dates from this period, although speakers of Proto-Indo-European (PIE) are believed to have inhabited Europe from *c.* 5000 BCE to *c.* 3000 BCE.

c. **1000–400** BCE   *The **First Sound Shift**, affecting all the stop consonants of PIE, is in progress. Grimm's Law and Verner's Law describe this unconditioned sound change, stating the relationship between Proto-Germanic consonants and their Indo-European predecessors: PIE voiceless stops change into voiceless fricatives, PIE voiced stops become voiceless stops, and PIE voiced aspirated stops become voiced fricatives and then finally voiced stops.*

c. **500** BCE   The **Celts inhabit Britain**. They are the first known speakers of Indo-European to settle there.

c. **200** CE   A **diaspora of Germanic languages begins** as speakers of Proto-Germanic leave their homeland.

---

1 This timeline draws from the information in this textbook, supplemented by the useful timeline in Mugglestone (2006) which is partly based on Baugh and Cable (2002). For a more complete discussion of the English literary tradition, see further Sanders (2004). For a detailed chronology of the global expansion of English during the modern period, see Table 13.1 *Timeline of the Transmission of English*, on pages 434–5.

43–410   The **Romans rule Britain** and its Celtic population.

410   When the **Visigoths sack Rome, the Empire recalls its troops from Britain**. Traditional accounts say that when Britain was left vulnerable to incursions from Scots and Picts, its chieftain asked Saxon mercenaries to defend the country in exchange for the Isle of Thanet, off the easternmost point of Kent in England. Whether or not an invitation was actually issued, the Germanic warriors took the opportunity to launch invasions of their own.

449   Tribes of **Angles, Saxons, and Jutes invade Britain**, according to sources reported in Bede's *Historia Ecclesiastica Gentis Anglorum* (731 CE).

c. **500**   *Old English emerges as a language from the mutually intelligible varieties of Low West Germanic brought by Germanic invaders across the North Sea to Britain. It is characterized, in contrast with Modern English, as an inflected language with a somewhat freer word order.*

c. **500–700**   *The Second (Germanic) Sound Shift is in progress. This unconditioned phonological change divides West Germanic, distinguishing modern High German from the Low German languages (Dutch, Flemish, Frisian) as well as from English. Relatively limited and incomplete, this shift begins in the mountainous region of southern Germany and spreads northward. In this change, the voiceless stops [p,t,k] become voiceless fricatives, the voiced stop [d] becomes a voiceless stop, and the voiceless fricative [θ] becomes a voiced stop.*

563   Arriving from Ireland, **St Columba introduces Christianity** to northern Britain. Along with the larger religious and cultural changes his missionaries initiate, Celtic monks bring the Insular hand (style of script) used to write Old English.

597   **Rome sends St Augustine (of Canterbury) to England** to convert its Germanic population to Christianity. Widespread conversion of Anglo-Saxon kings and their subjects follows.

664   The **Synod of Whitby adopts the Roman (as opposed to Celtic) Christian calendar** in England. The Roman Catholic Church will record and house documents, written both in Latin and in Old English, in its monastic scriptoria and libraries.

c. **670**   As Bede relates in his history (731), **Cædmon composes his 'Hymn'**. This poem is the only surviving work written by Cædmon, the first Old English poet whom we know by name. The story of this lay monk's extemporaneous performance of similar verse reveals the development of a new, English poetic form which incorporates biblical subject matter into a native-Germanic tradition of oral composition.

c. **700**   The **first written evidence of Old English** dates from this period.

731   **Bede writes the *Historia Ecclesiastica Gentis Anglorum* (*Ecclesiastical History of the English People*).**

780s   **Scandinavian raids begin**, destabilizing Britain.

796   The Mercian king, Offa, and the king of the Franks, Charlemagne, sign the **first-recorded English commercial treaty**.

832–1154   A collection of annals surviving in nine manuscripts, the **first *Anglo-Saxon Chronicle* is started** at Winchester (the *Parker Chronicle*) and maintained in copies held at monasteries elsewhere in England. The *Chronicle* kept at Peterborough continues into the early Middle English period. In its entirety, the *Chronicle* records major events in England during a period of significant change for the English language, thus providing linguists with a window into non-literary Old English.

850s   The **Scandinavians settle forcibly in England**.

871–99   West Saxon king **Alfred the Great consolidates part of England into a unified kingdom** and succeeds in repelling many of the Scandinavian invaders. During the relative peace that ensues, he fosters a renaissance of literature and learning in England. Called the father of English prose, Alfred either translates or orders translations of works meant to benefit his people. Among these we find excerpts from the book of Exodus, the *Pastoral Care* of Pope Gregory the Great, Bede's *Ecclesiastical History*, an historical compendium by Orosius, and *The Consolation of Philosophy* by Boethius. Other important books and manuscripts are copied at his scriptorium at Winchester.

878   **King Alfred establishes the Danelaw**, a region under Danish political and legal control in the north of England, after negotiating with the Scandinavians to end their invasions.

***c*. 930–60**   The **Junius Manuscript** dates from this period. It contains biblical paraphrases in verse attributed to the school of Cædmon: 'Genesis A', 'Genesis B', 'Exodus', 'Daniel', and 'Christ and Satan'.

937   King Athelstan, as part of a long-term campaign to conquer lands under Scandinavian rule, defeats an assembly of Scandinavian, Scottish, and British forces at the **Battle of Brunanburh**. This event is commemorated in the poem by that name.

970s   Important Old English poetry survives in two manuscripts dating from this period. The ***Exeter Book*** (including the poems 'Christ II', 'Guthlac', 'The Phoenix', 'Juliana', 'The Wanderer', 'The Seafarer', 'The Ruin', 'Deor', 'Wulf and Eadwacer', 'The Wife's Lament', and 'The Husband's Message', as well as charms and riddles) and the ***Vercelli Book*** (including the poems 'Andreas', 'Fates of the Apostles', 'Soul and Body I', 'Dream of the Rood', and 'Elene') both contain poetry attributed to the poet Cynewulf.

990s   Scholar and Benedictine monk **Ælfric of Eynsham composes saints' lives and homilies** (sermons and biblical commentaries) which circulate in manuscript throughout England. He also translates the Old Testament Heptateuch, works by Bede, and a Latin grammar into English.

991   The Anglo-Saxons are defeated by the Scandinavians at the **Battle of Maldon**; the English loss is commemorated in the poem by that name.

c. **1000**   Scholars generally agree that the ***Beowulf*** manuscript (*Nowell Codex* or *MS Cotton Vitellius*), which also includes 'Judith', dates from this period.

c. **1000**   *Late West Saxon becomes normative for written English. This dialect, previously the standard only within Wessex, comes to be used as a literary standard across England by people wishing to communicate in English.*

1016–35   **Cnut the Great assumes the throne of England**. At this time, Cnut is king of Denmark, which includes part of what is now Sweden; in time, he will also gain the throne of Norway.

1042   **English rule is restored** following Danish dominion when Edward the Confessor takes the throne.

1066   **Edward the Confessor dies without an heir**. There are three claimants for the crown: Harold Godwinson, Earl of Wessex; Harald III, king of Norway; and William, Duke of Normandy. Initially, Harold Godwinson seizes the throne, becoming King Harold II. He defeats the Norwegian king at the **Battle of Stamford Bridge**, but is himself soon defeated by William's forces at the **Battle of Hastings**. William's invasion begins the **Norman Conquest**. In the following years, a French-speaking monarchy, aristocracy, and church displace the native ruling class as King William I rewards his retainers and financiers with positions of power in England. *Whereas French dominates as the language of authority, culture, and literature, English becomes the language of a rural lower class (peasant farmers) who lack mobility and prestige. The language will change dramatically as a result.*

1066–*c.* 1450   In post-Conquest England, **laws are issued by the government in Latin and French**.

1086–7   **King William orders the Domesday Book**, an inventory of his new conquest. The record also yields census data: one and a half million people are reported to be living in Britain at the time.

c. **1100**   *The linguistic effects of the Norman Conquest initiate the **Middle English** stage of the language. Middle English may be characterized in contrast with Old English as having a significantly reduced system of inflections, increased lexical borrowings from French and Latin, and a less consistent spelling.*

1164   **King Henry II issues the Constitutions of Clarendon** as part of a reform of the legal system and the extension of royal authority over the Church. The archbishop of Canterbury, Thomas Becket, resists its ecclesiastical restrictions, provoking his own murder in 1170.

1176   **Henry II issues the Constitutions of Northampton** in an attempt to further reform the legal system and establish a common law throughout the kingdom.

c. **1170s**   The *Ormulum,* **a work of biblical exegesis, is written in metrical verse**. This work's author (Orm or Ormin) intended to represent English pronunciation through a system of phonetic orthography and strict poetic meter; scholars today are able to use this text to reconstruct aspects of early Middle English pronunciation.

1190   **King Richard the Lionheart embarks on the Third Crusade**. The largest and most successful of the early crusades, it generates a literature including various chronicles and the tales of Robin Hood. The crusades also bring vocabulary back to England in the form of loan words.

1204   **King John loses Normandy to France**, thus placing English estates there under foreign dominion. A growing patriotism favors England and English over France and French.

1215   **Magna Carta is signed**. Written in Latin, this 'Great Charter' requires King John to recognize that the king's will can be bound by law. Protecting the liberties and legal rights of the king's subjects, this document lays the foundation for the later writ of *habeas corpus*, which gave individuals the right to not be arbitrarily imprisoned and is the basis for the rule of constitutional law as well as English common law. It is the oldest valid legal precedent in English law.

c. **1225**   *Ancrene Wisse* (*'Guide for Anchoresses'*), an early Middle English devotional poem, addresses three aristocratic women leaving secular society to live in religious seclusion; it concerns the conflict inherent in the contemplative life as an interior, spiritual world meets an exterior, material world.

1258   The **Proclamation of Henry III** represents the first royal announcement (made under the great seal) to be written in English since the Norman Conquest.

1295   What came to be described as the **Model Parliament is called by King Edward I**; this parliament set a precedent for representations of subjects to the crown.

c. **1300**   The *Cursor Mundi* (*'Runner of the World'*), an anonymous religious poem, summarizes the history of the world within the context of salvation history. Its author announces that 'þis ilk bok es translate into Inglis tong/ to rede for the love of Inglis lede,/ Inglis lede of Ingland,/ for the commun at understand' ('This book is translated into the English tongue as advice for the love of English people, English people of England, for all to understand').

1337–1454   During this period, England and France engage in a protracted conflict known as the **Hundred Years War**. At the center of this dynastic turmoil is the issue of England's continental authority and competing claims to the French throne. When the English are finally expelled from all but Calais in France by the 1450s, the separate nationalism of the English is a *fait accompli. Hundreds of years after the Norman Conquest, the re-establishment of the English language in England is secured through its patriotic value.*

1340   The *Ayenbite of Inwyt* (*'Remorse of Conscience'*) **is recorded** (either composed or translated) in Middle English prose. A confessional tract 'Ywrite an englis of his oӡene hand' ('Written in English in his own hand'), by Michel of Northgate, the work is especially useful as a record of the fourteenth-century dialect of Kent.

c. **1343   Geoffrey Chaucer is born**. Although Chaucer brings French and Italian literary traditions to England, ultimately he demonstrates the literary capacity of the English vernacular as a poetic medium. Chaucer's works include *The Book of the Duchess*, *The House of Fame*, *The Parliament of Fowls*, *The Legend of Good Women*, *Troilus and Criseyede*, and *The Canterbury Tales*.

1348   The first waves of the European pandemic known as the **Black Death** hit England. Probably an outbreak of bubonic plague, the illness peaks between 1348 and 1350. Before it passes, the Black Death kills 30 to 60 per cent of Europe's population, creating a series of religious, social, and economic upheavals which dramatically affect Europe.

c. **1360–87   William Langland writes *Piers Plowman*.** This allegorical poem presents, within a series of dream visions and character studies (of Dowel 'Do-well', Dobet 'Do-better', and Dobest 'Do-best'), the narrator's quest for the true Christian life. The poem is written in alliterative verse broadly resembling that found in Old English (its style thus belongs to the Middle English alliterative renewal); it survives in three versions of very different lengths (the A, the B, and the C texts).

1362   *The Parliamentary **'Pleading in English Act'** stipulates the use of English in court proceedings. The act follows from the complaint that French, the language of the court in England, is neither common enough nor adequately understood for the majority of the people to be able to comprehend and defend themselves against the charges they face.*

1363   *The **chancellor opens Parliament with a speech in English**. Although this is the first time English is used in this capacity, the address is largely a symbolic act. English will not displace French in the legislature for many years, as French may be heard there as late as the seventeenth century.*

1381   The **Peasants' Revolt**, spurred by imposition of a poll tax, is one of a number of popular revolts against the unjust treatment of farm laborers in late medieval Europe. Although it fails, it comes at a time when serfdom in England is disappearing.

1383   The **earliest will we have extant in English** is recorded.

1384   **John Wyclif dies**. During his life, Wyclif was widely known as an Oxford professor of logic and theology, a biblical commentator, and a religious controversialist. In 1382, twenty-four of Wyclif's teachings were condemned as heretical or erroneous at the Blackfriars Synod in London. Wyclif advocated teaching the laity in the vernacular, and his followers, called Wycliffites or Lollards, produced many works in English, though no surviving English work can be safely attributed to Wyclif himself. He is thought to have encouraged the translation of the Latin (Vulgate) Bible into English.

1387   John of Trevisa translates the *Polychronicon*, Ralph Higden's chronicle of world history and theology. Of great popularity in the fourteenth and fifteenth centuries, Higden's chronicle is later translated several times between 1432 and 1450. Trevisa's version of the *Polychronicon* addresses the state of English in England from a contemporary point of view, and it is printed by Caxton in 1482.

c. **1390**   The **Later Version of the Middle English Bible is completed**. While the Early Version (finished *c.* 1385) follows the Latin wording and syntax closely, the Later Version reflects a more idiomatic English. Over two hundred and fifty manuscripts from both textual traditions survive in a variety of dialects. *Just as it contributes to religious reform, the Middle English Bible has ramifications for the language, encouraging literacy in English.*

c. **1393**   English anchoress **Julian of Norwich writes *Revelations of Divine Love*** (also called *Showings*), in which she records and interprets her visions of Jesus Christ. This set of sixteen mystical devotions is said to be the first book written by a woman in English.

Late 1300s   *Sir Gawain and the Green Knight* and *Pearl* date from this period. These poems, along with two others, survive in the late fourteenth-century manuscript *Cotton Nero A.x*. Both are written in the West Midland dialect of Middle English by an anonymous author (called the 'Pearl Poet' or the 'Gawain Poet') in keeping with the style of the Alliterative Revival.

1399   Henry Bolingbroke (Henry IV) seizes the throne from Richard II and begins the line of Lancaster.

1455–85   The **War of the Roses**, an internal dynastic conflict, pits the noble houses of Lancaster and York against each other in a struggle to occupy the throne of England.

c. **1400**   *The **East Midland dialect, especially that of London, becomes the basis of a written standard** in Britain.*

1400   Geoffrey Chaucer dies.

1400s–1600s   *The **Great Vowel Shift** is in progress. This unconditioned systematic shift reorients the long vowels of Middle English. All the long or lengthened (stressed) vowels are raised in articulation or, if already high, are diphthongized. Subsequent changes in the seventeenth and eighteenth centuries bring about our modern pronunciations. The Great Vowel Shift has a profound effect on English. It demarcates the vowel quality of Modern English from that of medieval English, and in the same respect it distinguishes English from other European languages like Italian and Spanish. In addition, to the extent that* *orthography becomes conventionalized before the shift, a disparity between the way a word is spelled and the way it is pronounced may result.*

1408   **John Gower dies**. Gower is best known as the author of *Confessio Amantis* (*'The Lover's Confession'*), a long narrative poem in English, as well as poems in Latin and French.

1417   In the king's name, the **Signet Office issues letters patent in English**.

1422   Like many other craft and business associations at the time, the **London brewers guild adopts English** as the language in which it will keep its records.

c. **1425–1550**   The **Scottish Makaris ('makers or poets') write in a northern Lowland Scots dialect** of late Middle or Early Modern English; the most prominent Makaris are Robert Henryson, William Dunbar, and Gavin Douglas.

c. **1430**   *At the Exchequer in Westminster, the **Chancery clerks adopt a Central Midlands dialect** of English as the standard for the state documents they prepare.*

c. **1450**   Monk and poet **John Lydgate dies**. He leaves behind *Troy Book*, *Siege of Thebes*, *Fall of Princes*, and many other works.

c. **1470**   **Thomas Malory dies**. He is best known as the author or compiler of *Le Morte d'Arthur* (*'The Death of Arthur'*). Malory's English rendition of Arthurian legend proves so popular that Caxton prints the romance in 1485.

1476   *William Caxton sets up his printing press at Westminster. He is the first person to bring movable-type printing from the continent to England. Compared to older methods of reproducing books (e.g. printing from engraved blocks, hand-copying manuscripts), this new technology creates texts more quickly and at a lower cost. As a result, printed books become accessible to a larger audience and the print revolution begets a revolution in literacy. Caxton's use of contemporary London English for his publications enhances the currency of that dialect; in time, the printing press promotes the development of a standard written language. The first book Caxton is known to print is Chaucer's* Canterbury Tales.

1476–1640   In England, **over twenty thousand titles are published in English**. The works range from short pamphlets to long books.

1485   At the **Battle of Bosworth Field**, the Yorkist king Richard III is defeated by Henry Tudor (Henry VII), founder of the Tudor dynasty.

1491   **William Caxton dies**.

1492   **Christopher Columbus lands in the Americas**. His original mission was to find an ocean passage from Spain to the 'East Indies' that was shorter than the current overland routes. Travel, trade, and colonization set the stage for language spread and exchange.

1497   On a voyage sponsored by the king of England, Italian explorer **John Cabot reaches Newfoundland**.

c. 1500   *The **Modern English** period begins. This stage of the language is charac-terized by reduced inflection and increased periphrasis, in contrast with earlier forms of English. It is conventional to subdivide Modern English into Early Modern English (c. 1500–c. 1700), Late Modern English (c. 1700–c. 1900), and Present-Day English (c. 1900–present).*

1509–1547   **Henry VIII rules** as king of England.

c. 1517–1648   The **Protestant Reformation** ensues with Martin Luther's attempt to reform the Catholic Church. Ultimately, widespread protest incites a schism that divides Christianity into Protestant and Catholic branches. During the English Reformation, the Church of England breaks from the Roman Catholic Church and papal authority. Through a series of legislative acts passed by Parliament from 1532 to 1534, King Henry VIII establishes a Protestant Church of England.

1526–30   Protestant reformer **William Tyndale translates the New Testament and part of the Old Testament into Early Modern English**. Tyndale is the first translator to use Greek and Hebrew sources, respectively, as the basis of his translation (medieval translations used the Latin Vulgate). Much of his Bible survives today, being incorporated into later versions, notably the King James (Authorized) version (1611). His simple syntax and plain style yield idioms that outlive him there.

1535   **Anglican bishop Myles Coverdale lightly revises Tyndale's Bible** and completes the Old Testament sections left untranslated by Tyndale (drawing not on Hebrew, however, but on Latin, English, and German versions and author-ities). Henry VIII places a **Coverdale Bible** in every church in England.

1536–41   **King Henry VIII oversees the Dissolution of the Monasteries**, in which he disbands over eight hundred monasteries, nunneries, and friaries across England, Ireland, and Wales, seizing their assets and appropriating their income. Thousands of books burn when monastic libraries are destroyed, compromising our knowledge of medieval language and literature.

1549   Archbishop of Canterbury **Thomas Cranmer compiles the Book of Common Prayer**. This text is the first prayer book to contain liturgy for daily and Sunday worship in English. Although it is revised two years later, the res-toration of Roman Catholic worship under Queen Mary and the English Civil War delay the next major version of the Book of Common Prayer until 1662. This prayer book remains in use by the Church of England today (along with modernized versions). Its impact is not limited to religious life—by way of allu-sion, its language will make its way into English literary texts and its idioms into popular culture.

1553–58   **Queen Mary reigns** in England.

1556   **Thomas Cranmer is burned at the stake** for heresy under the Catholic queen Mary I.

1558–1603 **Elizabeth I reigns** as queen of England.

1560 **Protestant scholars in Switzerland produce the Geneva Bible**, an English translation that sells in mass numbers in England after the complete Bible (with study apparatus) is printed there in 1576. It is the Bible of poets (e.g. William Shakespeare) and preachers until it is supplanted by the King James (Authorized) version.

1564 Church records register the **baptism of William Shakespeare**.

1577–80 British sea captain and privateer **Francis Drake sails around the world**. His circumnavigation of the globe furthers linguistic exchange.

1582–1610 The **Douai-Rheims Bible is published**. Translated from the Latin Vulgate into English and published with notes and commentary (the New Testament in 1582 and the Old Testament in 1609–10), this Bible offers Reformation Britain a version that upholds Catholic tradition. In style it is more Latinate than English.

1586 *William Bullokar publishes his* **Pamphlet for Grammar**, *the first published grammar of English. Written to demonstrate that English is as regulated as Latin in terms of its grammar, Bullokar's grammar is modeled on William Lily's Latin grammar, the standard school text for Latin. Employing the reformed spelling system he first introduced in his 1580* Booke at Large, for the Amendment of Orthographie for English Speech, *Bullokar sets out principles for the use of English.*

1588 **English naval forces defeat the Spanish Armada**, a fleet sent to support an invasion of England. The success guarantees the survival of the Tudor dynasty and the Protestant Reformation in England. The victory indicates the importance of sea power to the island kingdom and forms the precedent for a long-term commitment to maintaining a powerful navy.

1590–96 **Edmund Spenser publishes** *The Faerie Queene*, albeit in incomplete form; this allegorical epic poem celebrates Queen Elizabeth I and the Tudor dynasty.

1595 **Philip Sidney's** *Defence of Poesie* (*'An Apology for Poetry'*) **is published** (posthumously). In this essay, Sidney expounds the moral virtues of poetry. In his life, Sidney was honored as a poet and courtier, best known for his sonnet sequence, *Astrophel and Stella*.

1597 Jacobean philosopher **Francis Bacon establishes the inductive method for scientific inquiry** by which a philosopher proceeds from fact to derive axiom, then law. Bacon begins to explicate a system of ethics with his writings, including *Essays*, *Novum Organum*, *New Atlantis*, and *De Augmentis Scientiarum*.

1599 The **Globe Theatre is built by the Lord Chamberlain's Men**, Shakespeare's company of actors. The Globe burns to the ground in June 1613 when a cannon misfires during a performance. It is rebuilt on the same foundation shortly after.

1603   James VI of Scotland inherits the English throne as James I and begins a stormy period of rule by the house of Stuart.

1604   *Robert Cawdrey compiles* A Table Alphabetical, *the first dictionary of English. It contains a list of foreign and difficult words found primarily in Scripture and religious use. Providing an 'interpretation . . . in plaine English', this glossary is presented 'for the benefit and helpe of ladies, gentlewomen, or any other unskillful persons', whereby they 'may the more easily and better understand English wordes' (from the title).*

1607   The settlement in Jamestown, Virginia is established. It will become the first successful British colony in North America. The linguistic colonization of the new world results in further dissemination and development of the English language.

1609   All 154 of Shakespeare's sonnets are published.

1611   The King James Bible is completed. The project began in 1604 when James I instructed a committee of 47 scholars to translate the Old and New Testaments from Hebrew and Greek into English. Intended for a national audience, this translation is also meant to reinforce Anglican Church hierarchy and to limit the influence of the Puritans, followers of the theology of John Calvin who were committed to a more purely Protestant Church of England. Over the course of the seventeenth century, the King James (Authorized) version of the Bible supplants other Protestant translations as the standard version of Scripture. *This Bible plays an important role in the spread of literacy throughout England as people learn to read so that they can read the Bible.*

1616   William Shakespeare dies.

1616   Ben Jonson brings out his *Works* in a folio edition. By this time, Jonson is best known for *Volpone*, *The Alchemist*, and *Bartholomew Fair*; his latest comedy, *The Devil Is an Ass*, is first performed in this year.

1620   The Pilgrim Fathers set sail for America.

1623   The First Folio of Shakespeare's plays is published. Thirty-six plays are prepared and printed in folio format by Shakespeare's colleagues John Heminges and Henry Condell. Collected here are the comedies (*The Tempest*, *The Two Gentlemen of Verona*, *The Merry Wives of Windsor*, *Measure for Measure*, *The Comedy of Errors*, *Much Ado about Nothing*, *Love's Labour's Lost*, *A Midsummer Night's Dream*, *The Merchant of Venice*, *As You Like It*, *The Taming of the Shrew*, *All's Well That Ends Well*, *Twelfth Night*, and *The Winter's Tale*), the histories (*King John*; *Richard II*; *Henry IV, Part 1*; *Henry IV, Part 2*; *Henry V*; *Henry VI, Part 1*; *Henry VI, Part 2*; *Henry VI, Part 3*; *Richard III*; and *Henry VIII*), and the tragedies (*Troilus and Cressida*, *Coriolanus*, *Titus Andronicus*, *Romeo and Juliet*, *Timon of Athens*, *Julius Caesar*, *Macbeth*, *Hamlet*, *King Lear*, *Othello*, *Anthony and Cleopatra*, and *Cymbeline*). Two other plays, two narrative poems (*Venus and Adonis* and *The Rape of Lucrece*), and his poetry had been published earlier.

1631   John Donne dies. In his life, Donne, an Anglican priest and dean of St Paul's Cathedral in London, created numerous sermons and an important body of metaphysical poetry.

1633   The Welsh-born metaphysical poet **George Herbert dies**. An Anglican priest, Herbert is known for his religious poetry, some of which has been set to music as hymns and songs.

1641–51   The **English Civil War**, a series of armed political and religious conflicts between Parliamentarians and Royalists, results in the execution of King Charles I (for treason) and the exile of his son, Charles II. A republican government, the **Commonwealth of England** (1649–53), replaces the monarchy until political in-fighting forces the creation of a **Protectorate** (1653–59), ruled over by Oliver Cromwell, Lord Protector. Both governments constitute an interregnum, ultimately, for Charles II returns in 1660 after the deaths of Cromwell and his successor. Despite the failure of the republicans, the Civil War establishes the precedent that an English monarch cannot govern without the consent of Parliament. It bears legacies not only for law but also for letters and learning. **John Milton** plays an important role in English politics, acting as polemicist for Cromwell. Although he does not publish *Paradise Lost* until 1667, his epic poem about the nature of free will and the fall of man is the product of the religious and cultural interpretations of the Puritan Commonwealth. In 1651, **Thomas Hobbes** publishes *Leviathan*, a work of political philosophy defending rule by an absolute monarch.

1653   *Using Latin as a* lingua franca, ***John Wallis composes* Grammatica Linguae Anglicanae**, *a grammar meant to help foreigners learn English. Wallis is known especially for systematizing a set of rules—the Wallis Rules—for the use of* shall *and* will *(e.g.* will *in the first person promises,* shall *in the first person foretells). Wallis also points out that Latin grammar may not be appropriate as a model for English grammar, a warning that will go largely unheeded during the prescriptive movement that follows. His popular grammar remains in print well into the eighteenth century.*

1660   Charles II restores the monarchies of England, Scotland, and Ireland after the Commonwealth of England that follows the English Civil War.

1660–69   British naval administrator **Samuel Pepys keeps a detailed private diary** which comes to be an important source of information about the English Restoration. The record of his personal life alternates with eyewitness accounts of public events such as the Great Fire of London.

1660–1700   The **Restoration period** of literature follows the restoration of Charles II. This new movement is influenced by new social conditions, including the decline of Puritanism, and it encompasses a variety of styles and subjects in fiction, drama, and poetry. In 1678 **John Bunyan** publishes *The Pilgrim's Progress from This World to That which Is to Come*, an allegorical narrative about the Christian soul's path to heaven. Part II, completed in 1684, lays out the different path a woman must follow as Bunyan considers the Christian family more broadly. Explicitly Protestant in theology and anti-Catholic in sentiment, *The Pilgrim's Progress* is popular in both England and the Puritan colonies. Many English proverbial expressions like 'slough of despond' and 'vanity fair' are said to originate in this work. We may also trace the **development of the novel** to Restoration literature, in particular to the recognizably 'novelistic' long-prose fictions of **Aphra Behn**. With the Restoration, theaters, which had been closed by Oliver Cromwell during the Protectorate, are reopened. **Plays** performed during this period include William Wycherley's *The Country Wife* (1675), Aphra Behn's *The Rover* (1677), and William Congreve's *The Way of the World* (1700). The bawdy Restoration comedy becomes a recognizable form. **John Milton**'s *Paradise Lost* (1667) also dates to the Restoration, despite its roots in Commonwealth ideology. Composed in blank verse, the stated purpose of the lengthy poem is 'to justify the ways of God to men'. **Metaphysical poetry**, by Andrew Marvell and others, also circulates at this time. The leading poet of the period, however, is **John Dryden**, who writes verse satires such as 'Mac Flecknoe' and 'Absalom and Achitophel'.

1688   The **Glorious Revolution** brings to power the leader of the Dutch Republic, William of Orange, as King William III and his wife, Mary II. The joint sovereigns replace Mary's father, James II, who is forced into exile.

1689–95   Working in the realms of science and philosophy, **John Locke formulates his doctrine of empiricism**. Locke's investigation of the human mind and the self is presented in works such as *A Letter Concerning Toleration*, *Two Treatises of Government*, *An Essay Concerning Human Understanding*, and *Some Thoughts Concerning Education*.

c. **1700–***c*. **1900**   *Late Modern English develops out of Early Modern English.*

1700–40   The **Augustan period**, named after its English writers' reverence for the artistry of Rome under Caesar Augustus, sees the **rise of the novel** and the **expansion of satire** into genres such as poetry, among other developments. Within the first half of the eighteenth century, the essay remains a respected literary form. Through their expositions in the periodical *The Spectator*, for example, **Joseph Addison** and **Richard Steele** comment on political events and social behavior. **Jonathan Swift** exploits irony in his essay 'A Modest Proposal' (1729) in order to condemn the British ruling class for their treatment of the Irish. Fiction offers another vehicle for such critique; Swift is famous for his biting social commentary in *The Tale of a Tub* (1704) and *Gulliver's Travels*

(1726). Even poetry is brought into this service; modeling his poetry on Greek forms, **Alexander Pope** follows the mock-heroism of the *Rape of the Lock* (1712) with invective as he valorizes Britain's dullness in *The Dunciad* (1728).

Together journalism and satire act alongside drama as crucibles for the development of the novel, as is evidenced by the career of **Henry Fielding**. When censorship is imposed by the Theatrical Licensing Act of 1737, this well-regarded dramatist of the 1730s turns to writing novels such as *Joseph Andrews* (1742) and *Tom Jones* (1749). Earlier, greatly impressed by Cervantes' *Don Quixote*, **Daniel Defoe** completed *Robinson Crusoe* (1719). Nearly as popular in its day as Defoe's adventure story is **Eliza Haywood**'s *Love in Excess* (1719–20). After Fielding, **Samuel Richardson** marks the next turning point in the development of the novel; he follows *Pamela* (1740) with the lengthy *Clarissa* (1748). Contemporary with *Clarissa* is **Tobias Smollett**'s novel *Adventures of Roderick Random* (1748), an example of the picaresque thought to influence Charles Dickens. Technically, these later works lie outside the Augustan period, but they share many qualities with works of the period. Similarly, the writings of **Laurence Sterne** are closely tied to the Augustan period. For example, in *The Life and Opinions of Tristram Shandy* (1759), a fictional autobiography, Sterne foregrounds the necessity of context for interpretation.

1712 *Jonathan Swift publishes* **A Proposal for Correcting, Improving and Ascertaining the Language**, *originally written as a letter to the Earl of Oxford, Lord Treasurer of England. In this work, Swift suggests that in England an assembly similar to the French Academy might remedy the imperfections of its language by legislating English grammar and usage. Swift outlines the need for a dictionary and a grammar, on the authority of which the language could be settled, improved, and subsequently fixed in a permanent form. Although such a commission is never founded, Swift articulates a common anxiety about linguistic correctness; questions of usage trouble even learned writers like himself.*

1714 **Queen Anne dies** and George I (of the house of Hanover) inherits the throne. *With the death of Anne, the last of the Stuarts, the plan to establish and fund an English Academy loses impetus even while the publication of grammar books, rhetorical guides, and dictionaries by individual scholars obviates the need for institutional governance.*

1752 The **Gregorian calendar is adopted in Britain**. Decreed by Pope Gregory XIII in 1582 (reforming the Julian calendar), it set the vernal equinox on 21 March. The calendar gained acceptance gradually throughout Europe.

1755 *Samuel Johnson publishes his* **Dictionary of the English Language**. *Even at the time, his individual achievement is recognized as equivalent to the joint production of an academy. Despite its faults (e.g. weak etymology, unreliable pronunciations), Johnson's dictionary establishes modern lexicographic prac-*

tices such as the use of quotations from written texts to illustrate the usage of words and the range of their meanings. He is largely successful in settling orthography and establishing meaning for many of his entries.

1756–63   The **Seven Years' War**, considered the first global or 'world' war, reorients the balance of power in Europe. It also redraws the territorial holdings of its participants. The North American portion of the war, called the French and Indian War, begins in 1754. As a result of the Seven Years' War, Great Britain gains the French colonies in Canada along with Florida and Bengal, while France transfers Louisiana to Spain.

1760s–70s   Scottish inventor **James Watt improves the steam engine**, making it a practical source of power. Using steam—first from the burning of wood and then the burning of coal—the steam engine is part of a broad range of improvements in technology that lead to the **Industrial Revolution**. During the Industrial Revolution, the population of England soars and migrations from the countryside create industrial cities of unprecedented size.

1761   *Polymath **Joseph Priestley writes** The Rudiments of English Grammar as a textbook for the local school he established. Like Noah Webster, Priestley defers to actual usage, or the custom of speaking, as the first and only standard of a language. Further, he argues that a language inevitably changes for the expedience and usefulness of its speakers. Unlike contemporaries who claim to favor custom but abandon it in practice, Priestley is consistent in applying the principle of usage in his grammar of English.*

1762   *__Robert Lowth writes his__ Short Introduction to English Grammar as a pedagogical grammar, that is, a school textbook. Extrapolated from the model of Latin, his understanding of grammar and the resulting prescriptions and proscriptions which he delivers influence generations of writers. At least 22 editions of the* Short Introduction *appear during the eighteenth century. Many of the rules successfully established for Standard English are formulated there.*

1776   The **Declaration of American Independence** is signed. *Out of a new nation a new national variety of English will emerge and will itself be taken to other places in the world.*

1780   **Thomas Sheridan publishes a 'respelled'** *General Dictionary of the English Language*. Sheridan's work as a British stage actor and educator inspires his focus on elocution as a part of successful public speaking. The new spelling he gives words is intended to aid oral delivery.

1780–1830   Emphasizing the sublimity of nature over Enlightenment ideas of rationalism, the **Romantic period** elevates human emotions as a vehicle for aesthetic experience. In England, the period is ushered in with the joint publication by **William Wordsworth** and **Samuel Taylor Coleridge** of *Lyrical Ballads* (1798). In his preface to the second edition (1800), Wordsworth rejects poetic diction (a special language for poetry) and recommends language as it is used commonly in life. Coleridge contributes four poems to the collection, including his verse *The Rime of the Ancient Mariner*. Coleridge wrote many other well-known poems, including 'Kubla Khan' (1797) and 'Christabel' (1797–1800), as did Wordsworth (e.g. the semi-autobiographical poem *The Prelude*, published after his death in 1850). **William Blake**, who articulates the Romantic sensibility in his poetry, is among others worthy of mention. So, too, is George Gordon Byron (**Lord Byron**), who composes the long narrative poems *Don Juan* (1819–24) and *Childe Harold's Pilgrimage* (1812–18) along with shorter works like 'She Walks in Beauty' (1814). **Percy Bysshe Shelley** writes fine lyric poems like 'Ozymandias' (1818), 'To a Skylark' (1820), and 'Ode to the West Wind' (1819) and his longer pieces *Prometheus Unbound* (1820); *Alastor, or the Spirit of Solitude* (1816); and *Adonais* (1821). **John Keats** publishes short odes like 'Ode to Psyche' (1819) and 'Ode to a Nightingale' (1819), narratives like 'The Eve of St Agnes' (1820), and ballads like 'La Belle Dame sans Merci' (1819). In Scotland, **Robert Burns** incorporates Scots features into his poetry and folksong lyrics; he also writes in the Scottish vernacular.

Although Romanticism reaches its height in poetry, prose fiction also manifests its ideals, particularly the novels of the nineteenth century. **Jane Austen** sets her characters within the constraints of upper-middle-class society in *Pride and Prejudice*, *Sense and Sensibility*, *Mansfield Park*, *Persuasion*, and *Emma* (all published between 1811 and 1818). Around the same time, the historical novel is born with **Walter Scott**'s *Waverley* (1814), *Rob Roy* (1817), and *Ivanhoe* (1819). Earlier, and in a more specific vein, Romanticism gave rise to the Gothic as a literary construct. **Anne Radcliffe**'s *Mysteries of Udolpho* (1794) and **Matthew Gregory Lewis**'s *The Monk* (1796) form precursors to Mary Shelley's *Frankenstein* (1818) as well as later American Gothic works.

1789   *Noah Webster expresses his desire for a distinct language system in America, to create a nation independent 'in language as in government'. Specifically, as he asserts in his* Dissertation on the English Language *(1789), the basis of this standard must be 'universal undisputed practice and the principle of analogy'. Building upon his earlier* American Spelling Book *(1783), his* American Dictionary *of 1828 continues his attempt to establish an American national norm distinct from the British standard of usage.*

1791–1815   Britain fights long wars against France sparked by the radical political changes of the French Revolution and by the imperialist ambitions of the new French emperor, Napoleon Bonaparte. At the 1805 **Battle of Trafalgar**, the British Royal Navy defeats the combined forces of Napoleonic France and of Spain, giving unchallenged control of the seas to Britain. The final **defeat of Napoleon at Waterloo** in 1815 makes Britain the dominant political force in Europe.

1795   *American Quaker lawyer and textbook author* **Lindley Murray writes English Grammar, Adapted to the Different Classes of Learners**. *An imitator of Robert Lowth, Murray gives currency to the British prescriptions for English in the United States.*

1800   The **Act of Union** abolishes the Irish Parliament and gives Ireland representation in the British Parliament in Westminster. This legislative action, prompted by a rebellion in Ireland in 1798 against British Rule, meets with strong opposition and continuing conflict within Ireland.

c. **1807–55**   Early in the nineteenth century, Romanticism spreads from Europe to the United States. There, too, its manifestations are numerous. Rejecting rationalism in favor of intuition, the **American Romantic period** exalts the individual over society. It discovers goodness in the natural world as a balm for the corruption of human society.

Washington Irving ('The Legend of Sleepy Hollow' and 'Rip van Winkle', both from the 1819–20 work *The Sketch Book of Geoffrey Crayon, Gent.*) and **James Fenimore Cooper** (the Leatherstocking tales, published between 1823 and 1841) are among the first writers exhibiting Romantic style and subject matter in the United States. Later on, the popularity of **Edgar Allan Poe**'s detective fiction (e.g. 'The Purloined Letter' [1845]) and tales of the macabre (e.g. 'The Fall of the House of Usher' [1839]) shape more broadly the development of the short story in this country. The 'dark' Romanticism of **Nathaniel Hawthorne** is manifested in the writer's pursuit of morality and sin as a tangle of psychological and social constraints. Hawthorne's fascination with human psychology extends into short stories where the supernatural pervades. Best known are his works *Twice-Told Tales* (1837) and *The Scarlet Letter* (1850). Herman Melville's *Moby Dick* (1851) and *Billy Budd* (published posthumously in 1924) may be classified similarly.

During the mid-nineteenth century, American Romanticism gives rise to **Transcendentalism**. **Ralph Waldo Emerson** articulates the philosophy of Transcendentalism in his essay 'Nature' (1836). An ideal spiritual state transcends the physical and material world, according to this belief. Neither empiricism nor religious doctrine can guide the individual to such an awareness; intuition alone presents a path. In *Walden* (1854), the naturalist and historian **Henry David Thoreau** offers the experience of living simply in nature as a model for readers with this spiritual goal. Thoreau's essay 'Civil Disobedience' (1849) entertains the political implications of existence according to transcendentalist precepts. **Walt Whitman** participates in the transition between transcendentalism and realism. His major work, the poetry collection *Leaves of Grass* (1855), is intended as an American epic for the common person. **Henry Wadsworth Longfellow**, a lyric poet, leaves us his version of the epic in *Evangeline* (1847) and *The Song of Hiawatha* (1855).

1807   In Wales, the **Oystermouth Railway, the first fare-paying passenger railway service, opens** for business. Accessible transportation facilitates communication, not only in Wales but in other places which adopt the system.

1812–15   **War between Britain and the United States** promotes a sense of nationalism in the US similar to the nationalism felt in Britain as a result of the Napoleonic Wars.

1828   *Noah Webster publishes* **An American Dictionary of the English Language***, which represents to some extent an American counterpart to Samuel Johnson's dictionary. Webster intends to cultivate a different look for American, as opposed to British, English through its orthography. In fact, Webster's dictionary helps to establish spelling conventions for US English.*

1832   The **First Reform Bill is passed** by Parliament, beginning a process of liberal reform that brings the vote to more people and distributes parliamentary representation based on population.

1834   The **New Poor Law is passed** in order to reform the system of assistance for the unemployed. By forcing the poor into workhouses, this poverty-relief act is meant to distribute the cost to taxpayers more equitably. Opposition to the new and ultimately impractical system inspires social critique by writers such as Charles Dickens (cf. *Oliver Twist* and *A Christmas Carol*).

1837   **Queen Victoria accedes to the throne** of England, reigning for 63 years. During this period of industrial, scientific, and military progress, the United Kingdom gains the appellation, 'the Empire on which the sun never sets'. *With Britain's territorial expansion, English is taken all over the world. The language changes in its turn from cultural contact. The vocabulary is enriched by foreign loan words it borrows during this time.*

1837–1901   The British **Victorian period** corresponds generally to the time of Queen Victoria's reign. **Charles Dickens** is popular in his lifetime for the lengthy, serialized (weekly or monthly) works later published as single novels: *The Pickwick Papers* (1836–7), *The Life and Adventures of Nicholas Nickleby* (1838–9), *David Copperfield* (1849–50), *Bleak House* (1852–3), *Great Expectations* (1860–1), and *A Tale of Two Cities* (1859). **Thomas Hardy**'s novels—for example, *Tess of the D'Urbervilles* (1891) and *Jude the Obscure* (1894–5)—explore human character as the individual interacts with his or her environment. Perhaps unappreciated in their time, the **Brontë sisters** are now acknowledged for what has been termed 'female Gothic' fiction or romance: *Wuthering Heights* (Emily Brontë, 1847), *Jane Eyre* (Charlotte Brontë, 1847), and *The Tenant of Wildfell Hall* (Anne Brontë, 1848). **Victorian Gothic** gives us the prototypical vampire novel, *Dracula* (1897), by Bram Stoker and the Faustian horror gothic novel *The Picture of Dorian Gray* (1891), by Oscar Wilde.

For more than forty years of Victoria's rule, **Alfred Lord Tennyson** is Poet Laureate of England, publishing such lyrics as 'The Charge of the Light Brigade' (1854) and the blank verse *Idylls of the King* (1842). **Elizabeth Barrett Browning** also belongs to this era; she is best known for *Sonnets from the Portuguese* (1850). Victorian poetry features the dramatic monologue, mastered as a form in the 1842 piece 'My Last Duchess', by **Robert Browning**. Although the poetic oeuvre of **Gerard Manley Hopkins** is not published until 1918, making his impact on poetic tradition post-Victorian, he should be mentioned in the context of his lifetime. His numerous short poems (e.g. 'As Kingfishers Catch Fire' and 'The Windhover') test metaphysical imagery, sprung rhythm, and unconventional usage and syntax. **Matthew Arnold**'s poetry closes the Victorian period with his elegies on the death of faith at the beginning of the modern era—for example, 'Dover Beach' (1867). Arnold, who was a professor of poetry at Oxford, is remembered for his literary and cultural criticism in *Culture and Anarchy* (1869) and *Essays in Criticism* (1865–88). As we turn to Victorian drama to end our overview of Victorian literature, we once again find **Oscar Wilde**. Wilde's masterpiece of social satire, *The Importance of Being Earnest* (1895), embodies *fin-de-siècle* cynicism and verbal wit.

1860–61   The US **Pony Express horse relay transports mail** from Missouri to California. The short-lived experiment represents an attempt to link population centers on the east coast with the western United States.

1860–1900   The second half of the nineteenth century brings the so-called **Second Industrial Revolution** involving advances in chemistry, electricity, and transportation. *This series of improvements in technology and travel affect the language. When English speakers are brought into closer communication, linguistic conformity may result even while vocabulary may be exchanged.*

1861   A **transcontinental telegraph system is established** in North America.

1861–65   The **American Civil War** leads to the abolition of slavery—a goal promoted through literary as well as political channels for a century—throughout the republic. The power of the federal government also expands, as a result of the Union victory.

1866   The **transatlantic telegraph cable is completed**.

1867   **Canada is granted self-government**. In time, a national dialect of Canadian English becomes identifiable.

1869   The **Suez Canal opens**, dramatically shortening ship voyages from Britain to India and promoting the replacement of sailing ships by steamships.

1869   The **first transcontinental railroad is completed**; it runs across the United States from Nebraska to California.

1876   **Alexander Graham Bell introduces the telephone**.

1877   **Thomas Edison invents the phonograph**.

1884 *The **first fascicle of what will become the** Oxford English Dictionary **is published** (at this time, the work is titled* A New English Dictionary on Historical Principles*). This installment contains words ranging from* A *to* Ant.

1885 The **Canadian Pacific Railway is completed**, fulfilling a promise of Confederation. Eventually it stretches from Vancouver to Montreal, while also serving major cities in the United States.

1898 **Magnetic recording is used to capture sound**. This development leads to the invention of magnetic tape recording in the late 1920s.

Late 1800s **Internal combustion engines are adopted** to a variety of uses. With the commercial production of fuel petroleum after the mid-eighteenth century, engineering advances allow the development of automobile and aircraft engines. These technologies contribute to the English vocabulary and to divergence in the use of specific nouns for inventions. Meanwhile, new forms of transportation (first bicycles and then automobiles, along with railroads and steamships) continue to stabilize usage and grammar by improving communication.

Late 1800s The **first wire services are created** as newspapers cooperate to form associations for exchanging foreign and other news via telegraph.

c. **1900–20** *Present-Day English, the current stage of Modern English, develops out of Late Modern English.*

1901 The **first transatlantic radio signals are sent** between Cornwall and Newfoundland.

1901–14 The **Edwardian period** of literature begins with the death of Victoria and extends beyond the reign of King Edward VII (1901–10) to the outbreak of the First World War. British writers such as **Joseph Conrad** (*Heart of Darkness* [1902], *Lord Jim* [1900]), **Rudyard Kipling** (*Kim* [1901]), **Samuel Butler** (*The Way of All Flesh* [1903]), **H.G. Wells** (best-known for his earlier works, including *The Time Machine* [1895]), and **E.M. Forster** (*A Room with a View* [1908], *Howards End* [1910]) are active during these years. During this time, fiction enjoys a wide audience, both popular and elite.

1906 The **first public radio broadcast is made**. With this technology, signals are transmitted through the modulation of electromagnetic waves with frequencies below those of visible light.

c. **1910–39** In literature, the **modernist period** addresses the same kinds of aesthetic concerns explored in the plastic arts by painters and sculptors of the time. Indeed, inter-relationships among the arts are a feature of modernism, as is a ferment of movements, including Imagism, Cubism, Vorticism, and Dadaism. Literary modernism often attempts multiple perspectives and a variety of narrative modes in order to represent point of view, difficulty, and variety in human experience, particularly of the time. Important American modernist writers include **Gertrude Stein**, **Ezra Pound**, and **T.S. Eliot**, whose prose or poetry is experimental and innovative. All three writers move to Europe and become bridges between the old and new worlds during the flowering of modernism. Slightly later American modernists are **John Dos Passos** and **William Faulkner**, while Ernest Hemingway and F. Scott Fitzgerald, who both came to the fore in the 1920s, might best be described as modern rather than modernist in style and substance. A similar distinction might be made in England between **Virginia Woolf** and **Wyndham Lewis**, undoubted modernists, and D.H. Lawrence, E.M. Forster, and H.G. Wells, who were modern without being modernist. The international nature of literary modernism in English has often been remarked upon, with notable contributions from the Irish writer **James Joyce** and the Scots writer **Hugh MacDiarmid**.

Besides numerous anthologies, for example those of the Imagist poets, the renowned works of literary modernism include Ezra Pound's *Cantos* (c. 1925), T.S. Eliot's *The Waste Land* (1922), James Joyce's *Ulysses* (1922), William Faulkner's *The Sound and the Fury* (1929), Virginia Woolf's *Mrs Dalloway* (1925), and John Dos Passos's *U.S.A.* (1938). Important modern, though not necessarily modernist, works of this time include Ernest Hemingway's *The Sun also Rises* (1926), D.H. Lawrence's *The Rainbow* (1915) and *Women in Love* (1921), and F. Scott Fitzgerald's *The Great Gatsby* (1925). A towering literary figure difficult to constrain within any single literary category or movement is the Irish poet, playwright, and literary propagandist **William Butler Yeats**, often seen as the greatest poet writing in English in the twentieth century, by turns a symbolist, romantic, and modernist.

1914–18   **World War I** is one of the deadliest military conflicts in history, killing perhaps fifteen million people in Europe. Indeed, the losses of the 'Great War' are recognizable in the many war memorials seen in allied countries today. The war's effect on English appears in the language's acquisition of vocabulary. New words for the technology of battle (e.g. *air raid*, *tank*, *gas mask*, *camouflage*, *roadblock*) are introduced into English.

1919   The **first transatlantic flights take place**.

1921   With the exception of six counties in Ulster in the north, **Ireland is granted home rule** as an independent state within the British Commonwealth after a long and sometimes deadly struggle against British rule and among groups within Ireland.

1926   **Britain has its first and only general strike**. Although union members are forced back to work, the short strike signals the poor and deteriorating state of labor relations in Britain, a source of divisive conflict for the rest of the century.

1928   *The **Oxford English Dictionary** is published. As the one hundred and twenty-fifth and final fascicle of* A New English Dictionary on Historical Principles *is finished, the complete set of volumes is bound and published under this new title.*

1931   The **British Commonwealth is established**.

Late 1930s   Television becomes available on the commercial market. This technology uses high-powered radio-transmitters to broadcast a signal to a TV receiver.

1939–45   World War II, a global military conflict, leaves more than seventy million dead, a majority of them civilians, across the world. New vocabulary acquisitions preserve a memory of the war; words like *blackout*, *blitz*, *jeep*, and *radar* can be traced to the Second World War.

1939–   In part a reaction against modernism, in part a continuation and redirection of it, the **postmodernist period** can be seen emerging in English in the fiction of **Samuel Beckett** (early in *Murphy* [1938], later in his trilogy of *Molloy*, *Malone Dies*, and *The Unnamable* [1951–60]) and of **Flann O'Brien** (Brian O'Nolan) (in *At Swim-Two-Birds* [1939] and *The Third Policeman* [written in 1940, published posthumously in 1967]). The formal experimentations and earnestness of modernism are filtered through skepticism about Enlightenment ideals and often a dark and satirical humor, and there is an attempt through narrative layering to create a conscious metafiction. The relationship among texts (intertextuality) may be foregrounded. A further sampling of postmodernist writers may include **Joseph Heller** (*Catch-22* [1961]), **Ken Kesey** (*One Flew Over the Cuckoo's Nest* [1962]), **Kurt Vonnegut** (*Cat's Cradle* [1963]), **Vladimir Nabokov** (*Lolita* [1955]), **Thomas Pynchon** (*The Crying of Lot 49* [1966]), **John Barth** (*The Sot-Weed Factor* [1960]), **Donald Barthelme** (*Snow White* [1967]), **Alexander Trocchi** (*Cain's Book* [1960]), **Robert Kroetsch** (*The Studhorse Man* [1969]), and **Margaret Atwood** (*The Handmaid's Tale* [1986]).

1945   After winning a majority government in the closing days of World War II, the **British Labour Party brings in a government committed to social reform**. Through this party's efforts, a number of industries are nationalized and universal health insurance is introduced along with other measures that transform British society.

1945–   The **postwar period** of literature is closely aligned with the 'landscape of ruin' which provides a metaphor for broken lives and spirits in the aftermath of the war (Sanders 2004:586). **Graham Greene** (*The Ministry of Fear* [1943], *The End of the Affair* [1951], *The Quiet American* [1955]) inherits the mantle of Joseph Conrad, while **Anthony Powell**'s *roman-fleuve*, *A Dance to the Music of Time* [1951–75], attempts an almost Proustian perspective on British society.

Many texts and authors of the postwar period can also be classified as postmodernist, yet the period nurtures other writers deserving of mention in their own right. Many of these are playwrights. There are the Americans **Tennessee Williams** (*The Glass Menagerie* [1944]) and **Arthur Miller** (*Death of a Salesman* [1949]) and the British **Harold Pinter** (*The Birthday Party* [1958]) and **Tom Stoppard** (*Rosencrantz and Guildenstern Are Dead* [1966]). We should point also to the novels of **William Golding** (*Lord of the Flies* [1954]), **Iris Murdoch** (*The Black Prince* [1973]), **Muriel Spark** (*The Prime of Miss Jean Brodie* [1961]), **Doris Lessing** (*The Golden Notebook* [1962]), and **Malcolm Lowry** (*Under the Volcano* [1947]), all of whom are British, and to the Canadian **Alice Munro** (*Lives of Girls and Women* [1971]). The Beat writers of the 1950s and early 1960s—for example, **Jack Kerouac**, **Allen Ginsberg**, **Lawrence Ferlinghetti**, and **Gregory Corso**—also have strong connections with the post-war period.

c. **1945–90**   The **Cold War** develops between Western Democracies and Communist states. During this time, much political rhetoric feeds the conflict. An early example of such language use is Winston Churchill's 1946 speech, given in the United States, in which he describes the new Soviet sphere of influence in postwar eastern Europe as a region behind an 'iron curtain' of barbarism. The ideological conflict, which on occasion erupts in fighting (often between proxy client nations), is pursued through campaigns of espionage.

1947   **India and Pakistan become independent**. The independence of most British overseas colonies follows in the next two decades as the Empire wanes.

1947   The **transistor is invented**. This semiconductor device, which amplifies or switches electronic signals, will become the building block of modern electronic devices. The numerous technologies it enables contribute to communication and are reflected in the expansion of the vocabulary.

Late 1940s   The **first general-purpose electronic digital computers are used**.

Late 1950s   **Transatlantic jet service begins**.

1960s   Decolonization movements culminate in the **independence of former British colonies in Africa, Asia, and the Caribbean. Commonwealth literature** becomes a field of study which evolves into the area called World Literatures Written in English.

1960s–2000   **High-speed rail service is adopted** across the globe.

1969   **French and English are recognized as the official languages of Canada**.

1972   The **first public call on a personal, portable cell phone is made**.

1960s–   **Second-wave feminism** evolves out of earlier periods of feminism, beginning as early as the eighteenth century, in Britain and the United States; earlier feminist action focused on gaining for women civil liberties such as the right to vote. Many of the concerns that would become central to late-twentieth-century feminism are articulated by Simone de Beauvoir in *The Second Sex*, translated from French (1949) into English in 1953. There, for example, Beauvoir differentiates gender as a social role from the physical sex of the body. Important feminist texts follow, such as Betty Friedan's *The Feminine Mystique* (1963), Kate Millett's *Sexual Politics* (1970), and Juliet Mitchell's *Psycho-Analysis and Feminism* (1974). Feminism has an impact on literature and language in

English. It gives rise to spellings like *womyn*, designed to omit 'men' from the noun *woman*; to forms like *herstory*, meant to highlight the past achievements of women; and to the title *Ms*, intended to make a woman's marital status irrelevant to the form of her address. Similarly, vocabulary like *lady* and *girl* may be avoided as demeaning (although *gentleman* and *boy* may also be eschewed as socially limiting). The desire for a gender-neutral pronoun which does not discriminate (*he* is generally abandoned for inclusive reference) promotes the use of *they* with a singular referent (still non-standard), along with the split forms *s/he* and *his/her*. Alternatively, writers switch from the singular into the plural to avoid the gendered singular pronouns.

1973   Electronic mail is developed by the US Department of Defense as a method of exchanging digital messages through a network-based system. Later, email will become available for academic, government, and commercial use via the Internet.

1978   Edward Said publishes *Orientalism*, a critical work seminal in establishing the field of postcolonialism. Along with Said, **Homi Bhabha** (*The Location of Culture* [1994]) and **Gayatri Spivak** (*In Other Worlds* [1987]) are instrumental in articulating postcolonial theory. The **postcolonial period** of literature reacts to the discourse of colonization with a call to 'decolonize the mind', as Kenyan writer **Ngũgĩ wa Thiong'o** argued. More generally, postcolonialism may be seen as a global condition, a geographical category (emerging out of Commonwealth literature or World Literatures Written in English), or a strategy for reading literature written by individuals from former colonies. Postcolonial writers counter unequal power relations and re-establish new ones in literary and cultural works. A central tenet holds that context affects the production and reception of literature; artistic production must be understood in light of the ongoing discourses of globalization (including the legacy of colonialism), neoliberalism, and capitalism. The ideology of imperialism has been linked with the dissemination of culture in educational settings and in literature. A related debate about the status of national and regional varieties of English contrasts the notion of one English with that of separate Englishes. Recently, postcolonialism has been approached in association with globalization studies and diaspora studies.

Postcolonial writers may be surveyed by geographical region. From the Caribbean we may note **Jean Rhys** (*Wide Sargasso Sea* [1966]), **V.S. Naipaul** (*A House for Mr Biswas* [1961]), **Wilson Harris** (*Palace of the Peacock* [1960]), and **Derek Walcott** (*Omeros* [1990]). From Africa we might mention **Chinua Achebe** (*Things Fall Apart* [1958]), **Ben Okri** (*The Famished Road* [1991]), **Nadine Gordimer** (*July's People* [1981]), **J.M. Coetzee** (*Life and Times of Michael K* [1983] and *Disgrace* [1999]), and **Wole Soyinka** (*Death and the King's Horseman* [1976]). From South Asia we find **R.K. Narayan** (*The Man-Eater of Malgudi* [1961]), **Anita Desai** (*Clear Light of Day* [1980]), **Salman Rushdie** (*Midnight's Children* [1981]), **Amitav Ghosh** (*The Shadow Lines*

[1988]), and **Arundhati Roy** (*The God of Small Things* [1997]). From Australia and New Zealand come **Thomas Kenneally** (*The Chant of Jimmie Blacksmith* [1972]), **Alexis Wright** (*Carpentaria* [2006]), **Keri Hulme** (*The Bone People* [1983]), and **Mudrooroo** (*Master of the Ghost Dreaming* [1991]). From Canada we must note **Thomas King** (*Green Grass, Running Water* [1993]), **Dionne Brand** (*What We All Long For* [2005]), and **Rohinton Mistry** (*A Fine Balance* [1996]). British authors include **Hanif Kureishi** (*The Buddha of Suburbia* [1990]), **Zadie Smith** (*White Teeth* [2000]), and **Monica Ali** (*Brick Lane* [2003]).

Late 1970s   **Personal computers become available** for commercial sale.

1990   The **World Wide Web is developed** as a pool for information which can be shared by collaborators working at remote sites. It constitutes a system of inter-linked hypertext documents accessed through the Internet. Web pages contain text, images, video, and multimedia. *The system encourages the global spread of written English for Web use, introducing at the same time new words relevant to Web technology into the language.*

Mid-1990s   The **Internet is commercialized**. Originally developed in the United States in the 1960s, with funding from the US Department of the Defense, this global system of interconnected computer networks (a 'network of networks'), now carries the World Wide Web along with the infrastructure to support electronic mail and online chat services.

1994   The medium of **text messaging is introduced**. Texting allows the exchange of brief written messages between mobile phones over a cellular network. Typically, text messages are short and quickly written. Originally they employed number symbols found on the keypad to represent words and sounds. Because they are abbreviated, text messages may depart from standard spelling conventions. Linguists see text messaging, along with the development of **computer-mediated communication** through the Internet, as giving rise to a new, hybrid (oral and written) media along with a new kind of literacy.

2006   **Western Union discontinues its telegram services**.

2007   **Amazon Kindle introduces a software and hardware platform for e-books** and other digital media. Some people speculate that electronic readers will replace printed books in the future.

2010–   *English continues in use as a global language. While approximately 375 million speakers use English as a first language, millions more (perhaps as many as a billion) learn it as an additional language. The flourishing of national varieties allow us to speak of many Englishes today.*

Exercise Key

List of Exercises

12 Modern English

13 Varieties of English

Answers

Chapter 1

Exercise 1.1 Morphological and Semantic Concepts

1. a. handyman – *hand* (R) + *y* (S) + *man* (R)
    b. immobilization – *im* (P) + *mobile* (R) + *ize* (S) + *(a)tion* (S)
    c. fire-retardant – *fire* (R) + *retard* (R) + *ant* (S) [or *re* (P) + *tard* (R) + *ant* (S)]
    d. biodegradable – *bio* (P) + *de* (P) + *grade* (R) + *able* (S)
    e. worldly-wise – *world* (R) + *ly* (S) + *wise* (R)
    f. flightworthiness – *flight* (R) + *worth* (R) + *y* (S) + *ness* (S)
    g. owner-occupied – *own* (R) + *er* (S) + *occupy* (R) + *ed* (S)
    h. counterclockwise – *counter* (R) + *clock* (R) + *wise* (S)
    i. unforeseeable – *un* (P) + *fore* (P) + *see* (R) + *able* (S)
    j. icebreaker – *ice* (R) + *break* (R) + *er* (S)

2. (1) *-ed*, past participle: come*, decided, raised, submerged

   (2) *-ing*, present participle: lifting, submerging

   (3) *-ed*, past tense: said, lasted, swelled, rose*, sailed, perished, moved

   (4) *-s*, present tense: has, is, swarms

   (5) *-s*, plural: things, days, waters, mountains, birds, beasts, cattle*

   (6) *-'s*, possessive: men's

   (7) *-er*, comparative: more*, higher

   (8) *-est*, superlative: highest

   * NOTE: These forms are not entirely regular.

3. a. *cattle*: 'a member of the bovine class, cow, oxen, etc.'

   b. *efface* (denotation): 'to obliterate, rub out, cause to disappear'
      efface (connotations): consistently negative

   c. *bird* +ANIMATE −HUMAN, +AVIAN ±MALE, ±ADULT

Exercise 1.2 Periods of English

1. basic adjectives: god/good/good/good

   basic verbs: com/cam/cam/came; -bærn-/-brent/-burnt/-burned

   basic nouns: sæd/seed/seed/seed; -timan/tyme/tym/time;
   heofana/heuenes/heven/heaven

   pronouns: he/he/he/he; ic/Y/I/I

2. In OE, *sæd*, *hwæte*, and *coccel* are sown/grown. In ME, *seed, taris*, and *whete* are sown/grown. In EmodE, *seed, darnel*, and *corn* are sown/grown. In ModE *seed, darnel*, and *wheat* are sown/grown.

   Some basic words, like *sæd/seed* and *hwæt/whete/wheat*, remain relatively consistent throughout the history of the language, but other words (*coccel, taris, darnel*) change, perhaps because new ones are borrowed as old ones drop out or because of changes in cultural practices like farming. These differences may also reflect different interpretations of the original New Testament Greek by the English translators in each era.

3. In OE, 'heaven' comes before 'kingdom' (*rice*); in the other three passages, 'kingdom' comes first. In OE, 'like' (*gelic*) comes after 'man'; in the other three, 'like' comes first. The greatest changes occur between the OE and ME periods.

Exercise 1.3 Analyzing Shakespearean English

Here, forms of the pronoun *thou* and verb forms in -*st* which accompany them strike the modern reader. A more subtle difference is the use of *youngly* to mean 'early in life'. We also cannot rhyme *departest* and *convertest* (*conuertest*) as Shakespeare seems to; either it is not an exact rhyme or the sound of one of the words has changed.

Exercise 1.4 The Nature of Linguistic Change

1. Such a community would be accessible by many other communities, perhaps a trading center. There would be a dominant native (mother) tongue. There would be frequent political changes, perhaps even revolutionary upheavals. There would be a constant traffic of visitors and foreigners, often holding, perhaps, positions of influence and power. Finally, there would be very few written texts, perhaps only a rich oral tradition that prized creative and innovative verbal skill.

2. (1) Iconic: *humming* a tune; a *crackling* fire; she cycled *from* Main *to* Cambie *to* Oak

    (2) Indexical: *this* red book; put it *there*; it *went* away

    (3) Symbolic: *fire* (N); *cycle* (V); *red* (ADJ)

3. The words of language are *signs*, that is, things which represent or stand for other things. The relation between the sign and the thing it represents is arbitrary or conventional—there is no natural connection. It is a matter of agreement among the speakers of the language.

Exercise 1.5 Attitudes Toward Linguistic Change

The three typical views of language change are

    (1) language deteriorates from some perfect state;
    (2) language evolves toward a more efficient state; and
    (3) language neither progresses nor decays.

Generally speaking, people feel that language deteriorates and needs constant vigilance in order to maintain, or even to reacquire, its purity. The notion of language purity involves assumptions about corruption by foreign elements and by non-standard usage. Cultural and national chauvinism includes class discrimination based on dialect and literacy as well as pronunciation and accepted grammar. Prescriptivism defines what is acceptable and what is not. Even though they may be based on scholarship, prescriptive rules are imposed. A descriptive grammar, on the other hand, tries to record the varieties of usage it finds in a society without suggesting which usage is preferable.

Exercise 1.6 *Oxford English Dictionary*

1. The word *Sandwich* is capitalized because the word is said to be named after John Montagu, 4th Earl of *Sandwich* (1718–92), who once spent 24 hours at the gaming table without refreshment other than some slices of cold beef placed between slices of toast.

2. No, the word *booty*, n., is related to *boot*, n.[1], which means 'good, advantage, profit, use'. There is another noun, *boot*, n.[2], meaning 'a covering of the foot and lower part of the leg'.

3. Meaning 5a of the noun is 'A set of questions used to test knowledge or to promote learning'. It is said to be chiefly used in America. Sense 4b of the first verb is related to this meaning of the noun and has the general sense 'to question, interrogate'.

4. The word *slogan* is from Gaelic (Scottish/Irish). Its first meaning is 'a war cry or battle cry; *spec.* one of those formerly employed by Scottish Highlanders or Borderers, or by the native Irish, usually consisting of a personal surname or the name of a gathering-place'. The last use in this sense is 1879.

5. The word *stomach* derives ultimately from Greek through Latin into Old French and then was borrowed into English.

6. The first spelling for the word *eerie* was *eri*. It was first spelled *eerie* in 1792: 'Be thou a bogle by the eerie side of an auld thorn' (Burns, *Wks.* (1800) II. 403).

7. The *OED* lists several obsolete meanings of the word *nice*:
   • 1. a. Of a person: foolish, silly, simple; ignorant. *Obs.*
   • 2. a. Of conduct, behaviour, etc.: characterized by or encouraging wantonness or lasciviousness. *Obs.*
   • 3. c. Particular, strict, or careful with regard to a specific point or thing. *Obs.*
   • 3. e. Fastidious in matters of literary taste or style. *Obs.*
   • 4. a. In early use: faint-hearted, timorous, cowardly, unmanly. Later also: effeminate. *Obs.*
   • 5. Strange, rare, extraordinary. *Obs.*
   • 6. a. Shy, coy, (affectedly) modest; reserved. *Obs.*
   • 9. a. Slender, thin, fine; insubstantial. *Obs.*
   • 10. a. That enters minutely into details; meticulous, attentive, sharp. *Obs.*
   • 11. a. Critical, doubtful; full of risk or uncertainty. *Obs.*
   • 12. b. Of an instrument or apparatus: capable of showing minute differences; finely poised or adjusted. *Obs.*

8. *positive*: Having class, poise, or polish; smart, stylish, glamorous, 'classy'. *negative*: Of persons: haughty, pretentious, ostentatious; of things: flashy, pretentious looking.

Chapter 2

Exercise 2.1 Consonants

1. a. voiceless glottal fricative [h]
   b. voiced bilabial stop [b]
   c. labiovelar semivowel (or glide) [w]
   d. alveolar nasal [n]
   e. voiceless alveolopalatal fricative [š]
   f. voiced alveolar fricative [z]

2. a. [t] voiceless alveolar stop
   b. [s] voiceless alveolar fricative
   c. [k] voiceless velar stop
   d. [ð] voiced interdental fricative
   e. [r] alveolar retroflex
   f. [j] palatal semivowel (or glide)

3. a. shoot [š]
   b. kid [k]
   c. zone [z]
   d. notion [n]
   e. youth [j]
   f. jewel [ǰ]
   g. Jacques [ž]
   h. sugar [š]

4. a. raise [z]
   b. fire [r]
   c. reign [n]
   d. beige [ž]
   e. porch [č]
   f. allege [ǰ]
   g. mourning [ŋ]
   h. resign [n]

5. a. lotion [š]
   b. latter [ɾ]
   c. offer [f]
   d. leisure [ž]
   e. rugged [g]
   f. talker [k]
   g. yo-yo [j]
   h. sojourn [ǰ]

Exercise 2.2 Vowels and Transcriptions of Words

1. a. low front [æ]
   b. mid-back tense [o]
   c. high front lax [ɪ]
   d. low central [a]

2. a. [u] high back tense
   b. [ɛ] mid-front lax
   c. [ɑ] low back (unrounded)
   d. [y] high front tense rounded

3. a. low central to high back lax [aʊ]
   b. mid-front tense to high front lax [eɪ]
   c. high front lax to high back tense [ɪu]

4. a. [aɪ] low central to high front lax
   b. [ɔɪ] mid-back lax to high front lax
   c. [oʊ] mid-back tense to high back lax

5. a. sign
    b. wished
    c. build
    d. comb
    e. they
    f. crowded
    g. breathed
    h. air, heir, e're
    i. rich
    j. void
    k. junk
    l. huge

6. a. [sɑft]
    b. [pəroʊkiəl]
    c. [ənəf]
    d. [mæskjəlɪn]
    e. [ðoʊ]
    f. [mɪuziəmz]
    g. [kɑrv]
    h. [ɪnɛləǰəbəl]
    i. [haɪt]
    j. [dəbɑčəri]
    k. [kærəǰ]
    l. [mɔɪsčəraɪz]

    m. [ruf]
    n. [kwɪntəsɛnčəl]
    o. [dəm]
    p. [pɑrləmɛntəri]

7.   Error   Correction
    a. [θ]   [ð]
    b. [sh]   [š]
    c. [j]   [ǰ]
    d. [u]   [ə]
    e. [æ] (second one) [ə] or [ɪ]

Exercise 2.3 Stress

a. parénthesis
b. insènsibílity
c. pàrenthétical
d. áccent
e. absólve
f. accénted / áccented
g. àbsolúte / ábsolùte
h. accéntuàte
i. àbsolútion
j. númerous
k. tímeless
l. numérical

Exercise 2.4 Writing Systems

1. (1) Ideographic: there is a one-to-one correspondence between the sign and what it represents; no particular word is associated with the sign.

    (2) Logographic: develops from ideographic; a word becomes associated with the sign, the sign functioning as that word.

(3) Phonographic: a further development in which sounds become associated with a particular sign independent of the sign's original meaning.

2. The runic and the Latin alphabets both originated from Etruscan variants of the original North Semitic alphabet. Runes are an angular script suitable for carving on wood or stone. Examples still remain and are found over an extensive area, ranging from Scandinavia and the British Isles in the north to northern Italy in the south. When Christian missionaries brought their religion to England, they also brought the Latin alphabet, which took over as the method of writing, though Old English retained two of the runic symbols.

Chapter 3

Exercise 3.1 Causes of Change

1. a. the speaker's exerting the least effort in articulating sounds

   b. the hearer's requiring that sounds be maximally distinct

   c. the tendency of phonological systems toward structural balance

   d. certain tendencies of change common to all languages

   e. the limiting of redundancy and irregularities; the tendency to establish a one-to-one relationship between grammatical form and meaning

   f. the pronunciation of words as they are written

   g. the misapplication of a grammatical or phonological rule in order to correct a perceived mistake

   h. the generalization of a grammatical or phonological rule, often in error

   i. the alteration of a form because of perceived similarities to a related form, usually in order to remove irregularities

   j. the replacement of emphatic forms and euphemisms as they cease to overstate or understate their meanings

   k. a new understanding of the structure of a phrase, involving the reassignment of structural divisions

2. a. The more or less unconscious processes are (a, b, c, d, e).

   b. The more or less conscious processes are (f, g, h, i, j, k).

   c. Processes acting in opposition to each other are (a) and (b).

   d. Processes explaining similar changes are (g) and (h).

   e. When a child says 'She rided the bike' instead of 'She rode the bike', the process being applied is (i).

f. Processes describing the two pronunciations of *often* are (a) (loss of [t] after [f] for ease of articulation) and (f) (pronunciation of the *t* because it remains in the spelling).

g. The process explaining the pairing of such sounds in English as [t]/[d], [f]/[v], and [p]/[b] is (c).

h. The concept explaining the application of *-d* or *-ed* to create the past tense of new borrowings in Modern English is (i).

i. The process explaining the creation of new slang adjectives, like *harsh*, *rad*, or *random*, for emphasis is (j).

Exercise 3.2 Mechanisms of Phonological Change

1. a. [z] > [ž] voiced alveolar fricative becomes voiced alveolopalatal fricative; palatalization and labialization

    b. [u] > [aʊ] high back tense vowel becomes low central to high back lax diphthong; diphthongization

    c. [b] > [p] voiced bilabial stop becomes voiceless bilabial stop; devoicing

    d. [y] > [i] high front tense rounded vowel becomes high front tense vowel; unrounding

    e. [ɪ] > [ə] high front lax vowel becomes mid-central lax vowel; reduction

2. a. *February*: dissimilation; loss of [r]

    b. *yolk*: loss of consonant, [l], in medial position, diphthongization of vowel

    c. *irresponsible* (from *in + responsible*): complete regressive assimilation; [n] into [r]

    d. *every*: syncope (loss of medial vowel)

    e. *bright*: loss of sound symbolized by *gh*, compensatory lengthening and diphthongization of vowel

3. a. ME *claps* – ModE *clasp*: metathesis of [s] and [p]

    b. OE *andswaru* – ModE *answer*: loss of medial sounds [d] and [w], apocope of final vowel, reduction of penultimate vowel

    c. ME *kinred* – ModE *kindred*: intrusion of homorganic stop after [n]

    d. ME *launde* – ModE *lawn*: loss of medial consonant [d] and of final vowel (apocope)

    e. OE *hlid* – ModE *lid*: simplification of consonant cluster (loss of initial [h])

Exercise 3.3 Mechanisms of Morphological and Syntactic Change

a. the verb *sculpt* and the noun *sculptor*: back-formation, a kind of false analogy in which the *-or* ending is interpreted as an *-er* agent form; a conservative change

b. auxiliary verb *may* from the OE verb *magan* 'to be able': conversion of a full verb to an auxiliary; a conservative change; grammaticalization has occurred

c. EModE *skeates* (pl.) 'ice skates' in seventeenth century from Dutch *schaats* (sg.) 'skate, stilt': reinterpretation as plural of singular loan word with *-s* ending; false morphological analysis; a conservative change

d. *charterhouse* 'charitable institution', originally meant 'a Carthusian monastery': folk etymology; nothing to do with *charter*

e. OE *ic* (sg.), *wit* 'we two', *we* 'we all' have become ModE *I* (sg.), *we* (pl.): loss of number distinction (dual); an innovative change

f. OE *wīfmann* 'woman' and *wīfhād* 'womanhood' are masculine; their ModE equivalents are feminine and neuter respectively: loss of grammatical gender and replacement with natural gender; an innovative change

g. ModE *acorn* from OE *æcern* 'field fruit, mast (fallen nuts)' (OE *æcer* 'field' > ModE *acre*) by way of ME *akkorn*, which is believed to be a combination of *ake* 'oak' and *corn* 'kernel': folk etymology, false analogy

h. ModE *oakum* 'loose fiber often used in caulking' from OE *acumba* 'flax fibers separated by combing' (*a-* 'out' + *cemba* 'to comb'): folk etymology (nothing to do with oaks)

Exercise 3.4 Mechanisms of Semantic Change

1. a. *shroud* 'garment, clothing': specialization, pejoration

   b. *allergic* 'physical sensitivity to a substance': generalization, popularization of technical vocabulary

   c. *aisle* 'passage between pews of a church': generalization

   d. *brook* 'to enjoy, make use of' (now 'to tolerate'): pejoration

   e. *fame* 'rumor, report': amelioration

   f. *business* 'state of being busy': specialization

   g. *go* 'walk': generalization

2. a. *four sheets to the wind*: metaphor

    b. *turn over a new leaf*: metaphor

    c. *a sour note*: synesthesia

    d. *elect a new board*: metonymy

3. a. *STD* 'sexually transmitted disease': initialism

    b. *jesum crow* 'Jesus Christ': phonetic distortion

    c. *enjoys his drink* 'is a drunkard': generalization, semantic shift

    d. *confinement* 'the lying-in of a woman in childbirth': generalization

    e. *SAD* 'seasonal affective disorder': acronym

    f. *bowel movement* 'defecation': splitting features, technical borrowing

4. a. *flat foot* 'policeman': borrowing from lower-class usage

    b. *anal* 'inclined to fuss over details': borrowing from upper-class usage, technical lanuage

    c. *metaphysical* 'outside of immediate need or concern': borrowing from upper-class, prestige usage

    d. *loonie* 'Canadian dollar coin depicting a loon': borrowing from slang or lower-class usage

    e. *loony bin* 'asylum': borrowing from slang or lower-class usage

Chapter 4

Exercise 4.1 Classification of Languages

1. There are two systems of language classification. *Typological classification* describes linguistic features independent of their or their languages' derivation. Languages in this system resemble each other structurally. *Genealogical classification* describes historical changes in and relationships among languages. Languages in this system often have many differences. Neither system considers geographical distribution of the languages.

2. (1) *Isolating languages* are usually composed of discrete monosyllabic and invariable words. There are no affixes; there is one morpheme per word; and word order is very important.

    (2) *Agglutinating languages* have several morphemes glued together to make a word; each word contains a root with several affixes. Each morpheme is discrete and expresses a single meaning.

    (3) *Inflecting languages* have several morphemes per word, a root with affixes. These morphemes, however, can be changed in many ways and can have several different meanings.

Exercise 4.2 The Indo-European Language Family

1. Japanese   non-Indo-European

   Hittite   Indo-European; no modern descendants

   Flemish   Indo-European; closest to English

   Crimean Gothic   Indo-European; no modern descendants

   Portuguese   Indo-European

   Tamil   non-Indo-European

   Korean   non-Indo-European; isolate

2. William Jones was a British jurist and linguist who speculated that the structural similarities among Greek, Latin, Sanskrit, Gothic (Germanic), Celtic, and Old Persian implied a genetic relationship to each other and to a now lost common ancestor. These ideas launched the science of comparative philology and led directly to the reconstruction of PIE.

Exercise 4.3 Proto-Language and Reconstruction

1. A proto-language is a hypothetical ancestral language reconstructed by comparing similar morphological and phonological features of languages thought to descend from it. The four basic guidelines for reconstructing a proto-language are

   (1) to restrict cognate sets to core vocabulary;

   (2) to reject close or identical phonetic forms;

   (3) to know how and when language groups interacted; and

   (4) to determine the earliest attestation of a word.

2. *Cognates* are words in different languages that share a common ancestor. They may not appear very similar to each other, having undergone different sound changes in their respective languages. *Loan words* are often similar in morphology and spelling in the donor language and the borrowing language. A loan word may appear late in the history of the language.

   Set 1: Spanish *otoño*, Latin *autumnus* (English *autumn* is a borrowing from Latin), Romanian *toamnă*

   Set 2: English *harvest*, Old Norse *haust*, German *Herbst*

   Set 3: Russian *osen'*, Serbo-Croat *jesen*

Exercise 4.4 PIE Linguistic Features

1. *Ablaut* is the change in the root vowel of a word, which indicates a change in meaning or grammatical function.

   EXAMPLE: *sing/sang/sung/song*

2. A word consists of a *root* (the core meaning), a *derivational suffix* (affixes that express part of speech or modify the root's meaning), and an *inflectional ending* (expressing the grammatical category of the word). *Derivation* refers to changes in meaning (e.g. positive > negative) or changes in part of speech (N > V) made by changes in affixes. *Inflection* refers to changes in grammatical meaning or function (e.g. sg. > pl.) made by changes in endings.

Exercise 4.5 PIE Society and Homeland

The core vocabulary referring to body parts, eating, clothing, family relations, and group functions can suggest a great deal about the terrain and the collective behavior of the people using that vocabulary. Flora and fauna, farming, social hierarchies, law, traditions, and religion can all be read from the common words of a language.

Chapter 5

Exercise 5.1 Proto-Germanic

1. a. The traditional dates for the Common Germanic period are from approximately the tenth century BCE to the second century BCE.

    b. The geographical area currently accepted as having been inhabited by Common Germanic speakers is southern Scandinavia, from southern Sweden through Denmark into northern Germany.

    c. At the end of this period this group separated into three main sub-groups. The North branch migrated further north in Scandinavia, the East branch went east and south as far as the Black Sea, and the West branch moved west and south.

    d. The line of descent for Old English, beginning with Proto-Indo-European, is as follows: PIE > Germanic > West Germanic > Low West Germanic > Anglo-Frisian > Old English.

2.

		Lat.	**Go.**	**OHG**	**OE**	**ME**
a.	father	pater	(atta)	fater	fæder	fadir
b.	name	nomen	namo	namo	nama	name
c.	heaven	—	himinam	himile	heofonum	heuenes**
d.	hallowed	—	—	giheilagot	gehalgod	halewid
e.	will	uoluntas	wilja	uuillo	willa	wille
f.	evil	—	ubilin	ubile	yfele	yuel

** This set of forms shows the effects of dissimilation.

Exercise 5.2 Grammatical and Lexical Changes from Proto-Indo-European to Germanic

1. During the Common Germanic period, Germanic

   (1) changed from the aspectual system of PIE, based on whether an action is ongoing or completed, to a tense system, based on whether an action is past, present, or future with respect to the time of speaking;

   (2) further simplified the PIE verbal system to a two-way distinction between past and present indicated by inflected forms (and only later a future indicated by a periphrastic form);

   (3) innovated the ways the past was formed, retaining the PIE ablaut but also indicating past by a dental suffix, -d, -t, or -ed, which became the regular means of forming the past for most verbs and for all new verbs entering the language;

   (4) simplified the moods from five in PIE to three by conflating optative and injunctive with subjunctive, retaining indicative and imperative; and

   (5) changed the voices from active and middle to active and passive (though retaining the middle in Gothic in a very limited way).

2. In terms of the nominal system, Germanic simplified the cases from eight in PIE to five: nominative and vocative became nominative; dative, locative, and ablative became dative; and accusative, genitive, and instrumental remained the same.

3. In terms of the adjectival system, Germanic innovated a two-part adjectival system in which the original PIE endings were used only when the adjective alone modified a noun—the 'strong', or indefinite, form. When the adjective occurred with other modifiers, such as demonstratives or possessive pronouns, a 'weak', or definite, form of the adjective occurred.

Exercise 5.3 Germanic: Grimm's Law

	PIE	Gmc.	ModE
a.	*mūk- 'heap'	*mūxōn-	mow
b.	*mōd- 'assemble'	*mōtjan-	meet
c.	*gerbh- 'scratch'	*kerban-	carve
d.	*ghalgh- 'branch'	*galg-	gallows
e.	*agwesī- 'axe'	*akwesi-	axe
f.	*sleubh- 'slide'	*sleub-	sleeve
g.	*spel- 'recite'	*spellan	spell
h.	*tel- 'board'	*θil-jo-	deal (fir plank)

i. *tek- 'give birth to'   *θegn-   thane
j. *dhrēn- 'murmur'   *drēn-   drone

Exercise 5.4 Germanic: Verner's Law

1.   PIE   Gmc.   OE   ModE

   a. *ghaiso- 'stick'   *gairāz   gār – 'spear' garlic, to gore
   b. *teutā- 'tribe'   *θeuda-   - - -   Teuton
   c. *uperi- 'over'   *uberi   ofer   over
   d. *tekno- 'child'   *θegnaz   thegn   thane
   e. *skot- 'dark'   *skadwaz   sceadu   shade
   f. *dek- 'lock of hair' *taglaz   tægel   tail

2. Voiceless PIE stops in voiced environments become voiced fricatives (or stops) in Germanic when the PIE accent does not fall on the immediately preceding syllable.

Exercise 5.5 Germanic: Grimm's Law and Vowel Changes

PIE   **Gmc.**
a. *kʷrep- 'body'   *hʷref-
b. *albho- 'white'   *alba-
c. *kīgh- 'fast'   *hīg-
d. *modhro- 'a color'   *madra-
e. *treud-   *θriut- 'threat'
f. *west-   *west- 'west'
g. *plokso- 'flax'   *flaxsa-

Chapter 6

Exercise 6.1 OE Word Stock

1. (a) with little change in meaning or form: *heofon* 'heaven'

    (b) with some change in meaning or form or both: *dōm* 'judgment'

    (c) in local dialects, restricted contexts, or set expressions: *angnægl* (literally, 'painful nail') 'hangnail'

2. least important: Celtic
    more important: Old Norse
    most important: Latin

3. (1) *Continental period*: prior to 449 CE (the arrival of Germanic speakers in the British Isles); contact between Romans and Germanic tribes; approximately 200 words borrowed, mainly concrete and popular; e.g. *cēse* 'cheese' < Lat. *cāseus*, *weall* 'wall' < Lat. *vallum*; words are common to all Germanic language groups and later undergo the early sound changes of Old English and Old High German.

(2) *Celtic period*: early in the Anglo-Saxon era; possible borrowings through the British Celts, but also possible that Old English borrowed these words independently; e.g. *port* 'harbor, gate, town' < Lat. *portus*.

(3) *Christian period*: after conversion in 597 CE by Roman missionaries; usually learned borrowings concerning religion and scholarship; some entered general usage; e.g. *accent* 'accent' < Lat. *accentus*.

Exercise 6.2 OE Word Formation

1. a. *firencræft* 'wickedness' ('sin-craft'):
   noun, literal compound of two nouns: *firen* + *cræft*

   b. *herewǣd* 'armor' ('war-weed'):
   noun, kenning, compound of two nouns: *here* + *wǣd*

   c. *holdlīce* 'graciously' ('kind-ly'):
   adverb, derivation, *hold* (ADJ) + *-līce* (suffix)

   d. *ofercræft* 'fraud' ('over-craft'):
   noun, literal compound, *ofer* (ADV) + *cræft* (noun)

   e. *rǣdfæstnes* 'readiness to follow counsel' ('rede-fast-ness'):
   noun, literal compound and derivation, two roots: *rǣd* (N) + *fæst* (ADJ or V stem) + *-nes* (suffix)

   f. *sweordplega* 'battle' ('sword-play'):
   noun, kenning, compound of two nouns: *sweord* + *plega*

Exercise 6.3 Transcription of OE Consonants

a.	*hæcce* 'crosier'	[kk]	h.	*plega* 'play'	[j]
b.	*hægel* 'hail'	[j]	i.	*hafok* 'hawk'	[v]
c.	*prica* 'dot'	[k]	j.	*þaca* 'roof'	[θ]
d.	*smēþan* 'to smooth'	[ð]	k.	*nāht* 'nothing'	[x]
e.	*furðor* 'further'	[f]	l.	*sihð* 'vision'	[ç]
f.	*fūs* 'ready'	[s]	m.	*lǣce* 'physician'	[č]
g.	*fūse* 'readily'	[z]	n.	*burg* 'city'	[ɣ]

Exercise 6.4 Transcription of OE Vowels and Consonants

Sum man fērde fram Hiērūsalem tō Hiēricho, and becōm on þā sceaðan; þā hine
A certain man went from Jerusalem to Jericho, and came upon the thieves; they him
[sʊm mɑn fērdɛ frɑm hiērūzɑlɛm tō hiērɪkɔ ɑnd bɛkōm ɔn θū šæəðɑn θū hɪnɛ]

berēafodon and tintregodon hine, and forlēton hine sāmcucene. Þā gebyrode hit þæt
robbed   and tormented him, and left   him half-alive. Then happened it that
[bɛrēəvɔdɔn ɑnd tɪntrɛjɔdɔn hɪnɛ ɑnd fɔrlētɔn hɪnɛ sāmkʊkɛnɛ θū jɛbyrɔdɛ hɪt θæt]

sum   sācerd fērde on þǣm ylcan wege, and þā hē þæt geseah, hē hine forbēah. And
a certain priest went on the same way, and when he that saw,   he him passed by. And
[sʊm sūkɛrd fērdɛ ɔn θǣm ylkɑn wɛjɛ ɑnd θū hē θæt jɛsæəx hē hɪnɛ fɔrbæəx ɑnd]

eall swā se dīacon, þā hē wæs wið þā stōwe and þæt geseah, hē hyne ēac forbēah.
also this deacon when he was at the place and that saw   he him also passed by.
[æɑll swū sɛ dīɑkɔn θū hē wæs wɪθ θū stōwɛ ɑnd θæt jɛsæəx hē hynɛ æək fɔrbæəx]

Þā fērde sum   Samaritanisc man wið hine; þā   hē hine geseah, þā wearð   hē mid
Then went a certain Samaritan man   by him; when he him saw   then became he with
[θū fērdɛ sʊm sɑmɑrɪtɑnɪš mɑn wɪθ hɪnɛ θū hē hɪnɛ jɛsæəx θū wæərθ hē mɪd]

mildheortnesse ofer hine āstyred. Þā   genēalǣhte hē, and wrāð   his wunda,   and
compassion   for him stirred up. Then drew near he, and bound his wounds   and
[mɪldhɛɔrtnɛssɛ ɔvɛr hɪnɛ āstyrɛd θū jɛnǣəlǣçtɛ hē ɑnd wrūθ hɪs wʊndɑ ɑnd]

on āgēat ele and wīn, and hine on hys nȳten sette, and gelædde   on his lǣcehūs
poured on oil and wine, and him on his beast set,   and led   to his hospital
[ɔn ūjǣət ɛlɛ ɑnd wīn ɑnd hɪnɛ ɔn hys nȳtɛn sɛttɛ ɑnd jɛlǣddɛ ɔn hɪs lǣčɛhūs]

and hine lācnode;   and brōhte   ōðrum   dæge twēgen penegas, and sealde
and him medicated; and brought on the second day   two pennies,   and gave
[ɑnd hɪnɛ lūknɔdɛ ɑnd brōxtɛ ōðrʊm dæjɛ twējɛ pɛnɛjɑs ɑnd sæəldɛ]

þām læce, and þus cwæð, Begȳm   hys; and swā hwæt swā þū māre   tō gedēst,
to the doctor, and thus said, 'Take care of him and whatsoever thou more besides dost,
[θūm lǣčɛ ɑnd θʊs kwæθ bɛjȳm hys ɑnd swū xwæt swū θū mārɛ tō jɛdēst]

þonne ic cume, ic hit forgylde þē. Hwylc þāra þrēora þyncð   þē þæt
when I come, I it will repay you.' Which of the three seems to thee that
[θɔnnɛ ɪč kʊmɛ ɪč hɪt fɔrjyldɛ θē xwylč θūrɑ θrēɔrɑ θynkθ θē θæt]

sȳ þæs mǣg þe on   ðā sceaðan befēoll?
may be that one's neighbor who among the thieves fell?
[sȳ θæs mǣj θɛ ɔn θū šæəðɑn bɛfēəll]

Exercise 6.5 Sound Changes in OE Vowels

	Proto-Germanic	Old English	Sound Change
a.	*dāljan 'to divide'	dǣlan	umlaut
b.	*mūsiz 'mice'	mȳs	umlaut
c.	*erðe 'earth'	eorð	breaking
d.	*fōti 'to the foot'	fēt	umlaut
e.	*hælf 'half'	healf	breaking
f.	*nǣh 'near'	nēah	breaking

Exercise 6.6 Stress in Old English

a. hlín-duru 'grated door'

b. hréow-nes 'penitence'

c. béam 'tree'

d. déawig-feþera 'dewy-feathered'

e. ge-wrécan 'to wreak, avenge'

f. ge-wémmed-nyss 'corruption'

g. for-éaldian 'grow old'

h. ǽw-fæst 'devout'

i. be-sórg 'dear'

j. bífian 'to tremble'

k bétera 'better'

l. þéoden-stōl 'lord's throne'

m. tó-weard 'toward'

n. wálic 'lowly'

Chapter 7

Exercise 7.1 Pronouns

1.		Person	Number	Case	Gender
	a. *unc*	first	dual	acc./dat./instr.	all
	b. *ūs*	first	plural	acc./dat./instr.	all
	c. *ēow*	second	plural	acc./dat./instr.	all
	d. *him*	third	sg./pl.	dat./instr.	masc./neut.
		third	pl.	dat./instr.	all
	e. *þīn*	second	singular	gen.	all

2. a. him   d. ēower

   b. wit   e. ic

   c. hī

3. a. None.

   b. No.

   c. The ModE pronoun *it* comes from the third-person neuter nom./acc. *hit*, the *h* being lost in unstressed positions.

   d. The OE forms were replaced by ON forms in late Old English.

   e. Masculine/feminine/neuter dative, and masculine/feminine instrumental.

Exercise 7.2 Nouns

1. a. horn 'horn': masc./long *a*-stem
      heorte 'heart': fem./*n*-stem
      fēond 'foe': masc./root-consonant stem

   b. ǣl 'eel': masc./*a*-stem
      sacu 'strife': fem./*ō*-stem
      bæð 'bath': neut./short *a*-stem

2. The *a* of the name '*a*-stem class' refers to a stem vowel which existed in Germanic but is no longer found in Old English. The class contains masculine and neuter nouns.

3. ModE noun inflections are genitive with -'*s*, plural with -*s*, plural with -*en,* and plural with stem vowel umlaut. The plural and genitive -*s* inflections come from the *a*-stem noun class.

4. The OE noun *hlǣfdige* 'lady' belonged to the *n*-stem class. The reason that *lady* in the ModE words *ladybug* and *ladyfinger* is technically a genitive form is that the genitive ending *an* was lost over time. All feminine nouns in Modern English take the -'*s* genitive by analogy except in a few compounds such as *ladyfinger* (= 'lady's finger') and *ladybug* (= 'lady's bug').

Exercise 7.3 Demonstratives

1.		**Number**	**Gender**	**Case**
a.	*se*	singular	masc.	nom.
b.	*þā*	singular	fem.	acc.
		plural	all	nom./acc.
c.	*þǣre*	singular	fem.	gen./dat.
d.	*þās*	singular	fem.	acc.
		plural	all	nom./acc.
e.	*þissum*	singular	masc./neut.	dat.
		plural	all	dat.

f. *þæt*   singular   neut.   nom./acc.

g. *þisne*   singular   masc.   acc.

h. *þ̄ys*   singular   masc./neut. instr.

2. a. *þone*

    b. *þisses*

    c. *þisse*

    d. *þ̄æm*

    e. *þ̄æm*

3. a. *that* from neuter singular nom./acc. *þæt*
       those from nom./acc. plural *þ̄a*
       this from neuter singular nom./acc. *þis*
       these from masculine singular nominative *þes*

    b. Gender.

    c. ModE *the* comes from OE masculine singular nominative *se* which later changed to *þe*. ModE *a/an* comes from the OE numeral *ān*, meaning 'one' or 'a certain one'.

Exercise 7.4 Adjectives and Adverbs

1. The two classes of adjectives in Old English are weak and strong. The weak declension is used with other modifiers (a demonstrative, a numeral, or a possessive adjective); when the adjective is in the comparative or superlative degree; and when the adjective appears in direct address. The strong declension is used after the verb *to be* and in all other contexts.

2.

		Case	Gender	Number	Class
a.	*gōdra*	gen.	all	plural	weak/strong
b.	*heardes*	gen.	masc./neut.	singular	strong
c.	*untrumum*	dat.	all	plural	weak/strong
		dat.	masc./neut.	singular	strong
d.	*unforhtne*	acc.	masc.	singular	strong
e.	*̄æmtige*	nom.	neut./fem.	singular	weak
		acc.	neut.	singular	weak
		nom./acc.	masc.	plural	strong
		acc.	fem.	singular	strong
		instr.	masc./neut.	singular	strong

f.	*mǣru*	nom.	fem.	singular	strong
		nom./acc.	neut.	plural	strong
g.	*wīsan*	acc.	masc./fem.	singular	weak
		nom./acc.	all	plural	weak
		gen.	all	singular	weak
		dat.	all	singular	weak
		instr.	all	singular	weak

3.

Positive	Comparative	Superlative
a. *earm* 'poor'	**earmra**	**earmost**
b. **lēof**	**lēofra**	*lēofost* 'dearest'
c. **dol**	*dolra* 'more foolish'	**dolost**
d. *dēop* 'deep'	**dēopra**	**dēopost**
e. **sār**	*sārra* 'more painful'	**sārrost**
f. **sārlic**	**sārlicra**	*sārlicost* 'saddest'

Exercise 7.5 Agreement and Case Usage

A. AGREEMENT

1. In Modern English, agreement occurs in

   • number between demonstratives and nouns: *this dog/those dogs*;
   • person and number between subjects and verbs: *he is/they are*;
   • person and number between plural nouns and their pronouns: *the men . . . they*; and
   • person, number, and gender between singular nouns and their pronouns: *the boy . . . he*; *the girl . . . she*; *the train . . . it*.

2.   *þis earme folc* (neut.) 'this poor people'

   sg. nom. *þis earme folc*

      acc. *þis earme folc*

      gen. *þisses earman folces*

      dat. *þissum earman folce*

      instr. *þȳs earman folce*

   pl. nom. *þās earman folc*

      acc. *þās earman folc*

      gen. *þissa earmra folca*

      dat. *þissum earmum folcum*

      instr. *þissum earmum folcum*

B. CASE USAGE

    a. *me* – dative/instrumental, expressing means 'by me'

    b. *cyning* – nominative, direct address

    c. *lif* – nominative, subject *is gesewen*

    d. *eorðan* – dative, object of preposition *on*

    e. *tide* – genitive or dative, object of *wiþmetenesse*

    f. *us* – dative, object of adjective *uncuð*

    g. *þinum ealdormannum* – dative, object of preposition *mid*, expressing accompaniment

    h. *wintertide* – dative, object of preposition *on*

    i. *hus* – accusative, object of verb *þurhfleo*

    j. *tid* – accusative, object of preposition *on*

    k. *storme* – instrumental, object of preposition *mid*

    l. *wintres* – genitive, subjective

    m. *eagan* – genitive, subjective

    n. *wintra* – dative, object of preposition *of*

    o. *winter* – accusative, object of preposition *on*

    p. *fæce* – dative, object of preposition *to*

    q. *we* – nominative, subject of *ne cunnun*

Exercise 7.6 Verbs

1. a. strong, class 5

    b. weak, class 1

    c. strong, class 2

    d. weak, class 2

    e. anomalous

    f. strong, class 6

2. a. Weak Class I   'to tame' *temman/temede/temedon/getemed*

INDICATIVE

	Present	Preterit
ic	*temme*	*temede*
þū	*temest*	*temedest*
hē	*temeð*	*temede*
wē, gē, hī	*temmað*	*temedon*

SUBJUNCTIVE

ic, þū, hē	*temme*	*temede*
wē, gē, hī	*temmen*	*temeden*

IMPERATIVE

> *þū   teme*
> *gē   temmað*

PARTICIPLES

> *temmende   getemed*

INFL. INF.

> *tō temmenne*

b. Strong Class 7 'to blend' *blandan/blēnd/blēndon/geblanden*

INDICATIVE

	Present	Preterit
ic	*blande*	*blēnd*
þū	*bland(e)st*	*blēnde*
hē	*bland(e)ð*	*blēnd*
wē, gē, hī	*blandað*	*blēndon*

SUBJUNCTIVE

ic, þū, hē	*blande*	*blēnde*
wē, gē, hī	*blanden*	*blēnden*

IMPERATIVE

> *þū   bland*
> *gē   blandað*

PARTICIPLES

> *blandende   geblanden*

INFL. INF.

> *tō blandenne*

Exercise 7.7 Syntax and Word Order

a. S-AUX-V, passive construction with *from*

b. SOV, perfect periphrase

c. AUX-S . . . V, passive construction, auxiliary and past participle split

d. ADV-VSO, inverted word order in time clause with *þa*

e. SVO in main clause, with SOV (verb final) in subordinate clause

f. SOV in main clause; OV with impersonal verb in subordinate clause

g. VSO negative construction with *ne* and inverted word order

h. VSO question construction with simple inversion (no auxiliary)

i. VO imperative construction (no S)

Chapter 8

Exercise 8.1 External History

1. a. Proclamation by Henry III in 1258, the first official document in English after the Norman Conquest.

    b. Important adviser to King Edward the Confessor. Godwine's son, Harold, became king when Edward died in 1066, setting in motion the conflicting claims to the English throne that led to Harold's defeat at Hastings that same year.

    c. First king of England after the Conquest (1272–1307) to have a good command of English.

    d. One of the *Anglo-Saxon Chronicles*, maintained in English until 1154, showing the transition from Old English to Middle English at a time when there are very few documents in English.

    e. Period of intermittent fighting between England and France from 1337 to 1453 during which a series of important English victories created a sense of English nationalism.

    f. The majority of written texts in this period were French, which left English a predominantly spoken language. Without the regulatory influence of writing, English underwent rapid changes during this time.

2. Duke of Normandy who claimed the throne of England, defeating Harold at Hastings and inaugurating French rule in England for the next two hundred years.

Exercise 8.2 Word Stock of Middle English

1. a. negligent/negligee: B (earlier *versus* later borrowing), doublet

    b. case/chest: A (Norman *versus* Central French)

    c. folk/people: C (synonyms of English *versus* French origin)

    d. critic/critique: B, doublet

    e. wimple/guimpe: A, doublet

    f. horse/courser: C

    g. channel/canal: A, doublet

    h. ham/pork: C

2. | **English** | **French** | **Latin** |
    |---------|---------|---------|
    | hide | conceal | suppress |
    | begin | commence | initiate |
    | keen | fine | acute |
    | tine | barb | prong |

even (v)	level (v)	equalize
greedy	covetous	voracious

Exercise 8.3 Orthography

a.	cni͟h͟t	k, ʒ	knight
b.	þēah	th	though
c.	rēfa	ee/ie	reeve
d.	sceafan	sh, v	shave
e.	cēosan	ch	choose
f.	mu͟no͟c	o, k	monk
g.	brōc	oo	brook
h.	cūð	oo/ou, th	(un)couth

Exercise 8.4 Consonant Changes

a.	blōstma	blosme	loss of [t] in clusters with [s]	blossom
b.	folgian	folwen	vocalization of [ɣ] to [w] after [l]	follow
c.	hlāf	lof	simplification of consonant cluster	loaf
d.	cræt	cart	metathesis of [r] + vowel	cart
e.	lēohtlīc	līʒtli	loss of unstressed [č]	lightly
f.	behæs	behēst	excrescent [t]	behest

Exercise 8.5 Transcription

a.	shīres	[šīrəs]	'shires'
b.	bāne	[būnə]	'bane'
c.	weie	[wæɪə]	'way'
d.	reel	[rēl]	'real'
e.	yclipped	[ɪklɪpəd]	'clept' (obsolete, meaning 'called')
f.	strete	[strēt]	'street'
g.	chapelain	[čɑpəlæɪn]	'chaplain'
h.	withouten	[wɪθūtən]	'without'
i.	though	[ðɔʊx]	'though'
j.	wight	[wɪçt]	'wight' (obsolete, meaning 'person')

Exercise 8.6 Vowel and Consonant Changes

	OE	ME	Changes
a.	balu	bāle	(1) [ɑ] > [ā] lengthening in open syllable
			(2) [ʊ] > [ə] reduction in unstressed syllable
b.	flēon	flē	(1) [ēə] > [ɛ̄] monophthongization
			(2) [n] > Ø loss of unstressed [n]
c.	hrycgas	rigges	(1) [hr] > [r] simplification of a consonant cluster
			(2) [y] > [ɪ] unrounding
			(3) [ɑ] > [ə] reduction in unstressed syllable
d.	wegan	weie	(1) [ɛj] > [æɪ] new diphthong with vocalization of [j]
			(2) [ɑ] > [ə] reduction in unstressed syllable
			(3) loss of unstressed [n]
e.	hlæne	lēne	(1) [hl] > [l] simplification of a consonant cluster
			(2) [ǣ] > [ɛ̄] shift (raising)
			(3) [ɛ] > [ə] reduction in unstressed syllable
f.	stæfas	stāves	(1) [æ] > [ɑ] shift (backing)
			(2) [ɑ] > [ā] lengthening in open syllable
			(3) [ɑ] > [ə] reduction in unstressed syllable

Chapter 9

Exercise 9.1 Adjectival and Nominal Forms

			Old English			Middle English
a.	**strong**		MASC.		FEM.	
	sg. nom.	S	glæd	S	gladu	glad
	acc.	A	glædne	S	glade	
	gen.	A	glades	A	glædre	
	dat.	S/A	gladum	S/A	glædre	
	instr.	S	glade	A	glædre	
	pl. nom./acc.	S	glade	S	glade	glade
	gen.	A	glædra	A	glædra	
	dat.	S/A	gladum	S/A	gladum	

		Old English		Middle English
b. **weak**		MASC.	FEM.	
sg. nom.	S	glada	S glade	glade
acc.	S/A	gladan	S/A gladan	
gen./dat.	S/A	gladan	S/A gladan	
pl. nom./acc.	S/A	gladan	S/A gladan	glade
gen.	A	glædra	A glædra	
(alt. gen.	A	gladena	A gladena)	
dat.	S/A	gladum	S/A gladum	

2. nom.   *smal wōd*   small wood   *the smale wōd*   the small wood

   acc.   *smal wōd*   small wood   *the smale wōd*   the small wood

   gen.   *smal wōdes*   small wood's   *the smale wōdes*   the small wood's

   dat.   *smal wōd(e)*   small wood   *the smale wōd*   the small wood

Exercise 9.2 Pronominal Forms

a. (1) hē (3rd p. sg. masc. nom.)
   (2) his (3rd p. sg. masc. gen.)
   (3) hē (3rd p. sg. masc. nom.)
   (4) his (3rd p. sg. masc. gen.)
   (5) hi (3rd p. pl. nom.)
   (6) here (3rd p. pl. gen.)

b. (1) Hit (3rd p. sg. neut. nom.)
   (2) him (3rd p. sg. masc. obj.)
   (3) his (3rd p. sg. masc. gen.)
   (4) hē (3rd p. sg. masc. nom.)

c. (1) þou (2nd p. sg. nom.)
   (2) me (1st p. sg. obj. [dat. in
       Southern dialects])
   (3) my (1st p. sg. gen.)

d. (1) schō (3rd p. sg. fem. nom.)
   (2) schō (3rd p. sg. fem. nom.)
   (3) thaym (3rd p. pl. obj.)
   (4) thaym (3rd p. pl. obj.)
   (5) thaym (3rd p. pl. obj.)
   (6) schō (3rd p. sg. fem. nom.)
   (7) schō (3rd p. sg. fem. nom.)
   (8) hir(e) (3rd p. sg. fem. gen.)
   (9) schō (3rd p. sg. fem. nom.)
   (10) schō (3rd p. sg. fem. nom.)
   (11) hir(e) (3rd p. sg. fem. gen.)

Exercise 9.3 Verbal Forms

1. First-person plural present indicative personal ending on the verb. The *-es* ending is Northern and innovative. The *-eth* ending is Southern and derives from the OE *-að* ending through reduction of *a* to *e*. The middle form is from

the Midlands and shows variation, using the innovative Northern *-es* and the subjunctive plural ending *-en*. All these inflected endings are eventually lost.

2. Third-person singular present indicative personal ending on the verb. The *-es* ending is Northern and innovative, eventually becoming the standard third-person singular present ending and the only regular inflection in the present in ModE: *-s*. The *-eth* is Southern and conservative and is eventually lost. The Midlands dialects use both endings. (Note also the variant forms of the 3rd p. sg. fem. pronouns.)

3. Second-person singular present indicative personal ending on the verb. The Northern, innovative *-es* also occurs in the Midlands alongside the Southern, conservative *-(e)st* ending. All variations are eventually lost.

4. Two non-finite forms: the infinitive and the present participle. In Middle English there were three infinitive forms: (1) the bare infinitive, which in the North had an *-e* or sometimes Ø ending and in the Midlands and South had *-en* or *-e*; (2) the *to*-infinitve, which derived from the OE *tō*-infinitive; and (3) the *for-to*-infinitive, a Middle English innovation. Only the *to*-infinitive and the bare infinitive forms lasted into ModE.

   The *-and(e)* participle ending was Northern and also occurred in the Midlands with *-ende* and *-ing(e)*, which was the Southern ending and sometimes occurred as *-inde*. The *-nd(e)* forms derived from OE *-ende* and were eventually lost, the *-ing(e)* form becoming the regular ending. Its source is uncertain, though it may originate with the OE gerund ending *-ung*.

Exercise 9.4 Syntax and Word Order

1. SOV word order is found in Middle English in main clauses when the object is a pronoun, when the verb is impersonal, and when the verb is part of a periphrase (the AUX and the V split around the O); it is also found in subordinate clauses.

2. The word order is inverted (to VS) in Middle English when the sentence begins with adverbs of time or direction, when the object is put first for emphasis, and when there would be a *there* subject in Modern English.

3. The difference between the Old English and Middle English method of expressing the future is that Old English used the present-tense inflection and depended on context (e.g. use of future-time adverbs) to convey future meaning. In late OE some instances of periphrasis with *will* occur; in ME this, along with *shall*, plus the infinitive becomes the standard means of expressing the future.

Exercise 9.5 Synthetic to Analytic and Standardization

1. Generally a *creole* is thought to arise when a pidgin is learned by the children of its speakers. According to Nicole Dominique (1977), a pidgin must have been devised for communication between the English and the French after 1066, becoming creolized as Middle English during the following generations. There is little structural support for this theory despite the large French vocabulary in English.

2. Old English was a more *synthetic* language than either Middle or Modern English. It had far more inflected forms to express grammatical functions. These inflections fell away in Middle English, mainly because of the leveling and loss of vowels in the inflected endings. A more *analytic* language, depending on periphrastic forms and a more fixed word order, was developed through the Middle English period. Modern English is a heavily analytic language.

3. a. John Wyclif: religious reformer who translated the Bible into a readily accessible English dialect and spread this Bible throughout England.

   b. Geoffrey Chaucer: greatest writer in Middle English, whose dialect (basically a London dialect with some Kentish features), however, does not seem to have affected the development of a standard English.

   c. William Caxton: first English printer to use movable type, allowing for multiple copies of printed material to be distributed over large areas, requiring a common dialect readable by everyone.

   d. London: social, political, and commercial center located in the southern East Midlands. Its geographically central location and cultural importance drew people from all over England, creating a mix of dialects and giving rise to a London dialect that became the standard.

Chapter 10

Exercise 10.1 The Great Vowel Shift

1. a. down [ū]   d. throat [ɔ̄]

   b. grief [ē]   e. sound [ū]

   c. kind [ī]   f. race   [ā]

2. a. see/sea [ē] > [i] for *see*; [ɛ̄] > [ē] > [i] for *sea*

   b. great/grate [ɛ̄] > [ē] > [eɪ] for *great* (an exception to the Great Vowel Shift which did not shift to [i]); [ā] > [æ] > [ɛ̄] > [ē] > [eɪ] for *grate*

   c. hear/here [ɛ̄] > [ē] > [i] for *hear*; [ē] > [i] for *here*

3. The reason that *sweet* and *sweat* do not rhyme is that some ME words with [ɛ̄] occurring before a dental shortened the vowel before the Great Vowel Shift began; this affected *sweat*.

4. The first important consequence of the Great Vowel Shift is that long and short vowels come to be distinguished by quality instead of quantity in Modern English. The second is that the spelling of long vowels becomes partly confused; this is the result of the freezing of older vowel spellings because of the appearance of the printing press while the Great Vowel Shift was still in progress.

5. (We) (look)ed up and saw (head) (light)s directly in front of us.

   There was a (loud) crash and the car (veer)ed off the (road).

   By a (feat) of (good) luck, everyone (made) it (out) unhurt.

	ME	ModE		ME	ModE
we	[ē]	[i]	road	[ɔ̄]	[oʊ]
look	[ō]	[u]	feat	[ɛ̄]	[i]
head**	[ɛ̄]	[ɛ]	good	[ō]	[ʊ]
light	[ī]	[aɪ]	made	[ā]	[eɪ]
loud	[ū]	[aʊ]	out	[ū]	[aʊ]
veer	[ē]	[i]			

**shortened before a dental (and thus not affected by the Great Vowel Shift)

Exercise 10.2 EModE Vowels

1. a. sole/soul [ɔ̄] > [ō] > [oʊ] for *sole* by GVS (and then diphthongization); [ɔʊ] > [ɔ̄] > [ō] > [oʊ] for *soul* by monophthongization and GVS (and then diphthongization)

   b. pail/pale [æɪ] > [ǣ] > [ɛ̄] > [ē] > [eɪ] for *pail* by monophthongization and GVS (and then diphthongization); [ā] > [ǣ] > [ɛ̄] > [ē] > [eɪ] for *pale* by GVS (and then diphthongization)

   c. know/no [ɔʊ] > [ɔ̄] > [ō] > [oʊ] for *know* by monophthongization and GVS (and then diphthongization); [ɔ̄] > [ō] > [oʊ] for *no* by GVS (and then diphthongization)

2. The words *fir* and *fur* sound the same because [ɪr] and [ʊr] are centralized to [ər] when *r* is word-final.

Exercise 10.3 EModE and ModE Pronunciation

1.

		ModE	ME
a.	thigh [aɪ] < [ī] and loss of [ç]	[θaɪ]	[θīç]
b.	stalk [ɔ, ɑ] < [ɑl] with loss of [l]	[stɑk]	[stɑlk]
c.	nation [š] < [sj], [eɪ] < [ū], [ə] < unstressed [ɔ]	[neɪšən]	[nasjɔn]
d.	hustle [sl] < [stl], [ə] < [ʊ]	[həsəl]	[hʊstəl]

2.

		ME transcription	ModE transcription	ModE word
a.	gnawe(n)	[gnaʊən]	[nɑ]	gnaw
b.	lamb	[lɑmb]	[læm]	lamb
c.	knele(n)	[knēlen]	[nil]	kneel
d.	goune 'official's robe'	[gūnə]	[gaʊn]	gown

3. *Bangor* is a single morpheme. *Banger* is a combined form, joining *bang*, which is pronounced [bæŋ], with -*er*. In EModE, [ŋg] in final syllables is simplified to [ŋ]. Some regional pronunciations rhyme these words either with or without the [g].

Exercise 10.4 Renaissance Respelling

a. adventure: [ədvɛnčər] ME *aventure* from OF; etymological respelling based on Lat. *adventūrus*; spelling pronunciation (and palatalization of [t + j])

b. indict: [ɪndaɪt] ME *enditen* from OF *enditer*, etymological respelling based on Lat. *indictāre* with no change in pronunciation. [ī > aʊ] by GVS.

c. calk/caulk: [kɑlk] or [kɑk] ME *cauken* from French; etymological respelling based on Lat. *calcāre*; spelling pronunciation for some speakers.

d. adjust: [əǰəst] ME *ajusten* from OF *ajoster*; cf. Vulgar Lat. *adiūxtūre*; etymological respelling and spelling pronunciation (involving palatalization of [d + j])

e. palm: [pɑlm] or [pɑm] ME *paume* from OF; etymological respelling based on Lat. *palma*; spelling pronunciation for some speakers.

Exercise 10.5 EModE Nominal and Pronominal Forms

1. Initially, the plural forms, *you*, *ye*, and *your*, were used in addressing superiors in age, rank, or social class. They were also used among equals in the upper class who were not intimate. The singular forms *thee*, *thou*, *thy*, and *thine*, were used in addressing inferiors, and between members of the lower classes.

2. a. the kinges sone of Engeland: This is a split construction with genitive marked on the head noun (*kinges*); it was replaced by the group genitive ('the king of England's son').

   b. the Lord chamberlaine his seruants: This is a *his*-genitive, which gave rise to the apostrophe-*s* genitive form because the unstressed form [əz] was interpreted as a contraction of *his*.

   c. his, of it, it, its, thereof: These are all variants used at one time or another for the neuter possessive pronoun; *his* was inherited, the rest were analogical or periphrastic; only *its* remains.

   d. his fader ȝouþe 'his father's youth': This is an example of an old endingless genitive from the *r*-stem declension used for family relations; it was retained in limited contexts in EModE.

3. a. So shall you feele the loss, but not the friend <u>Which</u> you weepe for (Shakespeare, *Romeo and Juliet*)
      – The relative pronoun (*which*) is used with an animate noun (*friend*); in ModE *which* would be *who*.

   b. And dogged *Yorke*, <u>that</u> reaches at the Moone (Shakespeare, *King Henry VI, Part II*)
      – In this example, the relative pronoun *that* is used in a non-restrictive clause; in ModE *who* would be used.

   c. <u>Who</u> does he accuse? (Shakespeare, *Antony and Cleopatra*)
      – Prescriptive grammar requires *whom* as the objective pronoun in ModE (though it is not common in spoken ModE).

   d. there is no man Ø can tell me what (Shakespeare, *A Midsummer Night's Dream*)
      – The subject relative cannot be omitted in ModE.

Exercise 10.6 EModE Verbal Forms

a. hopest, hopedest
   – These are second-person singular present- and past-tense endings which were lost as the use of *thou* ceased.

b. shave, shove, shaved, shaven
– These are the principal parts of the strong verb *shave*, which became weak in EModE. The strong past tense *shove* was replaced by the weak past tense *shaved*. The strong past participle became exclusively an adjective.

c. ride(n), to ride(n), for to ride
– These are infinitive forms. The *for-to*-infinitive has been lost. The *to*-infinitive is the standard today. The plain infinitive is used in certain contexts, such as following modal auxiliaries and verbs of perception.

d. Let musicke sound while he *doth make* his choise;
Then if he loose, he *makes* a Swan-like end,
Fading in musique (Shakespeare, *The Merchant of Venice*)
– These lines include an example of the auxiliary form of third-person singular with Southern *-th* inflection. Both the auxiliary form and the Southern inflection were lost in favor of non-auxiliary form with Northern *-s* inflection as in *makes*.

Chapter 11

Exercise 11.1 EModE Syntax

a. When me list to sadder tunes apply me (Fletcher [*OED*]).
– Impersonal verb with objective first-person singular pronoun (*me list* 'it pleases me') and reflexive verb with simple pronoun (*apply me* 'apply myself'). *To sadder tunes* would follow *me* in ModE.

b. Tell him ther's a Post come from my Master (Shakespeare, *The Merchant of Venice*).
– *Ther's come* is ambiguously *there has come* or *there is come*. The latter would be a *be*-perfect. The verb and its auxiliary are split by the object. (Instead of *There is/has come a post . . .*, this construction might be analyzed by a modern reader as *There is a post which has come . . .*, i.e. a complex sentence with a relative clause.)

c. Let musicke sound while he doth make his choise;
Then if he loose, he makes a Swan-like end ... (Shakespeare, *The Merchant of Venice*).
– The dummy auxiliary *do* (*doth make*) is much more common in EModE, even in non-emphatic, positive, declarative sentences. (In this case, it might also be used for metrical purposes.) *Lose* is a remnant subjunctive in a conditional clause, which today is frequently indicative, i.e. *if he looses . . .*

d. While the second-service was reading at the Communion Table (L'Estrange, [*OED*]).
   – This shows the lack of the progressive passive in EModE. In ModE, this would be *was being read*.

e. Voyde sirs, see ye not maister Roister Doister come? (Udall, [*OED*]).
   – These lines include a negative question without an auxiliary. In ModE this would be *Don't you see . . . ?* There is also the use of nominative form *ye*, which in ModE is *you*.

Exercise 11.2 Eighteenth-Century Prescriptivism

a. prescriptivism and descriptivism: *Prescriptivism* is the view that language usage should adhere to a particular norm, that there are 'correct' and 'proper' ways of speaking. The role of the prescriptive grammarian is to regulate usage and prescribe and proscribe forms of language. Prescriptivism is opposed to *descriptivism*, which sees the task of the grammarian as recording usage objectively and formulating the principles upon which the language is based. Traditional grammar in the eighteenth century became highly prescriptive. This approach persisted in school grammars of the nineteenth and early twentieth centuries. In usage manuals, prescriptive tendencies and beliefs persist today.

b. vocabulary enrichment and spelling reform: Vocabulary reform is concerned with the enrichment of the vocabulary. Here there are two views that might be seen as conservative and innovative, respectively: (1) that a language can augment its lexicon from within, through reviving old native vocabulary or through coinages based on native words; and (2) that new words must come from other languages, such as Latin, Greek, or French. Competing approaches to spelling reform may also be characterized as conservative and innovative: either settling on one of a variety of spellings already in use or completely revamping the alphabet to reflect the real sounds of speech. Broadly speaking, in vocabulary, innovation wins out; in spelling, convention does.

c. universal grammar: The medieval concept of *universal grammar* was revived in eighteenth-century philosophy. It is the notion that underlying the diversity of language are universal principles (based on Cartesian logic). The fundamental principles of universal grammar are that language is logical, unambiguous, and unchanging, with one-to-one correspondences between meaning and form. Inventiveness and innovation work against the desire for strict order and control. (Universal grammar as it is understood today is quite different; it is related to the innateness of language and to the structure of the human brain—see Chapter 1.)

d. ascertainment and academy: In the eighteenth century, *ascertainment* referred to the effort to settle the perceived problems in English by standardizing, refining, and fixing the language. The first requires codification and the settling of disputed points; the second the removal of common errors; and the third a means of establishing language's permanent form. The English failed in their efforts to establish a language academy (such as had been established in France and Italy) to oversee these efforts. While this failure may reflect the weakness of these principles in dealing with forces of linguistic change, the notion of an academy failed more for social and political reasons. The many grammars and dictionaries of English published in the eighteenth century served much the same function as an academy.

Exercise 11.3 Eighteenth-Century Prescriptive Rules

1. a. My house is further down the street.
   – by differentiation of forms, *further* should be *farther*   **R**

   b. if I was you
   – mood is incorrect: conditionals take subjunctive, *were*   **L**

   c. to hopefully return
   – split infinitive   **L, R**

   d. She is as old as me.
   – case of the pronoun is incorrect: should be nominative *I*   **L**

   e. I don't care who he's a friend of.
   – sentence should not end with a preposition   **R**
   – case of the relative is wrong: should be *whom*   **L**

   f. Divest your coat.
   – improper meaning for *divest* (obsolete)   **E**

   g. It is her.
   – case of the pronoun is incorrect: should be *it is she*   **L**

   h. Lay yourself down.
   – trans. *lay* should be distinguished from intransitive *lie*.   **N**

   i. This house is more perfect than that house.
   – cannot compare absolutes such as *perfect*   **R**

   j. That book was unputdownable.
   – awkward and inharmonious word   **A**

2. a. Van Gogh's painting is more unique than Cezanne's.
   – *unique* cannot be compared—substitute another word, such as *unusual*

   b. I only ate a salad for lunch.
   – *I ate only* . . . (*only* should occur before the word it modifies)

c. He is so polite.
   – substitute *very* for *so* (*so* is not an intensifier: it can be used only in *so . . . that* constructions)

d. Is this assignment different than last week's?
   – substitute *from* for *than* (*different to* and *different than* are considered wrong)

e. They chose two officers, John and I.
   – substitute *me* for *I* (nouns and pronouns should be in the same case as those they are in apposition to)

f. After failing to make the appointment, I feel badly.
   – change *badly* to *bad* (a predicate adjective, not an adverb, is used after a copula verb)

Exercise 11.4 Eighteenth-Century Usage/Lexicography

1. Some authorities, such as Lowth, Johnson, and Campbell, noted the power of usage but still wished to control and direct it by imposing constraints based on authority and reason. Others, like Priestley and Webster, believed usage to be the first authority, and their job was to record and classify it without imposing changes. In practice, most eighteenth-century writers had preferences which sometimes violated their own maxims.

2. Webster was referring to the fact that usage changes. Though most writers theorized that language is or ought to be fixed and permanent, many of them acknowledged that it is in a constant state of flux. Some, like Priestley, believed in allowing usage to dictate its own standards and to resolve its own controversies in time.

3. The pivotal figure in English lexicography is Samuel Johnson. Before his *Dictionary of the English Language*, dictionaries were relatively small and not comprehensive, at first simply dictionaries of 'hard words'. His two-volume work matched those produced by the French and Italian academies and innovated the use of illustrative quotations. He fixed spellings and meanings and introduced many Latinate words. Finally, despite some weaknesses, his dictionary was so influential that it gave authority to dictionaries for over a century thereafter.

Chapter 12

Exercise 12.1 ModE Grammatical Changes

a. He was given the boot (i.e. fired) for poor performance.
   – indirect passive

b. He thought they were being ridiculous.
    – progressive with *be* and a predicate adjective

c. He figured he should be being considered for promotion.
    – modal progressive passive

d. He wanted to show them up.
    – transitive phrasal verb with particle in post-position

e. In no time, a plan got drawn up by him.
    – *get*-passive (with phrasal adverb)

Exercise 12.2 Modern Borrowings

1. a. taiga: 1888, < Russian *taiga* 'swampy coniferous forest area of Siberia'

    b. pastiche: 1866, < French *pastiche* < Italian *pasticcio* < Latin *pasticum*
        'pie, pastry'

    c. coyote: 1628/1793, < Mexican Spanish *coyote* < native Mexican Nahuatl
        cóyotl, name for a wolf-like animal

    d. plutonium: 1942 (its current sense referring to an element), < classical
        Latin *Plūtō* + *-ium* suffix < ancient Greek *Ploutōn*, name of the god of the
        underworld, learned

    e. hibernate: 1802, < Latin *hībernāre-* 'to winter', learned (apparently first
        used by Darwin)

    f. decathlon: 1912, < Greek *deka* 'ten' + *āthlon* 'contest' (from *pentathlon*),
        learned

    g. fauna: 1746/1771, < Late Latin *Fauna*, name of a Roman goddess, learned

    h. federalist: 1787, < French *fédéraliste* < Latin *foeder-* 'league, treaty'

    i. hammock: 1555, < Spanish *hamaca* (a loan from Taino)

    j. hangar: 1852, < Old French *hangard*, perhaps a Germanic loan

    k. souvenir: 1775, < French *souvenir* < Latin *subvenīre* 'to come into the
        mind'

Exercise 12.3 Neologisms

a. chocoholic: blend – choc(olate) + (alc)oholic

b. (on the) q.t.: initialism – q(uie)t

c. road rage: compounding – N + N/V, rhyme reduplication

d. do's and don'ts: functional shift – V > N

e. scuba: acronym – s(elf) c(ontained) u(nderwater) b(reathing) a(pparatus)

f. sucker (V): functional shift – N > V

g. hertz: commonization – (Heinrich Rudolf) Hertz

h. ROM: acronym – r(ead)-o(nly) m(emory)

i. rad: clipping – rad(ical)

j. alphabet: compounding – alpha + bet(a)

k. CD: initialisms – c(ompact) d(isk)

l. FIFO: acronym – f(irst) i(n) f(irst) o(ut)

m. ad: clipping – advertisement

n. sailplane: compounding – N + N *or* blend – sail + (air)plane

o. double-edged: compounding – ADJ + ADJ

p. herky-jerky: reduplication

Exercise 12.4 Grammatical Changes in Progress

a. 'Gods Cool' (painted on the window of a car)
    – missing apostrophe in contraction of *is* (*God's*): reduction of forms

b. I took my umbrella because I seen it was going to rain.
    – past participle *seen* used where past tense *saw* expected: conflation of forms

c. Who are you looking at?
    – subject pronoun *who* used where object (of preposition) *whom* expected: reduction of forms, change in usage

d. When a student arrives, they must be seated immediately.
    – plural pronoun *they* used where singular *he* or *he/she* expected: change in usage

e. The line-up at the book store was like an hour!
    – *like* used as a discourse marker

f. He went, 'Hi!' And I'm like, 'In your dreams.' So then we're all uncomfortable after that.
    – *went* used where *said* expected: quotative construction
    – *be like* used where *thought* expected: quotative construction
    – *all* used as narrative marker of action
    – some mixing of tenses: *went* (past) with *am* (present) and ambiguous contraction *we're*

Chapter 13

Exercise 13.1 British versus North American English

		BE	USEng	CanE
a.	class	[klɑs]	[klæs]	[klæs]
b.	lighter	[laɪtə]	[laɪɾɾ]	[ləɪɾər]
c.	primary	[praɪməri]	[praɪmɛri]	[praɪmɛri]
d.	park	[pɑk]	[pɑrk]	[pɑrk]
e.	white	[waɪt]	[waɪt] / [hwaɪt]	[wəɪt]
f.	router (tool)	[raʊtə]	[raʊɾər]	[rəʊɾər]
g.	conservatory	[kənsəvətri]	[kənsɑrvətɔri]	[kənsərvətɔri]
h.	crass	[kræs]	[kræs]	[kræs]
i.	plenty	[plɛnti]	[plɛni]	[plɛni]

Exercise 13.2 Vocabulary of National Dialects

	Word	**National Variety**	**Meaning**	**Source**
a.	sasquatch	CanE (and USEng)	hairy, manlike monster	Salish
b.	puckeroo	NZE	broken, useless	Maori
c.	dowf	SSE	dull	Old Norse
d.	natty	WISE	knotted hair	English
e.	kiva	USEng	ceremonial chamber	Hopi
f.	bodach	HE	peasant, churl	Irish Gaelic
g.	sangoma	SAE	witch doctor	Zulu (Bantu)
h.	bywoner	SAE	poor tenant farmer	Afrikaans
i.	coracle	WE	small boat	Welsh
j.	potlatch	CanE (and USEng)	tribal ceremony	Chinook Jargon < Nootka
k.	walkabout	AusE	periodic migration of Aboriginal peoples	Pidgin English

l.	joual	CanE	dialect of Canadian French	French
m.	hogan	USEng	hut	Navajo

Exercise 13.3 American Regionalisms

1. a. clophopper: a rustic; an awkward, stupid person; a large shoe; a large foot

    b. flapdoodle: imaginary food of fools

    c. dust bunny: soft roll of dust

    d. boogerman/bogeyman: the devil

    e. elbow grease: physical force

    f. get-go: the start, the beginning

    g. doohickey: anything whose name is unknown or forgotten

    h. fraidycat: timid or easily frightened person

2. a. davenport 'sofa, couch': This word is most common in Northern and Midland USEng, less common in Western and Mid-Atlantic USEng, and quite uncommon in Southern and Northeastern USEng.

    b. baby-buggy: This word is rare in Northeastern, Mid-Atlantic, and Coastal Southern USEng. It is common in Western, Inland Southern, Midland, and Northern USEng.

    c. creep 'crawl': This word is common in Northeastern USEng and fairly common in Northern USEng. It is rare elsewhere.

    d. frigidaire 'refrigerator': This word is found in Southern USEng, also less commonly in Midland and Northeastern USEng. It is rare elsewhere.

    e. ethyl 'high octane gasoline': This word is primarily Western. It also occurs in the western areas of Midland and Inland Southern US Eng. It is not found in Coastal Southern, Mid-Atlantic, Northern, or Northeastern USEng.

Glossary of Linguistic Terms

ablaut The systematic alteration or gradation of a root vowel in order to indicate the meaning or grammatical function of a word, as seen in ModE *sing, sang, sung.*

accent Acoustic prominence given to a particular syllable in a word. *See also* STRESS ACCENT, DIALECT.

accusative The case of the direct object, as in *I read the book.*

acronym The initial letters of words in a phrase pronounced as a word, as in *NATO < N(orth) A(tlantic) T(reaty) O(rganization).*

adjective A part of speech which qualifies or quantifies a noun, as in *blue sky.*

adstratum *See* SUBSTRATUM.

adverb A part of speech which modifies a verb or verbal, adjective, preposition, or conjunction, as in *speak loudly.*

affix A bound morpheme (*see* MORPHEME), in English either a prefix (e.g. *un-* in *unlock*) or a suffix (e.g. *-er* in *runner* or *-est* in *fastest*).

affricate A consonant sound created with the complete blockage of airflow characteristic of a stop, followed by the constricted outflow of air charac-teristic of a fricative, as in the initial sound in *cherry.*

agreement A process in which the grammatical information expressed in one form is repeated in other forms which accompany it, as in *these books are* (all plural forms) versus *this book is* (all singular forms).

allophone A predictable and non-distinctive variant of a sound which occurs in certain phonetic environments. For example, the [k] sound in *cool* is articulated further back in the mouth than the [k] sound in *cat*, but both belong to the same class of sounds, /k/. *See* COMPLEMENTARY DISTRIBUTION, PHONEME.

alphabet A system of writing which represents each of the sounds of a language by means of a discrete symbol.

alveolar A consonant sound created by bringing the tip of the tongue to the alveolar ridge (a portion of the roof of the mouth behind the upper teeth), as in the initial sound in *door.*

alveolopalatal A consonant sound created by bringing the front of the tongue to the roof of the mouth just behind the alveolar ridge, as in the initial sound in *sure.*

amalgamated compound   The fusing of two parts of a compound or the loss of one part as an independent word, as in *neighbor* from *nēah-gebūr* 'near dweller'.

amelioration   The acquisition of a more favorable meaning or an elevation in the value judgment associated with the thing named, as in *steward*, formerly meaning 'keeper of the (pig) sty'. *Compare* PEJORATION.

analogy   A process by which one form becomes like another form with which it is associated. On the basis of a pattern existing in the language, an old form is replaced or a new form is introduced. For example, the older plural *kine* has been replaced by *cows*, following the standard pattern of marking plurals with *-s*. Analogy serves to remove irregularities in the language.

analytic language   A language such as Modern English in which word order and function words rather than inflections are the primary indicators of grammatical relationships. *Compare* SYNTHETIC LANGUAGE.

anaphora   A kind of reference in which a form refers back to an expression occurring earlier in the discourse and is used to avoid repetition, e.g. the pronoun *he* in *the Dalai Lama . . . he*. The term means literally 'pointing back'.

anomalous verb   A verb that is irregular in its person and tense marking, such as *be* (e.g. *am, is, are*) and *go*.

apocope   The loss of a final vowel, e.g. the loss of *u* as OE *sunu* becomes ModE *son*.

approximant   A speech sound (liquid or glide) in which the articulators come close to one another but do not constrict the airflow, such as the initial sound in *yellow*.

arbitrary sign   A symbolic sign which is related by convention to the thing is represents. For example, the sequence of sounds constituting a word is not connected naturally or inevitably to the thing it names but only by means of social agreement.

archaic   Denoting a language feature which has changed very little in the course of time, preserving a characteristic believed to have existed in the parent language.

article   *See* DEFINITE ARTICLE, INDEFINITE ARTICLE.

articulation, manner of   The degree of restriction in the airflow in the oral/nasal tract during the production of a speech sound, e.g. stop, fricative.

articulation, place of   The part of the oral/nasal tract involved in the production of a speech sound, or the articulators used in producing such a sound, e.g. bilabial or velar.

ascertainment   An eighteenth-century term meaning 'to settle a matter and render it certain and free from doubt'. Ascertainment involved the codification, refinement, and fixing of the language in a permanent form.

aspect   A grammatical category of the verb which views the action as either ongoing or completed, as in the ModE contrast between the progressive *He was writing a poem* and the simple tense *He wrote a poem*.

assimilation   An articulatory change in which a sound becomes similar or identical to an adjacent sound in VOICING (*q.v.*), MANNER OF ARTICULATION (*q.v.*), or PLACE OF ARTICULATION (*q.v.*), such as in *husband*, where the [s] of *house* is voiced to resemble the voiced initial sound in *-band*. Assimilation is typically motivated by ease of articulation.

attestation The recorded instance of a word or language. *Compare* RECONSTRUCTION.

auxiliary verb A verbal element which cannot stand alone in the predicate of a sentence but must accompany a non-finite form of the verb, as in *He will pay*.

back-formation A process in which a segment believed to be an affix is removed to produce a morphologically simple word. For example, the verb *sculpt* is 'back-formed' from *sculptor* under the false assumption that *-or* represents the common English suffix *-er*.

backing The qualitative change in the articulation of a vowel to a relatively back position in the mouth, e.g. [æ] > [ɑ].

bilabial Articulation produced by bringing the lower lip up against the upper lip, as in the initial sound in *map*.

blend Two free words combined and blended, usually by clipping off the end of the first word and the beginning of the second word, as in *smog < sm(oke) + (f)og*.

borrowing *See* LOAN WORD. *See also* INTIMATE BORROWING, CULTURAL BORROWING.

bound morpheme See MORPHEME.

breaking A kind of diphthongization in Old English conditioned by certain consonant sequences following a vowel, e.g. [i] > [aɪ] in ME *kniʒt* > ModE *knight*.

calque A native word formation using the model of the form and meaning of a (morphologically complex and semantically transparent) foreign word. It stands in contrast to borrowing. For example, *spirit of the times* is a calque based on German *Zeitgeist*. *Also called* **loan translation**.

case An indication of the grammatical role of a noun or noun phrase in a sentence, typically by means of inflection, as in *the book's cover*, where *'s* signals genitive or possessive case.

clipping The deliberate dropping of part of a word, as in *fax < facsimile*.

closed syllable *See* OPEN SYLLABLE.

close *e* *See* OPEN *E*.

close *o* *See* OPEN *O*.

cognate Forms of the same word existing independently in related languages; they are direct continuations from a single original word in the parent language. For example, the cognates Skt. *rājā*, Lat. *rex* (*reg-*), and OE *rīce* all derive from *reg in Proto-Indo-European.

colloquial Designating everyday language used in familiar or informal contexts.

commonization The conversion of a proper noun into a common noun, verb, or adjective, as in *china*.

comparative *See* DEGREE.

comparative method A deductive linguistic method whereby extant daughter languages are compared in order to reconstruct forms in the proto-language that are otherwise unattested.

complementary distribution Mutually exclusive phonetic environments in which allophones predictably occur, e.g. the aspirated [t] in *top* (occurring syllable-initially before a stressed vowel) versus the unaspirated [t] in *stop* (occurring in all other phonetic environments).

composite predicates A verb of general meaning, such as *do, have, make, draw, give,* and *take*, in combination with a noun derived from a verb, as in *have a run*.

compound A process of word formation, characteristic in the Germanic languages, which involves the combination of two or more independent roots to form a single word, such as *blackboard*.

concord *See* AGREEMENT.

conditioned change A sound change occurring only in certain phonetic environments, such as flapping (voicing) of intervocalic [t] in *butter*.

conjugation The inflection of a verbal element for person, number, tense, and mood. *Compare* DECLENSION.

conjunction An invariable part of speech used to combine words, phrases, and clauses, e.g. *and*, *because*.

connotation The set of associations implied by a word, as in the case of *steed* (positive), *horse* (neutral), *nag* (negative). *Compare* DENOTATION.

consonant Speech sounds articulated with a certain amount of constriction of the outflow of air. Consonants generally serve to begin and end a syllable.

core vocabulary Vocabulary naming everyday objects, concepts, and actions, and including words that have grammatical functions.

creolization The process whereby a PIDGIN (*q.v.*) develops functionally and linguistically over time to become a native language (a creole).

cultural borrowing The name for a cultural item taken from another language group, as in the case of *tea* (from Chinese).

dative The case of the indirect object, as in *I gave the book to the student* (or *I gave the student the book*).

dead language A language that has no native speakers, such as Latin or Hittite.

declension The inflection of a nominal element for person, number, gender, and case. *Compare* CONJUGATION.

decreolization A process by which a creole is increasingly influenced by the standard language with which it is in contact and comes to resemble it more closely. The result of decreolization is a range of dialects known as a post-creole continuum.

definite article A noun determiner with anaphoric function, 'pointing' or referring backwards in the discourse to something which has already been mentioned, as in *Yesterday I read a book. The book was entertaining.*

degree The forms of an adjective or adverb expressing relative intensities: positive (e.g. *big*), comparative (e.g. *bigger*), and superlative (e.g. *biggest*).

deixis An indexical sign which refers to its object via proximity. *Deictic forms point out things in relation to the speaker, as in *now* 'the time of speaking' versus *then* 'before or after the time of speaking'.

demonstrative Noun determiners or pronouns with deictic meaning, one pointing to a referent close to the speaker (*this/these*) and one pointing to a referent far from the speaker (*that/those*).

denotation The literal, objective meaning of a word, or its dictionary meaning, e.g. *horse* 'a mammal belonging to the genus *Equus caballus*'. *Compare* CONNOTATION.

dental suffix The alveolar stops used to mark the regular past tense in English, i.e. [d, t, əd] in *love/loved*, *walk/walked*, *load/loaded*.

derivation The creation of new words by adding affixes, either prefixes or suffixes, to existing roots, e.g. *help*, *helper*, *helpful*, *unhelpful*, *helpless*.

descriptive grammar A grammar that explains or analyzes how language works and how it is used, without regulating usage. This approach is the basis of modern linguistics.

devoicing   The loss of vocal cord vibration on a sound, such as [d] > [t].

diachronic linguistics   *See* HISTORICAL LINGUISTICS.

dialect   A variety of a language, either regional or social, which is more or less mutually intelligible with other forms of the language. The term *accent* refers specifically to the phonological features of a dialect.

diglossia   A linguistic situation in which two languages coexist, one of which is a lower or socially stigmatized dialect and the other of which is a higher or prestige dialect, as in the case of English and French, respectively, during the English Middle Ages.

digraph   Two orthographic symbols which together represent a single sound.

diphthong   A vowel sound consisting of a vowel together with a glide (a *falling diphthong*), as in *ow* [aʊ], or a glide together with a vowel (a *rising diphthong*), as in [ɪu], forming the nucleus of a syllable.

diphthongization   The creation of a diphthong from a monophthong by the addition of a glide, as in [u] > [aʊ].

discourse marker   A words or phrase which structures the discourse and anchors it in the communicative context, such as *well*, *right*, *so*, *like*, *y'know*, *I mean*. They are generally seen as empty of semantic content.

dissimilation   An articulatory change in which a sound becomes less like an adjacent sound in voicing, manner of articulation, or place of articulation, such as OE *þeofþu* > ModE *theft* (where the final fricative is replaced by a stop to differentiate it from the

preceding fricative). Dissimilation is typically motivated by the need for perceptual clarity.

double genitive   A form containing both an inflected genitive and a periphrastic *of*-genitive, such as *a friend of my sister's*.

doublet   Two words in a language which have a common origin but which arrive in the language via different routes of transmission, such as native *shirt* and Old Norse *skirt*.

drag chain   A theoretical model of change meant to account for systematic shifts in which one change leaves a gap which is filled through a subsequent change, e.g. GRIMM'S LAW (*q.v.*). Compare PUSH CHAIN.

dual   Plural forms denoting 'two'. In OE, dual forms of the first- and second-person pronouns, meaning 'we two' and 'you two', existed.

dummy auxiliary *do*   A structural element (lacking semantic content) used in the formation of negatives and questions in Modern English, as in *Do you love dogs?*

ease of articulation   A motivation for sound change whereby a speaker exerts the least effort in articulating sounds.

enclitic   A weakly stressed form which cannot stand alone and is attached to the preceding word, as in the case of *-n't* or *'ll*. It often derives from a full word.

etymology   The history of the origin and development of the form and meaning of a word.

euphemism   A kind of understatement, or use of socially acceptable words, to avoid explicit reference to unpleasant or sensitive topics, as in the use of *pass away* for *die*.

extension   All of the possible referents of a particular word. The exension of *dog* is all of the possible members of the genus *Canis*, e.g. beagle, Pomeranian, shepherd.

external cause of change   Motivations for change which are external to the structure of a language but result from language contact or socio-historical influences.

extinct language   *See* DEAD LANGUAGE.

familiar forms   Forms used to address inferiors in age, rank, and social class generally, typically the second-person singular pronoun.

finite verb   *See* NON-FINITE VERB.

First Sound Shift   *See* GRIMM'S LAW, VERNER'S LAW.

fixed accent   Accent that always falls on the same syllable in a word. In Germanic, stress accent is fixed on the first or root syllable of a word.

folk etymology   The attribution of a new history, and often a new phonetic form, to a word through its association with a more familiar word. This occurs when a word has become unfamiliar for some reason. The meaning generally remains the same. An example is the use in some dialects of *sparrow grass* for *asparagus* (from Greek).

formal forms   Forms used to address superiors in age, rank, and social class generally, typically the second-person plural pronoun.

free accent   Accent that is movable, or floating, because it falls on different syllables in a word depending on the word's inflectional category.

free morpheme   *See* MORPHEME.

fricative   A consonant sound created by bringing the articulators close enough to produce turbulence or friction (a hissing sound) as air leaves the vocal tract, e.g. the initial sound in *sherry*.

fricativization   A process whereby a stop consonant is changed to a fricative, as in the final consonant alternation in *democrat* and *democracy* where [t] > [s].

fronting   The qualitative change in the articulation of a vowel to a relatively forward position in the mouth, e.g. [o] > [e].

frozen form   *See* REMNANT FORM.

functional shift   The conversion of one part of speech to another without the addition of an affix, e.g. *a parent* (noun) > *to parent* (verb).

function word   A word serving to mark grammatical relations rather than to express lexical meaning; function words include prepositions, articles, conjunctions, and auxiliaries.

future   The designation of the time of the action as subsequent to the moment of speaking.

gender   *See* GRAMMATICAL GENDER, NATURAL GENDER.

generalization   A widening in the scope of meaning of a word, as in *holiday*, formerly denoting 'sacred day', now denoting any day on which one does not work. *Compare* SPECIALIZATION.

genitive   The case of the possessor, as in *Mario's watch*. The genitive case also has a number of uses unrelated to possession, such as *the boat's hull*.

gerund   A verb functioning as a noun, e.g. *Swimming is good exercise*.

glide   A consonant sound created by moving the tongue from one position to another with a relatively unrestricted flow of air, as in the initial sound in *yet*. *Also called a* **semivowel**.

grammar   The set of constitutive rules or principles by which a language operates (or a book setting out either constitutive or prescriptive rules).

grammatical gender   A means of classifying nouns, often with little correspondence to the biological sex of the object. In OE, it includes masculine, feminine, and neuter genders. *See* NATURAL GENDER.

grammaticalization   The process by which a lexical word becomes a grammatical marker, either an inflection or a phrasal element, as in *be going to* as a future marker.

Great Vowel Shift   A series of non-phonologically conditioned vowel changes that occurred in all of the long vowels inherited from Middle English, which were raised in articulation, or if they were already high vowels, were diphthongized, e.g. [hūs] > [haʊs].

Grimm's Law   An unconditioned sound change, affecting all the stop consonants of Proto-Indo-European. Compare, e.g. Lat. *pater* and English *father*, showing [p > f] and [t > θ].

group genitive   A construction consisting of a nominal group (noun plus post-modifiers) with the genitive inflection attached to the last element of the group rather than to the head noun, as in *the Age of Reason's end*.

High German Sound Shift   *See* SECOND SOUND SHIFT.

his-**genitive**   An Early Modern English construction consisting of an uninflected noun followed by a third-person genitive pronominal form, usually masculine, as in *the count his gallies*.

historical linguistics   The study of language change over time.

homophone   Different words which sound the same but are spelled differently, e.g. *horse/hoarse*.

homorganic   Used to designate sounds articulated in the same place in the mouth: e.g. [m] and [b] are homorganic, since they are both bilabial.

hybrid   A complex word form which consists of a native part and a borrowed part, as in *faith* (Fr.) + *-less* (OE).

hypercorrection   The correction of a perceived mistake, as when a speaker says *between you and I* on the false belief that *me* is (always) incorrect.

imperative   The form used in making direct commands to a second person. Old English has an imperative inflection, e.g. *Gāð* 'Go!', while Modern English relies on syntax alone, e.g. *Shut the window!*

impersonal verb   A verb lacking a personal subject but with an experiencer expressed in a non-nominative case, as in *it seems to me*.

indefinite article   A noun determiner used for first mention of an item in the discourse, as in *Yesterday I read a book*. In English, the indefinite article derives from the numeral 'one'.

indicative   The verbal inflection expressing the mood of fact, used in making statements and asking questions.

infinitive   A non-finite form of the verb, appearing in ModE as both the bare infinitive (e.g. *eat*) and the *to*-infinitive (*to eat*).

inflecting language   A language type in which grammatical distinctions are expressed by morphological affixes, each affix expressing a number of different meanings; e.g. Latin, where verbal -*ō* expresses the first-person present tense indicative in *laudō* 'I praise', is an inflecting language.

inflection   An affix expressing the grammatical categories of a word, such as case (on nouns) or tense (on verbs).

inkhorn terms   A derisive sixteenth-century term for learned borrowings, considered overly pedantic and unnecessary, e.g. *demit* 'send away'.

instrumental   A case covering a range of meanings, including means, manner, cause, and accompaniment, roughly translatable by *with* in Modern English, as in *I opened the door with a key*.

intension   The dictionary definition, or denotation, of a word. The intension of a word is the linguistic means by which we make reference. *Compare* EXTENSION.

interdental   A consonant sound created by protruding the tongue slightly between the upper and lower teeth, as in the initial sound in *thick*.

internal causes of change   Motivations for change that are inherent to the system of a language, such as ease of articulation, perceptual clarity, and transparency.

interrogative pronoun   Any of the pronoun forms used for forming questions, including *who, what, why, where*, and *how*.

intervocalic   Used to denote a consonant sound falling between two vowel sounds, as in the [n] in *many*.

intimate borrowing   The borrowing of a word between languages spoken in the same geographical area at the same time.

intonation   The pitch patterns extending over sequences of sounds, generally used to distinguish different sentence types, e.g. the rising intonation of the question *Is he here?*

intrusion   The addition of a sound because of the difficulty of co-ordinating articulatory movements, as in the case of the insertion of [p] in *warm(p)th*.

inverse spelling   A kind of HYPERCORRECTION (*q.v.*) which occurs when a writer is aware that a written sequence represents a certain pronunciation but then uses that spelling in a word where it does not belong, as in the spelling *muzling* for *muslin*.

inverted word order   *See* WORD ORDER.

kenning   A metaphorical compound used in traditional oral compositions, such as *bānhūs* 'bone-house' for 'body'.

labialization   *See* ROUNDING.

labiodental   A consonant sound created by bringing the lower lip up against the upper teeth, as in the initial sound in *fun*.

labiovelar   A consonant sound which is pronounced as a velar stop with lip rounding, as in the initial sounds in English *quick* or *Gwen*.

language   A highly structured system of symbolic signs, primarily vocal, used for human communication with the express purpose of performing various speech acts. Language is innate and creative.

language contact   *See* EXTERNAL CAUSE OF CHANGE.

language death   A phenomenon that occurs when a more socially prestigious and politically powerful language supplants another language.

language family   A set of different languages that have a common origin, such as Hungarian, Estonian, Finnish, and Lappish (all members of the Finno-Ugric language family).

laryngeal   One of three fricative sounds (of uncertain pronunciation) believed to have existed in Proto-Indo-European.

laxing   The qualitative change from a tense to a lax vowel due to the relaxing of muscle tension in the tongue, e.g. [u] > [ʊ].

lax vowel   A vowel articulated with less tension on the tongue, thus lower and more centralized than a tense vowel, e.g. lax [ɛ] or [ʊ] compared with tense [e] or [u]. *Compare* TENSE VOWEL.

learned borrowing   A loan word adopted in a written form and typically of a formal or technical register.

lengthening   *See* QUANTITATIVE CHANGE.

lenition   A weakening of a consonant generally occurring between vowels, for instance a stop consonant > fricative, a fricative > approximant, voiceless > voiced, as in OE *fæder* > ModE *father*.

leveling of inflections   The merger of inflections into just a few distinct forms, resulting from vowel reduction and analogy.

lexicography   The practice of dictionary-making.

lexicon   The vocabulary of a language; a language's inventory of words either native or borrowed.

ligature   Two letters linked together as one, e.g. the combination of *a* and *e* as *æ*.

linguistic corruption   A view of language as having decayed from some earlier state of linguistic purity.

linguistic sign   Normally a symbolic sign (i.e. a word) that bears an arbitrary or conventional relationship to the thing it represents. *See* ARBITRARY SIGN.

linguistic variable   The set of variant forms that can be used with the same meaning, as in *I must have it* and *I have to have it* or *You should have seen it* and *You should have saw it*.

linking *r*   In non-rhotic dialects, the insertion of a word-final [r] in instances where the following word begins with a vowel (as in 'far away') but also in instances where it is not etymologically motivated (as in 'the idea(r) is').

liquid   A subclass of approximant consonants, including [l] and [r].

loan translation   *See* CALQUE.

loan word   A lexical item that is adopted from another language. Loan words are assimilated phonologically

and morphologically and do not fundamentally change the structure of the language.

long vowel   A vowel sound articulated for longer duration than a short vowel. Vowel length may be associated with tenseness (*see* TENSE VOWEL). Vowel length is distinctive in Old English (*gōd* 'good' versus *god* 'God') but not in Modern English.

lowering   The qualitative change in the articulation of a vowel to a relatively lower position in the mouth, e.g. [o] > [ɔ].

marked   Denoting a feature or characteristic that departs from what is expected, natural, or neutral (i.e. *unmarked*), such as the inverted word order in *Brussels sprouts I love*, in contrast with the unmarked *I love Brussels sprouts*.

merger   The collapse of two or more sounds into one, as in the case of [ɑ] and [ɔ] falling together as [ɑ]. *Compare* SPLIT.

metaphor   A process involved in figurative semantic shifts whereby the qualities belonging to the first referent become associated with the second, e.g. *bottleneck* comes to mean 'traffic jam'.

metathesis   The reversal or reordering of two sounds, e.g. *ask/aks*.

metonymy   A process involved in figurative semantic shifts whereby the name of an object associated with something is used for that thing, e.g. *the bar* comes to mean 'the legal profession'.

modal auxiliary   Any of the continuations of the preterit-present verbs of Old English which now serve as auxiliaries of mood, e.g. *shall, can, must*.

monophthong   *See* VOWEL.

monophthongization   The change of a diphthong into a monophthong by loss of the glide segment, e.g. [ɪu] > [u].

mood   An indication of whether the action is viewed as fact or non-fact (e.g. possibility, probability, desire, wish, or contrary-to-fact). The moods of English are the indicative, subjunctive, and imperative.

morpheme   The smallest meaning-bearing unit in language, e.g. *pre-, ordain, -ed*. Morphemes may be free (independent words) or bound (parts of words—bound roots or affixes).

morphology   The form and formation of words in a particular language as well as of word classes, or parts of speech.

mutation   *See* UMLAUT.

nasal   A consonant sound created by blocking the flow of air through the oral tract completely while allowing air to flow out the nasal tract, e.g. the initial sound in *mare*.

national variety   A kind of large-scale regional dialect spoken within a political entity, e.g. Australian English. *See also* DIALECT.

natural gender   A means of denoting the biological sex of the entity named, male, female, or sexless. *See* GRAMMATICAL GENDER.

nominal   Used to denote a noun or noun-like word, including demonstratives, adjectives, and pronouns.

nominative   The case of the subject, as in *Clarissa read the book*.

non-finite verb   A verb form which is not inflected for person, number, or tense, and hence does not agree with the subject and cannot stand alone in the predicate of a sentence; infinitives, participles, and gerunds are all non-finite verbs.

non-rhotic   Denoting dialects in which [r] is deleted pre-consonantally and word-finally, as in *ca(r)* and *ca(r)t*.

A *rhotic* dialect preserves [r] in these contexts.

noun   A part of speech denoting a person, place, or thing which may be modified for number in Modern English, such as *book/books, team/teams*.

number   A grammatical distinction of quantity, typically distinguishing between 'one' (singular) and 'more than one' (plural).

object   That which receives the action of the verb (direct object) or is the goal or recipient of the action (indirect object), as in *I read the book* (DO) *to her* (IO).

objective case   In Modern English, the combination of the Old English dative (indirect object) and accusative (direct object) cases.

open *e*   The mid-front lax vowel, found in the word *set* [ɛ], as distinct from close *e*, the mid-front tense vowel [e].

open *o*   The mid-back vowel, showing considerable variation, found in the word *port* [ɔ], as distinct from the close *o*, the mid-back tense vowel [o].

open syllable   A SYLLABLE (*q.v.*) that does not end in a consonant, e.g. *toe*, as opposed to a closed syllable that does, e.g. *cat*.

open syllable lengthening   In Middle English, the lengthening of a short stressed vowel in the open syllable of a disyllabic Old English word, e.g. OE ta-lu > ME tāle.

orthography   The writing system of a language, including its conventions of spelling.

palatal   A consonant sound created by bringing the front of the tongue to the high domed area of the roof of the mouth (the hard palate), as in the initial sound in *yes*.

palatalization   The articulation of a consonant more in the palatal region of the mouth, usually due to the proximity of another palatal sound, e.g. [s] > [š] (moving back from alveolar to alveolopalatal) or [g] > [j] (moving forward from velar to palatal).

paradigm A pattern comprising all of the inflected forms of a particular word.

participle A non-finite form of the verb used as part of the verb phrase or as an adjective. In form participles may be either present (e.g. *writing*) or past (*written*).

pejoration The acquisition of a less favorable meaning or a lowering in the value judgment associated with the thing named, as in the case of *poison*, which formerly meant 'potion, drink'.

perfect A verbal periphrastic form consisting of auxiliary *have* (and in earlier English *be*) and the past participle, used to express resultative past actions, e.g. *have spoken*.

periphrasis (*pl.* **periphrases**) A construction employing function words in place of inflectional endings to express grammatical meaning, as in the use of the *of*-genitive (e.g. *of the dog*) instead of the *'s*-genitive (*the dog's*).

person A designation of the participants in a speech situation: the speaker (first person), the addressee (second person), and the person or thing spoken about (third person).

personal ending An inflectional ending on the verb that indicates person and number, as in *sings* (where the *-s* ending indicates third-person singular).

personal pronoun A pronoun form used to designate either a person or a thing, e.g. *I, you, she, they*.

phoneme A distinctive sound of a language, as in the contrast between [k] and [p] in the minimal pair *cat* and *pat*.

phonemecization A process by which an allophone becomes a phoneme, thus increasing the number of distinctive sounds in the language.

phonemic spelling system A spelling system, as is found in Old English, in which each orthographic symbol represents a single phoneme.

phonetic alphabet A system for transcribing sounds in which there is a one-to-one correspondence between symbol and sound.

phonological environment The linguistic context which determines or conditions a sound change; the context may refer to such things as surrounding sounds or position in a word, e.g. the Verner's Law shift of [s] > [z] in a voiced environment (i.e. a voiced sound on both sides).

phonological symmetry The tendency toward structural balance within a phonological system, e.g. in pairing voiced and voiceless consonants or front and back vowels.

phonology The sound system of a particular language, including its inventory of distinctive sounds, possible sound combinations, and prosodic features.

phrasal verb A verbal construction consisting of a verb and a post-verbal particle, such as *beat up* (transitive) or *take off* (intransitive). *See also* VERB.

pidgin A contact language which develops in order to facilitate communication between peoples who do not share a common language. A pidgin is functionally limited, grammatically reduced, and typically short-lived.

popular borrowing A loan word adopted in an oral context and typically of an informal, colloquial register.

pragmatics Language use in its social context, especially the principles by which speakers co-operate when they communicate and the underlying beliefs and assumptions of speakers and hearers as they are encoded in language.

preposition   An uninflected part of speech which indicates the relation of the noun that follows to a verb, an adjective, or another noun, e.g. *in, by, with*.

prescriptive grammar   A grammar that prescribes (dictates) and proscribes (forbids) certain ways of speaking and writing in an attempt to establish and maintain a standard of correctness.

present   A tense inflection of the verb used to express the non-past (e.g. present habits and states, future events). *See* TENSE.

preterit   A tense inflection of the verb used to express past states and events. *See* TENSE.

preterit-present verb   A class of verbs in Old English which use strong preterit tense morphology (ablauted forms) in the present and weak preterit morphology (dental suffix) in the past. They are ancestors of the modal auxiliaries (e.g. *can/could*) in Modern English.

principal parts of verb   The forms of a verb from which the verb is inflected, e.g. the infinitive (e.g. *to walk*), the past tense (e.g. *I walked*), and the past participle (e.g. *I have walked*).

productive form   A regular or analogical inflection which occurs on the majority of forms existing in the language and is added to any new forms entering the language, e.g. the productive *-s* plural (*cows*) as opposed to the non-productive *-en* plural (*oxen*).

progressive   A verbal periphrastic form consisting of auxiliary *be* and the present participle used to express ongoing or continuous action, e.g. *be speaking*.

pronoun   A part of speech which substitutes for or stands in place of a noun or noun phrase, e.g. *I, it, that, our, mine, who, which, himself*. Types of pronouns include personal pronouns, interrogative pronouns, demonstrative pronouns, relative pronouns, and reflexive pronouns.

proto-language   The parent language, generally unattested and reconstructed, from which daughter languages have descended.

purism   *See* LINGUISTIC CORRUPTION.

push chain   A theoretical model of change meant to account for systematic shifts in which one form begins to encroach upon the position of another and eventually 'pushes' it into a new position; it is more common with vowels, which can shift in incremental amounts, and may have motivated the Great Vowel Shift. *Compare* DRAG CHAIN.

qualitative change   A sound change in which the position of the tongue is moved by raising or lowering or by fronting or backing, or by tensing or laxing; the position of the lips may also be changed by rounding or unrounding.

quantitative change   A change in which the length of articulation of the vowel (and sometimes consonants) is increased (lengthening) or decreased (shortening).

raising   The qualitative change in the articulation of a vowel to a relatively higher position in the mouth, e.g. [ɔ] > [o].

reanalysis   A new understanding of the structure of a phrase, often involving reassignment of structural divisions (rebracketing), as in the change from [according] [to him] to [according to] [him].

reconstruction   An hypothesis about the structure and vocabulary of a proto-language posited by means of the comparative method. Since forms in a reconstructed language are not recorded, we mark them with an asterisk (*).

reduced vowel   *See* SCHWA.

reduplication   A process in which the initial syllable or the entire word is doubled, exactly or with a slight phonological change, as in *ping-pong, wishy-washy.*

referent   The set of entities in the real world which a word denotes. A particular referent—a man, for example—may be denoted in a number of different ways (or with different intensions), as 'father', 'the doctor', 'the man mowing the lawn', etc.

reflex   The descendant in the daughter language of a sound in the proto-language, e.g. Gmc. *f is a reflex of PIE *p.

reflexive   A syntactic form in which the subject and the object of a verb have the same referent, in ModE expressed with reflexive pronouns, e.g. *John burned himself.*

register   A variety of language appropriate to or characteristic of a certain social situation, e.g. formal or informal, colloquial or literary, popular or learned, scientific or religious.

relative pronoun   A pronoun which introduces a relative (adjectival) clause and has reference to an antecedent. The pronoun serves a grammatical function within the relative clause and also connects the relative clause to the main clause, e.g. *The woman [who spoke] is my sister.*

remnant form   A form which preserves an older and now non-productive means of inflection, such as *oxen, five-foot long, cloven. Also called a frozen form.*

renewal   The replacement or supplementing of older forms by newer, more emphatic, more euphemistic, more expressive forms, as in the use of intensifiers such as *awfully, totally,* and *horribly* in place of *very, quite,* and *really.*

rhotacism   The change of a consonant, usually [s], into [r], as in the related words *was* and *were.*

rhotic   *See* NON-RHOTIC.

root   The base form of a word that cannot be further analyzed or divided (it contains no affixes); it carries the primary semantic content, e.g. *re-place-ment-s*, where *place* is the root. A root may also be the earliest historical form of the word, e.g. PIE *ped- 'foot'.

rounding   A qualitative change in which the sound is articulated with lip rounding, e.g. [i] > [y].

RP (or **Received Pronunciation**)   The prestige dialect of Britain, based on the dialect of the upper class as taught in the public schools, and formerly used on the British Broadcasting Corporation, now gradually being replaced by other dialects, such as Estuary English.

schwa   The mid-central lax vowel, as in the word *sun*. With the tongue in its most neutral, or rest, position, this vowel is sometimes considered a reduced vowel.

Second Sound Shift   An unconditioned consonant shift occurring in Old High German but not in the Low

Germanic dialects. Compare English *that* and German *dass*, showing [θ > d] and [t > s].

semantic differentiation   A gradual shift in meaning over time in which two (nearly) synonymous words gain distinct denotations; thus, *hound*, formerly 'dog in general', is now restricted to 'hunting breed of dog' and thus differentiated from *dog*.

semantic domain   A structured part of the vocabulary in which words within a certain area of meaning are related, such as the domains of kinship terms, food terms, and color terms.

semantic loan   The retention of the native form of a word but with the adoption of a meaning borrowed from the cognate word in a related language. Thus, the OE word *wið* (meaning 'against') acquires the meaning but not the form of the Old Norse cognate *við* (meaning 'in conjunction, company with'). *Previously called **semantic contamination**.*

semantics   Meaning in language, including meanings related to the outside world (lexical meaning, or dictionary meaning) and meanings related to the grammar of the sentence (grammatical meaning), e.g. tense or number.

semivowel   *See* GLIDE.

shortening   *See* QUANTITATIVE CHANGE.

short vowel   *See* LONG VOWEL.

sibilants   A subset of fricatives and affricatives characterized by high acoustic energy, or a hissing sound [s, š, z, ž, č, ǰ].

sign   A signal that refers to some object or state of affairs, including icons (as in a photograph denoting a person), indexes (as in thunder pointing to lightning), or symbols (as in a flag standing for a nation).

simplification of consonant cluster   The loss of a consonant adjacent to other consonants, such as the simplification of [kn] to [n] in *knee*.

smoothing   *See* MONOPHTHONGIZATION.

social dialect   A dialect which is shaped by factors such as the socioeconomic class, gender, age, education, and occupation of the speakers.

specialization   The narrowing in scope of the meaning of a word, as in the case of *girl* formerly meaning 'young person (of either sex)', now meaning a 'young female person'. *Compare* GENERALIZATION.

spelling pronunciation   The pronunciation of a word as it is written rather than as it is conventionally pronounced; for example, many speakers now pronounce the [t] in *often* ([t] had been lost at an earlier stage but had remained in the spelling). Compare *soften*, which has lost the [t] but not received a spelling pronunciation.

split   The separation of a single sound into two distinct sounds, as in the case of [ʊ] splitting into [ʊ] and [ə]. *Compare* MERGER.

standard language   A single form of a language, written and/or spoken, to be used throughout a country; the basis of the standard is typically a geographically central and linguistically compromise dialect. The standard becomes a prestige dialect and is artificially maintained through class and education.

stop   A consonant sound created by blocking the flow of air through both the oral and nasal tract; a stop is audible only when it is released by the opening of the articulators (called a ***plosive***).

stress accent Prominence given to a particular syllable in a word by increasing the volume of air expelled when articulating it and thus increasing its loudness.

strong adjective Any of a group of inherited Indo-European adjective endings retained in OE when the adjective constitutes the sole modifier of the noun or when the adjective follows the verb *to be*. The strong declension communicates indefinite reference, e.g. OE *godne cyning* 'a good king' (object). *Compare* WEAK ADJECTIVE.

strong verb A verb which forms its tenses by the Indo-European process of ablaut, or vowel gradation, such as *ride, rode, ridden*.

subject The doer of the action (e.g. *Mary ate the apple*) or that which is described in the predicate of the sentence (e.g. *Mary lives in Holland*); the subject controls verb agreement.

subjunctive Verbal inflection (in OE) or periphrasis (in ModE) expressing non-factual mood apart from direct command. *See* MOOD.

subordinate clause A clause (subject + finite verb) which cannot stand alone as an independent sentence (main clause) but is adjoined to a main clause via a subordinating conjunction, such as *Because he studied hard, he passed the course*.

substratum A phenomenon in which the language of the politically dominated group influences that of the dominant group, as is the case of Celtic on English spoken in Ireland. Compare *superstratum*, in which the language of the dominant group influences the language of the dominated group (as is the case of French on English in the Middle English period), and *adstratum*, in which there is a mixture of languages spoken by groups of equal political and social power (as is the case in the Balkan peninsula, where there are many shared features, among Albanian, Romanian, etc.).

superlative *See* DEGREE.

superstratum *See* SUBSTRATUM.

suppletive A paradigm comprising etymologically distinct roots, e.g. *good, better, best* or *go, went, gone*.

suprasegmental Denoting features of sound which extend over individual sounds, including stress and intonation.

syllable A unit in the phonetic continuum consisting of a nucleus (i.e. a vowel or vowel-like sound) and optionally associated consonants, which begin and/or end the syllable. The nucleus is the acoustically prominent part of the syllable.

syncope The loss of a medial vowel, such as in the pronunciation of *ev(e) ning*.

synecdoche A process involved in figurative semantic shifts whereby the whole is referred to by the part, as in the expression *new blood*, in which *blood* stands for 'a person'.

synesthesia A process involved in figurative semantic shifts whereby a word referring to one sense is transferred to another or to a non-sensual domain, as in *a flat note*, where *flat* is transferred from the visual to the aural dimension.

synonym Each of two or more words with identical or near identical meaning which often differ in register. Synonyms of English, French, and Latin origin tend to be colloquial, literary, or learned, respectively, as in the case of *rise/mount/ascend*.

syntax The arrangement of words into higher units such as phrases, clauses, and sentences. *See also* WORD ORDER.

synthetic language A language such as Old English where inflections rather than word order and periphrases are the primary indicators of grammatical relationships. *Compare* ANALYTIC LANGUAGE.

taboo word A word that is banned or strongly avoided for religious, political, or social reasons and is often replaced by a euphemism.

tense A linguistic category indicating the time of an event in relation to the moment of speaking (tense is hence a DEICTIC [*q.v.*] category). English has two tense categories expressed inflectionally: past (preterit) and present. Other temporal categories are indicated by PERIPHRASIS (*q.v.*), e.g. the future.

tense vowel A vowel articulated with more tension on the tongue, thus making it higher and less centralized than a lax vowel, e.g. tense [i] or [u] in contrast to lax [ɪ] or [ʊ]. *Compare* LAX VOWEL.

tensing The qualitative change from a lax to a tense vowel due to the increase of muscle tension in the tongue, e.g. [ʊ] > [u].

transcription The recording of speech using a phonetic alphabet. *Narrow transcription* records all the nuances of pronunciation, while *broad transcription* records only the grosser characteristics of speech.

transparency An ideal state of language in which there is a one-to-one correspondence of meaning and form; systematic, regular, and easily explicable rules; and a minimum of redundancy. If a language becomes overly opaque (complicated or irregular), an impulse for transparency may motivate language change.

umlaut A kind of regressive assimilation in which an original *i* or *j* causes the vowel in the preceding syllable to be fronted or raised, such as **gōsi* > *gēs*.

unconditioned change A sound change which is not conditioned by phonological environment; every instance of a particular sound changes, regardless of its context, as in the case of [ɑ] > [æ] (which has changed back and forth several times in the history of English).

unmarked *See* MARKED.

unrounding A qualitative change in which lip rounding is lost, e.g. [y] > [i].

usage The forms of language that are actually used or that are prescribed for correct usage, referred to as 'custom' by the eighteenth-century grammarians.

velar A consonant sound created by bringing the back of the tongue up to the back area of the roof of the mouth (the velum, or soft palate), as in the initial sound in *goose*.

verb A part of speech which expresses an event or state, and is inflected for tense, person, and number (in English). There are a number of subclasses of verbs, including transitive (e.g. *hit, buy*) and intransitive (e.g. *live, smile*).

verbal A verb or verb-like word, including verbs and AUXILIARIES (*q.v.*).

Verner's Law A set of exceptions to the operation of Grimm's Law explained by the position of the accent in Proto-

Indo-European. *See also* GRIMM'S LAW.

vocabulary   *See* LEXICON.

vocalization   A phonological process in which a consonant becomes a semivowel or vowel, as in OE *hafoc* > ModE *hawk*.

voice   An indication of the relationship between the subject and the action expressed by the verb, whether the subject of the sentence is acting (active) or is acted upon (passive), as in the distinction between *John drove the car* and *The car was driven by John*.

voiced aspirated stop   A consonant sound found in Proto-Indo-European consisting of a voiced stop with aspiration, e.g. *bh.

voicing   The state of the vocal cords, whether they are tense and vibrating (producing a voiced sound) or relatively open and still (producing a voiceless sound). Also, the addition of vocal cord vibration to a voiceless sound, as [p] > [b]. *Compare* DEVOICING.

vowel   A speech sound articulated with the air passing freely through the vocal tract (that is, with no constriction of the airstream); different vowels are produced by changing the shape and position of the tongue. A single vowel sound, with the pitch constant in a syl- lable, is called a *monophthong*. *See also* DIPHTHONG.

vowel reduction   The centralization and laxing of vowels to schwa [ə] in syllables other than those with primary stress.

weak adjective   A innovative Germanic set of adjective endings retained in OE to communicate definite reference and used when the noun and adjective are accompanied by another modifier (e.g. demonstrative, numeral, possessive) or when the adjective is in the comparative or superlative degree, e.g. OE *þone godan cyning* 'that good king' (object). *Compare* STRONG ADJECTIVE.

weak verb   An innovative class of verbs in the Germanic languages that form their preterit with a dental suffix, as in *trip/tripped*, constituting the regular, or productive, pattern in English.

word order   Generally, the position of the major elements in the sentence, subject (S), verb (V), and object (O). Across languages, the typical patterns are SVO, SOV, and VSO. *Inverted word order* refers to the reversal of the position of S and V which occurs in marked constructions, as is *Are* (V) *you* (S) *a teacher?* in an SVO language.

word stock   *See* LEXICON.

References

Abbott, E.A. 1966. *A Shakespearian Grammar*. New York: Dover [Reprint].

'About Australia'. 2008. Australian Government, Department of Foreign Affairs (http://www.dfat.gov.au/facts/Indigenous_languages.html).

Adamson, Sylvia, et al. (eds). 2001. *Reading Shakespeare's Dramatic Language: A Guide*. London: Thomson (for The Arden Shakespeare).

The Adventure of English: 500 AD to 2000 AD. 2002–3. Written and produced by Melyvn Bragg. London: LWT Production for Granada International.

Agard, John. 1990 [1985]. *Mangoes and Bullets: Selected and New Poems 1972–84*. London: Serpent's Tail.

Aitchison, Jean. 1996. *The Seeds of Speech: Language Origin and Evolution*. Cambridge: Cambridge University Press.

——. 2001. *Language Change: Progress or Decay?* 3rd edn. Cambridge: Cambridge University Press.

Algeo, John. 1998. 'Vocabulary'. In Romaine (ed.), 57–91.

—— (ed.). 2001. *The Cambridge History of the English Language. Vol. VI: English in North America*. Cambridge: Cambridge University Press.

——. 2010. *The Origins and Development of the English Language*. Based on the original work by Thomas Pyles. 6th edn. Boston: Thomson-Wadsworth.

——, and Algeo, A.S. (eds). 1991. *Fifty Years 'Among the New Words': A Dictionary of Neologisms, 1941–1991*. New York: Cambridge University Press.

——, and Butcher, Carmen Acevedo. 2005. *Problems in the Origins and Development of the English Language*. 5th edn. Boston: Thomson-Wadsworth.

Allen, Hope Emily. 1931. *English Writings of Richard Rolle: Hermit of Hampole*. Oxford: Clarendon.

The American Heritage Dictionary of the English Language. 2000. 4th edn. Boston: Houghton Mifflin.

Arlotto, Anthony. 1972. *Introduction to Historical Linguistics*. Boston: Houghton Mifflin. [Rprnt Lanham: University Press of America, 1981.]

Arnovick, Leslie K. 1999. *Diachronic Pragmatics: Seven Case Studies in English Illocutionary Development*. Amsterdam and Philadelphia: John Benjamins.

Avis, Walter Spencer. 1972. 'So *Eh?* is Canadian, Eh?'. *Canadian Journal of Linguistics / Le revue canadienne de linguistique* 17:89–104.

Australian National Dictionary. A Dictionary of Australianisms on Historical

Principles. 1988. Ed. by W.S. Ransom et al. Melbourne: Oxford University Press.

Ayto, John. 1999. *A Century of New Words*. Oxford and New York: Oxford University Press.

Babington, Churchill (ed.). 1865. *Polychronicon Ranulphi Higden Monachi Cestrensis*. 2 vols. London: Longman, Green, Longman, Roberts, and Green.

Bailey, Charles J., and Maroldt, Karl. 1977. 'The French Lineage of English'. *Langues en contact-Pidgins-Creoles*. Ed. by Jürgen M. Meisel, 21–53. Tübingen: Narr.

Bailey, Richard W. 1996. *Nineteenth-Century English*. Ann Arbor: University of Michigan Press.

———, and Görlach, Manfred (eds). 1982. *English as a World Language*. Ann Arbor: University of Michigan Press.

Baker, Peter S. 2003. *Introduction to Old English*. Malden, MA and Oxford: Blackwell.

Baldi, Philip. 1983. *An Introduction to the Indo-European Languages*. Carbondale: Southern Illinois University Press.

Barber, Charles. 1964. *Linguistic Change in Present-Day English*. Edinburgh and London: Oliver and Boyd.

———. 1976. *Early Modern English*. London: André Deutsch.

———, Beal, Joan C., and Shaw, Philip A. 2009. *The English Language: A Historical Introduction*. 2nd edn. Cambridge: Cambridge University Press.

Barney, Stephen A. 1985. *Word-Hoard: An Introduction to Old English Vocabulary*. New Haven and London: Yale University Press.

Barnhart, Robert K. (ed.). 1988. *The Barnhart Dictionary of Etymology*. Bronx, NY: H.W. Wilson.

———, et al. (eds). 1990. *Third Barnhart Dictionary of New English*. Bronx, NY: H.W. Wilson.

Baron, Naomi. 1984. 'Computer-Mediated Communication as a Force in Language Change'. *Visible Language* 18:118–41.

Bauer, Laurie. 1983. *English Word-Formation*. Cambridge: Cambridge University Press.

———. 1994. *Watching English Change*. London and New York: Longman.

———. 2002. *An Introduction to International Varieties of English*. Edinburgh: Edinburgh University Press.

Baugh, Albert C., and Cable, Thomas. 2002. *A History of the English Language*. 5th edn. Upper Saddle River, NJ: Prentice Hall.

Baumgardner, Robert Jackson (ed.). 1996. *South Asian English: Structure, Use, and Users*. Urbana: University of Illinois Press.

Beal, Joan C. 2004. *English in Modern Times: 1700–1945*. London: Arnold.

Bede. 1955 [731]. *A History of the English Church and People* [*Historia Ecclesiastica Gentis Anglorum*]. Trans. by Leo Sherley-Price. Rev. by R.E. Latham. Harmondsworth: Penguin.

Beekes, Robert S.P. 1995. *Comparative Indo-European Linguistics: An Introduction*. Amsterdam and Philadelphia: John Benjamins.

Benson, Larry D. 1987. *The Riverside Chaucer*. 3rd edn. Boston: Houghton Mifflin.

———. 2000. *The Canterbury Tales: Complete*. Boston: Houghton Mifflin.

Benveniste, Émile. 1968. 'Mutations of Linguistic Categories'. Trans. by Yakov Malkiel and Marilyn May Vihman. *Directions for Historical Linguistics: A Symposium*. Ed. by W.P. Lehmann and Yakov Malkiel, 85–94. Austin and London: University of Texas Press.

———. 1973. *Indo-European Language and Society*. Trans. by Elizabeth Palmer. Coral Gables, FL: University of Miami Press.

Biber, Douglas, Conrad, Susan, and Reppen, Randi. 1998. *Corpus Linguistics: Investigating Language Structure and Use*. Cambridge: Cambridge University Press.

——, Johansson, Stig, Leech, Geoffrey, Conrad, Susan, and Finegan, Edward. 1999. *Longman Grammar of Spoken and Written English*. Harlow: Pearson.

The Bible in English. 1996. Chadwyck-Healey (http://www.proquest.com/en-US/catalogs/databases/detail/bible_in_english.shtml).

Blake, Norman. 1983. *Shakespeare's Language: An Introduction*. London: Macmillan.

—— (ed.). 1992. *The Cambridge History of the English Language. Vol. II: 1066–1476*. Cambridge: Cambridge University Press.

Bloomfield, Leonard. 1933. *Language*. New York: Holt, Rinehart, and Winston.

Bosworth, Joseph, and Toller, T. Northcote (eds). 1898 [Supplement 1921]. *An Anglo-Saxon Dictionary*. Oxford: Oxford University Press.

Bright, James Wilson (ed.). 1906. *Euangelium Secundum Lucam: The Gospel of Saint Luke in West-Saxon*. Boston: D.C. Heath.

Brinton, Laurel J. 1996. *Pragmatic Markers in English: Grammaticalization and Discourse Markers*. Berlin and New York: Mouton de Gruyter.

——, and Bergs, Alexander (eds.). Forthcoming. *Historical English Linguistics* (*Handbücher zur Sprach- und Kommunikationswissenschaft/Handbooks of Linguistics and Communication Science*.) Vol. 2. Berlin and New York: Mouton de Gruyter.

——, and Brinton, Donna M. 2010. *The Linguistic Structure of Modern English*. Amsterdam and Philadelphia: John Benjamins.

——, and Fee, Margery. 2001. 'Canadian English'. In Algeo (ed.), 422–40.

Bryan, W.F. 1923. 'Notes on the Founders of Prescriptive English Grammar'. *The Manly Anniversary Studies in Language and Literature*. Ed. by J.M. Manly, 383–93. Chicago: University of Chicago Press.

Buck, Charles Darling. 1949. *A Dictionary of Selected Synonyms in the Principal Indo-European Languages*. Chicago and London: Chicago University Press.

Burchfield, Robert (ed.). 1994. *The Cambridge History of the English Language. Vol. V: English in Britain and Overseas*. Cambridge: Cambridge University Press.

Burnley, David. 2000. *The History of the English Language: A Source Book*. 2nd edn. Harlow: Pearson.

Burridge, Kate, and Mulder, Jean. 1998. *English in Australia and New Zealand: An Introduction to Its History, Structure, and Use*. Melbourne: Oxford University Press.

Butters, Ronald R. 1980. 'Narrative *go* "say"'. *American Speech* 55:304–7.

Bynon, Theodora. 1977. *Historical Linguistics*. Cambridge: Cambridge University Press.

Campbell, A. 1959. *Old English Grammar*. Oxford: Clarendon.

Campbell, George. 1963 [1776]. *The Philosophy of Rhetoric*. Ed. by Lloyd F. Bitzer. Carbondale and Edwardsville: Southern Illinois University Press.

Canadian Oxford Dictionary. 2004. Ed. by Katherine Barber. 2nd edn. Don Mills: Oxford University Press.

Cannon, Garland. 1990. *The Life and Mind of Oriental Jones: Sir William Jones, the Father of Modern Linguistics*. Cambridge: Cambridge University Press.

Carstairs-McCarthy, Andrew. 2002. *An Introduction to English Morphology: Words and Their Structure*. Edinburgh: Edinburgh University Press.

Cassidy, Frederic G., and Ringler, Richard N. (eds). 1971. *Bright's Old English*

Grammar & Reader. 3rd edn. New York: Holt, Rinehart and Winston.

Cawley, A.C. 1958. *The Wakefield Pageants in the Towneley Cycle*. Manchester: Manchester University Press.

Chambers, J.K. 1998. 'T.V. Makes People Sound the Same'. *Language Myths*. Ed. by Laurie Bauer and Peter Trudgill, 123–31. London: Penguin.

Cheshire, Jenny (ed.). 1991. *English around the World: Sociolinguistic Perspectives*. Cambridge: Cambridge University Press.

Clackson, James. 2007. *Indo-European Linguistics: An Introduction*. Cambridge: Cambridge University Press.

Clanchy, M.T. 1993. *From Memory to Written Record, England 1066–1307*. 2nd edn. Oxford: Blackwell.

Clark, Cecily (ed.). 1970. *The Peterborough Chronicle*. 2nd edn. Oxford: Clarendon.

Clarke, Sandra (ed.). 1993. *Focus on Canada*. Varieties of English around the World, Vol. 11. Amsterdam and Philadelphia: John Benjamins.

———. 2010. *Newfoundland and Labrador English*. Edinburgh: Edinburgh University Press.

Clark-Hall, J.R. 1984. *A Concise Anglo-Saxon Dictionary*. 4th edn. Toronto: University of Toronto Press and the Medieval Academy of America.

Cobbett, William. 1984 [1819]. *A Grammar of the English Language*. Intro. by Robert Burchfield. Oxford and New York: Oxford University Press.

Corrie, Marilyn. 2006. 'Middle English—Dialects and Diversity'. In Mugglestone (ed.), 86–119.

Coulmas, Florian. 1996. *The Blackwell Encyclopedia of Writing Systems*. Oxford and Cambridge, MA: Blackwell.

Coupland, Nikolas, and Thomas, Alan R. (eds). 1990. *English in Wales: Diversity, Conflict, and Change*. Philadelphia: Multilingual Matters.

Crotch, W.J.B. 1928. *The Prologues and Epilogues of William Caxton*. (EETS, 176.) Oxford: Oxford University Press.

Crystal, David. 1987. *The Cambridge Encyclopedia of Language*. 1st edn. Cambridge: Cambridge University Press.

———. 2003. *The Cambridge Encyclopedia of the English Language*. 2nd edn. Cambridge: Cambridge University Press.

———. 2006a. 'English Worldwide'. In Hogg and Denison (eds), 420–39.

———. 2006b. *Language and the Internet*. 2nd edn. Cambridge: Cambridge University Press.

———. 2008. *A Dictionary of Linguistics and Phonetics*. 6th edn. New York: Wiley Blackwell.

———, and Crystal, Ben. 2002. *Shakespeare's Words: A Glossary & Language Companion*. London: Penguin.

Curzan, Anne. 2000. 'The End of Modern English'. *American Speech* 75:299–301.

———, and Adams, Michael. 2009. *How English Works: A Linguistic Introduction*. 2nd edn. New York: Pearson.

Daniell, Christopher. 2003. *From Norman Conquest to Magna Carta: England, 1066–1215*. London and New York: Routledge.

D'Arcy, Alexandra. 2005. *Like: Syntax and Development*. Unpublished PhD dissertation, University of Toronto.

Davis, Boyd. 2000. 'Language and Digital Technology: Corpora, Contact, and Change'. *American Speech* 73:301–3.

Davis, Norman, et al. 1979. *A Chaucer Glossary*. Oxford: Clarendon.

Defoe, Daniel. 1697. *An Essay upon Projects* [Reprinted in W.F. Bolton (ed.). 1966. *The English Language: Essays by English & American Men of Letters 1490–1839*. Cambridge: Cambridge University Press, 91–101.]

Denison, David. 1993. *English Historical Syntax*. London and New York: Longman.

Diamond, Robert E. 1970. *Old English Grammar & Reader*. Detroit: Wayne State University Press.

Dictionary of American Regional English. 1985–present. Ed. by Frederic G. Cassidy and Joan Houston Hall. Cambridge, MA: Belknap Press of Harvard University Press.

Dictionary of Canadianisms on Historical Principles. 1967. Ed. by Walter S. Avis et al. Toronto: Gage.

Dictionary of the English/Creole of Trinidad & Tobago on Historical Principles. 2009. Ed. by Lise Winer. Montreal: McGill-Queen's University Press.

Dictionary of New Zealand English: A Dictionary of New Zealandisms on Historical Principles. 1997. Ed. by H.W. Orsman. Aukland: Oxford University Press.

Dictionary of Old English: A–G on CD-ROM. 2008. Ed. by Antonette diPaolo Healey et al. Toronto: Pontifical Institute of Medieval Studies, University of Toronto.

A Dictionary of South African English on Historical Principles. 1996. Penny Silva et al. Oxford: Oxford University Press.

Diringer, David. 1958. *The Story of Aleph Beth*. London: Lincolns-Prager.

———. 1962. *Writing*. London: Thames and Hudson.

Discovering the Human Language: Colorless Green Ideas. 1995. Part 1 of *Human Language Series*. South Carolina ETV; Equinox Films. Produced, directed, and written by Gene Searchinger. New York: Ways of Knowing.

Dollinger, Stefan. 2008. *New-Dialect Formation in Canada: Evidence from the English Modal Auxiliaries*. Amsterdam and Philadelphia: John Benjamins.

———. 2010. 'Written Sources of Canadian English: Phonetic Reconstruction and the Low-Back Vowel Merger'. *Var-ieties in Writing: The Written Word as Linguistic Evidence*. Ed. by Raymond Hickey 197–222. Amsterdam and Philadelphia: John Benjamins.

Dominique, Nicole Z. 1977. 'Middle English: Another Creole?' *Journal of Creole Studies* 1:89–100.

Dorian, Nancy C. 1981. *Language Death: The Life Cycle of a Scottish Gaelic Dialect*. Philadelphia: University of Pennsylvania Press.

Do You Speak American? 2005. Narrated by Robert MacNeil. New York: WNET.

Durkin, Philip. 2009. *The Oxford Guide to Etymology*. New York and Oxford: Oxford University Press.

Elyot, Sir Thomas. 1834. *The Governour*. Ed. by Arthur Turberville Eliot. London: John Hernaman.

Evans, G. Blakemore (ed.). 1997. *The Riverside Shakespeare*. 2nd edn. Boston: Houghton Mifflin.

Finegan, Edward. 1998. 'English Grammar and Usage'. In Romaine (ed.), 536–88.

———. 2006. 'English in North America'. In Hogg and Denison (eds), 384–419.

———. 2008. *Language: Its Structure and Use*. 5th edn. Boston: Thomson-Wadsworth.

———, and Rickford, John R. (eds). 2004. *Language in the USA: Themes for the Twenty-First Century*. Cambridge: Cambridge University Press.

Fischer, Olga. 1992. 'Syntax'. In Blake (ed.), 207–408.

———, and van der Wurff, Wim. 2006. 'Syntax'. In Hogg and Denison (eds), 109–98.

Fisher, John H., and Bornstein, Diane (eds). 1974. *In Forme of Speche Is Chaunge: Readings in the History of the English Language*. Englewood Cliffs, NJ: Prentice-Hall. [Rprnt Lanham: University Press of America, 1984.]

Fowler, H.W. 1965. *A Dictionary of Modern English Usage*. 2nd edn. Revised by Sir

Ernest Gowers. Oxford: Oxford University Press.

Foys, Martin K. 2003. *The Bayeux Tapestry on CD-ROM*. Woodbridge: Boydell & Brewer.

Freeborn, Dennis. 1998. *From Old English to Standard English: A Course Book in Language Variation across Time*. 2nd edn. Ottawa: University of Ottawa Press.

Frey, Leonard H. 1966. *Readings in Early English Language History*. Indianapolis and New York: Bobbs-Merrill.

Fromkin, Victoria, Rodman, Robert, and Hyams, Nina. 2007. *An Introduction to Language*. 8th edn. Boston: Thomson-Wadsworth.

Gamkrelidze, Thomas V., and Ivanov, Vjaceslav V. 1995. *Indo-European and the Indo-Europeans: A Reconstruction and Historical Analysis of a Proto-Language and a Proto-Culture*. Trans. by J. Nichols. Berlin and New York: Mouton de Gruyter.

Gelb, I.J. 1963. *A Study of Writing*. Rev. edn. Chicago and London: University of Chicago Press.

Gelderen, Elly van. 2006. *A History of the English Language*. Amsterdam and Philadelphia: John Benjamins.

Giltrow, Janet, and Stein, Dieter (eds). 2009. *Genres and the Internet*. Amsterdam and Philadelphia: John Benjamins.

Gimbutas, Marija. 1970. 'Proto-Indo-European Culture: The Kurgan Culture during the Fifth, Fourth, and Third Millennia BC'. *Indo-European and Indo-Europeans*. Ed. by G. Cardona et al., 155–97. Philadelphia: University of Pennsylvania Press.

———. 1982. *The Goddesses and Gods of Old Europe*. Berkeley and Los Angeles: University of California Press.

Godden, Malcolm (ed.). 1979. *Ælfric's Catholic Homilies. The Second Series*. (EETS, Supplementary Series, 5.) London: Oxford University Press.

Görlach, Manfred. 1991. *Introduction to Early Modern English*. Cambridge: Cambridge University Press.

Gramley, Stephan. 2001. *The Vocabulary of World English*. London: Arnold.

Grape, Wolfgang. 1994. *The Bayeux Tapestry: Monument to a Norman Triumph*. Münich and New York: Prestel.

Green, Jonathon. 1996. *Chasing the Sun: Dictionary Makers and the Dictionaries They Make*. New York: Henry Holt & Co.

Griffiths, Patrick. 2006. *An Introduction to English Semantics and Pragmatics*. Edinburgh: Edinburgh University Press.

Grimm, Jacob. 1826–65. *Deutsche Grammatik*. Göttingen: Dieterich.

Heaney, Seamus. 2000. *Beowulf: A New Verse Translation*. New York: Farrar, Straus & Giroux.

Hernández-Campoy, J.M. (ed.). Forthcoming. *The Handbook of Historical Sociolinguistics*. Oxford: Wiley-Blackwell.

Herring, Susan C. 2001. 'Computer-Mediated Discourse'. *The Handbook of Discourse Analysis*. Ed. by Deborah Schiffrin, Deborah Tannen, and Heidi E. Hamilton, 612–34. Oxford and Malden, MA: Blackwell.

———. 2007. 'A Faceting Classification Scheme for Computer-Mediated Discourse'. *Language @ Internet* 4. Article 1 (http://www.languageatinternet.de).

Heyd, Theresa. Forthcoming. 'English and the Media: Internet'. In Brinton and Bergs (eds).

Hoad, Terry. 2006. 'Preliminaries: Before English'. In Mugglestone (ed.), 7–31.

Hock, Hans Henrich. 1991. *Principles of Historical Linguistics*. 2nd edn. Berlin, New York, and Amsterdam: Mouton de Gruyter.

Hogg, Richard M. (ed.). 1992–2001. *The Cambridge History of the English Language. Vols I–VI*. Cambridge: Cambridge University Press.

———. 1992. 'Phonology and Morphology'. In Hogg (ed.), 67–167.

——— (ed.). 1992. *The Cambridge History of the English Language. Vol. I: The Beginnings to 1066*. Cambridge: Cambridge University Press.

———. 2002. *An Introduction to Old English*. New York: Oxford University Press.

———. 2006. 'English in Britain'. In Hogg and Denison (eds), 352–83.

———, and Denison, David (eds). 2006. *A History of the English Language*. Cambridge: Cambridge University Press.

Holinshed, Rafael, et al. 1587. *Chronicles of England, Scotlande, and Irelande*. London: Henry Denham (http://www.cems.ox.ac.uk/holinshed).

The Holy Bible. Authorized King James Version. Cambridge: Cambridge University Press.

Hope, Jonathan. 2003. *Shakespeare's Grammar*. London: Thomson (for The Arden Shakespeare).

Hopper, Paul J. 1982. 'Areal Typology and the Early Indo-European Consonant System'. *The Indo-Europeans in the Fourth and Third Millenennia*. Ed. by Edgar C. Polomé, 121–39. Ann Arbor, MI: Karoma.

Horace. 1978. *Horace: Satires, Epistles and Ars Poetica*. Trans. and ed. by Henry Rushton Fairclough. Loeb Classical Library. Cambridge, MA: Harvard University Press.

Horobin, Simon, and Smith, Jeremy. 2002. *An Introduction to Middle English*. New York: Oxford University Press.

Huddleston, Rodney, and Pullum, Geoffrey K. 2002. *The Cambridge Grammar of the English Language*. Cambridge: Cambridge University Press.

Hudson, Nicholas. 1994. *Writing and European Thought 1600–1830*. Cambridge: Cambridge University Press.

Hughes, Geoffrey. 1988. *Words in Time: A Social History of the English Vocabulary*. Oxford: Blackwell.

———. 2000. *A History of English Words*. Malden, MA and Oxford: Blackwell.

ICAME Collection of English Language Corpora. 1999. 2nd edn. Bergen: The HIT Centre, University of Bergen (http://www.hit.uib.no/icame/cd).

In Search of the First Language. 1994. NOVA with BBC Production, WGBH Educational Foundation.

Irvine, Susan. 2006. 'Beginnings and Transitions: Old English'. In Mugglestone (ed.), 32–60.

Jeffers, Robert J., and Lehiste, Ilse. 1979. *Principles and Methods for Historical Linguistics*. Cambridge, MA and London: The MIT Press.

Jespersen, Otto. 1922. *Language; Its Nature, Development and Origin*. London: G. Allen and Unwin; New York: H. Holt.

———. 1928–49. *A Modern English Grammar on Historical Principles*. 7 vols. London: George Allen and Unwin.

———. 1982 [1905]. *Growth and Structure of the English Language*. 10th edn. Oxford: Basil Blackwell.

Johnson, James Weldon (ed.). 1925. *Book of American Negro Spirituals*. New York: Viking Press.

Johnson, Samuel. 1977 [1755/1773]. *Samuel Johnson: Selected Poetry and Prose*. Ed. by Frank Brady and W.K. Wimsatt. Berkeley, Los Angeles, and London: University of California Press.

Jones, Charles. 1989. *A History of English Phonology*. London: Longman.

———. 2002. *The English Language in Scotland: An Introduction to Scots*. East Linton: Tuckwell Press.

Jones, Sir William. 1788 [1766]. 'The Third Anniversary Discourse, on the Hindus'. *Asiatick Researches* 1: 422ff.

Justice, David. 1987. 'The Lexicography of Recent Semantic Change'. Paper presented at the annual meeting of the Modern Language Association, San Francisco, CA.

Kallen, Jeffrey (ed.). 1997. *Focus on Ireland*. Varieties of English around the World, Vol. 21. Amsterdam and Philadelphia: John Benjamin.

Kastovsky, Dieter. 1992. 'Semantics and Vocabulary'. In Hogg (ed.), 290–408.

——. 2006. 'Vocabulary'. In Hogg and Denison (eds), 199–270.

Kay, Christian, Roberts, Jane, Samuels, Michael, and Wotherspoon, Irene. 2009. *Historical Thesaurus of the Oxford English Dictionary. With Additional Material from* A Thesaurus of Old English. Oxford: Oxford University Press.

Keen, Maurice Hugh. 1990. *English Society in the Later Middle Ages, 1348–1500*. London: Allan Lane, The Penguin Press.

Klein, E. 1969. *A Comprehensive Etymological Dictionary of the English Language*. Amsterdam: Elsevier.

Knowles, Gerry. 1997. *A Cultural History of the English Language*. London and New York: Arnold.

Krapp, George Philip, and Dobbie, Elliott van Kirk, (eds). 1936. *The Exeter Book*. New York: Columbia University Press/ London: Routledge and Kegan Paul.

Kreidler, Charles W. 1998. *Introducing English Semantics*. London and New York: Routledge.

Labov, William. 1972a. *Language in the Inner City: Studies in the Black English Vernacular*. Philadelphia: University of Pennsylvania Press.

——. 1972b. *Sociolinguistic Patterns*. Philadelphia: University of Pennsylvania Press.

Ladefoged, Peter. 2004. *Vowels and Consonants: An Introduction to the Sounds of Languages*. 2nd edn. Malden: Blackwell.

——. 2005. *A Course in Phonetics*. 5th edn. Boston: Thomson-Wadsworth.

Landau, Sidney I. 2001. *Dictionaries: The Art and Craft of Lexicography*. 2nd edn. Cambridge: Cambridge University Press.

Lanham, L.W. 1982. 'English in South Africa'. In Bailey and Görlach (eds), 324–52.

Lapidge, Michael, Blair, John, Keynes, Simon, and Scragg, Don. 1999. *The Blackwell Encyclopedia of Anglo-Saxon England*. Malden, MA and Oxford: Blackwell.

Lass, Roger. 1992. 'Phonology and Morphology'. In Blake (ed.), 23–155.

——. 1999. 'Phonology and Morphology'. In Lass (ed.), 56–186.

—— (ed.). 1999. *The Cambridge History of the English Language. Vol. III: 1476–1776*. Cambridge: Cambridge University Press.

——. 2006. 'Phonology and Morphology'. In Hogg and Denison (eds), 43–108.

Lehmann, Winfred P. 1994. *Historical Linguistics: An Introduction*. 3rd edn. London and New York: Routledge.

Leith, Dick. 1997. *A Social History of English*. 2nd edn. London and New York: Routledge.

Leonard, Sterling A. 1929. *The Doctrine of Correctness in English Usage, 1700–1800*. Madison: University of Wisconsin Press.

Lieberman, Antoly. 2008. *An Analytic Dictionary of English Etymology: An Introduction*. Minneapolis: University of Minnesota Press.

Lightfoot, David W. 1979. *Principle of Diachronic Syntax*. Cambridge: Cambridge University Press.

Lowth, Robert A. 1762. *A Short Introduction to English Grammar*. London: J. Hughs.

Lumby, J. Rawson (ed.). 1886/1901. *King Horn, Florizand Blauncheflur, The Assumption of our Lady*. (EETS, 14.) London: Kegan Paul, Trench, Trübner.

Lutz, Angelika. 2002. 'When Did English Begin?'. *Sounds, Words, Texts and Change*. Ed. by Teresa Fanego, Belén Méndez-Naya, and Elena Seoane, 145–71. Amsterdam and Philadelphia: John Benjamins.

McArthur, Tom. 2002. *The Oxford Guide to World English*. Oxford and New York: Oxford University Press.

McIntosh, Angus, Samuels, M.K., and Benskin, Michael. 1987. *A Linguistic Atlas of Late Medieval English*. Aberdeen: Aberdeen University Press.

McMahon, April. 2006. 'Restructuring Renaissance English'. In Mugglestone (ed.), 146–77.

Madden, Sir Frederic. 1967. *Laȝamons Brut or Chronicle of Britain: A Poetical Semi-Saxon Paraphrase of The Brut of Wace*. Osnabrück: Otto Zeller.

Magnusson, Magnus, and Pálsson, Hermann (trans.). 1965. *The Vinland Sagas: The Norse Discovery of America*. Harmondsworth: Penguin.

Mair, Christian. 2006. *Twentieth-Century English: History, Variation and Standardization*. Cambridge: Cambridge University Press.

Mallory, J.P., and Adams, D.Q. (eds). 1997. *Encyclopedia of Indo-European Culture*. London and Chicago: Fitzroy Dearborn.

Mehrotra, Raja Ram (ed.). 1998. *Indian English: Texts and Interpretation*. Varieties of English around the World, Vol. 7. Amsterdam and Philadelphia: John Benjamins.

Mey, Jacob. 2001. *Pragmatics: An Introduction*. 2nd edn. Malden, MA and Oxford: Blackwell.

Michael, Ian. 1970. *English Grammatical Categories and the Tradition to 1800*. Cambridge: Cambridge University Press.

Middle English Dictionary. 1952–2003. Ed. by Hans Kurath and Sherman Kuhn. Ann Arbor: University of Michigan Press. Available online at the Middle English Compendium (http://ets.umdl.umich.edu/m/mec/).

Miller, Thomas. 1890. *The Old English Version of Bede's* Ecclesiastical History of the English People. (EETS, 95/96.) London: N. Trübner.

Millward, C.M. 1996. *A Biography of the English Language*. 2nd edn. Fort Worth: Harcourt Brace.

Milroy, James. 1992. *Linguistic Variation and Change: On the Historical Sociolinguistics of English*. Oxford and Cambridge, MA: Blackwell.

——, and Milroy, Lesley. 1991. *Authority in Language*. 2nd edn. London: Routledge.

Minkova, Donka, and Stockwell, Robert. 2009. *English Words: History and Structure*. 2nd edn. Cambridge: Cambridge University Press.

Mitchell, Bruce. 1995. *An Invitation to Old English and Anglo-Saxon England*. Oxford and Cambridge, MA: Blackwell.

——, and Robinson, Fred C. 2007. *A Guide to Old English: Revised with Prose and Verse Texts and Glossary*. 7th edn. Malden, MA and Oxford: Blackwell.

Morenberg, Max. 2002. *Doing Grammar*. 3rd edn. Oxford and New York: Oxford University Press.

Mossé, Fernand. 1952. *A Handbook of Middle English*. Trans. by James A. Walker. Baltimore and London: Johns Hopkins University Press.

Mufwene, Salikoko S. 2001. 'African-American English'. In Algeo (ed.), 291–324.

——, et al. (eds). 1998. *African American English: Structure, History, and Use*. London: Routledge.

Mugglestone, Lynda (ed.). 2000. *Lexicography and the* OED*: Pioneers in the Untrodden Forest*. Oxford: Oxford University Press.

—— (ed.). 2006. *The Oxford History of English*. Oxford and New York: Oxford University Press.

Murray, K.M. Elisabeth. 1977. *Caught in a Web of Words: James A.H. Murray and the* Oxford English Dictionary.

Oxford and New York: Oxford University Press.

Mustanoja, Tauno F. 1960. *A Middle English Syntax. Part 1: Parts of Speech.* Helsinki: Société Néophilologique.

Nevalainen, Terttu. 2006a. *An Introduction to Early Modern English.* Edinburgh: Edinburgh University Press.

———. 2006b. 'Mapping Change in Tudor English'. In Mugglestone (ed.), 178–211.

———. 2006c. 'Synchronic and Diachronic Variation'. *Encyclopedia of Language and Linguistics. Vol. 12.* 2nd edn. Ed. by Keith Brown, 356–63. New York: Elsevier.

———, and Raumolin-Brunberg, Helena. 2003. *Historical Sociolinguistics: Language Change in Tudor and Stuart England.* London: Longman.

———, and Tieken Boon van Ostade, Ingrid. 2006. 'Standardisation'. In Hogg and Denison (eds), 271–311.

The New Jerusalem Bible. 1985. Ed. by Henry Wansbrough. New York: Doubleday.

Oizumi, Akio (ed.). 1991–2. *A Complete Concordance to the Works of Geoffrey Chaucer.* Hildesheim and New York: Olms-Weidmann.

O'Meally, Robert G. 1997. 'The Vernacular Tradition'. *The Norton Anthology of African American Literature.* Ed. by Henry Louis Gates, Jr, and Nellie Y. McKay. New York and London: W.W. Norton.

The Oxford English Dictionary. 1989. Ed. by J.A. Simpson and E.S.C. Weiner. 2nd edn. Oxford and New York: Oxford University Press. Available on CD-ROM (3rd edition online http://dictionary.oed.com/entrance.dtl).

Paolillo, John. 2005. 'Language Diversity on the Internet'. *Measuring Linguistic Diversity on the Internet.* Ed. by UNESCO Institute for Statistics. Montreal:

UNESCO (http://www.uis.unesco.org/template/pdf/cscl/MeasuringLinguistic-Diversity_En.pdf).

Pederson, Lee. 2001. 'Dialects'. In Algeo (ed.), 253–90.

Peirce, C.S. 1932. 'Speculative Grammar'. *Collected Papers of Charles Peirce. Vol. 2: Elements of Logic.* Ed. by Charles Hartshorne and Paul Weiss. Cambridge, MA: Harvard University Press.

Plummer, Charles. 1892. *Two of the Saxon Chronicles Parallel.* 2 vols. Oxford: Clarendon.

Pope, Alexander. 2000 [1711]. 'An Essay on Criticism'. *The Norton Anthology of Poetry. Vol 1.* 7th edn. Ed. by M.H. Abrams and Stephen Greenblatt, 2509–25. New York and London: W.W. Norton.

Poutsma, Hendrik. 1904–26. *A Grammar of Late Modern English, for the Use of Continental, Especially Dutch, Students.* 4 vols. Groningen: P. Noordhoff.

Prall, Stuart E., and Willson, David Harris. 1991. *A History of England. Vol. II: 1603 to the Present.* 4th edn. Fort Worth: Holt, Rinehart and Winston.

Priestley, Joseph. 1969 [1761]. *The Rudiments of English Grammar.* Menston: Scolar Press.

Prokosch, E. 1938. *A Comparative Germanic Grammar.* Baltimore: Linguistic Society of America.

Pullum, Geoffrey K., and Ladusaw, William A. 1996. *Phonetic Symbol Guide.* 2nd edn. Chicago and London: University of Chicago Press.

Quintilian. 1920–2. *The Institutio Oratoria of Quintilian.* Trans. and ed. by Harold Edgeworth Butler. Loeb Classical Library. Cambridge, MA: Harvard University Press.

Quirk, Randolph, and Wrenn, C.L. 1957 [Rprnt 1994]. *An Old English Grammar.* 2nd edn. DeKalb: Northern Illinois University Press

——, Greenbaum, Sidney, Leech, Geoffrey, and Svartvik, Jan. 1985. *A Comprehensive Grammar of the English Language*. London and New York: Longman.

Renfrew, Colin. 1988. *Archaeology and Language: The Puzzle of IndoEuropean Origins*. Cambridge: Cambridge University Press.

Rickford, John R. 1999. *African American Vernacular English*. Malden, MA and Oxford: Blackwell.

Rissanen, Matti. 1999. 'Syntax'. In Lass (ed.), 187–331.

Roberts, Peter A. 1988. *West Indians and Their Language*. Cambridge: Cambridge University Press.

Robinson, Orrin. 1992. *Old English and Its Closest Relatives: A Survey of the Earliest Germanic Languages*. London: Routledge.

Rogers, Henry. 2004. *Writing Systems: A Linguistic Approach*. Cambridge, MA: Blackwell.

Romaine, Suzanne. 1998. 'Introduction'. In Romaine (ed.), 1–56.

—— (ed.). 1998. *The Cambridge History of the English Language. Vol. IV: 1776–1997*. Cambridge: Cambridge University Press.

——, and Lange, Deborah. 1991. 'The Use of *like* as a Marker of Reported Speech and Thought: A Case of Grammaticalization in Progress'. *American Speech* 66:227–75.

Samuels, M.L. 1963. 'Some Applications of Middle English Dialectology'. *English Studies* 44:81–94.

——. 1972. *Linguistic Evolution, with Special Reference to English*. Cambridge: Cambridge University Press.

Sanders, Andrew. 2004. *The Short Oxford History of English Literature*. 3rd edn. Oxford: Oxford University Press.

Sapir, Edward. 1921. *Language*. New York: Harcourt, Brace, and World.

Saussure, Ferdinand de. 1986 [1915]. *Course in General Linguistics*. Trans. by Roy Harris. La Salle, IL: Open Court.

Schendl, Herbert. 2001. *Historical Linguistics*. Oxford: Oxford University Press.

Schmidt, Alexander. 1902. *Shakespeare-Lexicon*. 3rd edn. Rev. by Gregor Sarrazin. Berlin: Georg Reimer.

Schwyter, Jürg. Forthcoming. 'English and the Media: Radio'. In Brinton and Bergs (eds.).

Serjeantson, Mary S. 1935. *A History of Foreign Words in English*. London: Routledge and Kegan Paul.

Siegel, Robert. 2006. 'American Accent Undergoing Great Vowel Shift'. *NPR* (http://www.npr.org/templates/story/story.php?storyId=5220090).

Simpson, J.M.Y. 1979. *A First Course in Linguistics*. Edinburgh: Edinburgh University Press.

Singh, Ishtla. 2005. *The History of English: A Student's Guide*. London: Hodder Arnold.

Smith, Jeremy J. 2009. *Old English: A Linguistic Introduction*. Cambridge: Cambridge University Press.

Smitherman, Geneva. 2000. *Talkin that Talk: Language, Culture, and Education in African America*. London: Routledge.

Speaking in Tongues: The History of Language. 2007. Directed and researched by Christene Browne. Toronto: Syncopated Productions (http://syncopatedprod.com/index_files/Speaking_in_Tongues_The_History_of_Language_series_details.htm).

Spevack, Marvin (ed.). 1968–70. *A Complete and Systematic Concordance to the Works of Shakespeare*. Hildesheim: Georg Olms.

Stevick, Robert D. 1964. *One Hundred Middle English Lyrics*. Indianapolis: Bobbs-Merrill.

The Story of English. 1986. Part 2: *The Mother Tongue*, Part 3: *A Muse of Fire*,

Part 7: *The Muvver Tongue*. BBC-TV co-production with MacNeil-Lehrer Productions in association with WNET.

Stuart-Smith, Jane. N.d. 'Accent Change: Is Television a Contributory Factor in Accent Change in Adolescents?'. N.d. University of Glasgow (http://www.gla.ac.uk/departments/englishlanguage/research/researchprojects/accentchange/#d.en.27356).

———. Forthcoming. 'English and the Media: Television'. In Brinton and Bergs (eds).

Sundby, Bertil, Bjørge, Anne Kari, and Haugland, Kari E. 1991. *A Dictionary of English Normative Grammar 1700–1800*. Amsterdam and Philadelphia: John Benjamins.

Swift, Jonathan. 1957. *A Proposal for Correcting the English Tongue, Polite Conversation, Etc*. Ed. by Herbert Davis and Louis Landa. Oxford: Basil Blackwell.

Tagliamonte, Sali A., and Denis, Derek. 2008. 'Linguistic Ruin? LOL! Instant Messaging and Teen Language'. *American Speech* 83:3–34.

———, and Smith, Jennifer. 2006. 'Layering, Competition and a Twist of Fate: Deontic Modality in Dialects of English'. *Diachronica* 23:341–80.

Talking Canadian. 2004. Directed by Margaret Slaght. Toronto: Canadian Broadcasting Corporation.

Thomason, Sarah G. 2001. *Language Contact: An Introduction*. Washington, DC: Georgetown University Press.

———, and Kaufman, Terrence. 1988. *Language Contact, Creolization and Genetic Linguistics*. Berkeley, Los Angeles, and London: University of California Press.

Thurlow, Crispin. 2006. 'From Statistical Panic to Moral Panic: The Metadiscursive Construction and Popular Exaggeration of New Media Language in the Print Media'. *Journal of Computer-Mediated Communication* 11(3) Article 1 (http://jcmc.indiana.edu/vol11/issue3/thurlow.html).

Tieken-Boon van Ostade, Ingrid. 2009. *An Introduction to Late Modern English*. Edinburgh: Edinburgh University Press.

Townend, Matthew. 2006. 'Contacts and Conflicts: Latin, Norse, and French'. In Mugglestone (ed.), 61–85.

Trask, R.L. 1996. *Historical Linguistics*. London: Arnold.

Traugott, Elizabeth Closs. 1972. *The History of English Syntax*. New York: Holt, Reinhart, and Winston.

———. 1992. 'Syntax'. In Hogg (ed.), 168–289.

———, and Dasher, Richard B. 2002. *Regularity in Semantic Change*. Cambridge: Cambridge University Press.

Trudgill, Peter. 1999. *The Dialects of England*. 2nd edn. Oxford and Malden, MA: Blackwell.

———, and Hannah, Jean. 2002. *International English: A Guide to Varieties of Standard English*. 4th edn. London: Arnold.

University of Michigan, Humanities Text Initiative (http://www.hti.umich.edu/index-all.html).

University of Virginia, Electronic Text Center (http://etext.lib.virginia.edu/collections/languages/english/).

Van Herk, Gerard. 2009. 'Language in Social Contexts'. *Contemporary Linguistic Analysis: An Introduction*. Ed. by William O'Grady and John Archibald. 6th edn. Toronto: Pearson Longman.

Venezky, Richard L., and Healey, Antonette diPaolo. 1980. *A Microfiche Concordance to Old English*. Newark, DL and Toronto: University of Delaware.

Verner, Karl. 1967 [1875]. 'An Exception to the First Sound Shift'. *A Reader in Nineteenth-Century Historical Linguistics*. Ed. and trans. by Winfred Lehmann, 132–163. Bloomington: Indiana University Press.

Visser, F.Th. 1963–73. *An Historical Syntax of the English Language*. 4 vols. Leiden: E.J. Brill.

Waksler, Rachelle. 2001. 'A New *all* in Conversation'. *American Speech* 76:128–38.

Wald, Benji, and Besserman, Lawrence. 2002. 'The Emergence of the Verb-Verb Compound in Twentieth Century English and Twentieth Century Linguistics'. *Studies in the History of the English Language: A Millennial Perspective*. Ed. by Donka Minkova and Robert Stockwell, 417–47. Berlin and New York: Mouton de Gruyter.

Wallis, John. 1972 [1653]. *Grammar of the English Language [Grammatica Linguae Anglicanae]*. Ed. and trans. by J.A. Kemp. London: Longman.

Watkins, Calvert. 2000. 'Indo-European and the Indo-Europeans'. *The American Heritage Dictionary of Indo-European Roots*, vii–xxxv. 2nd edn. Boston: Houghton Mifflin.

Webster, Noah. 1806. *A Compendious Dictionary of the English Language*. Hartford: Sidney's Press.

———. 1951 [1789]. *Dissertations on the English Language*. Gainesville, FL: Scholars' Facsimiles.

———. 1968 [1783]. *A Grammatical Institute of the English Language, Part I*. Menston: Scolar Press.

Webster's Dictionary of English Usage. 1989. Springfield, MA: Merriam-Webster.

Webster's Third New International Dictionary of the English Language Unabridged. 1961. Ed. by Philip Babcock Gove. Springfield, MA: Merriam-Webster.

Wells, J.C. 1982. *Accents of English*. 3 vols. Cambridge: Cambridge University Press.

Whorf, Benjamin Lee. 1956. *Language, Thought, and Reality*. Ed. by John B. Carroll. Foreword by Stuart Chase. Cambridge, MA: The MIT Press.

Williams, Joseph M. 1975. *Origins of the English Language: A Social and Linguistics History*. New York: The Free Press.

Williams, William Carlos. 1938. *The Complete Collected Poems of William Carlos Williams*. Norfolk, CT: New Directions.

Winchester, Simon. 1998. *The Professor and the Madman: A Tale of Murder, Insanity, and the Making of the* Oxford English Dictionary. New York: Viking.

———. 2003. *The Meaning of Everything: The Story of the* Oxford English Dictionary. Oxford and New York: Oxford University Press.

Wolfram, Walt, and Schilling-Estes, Natalie. 2005. *American English: Dialects and Variation*. 2nd edn. Cambridge, MA: Blackwell.

Wright, Laura (ed.). 2000. *The Development of Standard English, 1300–1800: Theories, Descriptions, Conflicts*. Cambridge: Cambridge University Press.

Wright, William Aldis (ed.). 1887. *The Metrical Chronicle of Robert of Gloucester*. London: Eyre and Spottiswoode (http://www.archive.org/details/metrical chronicl02robe).

Index

NOTE: Some disciplinary terms not included here are defined in the glossary.